Ivan the Terrible

Ivan the Terrible

First Tsar of Russia

Isabel de Madariaga

Yale University Press
New Haven and London

For information about this and other Yale University Press
publications, please contact:
U.S. Office: sales.press@yale.edu   yalebooks.com
Europe Office: sales@yaleup.co.uk   www.yalebooks.co.uk

Set in Sabon by MATS, Southend-on-Sea, Essex
Printed in Great Britain by St Edmundsbury Press Ltd, Bury St Edmunds

Library of Congress Cataloging-in-Publication Data

De Madariaga, Isabel, 1919–
    Ivan the Terrible/Isabel de Madariaga.— 1st ed.
      p. cm.
    Includes bibliographical references and index.
    ISBN 0–300–09757–3 (cl.: alk. paper)
    1.   Ivan IV, Tsar of Russia, 1530–1584. 2.   Russia—Tsars and
rulers—Bibliography. 3.   Russia—History—Ivan IV, 1533–1584.
I. Title.
    DK106.D4 2005
    947'.043'092—dc22
                                                          2004029807

A catalogue record for this book is available from the British Library.

10 9 8 7 6 5 4 3 2 1

Contents

Illustrations

Maps

Foreword

The complex historiography of the reign of Tsar Ivan IV is usually expounded in detail in the first chapters of most late nineteenth- and twentieth-century works on Russian history.[1] It is a highly politicized historiography because at all stages since the beginning of the nineteenth century, historians have only too often forgotten that history is about human beings, and have been wedded to one or another theory of the interpretation of historical trends: Hegelianism, economic determinism, populism, historical materialism, Marxism, Eurasianism, economic materialism, Marxism–Leninism, most of which theories are at all times difficult to apply to a pre-modern society.

I have carried out no original research in Russian archives for this book, but have relied entirely on published sources and historical works. Among older historians I have drawn often on N.M. Karamzin whose *Istoria gosudarstva rossiikogo* appeared between 1814 and 1824 – the last of the Chronicles and the first of the histories, as Pushkin put it. It is invaluable not just for the simplicity and humanity of its moral approach, but also for the richness of the sources quoted in the footnotes, some of which have now been lost. I have also made ample use of S.M. Solov'ev's *Istoria Rossii s drevneishikh vremen* (1851–79), for he also quotes extensively from sources, though I do not share his reliance on the state as the motor of history. V.O. Kliuchevsky, one of the most balanced of Russian historians, does not attribute any ultimate political significance to Ivan's *oprichnina*, and sees it as the 'product of the excessively fearful imagination of the Tsar'. His conclusion that it was directed against persons and not against a system revived the conception of the moral rather than the political role of the Tsar, but though Kliuchevsky's judgments are always valuable, he has not devoted so much of his time specifically to writing about Ivan IV.

A 'bourgeois' historian stands out as bestriding the transition from anti-tsarist history to full-fledged Marxist history: S. Platonov developed the theory that Ivan set up the *oprichnina* in order to destroy the boyar and princely aristocracy and establish a new ruling class, the dependent military servitors, the future *dvoriane*, who served from the land and who would support the Tsar. It was an interpretation which made up for the deficiencies of Kliuchevsky, for it portrayed Ivan's policy as clearly directed not at persons but at the system, and in Platonov's view it led to a profound social, economic and political crisis, culminating in the Time of Troubles. It proved a very influential theory, and in one form or another continued in use until the fall of communism. But Platonov, one of the major historians of Russia, had not hesitated to stress the atrocities of Ivan and his moral culpability, and he succumbed to academic plotting against his position and was arrested in 1930, possibly at the instigation of the historian M.N. Pokrovsky, and exiled to Samara in miserable conditions, where he died within two years.[2]

While historiography floundered in ideological rapids, the Russian intelligentsia, and intellectuals in general, developed their own unprofessional, but human views of the Tsar. The Decembrist Kondratii Ryleev called him a tyrant, and Mikhail Lunin wrote of the mad Tsar who for twenty-four years bathed in the blood of his subjects. Belinsky wrote of a 'fallen angel . . . who revealed at times both the strength of an iron character and the strength of an exalted mind'.[3]

Soviet historiography presented particular problems, such as the need to apply rigid Marxist criteria to the analysis of what had actually happened, without agreement having been reached on what the Marxist criteria actually were or on what had actually happened.

Platonov's rival in the transition period was Pokrovsky himself, a committed Marxist and a bolshevik, who dominated the historical scene until the mid-1930s. His *Russian History from Earliest Times,* was published before the Revolution. He attributed the institution of the *oprichnina* to the victory of the monetary economy over the feudal natural economy, leading to an alliance between the service gentry and the merchant bourgeoisie and disregarding the personal influence of Ivan IV. By 1936 (after his death) he was denounced as anti-Marxist and anti-Leninist. More important, though difficult to classify, was the work of R. Wipper, which in different versions appeared in 1922 and in 1942, when it glorified Ivan as a leader and statesman. But it would be unjust to assume that historians and for that matter playwrights or historical novelists were all cast in one ideological mould, and new interpretations of Ivan's reign emerged into history and literature, reflecting individual judgments and the twists and turns of Soviet foreign policy and alliances.

Victim of these changes of direction was S.B. Veselovsky, one of the greatest scholars of mid-sixteenth century Russia, who reverted, mid-twentieth century, to the position of Kliuchevsky, that the *oprichnina* served no political purpose, and who was therefore attacked as non-Marxist and whose work was stifled.

At this point Stalin's interest in Russian history becomes more noticeable, and it culminated in his influence on the novels of A.N. Tolstoy and the films about Aleksander Nevsky and Ivan Groznyi, of Eisenstein, the second of which was commissioned by Stalin in 1941 before the German invasion of Russia, during the period of the Nazi-Soviet pact.[4] The treatment of the subject reflects the changing political situation, and Ivan, though a Tsar, is depicted, in Part I of Eisenstein's film, as a wise statesman, leader of his people, opposed by treacherous boyars and supported by the common people.

The trials which Eisenstein's film of Ivan met with have been analysed in an exemplary manner by Maureen Perrie,[5] and there is no point in recounting them here. However, there is one interesting feature in her account of Eisenstein's original screenplay, the emphasis on the sea, for which there is no evidence in the sixteenth-century sources. As a boy, Ivan's nurse sings to him the song:

> Ocean Sea,
> Sea of deepest blue
> Glorious sea
> The Russian rivers run towards you
> Towns stand on your shores
> There stand our ancient towns
> Captured by a dark foe . . .[6]

The musical theme and the song recur throughout the screen play, where Ivan's right to the Baltic Shore is emphasized repeatedly to its strains, right to the end where Ivan carries the dying Maliuta Skuratov in his arms to the sea shore, and the waves obey his commands. This reflects Stalin's personal commitment to the conquest of the Baltic states lost by Russia after the First World War and the Bolshevik Revolution,[7] but though access to a port seems an obvious Russian political aim, there is no specific mention of it in sixteenth-century sources, other than references to the efforts to keep or recover Narva. Ivan's atrocities are shown, up to a point, in the film (by permission: ' "yes, murders did happen" said Stalin'[8]) but they are justified as necessary in view of the constant treason which surrounded the Tsar. The first part of the film was shown publicly from January 1945. The second part was shown in the Kremlin in March 1946 and met with some criticism among the intellectuals but Stalin, when he saw it, was revolted and described it as a nightmare, with the *oprichnina* reminding him of the Ku Klux Klan, and Ivan as a weakling, a 'sort of Hamlet'.[9] The *oprichniki* were 'portrayed' as a gang of bandits, 'cannibals' who called to mind the Phoenicians and the Babylonians, whereas they were a progressive force which Ivan needed to forge the unification of Russia.

By now Ivan had to be portrayed as a 'state-building' ruler, a farseeing, wise statesman, and a brilliant war leader and diplomat, regardless of the previous critical attitude of all historians towards all tsars, who were *ipso facto* negligible and negative factors in history. Ivan's executions had to be explained as rendered necessary to uproot treason, a justification of Stalin's own terror, and the identification of Stalin with Ivan was encouraged openly though at times the authors subverted it by using Aesopian language – possibly including Eisenstein himself.

The image of Ivan as a 'progressive' ruler, was useful also during the Second World War, and it lasted until the death of Stalin, when it was undermined by the rejection of 'the cult of the individual', opening the way for a far more wide ranging debate on what was the correct Marxist interpretation of the policies of Ivan. Pokrovsky and Veselovsky were both gradually rehabilitated, and the image of Stalin as Ivan Groznyi served only to discredit Stalin. Historians free of the ideological burden of the 1920s, 1930s and 1940s, though in many cases still wedded to Marxism, came forward, and made good use of the increasing number of sources which were being discovered and edited. There is now genuine debate between historians, in part fuelled by the availability in Russia of English originals or Russian translations of many works published by Western historians, and of free communication on the internet.

In this book I have drawn to a great extent on the great Russian stalwarts of the history of Ivan IV who published in the twentieth-century. Veselovsky and Sadikov go back to the 1940s. The doyen of Russian historians of Ivan IV was for many years, until his death in 1988, A.A. Zimin; his major work on the *oprichnina* appeared in 1964, and was reprinted after his death in 1988, edited by A.L. Khoroshkevich, in 2001. There are some changes, of fact and of emphasis, in this new edition which have been carefully pointed out and assessed in a review by S.N. Bogatyrev.[10] Others who have taken up the torch are S.O. Schmidt, N.E. Nosov, I.I. Smirnov, R.G. Skrynnikov,

B.V. Kobrin and many more all of whom have contributed to the pursuit of the elusive truth. I have relied very greatly on their work for factual information, reserving my right to differ on interpretations. I have also drawn upon the work of American and German scholars in this field and here acknowledge my debt to them.

The present book is not about Russia in the age of Ivan the Terrible. It is an attempt, on the evidence at present available, to understand and explain Ivan the man and the ruler, whose personal reign, lasting from 1547 to 1584, had such a devastating impact on his people and his expanding country. Any such attempt faces formidable difficulties. First of all the uneven nature of the surviving evidence, so much of which has been destroyed by fire. There is no written trace of Ivan's personal relationship with any of his seven wives or his children. There is no original written record of any letter, or order, given by the Tsar; there are a few records of private discussions in which he took part, but they are mostly with foreigners, such as the Englishmen Anthony Jenkinson or Sir Jerome Bowes, or the Austrians Count Cobenzl and Daniel Prinz von Buchau, or the Jesuit Antonio Possevino. There are no records of meetings of the Boyar Council, or of any other administrative body, though there are formal records of Ivan's participation in public assemblies and in occasional formal discussions such as the sessions of the joint meeting of the Boyar Council and the Church *Sobor* to discuss the major reform programme of the Church and of canon law, known as the *Stoglav* (Hundred Chapters) in 1551. Formal documents are thus usually very impersonal, when compared with the lively exchange of letters between kings and their counsellors in other countries.

There are however very many records, which have survived in a haphazard way, of the organization of military campaigns, the raising of revenue, the distribution of estates, the execution of alleged traitors, and the barbarities committed by and for the Tsar. More source material is continuously being discovered and put into circulation, so that there is a vast amount of material to read. The scholarship, the ingenuity and the assiduity in interpreting this source material displayed by Russian historians over many generations, can only arouse admiration. Nevertheless, the uneven nature of what has survived conduces to a great diversity in its interpretation, and leads the historian to hesitate between possibilities, forcing him or her to lay a number of suppositions before the reader, thus weighing the narrative down with analysis. Much of this discussion has been relegated to the footnotes, which in this case are of greater relevance to the general tenor of the narrative than is usually so. Moreover excessive reliance has had to be placed on foreign sources, which have been discovered little by little. The accounts of the two Livonian nobles, Kruse and Taube, were already known at the end of the sixteenth century but were not translated into Russian until 1922.[11] The account of the German Schlichting was only translated into Russian in 1934.[12]

Foreign written sources have been supplemented by foreign prints and engravings, allegedly portraits of Ivan or illustrations of the atrocities committed by his troops. There is no authentic portrait of the Tsar in existence and all those reproduced in books about him are imaginary. The same applies to his father Vasily III. Portraits are printed allegedly of Ivan IV, but facing the other way they are used of the Jesuit Antonio Possevino.[13] The engravings of Russian atrocities are all imaginary. What they illustrate may well have happened, because warfare was terribly cruel everywhere at that time, and there is no doubt that Ivan was utterly ruthless towards his enemies, real or imagined. But pictures of atrocities can intensify the impact on the reader and leave a distorted picture on the mind. It is thus infinitely more difficult to study Russian sixteenth-century history than, say, that of Elizabethan England, where the correspondence between the Queen's advisers, Burleigh, Leicester and Walsingham, for instance, or between her enemies, has survived and enables the historian to associate personality with policy.

There has also been in the last thirty years a major assault, in the West, on one of the hitherto most important sources on which historians have depended, namely the correspondence between the Tsar and Prince Andrei Mikhailovich Kurbsky, and the *History of Ivan IV*, attributed to the latter. Professor Edward Keenan of Harvard University has argued at length that these two works are in fact forgeries, or 'apocrypha' as he prefers it, produced in the seventeenth century.[14] In addition Professor Keenan has argued that during the reign of Ivan the Terrible, as before and after, Russia was governed by an oligarchy, composed of members of aristocratic clans, closely interrelated by marriage; they governed in the name of the Tsar, who had no power and in the case of Ivan IV, was in fact illiterate. In addition an abyss separated the culture, such as it was, of the secular court society from that of church and monastic society. These latter arguments are expressed in an essay entitled 'Muscovite Folkways', originally drafted in 1976 as part of a Department of State contract, rewritten several times, and finally published in 1986, and 'meant to stimulate and provoke rather than to convince'.[15] However, Keenan has recently reiterated his view that Ivan was illiterate.[16]

This particular reader has not been convinced of the validity of any of these propositions. I am not qualified in linguistic and textual analysis. But as a practising historian I cannot accept the validity of Keenan's theories on historical grounds. There may be no evidence that Ivan was literate, but there is also no evidence that he was not. And there is no doubt that many boyars were literate – they had to be literate in order to negotiate treaties and truces.[17] I cannot accept either that Ivan was the illiterate tool of an oligarchy. It is really wildly improbable that the institution of the *oprichnina* in 1565, or the destruction of Novgorod and its inhabitants in 1570, were carried out merely on the initiative and authority of princes and boyars, and it certainly was not in their interests. Such policies would have to be imposed by someone with overwhelming authority. There is also too much similarity between the language of Ivan in his first letter to Kurbsky, of 1565, and the letters written to King Sigismund II, Augustus of Poland–Lithuania in 1567; these were ostensibly written by three great magnates in Russian service, and in fact by Ivan himself, and the texts have survived in the records of the Posol'sky Prikaz (Office of Foreign Affairs), and later in the archives of the Ministry of Foreign Affairs.[18] It is in my view quite probable that Ivan had learnt to read (it is after all not so difficult); it is equally probable that he did not write himself but dictated his most important missives, as most rulers did. Daniel Prinz von Buchau, imperial envoy in 1575, states positively that it was beneath the dignity of boyars to write themselves.[19]

The theory of the separation of the two cultures, religious and secular, is also unconvincing, when every line that was written in Russia as part of the formulation or implementation of policy by members of governing bodies is imbued with religious thought and feeling and couched in religious language. Even the lengthy disquisitions of ambassadors are replete with quotations from the Old and New Testaments. Priests were present at births, marriages, and deathbeds, they played a big part as confessors, and in pilgrimages to monasteries, often on foot, which were a frequent and normal part of life. They drew up wills. The Orthodox liturgy repeated familiar sounds to the faithful who probably knew much of it by heart. It is partly for this reason that I have included many quotations from writings attributed to Ivan, whether political or religious or, as so often, both. It is the way into his mind, the only way to understand his personality.

In the circumstances, I do not propose to attempt to refute Professor Keenan's theories, but will confine myself to referring the interested reader to the extensive literature covering the debate which he has launched.[20]

I have however adopted a few general principles of research and interpretation which I will state here. First of all, I have tried to write the history of Ivan IV, standing in Moscow and looking out over the walls of the Kremlin towards the rest of Europe, and not looking in – and down – into Russia, over its Western border, from outside. Adopting such an approach makes it easier to avoid supercilious judgments, to grasp what happened in Russia in Russian terms, to feel its full tragedy. This may explain why throughout I speak of Russia and not Muscovy. Ivan IV was *Tsar vseya Rusi*, of all Russia, and he considered himself to be the heir of Kievan Rus'. In the titulature of the Tsar, Vladimir came before Moscow. The emphasis on Moscow derives from the fact that it was the first big city which Westerners of all kinds came across, and by the time they became acquainted with Russia the history of Kievan Rus' was unknown to them, except of course to the Poles and Lithuanians. I do not believe one can read the present back into the past without distorting the past. Sixteenth-century Russians did not know that four centuries later the Ukraine would be an independent country with its capital in Kiev, nor that Russia would have conquered and then lost the Crimea.

At the same time I have pursued a comparative approach, for I think that many of the problems which faced Russia were of the same nature as those which France, Germany and, to a lesser degree, England had to contend with – though not necessarily at the same time as Russia. Both German emperors and French kings had had to struggle to have their authority accepted throughout their lands, a struggle in which Germany failed, and Russia had only partly succeeded by the sixteenth century. England had been forcibly unified under William the Conqueror, but it too had had to struggle to extend its borders to the coasts of the whole island, and to the whole archipelago, and was successful in Wales; partly so, for part of the time, in Scotland, and only partly so in Ireland.[21] The Trastámaras and the Habsburgs too had failed to unify the Iberian peninsula, where local *fueros* or constitutional rights survived, and the realm consisted of a union of crowns: it was a composite state.[22] The extension of a central royal authority throughout the realm was only achieved by the Bourbon dynasty in the eighteenth century. The Habsburgs and their predecessors on the imperial throne had dismally failed to unify the German lands. Sweden broke away from Danish control and asserted its independence. These various polities which emerged over time in Europe and turned into nations, share many common problems and it is up to the historian to detect them in the various disguises which they assume because of cultural, religious, geographical and political differences. England is an island and enjoys the blessings of the Gulf Stream; Russia has mainly infertile soil and an abominable climate; some European countries had been part of the Roman Empire of the West and formed a community which spoke Latin; others formed part of or were influenced by the Roman Empire of the East, practised their common Orthodox Christian religion, adopted much later, in the vernacular, and did not acquire a common language. But all these peoples have an underlying, common, Christian culture and shared political concepts, not always easy to detect, but which it is the duty of historians to seek out and define.

Finally I come to the question of the nature of evidence. Here I think that the advice given by Paul Bushkovitch in his 'The Life of Saint Filipp' is well worth following. He sets out a number of 'rules of reading', recommending them particularly for research into the study of Russian religion. The first and principal rule, which is most relevant to my research is: '*A text is what it says it is about*. Thus the life of Saint Sergei of Radonezh is not about the development of national consciousness in Russia. It is about the life of a monastic saint. It is about monasticism.' I have tried to follow this thoroughly sound recommendation. I can only hope that I will have satisfied my readers that I have done so.

I have also adopted a number of expressions which may seem idiosyncratic to my readers, but which are based on my determination not to mislead them by using words which distort what they meant at the time. The first of these is the word 'autocracy', used everywhere now as the translation of the Russian *samoderzhavie*. In the sixteenth century, and later, *samoderzhavie* signified sovereignty. *Samoderzhets* was translated into English as 'self-upholder'.[23] Secondly, I use Russia, not Muscovy to describe the realm of the Tsars, and Russian as an adjective for both Rus' and Russia. Muscovy was only one principality forming part of Russia, and its Riurikovich Grand Princes maintained their dynastic claims to the principalities on the Dnieper which had been absorbed by Lithuania after the Mongol conquest. Thirdly, I have tried to evade the use of the name 'Byzantium'. Thanks to Gibbon, It has become associated with deviousness, intrigue, and corruption, and leads readers to forget that Constantinople was founded by a Roman emperor, that for a thousand years it was the capital of the Eastern Roman Empire, using first the Latin, then the Greek language. Not that the Roman empire of Augustus, Tiberius, Nero, Heliogabalus was not also corrupt – but then we are less critical of our own fathers. Finally, faced with the real difficulty of finding suitable terms for the cavalry of Russia, I have borrowed from Professor Valerie Kivelson the designation 'service gentry' to describe the *boyarskiye deti,* and the later *dvoriane* of Russia because as a class they seem to me closest to the English landed gentry at a time when the latter were not at all genteel.

Highgate, 2004

Acknowledgements

It is with deep gratitude that I acknowledge all the help that I have been given in the preparation of this book. In the first place I must thank the Leverhulme Trust for a generous grant for research assistance to enable me to complete it. I also wish to thank Professors Michael Branch and George Kolankevich, successively Directors of the School of Slavonic and East European Studies, now part of University College London, for the facilities which they granted me, as an Honorary Research Fellow, and which enabled me to make use of the rich collection of the Library of the School. My thanks also go to the Librarian, Dr Lesley Pitman, and the staff of the Library, for their kindness and patience with me, and to Vladimir Smith Mesa for extra special attention. I must also record my gratitude to the London Library, a centre of excellence if ever there was one, and to Raj Khan who looked after my computer.

I must single out five people whose help was invaluable. My old friend and colleague, Professor W.F. Ryan, who helped me with offprints and suggestions, read the whole work, and saved me from many infelicities. Needless to say he is not to be blamed for any which remain. Secondly, my new friend (made on the Internet!) Dr Sergey N. Bogatyrev, who was generosity itself, supplying me with offprints, photocopies of his articles, and suggestions for reading, read the whole of my MS, and allowed me to pick his brains in endless conversations. He too, however, must be absolved of responsibility if I have occasionally wilfully refused to follow his lead. And to my old friend, Professor H.M. Scott, who also read the early chapters and gave me sound criticism and advice. Fourthly, Mrs Gwyneth Learner, who took on the chore of being my research assistant and gave me invaluable help in areas beyond my reach. And finally Mrs Vlasta Gyenes, Senior Library Assistant at SSEES, without whose constant friendly and kind assistance I would not have been able to complete my work in the Library now that I can no longer climb stairs or ladders. All these kind friends gave me enormous moral support, and sometimes physical support.

In Russia I am grateful to Professor R.G. Skrynnikov, who kindly gave me his book, *Tsarstvo Terrora*; to Professors A.B. Kamensky and S.A. Kozlov, who also sent me books, and to Dr Oleg Omel'chenko, who was more than kind in procuring books for me as well as photocopies of obscure articles. *Na dobruyu pamyat'*.

I am also grateful to Dr J. Lehtovirta, who gave me his book, to Dr Julia Gerasimova of Leyden University, for advice on illustrations, to Professor R. Frost, for much good advice, to Professor W.E. Butler for advice on Russian law, to Professor A. Pippidi, Director of the Institute of Modern History in Bucharest, who filled me in on the background to relations between Moldavia and Russia and sent me photocopies of articles, to Professor Averil Cameron who advised me on Byzantium, to Dr Susan Reynolds, who educated me in medieval history, to Professor John Guy who put me on the right track in English history, and to Dr N. Mears for information on the courtship of Queen Elizabeth by Erik of Sweden. I would also like to thank Robert Baldock at Yale University Press for his constant support, and Candida Brazil who coped with a difficult manuscript with unfailing patience and efficiency. Finally I am deeply grateful to Dr Stephen Sebag Montefiore, who gave me most useful help and information on sixteenth-century medicine and advised me and provided me with literature on the psychiatric problems of Ivan the Terrible.

Russia and Poland–Lithuania, mid-sixteenth century

0   200 km

N

BALTIC SEA

Helsinki

Narva

Lake Pskov

Lake Ladoga

Lake Onega

Monastery of Solovki

Archangel
St Nicolas   Kholmogory

Lake Beloozero

Sukhona

LANDS OF THE LIVONIAN ORDER

Pskov   *Shelon*   Lake Ilmen
Staraia Russa

St Cyril of the White Lake Monastery
Vologda

Sheksna   *Mologa*   *Volga*   *Kostroma*

NOVGOROD

Luga   *Msta*   *Volkhov*   *Slas*

Iaroslavl

Lake Seliger

Tver'tsa

Lake Seliger
Toropets   Staritsa   Tver'
Volga

Rostov
Nerl

Western Dvina

Velikaia   *Lovat*   *Kunia*

Velikie Luki

Aleksandrovskaia Sloboda   Nizhnii Novgorod
Suzdal   VLADIMIR

Yoshkar Ola

Kazan'

Trinity Monastery   *Kliazma*

Sviazhsk

Neman

Polotsk   *Mezha*
Vitebsk   Dorogobuzh

Monastery of Volokolamsk

MOSCOW   *Moskva*

Murom

Vilna

Dnieper

Protva
Tarusa

Kasimov

Radoshkovichi

Orsha   SMOLENSK   *Ugra*

Minsk

Sozh

Serensk   *Serena*
Zhizdra

Vorotynsk   Riazan

Odoev

Oka

R U S S I A

LITHUANIA

Pripet

Turov

Sna'   *Desna*   *Zusha*   *Don*   *Voronezh*

Volga

Western Bug
Warsaw

Wieprz
Kholm

VLADIMIR-IN-VOLYNIA
Ovruch   *Uzh*

CHERNIGOV

Kursk

Voronezh

POLAND
Cherven

Iskorosten
Dorogobuzh

Seim
Putivl

Oskol

Don

Peremyshl

Styr   *Goryn*
Zvenigorod

Vyshgorod
Belgorod   KIEV
Vasilev

Sula   *Psel*   *Vorskla*   *Orel*

Donets

Astrakhan'

GALICH   Terebovl

Dniester   *Southern Bug*   *Dnieper*

Don
Azov

MOLDAVIA

Siret

Bialad

Danube

Kerch

Kuban

B L A C K   S E A

Chapter I
The Historical Background

The world the Grand Prince Ivan Vasil'evich was born into in 1530 was still somewhat strange and mysterious to western Europeans, though better known to travellers from Italy, the Holy Roman Empire and the one-time imperial Roman lands in the Balkans and the Middle East, now under Ottoman rule. Until the Mongol conquest in 1238–42, the Orthodox Christian Slavo-Scandinavian[1] princes in Russia had maintained relations with the kings of Norway, Sweden, Denmark, Poland, Moldavia, Hungary and France, and the Holy Roman Emperor, and there had been frequent intermarriages. Harold Hardrada, king of Norway, married a daughter of Vladimir Yaroslavich; the first wife of Grand Prince Vladimir Monomakh, whom he married in 1067, was a daughter of King Harold Godwineson of England; and the Kievan princess Anna, daughter of Iaroslav the Wise, married Henry I, King of France, in 1051.[2]

The Mongol Conquest
The Mongol conquest profoundly affected the natural evolution of medieval, or Kievan, Russia, but there is no agreement among the experts as to the nature and extent of its impact.[3] It was a traumatic experience, coming only thirty-eight years after the fall of Constantinople to the Latin crusaders in 1204. This was also a considerable shock to the Orthodox Rus', whose religious capital was now in the hands of schismatics, and who had to look to Nicaea for ecclesiastical direction until 1296.

The Mongol conquest destroyed the remaining unity of Kievan Rus'.[4] A good deal of the south-western part of the old Kievan grand principality, including Kiev itself, which had been devastated, came under direct Mongol rule, and by the fourteenth century had been absorbed, mainly by conquest, into the Grand Principality of Lithuania. As a result

Kiev went one way and the city of Vladimir on the Kliaz'ma, founded in 1108 by Prince Vladimir Monomakh, went another, with consequences which will be discussed below. The principalities gravitating around the city of Vladimir, in the north-east, and the republic of Novgorod in the north continued under their own princes, subject to Mongol approval. The character of the north-eastern principalities defined the new community which arose around it. The climate was harsher, the winter was longer, the forest was denser, the days were shorter in winter though longer in the brief summer than in Kievan Rus'. Communication with the Eastern Roman Empire or central Europe was more difficult, and settlement was more recent in the north-east. The independent city republic of Novgorod was held by the Mongols on a somewhat loose rein, but it too formed part of the Mongol empire since its trade was of considerable importance to these rulers of the steppe.

Not only was the *zemlia* or land of Rus' thus divided, the north-east and the south-west losing touch with each other, but the fairly continuous contacts with eastern and central Europe which had marked the old ruling élite and the merchant class were much reduced – except for the city republics of Novgorod and Pskov, which continued to trade with the Hanseatic League, and the trade with the West which trickled through Smolensk. Vladimir and Moscow now participated more in trade ventures to the Middle East. There were no more Riurikid marriages with European royal and princely houses. There were some marriages with the Mongol ruling house, but not many after the conversion of the Golden Horde to Islam in 1340.

The Mongols did not settle in Rus', since the land was not suitable for the nomadic life which was the basis of the economy on which their huge cavalry army relied. Khan Baty established his capital in Saray, on the lower Volga, and summoned the Russian princes repeatedly to Saray, or sent them on to the Mongol capital Karakorum, in Mongolia, to have their *iarlyki* (patents to rule) renewed. This long journey was so exhausting that several princes, notably Alexander Nevsky, died on the way or the way back.

The khan of the Mongol empire had to be chosen among the descendants of Genghis Khan, the Golden Kin. Hence the Mongols were quite prepared to accept the Russian principle of confining the choice of princes to a ruling family, the Riurikids, descendants of the semi-mythical Scandinavian prince Riurik, and frequently accepted the choice made by the Russians, though they did not hesitate to reject it when they preferred another candidate. Their policy broadly was not to allow any principality to become too strong. They delegated the task of collecting the heavy tribute imposed on the Russian lands to the princes, and eventually to the ruler of Moscow, though the assessment was made by Mongol officials. It is estimated that in the late fourteenth century the principality of Moscow paid between five and seven thousand rubles a year, a very large sum bearing in mind that this was not the only financial burden.[5]

There has been much debate among historians on the scale of the physical destruction inflicted by the Mongol invasion, on the nature of Mongol influence on Russian social and political development, and the extent of Mongol responsibility for the perceived backwardness of sixteenth-century Russia. To understand the initial impact of this calamity on the Russians many factors must be considered: its suddenness, the destruction of the economy, the depopulation by death and enslavement and by the conscription of potential soldiers and craftsmen, the loss of skills, the plundered cities and devastated fields, all occurring with the speed of a whirlwind, and recurring whenever the Mongols thought the Russians needed a reminder of their subordinate status. The princes, who may well have been relatively protected from the worst effects of the conquest, had to learn to manoeuvre, to intrigue, lie and bribe, in order to achieve their ends, to submit to the demands of their masters, however humiliating.

Inevitably most of the Russian written sources dealing with this period are biased against a people whom they saw as a cruel and destructive oppressor belonging to an alien faith, the Ishmaelites or sons of Hagar.[6] Yet Russians and Mongols frequently cooperated on the battlefield, there was some intermarriage, and judging by relationships in the sixteenth century, there was no deep-seated racial prejudice. Moreover, the Russian *ulus*[7] was but a small and relatively unimportant part of the vast lands ruled over by the Golden Horde. Hence most of the political and diplomatic activity of the Khans was oriented towards the East, where their power originated. The portrayal of the Mongols at this time as barbarians living in tents does not do justice to the sophistication of the imperial administration in the west, based on the capital Saray, on the lower Volga, where there was a luxurious court, the streets were paved and there were mosques for the Moslem Mongols and a Russian bishop to minister to the Russian community of craftsmen and soldiers in Mongol service, as well as caravanserais to lodge the vast trading expeditions.

However, from the latter part of the fourteenth century the Mongol hold on Russia was affected by discord within the Golden Horde. The victory of Dmitri Donskoi, Grand Prince of Vladimir and Prince of

Moscow, supported by some other princes, over a Mongol force in 1380 at the Field of Kulikovo raised the prestige of Moscow among the Russian princes, though it was followed by a Mongol revival under Tokhtamysh, who razed Moscow in 1382. Tokhtamysh and his Russian allies in turn were destroyed by Tamerlane who, from his base in Samarkand, devastated Saray, but refrained from destroying Moscow. In the early fifteenth century the Golden Horde broke up into the Khanate of Crimea, the Khanate of Kazan' and the Great Horde. The two sons of the Khan Ulug-Mehmed of the Golden Horde became vassals of Grand Prince Vasily II, and founded, under Russian protection, the Khanate of Kasimov, on the Oka river. Its Mongol ruler helped Vasily II to regain his throne in the Russian civil wars of 1430–36 and 1445–53, which arose out of the conflict between the traditional Russian principle of lateral succession to the throne (to the next eldest brother) and hereditary succession from father to son, the principle which emerged victorious from the struggle.[8] It was against this background of conflict and confusion, of occasional alliances and occasional strife, that the final confrontation took place in 1480, on the River Ugra, between the remnants of the Mongol Great Horde, with its allies in the Crimea and in Poland–Lithuania, and a Muscovite army, with its Mongol allies, the khanates of Kazan', Astrakhan' and Kasimov, under Grand Prince Ivan III of Moscow. There was actually no battle, since both sides withdrew before the armies could engage. But from this date Moscow ceased to regard any Mongol horde as its overlord, though it continued to collect the tribute within Russia and distribute it as presents among its Tatar allies on a smaller scale.[9] Muscovite leadership in the two major confrontations between Russians and Mongols, at the Field of Kulikovo in 1380 and on the River Ugra in 1480, as well as its victory in the fifteenth-century civil wars, reinforced the Russian perception that the Grand Duchy of Vladimir/Moscow had become the leading principality in Rus', and Ivan III gradually asserted his sovereignty (*samoderzhavie*) over the remaining independent Russian principalities including, in a notional sense, those which now formed part of the Grand Principality of Lithuania (see below). The theological interpretation of this 'victory' also served to increase the authority of Moscow, for as the Tverian author of The Tale of the Death in the Horde of Michael Yaroslavich of Tver tells it, 'God gave Jerusalem to Titus not because he loved Titus but to punish Jerusalem'. Thus victory came to Moscow to punish the unbelievers.[10]

What, if any, influence did Mongol suzerainty have on the development of Muscovite absolutism? The idea of a universal empire instituted by God was fundamental to the Mongol conception of the world order and there was therefore, in their view, no point in resisting the Mongol army. Once the universal Mongol empire was established everyone would be compelled to serve it. The basic principles of Mongol rule were laid down in the Great Iasa, or Code, attributed to Genghis Khan, which regulated the universal service of subjects in the army and the administration, and proclaimed their duty to care for the sick and the old, to offer hospitality, and to produce their daughters in the beauty contests in which the 'moonlike girls' would be selected as wives or concubines of princes.[11] The code also dealt with civil, commercial and criminal law, naming as offences acts against religion, morals and established customs, and those against the life and interests of private persons. The usual penalty was death.

The practical aspects of Mongol administration and the etiquette in use at the Mongol court were familiar to the Russians who visited Saray; Russians learnt to speak Turkic, and the Mongols probably learnt some Russian. It was perhaps the arbitrary nature of Mongol decisions which most affected Russians, but it may be that this apprenticeship in subservience prepared them for the obsequiousness they are alleged to have shown to the tsars of Moscow. Moreover, Russian grand princes, and many appanage princes, learnt subordination to the Mongols the hard way: between 1308 and 1339 eight princes were executed in the Horde, including four who had become grand princes of Vladimir.[12]

The Mongol presence was not ubiquitous in Russia, and usually consisted of a limited number of officials, tax collectors, recruiting officers and platoons of cavalry. Yet by the sixteenth century many Russian princely families were stressing their descent from Mongol *tsarevichi* (sons of khans) or other nobles. The *tsarevichi* who descended from Genghis Khan took precedence over other princes in Moscow and ranked above or immediately below Riurikovichi until the end of the dynasty in Russia. Russian aristocrats could be proud of their descent from princely Mongol families, where they would have kept silent about descent from commoners.[13]

It is not easy to be precise about the nature of Mongol influence, for it extended over more than two centuries and the Golden Horde itself went through many changes during that period, including the vital conversion to Islam. But the Russian aristocracy did have fairly close contact with the nomads of the steppe, and by a process of osmosis may well have acquired many habits and adopted assumptions about the objects of a state, the nature of government, relations between lords and vassals, masters and servants, that are difficult to detect today. There are two specific aspects of this contact which may have rubbed off on the Russians, namely the degree of cruelty which they actually felt and saw in the executions or in the inflicting of punishment practised in the Golden Horde, and the absence of orderly judicial procedures (they did not usually *see* Byzantine practices). Not that the Riurikid princes of Russia (or their Viking ancestors) were not capable of great barbarity, but on several occasions, recorded in the Chronicles, such barbarity is clearly regarded as wrong in a Christian country.

The Russian Orthodox Church

When they conquered Russia in the thirteenth century the Mongols were pagans, and they seem to have treated all religions with tolerance.[14] The Russian Church did not suffer under the Mongol regime, but this did not make Christians tolerate Islam after the Mongol conversion in 1340. Inevitably the Russian ecclesiastical establishment was at first almost entirely composed of Greek churchmen from the Eastern Roman Empire. It was drawn from the celibate 'black' clergy or monks. Marriage was compulsory for the parish priests or 'white' clergy. The metropolitans were chosen and consecrated by the patriarch of Constantinople, and they in turn appointed and consecrated the bishops.

The Church was maintained by fees and contributions, by the proceeds of legal fines in areas under its jurisdiction, and by the income from original grants of landed property, which increased gradually as a result of princely and boyar donations to ensure prayers for the souls of the departed, and by monastic purchases. Many churches and monasteries were founded, the most famous of which was the Monastery of the Caves in Kiev. The Trinity monastery was founded in 1337 by St Sergius of Radonezh, not far from Moscow, as an isolated hermitage 'beyond the Volga'; it grew into the largest landowning community in Russia, with many churches and fortified walls. Another monastery founded on the same system was the Kirillo-Beloozersky (St Cyril of the White Lake), which in turn gave rise to many more such settlements in the northern lands. Further north still was Solovki, the formidable, fortified monastery in the Solovetsky islands in the White Sea which was used also as a prison, certainly by Ivan IV and equally certainly by the later tsars and by the communist regime.

Monks, and monasteries, played an important cultural role in Russia. The monks acted as scribes, letter writers, copyists and illuminators of manuscripts; they collected materials for and edited many of the Chronicles; they organized scriptoria, icon and fresco painting studios, and provided what teaching there was as well as some medical care and

a refuge for the poor, sick and destitute. The Church was also pre
all the main events of mortal life, birth, marriage and, above all, death.
Monasteries were places of pilgrimage. Sums were deposited for monks
to say prayers for the dead (though the Orthodox Church did not believe
in Purgatory) and to remember the departed on his name day with
services and feasting. Nunneries cared for women and girls, and
maintained schools of weaving and embroidery. There were no teaching
orders. Monks also built churches and oversaw their adornment with
icons and frescoes, and they surrounded the monasteries with elaborate
fortifications. As in western Europe, monasteries started out in poverty
and austerity, and gradually they grew rich and became lax about
observing the rules. They benefited from the respect shown by the
Mongols for religion, they were not taxed and they prayed for their
Moslem overlord.

The Church also played an important political role in Russia. It was
the only pan-Russian institution, after the Mongol conquest had split
Kievan Rus' in two. Indeed, the metropolitan of Kiev and All Russia (the
original designation of the see) was also the ecclesiastical head of all the
Orthodox population of the neighbouring Grand Principality of
Lithuania for a great deal of the time, though his see had ceased to be in
Kiev in 1299 and had moved to Vladimir and eventually to Moscow.

The Kingdom of Poland–Lithuania

A word must be said here about the complex relations between the two
grand principalities, Muscovite Russia and the Grand Principality of
Lithuania. A glance at the map on pp. xii–xiii will show the extent to
which Kievan Rus' lay on both banks of the Dnieper and how much
territory it lost to Lithuania as a result of the Mongol invasion. The
Grand Principality of Lithuania eventually comprised a nucleus of
Lithuanian lands, the *voevodstva*, or provinces, of Troki and Vilna
which, under a series of able rulers, extended slowly to the east and
south, conquering, annexing and absorbing ex-Rus' principalities.
Polotsk fell into Lithuanian hands when the Riurikid line died out in
1307, Kiev was conquered from the Mongols in 1362, and the
Lithuanian advance continued under Grand Prince Vitovt (1393–
1430), down the right bank of the Dniester until it reached the shores of
the Black Sea and was finally stopped by the Mongols in 1399. To the
east, Lithuania now had also swallowed the central basin of the Dnieper,
spreading from the old Kievan principality of Smolensk to Lutsk.

All these lands were now the property of Gediminovich[15] or Riurikid
princes of Lithuania, the latter sometimes holding on to their hereditary

lands, sometimes being granted new lands as patrimonies by the grand princes of Lithuania. The language of government was a form of Slavonic. As in Kievan Rus', succession from father to son was not automatic in the Grand Principality of Lithuania: a surviving brother or cousin of the reigning prince would often lay claim to the throne and factional wars were frequent and bloody. Relations with Muscovite Rus' were fairly close, though not always friendly. Novgorod often looked to Lithuania for princes; discontented Lithuanian princes would desert their grand prince and move to Russia or back to Lithuania, taking their lands with them or being granted lands there. There was in fact no reason why the unification of the Russian lands should not have taken place under Lithuanian leadership. But a decisive event, affecting the future of the whole area of Poland, Lithuania and Russia, occurred in the 1380s. A treaty of 1384 had provided for the marriage of Jagiello, the pagan Grand Prince of Lithuania, with a daughter of Dmitri Ivanovich Donskoi, Grand Prince of Vladimir Moscow. The marriage did not take place. In 1384 Jagiello turned west and was converted to Catholicism in order to marry the Catholic heiress to the crown of Poland, Jadwiga. The possibility that Russia might unite around the huge, mainly Orthodox, Lithuanian and ex-Russian lands, instead of around Moscow was lost for ever. The Lithuanian dynastic union with Poland precluded Lithuanian union with Russia, though Grand Prince Vasily I of Moscow later married Sophia, daughter of Vitovt of Lithuania. As long as Vitovt was alive (and he lived to be eighty) a certain stability prevailed, but he died in 1430, and the constant intriguing between various branches of the princely families in Lithuania, coupled with the civil war in Muscovite Russia, led many princes on either side to desert to the other, moved by religious or political reasons.

Although only a loose dynastic union at first, the Lithuanian union with Catholic Poland exacerbated religious differences within the Grand Principality which became more acute with the coming of the Reformation. To a great extent the conflict between the Gediminovichi, the Lithuanian Riurikid and the Muscovite Riurikid princes[16] reproduced for years features of the strife over the succession within the Riurikid dynasty itself, and all sides sought the assistance of outsiders like the Livonian Order[17] or, even more frequently, the Mongol khans and the khans of the Crimea, one of the successor states of the Golden Horde, who naturally enough pursued their own aims. What, by the sixteenth century, may have attracted the Lithuanian princes to Russia was a latent anti-Catholicism and anti-Polonism (fostered by the

Reformation); what may have attracted the Russian princes to Lithuania was the increasing power of the magnates as expressed in the Sejm and the *sejmiki*,[18] at the expense of the king. What attracted the grand princes of Vladimir Moscow (the official title of the principality) was the possibility of dynastic union with the Grand Principality of Lithuania, leading to a recovery of the Kievan lands in the south, something which Ivan III did not forget when he gave his daughter Elena in marriage to Alexander, Grand Prince of Lithuania, in 1495; nor did Vasily III forget it when on the death of Alexander in 1506 he took advantage of the elective nature of the Polish-Lithuanian throne to put forward his candidacy as prince at any rate of Lithuania.[19]

The grand princes of Lithuania attempted at intervals to obtain the consent of the Patriarch in Constantinople to the establishment of a separate metropolitanate for Kiev and Lithuania, or Kiev and Little Russia (the name given to the southern borderlands), in order to withdraw their Orthodox, mainly Russian, subjects from Muscovite religious control, but they achieved only short-lived successes. Several of the really powerful and forceful Russian metropolitans also threw their political weight, and sometimes even their spiritual authority, behind the policy of supporting the grand princes of Moscow at Saray in their pursuit of supremacy over the remaining free principalities of Rus'.

The Union of the Churches and the Fall of Constantinople

The Ottoman onslaught on Anatolia and the Balkans encouraged the rump of the Eastern Roman Empire to seek alliances in the West by pursuing the union of the Catholic and Orthodox Churches, which had been estranged since 1054. Union had already been discussed in a Church Council in Basel in 1433, and discussions were resumed in 1438 in Ferrara. The Metropolitan of All Russia, a Greek named Isidor, was appointed by the Patriarch of Constantinople, but he had not been the choice of the Russian bishops, who had proposed a certain Iona. Isidor proved to be willing to bow to the arguments of the Latins over the *filioque* clause – the clause in the creed which proclaimed the descent of the Holy Ghost from both the Father and the Son, in the Catholic version, as distinct from the Father only, in the Orthodox version – and to accept the Union of the Eastern and Western Churches. The Council moved to Florence in 1439, to avoid the plague, and the Act of Union with Rome was signed there in July of that year. The Union was unpopular, both in Constantinople and in Russia, and it did not help the Eastern Emperor to secure military assistance against the Turks (though Metropolitan Isidor was given a cardinal's hat). Isidor arrived back in

Moscow in 1441, but both the Union and the new cardinal were eventually rejected by Grand Prince Vasily II, and Isidor escaped through Lithuania back to Rome. Both imperial and ecclesiastical governments in Constantinople were in disarray, and in Moscow, Grand Prince Vasily sought to have Iona, the Russian bishop originally chosen, appointed metropolitan. But Vasily was caught up in the disasters of the Russian civil war with his cousin, and blinded, and he was only restored to his throne in 1447. Finally, in December 1448 Iona was appointed Metropolitan of Kiev and All Russia, including Lithuania and Little Russia, on the authority of four Russian bishops and the Grand Prince of Vladimir Moscow, without any reference to the Patriarch in Constantinople. The Russian Orthodox Church had now shaken off the authority of Constantinople and had become autocephalous, with fateful consequences in the long run.

The Russian rejection of the Union of Churches in 1439–41 deepened the cultural gulf between the Greeks and the Latins. The fall of Constantinople in 1453 was another great catastrophe and affected the relationship between the Russian Orthodox Church and the Grand Prince. The Emperor (Mehmet II) now reigning in Constantinople was no longer a Christian, and the relationship between the Church and the secular power could no longer be envisaged as a 'sinfonia' between two equal powers. And if the Russian Church was now autocephalous, the Grand Duchy of Muscovy was by far the most powerful and wealthy remaining Orthodox realm, able to weigh the scales down against the Church. The patriarchate still survived in Ottoman Constantinople, but it had no power. As the only independent, sovereign, Orthodox power (except for beleaguered Moldavia), Russia was in a position to step into the gap. Inevitably, the fall of Constantinople would enormously increase the prestige of the Grand Prince of Moscow in the whole Orthodox world. The Russian Orthodox Church could find in the concept of *translatio imperii* a Byzantine authority for an autocephalous church of which the Metropolitan of Moscow was the head.

The idea of the *translatio imperii*, of the transfer to Moscow of the role of religious capital of the Orthodox world (though not of its political domination), lurks behind the titles of tsar and sovereign (*samoderzhets*) used intermittently by Ivan III. This was not an automatic transfer undertaken immediately after the fall of Constantinople – it was a gradual assertion of the new status of Russia after it had thrown off the remnants of Mongol suzerainty. It could be argued that just as Constantinople had been punished by God for veering towards the Latin Church, so Moscow had been rewarded for rejecting the Union of

Churches. Moscow had also incidentally provided some financial assistance to the Orthodox Church within the Ottoman Empire in the last decades of the fifteenth century.

The first exponent of the new theory of Moscow as the third Rome was the Metropolitan Zosima, in the prologue to the new Paskhalia or calendar of religious events for the next millennium, starting in 1492, which he had drawn up in that year. He recorded that the Emperor Constantine had founded a city named Constantine after him, which is Tsargrad, the new Rome, and today God had blessed the new Constantine (Ivan III) and the new city of Constantine, Moscow. The next stage in the evolution of the religious status of Moscow occurred in the reign of Vasily III.[20]

The Consolidation of Moscow

A change had also come over the relative situations of the Grand Prince and the appanage princes in the course of the second half of the fifteenth century which further elevated the former above other princes. Ivan III had gradually succeeded in incorporating into the principality of Moscow most of the remaining independent principalities whose princes still enjoyed some sovereign rights. His most remarkable achievement was the destruction of the independent republic of Lord Novgorod the Great in two successive assaults, in 1471 and 1478. With his Tatar and Tverian allies, Ivan III defeated the forces of Novgorod and executed their leaders in 1471, forcing the defeated to pay a large tribute, to accept Muscovite rule and to cease any direct relations with foreign powers, i.e. Lithuania. In 1478 Ivan III attacked again. The defeated Novgorodians gave up their right to choose their prince, accepted the suzerainty of Ivan III, lost the great bell which had been used to summon the *veche* (popular assembly), and were eventually subjected to massive confiscation of private and church lands and to huge population transfers. The Grand Prince had now acquired enormous wealth in land, some of which he proceeded to distribute to men-at-arms in service tenure (*pomest'ya*; hence landowner, *pomeshchik*). He was to absorb the principality of Tver' by force in 1485.

Tver' had been the great rival of Moscow in the early fourteenth century, and it continued throughout the fifteenth century to consider itself as a grand principality on a level with Moscow. Its spokesman was the monk Foma, who had been the delegate of Tver' to the Council of Ferrara/Florence. Its Grand Prince Boris Alexandrovich was chosen by God, according to Foma. He was the great sovereign (*samoderzhets*), crowned with the tsar's crown; his city was the new Israel, or the new

Jerusalem. It was Prince Boris Alexandrovich who used a formula to describe his power identical with that used by Ivan III and which Ivan IV was to use later: 'I, Grand Prince Boris Alexandrovich am free to reward whomsoever I wish, and to execute whomsoever I wish.'[21] The similarity leads one to suppose that this formula expressed a general conception of the rights of a sovereign lord, and did not apply only to the ruler of Moscow. This same prince, Boris Alexandrovich of Tver', Ivan III's principal rival, was also known as *Groznyi*, and the words *groznye ochi*, or terrible eyes, are used of other princes, as, for instance, in the extremely moving lament for the destruction of Russia after the death of the Grand Prince Yaroslav. This dates from the period of the Mongol conquest, and describes the beauties of the Russian land, its great cities, its monastery gardens, its temples to the Lord, its awesome princes ('*knyazya groznye*', the word used of Ivan IV), its honourable boyars etc. The word *groznyi* is probably one of those many words which have changed their significance over time. We do not know precisely what it signified, therefore, in the time of its most famous bearer, Ivan IV.[22] But there is a nuance between dread and terrible: dread is what one is; terrible refers to what one does.[23]

Political Ideas

The closest the Kievan polity could come to an exposition of the nature and rights of governments was in the Old Testament accounts of the kingdom of Israel and in the history of David and Solomon, with Vladimir as David and Yaroslav the Wise as Solomon, or in the New Testament accounts of the rule of Herod and the relation of the kingdom of the Jews to the Roman Empire. The exposition of theoretical ideas on the East Roman conception of the derivation of power from God, and its relationship with ecclesiastical authority, came later, mainly in collections of Byzantine wisdom such as *Melissa* or 'The Bee', which were translated into Church Slavonic from the twelfth century onwards.

The change in the status of Ivan III as Grand Duke of Vladimir Moscow in relation to the remnants of the Horde and to other foreign powers, as well as to other previously independent Russian princes, obviously affected his conception of his power. After the fall of Constantinople and the encounter on the Ugra he assumed the title of *samoderzhets,* or sovereign, which had already been used by Boris Aleksandrovich of Tver'. Today *samoderzhets* is always translated as 'autocrat', which is, of course, closer linguistically to the original Greek, but completely distorts the sixteenth-century Russian sense of the word, which was 'sovereign', an independent ruler who has no overlord.[24] Yet, although the nature of Ivan III's power in internal matters remained as yet undefined, one can trace in him a gradually more authoritarian, even arbitrary exercise of power. This gradual change was supported by the Russian Church.

For some time the Church had been serving the political ends of the principality of Moscow (which seemed the best situated to protect it) and wished to increase its authority and power by adopting East Roman models. It was concerned less with the nature of power and more with how it was exercised, its moral rather than its political dimension. This trend is associated with the writings of Iosif Volotsky, the abbot of the monastery of Volokolamsk, who is often credited with being the father of Russian absolutism. He was one of the earliest to formulate his view of the power of the grand duke and of the relationship between the ruler and the people. Yet Iosif was not an unconditional supporter of the unlimited power of the ruler. In his view, the grand duke's power came from God, and was given by God to him. But if the grand duke allowed himself to be ruled by evil passions, anger, love of money, injustice, pride, violence and lack of faith, 'then he was not a servant of God, but of the devil, not a tsar but a torturer' ('*muchitel*', which also translates the Greek word *tyrannos*). There was no need to obey such a tsar. A true tsar had to observe the interests of the 'land'. For Iosif the power might be holy, but not the man, who could be unworthy. Moreover, power was not unlimited but had to be bound by 'precepts and justice' (*zapovedi i pravda*).

The concept of the king's two bodies had entered Russian religious and political thought from the Byzantine deacon Agapetus by the beginning of the twelfth century and it began to pop up in unexpected places.[25] In the funeral eulogy pronounced on the death of Vasily III in 1533, the orator exclaimed:

> We know that in his natural body our ruler is the same as all men; but in his power is he not the equal only of God? He is inaccessible in the glory of his earthly kingdom; but there is a higher, heavenly kingdom, for which he must be accessible and indulgent to people ... A real tsar rules his passions, in the crown of holy wisdom, in the purple of law and justice.[26]

The preacher was quoting almost word for word the saying of Agapetus.[27] Iosif died in 1515, but his followers developed his ideas later into a systematic support of the absolute power of the ruler as given by God.

The Court

The growing complexity of the administration in the course of the gradual annexation of Russian lands by the Grand Prince of Moscow had led to a considerable evolution of his court whence major decisions now issued throughout the realm. The relationship between the increasingly powerful Grand Prince and the political and social élite has, however, to be reconstructed from what actually happened, from what was tolerated by the magnates around him. His court was, in the words of one of the leading Russian historians of the period, A.A. Zimin, the fundamental social force on which rested the power of the rulers of Moscow. Courts had existed before, and they continued to exist in some of the appanage principalities for some time, where princes still had their own boyars. But the Grand Prince's court produced the military leaders and the administrative personnel now required to rule the country.

It is probably around this time, with the gradual incorporation of so many appanage principalities, and the accompanying loss of sovereign powers by the previously ruling princes, that the grand princes of Vladimir and Moscow began to claim the whole land of Rus' publicly as their *votchina*, or patrimony.[28] The appanage princes had owned and ruled over their appanages, exercising sovereign power in financial and judicial matters. These powers were taken over and used by the grand princes of Moscow as the appanages were absorbed. This process of integration was for some time the principal internal administrative problem which faced the grand princes of Moscow, and is usually described by Soviet and western historians as the 'centralization of the Russian state'.[29] It involved the extension of the prince's authority uniformly throughout the land in judicial, financial and military matters, at a time when most of the population was illiterate, communications were extremely slow and difficult, there was still considerable resistance to the Grand Prince's authority, and there was almost no administrative machinery. The problem was at this time (fifteenth and sixteenth centuries) common to most European polities, in many of which royal power was even less centralized than in Russia, because of constitutional structures (as in Poland–Lithuania), fragmentation (as in Germany), religious warfare (as in France and the Netherlands) or dynastic separatism and local rights (as in the Iberian peninsula). In fact the two most advanced countries in this respect were the Ottoman empire and England, in both of which power was in the hands of a new dynasty by conquest, and the power of the Crown was being extended.

The social pyramid resulting from the fusion of the principalities consisted of the appanage princes, in the north-east of Russia, who owned land by inheritance from a previous Riurikid princely ancestor, and who still occasionally enjoyed a degree of independent and sovereign power over their lands, and might even have a claim to the grand princely throne. A similar position was held by the 'upper' princes on the River Oka, who served the grand princes from the west Russian lands bordering on Lithuania (at times in Lithuania), both Riurikid and Gediminovich.[30] They sometimes served with their own forces, and preserved a greater degree of autonomy in their internal affairs than the Moscow princes; so did the one-time appanage princes of Suzdal' (the Shuiskys, Rostovskys, Yaroslavskys etc). In addition there were the non-titled nobles, of whom the highest in rank were the old Moscow boyars, who supplied the leading military commanders and the top governors, and as a group manoeuvred for position and precedence with untitled nobles from other principalities. The aristocracy as a whole was considerably weakened by the practice of partible inheritance, which led to the multiplication of title-holders and the division and subdivision of estates between siblings, until there was not enough left to divide. The lack of hereditary titles associated with posts, or of hereditary posts of any kind,[31] also considerably weakened the aristocracy and impeded its consolidation into a political class as distinct from a series of clans. The title of boyar was not hereditary, though the family might inherit a claim to be promoted to the rank. It depended on the grant of the tsar. The title of prince could not be granted; princes were born, and all their children inherited the title. Precedence at court and in service was regulated by the practice of *mestnichestvo,* which is dealt with below.[32]

Finally there were the so-called *deti boyarskie,* or boyars' children, called service gentry for convenience here. These were a mixed bag, originally comprising descendants of princely or noble families who had multiplied to such an extent that they were compelled by poverty to serve for a fairly low reward; minor landowners, foreigners and immigrants from other principalities who received allotments of land for their service; as well as occasional sons of priests or even ex-slaves.[33]

Institutions

A striking feature of Russian political structure was its lack of institutionalization. Carrying on from the early tradition of the prince consulting his war band, the grand princes' retinues had taken part in the duty of giving advice to the ruler in the commonwealth of Rus'.[34] These families of princes and untitled long-serving aristocrats were called by the generic name of boyar, which gradually became identified also with membership of the Grand Prince's Council, a body which grew out of the topmost level of the court. The practice of governing by council was traditional and still survived in some of the appanage principalities in the sixteenth century. The Grand Princess Sofia even had her own council, and so did many appanage princes in the reigning family.

The princely council is a most elusive body, which has left no record of its setting up, its functions, debates or decisions, its active membership at any time, or its constitutional status or role, if any. Its members were appointed by the grand prince and were placed in one of two ranks at its emergence in the late fifteenth century: the boyars proper, or highest rank, and the *okol'nichi*, a word which derives from *okolo*, or 'near', and evidently defined a man near the prince. The rank is first recorded in the thirteenth century, sometimes in conjunction with other court ranks such as cupbearer.[35] There were not many of these *okol'nichi*, and according to Herberstein, they were a 'sort of praetor or judge, placed near the lord' and always with him.[36]

Ivan III made more changes to Russian titulature, which reflect the maturing of a political conception and which probably developed out of his marriage to the niece of the last Emperor of the Eastern Roman Empire, Constantine Paleologus. He began to use, frequently, but not always, the title Tsar (Caesar), which may have indicated an intention of claiming imperial status. Now that there was no longer an Orthodox tsar in Constantinople, he could put forward a claim to inherit the religious mantle and almost a hereditary right to the imperial title (the *translatio imperii*). He adopted, possibly in imitation of the Habsburgs, the device of the two-headed eagle (believed by some to be the coat of arms of the Paleologi), and used it on his coinage. He added to his titles the words 'of all Russia' (*vseia Rusi*), stressing his dynastic claim to sovereignty over all the Russian principalities, and therefore the right to reconquer those principalities of Kievan Rus' which were now in Lithuania. He was even able to force acceptance of this claim on the Grand Prince of Lithuania in a treaty of 1494.[37] Ivan III also added to his title a long list of the various principalities and kingdoms over which he ruled. This is often interpreted as the self-advertisement of a parvenu among crowned European heads, but it is more likely to be an imitation of the general European practice.[38]

Grand Prince Ivan III firmly asserted his independence of all superior secular and ecclesiastical authority, on an occasion that has often been viewed as typical of Russian arrogance but is really perfectly understandable. When the imperial envoy Nicolas Poppel proposed in 1489 that his master the Emperor Frederick III should grant Ivan III the title of 'king', as an inducement to join an alliance against the Porte, the Grand Prince replied that he and his ancestors had been lords in their lands from time immemorial, that their lands had been granted by God, and that he needed no help from the Emperor.[39] Rus' had never after all been part of the Holy Roman Empire, nor even of the Eastern Roman Empire. It had now also, incidentally, ceased to be part of the Mongol Empire.

Sofia Paleologa

More difficult to explore adequately is the extent of the personal influence – if any – of Zoe Paleologa, the 'Despina' herself.[40] Many Russian historians have rejected any such influence for reasons that seem anachronistically nationalistic.[41] Having lost his wife, Princess Maria Borisovna of Tver', Ivan III sought a new bride. There was some talk of a Saxon princess, but after the fall of Constantinople to the Ottoman Turks, the niece, even of a dead Roman emperor, might provide an attractive proposition and would raise the position of the Grand Prince of Moscow even further above the shoulders of his kin and his rivals and strengthen his international position. Sofia, as she was called in Moscow, was the daughter of Thomas, brother and heir of Constantine Paleologus, the last East Roman Emperor, who died on the walls of Constantinople in 1453. Her father had been Despot of Morea and died in Rome in 1460, leaving also a son, Andrei. Born in 1440 or 1449, Sofia herself was brought up in Rome, and though Orthodox by birth she may have been a Catholic by upbringing. The initiative for the marriage came from Pope Paul II, through Cardinal Bessarion of Nicaea, a supporter of the Union of Churches.[42] The Pope, needless to say, hoped to secure Ivan III as a powerful ally against the Turk, as well as his consent to the Union of Churches. Agreement on the marriage was soon reached and Sofia left Rome in June 1472. She travelled with a large retinue by land and sea to Pskov', where she was greeted with a banquet, and where the first signs of strain between Latins and Greeks were noted when her escort, Cardinal Antonio Bonumbre, allowed himself to be preceded by a crucifix held aloft. (The body of Christ did not appear on Russian Orthodox crosses at that time.)[43] Sofia was evidently quite accustomed to public appearances and knew how to thank the Pskovites gracefully for their welcome. She arrived in Moscow on 12 November 1472, and the wedding took place the next day in order to evade the impending church fast. There was no coronation ceremony.

It took considerable courage and character for a young woman to embark on a marriage to the ruler of a country about which so little was known, and it is fair to assume that Sofia was a woman of parts. Ivan's physical presence was overwhelming: he was tall, lean and a fine figure of a man, but women looked away from him, frightened by his eyes. He was a formidable drinker, and after the long midday meal, lay in a drunken stupor, according to Herberstein's gossip (the traditional siesta, as recommended by Grand Prince Vladimir Monomakh).[44] It is also probable that Sofia evaded the complete seclusion imposed on high-born Russian women. She received foreign envoys, for instance. According to Herberstein, 'they say that she was a very cunning woman, and the prince acted very often on her suggestions'.[45] Certainly her arrival, accompanied by a number of Italians and Greeks who settled in Russia, led to a remarkable opening to the West in many fields. According to one account, she was ashamed to see her husband standing before the seated envoys of the Mongol Horde to pay the tribute, and it was she who urged him to make the final stand on the Ugra in 1480 which put an end to the official suzerainty of the Mongols over Russia.

S.M. Solov'ev puts forward the theory that the Church, anxious to assist the grand princes of Moscow in the achievement of sole power (*edinovlastie*), had for a long time been endeavouring to raise them above the other princes, but for the successful conclusion of their undertaking they had to draw on the traditions of the Roman Empire of the East. These traditions were brought to Moscow by Sofia Paleologa. 'He [Ivan III] was the first to be called Groznyi, because he seemed to the princes and to his *druzhina* like a monarch.'[46] He raised himself to an unattainable height, and compelled the descendants of Riurik and Gedimin to bow before him like the lowliest of his subjects. It was he who introduced the habit of kissing the grand duke's hand, of using the word '*kholop*' (bondsman or slave) to describe oneself in relation to the grand prince, and expected reports and petitions to be signed with the demeaning diminutive, for instance Ivashka, for Ivan. Ivan's contemporaries, continues Solov'ev, believed that this was due to Sofia's influence, 'and we have no reason to disbelieve them'.[47] It seems that perhaps we may have many reasons to disbelieve them, yet Prince A.M. Kurbsky, writing in the reign of Ivan IV, lamented that the devil had sowed evil habits in the excellent clans of Russian princes, just like the kings of Israel had done, by means of their evil and sorcerous wives, particularly those whom they took in marriage from foreigners. Elsewhere Kurbsky accuses 'the Greek' of having been instrumental in the death of Ivan III's eldest son.[48] But possibly a more perceptive critic of Sofia was Bersen' Beklemishev (of noble family but not officially a boyar), who in the reign of Vasily III allegedly said to the monk and man of letters Michael Trivolis, known in Russia as Maksim Grek (Maxim the Greek):[49] 'When the Greeks came here, our land fell into confusion. Until then our land had lived in peace and quiet. But as soon as the mother of the Grand Prince, the Grand Princess Sofia, came here with your Greeks our land fell into confusion and great disorder, like with you in Tsargrad [Constantinople].' When Maksim objected that Sofia descended on both sides from great families, Bersen' continued: 'Whatever she may have been she brought discord to us. A land which gives up its own customs will not stand for long, and the Grand Prince has changed the old customs here; what good can we hope for from that?'[50]

Ivan III's new political conceptions found visual expression in the remodelling of the city of Moscow on a far grander scale in brick and stone. He rebuilt the three cathedrals, to record births (Annunciation Cathedral), coronations (Dormition Cathedral) and death (Archangel Cathedral) within the Kremlin; he built himself a new palace fit for a tsar (the Palace of Facets); he reconstructed the walls of the Kremlin, using Russian builders as well as Italians who had come in the train of Sofia; and he drew on the best artists of the time to decorate the churches with frescoes. The new palace would also serve as the base for a new and far more elaborate and carefully regulated court, with new ranks, a far more ceremonious treatment of both Russians and foreigners and the extension and depersonalization of court service.[51]

Sofia almost certainly had her say in matters of the succession. She bore Ivan III five sons and three daughters, and there was doubtless some pillow talk, even if she lived in the women's quarters. We do not know where she in fact lived. She clearly helped to give external shape and form to Ivan's aspirations to sovereignty and provided him and Vasily III with information on court ceremonial in Constantinople and Rome. In the years from 1470 to the death of Vasily III in 1533 there were many foreigners in Russia, but Sofia was better placed than anyone to inform the Grand Prince and the court about the way things were done abroad.

The End of the World

The political crisis of the last decade of Ivan III's reign is shrouded in mystery and was played out against the background of a religious crisis which saw the appearance of the first translation of the Bible as a whole into the Church Slavonic language, and the first executions for heresy in Russia. Briefly summed up, in 1497 the Grand Prince, having lost his son and heir, Ivan, by his first wife, appointed his grandson, Dmitri Ivanovich, by his daughter-in-law the Princess Elena of Moldavia,[52] as his heir and had him crowned as co-ruler. Two years later the most prominent boyars at the Grand Prince's court, Ivan III's uncle by marriage, the ex-Lithuanian Gediminovich Prince Iuri Patrikeevich, and his son Vasily, were arrested. Others arrested at the same time were executed, but the Patrikeevs were spared though forced to take the cowl, Vasily under the name of Vassian. The arrests seem to have been connected with tension between the supporters of the young Dmitri, Ivan III's grandson, and Vasily, the eldest of his sons by Sofia, as heirs to the throne. The mother of Dmitri, Princess Elena, was in addition closely linked to a group of so-called 'Judaizers', heretics of a sort difficult to define. Russian scholars have argued endlessly about the interpretation of these events without reaching any satisfactory conclusion.[53]

The 'Judaizing' heresy, about which very little is known, was first detected in Novgorod, where according to the story a number of local people had been converted to Judaism by an alleged Jew, Zechariah, brought in the train of a Lithuanian prince, Mikhail Olel'kovich.[54] No one knows what the tenets of the Judaizers actually were, but it is very possible that they were influenced by latent anti-clericalism, rationalism and iconoclasm, a desire for simplification, and ultimately anti-Trinitarianism or even Arianism. There may have been some reflection of Hussite ideas. On the other hand there may also have been elements of Jewish mysticism, possibly even Kabbalistic studies or some acquaintance with the substantial quantity of translations from the Hebrew available in the Grand Principality of Lithuania.[55] Identifiable members of the heresy are very few, but it is known that there were converts at the court of Ivan III, where his daughter-in-law Elena of Moldavia seems to have been one of the most prominent, and where Fedor Kuritsyn, a leading diplomat, the man who is said to have transmitted the Tales of Vlad the Impaler to Russia, and even Ivan III himself were said to be sympathizers.

The apparent flourishing of heresy led the Archbishop of Novgorod, Gennadi, a man of considerable intellectual calibre, to pursue heretics with their own weapons and to set up a centre for the study of 'Latin', i.e. Catholic, culture while at the same time driving forwards the preparation of what he regarded as the main weapon against heretics, namely the translation of the complete Bible into Church Slavonic.[56] (His hope that Ivan III would introduce an institution on the lines of the Spanish Inquisition was disappointed.) Some, but not all, of the books of the Old and New Testaments and the Apocrypha were available in the form of separate manuscripts or collections of different and often incomplete books; among those that were not available were the

Chronicles (Paralipomenon) the first, second and third books of Esdras, parts of Ezekiel and other apocryphal books. [57]

The Judaizing movement flourished against a background of religious turbulence caused by the widely held belief that the world was coming to an end in the year 1492, the end of the seventh millennium in the Orthodox calendar, calculated from the creation of the world, and by the circulation of popular millenarian texts. The apprehension caused by the continuing advance of the Ottomans, culminating in the overthrow of the last remnant of the East Roman Empire, and the loss of Constantinople, was bound to have an extremely unsettling effect on all those living within the spiritual and physical radius of these dramatic events. By some the Ottomans were identified with Antichrist, as described in Revelations, and it had now become possible to draw upon the accounts in a Slavonic Bible to express these fears. Not less unsettling was the fact that the world did not come to an end in 1492.

Russia and Europe

The collapse of the Golden Horde, the advance of the Ottomans on the Black Sea and in Europe, and the Church Councils of Basel and Ferrara/Florence led in the second half of the fifteenth century to a considerable enlargement of the range of contacts between Russia and other European countries, particularly in south-east Europe, where the two dynastic houses, the Habsburgs and the Jagiellos, were in conflict over the lands of Bohemia, Poland and Hungary, all now threatened by the Ottoman advance. This explains the initiation of diplomatic exchanges with the Holy Roman Emperors (Frederick III and Maximilian I), the Papacy, the Ottomans and the semi-independent countries in the Balkans. Both emperors approached Russia in attempts to secure an alliance with the Grand Prince against the Ottomans. But Ivan was not to be diverted from his principal foreign policy problem: relations with Poland–Lithuania over their competing claims to the lands of the Dnieper basin, and the policy of each power of calling on the help of the khans of Crimea against the other. During the reign of Ivan III, the Grand Prince had managed to maintain an alliance with Mengli-Girey, Khan of the Crimea, which safeguarded his southern frontier during intermittent warfare with Poland–Lithuania. [58]

The diplomatic usages and ceremonial of Moscow had developed in relations with the Tatar Moslem khanates, which perpetuated the inferior status of Moscow and which exacted the exchange of elaborate gifts. Russian envoys abroad also frequently indulged in trade in goods they had brought with them – a practice regarded as beneath their dignity in the West. During the reign of Ivan III problems of precedence with Western countries were not frequent, though the Russian practice of conducting negotiations with Sweden and the Livonian Order through the governor in Novgorod and not in Moscow continued. Direct negotiations also occasionally took place between boyar members of the Russian Council and members of the Lithuanian Council, and negotiations with the Porte usually took place in Kaffa, not in Istanbul. By the death of Ivan III, Russia was well established on the diplomatic circuit, though its presence is largely ignored by Western historians.[59]

Chapter II
The Reign of Vasily III

Ivan III died in 1505, and his son Vasily acceded to the throne, as the result of his victory in a struggle for the succession between 1502 and 1505. On 14 April 1502, Ivan had transferred the Grand Principalities of Vladimir and Moscow to Vasily as *samoderzhets* (sovereign), thus depriving his grandson Dmitri, who had been arrested three days earlier with his mother, Elena, of his inheritance. This was clear proof of Ivan III's earlier assertion of the underlying instability of the principle of succession in Russia: 'Am I not free to decide between my children and my grandchildren? I will give my principality to whom I wish.'[1] Ivan's final will had apparently been written between late 1503 and June 1504. In it he had 'blessed his son Vasily' with the principalities which his father had left him and which God had given him, and he had left minor appanage lands to his younger sons, enjoining them to obey their elder brother. Sofia had died on 17 April 1503, and it is very probable that Vasily now became all powerful in a court in which his father's health was deteriorating, possibly to the extent of total incapacity.[2] Ivan III had strengthened Vasily's hold on the throne by preventing any of his own younger brothers (Vasily's uncles) from marrying and having children.[3] Sofia gave Ivan III five sons, and Vasily too, when he became Grand Prince, did not allow his younger brothers to marry until he had a son, and two of his brothers died in prison before him. The rules for the succession adopted by Ivan III clarified one issue: in order to inherit, the heir had to be the son of a Grand Prince (like Vasily).[4] There remains a curious doubt about the general acceptance of Vasily's legitimacy as ruler. According to Herberstein, Vasily came to the throne as regent until the death – in prison – of Dmitri in 1509, when he entered into his full inheritance, but without a coronation. Grand Prince Dmitri, who had been crowned, was still alive when Ivan III died, and his coronation evidently gave him some protection.[5]

One of the last concerns of Ivan III before he died was the marriage of Vasily, now in his early twenties, which was late for Russian dynastic marriages. Efforts to find a princely bride outside Russia failed, though until then grand princes had made dynastic marriages with princesses from appanage families and often from Lithuanian families in the hope of inheriting a principality, or at least making a claim to an appanage. The marriages of Ivan III's son and daughter to a Moldavian princess and a Grand Duke of Lithuania (Catholic at that) respectively were again clearly designed with foreign policy in view and to raise Russian prestige. But such marriages were now no longer possible: there were few appanages apart from those granted to immediate members of the grand princely family, which put them within the prohibited degrees, and Orthodox Europe was in Ottoman hands. It seems, therefore, that it was for Vasily that the practice was introduced of summoning a 'bride-show', or beauty parade of all suitable young ladies from noble families for him to choose among them. The logistics of such a beauty parade seem on the surface to make it a quite improbable performance. But Herberstein, who was in Russia twelve years after Vasily's wedding on 4 September 1505, reports that some 1,500 noble girls were brought together in the summer of 1505, and Vasily chose Solomonia Iur'evna Saburova, the daughter of a boyar from a relatively modest family. The thought of 1,500 nobly born young ladies being trundled through the muddy roads of Moscow in the huge wooden carriages without springs (*kolymaga*) used at the time makes one wonder if the numbers were not wildly exaggerated. The custom was probably recommended by Sofia as a solution to the problem of selecting a wife for a member of the grand princely family, though she died before the wedding. The marriage, alas, was not a success, for Solomonia failed to perform her principal function. She had no children.

The problem of Vasily's childlessness became crucial for the Grand Prince at almost the same time as a similar problem arose many miles away, and in both cases the solution profoundly affected the relationship between the Crown and the Church. Vasily was some twelve years older than Henry VIII of England, but it was roughly at the same time, in the early 1520s, that their common problem became acute.[6] However, Henry was faced with a far more complex situation, because not only was he in love with another woman, but his wife was the aunt of the Holy Roman Emperor Charles V. Moreover, he belonged to the Catholic Church and needed to obtain the approval of its ecclesiastical head, the Pope, who lived out of his reach, for an annulment. Vasily, too, was forced to manoeuvre carefully, for the Orthodox Church did not approve of the divorce of an innocent wife. According to one account, he sent to the Patriarch in Constantinople for consent, which was refused. The elders of Mount Athos also rejected his pleas. Thus Vasily needed to build up support in the Russian Church and to win the concurrence of the Metropolitan in office, Daniel, who would have to ensure that the Church Council summoned to pronounce the annulment would override the Patriarch of Constantinople.[7] A new marriage had also to be carefully considered because it would lead to the introduction into the magic circle of the court and council of members of the family of the new wife, and upset the existing balance between families and clans.

The divergences within the Church and in society already apparent under Ivan III now began to emerge in a new and more effective form. The heresy hunt against the Judaizers of the late fifteenth century had become associated with a theoretical dispute over landownership which had been rumbling for some time and which is usually regarded as having dominated the Church Council called in 1503–5 primarily to deal with heresy. Driven forward by Abbot Iosif Volotsky, the Council launched an intensive drive against the so-called Judaizing heretics. Many were arrested and tortured, and confessed. A number were burnt in Moscow on 27 December 1504, and a second batch were burnt in Novgorod in February 1505.

In Russian historiography the existence of an acute disparity of views between two monastic groups, the so-called non-possessors (*nestiazhateli*) and the possessors (*stiazhateli*), was allegedly posited and fought out in this same Church Council of 1503. 'Non-possessors' is the name given after the event to an ascetic monastic trend, which was said to regard landed property owned by monasteries as only a trust to be used for the welfare and the relief of the poor, and stressed that monks should not own any personal property. This trend was identified particularly with the monk Nil of Sora (Nil Sorsky), who had spent some time on Mount Athos, and who in Russia had established his hermitage across the Volga in the north-east. He was followed and imitated by many others, who thus became known as the Trans-Volga Elders. The possessors were considered to be followers of Iosif Volotsky, who had set up his cenobitic community in Volokolamsk, in the principality of Tver', and who held that ownership of land was necessary to enable the monks to carry out a wide range of religious and social functions in a disciplined and regulated way. Historians have held in determined fashion to this bipolar view of Russian church history, identifying either boyars or nobles as allied with the non-possessors or the possessors according to varying assessments of their economic needs, their desire for political power, their willingness to defend the absolute power of the grand prince, or their attitudes to heresy.

The traditional argument is that the Grand Princes Ivan III and Vasily III were anxious to secure more land in order to provide for the armed forces they were developing, by means of the distribution of service estates in central Russia as *pomest'ia*. Ivan III had of course already confiscated enormous quantities of ecclesiastical and secular land in the Republic of Novgorod and had used it to establish service gentry and junior members of noble families on service tenures. But Novgorod could be regarded as conquered country, and the notion of secularization as distinct from confiscation had not yet entered the thinking of Christian monarchs. (Most land confiscated from monasteries or Catholic churches during the Reformation was acquired by private owners.) But the grand princes are regarded as responding to powerful pressures from the service gentry and the lower nobility, and acting in the interests of the class of lower service men, though it is difficult to see what channels these groups could employ to make their collective views felt, nor does it seem likely that they could outweigh the opposing pressures from great landowners like the monasteries and the wealthy boyars. This interpretation is based on the concept of early sixteenth-century Russia as a horizontally organized class society, whereas a social structure based on kinship and clientele led rather to a vertically organized society.[8]

Since there is practically no evidence to substantiate any of these positions, it is safe to argue that at this stage, in the years 1510–50, while there may have been differences of opinion between monks on the morality of the ownership of estates, the concept of total secularization – as distinct from occasional confiscation – of church and monastic lands, as a government policy, had not yet arisen. There is evidence that Russian grand princes rarely hesitated to confiscate church or monastic land when they needed it or wanted it, but there is also evidence of the continuation of substantial gifts of land both to monasteries and to aristocrats, as and when the grand prince so wished, and all the historians who have written on the subject have stressed the paucity of the references to the subject at the time. Skrynnikov argues that no one dared mention the subject of confiscation of church properties, which is why the subject does not appear in the records of Church Councils and other works; others have argued that there was no pressure either for or against confiscation, and that the evidence of a dispute at the Church Council of 1503–4 is unreliable.

The early years of Vasily's reign seem to have been a period of some intellectual openness. Vasily was proud of his descent from an imperial family; he may have known Greek, he was literate, and he was a relatively cultured man by Russian standards, able to converse with educated monks. Notable among these was Vassian Patrikeev, disgraced by Ivan III in 1499 and forcibly shorn as a monk in the St Cyril monastery of Beloozero. Around 1510, Vassian was recalled to Moscow by the Grand Prince, who probably knew him as a young man, and the monk seems to have had considerable influence on the Grand Prince's spiritual life. Bonds of friendship may have existed between the two men, who were second cousins, and may have survived the downfall of the Patrikeevs. Vasily, for instance, appointed Vassian to be a witness to his draft will in 1523.

Another monk prominent in the circle of Vasily was Michael Trivolis, or Maksim Grek (Maxim the Greek), one of the few luminous figures in Moscow during his brief period of free intellectual activity. He came from a prominent Greek family settled in Corfu, and left to study in Italy in 1492. He was acquainted with both Marsilio Ficino and Pico della Mirandola; he lived through the ascendancy of Savonarola in Florence and in 1502 he became a Dominican monk in the monastery of San Marco. He admired the Catholic religious orders (Franciscan, Dominican and Carthusian). But in 1505 he reverted to Orthodoxy and entered Mount Athos as the monk Maksim. He was a distinguished Hellenist, and had worked on the Aldine Aristotle in Venice.

Maksim was summoned to Moscow from Mount Athos in 1518 at the age of about fifty to cooperate in revising Russian translations of the liturgy and the Psalms from the Greek, but he also wrote many other works. He was the first resident exponent in Russia of Italian Renaissance literary culture but was critical of humanism from the Orthodox standpoint. His knowledge of the works of Pico della Mirandola may well have introduced him to such unorthodox interests as Jewish Kabbalah.[9] But Greek in origin and training, he also brought to Russia a concept of the Christian Church founded on the Greek Orthodox model of the 'harmony' or 'symphony' between Church and State, neither dominating the other; he believed that monasteries should not own vast wealth, that monks should live by cultivating the soil as on Mount Athos, and that what they did own should be used for the benefit of the faithful. He believed that the tsar was instituted by God to fulfil the duty of ruling Christian folk and ensuring their salvation, but he held that even the tsar was bound to act within the laws established by the Church. In this he was in agreement with the Abbot Iosif Volotsky of Volokolamsk, though he specifically approved of conciliar government.[10]

From various of his writings it seems that Maksim Grek did not believe it was the duty of churchmen to advise rulers on constitutional forms. When asked how a ruler should plan his government, he is said to have replied: 'You have the books and you know the rules, get on with it.'[11] But he does seem to have favoured government by consensus among the élites. He admired the formula as expressed in the sixth novella of Justinian, which kept the religious and the political powers in equilibrium. Maksim could be critical of tsars – biblical and contemporary – who dispensed false justice and wasted their substance in festivities, but this did not lead him on to any statement of the right to rebel. There is nothing the least bit modern in this view of conciliar government, and no conception whatsoever of the representation of estates or interests.[12]

Although they were monks, Maksim Grek and Vassian Patrikeev received many visitors in their cells and seem for a while to have conducted what one might almost call an intellectual salon in which, according to at least one author,[13] speech was remarkably, indeed dangerously, free. Vassian, of course, was extremely well connected: many of his relatives were members of the Boyar Council at one time or another and the most distinguished general, Daniel Shchenya, was his cousin. Judging by the evidence later at their trial for heresy and for altering liturgical texts, Maksim and Vassian held somewhat unorthodox views on religion, whether on the dual nature of Christ or the relationship of Church and State.[14]

The eventual fate of many of these people has to be disentangled from conflicting chronicle fragments, many of which are extremely tendentious. Moreover, discussion of their ideas often starts from the assumption that because they were eventually charged with offences against the Grand Prince, therefore they were in 'opposition' either to some of his policies or to the nature and extent of his powers. Both Ivan III and Vasily III may also have caused deep resentment by their practice of exacting oaths of suretyship from princes who entered grand-ducal service, that they would never use the right of departure, oaths that were backed up by financial bonds often involving large sums of money and large numbers of people, who were made responsible for each other. In the reign of Vasily III, the behaviour of a Shuisky prince was once guaranteed by twenty-nine wealthy service people each putting up 50 to 150 rubles.[15]

Both Maksim Grek and Vassian Patrikeev opposed Vasily's divorce on religious grounds, when he broached the subject in 1523, and this is probably what led to their eventual disgrace.[16] Ever since the days of the

Emperor Leo VI the question of divorce and remarriage had been the subject of debate in the Orthodox Church in Constantinople, where divorce was in fact not infrequent. In Russia, however, it was a new problem, and the Russian clergy were more rigid and conventional than the clergy of Constantinople.

The Metropolitan Varlaam, in the circle of Vassian, was opposed to the annulment and Vasily III had to find a suitably pliable metropolitan; he removed Varlaam in a high-handed way in December 1522, without reference to the Patriarch of Constantinople, which distressed many of the hierarchy, and replaced him with Daniel of Volokolamsk, who had succeeded Iosif Volotsky in 1515 as abbot of his monastery. Maksim Grek was extremely unhappy about the appointment of a new metropolitan on the sole authority of a Russian Church Council, i.e. the Grand Prince, without the approval of the Patriarch of Constantinople. He clearly did not regard the more or less accidental declaration of independence of the Russian Church after the Council of Ferrara/Florence as permanent. Nor did he accept that the captivity of the Orthodox Church, now under Moslem rule, affected its supremacy as the universal Christian Church. Maksim did not hesitate to express his disapproval out loud and was denounced to Vasily III. He was also incautious in his expressions of contempt for the poor translation of Greek texts by Russian monks, which he was attempting to correct, and according to Herberstein he told Vasily in so many words that he was a schismatic who followed neither the Greek nor the Latin religion.[17]

As in the case of Henry VIII, Vasily's divorce became entangled in the conflict of ideas and interests over religion and property, though it did not lead to the assertion of the ruler's religious supremacy over the Church, the confiscation of ecclesiastical property, and the declaration of the king's right to appoint his heir (which already existed in Russia).[18] Some of the controversy over clerical ownership of landed property had revived in the 1520s. The alleged spokesman for the retention of church and monastic lands, Iosif Volotsky, who had died in 1515, had, in his last years, been close to Vasily III, and in the writings of these years he placed more faith in the power of the Grand Prince and was less critical of a possible tyrant.[19]

If Vasily was to get his divorce, he had to work with the Church, which theologically at least was powerful enough to resist the onslaught of the royal will, unlike the Catholic Church in England, where Parliament provided not entirely disinterested support to the king. Whether a bargain was ever struck, who knows, but Maksim Grek and Vassian Patrikeev, together with Bersen' Beklemishev, were charged with heresy, seditious speech and, in the case of Maksim, treasonable conversations with an Ottoman envoy, Skinder, then in Russia, in a trial conducted by Metropolitan Daniil in 1525. Maksim Grek was convicted and sentenced to close confinement, in chains, without access to books, pen or paper, in the Josephian monastery at Volokolamsk. It is unlikely that his talks with the Turkish envoy were treasonable in any modern sense of the word. He was probably hoping to secure Turkish support for his efforts to be allowed to return to Mount Athos. Vasily was unwilling to proceed to extremes against Vassian Patrikeev, who was exiled to the convent of Beloozero, but Bersen' Beklemishev and a clerk in the entourage of Maksim Grek were sentenced to death for treasonable speech by a boyar court, and executed.[20] Tried again in 1531, probably as a means of getting at Vassian Patrikeev, who had been loud in his condemnation of the 'possessors', Maksim was again pronounced guilty. Vassian was imprisoned in the monastery of Volokolamsk, where he died soon after. But Maksim Grek, now charged also with black magic and falsifying liturgical books, was sent to a monastery in Tver', where he was fortunate in finding in Bishop Akaky a kind and tolerant soul who treated him with consideration. Nevertheless, with the crushing of the intellectual and spiritual trends which Maksim and Vassian stood for, the authoritarian elements latent in the Russian Orthodox Church, which Iosif Volotsky had come to represent, came to the fore. A new, narrower, intellectual climate prevailed in Moscow.

Towards the end of 1525 Vasily secured his divorce from a Russian Church Council and proceeded to get rid of his wife Solomonia, first by charging her with witchcraft, on evidence kindly supplied by her brother. If she were convicted he would have been able to repudiate her canonically as a witch, but he clearly did not want to go to extremes and instead removed her forcibly to a monastery where, struggling violently, she was shorn as a nun, Sofia, and, according to some accounts, finally forced to accept her fate by the lash of a whip wielded by one of Vasily's courtiers. She attempted to free herself by spreading the rumour that she was pregnant, but was promptly removed from Moscow to a convent in Suzdal'.[21]

Apparently Vasily held a bride-show and chose as his bride Elena Glinskaia, a girl of fifteen (he was in his late forties) of Lithuanian origin, and the marriage took place on 21 January 1526.[22] But the circumstances of the bride's family make one wonder whether political considerations did not weigh more heavily in the balance than her looks. Elena's father, Vasily L'vovich Glinsky, was dead, but her uncle Mikhail L'vovich Glinsky had had a very unusual career. The family's origins were somewhat obscure, but it was said to be descended from the Orthodox Hungarian family of the Petrovichi, who had held high rank in the Hungarian kingdom in the first half of the fifteenth century, and from a Lithuanian family descended from the Mongol warlord Mamay (not a Genghisid). Mikhail Glinsky had, in his youth, spent twelve years, in Italy, become a Catholic, and fought in the army of the Elector Albert of Saxony and then in that of Albert's son Frederick, Grand Master of the Teutonic Order. In the 1490s he was very influential in the government of Lithuania but in 1506, after the death of King Alexander, he was disgraced, went over to the pro-Russian party, deserted Lithuania and entered Russian service in 1508 with his two brothers Ivan and Vasily (father of Elena). He received both estates on a service tenure and *kormlenie*, the allocation of the income of provinces or towns on a temporary basis. This was a new policy adopted with regard to incoming princes, which provided amply for their status and upkeep without granting them the sovereign rights inherent in an appanage. Mikhail Glinsky assisted Grand Prince Vasily in the conquest of Smolensk in 1514, which had allegedly been promised to him as an appanage, a promise which Vasily did not keep. The outraged Mikhail Glinsky then thought of returning to Lithuania but was suspected of secret talks with its king, Sigismund I, arrested and confined in a prison in chains. An indication of the regard in which Mikhail Glinsky was held is that the Emperor Maximilian I asked for his release through Herberstein, but Vasily III refused, though Glinsky had reverted to Orthodoxy, and he also at first refused his wife Elena's appeals to release her uncle. Mikhail Glinsky was finally freed in February 1527 and married into the Russian nobility. But a large number of boyars and nobles had to put up the enormous sum of five thousand rubles among them as a guarantee that he would not attempt to flee again.[23] Glinsky knew both Latin and German, most likely Italian as well, and had more information about the world outside Russia than any other magnate at that time, which he no doubt communicated verbally to Vasily and the Russian courtiers when he was not in prison.[24]

Elena Glinskaia's mother was also well connected. She was Anna, a daughter of the Serbian *voevoda* Stefan Iakshich. She married the Lithuanian Prince Vasily L'vovich Glinsky. Her sister Elena married Jovan, the Despot of Serbia, and their daughter, also Elena, known as 'despotitsa', later married Peter Raresh, the bastard son of Stephen the Great of Moldavia, and *voevoda* of Moldavia.[25] The two Elenas were thus first cousins. The Russian Grand Prince may have thought that maintaining the connexion with the Orthodox ruler of Moldavia might be useful, and Peter Raresh sent an envoy to Moscow in 1538 to discuss an alliance against Poland–Lithuania.[26] Russian relations with Orthodox Moldavia continued to play a part in Russian foreign policy under Vasily III and Ivan IV.

Vasily was unlike his father. He was not grim or forbidding and, though equally ruthless, could even be quite amiable. He was noble in appearance, with penetrating but not frightening eyes, and seems to have been slightly more moderate in his use of savage punishments than his father and his son. He welcomed foreigners to Russia, either as soldiers or as craftsmen, and though he personally enjoyed a country life, he kept up a magnificent court. He increased the numbers of court ranks and employees, and introduced the *ryndy*, young armed pages of good family and exceptional good looks, who stood around the Grand Prince and the throne in their white and gold robes, like a 'guard of angels'. One cannot envisage angels with beards, and one might note here in passing that in the miniatures that enliven the illustrated Chronicles very many young, beardless, men appear to be fulfilling various functions from waiting on the Grand Prince to executing his enemies. One explanation for their shaven faces has been offered, namely that it indicates that they are too young to be allotted responsible tasks to perform. The *ryndy* surrounding the Grand Prince must have belonged to this group. He too is said to have shaved his beard occasionally to please his new wife.

Vasily also put on specially lavish shows to welcome visiting ambassadors, ordering the closure of shops and the ceasing of all work, so that the common people could attend the Kremlin in their best clothes and be impressed by the grand princely power. The foreign envoys were solemnly received by the Grand Prince sitting on his throne, surrounded by his boyars in their rich clothes embroidered with pearls and their high fur hats (often loaned by the Grand Prince – Henry VIII also lent clothes to his courtiers). At the ensuing banquet, which might well last several hours, the first course was invariably roast swan. The Grand Prince might personally send food as a sign of distinction to a guest who would rise and bow in acknowledgement. To pass the time during these lengthy ceremonies the guests were allowed to speak freely to each other, which makes one wonder what happened at other times.[27]

As Russia extended its relations with central European powers, Muscovite bookmen joined in the European pastime of laying claim to ancient, classical descent as a means of asserting the right of precedence among the nations then beginning to take shape. The most important Russian attempt, both in literary form and in pictorial form, was the Tale of the Princes of Vladimir.[28] This literary composition dating from the early 1520s develops the legend that the grand princes of Rus' descended from Prus, the brother of the Emperor Augustus, and that the regalia for their coronation were presented by the Emperor Constantine Monomakh to his descendant the Grand Prince Vladimir Monomakh, an anachronistic and farcical claim since the Emperor Constantine died when Vladimir Monomakh was two years old. The historical element in this tale is splendidly imaginary. Alexander the Great was the son by Olympias of the Egyptian king and magician Nectanebo; after the death of her husband, Olympias returned to her father, the Tsar of Ethiopia, married a relative called Visa, and gave birth to a daughter, Antia. Visa founded 'Tsargrad', the city of the Tsar, and called it Vizantia after his daughter. Later, Julius, the Roman Emperor, sent his brother-in-law Antony to Egypt. Antony conquered Egypt and married its queen, Cleopatra. The Emperor Julius then sent his brother Augustus to put an end to this disorder, and Augustus killed Antony. But meanwhile Julius's generals, Brutus, Pompey and Crassus, rose against him and killed him, whereupon Augustus returned to Rome and became emperor, appointing his brother Patricius as king of Egypt and Herod as king of the Jews in Jerusalem. And 'Pion he made ruler in the Golden Lands today called the Ungarian lands'. He appointed various other rulers, and sent his kinsman Prus to rule in the lands of the Vistula and Niemen, and in Danzig. 'And Prus lived a very long time, until the fourth generation, and until now these lands are called the Prussian lands.' And a certain *voevoda* of Novgorod, Gostomysl, advised his subjects on his 'death bed to send to Prussia for a ruler, and they did so and found Riurik'. The tale now links up with the chronicle known as The Tale of Bygone Years, in which Riurik and his brothers, together with their nephew Oleg, arrive to take over the government of Rus', not from Prussia, but from Scandinavia.

At the same time a genealogy of the Lithuanian grand princes and the legendary story of the origin of the first Lithuanian Grand Prince, Gedimin, was produced. In view of the constant rivalry with Lithuania at that time for leadership over the lands of Rus', Gedimin is given a much more lowly origin. A certain princeling, Vityanets, was killed by lightning, whereupon his wife took as her second husband a servant, a groom called Gedimenik, and had seven sons. He was a brave man and brought order into the lands and became known as the Grand Prince Gedimin of Lithuania.[29]

In the reign of Ivan IV these fantasies were to take on real importance in negotiations with, for instance, Sweden and Poland–Lithuania, and the

Riurikovich descent from the Emperor Augustus was constantly stressed. Such genealogies served to give historical dignity to the grand princes of All Russia, to raise them in the eyes of their subjects and of other European powers, which were also busily creating mythological ancestors for themselves – drawn mainly from Greek heroes and Roman emperors.[30] The concept of 'tsar' as meaning emperor was already beginning to glimmer on the political horizon.[31]

Foreigners who visited Russia, starting with Herberstein,[32] were deeply impressed by the immense powers seemingly enjoyed by the Grand Prince, and there is no doubt that there were but few if any institutional barriers to his will, though there were undoubtedly intangible obstacles and an all-pervading need to solve conflicts by means of consensus and conciliation. Nevertheless, the historian should be aware that Herberstein's observation on the extent of the power of the Grand Prince, which has been reproduced by many subsequent travellers to Russia, and hence echoes down the *aulae* of history, deserves the same sort of analysis as any other historical source. What was Herberstein comparing Russia with?[33] One remark by one man is not enough on which to build a whole theory of government.

Herberstein was partly influenced by three Russian practices that he observed and which struck him as alien. These were the use of the formula 'I strike my forehead' (understood: on the ground) as a means of petitioning higher authority; the use of the diminutive – Ivashka, Fedka (Johnny, Teddy) – when speaking of oneself to the grand prince; and describing oneself as the 'slave' (*kholop*) of the tsar. If these formulae were taken literally they implied of course the existence of an enormous distance between the ruler and the ruled, and of the sort of slavery that was regarded as typical of, for instance, the Ottoman empire. (The fact that there were still slaves in Europe is often disregarded.) Yet these phrases give a misleading impression. To beat one's head (*bit' chelom*) when making a petition might have started out as a physical act of prostration on the ground, but it had long since declined into a ceremonial formula which, in the words of a modern student of the question, served to express a 'humble greeting', to request or make a complaint, or as a ceremonial form of expressing deference.[34] Physically it took the form of bowing low, and touching the ground with one hand. A number of modern non-Russian historians of Russia who are slow to perceive the many shades of meaning in words and actions regard the formula as expressing a real situation. But it came to be used between any two people when one was requesting a favour and on occasion it was used by Ivan IV to the Metropolitan Makarii.

The use of the word '*kholop*', usually translated as 'slave' today, was another feature of Muscovite life which shocked some foreigners. It is unfortunate that the word slave has been generally adopted to express what was a wider and far more varied concept. 'Slave', today, usually means, to the ordinary Anglophone, a victim of black plantation slavery. The Russian *kholop* was more often a domestic servant who did not work the land; he belonged to one of many different orders, including élite slavery (among the literate or the military), debt slavery or voluntary enslavement, lifelong, hereditary or limited. *Kholopy* were in any case psychologically quite different from chattel slaves in the New (and Old) World since both slave and master in Russia normally spoke the same language and practised the same religion.[35] Marshall Poe, in his article on the subject, makes much of the use of the word *gosudar*' (lord) as master or lord or owner of slaves in a 'patrimonial' regime. He seems to lose sight of the actual root of the word patrimonial, namely the Latin *pater* or father. In many contexts, particularly the context of the Christian religion, the lord was the father of the members of his household who were his children, his servants or his slaves. This does not imply that all masters behaved with Christian forbearance to those in their power, whether children or slaves, but the texture of their relationship was a domestic one.

Poe also, in accordance with current fashion, ascribes great importance to Tatar influence in establishing the Russian pattern of deference. However, he only briefly mentions the far more important current flowing from the Eastern Roman Empire, where the Greek word *doulos* had evolved away from its original meaning of 'slave' to signify a title applicable to someone who was acting for the emperor. The 'prince of princes' of Armenia, for instance, was said to be the '*doulos* of the emperor of the Romans', he was someone who served without being a servant. It could in fact mean a 'subject' of the ruler, something for which a word did not yet exist in Russian. *Kholop* could, of course, mean a slave in the literal sense, but it could mean many other things. There are innumerable shades of meaning on the slippery slope between slave and servant.[36]

Turning to institutions of government, there were very few. The Russian tradition, deriving probably from the Vikings, both in the Grand Principality of Moscow and in the appanage principalities, had been to consult with senior men of military reputation, rank, wealth and standing who formed a kind of council. Vasily, who was reported to have preferred to discuss policy in small groups, had allowed the number of boyars formally appointed to the Boyar Council to drop to six in

1521. He gradually increased the number to eleven after his marriage, in what has been described as a process of 'aristocratizing' the Council, namely increasing the relative weight of old princely and appanage families. But members of old Moscow boyar families, including Mikhail Iur'evich Zakhar'in, the uncle of Ivan IV's future wife, also belonged to the Council.[37] There were in fact not very many princely appanage families left after the havoc created by the fifteenth-century civil wars and the reigns of Vasily II and Ivan III. The most prominent princely families were now either relatives of the ruling dynasty (Andrei of Staritsa and Iuri of Dmitrov, brothers of Vasily), or of Lithuanian descent, like the Mstislavsky, Bel'sky and Glinsky families, who were given lands and *kormlenia*, like Mikhail Glinsky, but were not always appointed to the Boyar Council; or they might be Russian families who had redeserted from Lithuania to Russia with what remained to them of their own lands, or borderline families like the group of princes whose base was on the Upper Oka river – Vorotynsky, Odoevsky, Trubetskoy; or they might be Riurikids, like the princes of Suzdal', where the very numerous descendants of the founders of the city of Vladimir were concentrated and formed a solid, related group, 'united by a consciousness of a right to participate together with the monarch in the government of the country'. Among the latter the princes of Shuia (Shuisky) regarded themselves as the senior branch, because they were descended from Andrei, a brother of Alexander Nevsky from whom the princes of Moscow descended.[38]

Insofar as princes and boyars participated in the government of the country as a whole, it was through the Boyar Council. This institution is often wrongly portrayed as a representative body, which it was not. It was a Privy Council, varying in size according to the wishes of the grand prince, to which appointments were made by the grand prince on the basis of the status of individuals in terms of their birth and service rank, the services performed by their ancestors, the personal regard in which the grand prince held them, and their usefulness. The system was known as *mestnichestvo,* and served to integrate men of high rank originating in different principalities into the service of Moscow. A high-ranking noble might, as a first stage, be appointed to the lower rank of *okol'nichi*, a court rank. He could then be given the title of boyar, which normally made him a member of the Council.[39] The system was then extended to military appointments, where it created many problems, for senior boyars brought legal suits against appointments which did not reflect the existing status relationships, and refused to serve under a man whose family was of lower rank.

There were also a number of *d'iaki* (derived from *diakonos*) on the Council, who might belong to modest landowning families, or sometimes to merchant or clerical families, and who carried out administrative and secretarial tasks and were literate. They were frequently heads of *prikazy*, or government administrative bureaux. But not all boyars were members of the Council, and not all members of the Council were boyars, and many boyars were literate.

The Grand Prince, however, did not have a completely free hand in appointments to the Council. *Mestnichestvo,* the system of family precedence according to rank in service had not yet fully developed, but it was already sufficiently anchored to compel the Grand Prince at least to listen to complaints, even if he overrode them and occasionally made appointments 'without place'. In practice a system had developed whereby great families took it in turn to be appointed to vacancies in the military high command or in the Boyar Council, with strict attention to the rights of older generations. But within the actual administration based on the court, the Grand Prince had a free hand to appoint according to ability and experience. Quite how much power the Boyar Council exercised, as an institution, as distinct from the influence of individuals, is very difficult to assess. There is no record of a session of the whole Council, but then some members were often away from Moscow as *namestniki* or Lieutenants of the Grand Prince in the provinces. Laws, or edicts, according to the Chronicles, were issued by the 'the Grand Prince and his boyars'. When Nicolas Poppel offered Ivan III a throne on the part of the Emperor Maximilian, he was received by the Grand Prince and two boyars. Vasily III was reputed not to consult the Council as an institution, but this depends on the statement of only one disgruntled noble, who was eventually executed (Bersen' Beklemishev) – perhaps one of Herberstein's informants.

Boyars were consulted about Vasily's divorce in 1523, and they took part in the Councils that convicted Maksim Grek in 1525 and Vassian Patrikeev in 1531. Boyars took an important part in judicial matters in accordance with the Code of Ivan III of 1497, but decisions which were recorded as taken by the 'Grand Prince in conjunction with his boyars' were in fact often taken by him together with only a few boyars, or perhaps with *okol'nichi*, and sometimes merely with *d'iaki*. Boyars sometimes acted as members of ad hoc bodies, called 'commissions' by Russian historians, to which the grand prince delegated the power of decision in judicial matters. They also participated in the discussion of foreign policy and in the reception of ambassadors. But not all important matters went before the Council; the Grand Prince was free to choose his advisers and, like other rulers in other lands, he had favourites at any given time. Clearly the composition, function and powers of the Council fluctuated widely, and the Grand Prince decided whether to put matters before the Council or whether to discuss them with senior officials, or with favourites.[40]

There were no counts or dukes in Russia. There was in fact no nobility, in the sense used in the Latin world, but there was an aristocracy.[41] Boyar and *sluga* (servant) were the only titles grand princes awarded. The title *sluga* was given to high-ranking princes mainly from the western borderlands, such as the Vorotynsky princes or the Bel'skys, who as vassals of the Grand Prince lost their autonomy as appanage princes; but some Riurikovichi in the eastern lands also were given the title, for instance Prince Alexander Gorbaty-Shuisky. The *sluga* ranked above boyars on the *mestnichestvo* ladder.[42] Otherwise the highest social rank was enjoyed by appanage princes belonging to, or closely linked by marriage to, the ruling family, and by Riurikid princes who had not been impoverished by the continuous fragmentation of landed property and multiplication of claimants. But there were innumerable princes because of a feature of Russian social evolution which weakened the élite politically, socially and economically – this was the practice of partible inheritance.

Just as the grand princes divided their patrimony among their sons, so all the princes divided their inheritance among their sons, and all their children, male and female, inherited the princely title. There were thus as many as eighty Princes Iaroslavsky, which naturally devalued their rank.[43] Boyar nobles, descendants of old Muscovite boyar families, often ranked higher than these frequently landless princelings, or than the families which came over from Lithuania with but little land and no history.[44] Lower-ranking boyars, however, did not quarrel over precedence with service princes, i.e. princes who had no appanages, until they too began to invade the Council.

However, the aristocracy, and possibly to a greater extent the service gentry, had evolved a strategy for defending themselves against the impoverishment created by partible inheritance which has only now begun to be studied in some detail. The service gentry were protected by the entitlement of their sons to land from the Estate Office (Pomestnyi Prikaz) when they achieved majority and would be expected to serve. This helped to increase the total acreage available to a family. There was also an active market in land in which estates were exchanged or dowries sold, in order to consolidate lands for a family.[45]

Chapter III
Ivan's Birth, Childhood, Adolescence, Coronation and Marriage

Elena Glinskaia did not at once fulfil Vasily's expectations; he had to wait five years for the birth of her first son, Ivan, on 25 August 1530, during which she spent much time in religious pilgrimages, seeking divine intervention in the conception of her son.[1] (The delay did also give rise to some suspicions that Vasily might not be the father of the child.) Ivan's birth, and that of his brother Iuri on 30 October 1532, were marked by the appearance of three comets between 1531 and 1533, terrible storms and in 1533 a frightful drought, which lasted three months, during which neither the sun nor the moon could be seen for four weeks, travellers could not see their way, nor recognize each other, and birds could not spread their wings in the heavy air.[2] There is evidence that at the age of three Ivan suffered from what has been described as scrofula, but may well have been a carbuncle. Carbuncles and boils are evidence of vitamin B deficiency, scrofula of tuberculosis. Since Ivan was hale and hearty during adolescence and young manhood, the former is the more likely.[3]

Vasily III died, unexpectedly, on 4 February 1533, at the age of fifty-four, seemingly as the result of a hunting injury which became infected, leaving one son of three and a baby. Anticipating a dangerous situation for his heir he had made a new will,[4] setting up a Regency Council of seven members, some of whom were also members of the Boyar Council, though the two institutions were not the same. He added new members, including the boyar Mikhail Iur'evich Zakhar'in, who was close to him, and the latter's nephew, M.V. Tuchkov Morozov, and also Prince Ivan Vasil'evich Shuisky of the aristocratic Suzdal' princely clan. In addition he specifically appointed Elena's uncle Mikhail L'vovich Glinsky to the Regency Council in spite of his long period in prison, because he was of the family of the Grand Princess, had no claim to the throne and could therefore be relied on to take care of the personal safety of Elena and the young Ivan.[5] (Perhaps he remembered how he had himself treated the young Grand Prince Dmitri Ivanovich?) After touching scenes with his desolate wife and his children, Vasily turned his attention to the other world and asked to be shorn as a monk before his death. This traditional ritual had not been carried out by his father, Ivan III, who had firmly declared his intention of dying as a grand prince.[6] But Vasily, who may well have been influenced in his spiritual life by his second cousin Vassian Patrikeev, insisted at least in being buried as a monk, in spite of the opposition of some of the boyars, who even snatched away the monk's robe from the dying man. Finally the Metropolitan intervened, and in a voice of thunder proclaimed that he would not bless those who were trying to seize Vasily's soul from him, in this century or in the next, and that 'a silver dish was a good thing but a gilt one was better'. When Vasily was in his death throes, the Metropolitan produced the monastic garb just in time to enable the Grand Prince to be shorn as the monk Varlaam.[7] They say, concludes Karamzin the historian, that Vasily's face lit up at once and the terrible stench from his wound was dissipated.[8]

But with the accession of a young heir in the charge of a Grand Princess in her early twenties, the direction of the central government slackened. Whether on Elena's initiative or that of the boyars, a new member was added to the Council in January 1534, Prince Ivan Telepnev Obolensky, and it was soon rumoured that he was the Grand Princess's lover. Acting together with her, Obolensky proceeded to eliminate potential dangers such as the younger brothers of Vasily III, Iuri of Dmitrov and Andrei of Staritsa (who might well become rivals of the younger Grand Prince). Iuri was a popular prince and, in circumstances that remain obscure, a plot was devised to compromise him in a conspiracy to seize the throne. Whatever the truth, by 11 December 1534 he had been arrested together with his boyars and followers and lodged in that same palace prison where Grand Prince Dmitri had died in 1509. Iuri died of hunger three years later. Other princes fled to Lithuania. The Grand Princess's uncle, Mikhail L'vovich Glinsky, condemned her policies or her private behaviour, or both. He was accused of attempting to seize the crown and sent back by his niece to the very prison where he had already spent twelve years, and where he too soon starved to death. Andrei of Staritsa was the next to be trapped in an alleged plot, arrested and placed in irons, his wife and young son imprisoned, in 1537. His boyars were particularly ruthlessly treated, tortured in spite of their princely rank, and some thirty members of his retinue of service gentry were flogged and hanged at intervals on the road to Novgorod. But both Iuri and Andrei were solemnly buried as members of the Grand Prince's family in the Archangel Cathedral in the Kremlin. Thus potential rivals for the throne were quickly eliminated, leaving only Ivan's young cousin Vladimir Andreevich of Staritsa, at the time under arrest. The cruelty manifested by Elena's regime and the dishonour inflicted on a number of princes of noble family by public execution, without any form of trial, lowered her government in public esteem and led to an increasingly brutal treatment of the privileged élite.[9]

How much Elena herself actually influenced the government it is impossible to say. But as a government it undertook several positive measures, such as the introduction of elected officials in the provinces to deal with brigandage (*gubnye starosty*); the building of a new defensive wall around Moscow, this time enclosing what came to be known as the Kitaigorod (middle town); attracting settlers from Lithuania; ransoming prisoners; and introducing a currency reform and a new coin, the *kopek*. Then, seemingly without warning, according to Herberstein, this healthy and relatively young woman, who spent much time visiting monasteries, died in 1538. Inevitably, the rumour spread that she had been poisoned.[10] She was buried the same day, without much ceremony, apparently unmourned, except probably by her eight-year-old son.

Deprived of his mother's protection, and by her of the protection of his maternal and paternal uncles, the young Ivan's life seems now to have entered a particularly unhappy period. Prince Vasily Vasil'evich Shuisky, one of the executors of Grand Prince Vasily's will, took control of the Council and within seven days Ivan's governess, Agrafena Chelyadnina, a sister of Telepnev Obolensky, and Obolensky himself had been seized and were in chains in spite of Ivan's wails. Agrippina was sent to a convent in Kargopol', and Obolensky himself suffered the fate he had inflicted on members of Ivan's family: he was starved to death in the prison to which he had condemned Mikhail Glinsky.[11]

It is at this point that one can pick up Ivan IV's own story of what happened to him in the ensuing years, as he described it many years later in his first letter to Prince A.M. Kurbsky, dated July 1564.[12] There is no reason to suppose that Ivan's own account is more reliable than those of the surviving Chronicles, but it gives his own special slant on events. Once Obolensky had been eliminated, Ivan felt himself quite alone and unprotected, 'receiving no human care from any quarter'. His brother Iuri was too young to be of any help and in any case would have been unable to help him, for the child had been born deaf and dumb. It is possible that he was mentally quite normal, but at that time no one knew how to teach a deaf child how to speak. He was later to take part in

Ivan's coronation, being charged with flinging silver and gold coins in his brother's path on the way to and from the cathedrals in the Kremlin, and he sat 'one yard away' from Ivan when the latter received ambassadors in the Kremlin.[13]

The most senior and authoritative boyar, Prince Vasily Vasil'evich Shuisky, and his brother Ivan Vasil'evich, dominated the Council and together with their cronies seized and distributed posts and riches without any reference to the Council, let alone the youthful heir. In an effort to consolidate his relationship with the Grand Prince's family, at the age of fifty-four, Vasily Shuisky married the young Anastasia, daughter of the converted Tatar Tsarevich Peter, Vasily III's brother-in-law and one of the latter's most trustworthy and trusted friends. Vasily Shuisky moved into the palace of Prince Andrei Ivanovich of Staritsa (killed as mentioned above by order of Elena Glinskaia and Telepnev Obolensky) and behaved 'as in a Jewish synagogue';[14] one of the leading *d'iaki*, or officials, who was a member of the Regency Council appointed by Grand Prince Vasily, was executed in a humiliating and cruel manner without any trial; and Prince Ivan Fedorovich Bel'sky was released from the prison in which he had been thrown by the Regent Elena, but the Shuiskys locked him up again. Fortunately, Vasily Shuisky died suddenly at the peak of his power, leaving the senior position in the Council to his brother, Ivan Vasil'evich. The next victim was the Metropolitan Daniil, who was deposed without any consultation with a Church Council or the boyars, and who was replaced by Metropolitan Joseph. These court conflicts were not over policies or principles, but entirely concerned with power and the distribution of lands and riches.

Ivan describes the ill-treatment he and his brother Iuri suffered at this time, in possibly exaggerated terms, because the alleged lack of respect and the informality of the Shuiskys brothers' behaviour deeply offended his dignity as Grand Prince. According to his later recollections, Ivan and Iuri were ill-fed and hungry, and nothing was done as Ivan wished. He wrote: 'I . . .recall one thing: whilst we were playing childish games in our infancy Prince Vasily Vasil'evich Shuisky was sitting on a bench, leaning with his elbows on our father's bed, and with his leg upon a chair.' Shuisky treated the young Grand Prince rudely, he did not bow his head to him either in a fatherly manner or as a master or as a servant: 'And who can endure such arrogance,' exclaims the young Ivan. He describes how Ivan Shuisky, in the struggle to control the Boyar Council, arrested Grand Prince Ivan's own followers, such as Prince Ivan Fedorovich Bel'sky, exiled and even murdered them, drove out the Metropolitan Daniil, invaded his, Ivan's, dining-chamber and seized his favourite, the boyar F.S. Vorontsov, 'and having put him to shame, wanted to kill him'. Ironically enough, it was thanks to the intercession of the newly appointed Metropolitan Makarii that Vorontsov's life was saved, only for him to be executed at Ivan's orders not much later. 'Is it right', exclaims Ivan, 'for a servant to have intercourse with us, his lord, or for a lord to beg favours from a servant?'[15] In May 1542 Ivan Vasil'evich Shuisky died, last of the members of the Regency Council appointed by Vasily III. The only remaining Shuisky Prince Andrei Mikhailovich was unable to command the support of members of the Council and was beaten to death by the personal order of the thirteen-year-old Grand Prince in 1543.

Nothing is known of the education of Ivan except by inference. From a young age he was present with his mother when foreign envoys were received, and on one occasion he spoke to them in Tatar. Whether this was a phrase learnt by heart for the occasion, or whether he actually spoke the language as a child is not known. After the death of his mother and her lover (if he was her lover) there was no one man whose duty it was to educate the Prince for his role as a ruler, no male role model, to use modern jargon. It is not impossible that the children of the Tatar Tsarevich Peter at court were his playmates, and they would perhaps speak Tatar together. He almost certainly knew the language later in life because of the large number of Tatars at his court and in his service in the armed forces. It is also possible that the young Vladimir Andreevich of Staritsa, once he was released, was another playmate, as for many years the cousins were friends. Later, Ivan would often leave Vladimir in charge in Moscow when he left the capital for any reason, and Vladimir's mother, the formidable Princess Evfrosin'ya, may have had a role at court when she and her son were finally allowed back. The boy Grand Prince presumably had the usual cohort of dwarfs and fools and *skomorokhi* (minstrels, clowns, buffoons, etc.) to laugh at. Less agreeable, indeed ominous, was the boy's pleasure in throwing animals down from high towers to be smashed to pieces on the ground.

With adolescence the range of Ivan's activities increased. He was evidently fond of the chase and spent a lot of time hunting bears and other wild animals. A record of his travels in 1544, 1545 and 1546 shows that he was constantly on the move in spring and summer, nearly always with his brother Iuri, and often with his cousin Prince Vladimir of Staritsa. These hunting expeditions were combined with pilgrimages to many important monasteries, attendance at church services, and the giving of alms and gifts for memorial services.[16] On 21 May 1545 Ivan went to the Troitsky monastery, then to Pereiaslavl', and leaving his companions to return to Moscow, he continued to Rostov, to the Kirillov monastery at Beloozero, to the Ferapont monastery, to Vologda, Prilutsky, Kornilov, Pavlov, Boris and Gleb on the Ust'ia, then again on 15 September he was at the Troitsky monastery, in Aleksandrovskaia Sloboda, and in Mozhaisk for the hunting.[17] It is possible that on his travels in 1545 Ivan was in contact with Maksim Grek, who addressed two missives to the young Grand Prince at that time, with advice on how to be a good ruler: a genuine tsar strives after justice, issues good laws and tries to conquer his evil passions, namely malice, anger and the lawless caprices of the flesh; he closes his ears to slander.[18] Also around this time the priest Sylvester admonished the young Grand Prince, asking him to send young people guilty of sodomy away from his court.[19]

Judging by his letters to Kurbsky, and by his *poslania* (missives), which he had probably dictated, since writing was often at that time considered a menial occupation fit only for clerks,[20] Ivan was very familiar with both the New and the Old Testaments and with the Apocrypha. Indeed, he must have been surrounded by priests and have attended numerous church services every day, which imbued him with a deeply religious image of the world. Biblical language and dramatic symbolic images were ideally suited to his passionate, poetic and angry imagination. He was also familiar with many sermons and homilies by the fathers of the Orthodox Church, and must have been taught the catechism and the psalter, which he probably heard so often in church services that he knew it by heart. He appears also to have enjoyed singing in church. Was Ivan able to read? Or were tales read to him? Learning to read is not, after all, so difficult – even a sixteenth-century Russian manuscript.

At some stage Ivan must have become acquainted with the Tale of the Princes of Vladimir,[21] since it formed the subject of one of the most dramatic propaganda frescoes on the walls of the Dormition Cathedral in the Kremlin and the Russian princes' descent from the Emperor Augustus Caesar's brother Prus was worked into the liturgy for Ivan's coronation. Did he know the Tale of Dracula, based on *voevoda* Vlad Ţepeş Dracul, who ruled Wallachia from 1456 to 1462 and again in 1477?[22] It may well have been another influence on Ivan's attitude to his subjects, possibly connected with his family background through his mother. Around 1458–60 Vlad Ţepeş Dracul, already famous for his cruelty, had invaded Transylvania (then under Hungarian control). Stories of the atrocities he committed on that occasion against the Saxon towns were current in the court of King Matthias Corvinus of Hungary, and records of Dracul's lurid doings were carried away to the monastery of St Gallen in Switzerland by Catholic monks who escaped the Turkish advance. The invention of printing made the reproduction of tales of Dracul's real or imaginary atrocities into the best-selling horror stories of the age in the German-speaking world.[23]

When Fedor Kuritsyn was sent by Ivan III, in 1482–4, on an embassy to Matthias Corvinus of Hungary and Stephen the Great of Moldavia, he met the widow and children of Vlad Ţepeş Dracul in Buda, and could have found some things out for himself. A group of narratives of the Dracula tales, written in Church Slavonic, the only written language of Wallachia, found its way, probably by means of Orthodox monks fleeing from the Turks, possibly by means of Kuritsyn, to the monastery of Beloozero. They were then put together by Evfrosin, the well-known copyist and later abbot of the monastery, and cast a somewhat different light on Dracula as a ruler severe and cruel not for cruelty's sake but for the sake of his subjects.[24]

As we know, Ivan IV was a frequent visitor to this monastery, and it is not unlikely that he read these tales or had them read to him. On the whole they belong to the species folklore and propaganda rather than true stories: propaganda which proliferated in the wake of the constant and savage warfare between different national groups (Germans, Wallachians, Poles, Hungarians, Turks) breaking in great waves over people living in fear of what the next day and the next world might bring. Impaling his enemies may well have been a form of execution borrowed later by Ivan from the Ottoman Empire through Wallachia and tales of Vlad the Impaler. It does not seem to have been used by Russian rulers either earlier or later. It was not extensively used by Ivan, but mainly, it seems, where he felt particular personal vindictiveness, or against service gentry and boyars who fled to Lithuania. A moment's reflection will show that it was not a very practical form of execution on a large scale, and there are no reports of impalements in Russia similar to the equally unlikely reports of the executions carried out as Vlad Ţepeş sat down to his dinner. The English representative of the Russia Company, Jerome Horsey, reports one case, and for good measure throws in that the victim's wife was made to watch the death throes of her husband and was subsequently raped by a hundred gunners – again hard to believe.[25]

Tales of the heroic deeds of past princes, such as the Tale of Dmitri Donskoi's victory over the Tatars in 1380 and the *Alexander Romance* (dealing with Alexander the Great and widely read throughout Europe), together with *byliny* (heroic ballads) and fairy tales, probably formed the background to Ivan's childhood and adolescence. The coming of the last Emperor and of Antichrist, foretelling the end of the world, and the Last Time, were also subjects frequently dealt with, as well as the Homilies on the Second Coming of Christ, ascribed to Ephraim the Syrian, and the Tale of Christ and Antichrist, ascribed to Hippolytus of Rome. Fears of the end of the world were revived by the fall of Constantinople in, for instance, the Tale of the Fall of Tsar'grad, in which the returning emperor defeats the Ishmaelites and is crowned in the Church of St Sophia in the Last Days. At some stage Ivan probably saw the *Secretum secretorum*, a mirror of princes, said to have been written by Aristotle for the education of Alexander the Great.[26] Judging by his letters to Kurbsky, Ivan was familiar with tales from the *Iliad*.[27] He was also certainly familiar with the *chet'i-mineii* or menologies, comprising collections of extracts from the Bible, the Apocrypha, the writings of the Christian Fathers, sermons and homilies, grouped according to dates in the Christian calendar. At some stage, too, Ivan must have been introduced to the Chronographs, which dealt with world history, and to the Chronicles themselves, for which the material was collected in the court and some of which were composed in all probability in the Office of Foreign Affairs. Could Ivan write? No writing which has been identified as his has survived, but this proves nothing.[28]

In his first letter to Kurbsky, written in 1564, Ivan hints at unworthy pursuits, youthful vandalism, possibly chasing after women with a band of friends and failure to observe church rituals,[29] and in his *History of Ivan IV*, Kurbsky accuses the Tsar of committing real acts of brigandage and other evil deeds, 'unbefitting to relate, but shameful too'.[30] There is little evidence of Ivan's misbehaviour apart from his own confessions, but there is an obscure reference to something much more serious in a group of documents which suggest that in 1546 and early 1547, when Ivan was preparing for his coronation and his marriage, he also indulged in some of the most savage persecutions of those who had been his friends.

The source is a *vypis'*, or note, on the second marriage of Vasily III. Included in this document is a so-called 'prophecy after the event', attributed to an eastern patriarch who foretold that the son of an adulterous union, like Vasily's second marriage, would be a 'torturer, and a pillager of other people's property', and described the way in which a number of princes were cruelly put to death. In July 1546 Ivan was in Kolomna with his army, and executed three of his boyars in front of his soldiers, for their entertainment, including F.S. Vorontsov, whom Metropolitan Makarii had once saved by interceding for him with the

Shuiskys (see above p. 43). The patriarch's 'prophecy' is supported by entries in other regional chronicles to the effect that in 1547, while Ivan was inspecting the girls in his bride-show, he was also ordering the execution of Telepnev Obolensky's son, who was impaled opposite the walls of the Kremlin, and the beheading of Obolensky's nephew, 'at the request of his [Ivan's] uncle Mikhail Vasil'evich Glinsky and his mother Anna'. A fifteen-year-old princeling was also dispatched, to the disgust of Kurbsky.[31]

One person may have played a limited, if formative, part in the education of Ivan. This was Metropolitan Makarii. Born around 1480, Makarii, who was probably not from a military family, was created Metropolitan in 1542, when he was already over sixty. He started out in life as a monk in the Pafnut'ev-Borovskii monastery, which in the 1470s had been the centre of the school of icon-painting associated with the monk Dionisi. It is probably here that Makarii learnt icon-painting, and the monastery may have influenced his own spiritual and aesthetic conceptions. After a period in Mozhaisk, in 1526 Makarii was appointed – apparently by the wish of Vasily III – Archbishop of Novgorod, a see which had been left vacant for seventeen years. A fervent upholder of the primacy of Moscow, Makarii was a non-fanatical follower of Iosif Volotsky, who immediately introduced monastic communal living in Novgorod, and upheld the monastic right to own land. He also supported the construction of many churches in Novgorod, an activity which had seriously declined after Ivan III's last devastation of the city in 1478. As Archbishop of Novgorod, Makarii had exercised to the full the ecclesiastical privilege of interceding for prisoners, the poor and orphans, and those in disgrace with the government in Moscow, and thus won the esteem of the Novgorodians.

In his striving to raise the level of Russian culture Makarii, as he wrote himself, collected all the holy writings he could find and had them transcribed: the Holy Gospel, the Holy Apostol (Acts and Epistles of the Apostles), the three great psalters, the books of St John of the Golden Mouth (Chrysostom), and of Basil the Great and Grigorii Bogoslov, the Jewish Wars of Josephus, extracts from the works of Iosif of Volokolamsk, all the prophetic and apostolic books, the Apocrypha, the lives of saints and martyrs, the writings of the Church Fathers, and even the lives of the new saints whose canonization Makarii himself had arranged. He grouped them into twelve books of readings for the twelve months, which formed the *Great Menology* (*Velikii chet'i minei*). The first set of twelve books was prepared, Makarii explains, in the twelve years while he was Archbishop in Novgorod.[32] A copy was sent to the

Grand Prince, and there is evidence that Ivan IV later in life made use of the texts included there.[33]

It is also possible that, through Makarii, Ivan may have been introduced to the *Stikhi pokaiannye* (*Poems of Repentance*), which emerged in the course of the fifteenth and sixteenth centuries and became a self-contained form of literary expression: they were sung hymns to be used during the great fasts on the themes of the evanescence of life and the sinfulness of mortal man, and served to prepare the soul for the passage to the next world. They are very lovely poems, and would certainly appeal to one of Ivan's temperament, as far as we know it.

> Adam wept tears, sitting outside paradise
> Paradise, my paradise, oh my beautiful paradise
> For me, paradise, were you created,
> And because of Eve you were closed
> Woe to me a sinner
> Woe to me for not listening
> I have sinned lord, I have sinned
> And I disobeyed the command
> No more shall I see the heavenly food
> Nor hear the voices of archangels
> I have sinned lord, I have sinned
> Gracious God, have mercy on a fallen man.[34]

Raised to the position of Metropolitan of Russia in 1542, Makarii began to play an important part in the court of the young Ivan. It is extremely unlikely that a man of the cloth and of his scholarly temperament should have been indifferent to the welfare of the young prince, then about twelve years old, and should have failed to take steps to instruct him or have him instructed. There is no doubt that until at any rate 1560 Ivan treated Makarii with great respect and possibly even affection.[35] According to Uspensky, he was probably the most influential metropolitan in Russian history, being one of the few to continue in office until his death in 1563 instead of leaving it, whether voluntarily or not.[36] Once he moved to Moscow he drew upon a larger number of educated copyists and his work of scholarly diffusion went ahead.[37] He was also probably responsible for the appointment of Sylvester to the Cathedral of the Annunciation in the Kremlin.

Ivan came of age in 1545, when he was fifteen, but he did not yet rule. His grandmother, Princess Anna Glinskaia, and her two surviving sons,

Mikhail and Iuri, now dominated the court and proceeded to clear out Ivan's existing senior courtiers, his *dvoretskii* or majordomo, his *koniushii* or Master of the Horse, whose places they coveted, and others of his attendants, who were executed. The Glinskys also sought to avenge the death of their great-uncle Mikhail L'vovich.

Ivan's coming of age precipitated a meeting of the Boyar Council, the Church Council and the Grand Prince on 13 December 1546, to discuss his coronation, and in particular his title, and also his marriage. At the previous coronation, that of Grand Prince Dmitri in 1498, the young man had been crowned Grand Prince, Caesar to his grandfather's Augustus, and the crown had been placed on his head by Ivan III. The first and most significant departure was Ivan IV's coronation as 'Tsar', instead of Grand Prince, in a ceremony even more clearly based on East Roman practice than previously. On whose initiative this step was taken – on that of Ivan himself, deeply conscious of the need to assert his supremacy over his family and his boyars, by all valid means, or on that of Metropolitan Makarii, anxious to emphasize the role of Russia by giving religious sanction to a title hitherto used only intermittently, or even on that of the Glinskys, anxious to shore up his authority – is not known. It is not unlikely that the idea was sparked off by the desire to balance the Holy Roman Emperor as the secular head of the Christian world in the West by appearing as the secular head of the Christian world in the East, in a tenuous and unsystematic way for the time being, but nevertheless with a view to the future status of Russia in Europe.

A brief digression is necessary here on the problems created for the historian by the absence of exact translations for many Russian words descriptive of political concepts or institutions, and by the way in which Russian words can have many distinct meanings and uses in different places and times. One of the most elusive of these words is precisely the word *tsar'*. It derives from *tsesar'* or 'caesar', the title originally given to the Roman emperors after Augustus Caesar.[38] With the passage of time, the use of 'Augustus' was reserved for the senior emperor in Constantinople, and 'Caesar' could be used of the junior emperor when there were two. But in Russian the term *tsar'* was applied to the senior emperor, who lived in the imperial city, Tsar'grad, and also eventually to the ruler of the Golden Horde, to kings in the Old Testament, to the books of Kings in the Bible and to oriental potentates. (The Holy Roman Emperor of the West was called *tsesar'*.) Other European rulers were called *knyaz'*, usually translated as prince, but derived from Germanic **Kuningaz*, 'king'; or *korol'*, king, derived from Karl (Charlemagne). The primary meaning of *tsar'* was thus an independent ruler, with no overlord, who could be either a king of one particular nation or people, as in the Bible, or an 'emperor' ruling over several nations, such as the East Roman Emperor, a title pervaded by the charisma which emanated from a ruler chosen, crowned and anointed by God.[39] It was this kind of ruler who was '*imperator in regno suo*', the formula used by Philippe le Bel of France, and by Henry VIII.[40]

The fall of the East Roman Empire to the Ottomans had opened the way for the Russian Grand Prince, as the only independent Orthodox ruler, to contemplate calling himself tsar, and both Ivan III and Vasily III used the title occasionally, mainly in relations with minor powers such as Livonia. Vasily III did not use the title in his dealings with the Holy Roman Emperor, but once, in 1514, the Emperor Maximilian I was careless enough to address Vasily III as 'Kaiser', a precedent of which the Grand Prince duly took note.[41] Yet although the disappearance of the Empire of the East undoubtedly opened the way for the only remaining free Orthodox power to claim the title of emperor, and be recognized as such both in the East and in the West, such a step had to be carefully prepared since it would certainly be contested by other European powers. The growing assurance of the grand princely family, and the fact that many outside Russia failed to realize what the word *tsar'* meant, that it derived from 'Caesar' and was not some mysterious oriental term, coupled with the increasing spiritual ambition and political confidence of the Russian hierarchy, served to lead Metropolitan Makarii to propose or to agree to such a step.

On 16 January 1547, the coronation of Ivan took place in the Cathedral of the Dormition, the church of the Metropolitan, when he was sixteen. The rites were clearly modelled on the East Roman example, of which several texts had been translated from the Greek and had circulated in Russian monastic circles. A Russian deacon, Ignati, at that time in Constantinople, had written a description of the coronation of the Emperor Manuel Paleologus and his consort in 1392, and there was the precedent of the coronation of the Grand Prince Dmitri Ivanovich in 1498. Several versions of the rite of coronation of Ivan IV exist, written after the event, probably by Makarii, who devised the final form.[42] On the day of the coronation those with a role to play in the ceremony donned ceremonial robes and the regalia were carried into the cathedral, where Makarii blessed them and they were placed on a table on a dais twelve steps up from the floor, where there were also two thrones, one for the Grand Prince, one for the Metropolitan. Ivan was followed into the cathedral by his brother and family to the sounds of a sung *mnogoletie* ('many years') – no musical instruments were used in

Orthodox services. Makarii sat down on his throne, while Ivan stood before him. It is noteworthy that scholars always speak of the coronation of Ivan as Tsar of Moscow, but in fact when he stood before the Metropolitan he demanded to be crowned, as all his ancestors had been, as Grand Duke of Vladimir, Novgorod and Moscow and Tsar of All Russia, thus emphasizing the continuing dynastic claims of the Riurikids and the primacy of the city of Vladimir over all other Russian cities. He next announced that he wished to be 'anointed and crowned Tsar according to our ancient custom'. Makarii duly did so, proclaiming him 'crowned and anointed and titled Grand Prince Ivan Vasil'evich, God crowned Tsar and sovereign [*samoderzhets*] of all Great Russia'.[43]

Central to the Russian coronation were the regalia said to have been presented by the Emperor Constantine Monomakh to his grandson, the Grand Prince Vladimir Monomakh of Kiev. This included the cap of Monomakh (a kind of Mongolian jewelled and furred cap used as a crown), a sceptre, a cornelian cup, splinters from the True Cross, and the *barmy*, or shoulder capes. A few years after the coronation the 'throne of Monomakh', generally known as 'the Tsar's place', was erected in the Cathedral of the Dormition. It was a large carved wooden structure, raised on four lions, with bas-reliefs setting out the story of the envoys sent by the Emperor Constantine Monomakh to the Grand Prince Vladimir to ask for peace, and describing the gifts that he sent.[44]

After placing the cap of Monomakh on Ivan's head and handing him the remaining regalia, Makarii delivered a long lecture on the duties of a tsar, and expounded the basic theory of how the Russian Church now thought the powers of a tsar should be exercised. Makarii's 'precept' drew on a number of Biblical, Greek, and Russian sources and emphasized the co-equal powers of the Church and the Tsar: the crown came from God through the offices of the Metropolitan, confirming the Tsar's ancestral rights. There was no distinction for Makarii between a Tsar's obligations to the commonwealth and to the Church. He must rule his realm according to God's law, and use justice towards all from the highest to the lowest, rewarding and punishing in accordance with the laws of God. Makarii quoted from Agapetus's missive to Justinian, and from other Greek texts all designed to stress the divinity of the tsar as long as he ruled justly and mercifully and according to law, as well as his responsibility for defending the Orthodox religion and extirpating heresy.[45] Agapetus taught that the emperor received his power from God; he had been given the sceptre of the kingdom of this world and in the same way that of the kingdom of heaven. 'His mortal body was like that of any man but in terms of his power he was like God.' He must therefore be worthy of his power. The sins of the emperor harm not only himself but his whole realm; he must therefore struggle against his baser tendencies. 'God', says Agapetus, 'gave the emperor power in order to teach people to preserve justice, thus he must build his own rule on righteousness.' The whole point of supreme power was that it should educate subjects in the idea of law. To teach it, the emperor must himself be imbued with it, with both divine and earthly law. The tsar's power was indeed unlimited, since no one could compel him to observe the law. But he himself had to bow to the law in order to demand obedience to the law from others. There was, of course, no reference whatsoever to institutional limitations on the Tsar's power, but the Tsar must practise self-limitation.[46] In one respect, Makarii issued a specific injunction: the tsar should reward and protect his boyars and magnates (*vel'mozhi*) according to their lineage and be accessible and gracious and cordial, in accordance with his tsarist rank and status, to princes and service princes and service gentry, and to all Christ-loving men under arms.[47] Ivan certainly fulfilled these expectations as regards his family: his grandmother, the Princess Anna Glinskaia, was granted extensive lands as an appanage, his uncle Mikhail Vasil'evich was appointed Master of the Horse, and his uncle Iuri was made a boyar.[48]

But if Greek influence was strong, there was a fundamental difference between the East Roman and the Russian conception of the relationship between the Church and the Tsar. In the expressive phrase of Uspensky, in Byzantium the functions of the tsar and the patriarch (who was to be appointed in Russia in 1598) were defined by a special juridical ordinance, while in Russia they were accepted as the manifestation of a specific charisma, the charisma of power. Full powers expressed in juridical formulae became charismatic powers, the symphony of power became the symphony of charisma.[49]

Not content with the coronation by a mere metropolitan, Ivan strengthened his symbolic and practical position by appealing to the Patriarch of Constantinople for 'a blessing' of his right to the title of tsar, namely Caesar, and after long drawn out negotiations he finally received confirmation of his new title from the Patriarch of Constantinople in 1561. It came in a form which implied that a metropolitan had no right to crown a tsar, for only two patriarchs, that of Rome and that of Constantinople, had such a right. The missive invited Ivan to be crowned again by the Metropolitan of Chalcis, the patriarchal emissary who had carried it to Moscow. Ivan quietly suppressed this part of the missive and arranged for alterations to the Greek text in its Russian translation, which went to show that the Patriarch's approval had been given on his own initiative and not at the request of Ivan. It also introduced the argument that not merely his people were in duty bound to obey the Tsar but that his 'princes' were specifically bound to remain in obedience to him, a principle which was also put forward by the priest Sylvester in 1561.[50] Though in theory patriarchal approval may not have much affected Ivan's authority, it undoubtedly contributed to raising the spiritual aura of the Russian Tsar in the Orthodox world.

Makarii, who evidently enjoyed at this time considerable moral authority over the young Tsar, may also have been instrumental in pressing him to marry in order to keep him from base companions. On that same 13 December 1546 when Ivan's coronation was openly discussed in the meeting of the joint Council, the young Grand Prince stood up and declared his wish to be married. He had at first considered marrying abroad into some royal or imperial family, he said, but since he had no family of his own in Russia, he would be very lonely if he did not get on well with his foreign bride. Therefore, he had decided to marry a Russian.

A bride-show was at once organized. Inevitably it took time and careful planning. Suitable families in the provincial towns, princely and boyar, or belonging to the patrician groups in the towns, had to be notified so that their nubile daughters could be inspected. The daughters of court magnates and run-of-the-mill courtiers could be inspected in Moscow. Around 12–18 December 1546, orders were sent to *okol'nichi*, princes and boyars to proceed to some twenty-eight towns, ranging from Rostov to Kostroma, Yaroslavl' to Novgorod, in order to view the young ladies assembled there. Meanwhile, letters were sent out to the local princes and service gentry, announcing the forthcoming inspection as follows:

> When you receive this charter those of you who have daughters who are maidens, do you proceed without delay to our Lieutenants [*namestniki*] in [Novgorod] for an inspection [*na smotr*] and do not conceal your maiden daughters at home on any account. Those of you who conceal your maiden daughter and do not bring her to the Lieutenant, let him be in disgrace and punished. Send the charters from one to another of you without any delay.[51]

The response of the provincial nobles seems to have been somewhat half-hearted. Prince I.S. Mezetskoi and *d'iak* G. Shenka Bely reported in early January 1547 that they had been in Viaz'ma for two weeks and not a single prince or service man had brought in his daughters, while among the townspeople the girls were all too young. They were able to report on only one young lady. Such letters were evidently shown to Ivan himself, who followed the inspection with interest.[52] His choice eventually fell on Anastasia Romanovna Iur'ieva Zakhar'ina, niece of the boyar Mikhail Iur'evich Zakhar'in, who had been one of the witnesses to Vasily III's will and a member of the Regency Council, and who had died in 1539. One may wonder whether the decision had been taken in advance, and indeed whether Ivan already knew the young lady. The choice had the advantage of not introducing a new boyar family into the delicate balance at court, since it was already there. What led Ivan to choose Anastasia is not known, but it was from the personal point of view an excellent choice, though of course it altered the existing balance between the Iur'ev Zakhar'ins and the Glinskys.[53]

The wedding was celebrated with all due solemnity on 3 February 1547. In accordance with usual Russian ceremony, the proceedings lasted three days. Weddings were one of the occasions when married women took an active part in court life. Princess Evfronsin'ia of Staritsa had a prominent role, as did her son and various important princes and boyars and their wives. Places by the bed were occupied by two figures who were to play an important part in the future, Aleksei and Daniil Adashev. Aleksei, with many other high-ranking boyars, also accompanied the Tsar to the bathhouse on the eve of the wedding. Metropolitan Makarii issued an admonition to the newly-weds in which he adjured the young couple to visit churches and prisons, love their families, respect priests, be generous to boyars and people, refrain from listening to slanderers, observe Sundays and all saints' days and all fasts, and to couple only on favourable days.[54]

Evidently Ivan felt his marriage to be so successful that he wanted to share the experience with his brother, the fifteen-year-old Iuri. Aleksei Adashev's closeness to Ivan at this time is further documented by his presence together with his wife at the wedding of Iuri on 3 November 1547. Iuri was undoubtedly handicapped but he was not unfit for marriage. Already in September, after consultation with Makarii, Ivan had summoned the boyars and princes to bring their daughters to his court, and after inspecting the girls Iuri expressed his preference for Princess Ul'iana Paletskaia. The Tsar appointed the best men, one of whom was a boyar, and their wives were appointed matrons of honour to the Princess. Two prominent officials and three prominent ladies were to be by the bed, one of whom was the wife of Adashev; other boyars were appointed to bathe with the bridegroom, and to prepare the bed, where again we find Adashev and his brother Daniil. What is striking in the description of these weddings is the active participation of women of boyar rank, and in the case of Iuri's wedding of the Tsaritsa herself, who dressed the hair of the bridal couple, while Ivan embraced them and lavished gifts on them, and after dinner the next day, they made merry.[55]

In November the Tsar authorized the marriage of his first cousin, Prince Vladimir of Staritsa (even though the Tsar still had no male heir), but the wedding was postponed because of the impending campaign against Kazan'. The boyars and princes were again ordered to produce their daughters, who were inspected on 24 May 1550. Prince Vladimir chose a girl from the Nagoy clan and the wedding took place on 31 May with similar celebrations in the presence of several boyar and princely ladies.

There is no study of the Russian court as a political or social institution such as exists in French or English historiography, and there is no intimate portrayal of a day in the life of the Tsar.[56] There is thus an extensive gap in our knowledge of the life of Ivan. Some court lists have survived, with the names of some of his personal servants, which show that many of them served him for many years. One of his gentlemen of the bedchamber, Istoma Osipovich Bezobrazov, served him for twenty-one years. The courtiers who served the Tsar in a personal capacity, as cupbearers, carvers, servers, waiters, tasters, body servants in the bed-chamber, gentlemen-at-arms, keepers of the treasure, and purveyors of food, jewels and clothing, had titles that do not translate easily from Russian into English, but which correspond roughly with the same functions performed in Western courts. The personal attendants of the Tsar comprised the *postel'nichi*, or gentlemen of the bedchamber, the *spal'niki*, or bedroom attendants, the *stol'niki*, who served at table in the banquets for two or three hundred people, the *chashniki*, or cupbearers. But there were others – tasters, washerwomen, cooks – about whom we know nothing. There was certainly a very large staff necessary to procure and produce food for the Tsar's family, for banquets and for contingents of troops guarding the palaces. There were also many outdoor court servants, grooms, huntsmen, houndsmen, falconers, coachmen etc., and some three thousand *zhiltsy*, senior service gentry, the lowest court rank, charged with the defence of the Kremlin, who also acted as the private soldiers in the Main Regiment of the armed forces. The Master of the Horse was responsible for the care of the vast number of horses.

The Tsaritsa also had her ladies-in-waiting, the mistress of her robes, the mistress of her court and of the nursery and even her own boyars. She and her women rarely ate in public, usually only on the occasion of weddings and christenings, but they travelled extensively, in company with the Tsar, sometimes even on foot, on pilgrimages, and in considerable discomfort. The principal residence of the Tsar was inside the Kremlin, a fairly large walled area comprising within its boundaries the three principal cathedrals, many other churches and several monasteries, and the palaces of the Tsar and of many of the magnates. Typical of Russian palace construction was its disjointed higgledy-piggledy character in comparison with Western architecture. Separate buildings were erected, each for its own purpose and with its own style of windows and roof, which were joined together by halls, landings, corridors, galleries and stairs. The most typical of this kind of building was the much later wooden palace of Kolomenskoe. Stone had begun to replace wood in the Kremlin, notably in the Granovitaia (or Facet) palace, built in the reign of Ivan III, where banquets took place. There was also a dining hall, and a number of official buildings. In an adjacent palace, was the *brusiannaia* (beamed) chamber in which Ivan received foreign ambassadors and envoys informally and where the Boyar Council met, and the Golden Chamber (so called because the frescoes decorating the walls had a golden background), where foreign envoys were also received. In each room a throne was set up on a richly carpeted dais for the Tsar, located near the corner in which the icons were displayed, reminiscent of the place occupied by the throne in an imperial throne-room in Constantinople – which suggests that the ceremonial might have been brought over by Sofia Paleologa, or possibly introduced by Ivan III under Ottoman influence.[57] In the Golden Chamber, to the right of Ivan's throne, was an icon of the Lord of Hosts, with a sceptre, and to the left a painting of Joasaf talking in the desert with Varlaam.[58] There were benches along the walls, covered with velvet or damask, on which the boyars took their seats in the strictest order of precedence dictated by the system of *mestnichestvo*. The boyars maintained a motionless silence during the audiences of foreign envoys, which deeply impressed the latter. Tatar tsarevichi were often present at these audiences, particularly if Tatar envoys were being received, in order to underline the reversal of situations, for it was Russia which now disposed of the Tatar thrones to the various claimants. Four, sometimes two, *ryndy* or armed pages in their white garb were placed around the Tsar, at a distance calculated according to their rank in the *mestnichestvo* placing. The presence of armed men on such occasions was unusual in diplomatic practice, but as was explained to the papal envoy Antonio Possevino in 1579, this was a habit taken over from the Emperor Manuel Paleologus – not in self-defence, but to impose.

The Tsar received foreigners dressed in his great habit or his lesser habit; both were lavishly ornamented with jewels and weighed down with gold, but the lesser habit was lighter. He also always wore a jewelled crown, and might have beside him on a bench the crowns of some of his subsidiary realms, such as eventually the crown of Kazan', so that he could change crowns during a banquet. Foreign envoys were not expected to prostrate themselves or even to kneel, merely to bow.

Ceremonial banquets for foreign embassies played a big part in the life of the court. As many as two hundred boyars and lesser ranks might attend in rich golden garments, sitting on benches all around the banqueting room, with Ivan on a raised dais, alone at first, later in life accompanied by his sons. Tablecloths were spread over the tables, but there were no napkins or plates, the only cutlery was a spoon, and a drinking cup was also provided. Guests brought their own knives. Three or four guests ate straight from one large, usually golden, dish placed before them, which was carried in by three or four men. Meat was carved into pieces, and guests ate with their fingers – as elsewhere in Europe at that time. Forks were not yet in general use in courts. Food was said to be very monotonous in Russia, consisting of baked, boiled or roast meats, pies of many kinds, fresh and salt fish and 'roots', the usual name for vegetables, overwhelmingly flavoured with garlic and onions. Poultry and eggs were widely used, though not on fast days, and there were sweets of various kinds based on honey, flour, fruit and berries.[59] Sour cream took the place of lemons. During the great fasts no dairy produce was consumed.

The *terem*, or private apartments of the Tsar were usually on the upper stories and the buildings reserved for the tsaritsas and the children were usually of wood – which is much warmer than stone. They had their own chapels and their own baths. On the ground floor vast quantities of stores were kept, including the rich robes in cloth of gold which were lent to boyars for official receptions. The living quarters were hung with tapestries or carpets; there were, of course, many icons, but also other wall paintings and frescoes of scenes drawn from the Bible, or historical scenes, or scenes depicting the seasons, and some rudimentary portraits. There were canaries, other singing birds and parrots.

Was there a library? Not in the sense of a room specially designed for keeping books on shelves and reading them in comfort. But there seems to have been a collection of manuscripts, often in Greek, such as the ones Maksim Grek worked on, but also of course in Church Slavonic and in contemporary Russian. Manuscripts had been collected by Ivan's predecessors, and possibly Sofia Paleologa had brought a few. Ivan received manuscript books as presents from foreign envoys and visitors, and he ordered books to be copied for his use. There were manuscripts of various books of the Bible, the Apocrypha, the prophecies of Enoch or Esdras, all of which may have been kept in Ivan's private *kazna* or treasury, housed in his private apartments, from which he could send for whatever he wanted to read or consult – if he could read. The Greek text of the Donation of Constantine, mentioned *in extenso* in chapter sixty of the *Stoglav* (see Chapter V), was looted by the Polish forces from the Tsar's treasury in the Kremlin in 1611, and handed over as a present to the Pope by the King of Poland in 1633. Manuscripts were, of course, also widely held in monasteries, from which the Tsar could borrow and to which he presented copies.[60] Lists of Ivan's personal property at his death, and of the contents of his archives in the 1570s have survived, but they give no indication that he owned any books, while the list of 1611 of the contents of the private treasuries of Tsars Fedor Ivanovich (r:1584–98), Boris Godunov (r: 1598–1605) and Vasily Shuisky (r: 1606–11) comprises a total of fifty-three manuscripts and printed books.[61]

One of the most striking differences between Russia and the West was the lack of daylight in Russia. In winter, darkness covered the land by three o'clock; during the day some light might pass through mica windows (glass was little used as yet), but at night lamps and chandeliers were widely used – the consumption of beeswax was huge. Access to the Tsar's residence, up the Red staircase, was limited to boyars and others with official positions and Council ranks, and guards were always on duty. Religious services took up a good deal of the Tsar's time. Ivan was personally devout, indeed he seemed to have had a kind of exalted spirituality, which sought an outlet in church services in times of personal or political crises.

The Tsar also spent a lot of time travelling between various monasteries, villages and estates, either his own or those of his relatives, or those he had confiscated and kept for himself. He would inspect the quality of their administration and consume their produce, staying in monasteries which had to be equipped with the necessary accommodation and supplies, since he usually brought his wife and children and attendants with him, as well as other members of his family such as his brother Iuri with his wife and attendants, and sometimes his cousin Vladimir of Staritsa and many boyars. His travels were punctuated by hunting expeditions. As in England and most other countries, travel from one estate to another was not merely undertaken in order to consume its produce locally. It was essential after a few weeks in any one place to clean and refresh with herbs the accommodation used by large numbers of courtiers and men-at-arms at a time when sanitation was primitive.

Chapter IV
The Era of Aleksei Adashev

Ivan was now crowned and married. But he was still only seventeen, and it remained for him to assert his authority as Tsar and impose his will on the surrounding boyars. It is interesting to compare the way the young Ivan reacted to power with the way of his almost-contemporary, the short-lived King Edward VI of England. Edward was only nine when he came to the throne, and he was surrounded by his overpowering uncles, the Duke of Somerset and the Lord Admiral Thomas Seymour. But the intrigues among the English 'boyars' led first to the execution of the Lord Admiral and then, after the victory of Dudley, the future Duke of Northumberland, to the execution of the Duke of Somerset. Edward may have been fond of one or both of his uncles, but he seems to have signed their death warrants without a murmur. And standing over him there was an influential priest, Cranmer to Ivan's Makarii.[1]

It is unlikely that Ivan himself thought in terms of a reform pro-gramme, or that his role presented itself to him in terms of problems to be solved on the way to a teleological end, nor had his education prepared him for governing. It was more a question of what life would throw up at him, and the extent to which he could, at such a young age, act independently of the advice of the boyars. This is not the approach of some of the Russian and Soviet historians of the 1920s up to the 1970s who conceived of the Tsar's activity in terms of a programme of *zakonomernyi* ('in the order of things', but perhaps here 'historically inevitable') – action imposed on him by the laws of history, the ineluctable advance of the historical process, driven forward by the class struggle towards a pre-ordained end, the establishment of Russian absolutism as the progressive way of overcoming feudal fragmentation. Others, however, have assumed that Ivan at the age of seventeen was limited in the exercise of power by ignorance, deference to boyar authority, and a lack of the maturity which might have enabled him to concentrate on matters of state rather than on roistering in the streets and jostling innocent civilians. What the young man had already seen, the way people behaved to each other and to him, was likely to give rise in him to fear, suspicion, distrust, self-defensiveness and cruelty. There was no adult man in his entourage, or member of his family, whom he could look up to, whom he could regard as a model, whom he could even regard with affection, as far as is known (except possibly Makarii, Aleksei Adashev, and his brother, Iuri). But he had a profound sense that the ultimate power was his and that he should be free to exercise it.

Karamzin, who more than most Russian historians sees Ivan as a human being, though a very wicked one, describes him at this stage of his life as an unbridled colt, given over to idleness, noisy festivities, using his powers as Tsar to play capriciously with disgrace and rewards. He was tall, well made, physically powerful, light on his feet, 'like a leopard', and in everything like his grandfather Grand Prince Ivan III.[2] But political power was in the hands of his Glinsky uncles, and woe betide those who complained against the mighty to the Tsar. In spring 1547, seventy-five citizens of Pskov complained in Moscow against their governor. The Tsar did not heed them and, seething with rage, poured boiling wine over them, singed their hair and beards, and ordered them to be undressed and laid on the ground. They thought that their last hour had come, but at this moment the great bell in Moscow fell down, and the Tsar rushed off to see what had happened, forgetting about his victims. The point of this sad story is that neither marriage nor power had served to teach Ivan to restrain his savage impulses, which already at this tender age had become uncontrollable. Whether he already felt that any advice which ran counter to his own inclinations was a limitation of his sovereignty, as consecrated in his coronation, we cannot tell, but his unpredictability was already manifest. The next lesson he was to learn was that he could not control people.

The summer of 1547 was very hot and a number of fires occurred in the capital. Fire was always the main danger in this largely wooden city and it needed only a spark to set it off. On 24 June Moscow went up in flames. The fire swept into the Kremlin, blew up the gunpowder stores in several of the towers on the walls, and destroyed stocks of goods and food. Many of the official buildings and records were reduced to ashes, and Metropolitan Makarii nearly lost his life and was badly bruised in a well-meant attempt to rescue him from the Cathedral of the Dormition by smuggling him out through a recess in the Kremlin wall and lowering him down by a rope into the Moscow river. He seems never to have fully recovered from the shaking. He was taken to a safe monastery, where

Ivan and the boyars came to his bedside for a Council meeting.[3] Anything between 2,700 and 3,700 people died in the conflagration (aside from children) and some 80,000 were left homeless. Ivan himself and the magnates took refuge in his hunting lodge on the Vorob'evo hills, outside the town.[4]

The disaster may have been used (or even provoked) by rivals of the Glinsky family, notably the Zakhar'ins, who were relatives of the new Tsaritsa and of non-princely boyar rank. They might have been plotting to dislodge the Glinskys from power by instigating an outbreak of rioting directed against them. Ivan's uncle Prince Iuri Vasil'evich Glinsky, who had taken refuge in the Cathedral of the Dormition in the Kremlin, was seized by the rabble and stoned to death within the church in front of Metropolitan Makarii, who was conducting matins. This, of course, amounted to sacrilege.[5] The rioters then turned on the boyars and the retainers of Iuri Glinsky. The Tsar set up a body to discover those guilty of the arson which all assumed had taken place. When the authorities asked the people who they thought responsible for setting fire to Moscow, the rumour spread that the fire had been caused by witchcraft, the main witch being the old Princess Anna Glinskaya, Ivan's grandmother, who was accused of stripping the hearts out of the dead bodies and soaking them in water which she sprinkled on the streets of Moscow. The authorities took severe measures, and those suspected of being responsible were tortured, beheaded, impaled or thrown into the fires.[6] On 26 June the crowd, in what appeared to be a clandestinely organized demonstration, marched to Vorob'evo, where Ivan had taken refuge with his family, and clamoured for Princess Anna, her children and her servants to be handed over.[7] But at Vorob'evo, Ivan, the boyars and the men-at-arms with him proved able to put down the revolt.[8]

Soviet historians have spilled much ink in the attempt to link this popular revolt with specific individual boyars or social groups, such as the service gentry rising against the misrule of the boyars and the neglect of their own landed interests, notably the abuse of justice when they were forced to go before boyar courts in the provinces; or the people as a whole rising against the service gentry in defence of their class interests. Present-day historians have discarded these interpretations as far-fetched and consider the outbreak of violence as a straightforward primitive revolt inflamed by the catastrophe of the fire and by tales of witchcraft, a revolt which had but little effect on the balance of power at court between the aristocratic boyars and the service gentry and did not in any way reflect a conflict of interest between those, namely the boyars, assumed to favour 'reactionary' decentralization and the service gentry, assumed to favour centralization and the 'progressive' strengthening of the absolute power of the Tsar. But it provided an opportunity for a fresh round of the conflict between the boyar and princely clans over the division of power around the throne, regardless of policy.

There remains the question of the impact of these events on the young Ivan. He had been faced with the frightening spectacle of popular clamour for his grandmother to be delivered to the mob, and of the murder of his uncle at the hands of an incensed crowd, as well as popular disregard of his authority. Historians of Peter I have often remarked on the psychological effect on the ten-year-old Peter of the horrible death of the elder statesman, A.S. Matveev in 1682 at the hands of the *strel'tsy* (musketeers) in Moscow, and the possibility that this may have left him with the tic to which he was always subject and inured him to spectacles of cruelty. Ivan IV had already shown himself unbalanced and cruel in his relations with human beings. He had now experienced fear, and probably also outrage at the sense of his powerlessness when faced with a howling horde which, he probably suspected, was being directed against him by a hidden hand. This episode may well, in his case, have fostered an incipient paranoia. In an address to a meeting of the Church Council four years later, in 1551, Ivan remembered these events and described his own reaction to the threatening multitude: 'and fear entered into my soul and trembling into my bones'.[9]

In his letter to Prince A.M. Kurbsky dated 1564, seventeen years later, Ivan describes these events in burning language, blowing them up into a suspected attack on his own life in order to force him to hand over his grandmother.[10] At any rate the rising spelt the end of the power of the Glinskys. The remaining brother, Mikhail Vasil'evich, attempted to flee to Lithuania, was intercepted, arrested and then forgiven, but he lost the post of Master of the Horse, which he had briefly held. The winners in the struggle for power were the non-princely relatives of the Tsaritsa Anastasia, the Yur'ev-Zakhar'in Romanov clan, two of whom were promoted, Danila Romanovich, her brother, to the rank of boyar, and her cousin, Vasily Mikhailovich, to the rank of *okol'nichi*.

One cannot do better than turn to the description given by the historian Karamzin of the ensuing events, for he imparts to them an atmosphere of drama which brings out their flavour:

> In these dreadful times . . . there appeared a certain remarkable man by name Sylvester, by rank a priest, by origin from Novgorod; he approached Ivan with a raised and menacing finger and the

appearance of a prophet and in a convincing voice told him that the judgment of God was thundering above the head of the light-minded Tsar, driven by his evil passions [*zlostrastnyi*], that fire from the Heavens had turned Moscow into ashes, that a higher Power had stirred up the people and poured the vials of its wrath into their hearts. Opening the Holy Scriptures, this man showed Ivan the commandments, given by the All-Powerful, to the body of tsars on earth.

Sylvester's powerful oratory won the young Tsar over to the desire to fulfil these divine injunctions, impressed his heart and soul, inflamed his imagination and achieved a miracle: Ivan became a different man and begged Sylvester to help him.[11] But it was not quite like that, as will be shown.[12]

There was evidently a government in Russia in the sense that a number of people were charged with making and implementing decisions bearing on the military, judicial, financial and political needs of the nation. How much time and attention Ivan himself gave to problems of government at this time we cannot tell. Government and administration both proceeded from and took place in the court, which had evolved over the years but was still strongly marked by its origins in the appanages. When appanages or non-sovereign principalities of importance were taken over by Moscow, they were not incorporated into a unified administration, for it did not exist. For each new unit (unless the appanage was re-created for a member of the tsar's family) a new chamber or *dvorets*, under a *dvoretskii* (majordomo, *maire du palais*), usually of the rank of *okol'nichi*, was set up in Moscow which dealt with those parts of the administration which had been taken over by the centre. There were thus many of these *dvortsy*, one each for Tver', Ryazan', Uglich, Dmitrov, Nizhny Novgorod and eventually Kazan', and many others.[13] But there were princes who still retained some part of the attributes of sovereignty, particularly their own boyars, service gentry, men-at-arms, retinues and extensive lands, notably Prince I.F. Mstislavsky, who owned two fortified southern towns, which constituted a miniature state. In one *uezd* (district) he owned 524 peasant households, and in another over a thousand; in both he maintained Cossacks and *strel'tsy*.[14] The Vishnevetskys and the Bel'skys also owned miniature states, as did the princes of the Upper Oka, such as the Vorotynskys, Odoevskys and Trubetskoys, and the occasional solid blocks of 'lineages',[15] like the Shuiskys, Princes of Shuia in Suzdal', who formed a strong, interrelated group, 'united by a consciousness of a right to participate together with the monarch in the government of the country', because they were descended from Andrei, a brother of Alexander Nevsky's.[16]

The structure of the administration, as distinct from political decision-making, was beginning to take shape in the sixteenth century in response to the increasing needs of the government of an expanding realm. But it still was based on a distinctive feature which pervaded Russian administration and society, the system of suretyship and collective responsibility. In one form or another it seems to have existed in most European countries and in many non-European ones. In England it was known as frankpledge, the responsibility of the individual for the group, and of the whole group for the individual.[17] It is a system typical of the organization of power where the state is undeveloped and has few administrative tools at its disposal. By delegating the exercise of power down to the lowest social groups and making all groups at all levels responsible for the fulfilling of duties laid on them, the central administration is discharging its obligations while keeping free of any financial or manpower commitments. The *krugovaya poruka*, as it is known in Russia, applied equally to the local group charged with conveying a criminal to the law court which was to try him, to the family of a criminal, or to the princely sureties who guaranteed that one of their number would not be disloyal to the Tsar and escape to Lithuania.

In Western Europe, as the state grew stronger it dispensed with collective suretyship, and the individual gradually emerged from the group and bore his own burdens.[18] But in Russia in the sixteenth century collective responsibility was essential for the fulfilment of government tasks at every level, and it continued to be so in the seventeenth century.[19] It did not begin seriously to unravel until the eighteenth century, and even then remained in force in many areas of life.

In the reigns of Vasily III and Ivan IV collective suretyship has been studied in most detail in relation to the aristocracy, about which some written evidence has survived. Though an individual might find himself incriminated by the actions of those he could not control, he was also to some extent protected by belonging to a group which would share his responsibility for administrative actions. But because he was responsible for his kin and his surety group, he was also closely concerned in preventing treasonable action, which might rebound on him. This explains the frequent comments by foreigners on the culture of denunciation in Russia, which was particularly evident in cases of political suretyship. Bonds signed by members of the aristocracy would commit them to serve the grand prince and his sons, 'and to report to them anything that anyone else said, favorable or unfavorable, pertaining to the Grand Prince and his sons'.[20] The texture of Russian society was thus still much more closely woven than elsewhere in Europe, though suretyship probably had a common, possibly Viking, origin.

The magnates and officials who formed the government or manned the administration were part of the court, and the court ranks were strictly graduated. The highest rank at court, granted by the tsar, which very few enjoyed, that of *sluga* was non-hereditary and may have been awarded mainly to distinguished soldiers.[21] The title of 'boyar' too was granted by the tsar, usually to the highest aristocrats, from princely or old noble clans, appointed to the Council, who would expect to be given the senior army commands in time of war or to be supplied with the income from a province or a town as a reward for present or past service (*kormlenie*). (But not all boyars were members of the Council.) The *okol'nichie* often carried out the duties of a *dvoretskii* in the central Moscow office (*prikaz*) of a province. The *dumnye dvoriane*, or duma nobles, came next, when the rank was finalized in the 1550s. They could be of gentry or even of non-landowning origins, and maintained and developed the incipient bureaucracy. However, by the sixteenth century the numbers of *d'iaki*,[22] and of subordinate clerical posts, were increasing and the evolution of the bureaucracy in Russia was not so different from that which was taking place in France, except that there was no necessity for the Crown to introduce the venality of office, because it could count on service from the community. But with the increase of departments dealing with specific geographical areas or branches of the administration such as the Treasury or the regulation of the armed forces, the number of permanent officials was bound to increase. The *d'iaki* who were the lynchpin of the administration, and ran the various *prikazy* or offices, disposed of a subordinate clerical staff. The *d'iak* himself might be well born, even a landowner.[23] The best known *d'iaki* of the sixteenth century, Ivan Mikhailovich Viskovaty and the Shchelkalov brothers, all came from landowning families. Had Peter I not intervened in the eighteenth century by tying landowning to nobility, Russia might well have developed a *noblesse de robe* on the lines of the French, Spanish and English models.[24]

The *striapchie* or 'special attendants', the treasurers or *kaznachei*, the *pechatniki* in charge of the seal, the junior clerks or *pod'iachie* also formed part of the court but were already primarily associated with the administration. Those in the court ranks could be raised to a higher rank, but the concept of 'ennoblement' did not exist for there was no legally defined noble status. There were military ranks but no knights or squires, or coats of arms, no ethos of chivalry, no jousting (only fisticuffs), no military orders, whether secular or religious, and the only woman who was worshipped was the Mother of God.

It was the weakness of the notion of inheritance from father to son, as distinct from the much better established practice of inheritance from elder brother to next brother, which, coupled with the partible inheritance of land, weakened the aristocratic élite.[25] Men in or raised to high military posts as commanders of garrisons in vulnerable cities, or as governors in charge of public order, tax collection and justice, had not been able to turn these functions into hereditary positions and establish firm regional bases after the appanages were destroyed, by extending their 'affinities' as in England, or becoming semi-independent dukes, counts or even barons as in France or Germany. Hence the reliance on *mestnichestvo* as a means of perpetuating high status.

The career of Aleksei Adashev serves to illustrate the nature and the pitfalls of court service. Adashev came from a fairly prosperous gentry family in Kostroma which had not yet achieved boyar rank, but was highly regarded. His father, Fedor, was sent on a mission to the Ottoman Porte in 1538–9; he was accompanied by Aleksei, who stayed on for a further year, 1539–40, on grounds of ill health.[26] Aleksei had, therefore, a far better opportunity to study Ottoman civil and military organization than had Ivan Peresvetov, of whom more below. His father was raised to *okol'nichi* in 1547 and to boyar by 1553, and insofar as we can follow his career Aleksei started his life at court either as a trusted *rynda* and personal guard of Ivan's, or as a *striapchi*, or court attendant. Whether this post ranked above or below a *rynda* is not clear.[27] It is possible that the Adashevs were linked by marriage with the family of the Tsaritsa Anastasia, the Iur'ev Zakhar'ins, which may explain Aleksei's promotion at court.[28] The Adashev estates lay not far from those of the Iur'ev-Zakhar'ins in Kostroma.

S.O. Schmidt explains the eventual promotion of Aleksei Adashev by his closeness both to the boyars and to the run-of-the-mill service gentry, that is to say by his political capacity to mediate between the demands of these two social groups. Yet it is far more likely that this relatively young man achieved prominence because of his role as a favourite personal servant of Ivan's. A later chronicle of the seventeenth century relates that on his return from Constantinople the Tsar viewed Aleksei's father, Fedor, with great favour, and on Aleksei's return from the Porte a year later he too was brought into the intimate circle of the Tsar and remained there for many years, until the *oprichnina* was founded.[29] He was a member of the thousand specially appointed guards allotted lands near Moscow in 1550 which formed part of Ivan's personal military household, serving on a rota basis. Aleksei owned a large estate, the village of Borisoglebsk, in Kostroma, and probably estates elsewhere.[30] Ivan himself exclaimed in his raging denunciation of 1564 that in his young days he had raised Adashev up out of the mire,[31] he knew not how. But there is no doubt of Adashev's closeness to the Tsar, certainly from 1547, when he is listed as being present, together with his brother Daniil, as one of those performing personal services at Ivan's wedding, such as making the bed, and he is named in the official record as a *spal'nik* (in the same bedchamber service but in a slightly lower rank than a *postel'nichii*).[32] Both these ranks of *spal'nik* and *postel'nichii* imply service in the bedchamber, and in Russia, as in England or France, gentlemen of the bedchamber had exceptional opportunities of making use of physical proximity to the ruler to acquire influence or to achieve promotion.[33] Adashev's closeness to Ivan is further documented by his role, together with his wife, at the wedding of Ivan's brother, Iuri, on 3 November 1547, and on 31 May 1550 at the wedding of Prince Vladimir of Staritsa. By 1548, both Adashevs, father and son, were prominent enough at court to be on the list of recipients of Christmas presents sent by the abbot of the Trinity monastery, though Aleksei was only thirty-fifth on the list. The priest Sylvester received nothing.[34]

The first external sign of a new way, inspired by the moral authority of Sylvester, was the summoning of a meeting, called 'the assembly of reconciliation' by historians, in the autumn of 1549. It cannot be said that this gathering was an embryonic representative political institution, since as far as one knows, no one was elected to it, its size is unknown, and as a body it did not discuss any issues of public concern, it merely listened. It was summoned in order to pacify the public. But changes in the court did indicate that the Tsar was bent on new policies and new advisers.

The years 1549–60 are roughly identified in Russian historiography as the period of the so-called Chosen Council (*Izbrannaia rada*), or 'the government of Sylvester and Adashev'. The priest Sylvester, Karamzin's hero, who had so impressed Ivan, according to chronicles written well after the event, and so dominated him, according to Ivan's own letter to Prince Kurbsky,[35] was not Ivan's confessor. His early history is much debated; some historians consider him to have been a follower of Makarii, and therefore of the Josephians, others consider him to have been a sympathizer with the 'non-possessors'.[36] The date of his move from Novgorod to Moscow is uncertain, but in 1545–6 he is recorded as priest in the Cathedral of the Annunciation in the Kremlin. Sylvester was an expert copyist and trader in manuscripts, and had apparently run a workshop in Novgorod with his son Anfim, employing free labour, and attached to the Cathedral, to train copyists. He was also an experienced icon-painter. Icon-painting was not only a skill, it required theological understanding of the traditional ways in which saints and apostles, let alone Christ himself and the Virgin, were portrayed in accordance with ecclesiastical rules.

Sylvester was a man of some education, who knew Greek, perhaps Latin, possessed a small library, and made no effort to secure ecclesiastical promotion. Some historians have suspected him of being a narrow-minded fanatic, others recognize that very little is known about his personal views (though he may have been a very good businessman). As is so often the case in sixteenth-century Russia, it is not easy to obtain a clear picture of a personality, particularly someone who had no official position at court. Sylvester, on the evidence of one letter in 1553, is said by some historians to have been close to the Shuisky clan, notably Prince A.B. Gorbaty-Shuisky. And according to A.A. Zimin, on very slender evidence, he was also close to Prince Vladimir Andreevich of Staritsa and his mother, Princess Evfrosin'ya.[37] One written work of considerable importance is attributed by some historians to Sylvester, namely the 'Missive to Ivan Vasil'evich' found in a collection of sixteenth-century manuscripts in Sylvester's possession. In language reminiscent of the priest's admonition described above, Sylvester attempts to frighten the Tsar by drawing attention to the fate which overtakes wicked rulers, such as Nebuchadnezzar, reduced to the level of a brute beast grazing on grass for six years, until he repented, or Manasseh, King of Judah, a bloodthirsty idolater taken captive by the Assyrians for his many sins, who later repented and became a wise king in Jerusalem.[38] Sylvester warns Ivan of the universal flood, of the destruction of Sodom, and of the fire of 1547 in Moscow as punishments for wicked kings, and particularly for those who practise sodomy.

More doubtful is the attribution to Sylvester of the *Domostroi*, the book of household management that began to circulate in the mid-sixteenth century, though the present text incorporates sections dating from the seventeenth century. The book deals with the running of a substantial household, from a man's, possibly from a priest's point of view, or even possibly from the point of view of a high-ranking official, who would in all probability be literate. Apart from its detailed and strictly practical instructions on the control of bonded labour and servants, the storage of goods, the brewing of mead, the preparation of food and sweetmeats, the *Domostroi* dwells on the religious duties of the wife, who shall obey her husband in all things. It is this book that is one of the sources of the myth of the universality of uniquely severe corporal punishment prevailing in Russia.[39] A wife is enjoined to strike a servant if he does not heed her; if she in turn fails to live up to her duties, her husband should 'beat her when you are alone together; then forgive her and remonstrate with her. But when you beat her, do not do it in hatred, do not lose control. A husband must never get angry with his wife; a wife must live with her husband in love and purity of heart.' Similarly, when disciplining servants, beat them, but then forgive them; a wife must 'grieve over her servant's punishment, insofar as that is reasonable, for that gives the servants hope'. The author further recommends that no one should box the ears or hit another about the eyes or around the heart. These admonitions, possibly more honoured in the breach than in the observance, fit in well with the general tone and context of similar books of manners and household management in use elsewhere in Europe at the time.[40]

Sylvester's overpowering rhetoric and possibly his threats of damnation certainly seem to have had a profound moral and spiritual influence on the Tsar and to have led him to repent publicly, and dramatically, of many personal and political misdeeds. Sylvester was evidently a man of strong personality, who may have exercised an influence on Ivan's personal behaviour and private thoughts which the Tsar came in time to resent. During the years of the priest's ascendancy there are few if any references to licentiousness and drunken behaviour at court. Even Ivan's innate cruelty seems to have been held somewhat in check. The years 1549–59 saw the smallest number of executions among the magnates of the court and in the Tsar's own family, in spite of occasional serious political crises.[41] The Chronicles reflect a relatively peaceful decade in domestic matters perhaps because Ivan was for much of the time actively engaged in war and legislation.

Ivan does seem to have been very much attached to his wife, Anastasia. The couple were childless for two years and spent much time on pilgrimages in accordance with the Russian tradition of asking for divine intervention, a tradition followed by Grand Princess Sofia, who waited a long time for a son, and by Grand Princess Elena Glinskaia, who also had to wait after her marriage to Vasily III.[42] Ivan and Anastasia then had two short-lived daughters, Anna (1549–50) and Maria (1551–4), before their first son and heir, Dmitri, was born in 1552.

Of Sylvester's relations with Anastasia we know nothing, but there is an intriguing suggestion that she did not like him, and that he did not like her, possibly because he interfered too much between husband and wife. In his second letter to Kurbsky, Ivan charged Sylvester with likening Anastasia to the Empress Eudoxia (AD 395–404), wife of the Emperor Arcadius. Eudoxia became extremely hostile to St John Chrysostom, who attacked her virulently from the pulpit, seeing in her the incarnation of Jezebel and Salome.[43] Had Anastasia ever compared Sylvester with the golden-mouthed Archbishop of Constantinople and fretted at his hold over her husband?

Possibly – though we have no evidence of this – Sylvester was also able to influence the Tsar's views on policy. His moral ascendancy was so deeply felt that Ivan, again according to his own later account, raised him to the position of a favourite (whatever that might mean in sixteenth-century Russia), though he had no official governmental rank or status. He is said by A.A. Zimin to have represented the interests of those boyars who, though boyars, were nevertheless inclined to introduce some reforms in order to strengthen the central government. Sylvester was not corrupt, and when his influence ceased, he simply withdrew around 1560 to a monastery.

Sylvester is almost never mentioned without his alter ego, Aleksei Fedorovich Adashev, indeed the two are frequently mentioned together as 'the government of Sylvester and Adashev' and their supporters, friends etc. Ivan implies that he had known Adashev, who was a couple of years older, since adolescence and it is therefore possible that he was one of the young men brought into the palace to provide companionship for the young Grand Prince. He might also have attracted the young Tsar's attention by his knowledge of the Ottoman Empire.

Karamzin's dramatization of events, based on the accounts given respectively by the Tsar himself and by Prince A.M. Kurbsky, has launched one of the most controversial episodes in the history of Ivan IV on a long and complicated historiographical life. It is assumed by Karamzin, and by most subsequent Russian historians, that around 1549 Russian government was entrusted by Ivan into the hands of the priest Sylvester and the young Adashev, who represented a 'holy union' of chosen, experienced and virtuous men, including incidentally Metropolitan Makarii and Prince D. Kurliatev. The name 'Chosen Council' (*Izbrannaia rada*) was first launched by Prince A.M. Kurbsky in his *History* of Ivan IV,[44] written probably in the late 1570s. It does not appear in either of the first two letters which Kurbsky addressed to Ivan, but the existence of such a council is implied in the first letter of Ivan to Kurbsky.

The notion of a specific party, ruled by Sylvester and Adashev, was given enormous weight and importance by Solov'ev in his *History of Russia since Olden Times*. Without further explanation, Solov'ev stated as a fact that Sylvester and Adashev ruled Russia at the head of a 'vast clique', a powerful and multitudinous party; sometimes Sylvester is mentioned without Adashev, but with many unnamed advisers, followers, adherents. This all-powerful party has been described for instance as 'a close circle of men, with Sylvester at its head, a circle which managed everything; and acting carefully, and slowly, was able to conceal from the eyes of the Tsar its real purpose, which was, acting in concert with the great boyars, to overthrow all that the Tsar's predecessors had achieved'.[45]

V.I. Sergeevich, one of the great Russian legal historians, writing in 1900, developed the idea of the existence and the constitutional significance and powers of the Chosen Council even more. According to him, the Chosen Council had converted the pre-existing Duma or Council from an advisory body with a fluctuating membership, appointed by the Tsar, into a permanent, executive, representative body whose decisions were binding on the Tsar, who was merely its chairman. He then provided the names of people he thought had been appointed members of the Chosen Council, without any evidence that this was so.[46]

It is true that at the beginning of Ivan's reign the only policy-making body, the Boyar Council, had become unwieldy: it was composed of thirty-two people, after the riots of 1547, of which ten were appointed after February 1549 (leaving aside the large number of additional *okol'nichie* appointed in these years).[47] The effort to renew the membership of the Council by introducing new blood could not get very far because of the *mestnichestvo* system, which defended the right of the next ranking boyar family to a post in the event of a new appointment.[48] Moreover, Ivan's marriage had not been popular in some princely circles. Until the first marriage of Vasily III, Russian grand princes had always married either into Russian princely houses or into foreign ones, such as Lithuania or Moldavia. The new system of choosing a bride at a bride-show made it possible for the tsar to choose according to looks and not according to status. This is possibly what Ivan did, and it was to cause trouble. For it led to the appointment of several of the Tsaritsa's male relatives to the Boyar Council. This was far too large a number for efficient consultation and administration, and it has been suggested that the 'Chosen Council' was just another name for a smaller group of some nine to twelve people, the so-called

Blizhniaia Duma, which could be viewed as a closet council, carved out of the Duma and composed of many of the same people.[49] Many of these were associates of Aleksei Adashev, states the leading historian of this period, A.A. Zimin. But in the period 1547–53 Adashev was a mere guard (*rynda*) or at most a gentleman of the bedchamber (*postel'nichii* or *spal'nik*), while among his so-called 'associates' there were boyars of long standing, for instance, the princely descendants of Gedimin, Prince Ivan Dmitrievich Bel'sky (son of a great survivor Prince Dmitri Bel'sky), who had married a niece of Ivan III, Princess Anna of Ryazan', and Prince I.F. Mstislavsky, a *rynda* in 1547 but already a boyar in 1549, who occupied important military posts in the 1550s, another survivor if ever there was one, and largely because he too was closely related to the Tsar (his mother had been a niece of Vasily III); and the boyars I.V. Sheremetev Bol'shoi (major), and M. Ia. Morozov, D.R. Iur'ev Zakhar'in, the nephew of the Tsaritsa, and V.M. Iur'ev Zakhar'in, her cousin.

It is inconceivable that in a society deeply imbued with the consciousness of rank and clan a mere stripling whose father was not yet a boyar, and a priest, should be accepted as equals, let alone superiors, by magnates and descendants of Riurik and Gedimin. Moreover, although the political authority of a metropolitan was acceptable, and Ivan sometimes delegated tasks to Metropolitan Makarii, the whole notion of government by priests was alien to Russian Orthodoxy, as Ivan made clear in the long diatribe in his first letter to Kurbsky against the spiritual ascendancy of Sylvester, whom he likened to the priest Eli in the Old Testament. Eli, a good and just man, had taken upon himself the role of ruler and as a result Israel was conquered and the Ark of the Covenant of the Lord was in captivity unto the days of David the King. 'Do you not then see', exclaims Ivan, 'how the authority of priest and governor are incompatible with royal power?' Even Moses had not been allowed by God to be both king and priest, and had been forced to hand over the priestly office to Aaron.[50]

Ivan has a great deal to say on the misdeeds of Sylvester and Adashev, but the question that must be dealt with now is who actually composed the Chosen Council – who were its members if it existed? At one point Ivan accused Prince A.M. Kurbsky of having been a member, but it is obvious from his career – constantly on the move as a senior general – that Kurbsky could not have been sitting in Moscow. The trouble is that when the Chosen Council is mentioned it is always said, in the sources or in the work of subsequent historians, to be composed of Adashev and Sylvester and their associates, their fellows, their supporters, people who thought like them, their clique. Only one other member is ever mentioned by name: boyar Prince D.I. Kurliatev-Obolensky, who had a fairly distinguished military career and who was said later by Ivan IV to have been imported by Adashev and Sylvester in order to help them to seize power. (How could underlings appoint a boyar, one wonders?)

The sources are of course extremely exiguous and partisan. One must remember that the only person to use the phrase 'Chosen Council' was Prince Kurbsky – Ivan himself never uses it. So was it a council at all? Or was Kurbsky merely referring to a group of influential moral advisers who gave encouragement and backing to Ivan at a time when the Tsar was interested in taking positive political action in various spheres? Different historians have viewed it differently: as a restricted council superimposed on the Boyar Council; or as a Privy Council, a *Blizhniaia Duma*. Nineteenth-century historians seized upon the phrase '*Izbrannaia rada*' to describe an institution which allegedly existed and ruled the country from about 1549 to 1560. But the whole concept of such an institution is riddled with inconsistencies, some of which have now been pointed out by Russian historians, and which came under a withering attack by A.N. Grobowski, in 1969.[51] The evidence suggests more and more clearly that it did not exist as a separate political institution.

From a purely practical point of view the Tsar needed to draw on advice, information and knowledge from his advisers, and he needed competent generals and officials to carry out his policies, or the policies agreed upon in council. But to work with and through advisers does not make them into a formal council, nor does it limit his authority at its source, since the ultimate decision-making power is his. Moreover, all the evidence of the existence of this Chosen Council comes either from Ivan or from Kurbsky and dates from a period when the Tsar was already showing signs of the paranoia that was later to overtake him, and which led him to see all his one-time friends as enemies.

Why, then, have Russian historians been so anxious to make of the Chosen Council an institution of a new and effective kind? It may well be because of a historical inferiority complex which sees Russia as a latecomer in the development of political (and social) institutions able to formulate and channel the interests and needs of the people. There are even historians who have argued that Ivan introduced a certain 'democratism' into the government of Russia, a most anachronistic concept in the sixteenth century, and doubtless meant to represent what in modern English is described as populism, equally inaccurately.

Chapter V

The 'Government of Compromise'

The 'government', allegedly, of the 'Chosen Council' has also been called by historians the 'government of compromise', meaning that neither side in the class war said to be raging between the boyars, anxious to keep their lands, and the service gentry, anxious to acquire more land at their expense, was able to dominate policy. It was Adashev's position, halfway between these two social groups, which enabled him to become the instrument of compromise. He is said to have 'joined the government' in 1547, though at that time his official rank was still that of an armed *rynda* or guard and his father was still an *okol'nichii*.[1]

During the period 1547–58 the Tsar and the Boyar Council were able to introduce a number of useful policies in the domestic field and to accomplish one of the main foreign policy aims of the previous grand princes of Moscow, namely the conquest of the Khanate of Kazan', which controlled both banks of the Volga down to the Caspian Sea.[2]

It is difficult to tell to what extent Ivan himself initiated any of the domestic policies which marked these years. Assuming that the new policies were not imposed by his domineering guardians on a reluctant young Tsar, mainly interested in amusing himself, they seem to have been the result of personal rather than political compromises between different forces and clans at court which were on the whole in broad agreement on the policies to be pursued. These were concerned with law and the administration of justice, the extension of the control of the central legal system to territories acquired since the previous law code of 1497 was drawn up (Ryazan', Pskov, Smolensk), the reform of local government, the recasting of property rights in land to ensure the performance of military service, some reduction in ecclesiastical land-holdings, and improvement in church discipline. It is difficult to discern in this list, concerned mainly with 'tidying up', a clear pattern of class-inspired positions. According to the most influential historian of the period,[3] the basic conflict was between the progressive Tsar, attempting to centralize the administration of the country, and the reactionary boyars, anxious to preserve the decentralized 'feudal' structure. Since neither side was systematic in the pursuit of its alleged aim, and the boyars in any case were not united, it is difficult to sustain this interpretation.

The new spirit in which the Tsar proposed to govern was expounded in an allocution pronounced on 27 February 1549 to a large public gathering composed of the Metropolitan, the Church Council, the Boyar Council and the boyars in general, service gentry, and possibly some popular urban elements, since it met in Moscow. According to contemporary accounts Ivan – who evidently could never resist a dramatic scene – is said to have summoned selected people from every rank and station in every town (unlikely), and, having withdrawn to pray and to commune in silence, he went on a Sunday after mass, in procession with his boyars, the Church hierarchy and the armed forces, to the *lobnoe mesto* (which was to acquire fame as the place of execution) just outside the Kremlin, where the people had gathered in deep silence. Here he solemnly addressed the Metropolitan Makarii, begging him to support a Tsar who had been left fatherless and motherless, and whose nobles had taken no care of him. He begged the people's pardon for the offences he had committed in his unregenerate days, through no fault of his own, and he prayed them to forget the past and to unite in the love of Christ, bowing in all directions to the people.[4]

Ivan then accused the boyars of having, while they ruled on his behalf, oppressed and injured the service gentry and nobles, as well as the peasants, and he warned that any such future oppression would lead to disgrace and punishment. The boyars in turn begged the Tsar to bring to trial anyone charged with such behaviour. The same speech was repeated by the Tsar to an assembly of army commanders, senior officers and service gentry on the following day. The Tsar then decreed that in future service gentry in the towns and provinces were no longer to be tried before the courts of the lieutenants (*namestniki*) in the provincial centres, except for murder, theft and brigandage, when caught in the act, and orders were duly sent out. Both the political élite and the administration in the 'court' or *dvor* were conciliated by this new approach which placed the service gentry under the jurisdiction of the officials in the capital, even of the Tsar himself, and removed them from the jurisdiction of the provincial governors.[5] This order can therefore be seen as the result of a process of balancing of interests.[6]

The Assembly of 1549 ranks in Soviet historiography as the first in a long chain of so-called 'assemblies of the land' or *zemskie sobory*, which allegedly brought together selected (or elected) representatives of the various estates, the Boyar Council, the Church Council, the higher court ranks and the top level of the merchantry. It is held to be the ancestor of the Russian version of the assemblies of estates which existed at the time in France, Spain, Germany, Sweden and, of course, Poland–Lithuania.[7] Russian historians also include the English Parliament among the models of the *zemskii sobor,* but this reflects a modern misunderstanding of the nature of the sixteenth-century English Parliament, of which more will be said below.[8] The assembly of February 1549 has acquired a quite spurious importance owing to the determination of Russian nineteenth- and twentieth-century historians to detect in it the meeting of a Russian Estates General. They were at the time obsessed with representative institutions and democracy, concepts which were all the rage when they wrote, as symbols of a modern political system. 'The February assembly was the first *Zemskii sobor.* Its summoning was the indication that the Russian state had now been converted into a "monarchy governed by representative estates", a central estates institution had now been founded.'[9] The author of this statement, A.A. Zimin, admits that the institution was not as yet fully fledged, since the towns were not represented, and no one was elected, but he argues that there was a substantial change in the nature of the Russian constitution since legislation had now to issue from and be approved by a representative body. Subsequent events will show that this was simply not the case. As before, and later, the Tsar could just issue orders when he wished, though he did at times issue what one might term orders of national significance after formal discussion with members of his Privy Council.[10]

The political nature of the 'assembly' is better explained by a suggestion put forward by the historian G. Vernadsky. He argued that the original popular gathering of 1547 – which organized the riot after the fire in Moscow, and the murder of Iuri Glinsky – may have derived from some latent communal memory of the past role in political life of a popular *veche,* the medieval, unelected, town assembly of all the heads of free families, and that the gatherings which took place in 1549, 1550, 1551 etc. should rather be envisaged as *tserkovno-zemskie sobory* (Church and Land Assemblies).[11] These early *sobory* were not 'representative', they were transient, summoned at the will of the ruler; there were no legally incorporated estates or other orders or bodies to serve as electorates. To quote an English historian on England, 'the development of parliament from an extension of the *curia regis* into something like a national assembly – from an "occasion" into an "institution" – was probably the most important political legacy of the late Middle Ages.'[12] This did not happen in Russia until the seventeenth century. The meeting of an 'assembly of the land' in 1566 was still an occasion, not an institution. The first assembly to qualify as a genuine political institution was the assembly of 1598, which elected Boris Godunov to the throne of Russia.[13] But the concept of two distinct political organisms, the Crown and the land, was now beginning to emerge. Previously all state affairs had been *gosudarevye dela*, affairs of the Crown, there were now also *zemskie dela*, affairs of the land.[14]

Soon after Ivan's speech to the people of Moscow in February 1549, Aleksei Adashev was allegedly appointed head of a new office for receiving petitions for the redressing of wrongs (*chelobitnaia izba*), in response to Ivan's assurance that he would provide justice to the common people against the boyars (an office roughly corresponding to the Master of Requests or the *maître des requêtes* in England and France).[15] The *chelobitnaia izba* is said to have been located in a building opposite the Cathedral of the Annunciation, in which Sylvester served. From here, according to the early seventeenth-century Piskarevsky Chronicle, Adashev 'ruled the Russian land', and Sylvester with him.[16] The reference to the presence of Sylvester in this *izba* in this early seventeenth-century chronicle has led historians to assume that he played a major part in its activities all along. It must be said, however, that not all historians agree that this institution was founded at this time, nor do they agree on the importance of this particular office as the centre in which all wrongs were redressed, nor on its location.[17] In any case, an ordinary priest was unlikely to act as an official.

Makarii was in fact often left in charge of Moscow when Ivan travelled outside the city. This was the case in the second half of 1549, when the Tsar, with a large military contingent, left on the first of several attempts to conquer the Khanate of Kazan', and his cousin Vladimir of Staritsa (then aged only thirteen) was left in nominal charge under the aegis of the Metropolitan in Moscow. Policy was discussed in Makarii's rooms, he was evidently present at some meetings of the Boyar Council, and in Ivan's absence he sometimes received ambassadors and discussed foreign policy.[18]

A second major undertaking of the new 'government' was the revision in 1550 of the law code of Ivan III, dating back to 1497. Here again Russian and Soviet historians have differed on its significance. There was no judiciary in the English sense of the word (and no public teaching of law) in Russia, though canon law – as expounded in the *Nomokanon*, in use in ecclesiastical matters – gave some training in legal thinking. The heads of government offices were judges (*sud'i*) as well as administrators, and the Boyar Council had both judicial and executive functions; members acted as judges over the Council's members and over issues arising within the range of their responsibilities. Adashev may have played a part in the preparation of the new code; he was at the time *kaznachei* or treasurer in the *bol'shaia kazna*, which was both the Tsar's public treasury and his central chancery, but no one had any real knowledge of law and it is impossible to pinpoint the guiding hand.[19]

The new code repeated many of the clauses of the old. It attempted to bring order into the existing maladministration and corruption in the field of justice; to deal with the problem of brigandage and public order and with the status of the various social groups, including the graduated compensation for injury to the honour of members of the various ranks; it regulated the conditions for the departure of peasants from their masters on St George's Day (26 November), and dealt with the various types of bondage (*kholopstvo*), landownership, taxation, and local government. The promised removal of the service gentry from the jurisdiction of the provincial governors was confirmed. The code was in general harsher than the code of 1497: crimes against the Crown, such as treason, were punished by death (art. 61). Ominously so was the surrender of a town to the enemy. The regulation of justice in the provinces increased the responsibilities of the local elders (*gubnye starosty*) in the maintenance of order in the core region of Russia, as enacted during the regency of the boyars (1539). Taxes and fees payable to the local administration now began to be regulated by individual charters issued to the localities.[20]

One of the most important articles was no. 85, which had no model in the previous code. It laid down the law regarding the right to repurchase ancestral allodial land which had been sold, setting down the conditions in which relatives would be allowed to repurchase it. To this extent it was a limitation on the free use of boyar and noble land. (It should be borne in mind that owners of allodial land could not in any case dispose of it freely, since it was usually burdened by family and clan claims.)[21]

Did this policy represent the victory of the service nobility over the boyars? Or did it represent the victory of the ruling class as a whole – anxious to consolidate its ownership of property in land – over the Tsar? Or did it represent a consensus in Russian society? The principality of Vladimir Moscow had swallowed up many appanages and princely estates, had absorbed a number of important cities since 1497 and had annexed lands in Lithuania. Titles to land remained very confused and confusing. There was land belonging to the Tsar, confiscated land, appanage land held of old by Riurikid princes, new grants of land as appanages, with occasional judicial or military privileges attached to suzerainty, made by grand princes (Ivan III, Vasily III) to members of the ruling family or their relations, or to Orthodox princes deserting Lithuania for Russia.[22] The administration of the country by means of the *dvortsy* or chambers responsible for individual principalities contributed to the perpetuation of the fragmented judicial system. Here again Russian and Soviet historians have differed on its significance.[23]

The new code thus covered criminal law, civil law, bondage and some aspects of the law on property. Of more interest is the constitutional nature of the document: it was declared to be binding throughout the whole country. 'In future all affairs throughout the land are to be judged according to this code.' For the first time in Russia, law (*pravo*) in the sense of the norms to be followed in obtaining and dispensing justice was declared to proceed solely from law in the sense of legislation. If some dispute arose for which the law provided no solution, then the superior power should be informed. The code does not specify by whom, plaintiff, defendant or judge, but in general Russian procedure was inquisitorial, not accusatorial, though a prosecution had usually to be initiated by the victim and was not initiated by the tsar except in cases of public order, brigandage, treason etc. If a new law was required it would be promulgated 'by the tsar with the assent of all the boyars' and would be appended to the code, which was thus a growing and flexible instrument. But it remained, as in most countries, very difficult to apply the law where there was no control over its implementation, and the judicial duel could still be used in Russia to decide on guilt or innocence (clauses 6–7 in 1497, 11–14 in 1550). Moreover, as in France or England, the final instance in the event of appeal was the ruler.

Russian historians have of course been concerned to define the extent of the role played by the Boyar Council in legislation at this time. The Council was not a representative body, however embryonic, but an advisory body, with some judicial and some executive functions (rather like the English Privy Council under the Tudors).[24] Zimin held that the Boyar Council was 'representative' and drew the conclusion that the Tsar could not issue a law without its consent.[25] And in fact many major enactments were issued jointly by the Tsar and the boyars, but this did not represent a limitation on the power of the Tsar by a representative body. The statement that a law had been issued by the Tsar and approved by the boyars in the Council was merely a conventional formula. Any order from the Tsar alone had the force of law. On the whole, the Tsar and the boyars acted together in the interests of a greater whole and it is more than likely that the bulk of the thinking, the research and the drafting behind important legislation was carried out by the increasingly competent officials, the *d'iaki*, who remained behind the scenes or sometimes advanced on to the centre of the stage, and were promoted to be councillors and even executed.

The new code was to take effect in the whole territory the moment it was promulgated (but was not to be retrospective); should new cases arise for which the code made no provision, then these matters should be reported to the Tsar who, with the consent of the boyars, would add to the code. This important proviso underlined the code's nationwide significance, and it has also been regarded by some historians as establishing the right of the boyars to share in the act of legislation by 'approving' the laws, i.e. as giving them a constitutional role. But this attributes too much weight to a formula which existed long before any institution had developed to embody the principle. The code was then presented to a Church and Land *sobor* or Assembly in 1551 for approval.[26]

Meanwhile a number of joint Church and Land Assemblies, at which members of the Boyar Council were also present, took place. A Church Council was first called in the period September 1548 to February 1549 at which Ivan was not present.[27] One of its main tasks was to proceed to the canonization of thirty-nine Russian saints, both religious and secular. This was in fulfilment of Makarii's policy of 'nationalizing' the body of saints which presided over the spiritual welfare of Russia. 'Canonization' was not a very formal process, and many a local warrior prince or holy monk or nun had acquired an informal halo. Makarii evidently wished to bring together under one Muscovite roof the patrons to whom the faithful might pray in the new, united tsardom. It has been pointed out, however, that he did not include many Muscovite saints in his new pantheon. Makarii was also convinced of the need to introduce some order into the liturgy in use in the Russian Church, where seemingly every prince and every bishop had allowed deviations from the rubric. At a time when religious conflict was rampant all over Europe it was also incumbent on the Russian Church to bring order into its own house, which had aroused much criticism for lack of discipline and improper conduct.[28]

The first Church Council was followed by two more which were certainly summoned by Makarii, and in February 1551 a meeting of a full Church Council was called to discuss a series of questions on religious matters, evidently prepared in advance and drafted by a number of different people, including possibly the Tsar and Sylvester.[29] Ivan, always happy to dramatize his public appearances, made use of the opportunity of addressing a large gathering, begged their pardon again and repeated his criticisms of boyar rule in his minority, and particularly of the ruthless way the boyars had dared to seize and destroy his uncles, Princes Iuri and Andrei Ivanovichi.[30] But the *Sobor* had more serious business to deal with.

The authority of the monasteries, in spite of (or perhaps because of) the enormous influence of the monastery of Iosif of Volokolamsk, had been in decline in the sixteenth century, and that of the church hierarchy had been rising. This was perhaps partly as a result of the debates, being held with increasing intensity, over the propriety of monasteries owning vast amounts of land. (The subject became more and more burning in the 1530s–40s, and one may speculate whether the confiscation of church lands and the destruction of the monasteries in Protestant Europe and in England passed unnoticed in the Russian Church, though there is no written evidence of their reaction to it.) By the mid-sixteenth century the Church owned about a third of the populated land, though some monasteries were so poor that the monks went about in rags, even begging in the streets.[31] There was of course in principle no legal obstacle to monastic ownership of land in Russia, since landownership was not confined to a particular class or social group, as occurred in the eighteenth century. Monasteries had indeed always been based on land rather than money. Both the possessors and the non-possessors believed that land and other wealth belonging to monasteries should be used for charitable or religious purposes, but there was a distinction between those who believed in a monastic life of eremitical poverty, and those who believed that the Church needed adequate funds to carry out its religious duties. Much of the land they owned had been acquired as payment for prayers for the dead, though some monasteries had also accumulated enough wealth to act as moneylenders. In mid-sixteenth-century Russia the issue was the limitation of ecclesiastical landownership in the interests of distributing land to the new military service men, rather than the confiscation of all church land.

One major figure in Russian monastic life, Maksim Grek, still played an important part in the background of this discussion at this time. His situation had gradually improved after the death of Elena Glinskaia in 1538. Metropolitan Iosif, who had followed Metropolitan Daniil, was benevolent, and even more so Metropolitan Makarii. Though allegedly a follower of Iosif of Volotsk, Makarii evidently did not approve of the treatment meted out to Maksim, who had not been allowed to take communion for seventeen years.[32] But the elderly monk (he was then around eighty) was not allowed his heart's desire, namely to return to Mount Athos. Maksim also appealed to the Tsar, other churchmen and secular people spoke up for him, and at last, in 1551, after the Church Council, the abbot of the Trinity, Artemy, procured his removal from Volokolamsk to the Trinity monastery, much nearer Moscow. Maksim is said to have sent an admonition to Ivan condemning monastic greed and the appropriation of land, and he remained the spokesman behind the scenes of the non-possessing trend, which was in a minority in the Council, though as usual those who rejected possessions had greater moral authority.[33]

Into what was, up to a point, a vacuum, Metropolitan Makarii stepped, with the aim of increasing the authority of the Church hierarchy over the monasteries and the priesthood, and restoring a proper observation of the rules of poverty, obedience, sobriety and chastity. Quite in what way Ivan himself took the initiative in airing these matters is not clear, nor is the extent to which he took part in formulating the questions to be submitted for discussion – though they sometimes reflect his ironical cast of mind – but the consideration of many of these problems was bound to lead to tensions and personal clashes. It is also suggested by many historians that Sylvester took an active part in the drafting of the questions, and possibly in the drafting of the replies – but modern research suggests that he was not the only cleric involved. There is no evidence whatsoever of his participation or even of his presence.

The whole document submitted to the Council is divided into a hundred chapters (hence its usual name, *Stoglav*) issued in the name of the Tsar. The issues dealt with fall into a number of groups: church–state relations, including state revenues from the Church and the maintenance of the judicial independence of the Church and ecclesiastics, and the immunity of their lands from tsarist confiscation; the elimination of disorderly behaviour and financial and sexual corruption in monasteries and parishes; establishing a common liturgy; defining the social duties of the Church, for instance ransoming of prisoners (a major and costly undertaking), alms-giving and education; improving the spiritual and moral behaviour of the faithful and combating heresy and witchcraft. A number of questions submitted by Ivan himself were divided into a group of thirty-seven in the fifth chapter and a group of thirty-two in the forty-first chapter, and the replies are given in later chapters.

The Tsar opened proceedings by referring to the recent promulgation of the legal code and to the reforms in local administration and justice. He now appealed to the hierarchy to carry out the same improvements in the life of the Church.[34] In the first question he begged the assembled company to examine whether in their homes and churches the bells were properly rung and the liturgy sung according to the holy rules. This gives an indication of the nature of many of the questions, which affected the public and private behaviour of priests and monks and of painters of icons who should be living virtuously and teaching their pupils. Copyists and translators of service books were charged with making mistakes which were perpetuated in the church services, and the teaching of literacy was negligent. It was not, however, the monasteries which were urged to take on the task of teaching the outside world, but the white clergy in the parishes.[35] They were specifically enjoined, in chapter 26 of the *Stoglav*, to choose good married priests and deacons in Moscow and all cities, honourable and with the fear of the Lord in their hearts, able to teach reading and writing, who would receive children into their homes and teach them psalm-singing and reading from a lectern.[36]

Questions 1 to 37 in the fifth chapter raised the specific issues of clerical misbehaviour or negligence, both among the black and the white clergy, and answers were supplied later in the document. Their interest lies in their portrayal of popular attitudes on events in the life of the Church, such as drunkenness (qu. 17), the wearing of a *tafia* (the Moslem skullcap) or a hat in church, which the corresponding answer naturally forbids as a godless Moslem tradition (ch. 39), and the indulgence in drinking, feasting and merriment in a building erected for prayer and the remission of sins (qu. 21).[37] Many matters of church ritual were dealt with as well as rules for entering the religious life, forbidding nuns and monks to live under the same monastic roof, or to wander the streets begging for charity. In question 15, the document notes the extent of the donation of land to monasteries for the monks to remember the donors in their prayers, and the extent of their purchases of land. It asks: is it right that monks should concern themselves with land and trade in towns? Who will be subjected to torment for this on the day of judgment? And is the lending of money at interest compatible with Holy Writ?

The shaving of beards by laymen and the wearing of foreign-style clothes were dealt with in question 25. 'At the present time men who call themselves Christians, thirty years of age and older, shave their heads, beards and moustaches and wear the garments and dress of an alien faith; how then is a Christian to be recognized?' It is generally assumed that Russians were profoundly attached to their beards, but it is also permissible to ask how true this was. It is a striking fact that the miniatures which illustrate some of the Chronicles, many of which have been reproduced in books, show a large number of beardless men. They convey the impression of being young men, whereas the bearded are elderly, and all clerics are bearded. A miniature of Tsar Ivan issuing a decree in 1556, surrounded by ten figures whose faces are visible, has been reprinted in one of the sourcebooks drawn upon here.[38] Of these ten figures six, including the Tsar, are beardless – in fact the Tsar never appears with a beard. In the few portraits which are reputed to represent real human beings (the *d'iak* Mishurin, Boris Godunov), the sitters are beardless. It may well be, therefore, that the practice of shaving was much more widespread than is generally believed and that the constant reiteration of the prohibition of shaving was really necessary in order to ensure conformity.[39]

Shaving the beard and moustaches was closely connected with sodomy, a problem which particularly agitated the clerical conscience and which is dealt with in chapter 5, question 25 of the *Stoglav* and the whole of the quite short chapter 33, threatening those who continue to sin with excommunication and exclusion from the Church. Question 29 in the fifth chapter charged the faithful with failure to repent of their many and serious sins: fornication, adultery, sodomy, injustice and pride, and envy. Why had the Lord of old drowned the whole world in a flood with the exception of Noah? Why had Sodom and Gomorrah perished in flames? And why had the Lord given Tsargrad (Constantinople) to the alien and godless Turks? Sodomy was regarded as a vice of the wealthy, and was viewed as particularly dangerous because the whole community might be punished for the sins of individuals.[40] Shaving was regarded as conducive to sodomy, since it gave men a round, smooth face like a woman's.[41]

The *Stoglav* also laid down the age for marriage – fifteen for men, twelve for women, and reasserted the prohibition, dating from the Emperor Leo VI, of marrying more than twice.[42] The maintenance of the separate jurisdiction of the Church over clerics and in fields connected with religion, such as marriage or wills, was upheld by the simple device of a reference to the Donation of Constantine to Pope Sylvester in the fourth century.[43]

A further policy change introduced at this time was of major importance in the evolution of the relationship between the Tsar, the landowning class and the armed forces. For most of the fourteenth and early fifteenth centuries the main fighting force had been composed of cavalry, largely based on the princely appanages with little centralized organization. By the mid-sixteenth century these princely private armies were to be found only, if at all, in the appanages of Lithuanian origin, such as those of the Bel'skys and Mstislavskys, and in the retinues of the Russian 'service' princes of the Upper Oka, such as the Odoevskys and the Vorotynskys.[44]

The development of a Russian army dependent on the grand prince alone began in the reign of Ivan III, who had already extended the grand prince's control over the armed forces where he had been successful in absorbing a principality and destroying its separate identity. Princes and boyars, when not acting as governors and local commandants, were usually absorbed as commanders and senior officers in grand princely regiments, in accordance with the ranking laid down by the code of precedence, or *mestnichestvo*. The general run of service gentry, originally of mixed social origins, was gradually sorted out into those who served the grand prince directly, as members of his *dvor*, received estates in service tenure (*pomest'ia*), and were merged into the *dvoriane* or future service gentry, and those who had served local princes and boyars and who continued to carry out their service as *pomeshchiki* on a provincial basis. Lower-ranking cavalry officers were thus attached to provincial towns, resided on their estates and were summoned when required by the grand prince, bringing their servants with them. Both these groups received lands on a service tenure which in the early days of the system could not be sold or pledged, but could be passed on the death of the holder to a son or son-in-law fit to perform service. The service to be given was strictly calculated in terms of the amount and quality of land.

The system of *pomest'ia* was devised to enable cavalrymen to serve when called upon, and was to remain the basic way of paying for the cavalry army until the reign of Peter the Great.[45] The Pomestnyi Prikaz, or Estates Office which administered the recruitment and the provision of land to the mounted cavalry, was founded in 1475. Further distribution of lands as *pomest'ia* took place under Vasily III and Ivan IV from a variety of sources. The estate was not regarded as the private property of the *pomeshchik*; it provided a fixed income for his maintenance and his equipment, and he was not expected to concern himself with its exploitation. He was not therefore a landowner in the Western sense of the word, but a land user entitled to a certain income from the land. It was thus quite distinct from the *votchina* or the patrimonial estate which formed the basis of the wealth of the aristocracy and the service gentry, which many *pomeshchiki* owned in addition to the land granted by the government.

The first major initiative in the remodelling of the armed forces taken in Ivan IV's reign occurred in 1550. The Tsar's *dvor* numbered some three thousand all told, and a specific group of one thousand cavalrymen, divided into three categories, was now provided with *pomest'ia* in the central provinces to enable them to lodge in Moscow and provide all their supplies from lands relatively near to the capital. They were to be available for immediate service as required, serving on a rota. The estates they were allotted were provided mainly from the Tsar's own lands or from lands of free peasants around Moscow.[46] Aleksei Adashev was one of these cavalrymen.

A corps of infantry equipped with firearms was also formed by Ivan, *pishchal'niki*, or 'harquebuzzers', as Jerome Horsey, a later English visitor, called them, who had already been used in 1480 in the non-existent battle of the Ugra and who were replaced in 1550 by musketeers or *strel'tsy*, also on foot. These, together with Ivan's chosen one thousand cavalry corps, formed his personal guard, 'the forerunners of Peter I' s guards regiments', presumably to protect him against the sort of rioting which had so frightened him in 1547.[47] The *strel'tsy* were to be part of the military scene until the reign of Peter the Great. Their function was not to fight with cold steel or pikes in hand-to-hand combat, but to use firepower. Their numbers fluctuated and probably reached some twenty thousand by the end of the sixteenth century. They were, unlike the cavalry levy, a permanent uniformed corps. Unlike the Ottoman janissaries they were free men; they received salaries in money and goods according to rank, but also maintained themselves and their families partly by artisan production and small-scale trading activities. Their officers belonged to the gentry and were allotted *pomest'ia* as well as salaries. The whole corps came under the authority of a new Streletskii Prikaz.

Artillery was also extensively and effectively used in Russia, and Ivan may have taken a personal interest in the manufacture of guns – from Russian-produced iron ore – and their utilization by his army. Each regiment was allocated a certain number of guns in the 1550s. Ivan took 150 heavy and medium pieces of artillery to Kazan' with him in 1552, and in this respect Russia was not inferior to her Western enemies, though supplies of gunpowder and lead had to be imported and could therefore be subject to enemy blockade on land.[48]

The origin of the idea of this corps of *strel'tsy* has been much debated in Russia. Clearly Russia needed more modern weaponry, namely firearms and heavy artillery, for her wars against Poland, Sweden and in Livonia, rather than cavalry armed with bows and arrows.

Contemporaries and many military specialists have speculated on whether the new formations were borrowed from the Ottomans through the writings of a certain Ivan Semonovich Peresvetov, which may perhaps have been known to Ivan IV. For a long time Peresvetov's very existence was in doubt and he was thought to be an assumed name or a collective personality. Not until the beginning of the twentieth century was his existence actually established.[49] In the 1950s he was unfortunately treated as one of the powerful humanist thinkers of sixteenth-century Europe, comparable to Machiavelli or Bodin. A revision of his human and intellectual qualities has not yet been undertaken, nor is it certain that all his alleged writings can be attributed to him; thus his influence still needs to be questioned.

Born and bred in Lithuania, conditioned by life in this borderland, divided between Polish Catholicism and Russian Orthodoxy, offering his sword as a Polish cavalryman now to the Hungarian Jan Zapolya, a vassal of the Ottomans, now to the Habsburg King of Bohemia, now to the *voevoda* Peter IV Raresh of Moldavia,[50] Peresvetov was a fairly senior officer serving with six or seven horses and the corresponding number of grooms and servants. Evidently resentful at his failure to make good in service, and distrusting boyars and their ilk, he attempted to enter Russian service in 1538, during the regency of Elena. He may have been attracted to Russian service by his connexion with Peter of Moldavia, whose wife was Elena's cousin by marriage. He tried to interest the Russian court in a model shield 'in the Macedonian manner' which he had invented, and was taken up by the boyar M. Iu'rev Zakhar'in, the uncle of the future Tsaritsa Anastasia, and provided with a workshop and a *pomest'ie*. Unfortunately for Peresvetov, Zakhar'in died, he lost his patron, and all interest in his patent shield evaporated.[51]

Peresvetov continued in increasingly impoverished circumstances for some ten years, after which all traces of him vanish. This was not surprising since he had no connexions in Russia with any of the boyar clans, or even with the gentry, who tended also to be united by fairly close local associations. Reduced in his own eyes to poverty, in 1549, at the time of the gathering of the so-called 'assembly of reconciliation', he personally submitted a petition, together with a number of other written works, to Tsar Ivan, accusing the 'great' of having despoiled him of his land, leaving him naked and destitute, without even a horse. Peresvetov's not unjustified hope of achieving more in Russia, where a simple horseman could now count on some support as a *pomeshchik*, was not to be fulfilled, and as a man he disappears from sight. But the various writings attributed to him survived in a number of manuscript copies of the early seventeenth century and have led to a belated acceptance of his existence as a man and his importance as a 'spokesman' of the gentry or the holders of *pomest'ia*, as against the rich and powerful, in the sixteenth century.

It is this interpretation of the 'class' role of Peresvetov, considered to have been insufficiently appreciated by pre-revolutionary historians, which has contributed to his great importance in Soviet historiography. The relevant texts attributed to Peresvetov are 'On the conquest of Tsar'grad by the godless Tsar Magmet Amuratov, son of the Turkish Tsar', 'The Tale of Magmet Saltan', and 'The Great Petition', which contains Peresvetov's account of the five months he spent in the service of Peter IV Raresh, his only Orthodox patron.[52] Mehmet II's victory over the last Paleologus emperor, Constantine, was in great part attributed by Peresvetov to the selfishness, cowardice and incapacity of the 'great' men surrounding the Emperor and his failure to support the more lowly men-at-arms. ('The rich never think of fighting, they think of peacefulness and gentleness and rest.') He argued in favour of a centrally recruited, controlled and paid army, like the Turkish janissaries, but he also argued that free men fight better than slaves, and the Russian cavalry was free, while the janissaries were slaves as were all the civil employees of the Ottoman court. In Russia the *kholopy* or bondsmen of various kinds in the armed forces were at this time mainly employed either in the transport of food, fodder and munitions, or in labouring on engineering projects.[53]

Another great virtue of the Ottoman system in Peresvetov's eyes was its concentration on *pravda* rather than *vera* – truth or justice, rather than faith. This makes one wonder whether the long years in foreign parts, before he came to Russia, had somewhat dented the purity of Peresvetov's Orthodox faith. The sense of the Russian word *'pravda'* is impossible to convey in English, where in dictionaries the emphasis is almost always on the notion of truth, whereas in Russian the notion of justice or righteousness is fundamental.[54] The most articulate expression of Peresvetov's ideas (if they were his ideas) comes in his version of the tale of Prince Peter IV of Moldavia, where the Prince praises Mehmet the Conqueror for having restored justice to Constantinople, and explains that 'God does not love faith, but *pravda* or justice'. Through his Son he left us the gospel of truth (*pravda*), loving the Christian faith above all other faiths, and showed us the path to heaven. But the Greeks, though they honoured the gospel, listened to others and did not carry out the will of the Lord and fell into heresy (i.e. the decision to unite with Rome, taken at the Council of Ferrara/Florence).

But Peresvetov was primarily concerned with the practical problems of governing a warlike society. He favoured the institution of a professional army (like the Ottoman janissaries), but free, government by state employees, and the bridling of the high nobility. It is difficult to see in him the spokesman of the gentry, he seems rather to place his faith in a state ruling by '*groza*', terror or awe. Mehmed was again quoted as an example, for when he discovered that his judges were being dishonest he had them flayed alive, saying:

> if their flesh grows back again their crime will be forgiven. And he ordered their skins to be stretched out and ordered them to be stuffed with cotton and ordered them to be affixed with an iron nail in places of judgment and ordered it to be written on the skins: without such terrors, justice and sovereignty cannot be introduced.[55]

Mehmed was also praised for being dread, or terrible, in fact '*grozen*': 'If a tsar is mild and peace-loving in his realm, his realm will become impoverished and his glory will diminish. If a tsar is dread and wise, his realm will expand and his name will be famous in all lands.'[56] 'A kingdom without terror [*groza*] is like a horse without a bridle.'[57] Peresvetov's admiration for the efficiency of Ottoman rule is by no means unique at that time, when it was very much a *lieu commun* in that part of Europe which had had dealings with the Porte.

To be 'dread' Ivan did not need any advice from Peresvetov, and there is not in fact any evidence that Ivan IV ever read anything written by Peresvetov; and if the idea of creating the corps of musketeers came from outside Russia, a more convincing source is in fact Moldavia, where *voevoda* Peter Raresh[58] had introduced a corps of musketeers who were not slaves like the janissaries, but free like the *strel'tsy*, and with which of course Peresvetov would have been familiar.[59] It seems, therefore, unlikely that Peresvetov exercised any influence on Ivan's policy in the 1550s as a spokesman for the gentry.

The demand for land for distribution as service estates colours much of the underlying politics of sixteenth-century Russia. The need to supply the armed forces with land allegedly aroused the interest of the grand princes in confiscating the lands of the Church and the monasteries, and even that of the rich princes and boyars, and similarly created a pressure among the service gentry to acquire land and divided them politically as a result from the magnates who owned vast estates, or appanages, from which lands could also be confiscated. These various political positions have been discussed at length by Russian historians and many different and often incompatible conclusions have been reached on an extremely slender basis of fact. The assumption that the main political divide throughout the sixteenth century was between the 'reactionary' or 'conservative' boyars, anxious to preserve the land in their hands and to prevent the 'centralization' of the state, which existed in a condition of blissful fragmentation, and the service gentry, who supported an absolute ruler in his progressive struggle for centralization against the boyars, has in the more recent historiography been very largely discarded. Both the boyars and the service gentry wanted land in both forms, as *votchina* (in outright ownership), by far the most valuable, and as *pomest'ia* (in service tenure), and both social groups, which overlapped to some extent, since they came from linked family clans, favoured a concentration of power in the central government. But *pomest'ia* were issued not only to descendants of noble servitors in the Tsar's court and various appanage courts, but also to court servants of no rank, to any free man, or even to bondsmen or *kholopy*, and foreigners, when the Tsar was attempting to increase the numbers of his cavalry. Ultimately the losers were the peasants.

As the manpower needs of the Russian state expanded and the armed forces settled into new patterns, the cavalry to which *pomest'ia* were granted fell into two broad categories, those who served as individuals *po otechestvu*, by hereditary social rank, and those who served *po priboru*, or collectively on lists attached to provincial centres. Was this feudalism? It is generally argued that it was not, because there was no contract binding on both sides, on lord and vassal; only the vassal was bound to serve for the upkeep he received from the land. Nevertheless, in practice as distinct from theory, in its impact on the life of an individual, the Russian cavalry levy was not so different from the levy on land held from a baron or directly from the king in early medieval England, though there was no mechanism, such as scutage in England, to enable a holder of a *pomest'ie* to commute his service duty for a money payment.

Chapter VI
The Conquest of Kazan'

While Ivan IV was struggling in the 1550s with his first experience of ruling, he was also facing his first experience of the complexities of war and foreign policy. Russia was a landlocked power, with a toehold on the Gulf of Finland at Ivangorod, opposite Narva. To the southwest was the vast Polish-Lithuanian Commonwealth, which had absorbed so much of the Dnieper basin and so many principalities of Kievan Rus'. It was no longer as powerful as it had been in the fourteenth and fifteenth centuries, since Ivan III and Vasily III, in the course of various wars, recovered some of the principalities, notably Smolensk, which had once belonged to the Grand Principality of Kiev, though they did not recover Kiev itself. To the north, access to the Baltic was almost entirely shut off by the Order of the Livonian Knights, the northern remnant of the Teutonic Knights, whose lands in East Prussia had now been secularized. To the south, Russia was hemmed in by the Khanate of Crimea, which held the northern shore of the Black Sea, and to the east, extending along the Volga, were the Khanates of Kazan' and Astrakhan' and the lands of the Tatars of Kabarda. The three Tatar Khanates were the remainder of the fearsome Mongol Golden Horde, which had finally disintegrated in 1502, leaving these three unstable Moslem principalities with indeterminate borders between themselves, with Russia and to the east.

Each separate realm had its own political aims, Poland–Lithuania, under the Jagiellonian dynasty, hoped to recover the lands lost to Ivan III and Vasily III. Russia hoped to recover even more of the heritage of Kiev,[1] to achieve access to the Baltic Sea, which would enable her to break through the barrier presented by Poland–Lithuania and Livonia to communication with the West, and to put an end for ever to the instability on her western and southern border and to the perpetual and damaging Tatar slave-raids to which she was so vulnerable. Poland–Lithuania had for long been the strongest enemy, and both Russia and

Poland intrigued actively for the alliance of the Tatar khanates in the wars against each other. A new dimension was introduced into the shifting pattern of alliances in the south by the fall of Constantinople and the establishment of the powerful Ottoman empire, which would inevitably attract the allegiance of the Moslem enemies of Russia. The Khanate of Crimea had already become a Turkish vassal state.

Ivan III as Grand Prince played on these different strings in his foreign policy with skill and care, and took advantage of the internal weakness of the Khanate of Kazan', which was not a homogeneous Tatar realm but a conglomeration of tribes, some Tatar, some not, and riven by dynastic conflicts. The Volga divided the land into the meadow side and the mountain side (left bank and right bank) and there were settlements of non-Tatar peoples and various Finnic tribes who were neither Christian nor Moslem and thus had no particular attachment to Kazan'. On the death of Khan Ibrahim, Ivan III was able to intervene and, acting with one of the candidates to the throne, Mehmet Emin,[2] to conquer the city in 1487. It was not a permanent conquest, but it established Ivan III for the first time in the role of an overlord who 'invested' the Khan of Kazan' with his throne, inverting the situation which had existed since the Mongol conquest, when it was the Tatar khans who decided which Russian prince was to rule in which Russian city. The Khanate of Kazan' was now in a situation of intermittent dependency. The players in the game included also the Khan of Astrakhan', the chiefs of the Nogai Horde and, further east, the Khanate of Sibir'. The patterns of alliance shifted between these various rulers according to commercial, and often dynastic, factors, as mortality took its toll.

The religious and political flexibility demonstrated by all the Russian grand princes in their relations with the Tatars had allowed many of the latter to settle in Russia, in groups, keeping their faith, being allotted towns and taking service with the Grand Prince, or entering Russian service as individuals, converting to Christianity and marrying Russian women. The most prominent of these Tatar appanages was the Moslem Khanate of Kasimov on the River Oka, established by Tsarevich Kasim, a son of Khan Ulug Mehmed of the Golden Horde, in mid-fifteenth century, by agreement with Grand Prince Vasily II. The Khan of Kasimov was a Genghisid, and therefore qualified to reign in the various Tatar khanates should their dynasties die out.[3] In these Tatar appanages[4] police, justice and administration were in the hands of the Tatar rulers, even when Russian Orthodox subjects also lived there, but their rights over the indigenous people were somewhat different; they enjoyed the same rights over the Moslem population as the appanage princes in Russia enjoyed over the Orthodox population, but only the rights of *kormlenie* over the Orthodox.[5]

Mehmet Emin, who had lasted many years in Kazan', most of them in alliance with Russia, died in 1518, leaving no direct descendant. Vasily III tried to impose the thirteen-year-old Shah Ali (Shigali in Russian sources) from the Khanate of Kasimov. But he was deposed by a rival khan sponsored by the Khan of Crimea, with the support of Poland–Lithuania, while the Khan of Crimea launched an offensive which reached Moscow in 1521. Peace negotiations were undertaken between the Khan of Crimea and the governor of Moscow, Vasily III's brother-in-law, the converted Genghisid Tatar prince known as Tsarevich Peter, who was married to Vasily's sister.[6] Vasily III realized that a military base had to be set up closer to Kazan' than Nizhnii Novgorod (at the time the nearest base on the Volga), if the Russians were ever to achieve victory, and a fort, Vasil'sursk, was eventually built at the junction of the River Sura and the Volga; this, since it was on lands belonging to Kazan', was the first actual annexation of land. Renewed conflict reversed the balance between the Crimeans and the Russians, though the throne of Kazan' remained in the hands of a khan of the Crimean dynasty during the regency of Ivan's youth.

Could this unstable situation last? Both the khans of Kazan' and the khans of Crimea were interested in extending their authority in the east, but as regards Russia, they were concerned not so much with the conquest of territory as with slave-raiding, since the trade in slaves and the ransoming of prisoners was one of their principal sources of wealth. The Russian frontier was open and extremely vulnerable to invasion by large Tatar cavalry forces, and the Crimean Khanate was no minor succession state but a powerful and well-armed nation which preserved its independence until 1783. The frequent changes of alliance between Kazan', Crimea and Poland–Lithuania subjected Russian towns and villages to constant destructive inroads.

It is also possible that Russia was launched on a path of conquest by a general awareness of the religious polarization in Europe brought about by the Reformation, by a new, crusading anti-Islamic fervour, evident since the fall of Constantinople and by the threatening Ottoman advance in the Balkans. Belgrade fell in 1521, Rhodes in 1522; the battle of Mohacs in August 1526 destroyed the Hungarian kingdom and killed the Jagiellonian king. In 1529 Sultan Suleiman the Magnificent laid siege fruitlessly to Vienna in a terribly destructive campaign which ended in a truce between Ferdinand of Habsburg (the brother of Charles V) and Suleiman in 1533 and which confirmed the loss of Buda to the Turks. In

1538 Peter Raresh, the *voevoda* of Moldavia, sent an envoy to negotiate – in vain – for help from Russia,[7] but Suleiman invaded Moldavia, dislodged the *voevoda* and replaced him with new and more subservient client rulers.

More to the point as regards Russia, the fall of Constantinople and the final elimination of the last remnants of the Roman Empire of the East left the Orthodox Church in captivity, with no other free protector but Russia. The theory of 'Moscow the third Rome' was in the air.[8] It does seem that at this time what had for years been a tolerated *modus vivendi* between many races and religions was under increasing strain, and all the powers involved were determined to reach a final solution rather than to live from truce to truce. The threat of Islam was much more immediate and visible than it had ever been – most of the lands that had once been under the sovereignty of the Christian East Roman Empire were now ruled by the Moslem Turks.

From the point of view of the other central European powers, Russia had now emerged from diplomatic obscurity and had become an unknown quantity which had to be taken into account. The Holy Roman Emperors, in the persons of Maximilian I and Charles V, dominated western European politics of the age in terms of prestige rather than power. They were viewed with constant hostility by the kings of France, who sought safety in alliance with the powers which might attack the Habsburgs from the east. The pattern of sixteenth- and seventeenth-century diplomacy could already be discerned, with France seeking friendly relations with Poland–Lithuania and alliance with the Ottoman sultans. The Jagiellos of Poland–Lithuania in turn, rivals of the Habsburgs for the thrones of Bohemia and Hungary, and for control of the Danube, were hemmed in from the east by the Grand Principality of Moscow, nibbling away at the Lithuanian lands and increasingly subject to the devastating attacks mounted by the khans of Crimea.

To the north of Russia, the crisis caused by the collapse of the Order of the Livonian Knights, under the impact of the Reformation, intensified the rivalry between its neighbours for its inheritance. The Poles and Lithuanians met with the hostility of the Habsburgs, since Livonia was a dependency of the Holy Roman Empire. They also faced the enmity of the Grand Principality of Moscow, anxious to acquire land and ports in Livonia; and of Sweden, similarly desirous of protecting the shores of Finland by occupying Livonian lands and ports. Russia was not at this stage an initiator of policy, but Ivan III and Vasily III manoeuvred quietly and skilfully between Crimea, Poland–Lithuania and the Empire – maintaining good relations with the latter – and thus increased their diplomatic importance and widened the range of their relationships, while rejecting all attempts, by the Empire or the Papacy, to establish Moscow's rank in the pecking order of European states by the offer of papal or imperial crowns, and indeed claiming superiority of status.[9]

Under Ivan III and his forerunners Russia had already mastered the ways of international negotiation with the East Roman Empire and the Tatar states to the east, and the Grand Prince had also learnt to conduct diplomatic relations with the neighbouring powers in western Europe. As the range of Russian contacts increased, so Ivan III and Vasily III began to develop not only a certain skill and continuity in international relations but also a staff of secretaries experienced in conducting international affairs and qualified to some degree in language and diplomatic practice – a practice which varied widely from country to country. In the build-up of the rituals of diplomacy, Russia ended up astride East and West, influenced by long experience of Mongol/Tatar manners, while learning to adapt to Western ones. For instance, the custom of exchanging gifts between rulers, between ambassador and ruler and between ambassador and local magnate was most carefully regulated to take account of all possible implications. Gifts of money, or even of gold and silver currency, were frowned upon, for, as Montaigne noted, Sultan Bajazet never accepted gifts from envoys because the giver, as a result, is always raised above the receiver. In general the Mongols and Tatars did not distinguish between gifts and tribute.[10] Gifts of furs, usually in bundles of forty skins, were common – sables were the most highly prized. Nothing was wasted. Even the skins of the sheep eaten by ambassadors on the way to the Russian border, where the foreign country would take over the supply of food, had to be returned to the tsar, as did the skins of the sheep eaten by the foreign envoys in Russia.[11]

In the West too, in the sixteenth century, the manner of conducting relations with other powers was only just beginning to acquire consistency, to be established in the law of nations (the words 'international law' did not exist, though the concept was vaguely adumbrated)[12] and to be expounded in textbooks, the first of which seems to be that written by Bertrand du Rosier, dating from around 1500.[13] A common manual served for western European countries, for in theory they all belonged to the *res publica christiana*, the community of Latin Christendom. It was indeed not an inclusive Christian community, for the Orthodox Christians did not 'belong' to it, in practice if not in theory. They were schismatics, not 'one of us', and even their long obedience to the Roman Empire of the East in religious matters earned them no merit.[14] As a result the Grand Principality of

Moscow had no precise rank in the European order of precedence, and the Russians were anxious to work out where they stood. For the Russians this also implied working out which sovereign rulers were addressed by the grand prince (or tsar) as 'brother', and which were too low in status to merit such a distinction.[15]

A Russian version of what was probably an Italian list of European states placed in order of rank, dating from the early sixteenth century, and in all likelihood originating in the Office of Foreign Affairs, has been found in Russia and gives some indication of their view; though as Russia does not figure on the list, one cannot judge of the Tsar's standing and there is no indication of where western countries placed the Grand Principality of Moscow.[16] The Holy Roman Emperor obviously came first, followed by the 'king of the Germans', i.e. the heir to the Holy Roman Emperor, then the kings of France, Hungary, Spain, England ('Negliter'sky'), Portugal, Naples, Bohemia, Scotland, Denmark–Sweden, in that order, and finally Poland–Lithuania. Precisely which qualifications decided the order of precedence is hard to tell, but judging by other, later, lists it was such things as the antiquity of a crown, the date of the ruler's conversion to Christianity, when a country achieved its independence etc.[17] Where exactly the Office of Foreign Affairs thought that Russia belonged is not clear, but Ivan IV probably considered that his place was immediately after the Holy Roman Emperor, since he was descended, as everybody knew, from Augustus Caesar. (This placing was somewhat odd, because Ivan IV regarded all elective monarchies as inferior to hereditary ones. But the elective quality of the Holy Roman Empire went back to Rome 'on the plea that to allow the throne of Caesar and the temporal lordship of the world to pass by inheritance like a farm, was unbecoming its peculiar dignity'.[18])

Precedence was important not only in the signature of treaties, in the forms of address and ceremonial (who dismounted first and who remained on his horse, who took off his hat and who kept it on) used on public occasions between ambassadors and sovereigns, and in the nature and quality of the gifts exchanged, but also in the etiquette prescribed for the ceremonial in use at receptions according to the rank of the power concerned, the rank of the envoy and the nature of the relations between their respective governments, whether friendly or hostile at a given moment. Even the display of silver (much of which eventually was English) at Russian official banquets for foreign envoys was regulated by the status of the power concerned in the diplomatic pecking order.[19] The sort of misunderstanding that might occur is illustrated when Queen Elizabeth, on a warm summer's day, made the mistake of receiving the

Russian ambassador walking up and down in her private garden, and not in full panoply, sitting on a throne under her canopy of estate. Ivan complained at the lack of ceremony shown to his envoy and was assured in reply that the garden was the Queen's own privy garden and that vegetables like onions and garlic were not grown there.[20]

Traditionally, crowned heads, or kings, addressed each other as 'brother' (*brat*).[21] But some kings were more equal than others, and acknowledgement of the status of brotherhood was a bargaining counter to be used in negotiations. Essential for the acceptance of the rank and quality of a royal house was the recognition of a God-given hereditary right to reign, and an ancestral claim by descent to outright ownership of hereditary lands; thus Ivan IV regarded information about the genealogy of the Riurikovichi as a state secret, which it was treason to penetrate or disclose, and did not acknowledge elected rulers as his equals. As a result of the break-up of the Union of Kalmar between the three northern crowns in 1521, Grand Prince Vasily III had refused to recognize the new King of Denmark–Norway, Frederick II, and the new King of Sweden, Gustavus I Vasa, as his brothers. The elected king of Sweden, a minor noble, was not even a noble, according to the Russians, but a merchant and a trader, and the ruler of Denmark was a king of 'salt and water'.[22] In 1559, when the envoys of the new King Christian III of Denmark attempted to impose equal treatment of their king on the Tsar, the Russian boyars refused even to discuss the subject, and insisted that Christian III should address Ivan not as brother but as father. When Ivan heard that Sigismund Augustus of Poland–Lithuania had used 'brother' to a later king of Sweden, Erik XIV, he exclaimed contemptuously 'he is free to call his coachman brother if he wants to'. The same problem arose in an even more acute form in relations with the Tatars and specifically the Crimeans. As descendants of the Golden Kin who continued to regard the Russians, who addressed them as 'tsars', as their vassals, the Crimeans made their recognition of the grand princes as brothers conditional on gifts of gerfalcons, sables and walrus tusks, or on the ransom of prominent prisoners.[23]

Hence also Ivan's constant insistence on being recognized as Tsar, instead of Grand Prince. The demand to be addressed as Tsar formed part of all Ivan's negotiations with Sigismund Augustus, and was met throughout with a blank refusal. Like all practitioners of international relations, Ivan was of course willing when necessary to compromise on titulature – he would not sacrifice a useful treaty for a name. But his attitude reflects the bred-in-the-bone conviction of the high standing of his dynasty in Europe.[24]

Recently the argument has been advanced that the Russian conquest of Kazan' was motivated by an 'ideology of imperialism'. These arguments are not very convincing because the words 'ideology' and 'imperialism' convey concepts which were not current at the time, were indeed meaningless, in sixteenth-century Russia or Europe, and thus distort the mental cast, the *mentalité*, of the period. Such an approach is a reading back into the past of the obsessions of the twentieth and twenty-first centuries.[25] The very word 'state' was not yet in general use, let alone 'nation-state'.[26] Expansion at the expense of Poland–Lithuania was quite simply regarded as the achievement of legitimate dynastic claims.[27] And there were also several very good reasons why Russia should attempt the conquest of Kazan' now that it was so weak: the first, and probably the most deeply felt, was the urge to turn the tables on the power to which Russia had for so long paid tribute. Equally important was the fact that Kazan' was only some two hundred miles down the Volga from Nizhnii Novgorod, and the desire to control the mouth of a river and an outlet to a sea was very powerful.

It has been argued that in the Chronicles and other writings of the time Moscow claimed that it had a legal right to Kazan' as a Russian *votchina* since earliest times (untrue) and that the Khanate was Russian by the law of conquest (as Sultan Suleiman argued that Hungary was his and as both William I and William III argued that England was theirs); that it was Russian by historical and dynastic right; that it belonged rightfully in the forward march of Christianity (the theory of Metropolitan Makarii); and that its conquest was justified by the ideology of imperialism. But can the English conquest of Wales and attempts to conquer Scotland be explained too as a consequence of an ideology of imperialism? Or is it just a natural urge to expand to the limit of one's borders? Or to control one's waterways? Kazan' had never of course been Russian, nor had Wales been English. But a glance at the map will show how dangerous to Nizhnii Novgorod was the proximity of the Khanate of Kazan'. Economic arguments, however, are not convincing except as additional factors in motivating the conquest, notably the control of the eastern trade down the Volga and through the Caspian, provided Astrakhan' was secured as well.

The word imperialism, with all the negative nuances attached to it today, simply does not apply to the idea of empire in the sixteenth century, when, as far as Europe was concerned, there had been for a long time only two supranational empires, both descended from the Roman Empire, which had been the cradle of the Christian religion: the Roman Empire of the East was the continuation of the Empire of Augustus

Caesar, and is always and misleadingly called Byzantium nowadays, though in the sixteenth century that name was only just beginning to be used;[28] the Holy Roman Empire was an attempt to re-create the Roman Empire of the West, which had perished in AD 470 under the assault of the Germanic tribes, by the descendants of those same tribes, Charlemagne and Otto I. Both these empires were imbued with the belief that they were the commonwealth of all Christian nations, and though the formula of *cujus regio ejus religio* had not yet been devised, nevertheless the massive advance of Islam into eastern Europe, the breach between the Catholic and the Orthodox Churches and the assault of the Reformation in its various guises on the older forms of the Christian religion had led to intensified religious tension and even fanaticism and hence to the attempt to impose uniformity, often in the interests of public order. In the new Protestant communities, those who held to the old Catholic religion were to be prevented by violence from practising it in the churches which had in the past always been theirs; and where Catholicism (or Orthodoxy) won the upper hand, the Protestants often went to the stake, and so did many Jews.

The concept of the *translatio imperii* moved in tandem with that of 'Moscow the Third Rome'. The adoption of the title of 'Tsar' followed on the disappearance of the East Roman Empire, but Russia never put forward any claim to suzerainty over previously imperial lands (Bulgaria, the Balkans). Similarly, the concept of 'Moscow the Third Rome' seems to have been confined to ecclesiastical matters, and even there it was used very cautiously by Ivan.[29]

There were of course other uses for the name empire. In its Russian form '*tsarstvo*' it was used for the words 'realm', 'kingdom' or 'empire' in Western languages or Latin. 'Tsar' was the recognized Russian appellation of the Tatar khans and Ottoman sultans as well as of the emperors in Constantinople and the kings in the Bible and in the Middle East. Holy Roman emperors were known as '*tsesar*' (caesar). Western European rulers were usually known as '*korol'*' or king, and their domain as '*korolevstvo*'. The lack of precision in the use of these terms, both in the West and in the East, is nowhere clearer than in the well-known phrase, 'Rex est imperator in regno suo', used by Philippe le Bel and Henry VIII and even in Russia.[30]

The one argument which seems to convey most clearly the essence of the Russian determination to conquer Kazan' was the deeply felt desire to be free from the humiliating vassalage that had been endured for more than 250 years, and to turn the tables on those who had once been the Russians' masters. This argument can be found in the Chronicles. It was not, as far as one can determine, racist, as modern colonialism became later, but political, and intensely religious.[31]

Modern Western historians of Mongol influence on Russia[32] have carefully analysed the Chronicles in order to pinpoint the dates of the interpolations in them which might support the view that anti-Islamic remarks were inserted after the events rather than before, notably in the *Kazanskaia istoria*,[33] which is regarded as a chapter in the Chronicle of the Beginning of Tsardom, dating from after the conquest. They thus suggest that religious fanaticism did not naturally inspire the crusade against Kazan', but that it was deliberately cultivated by the spokesmen of the Church, regardless of the fact that the Church had been quite exceptionally well treated by the Mongol overlords. However, it seems rather too rigid to expect perfect consistency of outlook in an age of violent religious controversy raging over the whole of Europe and the Middle East. Human beings have often been able to think one thing and feel another, or to keep two opposing ideas going in their minds, and to cohabit peacefully with a much hated religion seems to have been more easily achieved at that time in the very multiracial East than in the more racially uniform West. However, the Patriarch of Constantinople, Gennadios, appointed by Mehmed the Conqueror, though duly grateful for the Sultan's favour, spoke in private of the Turks as 'the bloody dogs of Hagar', just as Makarii, Ivan IV and for that matter Prince Kurbsky spoke of them as 'the Hagarenes'.[34] The driving force behind the campaign against Kazan' was undoubtedly Metropolitan Makarii, as is evident from his writings, though Maksim Grek also was a strong advocate. But Ivan seems to have been a convinced supporter of the policy, and it was popular with the boyars and the service gentry who could hope to acquire land.

In 1549 the Khan of Kazan', of the Genghisid Crimean dynasty, died, leaving a two-year-old infant as heir. The opportunity for intervention was too good to miss. The first of Ivan IV's campaigns against Kazan' took place in that year, but it became bogged down owing to an unseasonable thaw which prevented Ivan's forces from crossing the Volga.[35] Ivan himself did not take part in the campaign of 1549 and was very cast down at its failure, but he embarked on a further campaign in 1550 which was equally indecisive owing to an unexpected thaw. It was then decided to follow the example of Vasily III and build a fort which would dominate the river above the city, at Sviiazhsk. Many of the non-Tatar peoples of Kazan' deserted to Moscow, where Ivan received them well, rewarded them with furs, horses and money and promised them his favour. The garrison of Kazan' numbered only some twenty thousand,

and Suiunbek, the mother of the baby Khan, could not control the government. Hoping to avoid war, the people of Kazan' agreed to the restoration of a previous Russian nominee, Shigali, Khan of Kasimov as their tsar; but there was a dispute over the terms of the truce negotiated by Aleksei Adashev. Suiunbek and her son were sent to Moscow, and part of the land of Kazan' was assigned to Russia. The weeping 'Khansha' departed on a boat on the Volga, escorted by all the people and lamenting her sad fate. Meanwhile, Shigali procured the release of up to sixty thousand Russian prisoners, who were repatriated to Russia 'like a new Exodus', according to the chroniclers. But having heard of treasonable talk against him, Shigali invited the supposed traitors to a banquet and had their throats cut – seventy in all. The murders were carried out by Shigali's own men and by *strel'tsy* from Moscow. Ivan sent Aleksei Adashev twice to renew negotiations and to remove Shigali, and by 1552 the latter had abdicated, refusing to act as Ivan's Trojan Horse within the city. The people of Kazan' no longer believed in Russian assurances, and war became inevitable.

There was for once no danger from Sweden, Livonia or Poland–Lithuania. The old King Sigismund I of Poland–Lithuania had just died, and the new King Sigismund II Augustus was still feeling his way. The war was encouraged by Metropolitan Makarii and by the Archbishop of Novgorod, Pimen, who proclaimed the religious inspiration which lay behind it in missives to Ivan, urging special prayers to the Virgin of the Don (who had succoured Dmitri Donskoi in his time). In an epistle delivered at Sviiazhsk, Makarii stressed that the Russian people were called upon by God to defend the true faith, in the words engraved on the crown above the throne in the Archangel Cathedral quoted from the Bible: 'I have raised you to be Tsar saith the Lord and taken you by the right hand.'

On 16 June 1552 Ivan started out on his fourth campaign against Kazan'. He took a touching farewell of his pregnant wife in Moscow, who fell at his feet praying for his safety. He then went to the Cathedral of the Dormition to pray. He dealt with new threats from the Crimean Tatars as he advanced on Kolomna, while Princes Shcheniatev and Kurbsky defeated a Crimean corps advancing on Tula in a battle in which Kurbsky received serious injuries, a large number of Russian captives was freed and the Crimean Khan lost many herds of camels. In July Ivan's army at last advanced on Kazan'. The Russians were well supplied with artillery, while the Tatars were unable to use more than their muskets and arquebuses.[36] The twenty-two-year-old Tsar was in theory the commander in chief of the Russian forces and he had been very active in their inspection and in the various councils of war in Moscow.

Ivan was, however, disturbed by reports of orgies worthy of Sodom and Gomorrah taking place in the fort of Sviiazhsk and sent a priest to admonish the warriors. The priest, Protoerei Timofei, reported that some warriors had even shaved their beards.[37] Ivan, who was a firm believer in magic, countered the evil Tatar spells by sending for a potent counter-magic, namely the splinters of wood from the True Cross, which formed part of the Tsar's regalia and which were brought with all speed from Moscow. Kurbsky, who was also a firm believer in magic and evil spells, describes the part played by Tatar magicians in the battles by bringing on intense rainstorms. This was achieved by the very old men and women in the fortress who appeared on the walls at sunrise, shouting out Satanic words, waving their clothes at the army and turning around in an 'indecorous manner'.[38] The wind would rise and the clouds form and the rain would fall only on the Russian forces. The priests went in procession around the army, bearing the holy relic and performing Christian rites, and the signs of Tatar magic ended.

On 23 August 1552, the seven-week siege of Kazan' began, directed by an experienced and talented general, Prince Alexander Gorbaty-Shuisky, while the twenty-four-year-old Prince A.M. Kurbsky was appointed one of the commanders of the right wing.[39] At last the underground explosive charge placed by a foreign engineer under the walls of the city exploded and the Russian assault began. While the Russians stormed the city Ivan, who – following the practice of Joshua before Jericho – had been attending a church service, returned to the church and listened to the interrupted liturgy, punctuated by further explosions, leaving Kurbsky, at least, with an unfavourable impression of his military capacities. It was still a time when a ruler was expected to take a personal part in a battle. But Ivan was fulfilling the even more important religious duties of a tsar.

The fighting was very fierce, and casualties piled up on both sides. As Tsar Ivan, having heard the liturgy to the end, took communion, and then mounted a charger to advance into the field of battle, his banner already flew over the fortress. The Russians turned aside for a while to indulge in killing and looting, in spite of Ivan's orders. The principality of Kazan' collapsed, only a small contingent of horsemen succeeding in getting away, while those remaining in the city were dispatched by the victorious Russians, who collected a huge amount of loot. Ivan marked the occasion by further prayers, and indicated the place where a Christian church was to be built to commemorate the occasion. The prisoners and the treasure were handed over to the fighters, and Ivan kept only the actual regalia used by the 'tsars' of Kazan'.[40]

The Tsar attempted to win over the surrounding population by assurances of good government, and many of the people swore allegiance to him. The Nogai Horde was now in friendly hands, and some of the Kabardian princes also accepted Russian overlordship. But the fighting was not at an end.

Vast numbers of prisoners were taken; some were deported to Russia and forced to convert, whereupon they could be incorporated into the Russian armed forces – or they were simply killed. Their lands in Kazan' were placed in the hands of the new Russian governor of Kazan', Prince Petr Ivanovich Shuisky, an energetic and efficient commander appointed in 1555 (a correspondent of Maksim Grek), and the newly established archbishop of the city, who were jointly charged with its government. The lands were widely distributed to the Russian service gentry in 1557.

Having given orders for the removal of the corpses from the streets, Ivan himself left Kazan' and returned to Moscow. On the way back he was greeted by the news of the birth of his first son, Dmitri, and in an outburst of joy he gave the horse he was riding to the lucky messenger. As he approached Moscow he was greeted by rejoicing multitudes, who kissed his hands and feet as he advanced among them. The Metropolitan, surrounded by the hierarchy and bearing icons, greeted him. Ivan thanked them for their prayers and gave an account of the battle in which he more than once paid tribute to the courage of his cousin Prince Vladimir Andreevich of Staritsa. Like a warrior chief of old, he addressed his troops, thanked them and promised good government in the future. The Metropolitan replied in kind, and finally Ivan shed his soldier's clothes and donned the rich purple over his shoulder, the miracle-working cross around his neck and breast, and the cap of Monomakh on his head. He appeared before his subjects as the triumphant king who had led his people to victory in the battle for the purity of their religion and their freedom from the oppression of the Moslems. Then a few days later, he gave his forces a splendid banquet which lasted three days. Never, says the chronicler, was there such a lavish display, such magnificence, such rejoicing, seen at the Russian court. The commanders and *voevody* were showered with beautiful furs, golden bowls, horses and money, all together worth forty-eight thousand rubles, as well as *votchiny* and *pomest'ia*.[41] It was the apogee of Ivan's reign so far and he was himself in a state of exultation and exaltation at the fulfilment of his role as a Christian conqueror.

The Tsar had allegedly been persuaded by the brothers of the Tsaritsa to leave Kazan' and return to his wife, against the advice of his military specialists, notably that of Prince Kurbsky, who believed that the situation around Kazan' was still precarious, the presence of the Tsar necessary, and that Russia should assert its control by force over all the tribes previously subordinate to the Tatars. Indeed, the leaders of the various tribes which made up the population of the Khanate soon rose in open revolt and continued unsubdued for a number of years, which made it necessary for Russia to keep troops in the area and led to many casualties on both sides. The fall of Kazan' inevitably altered the situation of the Tatars settled in Russia, and increased their number. A number of Tatar tsarevichi, whether converted or not, now played a part in the Russian court, and a considerable number were recruited into the armed forces. Ivan also arranged for the baptism of two leading Tatar princes. The young Khan of Kazan', Utemish Girey, the son of Safa Girey, was given the name of Alexander and taken by Ivan into his own household, where he was to be taught his letters and the tenets of the Christian religion. His mother, Suiunbek, was married off, apparently much against her will, to Shigali of Kasimov. A little later Ediger Mehmet, also a *tsar'* of Kazan', who had been taken prisoner, declared his wish to become a Christian and was baptized Simeon by Metropolitan Makarii, in a lavish public ceremony attended by Ivan's brother Iuri, his cousin Vladimir, many boyars and the whole Holy *Sobor*. He was provided with a household and boyars of his own, and was kept not like a prisoner but like an appanage prince.[42] As a result of their conversion these Tatar princes lost some of their authority over their own people, but they also became useful to Ivan as military commanders.

On his return to his capital Ivan arranged for the commemoration of his victory by the building of a church which has remained one of the most striking in Moscow, familiar to all tourists as the very emblem of Muscovite Russia – namely the Cathedral of the Protection (or Veil) of the Virgin, better known as the church of St Basil the Blessed, with its nine multicoloured domes, situated just outside the Kremlin.

A second dramatically vivid memorial to Ivan's victory is the icon dedicated to St Michael, known as either the 'Church Militant' or the 'Blessed Host of the Tsar of Heaven', which is placed opposite the 'tsar's place' or throne in the Dormition Cathedral in the Kremlin. It is generally held to have been painted to commemorate the conquest of Kazan' at some time in the 1550s, though the exact date, as usual, is not known. Warriors in three separate processions move forwards leaving far behind them a city in flames (said to be Kazan'). In the middle of the central procession a dominant figure, possibly the Grand Prince Vladimir Monomakh, advances on a towering horse, led by a solitary horseman who turns towards him and is identified as Tsar Ivan IV himself, who is preceded in turn by the Archangel Michael on a winged charger, urging him forwards and showing the way on to Jerusalem, where the Virgin with the baby Jesus in her arms awaits him. Two of the three processions are composed of warriors on horseback, with haloes and emblazoned shields. They are warrior saints of Russian history, ancestors of Ivan in the performance of heroic deeds, such as Alexander Nevsky and Dmitri Donskoi. In the middle procession the horseman is evidently an emperor, but the warriors are on foot, and do not have haloes. One Russian expert on this icon has suggested that it may be a symbolical representation of Ivan's return to Moscow after the conquest of the Tatar city. But an alternative version has been put forward in which the third and largest figure is not Vladimir Monomakh, but Ivan himself, clothed in imperial garb. The presence of Ivan in an icon of this kind would in any case be unusual, since it was against Russian practice to represent living beings on icons.[43]

Chapter VII

The Dynastic Crisis of 1553: Domestic and Military Policy, and the Arrival of the English

After his triumphant return from the conquest of Kazan' in late autumn 1552 Ivan stayed in Moscow and took up the threads of domestic policy again. However, early in 1553, an incident occurred which sowed the seeds of Ivan's suspicions of incipient treason among his boyars. The outline of events, as first related in the Chronicles,[1] is as follows: on 1 March 1553, the day after the christening of the Tatar Khan Simeon of Kazan', Ivan fell seriously ill of an unspecified fever. He was at times unconscious, at times delirious, and his life was feared for. His only son, Dmitri, was barely six months old, still in swaddling clothes. For the members of the Tsar's court, the problem of the succession was acute. With an infant on the throne, a regency was inevitable, and at the time Ivan himself was too ill even to appoint one. In the circumstances, if his baby son inherited the throne, power would inevitably be concentrated in the hands of the Tsaritsa's relatives, the Iur'ev Zakhar'ins, since Ivan's brother, Iuri, was incapable. One must remember that primogeniture was only fairly recently established in Russia (as in Lithuania) and there were many advantages for a country as vulnerable as Russia in being ruled by a grown man capable of commanding armies and whose authority was indisputable.

The court divided along a number of different fault lines: there were those who maintained the absolute right of the baby Dmitri to inherit the throne. These were mainly the Iur'ev Zakhar'in relatives of the Tsaritsa, and their supporters, who could expect to monopolize positions of power at court and to benefit in rank and wealth should Dmitri become tsar. But there were also powerful boyars who, remembering the childhood of Ivan himself, thought that one experience of a minority was enough and, resenting the status and power the Zakhar'ins might acquire, threw their weight behind Vladimir of Staritsa, Ivan's first cousin and only adult male relative, who, if he were ever to rule, would remember those who had first supported him. Moreover, Vladimir was only seventeen years old and was regarded as not very bright, which would enable his boyar supporters to dominate the political scene. On the other hand, there was an unpredictable factor in his ambitious and formidable mother. Finally there were a number of prominent courtiers who adhered not particularly enthusiastically to the principle of primogeniture and supported the young Dmitri.

The illness of Ivan was so serious that he was urged by a prominent *d'iak*, Ivan Mikhailovich Viskovaty (we shall meet him again), to make his will. A will was undoubtedly written, appointing guardians for Dmitri, but no trace of it has ever been found, nor is there any mention of its possible contents in the Chronicles. Strangely enough, there is no mention throughout Ivan's illness of the presence of Metropolitan Makarii, or of Ivan's confessor, the priest Andrei,[2] though it was normal for a confessor to be present at a deathbed and for a metropolitan to witness the tsar's will.

The accounts of what now happened vary according to who wrote them and when they were written. Substantial additions were made to the principal chronicle long after the original contemporary entry, as well as to a later chronicle; it is generally accepted that these interpolations were either dictated by Ivan himself or added with his approval.[3] According to this revised version at one stage Ivan recovered consciousness enough to require the courtiers to swear allegiance to his son as heir, and this brought the divergences to a head. On the day he signed his will, he himself, already somewhat recovered, brought a number of prominent boyars to the cross to swear their fealty; these may possibly have been the boyars mentioned as guardians in his will.[4] Feeling too weak to proceed further, Ivan now handed over the task of collecting the oaths from the boyars to the Princes I.F. Mstislavsky and V.I. Vorotynsky (who had already sworn), while the *d'iak* Ivan Mikhailovich Viskovaty held the cross.

The circumstances were very confusing. Swearing allegiance was traditionally performed to a living grand prince, in his presence, not to a future heir, as Prince I.M. Shuisky pointed out.[5] A number of boyars the next day manifested reluctance to swear allegiance to a baby who might die at any time. Ivan himself seemed to be aware that the Zakhar'ins did not have enough authority and support even to provide protection for Anastasia and her son in the event of his death, and in the later interpolations in the Chronicles he is recorded as advising those boyars who had loyally sworn allegiance to his son on the first day to flee with the infant Prince to a foreign land, wherever God might send them, for safety. Ivan in 1564 accused the boyars, led by Sylvester and Adashev, of 'having wanted to raise Vladimir of Staritsa to the throne and, like Herod, of trying to destroy his God-given son'.[6]

In fact Sylvester played a very modest part in these events. But Ivan later cast him, in the interpolations in the Chronicles added under his aegis, as one of the arch plotters in favour of Vladimir, and subsequent historians have accepted, on very slender evidence, the accusations that Sylvester had in the past intrigued to have Vladimir's appanage returned to him by Ivan, that he was a friend of Vladimir's mother, the Princess Evfrosin'ya, and that he was one of Vladimir's 'party'.[7]

Pressed to swear allegiance, Vladimir himself backed away; Ivan withdrew to his chamber, saying: 'you know well, if you do not want to kiss the cross, on your soul be it, what happens to it will not concern me.' At this point a number of boyars intervened and said they would not allow Vladimir of Staritsa into the chamber to see the Tsar until he took the oath, while Princess Evfrosin'ya made matters worse by complaining that an oath was not worth anything unless it was freely given. Mother and son were later charged with calling up their armed retinue and distributing money to possible supporters.[8] Vladimir reluctantly took the oath on 12 March (the text survives), and at this point Sylvester intervened to say to the boyars: 'Why do you not let him [Vladimir] in to the Tsar, he wishes him well . . . and from then on there was enmity between Sylvester and the boyars.'[9] This is the only actual evidence of Sylvester's attitude to Vladimir, and to his claims to the throne; everything else that is adduced is mere assumption.

Fedor Adashev, the father of Ivan's favourite Aleksei and not yet a boyar, expressed the doubts of some of the boyars when he said to the Tsar: 'We will kiss the cross to you, Lord, and to your son, the Tsarevich Dmitri, but we will not serve the Zakhar'ins; your son is still in swaddling clothes, and we saw many misfortunes already from the boyars before you came of age.' This suggests not that Fedor Adashev wanted Vladimir of Staritsa to inherit, but that he hoped Ivan would appoint a regency sufficiently strong to prevent the Zakhar'ins from seizing power. Aleksei Adashev took the oath on the first day. So the question arises: was there a boyar plot to place Vladimir on the throne, according to the first account in the chronicle? Or did a plot only begin to take shape years later when Ivan arranged for the rewriting of the past?[10] And who took part in it?

What does appear evident is that Ivan's illness caused a good deal of chaos and confusion at court at the time, and many imprudent words were uttered as boyars spoke angrily and incautiously to one another, recalling past misdeeds.[11] Among these was Prince Semen Lobanov Rostovsky, whose words were repeated to Ivan by one of the major figures at court, the Master of the Horse Ivan Petrovich Fedorov Cheliadnin (of whom more will be heard).[12] The crisis lasted twelve days, but the boyars were all brought to swear allegiance, and just as Vladimir of Staritsa was finally induced to take this step, so, after three visits to her, was his mother, Princess Evfrosin'ya.[13]

The historian of the career of Ivan Viskovaty casts some light on these murky events. He points out that of the twelve councillors who first took the oath, seven were closely related to the heir to the throne, and three were related to the Zakhar'ins, the family of the Tsaritsa. In his view, the behaviour of Prince I.M. Shuisky or Fedor Adashev, who hesitated, does not seem likely to have been conditioned by concealed factional ambition, but by genuine differences of political orientation.[14] It is worth noting the fate, in the immediately following years, of those alleged to have taken part in a plot against Dmitri, though of course it is quite possible that Ivan, who could be both devious and vindictive, concealed his real feelings towards all those present until the time was ripe. Fedor Adashev was raised to the rank of boyar in 1555; Aleksei Adashev, according to some accounts, a *dumnyi dvorianin*[15] in 1553, was raised to the rank of *okol'nichi*, a step on the ladder to *boiarstvo* (a rank he never reached), in 1555. The twelve princes, boyars and duma *d'iaki* listed as swearing allegiance to Dmitri on the first day appear in the records as regularly in attendance on the Tsar and are therefore assumed to have belonged to a small unofficial Privy Council which advised him. In 1554 the same men are there, only one of them is missing.[16] No one has been disgraced for his behaviour during the Tsar's illness.

However, in his first letter to Prince A.M. Kurbsky (5 July 1564), Ivan spewed forth all his venom against those he now suspected of having betrayed his trust. He accused them of rising up like 'drunken men' led by Sylvester and Adashev, of intending to destroy his son, 'for Tsar does not bow down to Tsar, but when one dies the other rules'. Ivan had recovered, but Sylvester and Adashev continued to 'counsel all that was evil, to persecute him, while complying with every whim of the Prince of Staritsa'.[17]

Russian scholars have endlessly analysed the authorship and the date of the interpolations in the chronicles, but less attention has been devoted to the question of how true is their portrayal of the events during and after Ivan's illness. The account given by one historian, I. Gralia, in his life of the *d'iak* Viskovaty, is distinguished by its common sense. He points out that only three of the boyars present at Ivan's bedside were reluctant to swear allegiance to Dmitri, namely Prince Ivan Pronsky Turuntai, Prince Petr Shcheniatev and Prince Semen Lobanov Rostovsky. The first was attached to the household of Vladimir of Staritsa, the second was of Lithuanian descent (a Patrikeev), the third, Rostovsky, belonged to the Suzdal' group of princes and had been made a boyar in 1553. The Suzdal' princes regarded themselves as the highest ranking among the Riurikovich clans and objected to having to serve the Zakhar'ins if the latter were appointed regents for Dmitri.[18] All these, therefore, were what one might call natural contenders with the Zakhar'ins for power and therefore reluctant supporters of the Tsar. Behind all the verbiage it seems that the discord had really centred on the age-old conflict in Russia between succession from father to son and lateral succession from elder to next brother, a conflict in which the ruler, ever since Vasily III, was more and more determined to secure hereditary succession in his own house. It is also probable that many boyars realized that hereditary succession was better for the stability of the dynasty.

Ivan eventually recovered and set off on a pilgrimage to the distant monastery of St Cyril of Beloozero to give thanks for his recovery, accompanied by the Tsaritsa, his family, Aleksei Adashev, Prince A.M. Kurbsky and other courtiers. It was also an opportunity for Ivan to withdraw from court life and unwind in the calm monastic atmosphere in which he found comfort. He visited Maksim Grek at the Trinity monastery on the way, possibly their only meeting, and Maksim warned the Tsar not to proceed to the White Lake, for fear of endangering the life of his son in the harsh travelling conditions.[19] And indeed, the gangway of a boat they were travelling in overturned and the baby was dropped by his nurse into the river and drowned. This was no doubt both a grievous personal loss to Ivan and a dynastic blow. There was now no heir to the throne, other than Vladimir of Staritsa, but Anastasia fortunately was soon pregnant again. Her second son, Ivan Ivanovich, was born in March 1554, and Tsar Ivan took advantage of the strengthening of his position to force Vladimir of Staritsa to take a fresh and far more wide-ranging oath of allegiance to his son and any other heir he might beget, and to denounce anyone he heard plotting against the Tsar, even his own mother. Vladimir was forced to undertake to live in Moscow with no more than 108 armed men in his retinue, and to refrain, with many sureties, from recruiting service gentry and *d'iaki*.[20] But Ivan neither forgave nor forgot the turmoil his illness had created.

Sylvester and the *d'iak* Ivan Viskovaty were involved in June 1553 in a rather obscure dispute over the alleged heretical, possibly anti-Trinitarian, views of a noble, Matvei Bashkin, and a bondsman, Fedor Kosoi. This was linked in October with a denunciation by Viskovaty of the allegedly unorthodox, even heretical, character of some of the icons which had been restored, under the overall direction of Sylvester, in the Annunciation Cathedral after the fire of 1547. The heretical views of Bashkin, reported to his confessor Simeon, were denounced by the latter to Sylvester and by them both to the Tsar, who ordered an inquiry. A number of other priests were implicated, including Artemii, who had briefly been abbot of the Trinity monastery. Viskovaty had also criticized the repainted icons in the Golden Chamber which showed signs of 'Latinism', and of the influence of Western models filtering in through the use of painters from Pskov and Novgorod, patronized by Sylvester and Metropolitan Makarii, and ultimately approved by Ivan himself. God the Father had actually been portrayed in one icon, which was against the traditions of Orthodox icon-painting.[21] Viskovaty's censure of Sylvester's choice of themes and style was, however, not accepted by the Tsar and the *d'iak* suffered a three-year ecclesiastical penance (*epitemia*) for having taken an incautious initiative, while Sylvester was cleared of the charge of heresy.

The incident of the icons blew over, but the so-called heretics were subjected to a full-scale inquiry by a Church Council. Artemii, whose tenure as abbot of the Trinity monastery had lasted barely six months, since he proved too tolerant, was judged to have failed to condemn the heretics sufficiently harshly and sentenced to reclusion in the Solovki monastery. Not long after, he escaped, doubtless with the connivance of supporters in the monastery, and reached Lithuania, where he remained active as a faithful Orthodox follower of the tenets of the Trans-Volga elders. The more serious heretics, Bashkin and Fedor Kosoi, were sentenced to imprisonment in the monastery of Volokolamsk, where Bashkin died, while Kosoi managed to escape to Lithuania. Neither the heresy nor the prosecution was of major significance. But it was the first prosecution for heresy in which the young Tsar took a personal part, and it launched him on the path of intolerance and the development of the punitive powers of the government.[22]

Viskovaty escaped with a relatively minor penalty by Ivan's standards. But one may wonder whether the real target, both of the heresy trial and of the attack on new styles of icon-painting, was really Makarii, an attack possibly initiated by Ivan himself, sheltering behind Viskovaty. It may have been intended to reopen the debate in the Church Council on article 98 of the *Stoglav*, on the problem of the delimitation of ecclesiastical and secular jurisdictions in new and old town suburbs (*slobody*). If founded by archbishops, they were not subject to tsarist taxation, while those belonging to priests were taxed, in order to prevent taxable people from changing their residence from one area to another to avoid taxation. The decision of the Council had been that the metropolitans and archbishops, while retaining their existing jurisdiction, would agree not to set up new settlements or allow taxable people to move into existing ecclesiastical ones in future. In fact it was a way of limiting ecclesiastical income and a tacit victory of the Tsar over the Church.[23] There was no hope of forcing through confiscation of church estates through a Church Council, however. Nevertheless, Ivan may have been affronted by the underlying opposition of the Metropolitan on this particular issue of Church–state relations.[24]

Further evidence was discovered in the following year (1554) – according to a later chronicle[25] – that there had been a genuine attempt to alter the succession during Ivan's illness. This was the result of the attempted flight of Prince Semen Lobanov Rostovsky to Lithuania in summer 1554. He was caught on the border in July, arrested, interrogated and tortured. Rostovsky attributed his intention to fly to his mental crassness, his meagre way of life, idly and pointlessly eating him out of his tsarist award and his inheritance. Whether he was the ringleader of a conspiracy cannot be ascertained, but like many Russian princes and boyars he was aware of the different constitutional organization prevailing in Lithuania, where men like him were entitled to take part in electing the king. His servants confirmed that he had spoken ill of the Tsar, that he had treacherously consulted the Polish Lithuanian envoys at the time negotiating a truce in Russia and advised them not to make peace. He had informed the Lithuanians about conditions in Russia and had told them that the Tsar would be unable to keep conquered Kazan'. He had even spoken ill of the Tsaritsa, complaining that the Tsar dishonoured princely families by failing to appoint them to the highest posts and surrounding himself with young people, that he had persecuted the descendants of Riurik and had raised up a servant (*rab*) by marrying the daughter of an untitled boyar.[26] 'How can we be expected to serve our sister?' he had exclaimed. It is evident from what happened later that under torture he denounced many boyars and others for having plotted against the young Tsarevich Dmitri Ivanovich during Ivan's illness in 1553.[27]

Ivan set up a tribunal composed of members of his Privy Council[28] to investigate Rostovsky's treasonable intent, and to judge him, whereupon Rostovsky – in the new version of the entry interpolated in the chronicle

– admitted that he and many others had planned to leave Russia at the time of the Tsar's illness in 1553, when the choice seemed to have been between being ruled by the Zakhar'in relatives of Tsarevich Dmitri or by Vladimir of Staritsa. He named many of the plotters, including Vladimir himself, who had invited Rostovsky to take service with him.[29] The father-in-law of Ivan's brother, Iuri, had also been approached. When the Tsar had recovered from his illness Semen Rostovsky had attempted to conceal the whole plot, but fearing to be betrayed he determined to flee to Lithuania, a proceeding which he justified by the traditional 'right of departure' of the boyars to seek service with another prince, a right which had been rejected by the grand princes since the days of Ivan III. Condemned to death by the Tsar and the boyars, and brought to the place of execution, Semen was reprieved on the intercession of Metropolitan Makarii and other church hierarchs and sent to the prison cells of the monastery of Beloozero.

But the evidence that there really had been a serious plot against the Tsar in 1553 left its mark on Ivan and increased his distrust of the princes and boyars who surrounded him.[30] Clearly the Zakhar'ins did not have sufficient weight at court to destroy the Staritsky faction, and in 1554 Ivan quietly dropped a number of them from the Boyar Council, though they had maintained their loyalty in 1553.[31] What is also noticeable in the accounts of these events is a discrepancy between the more moderate early account of Ivan's illness and its consequences and the more agitated tone of the later account.[32] And finally the presence or absence of Makarii at what might well have been a deathbed is never once mentioned.[33] It is extremely unlikely that he was absent the whole time, since his presence would normally be required. So the failure to mention his presence must reflect some of the deliberate obfuscation which surrounds this incident in the chronicles.

The turmoil over the succession of Dmitri, followed by the child's death, left its mark on Ivan. At the time it may have led him to distrust the Zakhar'ins, who had been in too much of a hurry to presume his inevitable death and hence to exact the oath of allegiance to the baby Dmitri. But there is no agreement among historians, for sheer lack of evidence, on the new balance at court. According to one account, several members of Anastasia's family lost their posts in the mid-1550s, and a number of princes were appointed to the Boyar Council. On the other hand the crisis seems to have added weight to the position of Adashev. It is usually stated that Sylvester shared in his authority, but the only evidence dates from after the event. It is to be found in Ivan's own diatribes against the priest in his letter of 1564 to Andrei Kurbsky, and in an interpolation in a chronicle of the late 1570s/early 1580s which states that in 1553 Sylvester was in great favour with the Tsar, that he was all-powerful, gave orders to the Metropolitan and to military commanders, and in fact governed everything. It is also found in an early seventeenth-century chronicle entry.[34] Adashev was certainly active in the diplomatic discussions of these years, where his name is usually mentioned together with that of the *d'iak*, Ivan Viskovaty. The favourite is said to have been in charge of reporting to the Tsar, taking down his decisions and seeing them acted upon, and issuing occasional charters.[35]

It may have been the strain placed on Ivan's military resources both by the conquest of Kazan' and the subsequent pacification of the surrounding lands and by the extension of Russian ambitions to the conquest of Astrakhan' which led to further major changes in the nature of the Russian service levy which affected the form of landholding. The consolidation of the Russian hold over Kazan' and the eventual conquest of Astrakhan' made great demands on manpower. In Kazan' the Russians had to fight the local people and expel much of the native population of the city and surroundings. In 1550, while he was campaigning against Kazan', Ivan had sent a series of questions to Makarii in Moscow, many of which dealt with problems of military organization and show the way his mind worked. The questions put forward policies for discussion which were by no means all implemented. Among them was the further regulation of *mestnichestvo*, of which the inconveniences in wartime were obvious; the problem of monastic land as regulated in the *Stoglav*; and the establishment of strong frontier posts on the borders of Lithuania, 'Germany' (i.e. Livonia) and the Tatar khanates, to guard against fugitives, raids and forbidden goods. The efficiency with which the Russian frontier guards at this period were able to seize anyone attempting to desert, particularly to Lithuania, is striking.[36] Other important topics were raised by Ivan, such as the need to keep written records (in books) of the size and quality of allodial[37] lands, whether they were arable or meadow, the existence of rivers, lakes and so on. Similar records should be kept of service lands. Finally Ivan was also anxious about the fate of service lands if the *pomeshchik* should die, and proposed all sorts of alternative solutions mainly based on compelling the widow to remarry a new owner if she was young enough to have children, or compelling a sister or niece to marry the new owner if there was no widow. If she was too old, however, he suggests that the widow should be sent to a monastery, while the new holder of the estate cared for her children and family; and if she did not want to be a nun then she was to be given enough land to feed her, and her estate would be escheated to the Tsar.[38] In his final question, Ivan expresses the wish for a detailed survey of the land at his disposal and already granted, so that there should be no quarrels over lands and water in future. There is no evidence of discussions on these subjects among leading boyars, or at all; there are only the resulting edicts.

To what extent did the Tsar acquire military knowledge, and to what extent was he dependent on his commanders? It is worth asking this question, for the 1550s proved to be a period of great changes in the social organization of the Russian army, and in its technical equipment and methods of fighting. The service gentry cavalry remained an undisciplined body which fought in no particular formation, and which was badly affected by absenteeism. The troops could be ordered to dismount and fight on foot. The *strel'tsy* were uniformed, centrally armed and trained. Their service was hereditary, and they were granted plots of land to supplement their wages. In peacetime they engaged in various crafts. The *gul'iai gorod*, or mobile fortress, which could be quite sizeable, continued to be a feature of Russian assault tactics, giving protection to the harquebusiers and the artillery. The force was usually divided into five main regiments – advance, centre, left and right wings and rearguard – commanded by *voevody* in strict *mestnichestvo* rank, which created a lot of difficulties when senior commanders refused to serve under talented generals of lower rank. It became usual for the Tsar to insist on service 'without rank' (*bez mest*) to ensure his right to appoint men of his choice.[39]

The financing of the war effort was improved in 1555, by an edict which laid down that all lands and agricultural properties forcibly taken by monasteries in repayment of debt from *pomeshchiki* and peasants or by illicit expansion were to be returned to the owners; lands granted by boyars to monasteries were to be returned to the situation they were in at the death of Vasily III. This was clearly an effort to recover some lands from the monasteries, but it could scarcely be called a victory for the non-possessors. In turn, princely landowners in a certain number of principalities were not to sell or bequeathe their lands or give them to monasteries without the permission of the Tsar on pain of confiscation; and allodial estates given to monasteries were to be taken back and used as service estates. It was a policy aimed particularly at areas thick with minor princes of the ruling dynasty or at areas only fairly recently incorporated, such as Tver' and Ryazan'.

The most fundamental change, however, to the organization of military service and the status of landownership was the *ukaz* called the

Code of Service (Ulozhenie o sluzhbe) of 20 September 1555, which formed part of the *ukaz* which abolished *kormlenie*. The code laid down the service to be performed in relation to the amount of land received in a *pomest'ie* and consolidated the Russian cavalry army as a centrally recruited body paid by the state in the form of income from land, and in cash when on duty. The standard allocation was 100 quarters of land (*chetverti*, approximately half a hectare), to which every service man was entitled, the equivalent of a fully equipped horseman including armour to the value of 4.50 rubles. There were some six different levels of entitlement to land, ranging from 100 quarters to 350. Such a policy had to be based on knowledge of the extent of the land fund and a *perepis'* or land survey was set in hand to determine the quantity of free land belonging to the Tsar. Quite the most important novelty introduced by the Code of Service was the principle that 'all land must serve'. Princes and boyars had been the outright owners of their allodial lands, the former as descendants of sovereign princes. As the Chronicle of the Beginning of the Realm now put it, the Lord (*gosudar'*) 'ordered the service laid down in the code to be performed from *votchina* and *pomest'ia* land' ('*s votchin i s pomest'ya ulozhennuyu sluzhbu uchini zhe*').

Surprisingly little attention was paid by the aristocracy at the time and has since been paid by Soviet and Russian historians to this fundamental change in the status of allodial land and to the relationship of the boyars to the Crown brought about by it. Until the early fifteenth century boyars had theoretically been entitled to leave the service of the Russian grand prince, taking their lands with them, even if of late they only dared to do so in very few cases. This right implied that the grand prince had no property rights in their land. It must be noted that the Russian grand princes similarly insisted on the right of Lithuanian princes to leave Lithuanian for Russian service bringing their lands with them. This was a somewhat unusual situation in Europe, where kings mostly endeavoured to assert a residuary right of ownership of land, and often succeeded, as in the case of England since William the Conqueror, where all land belonged to the king and was distributed by him to a small number of tenants in chief. Muscovite Russia had been unified bit by bit, and the right of departure could now be claimed only in the case of princes who were likely to be supported by those whose service they entered, notably the Russian princes who left Russian service for that of Lithuania. Yet in 1555 the princes seem to have given up the right to own land unencumbered by service without a murmur, though it was precisely this unencumbered land which might have given them the power to resist the demands of the Tsar. Now, since all land must serve, all landowners must serve too, and were thus bound to service.[40] Now, not only service land could be confiscated for failure to perform the service due, so could allodial land. For those like the political philosophers of seventeenth- and eighteenth-century England who saw such a close link between property and freedom, the failure of the Russian aristocracy to detect the fatal weakening of their position which they had allowed to happen with such facility argues a superficial understanding of the realities of power. But was the failure to establish hereditary posts not even more debilitating?

Important as this enactment was, it was not embodied in any specific law and was simply introduced as the Tsar's decision (*prigovor*) on *kormlenie* and service, and is believed to have been drafted by Adashev and written up by him in the chronicles. This refutes the frequent attempt by Russian historians to assert that laws had to be approved and issued by the Boyar Council as a legislative institution. The larger-scale *kormlenie* had already been abolished in the earlier 1550s; the extension of its abolition was introduced by a simple verbal order from the Tsar and not by a law approved by the boyars. It was replaced by the election of local officials, mainly in northern Russia at this time. Moreover *kormlenie* was not done away with everywhere and all at once.[41] In the opinion of Skrynnikov the policy at this time did not favour either the boyars or the service gentry. The whole landowning class benefited, but inevitably the more powerful boyars and princes in the *dvor* benefited most, because they were closer to the Tsar.

War had undoubtedly exercised its fascination over Ivan, and his personal experience of campaigning may have been responsible for the intensive programme of military reforms of the mid–1550s. The sources give some clues as to who, among Ivan's close advisers, was primarily responsible for devising them, or even implementing them. Aleksei Adashev is of course frequently mentioned in the chronicles (which he may have been responsible for overseeing) as carrying out commissions for the Tsar. Inevitably, it took some time for new structures to be put in place, and again we do not know who was responsible for doing so or exactly when. One of the most recent students of the period has outlined a change in the personal composition of the court which reflects a new set of influences. The Iur'ev Zakhkar'ins, Anastasia's relatives, lost ground and they and the territorial *dvortsy*, or government agencies, in charge of regions like Tver' or Nizhnii Novgorod were replaced by the *d'iaki*, or non-boyar secretaries. Nine new boyars were appointed and several new *okol'nichi*. The new central functional bureaux (*izba*) were founded or expanded in these years: *Razboinaia* (brigandage), *Pomestnaia* (service estates), and the Razryad or Military Register, which brought together the calling up, inspection, and deployment of the service cavalry. This signified the gradual transfer from the territorial to the functional principle in the developing bureaucracy. Metropolitan Makarii, too, ceased to have such a dominant position, while the role of Aleksei Adashev became ever more prominent, coinciding in the years 1555–8 with the apogee of the reforming activity of the Boyar Council. Moreover, the late 1550s were a crucial moment in Ivan's personal development, since there was clearly a divergence of opinion in the Russian court about the direction Russia's next campaign of conquest should take.

Russian trade with the East benefited greatly from the conquest of Kazan', which was soon followed by the conquest and annexation of Astrakhan' on the Caspian Sea. The Russians had abandoned the old Tatar city in favour of a new fortress further downstream which was fortified by earthworks and defended by a well-armed garrison. A monastery was built nearby to care for the spiritual health of the Russian residents. The outcome of conflict between two factions among the Nogais led to one recognizing Moscow and the other supporting the Ottoman Turks. In 1556 Russian forces overthrew the Khan and annexed Astrakhan', bringing Russia physically nearer to the Porte, which began to show an interest in defending the area against the miscellaneous raiding of Don Cossacks, Dnieper Cossacks under Prince D Vishnevetsky, in alliance with Ivan IV, and various Circassian tribes.[42] The whole of the Volga was now in Russian hands and they controlled the trade through the Caspian.

Russian trade with the West was considerably hampered because its routes lay through potentially hostile territory, namely Poland–Lithuania and Livonia, with in the background the potential threat from Sweden, and further west the costly procedure of paying the Sound tolls to Denmark and then facing the obstacles to Russian trade created by the members of the Hanseatic League. Freedom of trade was becoming of more importance to Russia because of the increasing need for munitions and the wherewithal and skills to manufacture them. Not only might Russia have to pay tolls, but the passage of goods might be totally prohibited, just as the passage of Russian envoys to Western countries to pursue diplomatic negotiations and the passage of skilled craftsmen could be totally prevented.[43] Similarly, Ivan wanted safer communication with the West, though there is no evidence of a particular interest in the sea as such, and he was anxious to recruit technicians from abroad. Their passage could be obstructed, as in the well-known incident of the recruiter Hans Schlitte.

Schlitte was a merchant from Goslar, in Saxony, who traded on a large scale with a governor of Pskov. But the Russian's enterprise foundered, and he ended up under arrest in Moscow and was eventually executed. Schlitte persuaded the Emperor Charles V in autumn 1549 to give him a recommendation to the Tsar so that he could endeavour to recover his confiscated gold by promising to procure for Ivan skilled craftsmen who could cast heavy guns, and to provide instructors in their use. Schlitte proved so convincing that Ivan, in turn, gave him a recommendation to the Emperor Charles V, and the enterprising merchant converted this document into a credential, which presented Schlitte as an accredited agent of Ivan's. The whole episode became more and more mystifying, as it became involved with Charles V's hopes for the conversion of Russia and the efforts of the spokesmen for Livonia earlier, at the diet of Augsburg in 1547, to oppose the sale of any armaments to Russia. Lübeck was now also roped in to frustrate Schlitte's plan to supply Ivan with armaments, by preventing the embarkation of the large numbers of people he had recruited, while the Livonians tried to intercept them at sea. Schlitte was arrested for debt in Lübeck, and appealed to the Emperor, whereupon the Grand Master of the Livonian Order also appealed to Charles, who now supported the Grand Master on the grounds that Schlitte had not acted on behalf of Ivan but on his own. The whole story is both confused and ridiculous, and its ripples went on well into the 1570s.[44]

The rulers of Livonia were among the most determined in barring Russian access to the West through their lands, and they warned the Emperor Charles in 1551 that all the Tsar's neighbours went now in fear of him and bent their heads to him and that the Livonians dreaded to be brought under his *grausame Gewalt* (cruel power) and to be compelled to change their religion; and if craftsmen and artists were allowed to stream into Russia, they would be followed by thousands of evil Anabaptists, Sacramentists and others expelled from the German lands. For the time being Ivan contented himself in 1554 with a renewal of the existing truce with Livonia on payment by the latter of the tribute allegedly due to Russia since 1503, including the arrears, and the restoration of the Orthodox churches destroyed, together with the Catholic churches, by Lutheran fanatics in Livonia. The negotiations were carried out by Aleksei Adashev and Viskovaty. Trade was to be free for Russian imports and exports, but the Livonians still refused to allow the free passage of foreigners into Russia.[45]

Ivan's interest in direct communications and trade with western Europe was strengthened by the totally unexpected arrival on the shores of the White Sea, in summer 1553, of an English sea captain, Richard Chancellor, seeking a northern route to the Indies. The expedition had been financed by a group of English merchants, with government approval, and bore a letter from King Edward VI addressed to 'all kings, princes, rulers, judges and governours of the earth', in the hope of discovering a new, northern sea route to the Indies, free from Spanish and Portuguese control. Three ships were commissioned, but two were lost at sea.[46] Chancellor, with the *Edward Bonaventure*, made land near the mouth of the Northern Dvina river in the White Sea, on 24 August 1553, where local fishermen informed him that he was in the dominions of the Tsar of Russia. The northern route to Russia was not unknown, but Chancellor was the first Englishman to arrive in Russia by it, and he was eventually met by Russian officials (*pristavy*) and escorted to Moscow in November. Chancellor's letter from Edward VI opened the way for him in Moscow, and when he left for England in February 1554, he had secured Ivan's consent, in a letter addressed to Edward, to more English ships visiting his ports, and the Tsar had declared his willingness to open negotiations for the regulation of trade between the two countries.

From the very beginning Chancellor viewed the inhabitants of this strange land as 'the barbarous russes', though he was in many ways less prejudiced than later English envoys from the Russia Company. He had travelled in the Middle East, and possibly France, and was less supercilious than most Protestant Englishmen. He provided the first, and in many ways the most perceptive and sympathetic, of many accounts of Russia as seen by Englishmen, as well as information about Russian products, weights and measures, and trade. His description of northern Russia is in striking contrast to the devastation recorded by Giles Fletcher thirty years later.

Chancellor was impressed by the size but not the beauty of Moscow, and he thought poorly of the Kremlin, where the public buildings lacked the external ornamentation and internal decoration customary in Tudor palaces. But when he was finally received at court, he realized that finery in Moscow was worn, not hung on walls. The hundred courtiers who welcomed him were all dressed in cloth of gold to their ankles, while in the actual presence chamber Ivan was seated on a high throne with a 'diadem or crown of gold, appareled with a robe all of goldsmith's work' and a sceptre inset with precious stones, surrounded by his principal officials and members of his council, and flanked by two men who were probably Aleksei Adashev and Ivan Viskovaty, the two men in charge of Russian foreign relations with the West at this time. Chancellor was deeply impressed by the riches and the majesty of the Tsar, and after the usual formal exchanges, he withdrew into an adjoining chamber where he was looked after by Aleksei Adashev before proceeding to a banquet in the Golden Chamber starting as usual with roast swan.[47] Ivan was now clothed in a robe of silver and wearing a different diadem. The food was served on golden dishes, the tablecloths were spotless, and in the middle of the room there was a 'mighty cupboard' with the most elaborate display of gold and silver plate. Chancellor was also struck by the fact that Ivan greeted all his guests and nobles by name when he served each one with bread.[48]

Like Christopher Columbus, Chancellor started out to find one place and found another, in his case Russia. But trade was the immediate object of the English Company of Merchant Adventurers which sponsored his voyage, and Chancellor made the best use of his opportunities. When he reached home, however, the letters he carried, addressed to Edward VI, were delivered to Queen Mary I. From Ivan's point of view, Chancellor's landfall in the White Sea showed that direct access to the West could be opened, dangerous for sailors, but only liable to political interference by sea from Denmark–Norway. Access to the Holy Roman Empire, Italy and the West would remain precarious.

Chapter VIII

The War in Livonia and the End of the 'Chosen Council'

As usual there is no agreement among historians about what Ivan intended to do after the conquest of Kazan' and Astrakhan'. Was his first assault on Livonia in 1558 part of a campaign to acquire an opening on the Baltic, as is usually maintained, or was it merely an effort, at a time when he was strapped for cash, to collect tribute allegedly due to him from part of Livonia, namely the city of Dorpat?[1] Or was he hesitating between the Livonian option and a push to conquer the Khanate of Crimea, put an end to Tatar slave raids into Russia and perhaps acquire an outlet to the Black Sea? There is no evidence but his deeds.

Russian negotiations with the Livonian Order usually took place between Novgorod and the Order, or between Pskov and the Order or in the form of a treaty between the bishop of Dorpat and Pskov. Negotiations took place in Novgorod or Pskov, not in Moscow.[2] Livonia had been disrupted by religious and political conflict for some time, and the province was open to invasion from all sides. Authority was now divided between the remnants of the Teutonic or Livonian Order headed by Prince Wilhelm von Fürstenberg, the Archbishop of Riga and the leaders of the major commercial cities like Riga, Reval, Narva and Dorpat, now mainly Lutheran, who did not all view Russia with the same distrust. In Dorpat, for instance, many Russians had been settled for some time as traders or craftsmen, and there had even been an Orthodox church for them, which had allegedly suffered from vandalism during the religious turmoil in the province. Other cities were still closely linked with the German towns of the Hansa.[3]

Ivan's broader aims were quite clear: uninterrupted access to the West via a Baltic port would create a direct commercial link all the way from the Baltic to the Caspian, now that Kazan' and Astrakhan' were in Russian hands. Imports from the West, particularly of arms and military supplies, were ever more necessary now that Russia was embarking on hostilities with Western powers, requiring a more sophisticated type of armament. At present Russia's only outlet on the Baltic was the shallow and unsatisfactory port of Ivangorod, built over against Narva. The benefits to be drawn from the northern route explored by Chancellor could not yet be assessed. Frontier disputes between Russia and Sweden in Karelia had been settled by a truce of sixty years concluded in 1510.[4] Recent conflicts with Livonia over Russian trading rights and the free passage of craftsmen and supplies to Russia had been temporarily shelved by means of a five-year truce between the two sides in 1550. But in 1551, long before the expiry of the truce, the Livonian towns again obstructed direct Russian trade relations with the West, forcing the Russians to trade only through Livonian merchants. War was not yet implicit in the situation, but a pretext now existed.

In further discussions in 1554, Ivan IV reminded the Livonian envoys that, from the Russian point of view, the Order was in Livonia only on sufferance, and that if they did not comply with his demands, the Tsar would come for them in person. Russian diplomacy, in the persons of Aleksei Adashev and Ivan Viskovaty, now produced ancient claims to Russian suzerainty over the city of Dorpat, which had paid a tribute to Pskov of one mark per adult male dwelling in the city and its surroundings, or about six thousand marks, as far back as the time of Ivan III, when Pskov was an independent city republic.[5] The Livonians climbed down and agreed that all males in the bishopric of Dorpat would pay the agreed tribute by 1557, and they consented to allow Russians to buy all the goods they needed in Livonia except armaments, and to permit the passage of craftsmen. In the event, when the Livonian envoys arrived in Moscow early in 1557 they brought no money, and were sent packing by Ivan.

In the meantime a glimmer of light showed in the West, where Chancellor had returned to England with news of his auspicious reception in Moscow and of the permission given by the Tsar to open up trade between the two countries on very favourable terms for English merchants. Edward VI had been succeeded by Queen Mary and King Philip, who now granted a formal charter to the Russia Company. The company decided to send Chancellor back to Russia to attempt to establish trading relations on a stable footing.[6] Anglo-Russian trade could now become independent of the Danish-imposed Sound tolls,[7] the Hansa and the interposition of middlemen.

Events in Livonia developed in parallel with events in Kazan', where the Russian forces were still deeply engaged in mopping-up operations. Moreover, until Russian relations with the Khan of Crimea and the

Grand Prince of Lithuania–King of Poland were established on a firm basis, Ivan could not afford to advance deep into Livonia. But in 1557, the pacification of Kazan' and the conquest of Astrakhan' seemed relatively complete and many detachments from the various local tribes around Kazan' joined the Russian armed forces drawn up on the Livonian border. In the meantime yet another Livonian embassy arrived in Moscow in December 1557, again without any tribute money.

A little while earlier, in 1555–6, a feint, or possibly a more determined, operation had been launched in the south against the Khan of Crimea, now a vassal of the Ottoman Sultan, who had not recognized Ivan IV's newly proclaimed sovereignty over Kazan'. Its leader was Prince Dmitri Vishnevetsky, the Orthodox Lithuanian magnate whose base was in the Ukraine, around Kiev and the lower Dnieper, and who offered to cooperate with Russia. To what extent it was an independent undertaking and to what extent it was ordered by Ivan as part of a general strategic plan is difficult to establish. In military sorties of varying success, acting together with Cossack detachments which were beginning to acquire consistency, Vishnevetsky harassed the Crimeans, occupying the island of Kortitsa in the rapids of the Dnieper, which was later to become the headquarters of the Zaporozhian Cossacks. This led to a formal breach between the Khan of Crimea and Russia.[8]

Ivan had also been successful in warding off an attack by Sweden. The Grand Prince of Vladimir-Moscow did not have direct diplomatic relations with the ruler of Sweden, which were carried on through the *namestnik* or governor of Novgorod. This was a tradition going back to the days of the independent city republic, when Novgorod negotiated in its own name; it now enabled Ivan to bring pressure to bear on Sweden by continuing to refuse to treat her as a sovereign state. Indeed, in the diplomatic documents exchanged in this period, Ivan is very careful to stress the difference between himself as the hereditary Tsar of his lands and the base-born, non-royal, 'elected' King Gustavus of Sweden.

Gustavus had attempted in 1554 to construct a coalition between Sweden, Denmark, Poland–Lithuania and Livonia against Russia and had made his plan public at the Diet of Wolmar in Livonia in 1554, using the threat that if Livonia rejected his plans he would be forced to make peace with Moscow, leaving the province to the tender mercies of the Tsar. Sweden's projected coalition was of course regarded as hostile by Russia, who in 1555–6 twice attacked and ravaged Vyborg, while the Swedes attempted to seize Oreshek at the mouth of the Neva. This was clearly not a serious campaign, and, moreover, Livonia refused to follow the Swedish initiative. Hence in the following year Gustavus backed down and sent envoys to the then governor of Novgorod, Prince. M.V. Glinsky, to discuss peace with Russia. Ivan eventually consented to talks with the Swedish envoys in person, who were sent on to Moscow, formally received by the Tsar and treated to a proper banquet in the presence of the boyars and other members of his court.[9] In March 1557 a truce, to last until 1597, was signed between the King of Sweden and the governor of Novgorod, in which Sweden had to agree not to support either Livonia or Poland–Lithuania in a war with Russia. But Ivan still refused, in very rude language, to meet Swedish envoys himself in future, and they were again relegated to the governor of Novgorod.[10]

Meanwhile relations with England were taking shape. The newly formed Merchant Adventurers Company landed the cargoes of three ships in 1556, in the port of St Nicholas on the White Sea. They were forwarded by river down to Vologda, then by land to Iaroslavl' and on to Moscow. On the return journey in July 1556 (only one outward and one return journey could be undertaken before the port of St Nicholas became ice-bound) four ships sailed with cargoes of wax, train oil, tallow, furs, felt, yarn and so on, some of which probably belonged to a Russian envoy, Osip Nepea, sent by Ivan to Queen Mary. The voyage was disastrous: only one ship reached Britain, the *Edward Bonaventure*, belonging to Chancellor, and it was wrecked off the coast of Scotland. Chancellor lost his life in saving Nepea, and the cargo was pillaged by 'the rude and ravenous people of the country'. Rescued from the Scots, Nepea and the nine surviving members of his suite were given a lavish welcome in London, where Philip and Mary presented him with a lion and a lioness for Ivan. Nepea was informed that Russians would be allowed to trade freely in England, but unlike the English in Russia, they would have to pay customs dues. It was widely believed at this time that English ships were carrying arms to Russia, and the Emperor Ferdinand I interceded later with Queen Elizabeth to beg her not to supply such a dangerous monarch with weapons.[11]

There remained Poland–Lithuania. The Polish-Lithuanian Commonwealth needed outlets to the Baltic Sea just as much as Russia, if not more, because her trade was more bound up with Europe than that of Russia, which also traded to the Near and Far East. Control of the river Dvina and the great port of Riga would enable the Commonwealth to break through the German encirclement which extended north along the Baltic shore to the Russian border at Narva, and south to the now secularized lands of the Teutonic Knights in East Prussia. Ever since the collapse of the central authority of the surviving Order of the Livonian Knights, the Polish-Lithuanian kingdom had been conducting secret negotiations with the Archbishop of Riga on the future of the city, and on the choice of a successor who might be able to transform the bishopric into a lay principality on the East Prussian model, behind the back of the merchants and the city council, who supported the continuation of the rule of the Order, as it secured their monopolistic hold on Russian trade.

There was in addition a standing cause of war between Russia and the Commonwealth in the claim, first formally put forward in diplomatic negotiations by Ivan III, and recognized by King Alexander of Poland–Lithuania in 1503, that many of the Ukrainian lands which had once formed part of Kievan Rus' belonged as of right to the house of Riurik.[12] This is a claim which has been disputed by nineteenth- and twentieth-century historians who, in accordance with the dominant ideology of the times, in their approach to historiography, placed the demands of nationality before those of a dynasty. But Ivan III thought in terms of his dynastic rights, and the fact that Moscow had never ruled over Kiev was irrelevant to him, since his ancestor, Grand Prince Vladimir Monomakh of Kiev, had once ruled over what was one day to become Moscow. After all Vladimir Monomakh had been Grand Prince of both Vladimir and Kiev, and Vladimir was senior to Moscow and came before it in the Russian titulature.

Since 1552 a five-year truce between the two countries had maintained peace, but it was too unstable to last, since Poland–Lithuania firmly refused to recognize Ivan's new title as tsar and continued to address him as Grand Prince. Anxious to maintain the defence of their trade once the Order was unable to deliver, the cities of Livonia too turned towards the Commonwealth for protection, though Riga stood out for its independence. In September 1557, the Livonian Order concluded an alliance against Russia with Poland–Lithuania, the treaty of Pozvol, which placed the remnants of the Order under Polish–Lithuanian protection. The treaty clarified the situation in Livonia and was of course regarded as a *casus belli* by Ivan IV, who decided on war with Livonia before Poland–Lithuania could mobilize its forces to intervene in the province.[13]

War began in January 1558, when the main Russian army, together with a large contingent of Tatar cavalry led by a number of Tatar tsars, *tsarevichi* and nobles, Kabardian princes and nobles, and large numbers of Cheremis, Circassians, Bashkirs and Kazan' Tatars, invaded Livonia, under the supreme command of the one-time Khan of Kazan' who had now reverted to his previous role as Shigali (Shah Ali), Khan of Kasimov and vassal of Ivan IV. The countryside was duly plundered and ravaged, but Ivan was more concerned with the cities; in May 1558 the port of Narva surrendered to the Russian forces. Aleksei Adashev and Ivan Viskovaty carried out negotiations with the city's representatives to determine the conditions of its transfer to Russian sovereignty,[14] since Ivan hoped to open it up at once to direct European trade with Russia. The Russian conquest of Narva indeed altered the terms of trade in the eastern Baltic, freeing it from Livonian control and opening it up to Dutch and north German ports, to the extent that privateering now also became a lucrative business for the Livonian fleet in the Finnish Gulf.[15] On 19 July, Dorpat fell to Ivan's Tatar allies, who seem – at any rate in the cities – to have been fairly disciplined at this stage, in order not to alienate the future subjects of the Tsar.

Ivan also left a door open for talks, ordering the commander in chief, Shigali, to proclaim the Tsar's willingness to listen to what the Livonians might submit to him, while the authorities in Dorpat set about collecting the tribute allegedly due to the Russians, and originally paid to the independent city of Pskov.[16] There was a temporary respite in operations later in 1558, while Ivan switched troops under Prince I.D. Bel'sky to defend the line of the River Oka against a renewed Crimean attack. But operations in Livonia continued, for the time being, directed primarily against the port of Reval (Tallinn), which held out against a long siege. With Narva in Russian hands, however, direct Russian trade with the West had now been achieved. So dangerous was this for the other Baltic powers that an embassy sent by King Gustavus of Sweden to England in 1557 now appealed to Queen Mary to forbid her subjects to sail to the Russian port of St Nicholas in the White Sea.

It was after the return of this embassy to Sweden that the idea began to gain currency in that country of a possible match between the heir to King Gustavus, Prince Erik of Sweden, and the Princess – not yet queen – Elizabeth of England. Erik and his half-brother John may have been base born in Ivan's eyes (though Erik's mother was a European princess), but they were very personable, cultured and well-bred young men in the Renaissance manner, handsome, good linguists and good musicians. Elizabeth certainly might have done much worse than the future Erik XIV were it not for the fact that he went mad north-north-west about ten years later. Elizabeth refused the offer made to her on Erik's behalf by his brother John, now Duke of Finland, in spring 1560, but John succeeded in winning his father over to the idea that Erik should make an attempt in person, and the Swedish prince sailed for London to woo Elizabeth, now Queen of England, with the formal blessing of the Swedish Council of State, in June 1560.[17]

Meanwhile, a new Russian envoy, P. Alfer'ev, was sent by Ivan to Vilna in spring 1558 to discuss the possibility of a joint Russian and Lithuanian crusade against the enemies of Christianity. This Russian revival of the concept of an anti-Crimean, indeed anti-Turkish, alliance of Russia with Poland–Lithuania, and possibly other Catholic powers, was the consequence of Russian fear that Lithuania might participate in the Livonian war against her, at a time when the existing five-year truce between the two countries had run out. It also fell in with the anti-Moslem crusading spirit of Metropolitan Makarii. On 8 March discussions took place in Vilna, between Alfer'ev and King Sigismund Augustus, with a view to achieving a perpetual peace between the parties and keeping Poland–Lithuania out of the Livonian imbroglio. The terms offered by Ivan were surprisingly generous, so much so that one is inclined to ask how sincere he was. If a perpetual peace could be achieved he was prepared to forgo his claims to his patrimonial lands now in Lithuania, the city of Kiev and other towns, that is he would give up the traditional Riurikovich claims in order to win Livonia.[18] But, one wonders, who was deceiving whom? Was Ivan really prepared to abandon all claims to his 'hereditary lands' in order to obtain Livonia? And did Sigismund Augustus have any intention of participating in the destruction of the Crimean Khanate, which was far too useful to him as a counterweight to the power of Russia now that the latter was no longer threatened by the Tatar kingdoms of Kazan' and Astrakhan'?

Lithuania responded promptly to the Russian initiative, sending her own envoys to Moscow for talks which lasted from 5 June to 1 July 1558 and were conducted by Aleksei Adashev and Ivan Viskovaty, who assured the Lithuanian envoy that Russia was prepared to receive a 'grand embassy', in accordance with Russian diplomatic practice, to finalize the negotiations. The Lithuanian envoy was even allowed by Ivan to attend the Orthodox mass in the Cathedral of the Annunciation in the Kremlin. Meanwhile, the Russian advance in Livonia continued unchecked.

Ivan submitted new peace proposals to the Livonians, and when they were rejected his forces – this time under another Tatar commander in chief, Tokhtamysh, assisted by two princes from the Horde and the Princes Cherkassky (the name by which the Caucasian princes of Kabarda were known), as well as many Tatar princes and nobles – invaded the province again in January 1559, occupying towns, burning settlements, taking many prisoners and advancing as far as Courland.[19] Chaos reigned in the lands of the Order, but Ivan was now induced by the threatening moves of Denmark, Sweden and Poland–Lithuania to order an armistice from May to November 1559. This armistice enabled Russia's rivals in the Baltic to arm and organize their campaign, and it lost Russia all that she had so far gained by war and diplomacy.

Anxious for the future of Livonia, in summer 1559 the Grand Master and the remnants of the Livonian Order surrendered their independence to Poland and concluded a treaty with the Commonwealth in which the Order agreed to military cooperation with Poland–Lithuania, the sharing of any conquests they might make, and *de facto* placed what remained of the Order under Polish–Lithuanian protection at the cost of ceding some of its lands. The treaty of Vilna, to that effect, was signed on 31 August 1559. Soon after, the old, and pro-Russian, Prince Wilhelm von Fürstenberg was replaced by Gotthard Kettler as Grand Master. Denmark now seized the island of Oesel.

Meanwhile, in March 1559 a new, 'grand embassy' from Sigismund Augustus had arrived in Moscow to discuss the earlier Russian proposals for an alliance against the Crimean Khanate, which the King had decided to turn down, encouraged by a Turkish decision to restrain Crimean attacks on the Commonwealth. The envoys were invited to dinner with Ivan and talks were held with Aleksei Adashev and Viskovaty, but the Polish envoys now insisted to the Russians that there could be no permanent peace with Russia until Poland–Lithuania's territorial claims against Russia were settled, such as the return of Smolensk and a number of other towns to Lithuania. They proved impervious to argument and even compared Ivan to a snake which having devoured a man's wife and children now wanted to marry him.[20] When the Russians turned down their proposals, the Lithuanians suggested a prolongation of the existing truce, which Adashev rejected. A few days later the Lithuanians accused Ivan of declaring war on a Christian prince, namely the Archbishop of Riga, Christoph von Mecklemburg (who was a relative of King Sigismund's). Outraged, Ivan sent them away without any *med* (mead, the most modest of the offerings in kind made to an embassy), and Adashev withdrew (or was withdrawn) from the talks, which were handed over to the *d'iak* Viskovaty. The situation was clouding over for Ivan, for both Denmark and Sweden now began to press claims to parts of Livonia.[21]

As a result of Ivan's rejection of further talks, the Lithuanians very secretly began to prepare an alliance with the Crimea against Russia, to back up their forward policy in Livonia. The Russian hope of winning Poland–Lithuania over to a joint anti-Moslem crusade which Adashev and Viskovaty had been pursuing was now revealed as a total illusion: Poland–Lithuania would intervene in the Livonian conflict as the protector of the Order, if it intervened at all, and as the enemy of Ivan, thus widening and prolonging the conflict. This was a crushing blow to Ivan. Behind the weak and disorganized Livonia now stood the powerful Polish-Lithuanian Commonwealth, and Denmark was beginning to put in her claims. In November 1559, Kettler, at the head of Livonian troops which had been reinforced during the truce with Russia, destroyed a Russian army near Dorpat, a defeat due entirely to the negligence of the Russian commanders, who were involved in a suit for precedence.[22]

A renewed threat by the Crimeans forced Ivan to send reinforcements to the south and to man the defensive line on the River Oka. In 1558–9 two Russian detachments were sent, one under Daniil Adashev, Aleksei's brother, and the other under Ivan's gentleman of the bedchamber, Ignatii Veshniakov, to build a fort on the Donets River as a base for an advance on Crimea to be led by Ivan himself. The idea of building ships on the Donets was launched at that time, but of course Ivan never went there, and the Russian armies served mainly to keep the Khan of Crimea busy at a time when the Sultan in Constantinople had refused to support his Crimean vassal, and when the Khanate was suffering badly from an epidemic of the plague (as was Pskov). Prince D. Vishnevetsky, the Lithuanian magnate, who was intermittently Ivan's ally, carried on operations on the lower Dnieper, and Russian forces which had sailed down the Dnieper under Daniil Adashev raided the coasts of Crimea. Ultimately the plan was to lure the Crimeans into a set battle in the open, but nothing came of it.

Meanwhile, Ivan's life was beginning to be overshadowed by a great personal anxiety. Never a considerate husband, though evidently very uxorious, he insisted on taking his wife and children, and other members of his family, with him wherever he went on his combined pilgrimages, hunting expeditions and military inspections. This had already led to the loss of his first-born son, Dmitri. After twelve years of marriage, Anastasia had by 1559 borne Ivan six children – three girls and three boys, of whom all the girls and one boy had died in infancy. Of her two surviving sons, Ivan, the eldest, seemed to be strong and healthy; but the signs of what may have been Down's syndrome were already apparent in the youngest, Fedor, born on 31 May 1557.

On 25 September 1559, in accordance with the tradition in the grand princely family, Ivan, who loved visiting monasteries, went to pray at the Trinity monastery with all his family – and to hunt – and returned at the end of the month to Moscow. At the beginning of October the Tsar set off again to Mozhaisk with all his family, including Anastasia, who was beginning to ail. It was here that the news reached him that the Livonian

Order had broken the truce and placed itself under the protection of the Commonwealth, and that the new Grand Master, Gotthard Kettler, with a Livonian force, had defeated the Russians outside Dorpat in November 1559. Reinforcements had to be sent immediately to Dorpat. The Tsar attempted at once to return to Moscow but found the roads completely impassable because of exceptional rain and flooding. The Tsaritsa's health grew steadily worse, but in spite of the weather he brought her back to Moscow, which they reached on 1 December. 'How shall I recall the merciless journey to our ruling city with our ailing Tsaritsa Anastasia,' wrote Ivan to Prince Kurbsky in 1564.[23] From then on, she faded gradually away.

The rashness of Ivan's hope of winning over Lithuania to an anti-Moslem crusade was brutally revealed to him in that same autumn 1559 when Daniil Adashev delivered to Moscow dispatches addressed by the Lithuanians to the Khan of Crimea. The messages had been captured by a Russian detachment at a crossing point on the Dnieper. In these reports, King Sigismund Augustus notified the Khan that he was prepared to cooperate with him against the Tsar. Thus did Daniil, without knowing it, destroy the policy his brother Aleksei had allegedly been pursuing, with or without the Tsar's approval.[24]

The policy of attempting to secure an alliance with Poland–Lithuania in order to avoid a war on two fronts, the assumption that the Commonwealth was as concerned as Russia to put an end to the Crimean Khanate's raids on Christian lands, had ended in total failure. Aleksei Adashev may have sponsored it and had been in charge of implementing it. He is usually considered to have opposed the advance into Livonia, but there is really no evidence of his own personal opinion.[25] If he was responsible for the armistice of May–November 1559, then Ivan may well have borne him a grudge, which was to grow and fester, for what was to prove a fatal mistake.

Yet again an embassy from Sigismund Augustus arrived in Moscow on 7 December 1559. Negotiations with Lithuania became more and more tense. At the Lithuanian envoys' audience with Ivan on 30 January 1560, Adashev was not present. The envoys asked for 'private talks' with the Russian negotiators, and with Adashev, which conveys the impression that they hoped to go behind Ivan's back on the assumption that they could speak to a so-called 'peace party'. But attempts to speak with the envoys of the other party seem to have been a policy practised by both Russians and Lithuanians, for when Russian envoys were in Lithuania, they also asked to speak privately to Lithuanian officials or nobles, implying here too an attempt to separate the King from his officials, to reach an agreement behind his back. So it may merely have been an old and accepted ploy, a way of saying what could not be said officially. Viskovaty; for instance, promptly repeated to Ivan all that was said to him. (Viskovaty is several times referred to by Russian historians as head of the Russian *razvedka* or security service, in fact a sort of Francis Walsingham, more it seems on the basis of how he behaved than of any evidence of the existence of such a service.)

Thus far the Russians had been successful in most of their military undertakings in Livonia proper, but according to some Russian historians the war divided the Russian aristocracy, who were not so much at loggerheads about the aims as about the timing of a campaign which was bound to lead to the involvement of major powers such as Sweden and, above all, Poland–Lithuania.[26] Internal reform which had marked the years 1555–8 had been postponed or abandoned; Russia was not, in the sixteenth century – indeed was almost never – in a position to embark on major political or social reforms in time of war. As a result there had allegedly emerged a war party, that of the Tsar himself, and a peace party, that of Adashev (and of Sylvester, the only person ever actually mentioned by Ivan as having opposed the war) though possibly not of Viskovaty.[27] The consequences of this division became evident in the crisis of the years 1559–64, and may have contributed to the eventual disgrace of Aleksei Adashev and of his brother Daniil, whose exploits against the Crimea were praised by Aleksei – who was at that time in charge of compiling the official Nikonovskaia Chronicle – as substantial victories. But the Tsar was not deceived. He wrote in 1564 to Prince Kurbsky, referring to Daniil's raids on the Crimean coasts in 1558–9, 'What of your victory on the Dnieper and the Don? How much sore affliction and destruction was brought upon the Christians, while the enemy suffered not even the slightest discomfort?'[28]

The Lithuanian envoy urged Aleksei Adashev, when he spoke to him alone, to remind the Russian boyars to persuade the Tsar to make peace, on the Lithuanian terms. Ivan was so outraged that he sent them away without even a banquet, which was positively insulting.[29] Still another Lithuanian envoy arrived in Moscow and on 23 January 1560 issued an ultimatum to Ivan to stop the war in Livonia, which, he asserted, belonged to the Grand Principality of Lithuania. In private talks with Adashev and Viskovaty he too endeavoured to give the impression that there was a disagreement between the Poles, the dominant party, and the Lithuanians, the former being anxious for war, while the Lithuanians were more amenable to negotiations. But this was merely a ploy to get Ivan to send an 'embassy' to Lithuania to conclude peace on Sigismund's terms. When Adashev showed the Lithuanian envoy the charters setting out the tribute paid by Dorpat of old, he exclaimed that this was competely new to him.

On 30 January 1560, Ivan received the Lithuanian envoy in an audience at which Adashev was not present, and sent him away empty-handed, again not even inviting him to a meal; the envoy left on 2 February. In the same month an envoy also arrived from the Emperor Ferdinand, in the hope of mediating between the two parties, but the Russians stressed that there was no point in further talks, since the Lithuanians had already entered 'our Livonian lands and occupied a number of towns', to which the Lithuanians repeated that Livonia had always belonged to the Commonwealth, having been granted by the Holy Roman Emperor. The final breach occurred early in July 1560, when couriers were again exchanged between Russia and the Commonwealth. Discussions took place between Viskovaty and the Commonwealth envoy, but neither these attempts at peacemaking nor a renewed attempt by Sweden to mediate served any purpose.

The year 1560 is usually regarded as the year in which the so-called 'Chosen Council' fell from power and its principal members were disgraced by Ivan IV, reflecting a complete change of character in the Tsar himself and leading to a complete change of government. Clearly, by the early 1560s Ivan had decided that in order to pursue the policy on which he had determined, he must surround himself with new advisers. The first external sign of the new course was the dismissal of Aleksei Adashev from his post in the court in Moscow (whatever it was) and his appointment as third *voevoda* of the army in Livonia, serving under Prince I.F. Mstislavsky.

Ivan now determined to launch a stronger campaign. He appointed Prince A.M. Kurbsky as second *voyevoda* 'to stiffen the troops', and a substantial force under Prince I.F. Mstislavsky advanced against the Livonian army, inflicting a major defeat on it in the battle of Ermes on 2 August 1560 and capturing Fellin, the great fortress of the Order, where the old Grand Master Wilhelm von Fürstenberg was still living. Fürstenberg was taken prisoner to Moscow, where he was held in reasonable conditions and eventually died. The Landmarschall Philip von Bell and three other high officers, perhaps because Adashev interceded for them, perhaps because Bell was rude to Ivan, were all executed.[30]

Adashev had never served as a *voevoda* on active service before, though he had taken a prominent part in the diplomacy of the campaign against Kazan'. He took part in the battle of Ermes and in the capture of the fortress of Fellin; Daniil Adashev, who was a professional soldier, was also now sent to the army in Livonia, where he commanded the artillery.

The reason usually given for the fall of the so-called 'government of Sylvester and Adashev' is their disagreement with Ivan's policy of expansion at the expense of the disintegrating Livonian Order before the conquest of Kazan' had been properly consolidated as a base for further expansion against the Tatar Khanate of Crimea. This implied the turning away of Russia from expansion at the expense of the non-European world of Islam towards expansion in the Christian world of the West. The source for this explanation is the correspondence between Prince A.M. Kurbsky and the Tsar, begun by the former in 1564, and it is based on the assumption that Sylvester was in some way influential in the administration and that Aleksei Adashev had occupied a prominent post in the 'government' for a number of years and was a member of the so-called *Blizhniaia Duma*, or Privy Council carved out of the main Boyar Council, composed at times of over twenty members. According to S.O. Schmidt, in an article first published in 1954[31] describing Adashev's career, Adashev was appointed to a new *chelobitnaia izba*, or Chamber of Requests, in 1549, after the famous *Sobor primirenia* or 'assembly of reconciliation' which took place after the fire of 1547 and the elimination of the Glinsky princes from power (see Chapter IV).[32]

Ivan's attack on what he described as the partnership between Sylvester and Adashev dates from 1564; he accused them of 'holding counsel in secret', issuing orders without consulting him, giving worldly instead of spiritual advice, and 'taking the splendour of our power from us'. He charged the two with distributing estates to their supporters, scattering them in the wind in an unbefitting manner; with 'strengthening their position with friendships' and acting in their interests with a total disregard for his authority and interests. Ivan was particularly angered at the fact that all this oppression from which he suffered was enforced in the name of God and religion.

For S.O. Schmidt, the social position of Adashev, halfway between the boyars and the service gentry, made him the ideal person to carry out, on behalf of the Tsar, the 'policy of compromise' between these two forces which, again according to Schmidt and many other Soviet historians, dominated the early 1550s. The possibility that the Tsar might simply have liked and trusted Adashev at that time cannot be considered seriously in Marxist historiography, since history is moved by social forces and not by people. On the other hand, in his letter to Kurbsky of 1564[33] Ivan speaks with great contempt of Adashev's origins, referring to him as 'that dog Adashev who in my youth served only to walk in front and clear people out of my way'.[34] Yet Adashev formed part of Ivan's escort drawn from members of the Privy Council on various journeys in 1553, after Ivan's illness, and in 1554; he was at the council meeting that took the decision concerning brigands in January 1555, and took part in the Tsar's march to Kolomna in summer 1555.[35] But his official rank was still no higher than *okol'nichi*, to which he was raised in 1553.

However, according to a later historian, Filiushkin, writing in 1999, there is no evidence that Adashev was ever appointed to the rank of gentleman of the bedchamber, even though he was so frequently in Ivan's company and seems to have carried out the functions associated with that post; nor is there any evidence of the existence of the Chamber of Requests in 1549. According to A.A. Zimin, the Chamber of Requests was an extremely important institution because all complaints against officials of any kind came before it, and it was Adashev who was supposed to decide on them, either after referring them to the Tsar or on his own initiative. He was thus at the centre of the 'judiciary'.[36] It is worth noting that the official title of the head of a government office was *sud'ya* or 'judge', which confirms the extent to which administrative and judicial functions were perceived as interrelated, as were the abstract concepts of ruling and dispensing justice. But no trace has been found of any documents purporting to issue from the Chamber of Requests until the 1560s, so historians have now cast grave doubts on its existence in the 1550s. There is, however, evidence that Adashev was closely concerned with a number of policies implemented by the Boyar Council and the Treasury (*kazna*).

Lists of the boyars and other council ranks, and military leaders who were closest to Ivan at this time suggest that there was a change of personnel about him in the years 1555–8, and that within the new and most high-ranking group there was a core of active agents of Ivan's will, including the three *okol'nichi*, namely Aleksei Adashev, L.A. Saltykov and F.I. Umnoi Kolychev, whose names appear more frequently than anyone else's on documents issued on behalf of the Tsar. But Adashev rarely appears as the initiator, only as the executor of a given order, and therefore to identify him with the leader of a government is far-fetched.[37]

The death of the Tsaritsa Anastasia in August 1560 was the signal for the final downfall of Adashev. He had participated in several successful military operations in Livonia since joining the army under the overall command of Prince I.F. Mstislavsky; nevertheless, he was removed from his post as third *voevoda*, and appointed *voevoda* of

Fellin, a form of honourable exile. Moreover, almost immediately after Adashev's new appointment, on 9 October 1560, Ivan issued an order confiscating all his lands in Kostroma (where they were very extensive – the whole village of Borisoglebsk, comprising some fifty-five estates), and also the patrimonial estates of his mother in Pereiaslavl' (his father had meantime become a monk in the Beloozero monastery and may have died in 1556),[38] which were handed over to the boyar I.V. Sheremetev Men'shoi (junior). Adashev was allocated instead larger, but less productive, estates in Novgorod district, a clear indication that he would not be serving in the court in Moscow again.[39] In Fellin he was promptly involved in a local precedence suit with a noble, junior in rank and standing to himself, who appealed to the Tsar. Ivan was not going to take the side of his ex-protégé and removed Adashev from Fellin to Dorpat, under the *voevoda* Prince D.I. Khilkov, who also subjected him to a number of humiliating pinpricks.

Not much more is known of Adashev's life, except that he caught a fever and died in Dorpat some time in late 1560 or early 1561. After his death Prince Andrei P. Teliatevsky was sent to Dorpat to take charge of his papers, which included rough notes for the preparation of entries in the chronicles. Whether or not Adashev took a prominent part in drafting or redrafting the chronicles cannot be proved, but it seems unlikely that he had more than notes for future entries with him in Dorpat.[40] Adashev's epitaph may be summed up in the remark of the nineteenth-century man of letters A.I. Turgenev, to the poet and tutor of Alexander II, V.A. Zhukovsky: 'You do not belong to yourself: your name will be known to posterity. Your role will be *à peu près* that of Adashev.'[41]

Daniil Adashev did not long survive his brother. One of his relatives was suspected of treason in 1563; two *voevody* were arrested and as the investigation widened almost all the surviving relatives of Aleksei Adashev were arrested including Daniil, Daniil's father-in-law, P.I. Turov, and Aleksei's father-in-law. Kurbsky, who had been transferred from Polotsk and appointed *voevoda* in Dorpat in Livonia, heard of the arrests and went first to Moscow, where he met Turov, who was a friend of his and who warned him of what was coming. A month later Turov had laid his head on the block. Probably in connection with this affair, Daniil Adashev and his twelve-year-old son Tarkh, were also executed, together with two other related families and their children.[42]

Sylvester as a priest had more independence than Adashev, and he was also considerably older, probably by now in his late sixties. Evidently, when he saw which way the wind was blowing he made up his mind to take the cowl and to withdraw to the monastery of Beloozero, with which he had been keeping up connexions for some time, and where he became a monk under the monastic name of Spiridon. He took his library and other effects to the monastery with him: his name is entered in some of the books. The monk Spiridon lived for some ten years in the monastery and probably died there around 1568 or 1570.[43] His name is found in the monastery's official *sinodik* (the list of names of those who have died and should be prayed for).

Sylvester is assumed to have been a supporter of the non-possessors, because of his close relations with the monastery of St Cyril of Beloozero, one of their original outposts, and because he finally withdrew there. He was also in communication with Maksim Grek when the latter was transferred to the Trinity monastery. He was therefore, according to Zimin, who expounds this theory, bound to be attacked and undermined by a powerful group of Josephians. Ivan in turn accuses Sylvester of being responsible, together with Adashev, after the breach with him, for the murder by stoning at their orders of the Josephian Bishop of Kolomna, Feodosii.[44] It seems, however, very unlikely that Sylvester, with or without Adashev, could give orders leading to the murder of a bishop. Such an analysis of his political orientation leaves out of account his relations with the Metropolitan Makarii, who was undoubtedly a Josephian, and leaves one under the impression that the political outlook of most of the major figures at the court of Ivan was not nearly so cut and dried as historians have made out in the effort to clarify their stand in the class war. The evidence is as usual very slender, and is in the nature of what they ought to have thought and done rather than of what they actually did.

The final act in the tale of the 'Chosen Council' occurred sometime towards the end of August, before Adashev was sent away as *voevoda* to Fellin in Livonia.[45] The Tsaritsa's brothers, the Iur'ev-Zakhar'ins, had always been opposed to Sylvester and Adashev (the dislike was apparently mutual), and after her death they circulated reports that she had been poisoned by her enemies at court and persuaded Ivan to set up a formal trial of Sylvester and Adashev. The evidence that such a trial took place seems to lie exclusively with Kurbsky in his *History of Ivan IV*; he states that the Tsar immediately believed in the accusations of witchcraft brought against 'these good and holy men' by his brothers-in-law and, deceived by their flattery, he 'summoned a council, composed not only of his secular senate, but of all the clergy', that is to say the Boyar Council, the Metropolitan and the bishops and all the higher clergy. The main charge of sorcery was directed at a certain Maria Magdalina, a venerable Polish lady with five sons, who was said to live in Adashev's house. She was 'a great faster' according to Kurbsky, who is the sole source to mention her, who mortified herself even further by wearing heavy chains. She was charged with being a witch and a confederate of Aleksei Adashev and was put to death with all her children.

The existence of a council called to try Sylvester and Adashev is accepted by one of the leading Russian scholars, R.G. Skrynnikov, because in his view, as an *okol'nichii* Adashev had to be judged by his peers, i.e. the Boyar Council. There is no evidence for this requirement in Russian sixteenth-century judicial procedure (the concept of 'peers' did not exist), but the Tsar may have felt the need to secure a public proclamation of the guilt of his previous councillors. Kurbsky does express outrage at the procedure adopted by Ivan, namely a so-called trial, *in absentia*. 'Where under the sun is such a judgment – without confrontation – heard of?' he exclaims. And he quoted from John Chrysostom's letter to Pope Innocent I, in which John protested against the accusations made against him in Constantinople: 'Neither in pagan law-courts nor in barbarian places of justice have such things ever happened. Neither Scythians nor Sarmatians ever gave judgment on one side only, in the absence of the accused.'

Only the Metropolitan Makarii urged that the two men (Adashev and Sylvester) 'should be brought before' the Council 'so that the charges may be brought against them in their presence for it is indeed right that we should hear what they have to say in reply'. But the flatterers of the Tsar shouted him down: 'It is not right, O bishop, these men are recognized evil-doers, and they will bewitch the Tsar and destroy us if they come.' Kurbsky then states that Sylvester was sent to the Solovki monastery, while Adashev, then in Dorpat, was arrested and ended up in prison.[46] There are, however, substantial inconsistencies in Kurbsky's story, notably his assertion that in October 1560, after the so-called trial took place, Adashev was given the substantial land grant in Novgorod province to replace his confiscated estates, an unlikely event had he been condemned for witchcraft; while Sylvester's son Anfim, a highly placed *d'iak*, was merely removed to a provincial post. It seems, therefore, that Kurbsky, writing in Lithuania and in the 1570s, may have confused some of the detail and the timing of events; he had been in Moscow in 1563, when he saw P.I. Turov, the father-in-law of Daniil Adashev, who warned him of the visions he had had of the executions to come and could well have informed him of the conviction of Adashev and Sylvester for witchcraft had they taken place. Moreover, Kurbsky is clearly wrong about the exile of Sylvester to Solovki. But what he wrote is very good evidence of his own passionate hatred of what Ivan IV had become.[47]

Was it the failure of the foreign policy of Adashev and Viskovaty that caused their disgrace (*opala*) – permanent in the case of Adashev, temporary in that of Viskovaty, who had been so closely associated in its conduct from the beginning, in Kazan'? (Viskovaty was after all only sent on a brief mission to Denmark before returning to his post.) Or had Ivan come to resent what he sensed as criticism, and which to him was treason? The dominant role of Aleksei Adashev, Sylvester and the 'Chosen Council' in policy-making in all fields has been constantly stressed in Russian historiography, but in fact traces of the activity of Adashev himself, in this period, are found mainly in the conduct of foreign policy. We do not know what Adashev actually thought, or whether the foreign policy he was pursuing, usually jointly with Ivan Viskovaty, was their own or that of the Tsar – although the language noted in the reports of the conferences held with representatives of foreign powers suggests that though the Tsar might not actually have been physically present he was undoubtedly there in spirit. There is nothing in the contemporary chronicles or surviving official records to confirm the portrayal by Ivan of the domination exercised over him by Sylvester and Adashev, of their plotting together against him, or attempting to conceal from him what was happening in the country.[48]

In fact there is nothing to confirm the existence of an institution called the Chosen Council at all. It is never mentioned except in Kurbsky's letters to Ivan IV. But Kurbsky does not mention either Sylvester or Adashev or the Council in his first letter to Ivan. The idea of such a body owes its origin to the diatribes of Ivan IV, in his first letter to Kurbsky, against two people who were at one time close to him, served him and in the case of Sylvester preached at him very powerfully, telling him how to behave, what to wear, how many church services to attend, how often to fast and possibly how often to make love to his wife. The diatribes against individuals were seized on by Kurbsky and returned in kind, but not in the context of an institution. The Chosen Council, for him, is composed of 'select' men, of good, even saintly character, the 'strong in Israel' who are being destroyed by the beast of the Apocalypse. There were chosen men about Ivan, but no Chosen Council. Similarly (if on a lower level of importance), there was no trial in 1560, though there may have been a meeting of some of Ivan's advisers which condemned the two men, thus justifying the confiscation of Adashev's lands, but taking matters no further. The misunderstandings arising out of Kurbsky's letters and his *History* are of the same nature; his anger leads him to such violent invective against Ivan that he fails to be precise about what he is actually describing.

Chapter IX

The Death of Anastasia, and Ivan's Second Marriage

There were several serious fires in Moscow in July 1560, and the Tsar removed Anastasia from the city to his palace in the country at Kolomenskoe, while he, together with his cousin Vladimir of Staritsa, worked hard to extinguish the fires.[1] Some three thousand Crimeans raided Moscow on 2 August and were put to flight. But the shock and the smoke were too much for the failing Tsaritsa, and she died on 7 August 1560 at the age of twenty-nine. Thus passed away the first Tsaritsa of the whole Russian realm. An apparently gentle and unassuming person, she was evidently much loved, not only by Ivan, and her funeral was the occasion for a huge popular demonstration, for she was merciful and bore no malice. The Tsar followed her bier, wailing and groaning, upheld by his brother Iuri, his cousin Vladimir and two Tatar tsarevichi, and accompanied by the people from the whole city, who came not in order to receive alms, but from their sorrow at her death.[2] The Tsaritsa had no doubt succumbed to the fate of so many women at that time in all countries, the anaemia and exhaustion brought on by repeated pregnancies, added to grief at the death of four of her children, and by the physical effort to keep up with her husband's activities[3] in a very hostile climate. Nothing is known about her relations with Ivan directly. Instead, she is mirrored in his correspondence, in various chronicles and in the writings of others. Ivan later accused Aleksei Adashev and the priest Sylvester of contributing to her death by urging him not to take her on pilgrimages to visit holy shrines and relics, which would have enabled her to recover her health. And he was convinced that they had used magic against her. Karamzin puts it in a nutshell: for those who believe in the existence of 'two Ivans', the good and the evil: 'This was the end of the happy days for Ivan and for Russia; for he lost not only his wife, but his better nature [*dobrodetel'*].'[4]

Thus far Karamzin's human and kindly portrayal of these events, but there are other views. For a long time some historians of Russia have held that Anastasia was poisoned, and examination of her exhumed bones at various times has often confirmed scholars in their conjecture that she (and several of Ivan's relatives and nobles) suffered this fate. A recent analysis of the amounts of arsenic and mercury, the poisons surmised to have been used, found in her bones indicates the presence of 0.8 mg of arsenic per 100 g of bones, and 0.13 mg of mercury. This compares with the same level of arsenic in the bones of Grand Princess Elena Glinskaia, Ivan IV's mother (d. 1538), and Tsar Fedor Ivanovich (d. 1598). But even assuming that Anastasia was poisoned, which this evidence does not confirm, who had an interest in killing this entirely inoffensive young woman? Certainly not Adashev, already exiled to Fellin, nor Sylvester. And surely not Prince Kurbsky? The general conclusion one can draw from this evidence is that Anastasia was not poisoned, and that Ivan's later determination to believe that she was formed part of the paranoia which was gradually gathering within him and obscuring his vision.[5]

Only about a week after the death of Anastasia, on 14 August 1560, Metropolitan Makarii, the bishops and the boyars appeared before Ivan with a somewhat unexpected petition. They begged the Tsar to stop grieving and, placing his hopes in God, to remember that he should not put off remarrying, because he, the ruler, was still young and had not yet reached the years when he could live without a spouse. Thus he should marry soon in order not to suffer from privation. Ivan took a little time to reflect, but decided that it was better to marry than to burn, and almost at once he announced that he would take a new wife.

This decision has surprised many historians, particularly those influenced by contemporary attitudes to love, many of whom believe that Ivan's devotion to Anastasia required him to mourn her for a longer time. In particular the otherwise sober S.B. Veselovsky was outraged at the suggestion that a man who led such a dissolute life and was so selfish in the demands he made on his wife could have had any feeling for her.[6] He suggests that Makarii's proposal that the Tsar should remarry was motivated by disapproval of his dissolute behaviour since his wife's death. Undoubtedly Ivan was a highly sexed man, and if Anastasia's illness had inflicted a period of compulsory chastity on a very passionate nature, he may have found relief in wandering from the marriage bed. Karamzin notes an entry in a manuscript of one of the chronicles to the effect that 'on the death of the Tsaritsa Anastasia, the Tsar began to fly into rages and be adulterous'.[7] There is every likelihood that this was true, and even that Ivan was unfaithful before Anastasia's death, whether he loved her or not. When Kurbsky reproached him much later with what in this context they called 'sacrifices to Cronus', namely betraying the Tsaritsa during her lifetime, Ivan replied: 'And if you say that I did not hold out and did not remain pure, well, we are all men.' And he pointedly, if obscurely, inquired of Kurbsky: 'Why did you take the soldier's wife?'[8] The Chronicles too remarked on the change in Ivan's character with the death of Anastasia. He became totally uninhibited in his behaviour. Her death caused a raging turmoil in the depth of his nature, changed his sagacious character into a frenzied temper, and he began to crush many of his relatives and his counsellors.[9]

The intensity of the crisis following on Anastasia's death leads one to wonder whether it caused some kind of psychological breakdown in the Tsar's mind, increasing his paranoia to a degree of panic which he could master only by dissolute orgies and the widespread slaughter of his presumed enemies. He had always been cruel and sadistic, but the loss of control, the extent and precipitate nature of the operations he began now to embark on were new, and the degree of sadism unprecedented.

There were, however, other considerations which were bound to induce the Tsar to marry again. First of all, although Ivan had two sons, the younger, Fedor, was not a very promising candidate for the throne so that all hopes were concentrated on the elder son, Ivan Ivanovich, who might not live. The Tsar's brother, Iuri, was never even considered as a possible heir (Iuri's son, Vasili, born in 1560, died at the age of eleven months to Ivan's great grief),[10] so that the nearest successor now was, inevitably, Vladimir Andreevich of Staritsa, who, though not a strong character, was in a good position to win over many of the appanage princes in order to forestall a minority with a regency under Anastasia's relatives, the Iur'ev Zakhar'ins. Ivan naturally enough preferred to leave his realm to a son of his own.

The second consideration concerned the balance of power between factions in Ivan's court. As long as Ivan was unmarried, the influence of the brothers of Anastasia would remain powerful, perhaps even increase. By marrying he would introduce new elements and reposition the old. Many boyars who opposed the influence of Anastasia's brothers were therefore anxious for him to marry suitably.

But Ivan did not intend to marry into a Russian family this time, a policy which would surround him again with relatives of his bride. Moreover, in the past Russian grand princes had married into foreign ruling houses, and it befitted him to do the same. Thus he sought for a consort in a foreign royal family. There was to be no bride-show. Marriage was to form part of foreign policy. But Ivan exacted a certain degree of choice. He ordered his envoys to inspect possible Swedish and Polish girls, but Tatar girls were to be brought to Moscow for him to choose among them.[11] Ivan turned first to Poland–Lithuania, in spite of the tense relations between the two countries. War had not yet in fact broken out between Poland–Lithuania and Russia; Russian forces were advancing from Dorpat in Livonia, and Sweden was besieging Reval, but Sigismund Augustus was still negotiating with the new Grand Master of the Order over the division of the spoils when the Order should finally collapse.

Sigismund Augustus had two sisters, both marriageable, Anna (the elder) and Catherine, and Metropolitan Makarii assured Ivan that they were not within the prohibited degrees.[12] The negotiations were carried on with the Lithuanian half of the Commonwealth and on 18 August a Russian embassy departed for Vilna to propose a treaty of peace between the two countries guaranteed by the hand of the Princess Catherine. The Tsar did not yet know how old she was, but he had decided on the younger sister, probably as the most likely to bear a child. Ivan made it a condition that Catherine should convert to the Orthodox faith, and ordered the envoys to speak privately to the Lithuanian nobles to ensure that the treaty should be drawn up in its final form in Moscow, and modelled on the treaty of marriage between the Grand Princess Sofia Vitovtovna of Lithuania and Grand Prince Vasily I in 1390. Already at this early date, Ivan's instructions laid down where the Polish princess was to be met and escorted to Moscow and where she was to be lodged in the Tsar's private apartments in his palace. It seems as though it did not cross Ivan's mind that he might be refused. But if the Lithuanians insisted on her keeping her religion then the marriage was off.[13]

In the long instruction to his envoys Ivan was delightfully open about his reasons for seeking a perpetual peace with Sigismund: 'by the will of God and for our sins, our lord Tsar and Grand Prince has lost his Tsaritsa, and he is not yet of an age to be able to live without a wife.' The envoys then asked to see the lady's 'eyes'. The Lithuanian spokesmen naturally insisted that Catherine should be allowed to keep her religion and that negotiations for the treaty should take place in Vilna. They declared that it was not customary for rulers to show their daughters or sisters to envoys, though they might allow them to catch a glimpse of the Princess in church. The well-coached Russians then pointed out that in all previous marriages between the two houses the actual marriage treaty had been concluded in Moscow, thus maintaining the primacy of Moscow over Lithuania. They asked for details about the age and health of the sisters of Sigismund and that a *parsuna* or portrait should be provided. Envoys travelled back and forth between Moscow and Vilna, but Sigismund was clearly placing obstacles in the way of an agreement. He was in fact aware that it would not serve his purpose, that it might lose him Livonia, which he was just as keen to acquire as Ivan. He now raised the question of the withdrawal of Russian troops from Livonia as a necessary precondition.

Ivan was of course seeking more than a wife. A marriage with a sister of Sigismund would strengthen the Russian position in Livonian diplomacy, notably against Sweden, and would also enable him to cultivate his own party in Poland and isolate the more bellicose Lithuanian nobles from the more indifferent Poles. Sigismund in the meantime continued reluctant to strengthen Russia's position. He still refused to use the title of Tsar, though he did agree to call Ivan 'brother'. He put forward objections such as the need to consult the Sejm, the Holy Roman Empire and his brother-in-law the Duke of Brunswick and stressed that in previous marriages Lithuania had been a grand principality, while it was now a kingdom and should be treated accordingly. In fact Sigismund was convinced that he would not be able to acquire his share of Livonia without war with Russia. Ivan, as always when he met with obstacles, became more contumacious, repeating his claims to the ex-Kievan lands and to Livonia as his *votchina* or ancestral land, and proclaiming that the Holy Roman Emperor alone among rulers was his equal in status.

The Lithuanian envoys in turn were concerned with the rank of any children of a marriage between Ivan and Anna or Catherine Jagiellonka, in view of the precedence demanded by the Russian negotiators for the children of Ivan's first marriage. Relations between the two rulers were not improved when Ivan was able to confront Sigismund with the dispatches captured by Daniil Adashev, showing that the Polish King had been attempting to persuade the Crimeans to declare war on Russia.[14] The talks went on until 16 February 1561, when Ivan dismissed the Lithuanian envoys and abandoned the idea of the marriage, though he never forgot the insult.

Talks about a future truce which both sides needed continued,[15] during which the Lithuanian envoys even attempted to use Makarii as an intermediary. But the wily Metropolitan was not to be drawn, though he did remind the envoys of the Commonwealth that even Lithuania belonged to Ivan as his 'ancestral land'. Equally extravagant claims were put forward by Sigismund to Novgorod, Pskov and, of course, Smolensk.

Ivan's hopes for a Swedish marriage fell through completely because of the death of King Gustavus Vasa in September 1560. This forced Prince Erik to curtail his courtship of Queen Elizabeth and return to his country. But the third Russian embassy sent abroad to find a bride for the Tsar was more successful. Envoys were sent to the Khan of Kabarda, Temriuk, who had already declared himself a vassal of Ivan's and who had been conducting military expeditions against the Crimea together with Ivan's forces. Temriuk had sent his son Salmuk to Moscow in 1558, as a youth, and Ivan had taken a liking to him.[16] He was eventually baptized and took the name of Mikhail with the surname Cherkassky (Circassian), and Ivan ordered him to be taught his letters. The Cherkassky, as a large clan of Kabardian origin, survived the reign of Ivan – though Mikhail Temriukovich did not – and became one of the wealthiest princely and boyar families in seventeenth-century Russia.

The Russian envoys looked at Temriuk's daughters, and they returned with one, thus allowing the Tsar no choice. She was the Princess Kucheney, aged about fifteen, to whom Ivan fortunately took a fancy. She was converted by the persuasions of Metropolitan Makarii and took the name Maria before her marriage on 21 August 1561.[17]

It is possible that there was considerable opposition to this marriage at court. Not long before it took place, prince Vasily Mikhailovich Glinsky, Ivan's first cousin on his mother's side, appealed to Ivan for leniency for some unknown offence, through Metropolitan Makarii and the whole ecclesiastical council, and was forced to sign a surety bond guaranteeing that he would not flee to Lithuania, nor carry out any independent negotiations with the King of Poland.[18] But we know very little about this marriage except for what the agent of the Muscovy Company Sir Jerome Horsey wrote later, doubtless repeating gossip he had picked up in Moscow: 'The manner and solemnity of this marriage was so strange and heathenly as credit will hardly be given to the truth thereof.'[19]

Most historians reject the idea that Tsaritsa Maria ever exercised any influence over Ivan – indeed many also reject the idea that Anastasia had any influence at all, or that Grand Princess Sofia had ever influenced Ivan III. Whether this is the result of an innate Russian hostility to women or disbelief in their capacity, or whether it arises from the materialistic interpretation of history is hard to tell. A year after his marriage to Maria, Ivan sent a gift of 1,000 rubles in August 1562 to the Trinity monastery for prayers to be said for Anastasia; however, when Maria died, in 1569, he sent 1,500 rubles and a golden dish. To the historian Floria the discrepancy in the amount shows that he was more attached to Maria than to Anastasia.[20] But maybe Ivan felt that Maria might be in more need of prayers. 'It is hard to understand what he [Ivan] could gain from an alliance with a savage,' wrote Solov'ev,[21] and according to contemporary opinion Maria was wild and cruel by nature, encouraging Ivan in his evil inclinations but unable to keep his love.[22]

Indeed the mores of the Russian court had changed considerably since the death of Anastasia. Almost at once Ivan had given way to wild bouts of dissipation, drunkenness, fornication and sodomy, which horrified the straitlaced Kurbsky who reported them. In his first letter to Ivan of 1564, Kurbsky castigates the Tsar's evil advisers and warns 'against a destroyer conceived in fornication, the Antichrist', referring to one of Ivan's advisers as having been 'born in adultery' (possibly A.D. Basmanov).[23] And he concludes: 'It is not befitting O tsar to show indulgence to such men! In the first law of the Lord it is written: A Moabite and an Ammonite and a bastard to the tenth generation shall not enter into the congregation of the Lord.'[24] In his *History*, written in the 1570s, Kurbsky refers to the 'flatterers and evil destroyers', who 'began with frequent feasts and much drunkenness from which all kinds of impurities sprang'. Great beakers pledged to the devil, filled with extremely heady drink, were pressed on the Tsar until he drank himself into a stupor. Those who refused to take part in these drunken orgies were secretly denounced as foes of the Tsar. 'O new idolatry, in truth a pledge and an offering not to the statue of Apollo and others but to Satan himself and his devils.' Kurbsky continues with a litany of the disasters brought on Ivan because he had substituted for his chaste and holy life impurities filled with all kinds of filth; instead of displaying his strength and royal justice his flatterers had urged him on to acts of ferocity and inhumanity, to idleness, and to long sleeping and yawning after sleep. Ivan was also accused of cowardice in fleeing from battle with the Moslems. 'Was it not time to come to your senses', wrote Kurbsky, 'and to repent before God like Manasseh, and turn according to your natural free will to your Creator . . .'[25]

The 1560s saw indeed a 'great persecution', as Kurbsky put it, an explosion of dissipation accompanied by intermittent bouts of cruelty and injustice, as though Ivan had been suddenly released from the immense pressure brought to bear on him by the moralizing of Sylvester and the example of the good life led by the angelic Adashev. The 'evil-inspired flatterers' (the Iur'ev Zakhar'ins), according to Kurbsky, pointed out to the Tsar that he had been held in chains by Sylvester and Adashev, who had ruled him, telling him what to eat and drink and 'how to live with his Tsaritsa'.[26] The Tsar danced with his friends, wearing masks (a practice forbidden by the Church) and attended by *skomorokhi*, the disreputable wandering clowns, minstrels and jugglers who entertained the lower orders.[27] This too horrified the older and more conservative boyars. Prince Dmitri Obolensky Ovchinin was killed for an incautious word; he reproached Fedor Basmanov, the Tsar's new catamite: 'we serve the Tsar in useful ways, and you in your filthy sodomitical affairs'. Basmanov complained to Ivan, who first emptied a boiling hot dish all over Obolensky Ovchinin, and then stabbed him.[28]

To what extent did this violent outburst, almost a change of character, arise from the psychological shock of the actual death of Ivan's wife, even if she had clearly been dying for some time? It is not merely a question of the loss of someone he may, or may not, have loved, but of someone who belonged to him, who was his. It surely led also to a renewed sense of his vulnerability, the fear induced in him by what he saw as a successful attack on someone close to him, by someone close to him, probably by means of witchcraft.

In early 1562, Prince I.D. Bel'sky, the extremely well-connected Gediminovich prince, and close relative of the Tsar's family, attempted to flee to Lithuania. He was placed under house arrest and two of his military servitors were executed. But his disgrace did not last long, and he was forced to give a collective surety bond by which the guarantors, six boyars and 119 service gentry from various parts of the country, agreed to pay ten thousand rubles should he attempt to flee again. Bel'sky himself had to swear a fresh oath of loyalty.[29] By spreading the financial responsibility down into the ranks of the service gentry, Ivan was ensuring that they would keep a sharp eye on any indications of Bel'sky's disloyalty. In any case the Prince was soon released, though the guarantee continued in operation.[30]

The next to suffer were the two Vorotynsky brothers, Mikhail Ivanovich, the most distinguished and high ranking of Ivan's generals, who had been awarded the title of '*sluga* (servant) and boyar' for his services in the conquest of Kazan', and Alexander. Mikhail was a strong, brave and very skilled general, according to Kurbsky, and the brothers were among the few survivors of the small group of 'Upper Oka princes' whose estates, bordering on Lithuania, were closer to appanage principalities than to those of service princes. In the summer of 1562 they had been entrusted with the defence of the Oka line at Serpukhov against the Crimean Tatars, but had been unable to force a battle on them. Serpukhov was not far from their own appanage at Vorotynsk, and as princes they had their own retinue of over one thousand men-at-arms and might therefore have seemed threatening to Ivan.[31] Alexander was exiled to Galich in 1562 and made to sign a surety bond: eight boyars, together with one hundred princes and service gentry put up fifteen thousand rubles; but the service gentry were of even lower category than those who had signed for Bel'sky, thus showing that Ivan was reaching out into even lower social classes to achieve control over the élite. Alexander brought a precedence suit before the Tsar which Ivan curtly brushed aside: 'You deserve to stand below Prince Pronsky, and you should know your own value, and serve us according to our instructions.' Alexander may have found this too humiliating for he soon took the cowl and died.[32]

Mikhail Vorotynsky, the hero of Kazan', suffered a different fate, which suggests that Ivan was still keeping some sort of control over himself and also provides an interesting sidelight on exile to a monastery. He was sent to the monastery prison of Beloozero in 1562, with his wife and two of his children, and some of the circumstances of his detention are illustrated in a report from the *pristavy* or guards who were set over him in the monastery. He was granted an annual subsistence allowance from March to March, which evidently was not punctually paid. The total for the family and their twelve retainers was ninety-eight rubles twenty-seven altyn a year (fifty rubles for the princely family, forty-eight for the twelve retainers), plus a clothing allowance of twelve rubles per person for the princes with an additional fourteen rubles seventeen altyn for servants (two men and two women). But the Prince petitioned the Tsar, through his guards, at the end of the first year, asking for clothes and underwear for himself and his family, and also for tablecloths, as he had none left, and dishes and cauldrons, since those he had were worn through and he had nothing to buy new ones with, and also frying pans, dishes and wine bowls. He also needed a pail of Bastru,[33] a pail of Romanee (Spanish wine) and one of Rhine wine, one hundred lemons, three *grivenki* of ginger, two fresh sturgeons, and two fresh sterlets due to him and which he had not received, together with half a *pud* of grapes, half a *pud* of raisins and three pails of cream, more lemons, wax, saffron, pepper, cloves, four fur coats and clothes, and lengths of taffeta and other silks, because the 'young princess has outgrown her clothes'. We do not know whether Prince Mikhail ever received the arrears of the supplies he demanded, but that he should have had the confidence to ask for them shows that his exile was not so physically oppressive as one might have supposed.[34] The list is also informative about the Russian aristocratic diet.

Another magnate, more clearly associated with Aleksei Adashev (his is the only name ever mentioned as forming part of Adashev's so-called government), was also disgraced, on 29 October 1562, namely Prince

Dmitri Ivanovich Kurliatev Obolensky, who was ordered to take the cowl together with his wife and two sons. Kurbsky, who regarded him as a man of integrity and good counsel, was outraged at the forcible tonsure, calling it an unheard of crime that a whole family should be forced in this way to become religious, even though forcible tonsure was not unknown in the case of individuals.[35]

While the Tsar busied himself with the further organization of his private life, the war in Livonia – which had so far been primarily a war between Russia and the Livonian Order – was spreading more widely and beginning to involve all the Baltic powers. Denmark, under its new king, Frederick II, was claiming the island of Oesel.

The various Baltic maritime powers were at this time deeply divided by their conflicting policies towards Russia. All of them wanted to control trade with Russia and to prevent the import of munitions of war by the Tsar through Narva, and indeed on English ships through the White Sea. The propaganda against such a dangerous trade was directed from the Hanseatic League and the remnants of Livonia, but all the Baltic powers were convinced that Russia could only wage war against them if she received substantial cargoes of armaments, munitions and food – even salt and herrings – to keep her armies supplied and her soldiers fed. Intense pressure was brought to bear by the Livonians and the Hansa through the Imperial Diet, and by Sigismund Augustus even on Queen Elizabeth, to curtail trade with Russia. All believed that armaments were somehow reaching Ivan IV, since in German opinion the Russians were quite incapable of providing their own.

The Emperor, now Ferdinand I, supported a ban, and Sigismund Augustus informed Elizabeth of England in 1560 that he would detain ships trading with Narva, because she was bound to know that the Russians were 'enemies to all liberty under the heavens' and if Ivan were provided with weapons at present unknown to him he would vanquish all other nations. Elizabeth well knew how cruel and powerful Ivan was, what tyranny he used on his subjects and 'in what servile sort they be under him'. In fact it was the duty of all good Christians not to supply the Tsar with munitions. Elizabeth of course denied that she was supplying Ivan with arms, and if she did send any, it was probably not often and not much. For in fact the Russians did not need to import arms, and most of the ships captured in the trade with Narva were carrying exports from Russia, not imports to Russia. But the whole episode is an interesting example of the use of propaganda, influential to this day, devised in this case by Russia's commercial rivals to exclude her from direct trade with the West.[36]

The Grand Master of the Livonian Order appealed in vain for help to all those who might have an interest in perpetuating their control of the Baltic: the Holy Roman Emperor, the Hansa, Lübeck in particular, but all were more interested in obtaining their share of Livonia. On 28 November 1561 a convention was signed between Sigismund Augustus and Kettler dissolving the Order. Kettler converted to Protestantism and became Duke of Courland, as a vassal of Sigismund's, and considerable pressure was put – unsuccessfully – on the burghers of Riga to consent to the occupation of the city by Polish forces. The final treaty ratified in March 1562 between Sigismund and Kettler still excluded Riga from Polish control, and the Commonwealth was compelled to fight for this most important and strategic port.

Meanwhile, the twenty-year truce between Sweden and Russia was going to reduce the pressure on Russia considerably, since it left Ivan to face only Poland–Lithuania. In March 1562 the existing Russian truce with Sigismund Augustus ran out, and Ivan sent a force under I.V. Sheremetev and I.M. Vorontsov and a number of Tatar princes to carry out a destructive raid on the borders between Russia and Lithuania, while Prince A.M. Kurbsky undertook a raid on Vitebsk, thus carrying the war into Lithuanian territory. Ivan himself took part in May in an unsuccessful operation which had to be cut short to cope with an attack from the Crimean Tatars in the south, concerted with King Sigismund Augustus. In August 1562, Kurbsky was wounded in a battle which Ivan later reproached him with having failed to win, and Russian forces had to give up a number of previous conquests to the Lithuanians. In September 1562 the Tsar returned to Moscow. Hostilities broke out again with the seizure by the Lithuanian General Radziwill of the Livonian fort of Tarvast, later abandoned to Ivan and razed by him.

Ivan's concerns fluctuated at this time between keeping a watchful and repressive eye on possible defections, and pursuing his military objectives in attacks which were concentrated against Poland–Lithuania and which culminated in one of the greatest Russian successes of the war, the capture of the key city and centre of communications, the one time Riurikovich city of Polotsk, which controlled the western Dvina and the road to Riga. At the end of November 1562 the Tsar in person led a vast array, said to be of some 280,000 armed men and two hundred guns, accompanied as usual by his cousin Vladimir of Staritsa, by the two baptized Tatar *tsarevichi* Alexander and Simeon (described in the chronicles as the Tsar's brothers), and by four other Tatar *tsarevichi* (Ibak, Tokhtamysh, Bekbulat and Kaibula). Stopping on the way to batter a prince Ivan Shakhovskoy to death with a mace, Ivan laid siege to Polotsk on 31 January 1563.[37] After three weeks it capitulated.

For Ivan this was not only a major military success, it was also the recovery of a *votchina* which had belonged to his ancestors, a step on the road to the recovery of Kiev, and he now added 'Polotsky' to his title. During the campaign the Tsar's headquarters had been in the monastery of SS Boris and Gleb, near the town, and prayers had been offered to the princely martyrs of the old Kievan dynasty. It was also the recovery of a city for the Orthodox Church, and the freeing of the cathedral of St Sophia, the source of whose cult was located in Kiev.[38] Ivan promised the citizens of Polotsk personal freedom and security of their property, but did not keep his promise. He seized the property of the prominent and rich people, dispatched the bishop, many important citizens and the *voevoda* to Moscow as prisoners, ordered the Latin churches to be pulled down and the Jews to be converted to Christianity or thrown into the River Dvina to drown. He spent several days celebrating the recovery of this ancient city of his ancestors, saved – as Karamzin puts it sardonically, by its early subordination to Lithuania – from the ravages of the Mongols.[39] Russian accounts stress the welcome given to Ivan as the head of the Orthodox community by the many Orthodox Lithuanians. This overwhelming Russian victory led Sigismund, fearful of a Russian advance on Vilna, to negotiate through his councillors with the Russian boyars for a truce, which Ivan granted until the end of 1563; it also led to the successful conclusion of Russian talks for a truce with the Khan of Crimea.[40]

So pleased was Ivan with the conquest of Polotsk that on his return to Moscow he stopped in Staritsa to attend a splendid banquet arranged by Princess Evfrosin'ya, the mother of his cousin Vladimir, and to reward his cousin, and soon after he had the joy of hearing of the birth of a son, Vasily, to the Tsaritsa Maria; thus the events after the conquest of Kazan' were repeated. (Alas, the baby died on 3 May.) Ivan then went off on an extensive tour of the lands he had confiscated from the Vorotynsky princes, and then returned to what had become a favourite residence of his, namely Aleksandrovskaia Sloboda, in the district of Pereiaslavl'. This picturesque, wooded property on the banks of the River Sera had once been a hermitage and was supplied with an abundance of hares, bears and wolves.[41] It had been the happy hunting ground of Grand Prince Vasily III, who had built a palace and a church, and used it as a hunting lodge.

The general cessation of hostilities may, however, have been the result of a deep-rooted division of opinion at the Russian court: should Ivan now concentrate on fighting the Crimean Tatars to secure his southern border and achieve an opening on the Black Sea, or should he accept the truce with the Tatars and concentrate on fighting Sigismund, to outside appearances the most dangerous of his enemies, to secure Livonia and the Baltic shore? Most historians consider that the court was deeply divided, and that the exile and eventual disgrace of Adashev was due to Ivan's loss of confidence in an adviser who took a line opposed to his own, in contrast to Ivan Viskovaty. As usual, however, there is really no evidence of Adashev's opinion. It is assumed that because he was disgraced he must have opposed Ivan's forward policy in Livonia, whereas his fall may have been caused by a sudden revulsion in Ivan against his closest advisers, as the domestic structure of the last fourteen years crumbled around him.

Only three months later the first stage of the underlying conflict between Ivan and his cousin Vladimir of Staritsa came to a head. Always suspicious of him, though able to conceal it under a friendly exterior, Ivan was given the pretext he needed. A clerk of Vladimir's, imprisoned by him on some pretext, found a way to denounce his master to the Tsar, already in his quarters in Aleksandrovskaia Sloboda, for plotting to poison him. Ivan demanded that the man be produced, launched an inquiry with all the usual tortures, and called upon Makarii and the Holy *sobor* to intervene to judge Vladimir. Makarii as usual warded off the lightning, and the Princess Evfrosin'ya defused the situation by declaring her intention to become a nun. Whether she chose to or was compelled to take the veil is uncertain.[42] She was allowed to depart, her dignity intact, and properly escorted by her own boyars' wives, and military servitors, who were granted land in the vicinity of the convent which she had founded near Beloozero and to which she retired, while Ivan removed all Vladimir's boyars and service gentry and exchanged them for others under his own control and confiscated a great deal of his property.[43] Skrynnikov suggests here, again, that in accordance with Russian laws at the time members of the Boyar Council could not be subjected to punishment unless a properly conducted trial was carried out by the judgment of their peers, the boyars. But the Staritsky 'affair' created such a tension between the Tsar and the boyars that the former did not want to have recourse to the proper procedures – if any actually existed. It is difficult to accept Skrynnikov's portrayal of the Russian judicial process and the respect in which it was held, in view of the endless arbitrary executions, notably of the remnants of the Adashev connexion, which were taking place at this time.[44]

The outgoing year 1563 saw two natural deaths of great significance in Ivan's immediate surroundings: the first was that of his brother, Iuri, on 24 June 1563.[45] Iuri was always treated by Ivan with consideration, even affection, as a tsar's brother who posed no danger; he was given his own household, boyars and men-at-arms. His funeral was attended by boyars and magnates; only the dying Metropolitan Makarii was absent. Iuri was extremely fortunate in his wife, who on his death retired to the Novodevichii convent and maintained a great name for devotion and charity in the luxurious quarters Ivan insisted on having prepared for her.[46] Ivan inherited all the childless Iuri's appanage. It is impossible to assess the extent of Ivan's loss, because we do not know the extent of Iuri's disability.

On the last day of 1563 Metropolitan Makarii, in the fullness of years, died. He was probably already over eighty, and had never quite recovered from the accident he suffered during the fire of 1547 (see Chapter IV, pp. 61ff., above). Although he was very active in the 1550s his influence had been declining, possibly since Ivan's serious illness in 1553, possibly because he had vexed the Tsar by his systematic – and very often successful – use of his right of *pechalovanie* or intercession in favour of those whom the Tsar wished to disgrace.

The Metropolitan's influence on the religious, political, intellectual and artistic life of Russia had been considerable. He had, for instance, encouraged the introduction of printing.[47] Printing had begun to penetrate into Russia by 1553, and the first book printed in Russian, in Russia, an elaborately decorated edition of the *Apostol* (or readings from the Acts and Epistles of the Apostles used in the liturgy) appeared in March 1564, after the death of Makarii, by order of the Tsar and the new Metropolitan, Afanasii. It was intended to be a witness to Russian ecclesiastical merit by being widely distributed in captured Polotsk. The Tsar in 1564 ordered the setting up a of printing house (at his expense) under a master printer, Ivan Fedorov, a Russian educated at Cracow University, and it rapidly produced the required texts. Printing of course gave rise to problems about the reliability of the manuscripts used, and the danger for the editor and printer in making unauthorized alterations to the text by mistake. In any event, Fedorov and his assistant both left Moscow in 1565, as Fedorov explained later, in 1574, as a result of 'great persecutions which we frequently suffered, not from the Lord himself [Ivan] but from many officials and ecclesiastical powers'. Fedorov goes on to make clear that they were accused of heresy by ignoramuses, and having suffered such hatred and envy they chose exile and left for unknown lands.[48] Printing, however, continued under Ivan's own eye, in Aleksandrovskaia Sloboda.

One additional service was performed by Makarii as part of his policy of raising the status of the metropolitanate and its ascendancy over the whole of Russia: he brought the 'white cowl' worn by the Archbishop of Novgorod with him to Moscow. The legendary white cowl was a gift from the Emperor Constantine the Great to Pope Sylvester I, symbolizing the primacy of the spiritual power over the secular power (a further dimension of the Donation of Constantine); at first highly revered by the Popes it was nearly destroyed at the time of the schism beginning in the ninth century. But it was saved and sent to Constantinople with the instruction that it was to be forwarded to the Archbishop of Novgorod, where the true faith subsisted. Its fate now became linked to the theory of the Third Rome, because it was foretold that the imperial city (Constantinople) would fall to the Hagarenes, and the true faith would perish there. But in the Third Rome (Russia), though the imperial crown would be given to the Tsar, the white cowl must be given to the city of Novgorod the Great.[49] Makarii of course wore the white cowl when he was Archbishop of Novgorod, but by taking it with him to Moscow he was making a statement about the growing authority of the see of Moscow over that of Novgorod. At a Holy *sobor* held jointly with a session of the Boyar Council in February 1564 the new status of the white cowl was approved. The Archbishop of Novgorod did not lose the right to wear it, but the Metropolitan acquired it.[50] One of Makarii's further services to Ivan came to fruition just before his death, namely the endorsement by the Patriarch of Constantinople of Ivan's title of Tsar.

Makarii was a man of great moral authority, though he has been accused by some historians of moral cowardice. He was impressive as a speaker and preacher and probably one of the few men of integrity and culture in Ivan's entourage in his youth. More than anyone else he had contributed to the cultural formation of the young ruler, above all with his conception of Ivan's high station and God-given power. But power, in Makarii's view, went with responsibility and there is some suggestion that at the end of his life the Metropolitan wished to retire to a monastery, sickened by Ivan's cruelties which he could do nothing to control. Whether he was instrumental in bringing Sylvester to Ivan's notice cannot be confirmed, but certainly both men provided a formidable moral obstacle to the indulgence of Ivan's capricious whims. Some historians (for example Karamzin) criticize Makarii for being vainglorious, lacking in the courage to stand up to Ivan, yet all admit that he did not hesitate to reproach the Tsar for his dissolute life and for the cruelty of his repressions, and that his intercession saved many lives – if only for a time. Makarii was also not a fanatic, and his treatment of heretics was milder than that of his predecessors (his contemporaries attributed Ivan's fanaticism rather to Sylvester). But he was a consistent champion of the anti-Moslem crusade and a firm supporter of the symphony between ecclesiastical and secular authority and of church ownership of landed estates.

In his last days, Makarii hoped to be released and allowed to withdraw to a monastery, but Ivan did not allow him to go. However, he did, according to one late chronicle, make a final attempt to frighten Ivan with the thought of death and the Last Judgment. When the Tsar asked Makarii to send him suitable devotional works, the Metropolitan sent him a book of funeral prayers. This angered the Tsar, who exclaimed that such books were not allowed in his tsarist apartments. Makarii replied that having been asked for suitable devotional books 'he had sent the most satisfying for the soul, for he who reads it attentively will not sin'. He was said to have had a vision of the horrors to come on Russia and prayed to God: 'Dishonour and the shedding of blood and the division of the land are coming upon us . . . Oh God have mercy on me, turn aside thy wrath. If thou canst not forgive us our sins let it not happen when I am alive, do not let me live to see it . . .' His death removed the last moral obstacle from Ivan's path to unlimited power.[51]

Archpriest Andrei, who had worked with Makarii on the *Stepennaia kniga* or Book of Degrees (a chronicle of the joint activity of the heads of the Church and the state in Russia, started by Makarii in the 1560s and going back to the beginning of the Riurikovichi, indeed to the mythical Prus, the brother of Augustus, emperor of Rome), had been appointed Ivan's confessor (not purely an easy task) in 1549. He had taken the cowl under the name of Afanasii in 1563, retreated to the Chudov monastery in the Kremlin, and was appointed Metropolitan after the death of Makarii, on 24 February 1564. His appointment was clearly engineered by Ivan, who wanted a change of style from Makarii and Sylvester. Afanasii as a confessor had evidently been gentle and unassuming, but as a metropolitan he was to prove unexpectedly strong. He had hoped to achieve the canonization of Makarii, but it did not happen. In the new world that Ivan was introducing there was no room for such as he – and Afanasii soon left his post.[52]

Chapter X
Tsar Ivan and Prince Andrei Kurbsky

Throughout 1563 Ivan must have been turning over in his conscious and subconscious mind new conceptions of the theory and practice of power, of what he had the right to do and what he had the power to put into practice. For a man of his uncontrollable temperament, obsessed with power, the last few years must have been frustrating. He met with treason and betrayal at every turn, yet whenever he tried to eradicate it, he came up against the opposition of the Metropolitan, the Church Council, the boyars, the senior *d'iaki*.

Executions of any likely opponents or critics of Ivan's behaviour multiplied in the first half of 1564. Prince Mikhail Repnin Obolensky, for instance, who had distinguished himself at the conquest of Polotsk, was unwise enough to protest when he saw Ivan indecorously 'dancing in masks', but the Tsar responded by urging him to join in and forced a mask onto his head. This was a practice condemned by the Church.[1] When Repnin tore the mask off and trampled on it, the Tsar was furious, banished him from the feast and had him murdered some days later in church (or in a cellar), at the same time as another boyar, Prince Iuri Kashin Obolensky, was also dispatched as he attended a service. A slightly different version of this incident suggests that Ivan had always hated the Obolenskys because one of them was alleged to have been the lover of his mother, the Grand Princess Elena, and he turned on Repnin Obolensky because he was constantly quarrelling with Fedor Basmanov whom he accused of being Ivan's paramour. It was also said that Ivan was jealous because the two men had distinguished themselves at the siege of Polotsk. There is a further suggestion that the two Obolenskys were executed four days after a courier brought news of a severe defeat of a substantial Russian corps by Lithuanian troops on the River Ula, on 26 January 1564. Ivan may have suspected them of having provided secret information to the Lithuanians, thus contributing to the Russian setback. One of Ivan's best generals, Peter Ivanovich Shuisky was killed in this engagement, a serious loss, and many *voevody* were captured.[2]

It was essential for Ivan to find a scapegoat for the defeat, and to negotiate a truce. But the terms he had previously put before a large embassy from Lithuania which had arrived in December 1563, for a ten-year truce, leaving Polotsk and all the Livonian lands conquered by Russia in Russian hands, were now totally unacceptable to the Lithuanians. Their embassy had departed from Moscow three weeks before the murder of the two princes. A third Obolensky, Dmitri Fedorovich Ovchina Obolensky was thrown to Ivan's huntsmen with orders for him to be strangled, for quarrelling with Fedor Basmanov and accusing him of being the Tsar's catamite.[3]

It would be tedious to list every one of the boyars, often princes, who suffered now, with total disregard to such legal procedures as existed. Some victims had close or distant connexions with Adashev, some were rich, like Prince Dmitri Khilkov (whose lands were confiscated by Ivan), or the two Sheremetev brothers, Ivan bol'shoi (major) and his brother Nikita, distinguished commanders, members of an old boyar family. The latter was strangled, possibly in connexion with the battle on the River Ula. Ivan bol'shoi, 'a sharp and wise man', was loaded with the heaviest iron hoops and chains and kept in an airless dungeon to force him to tell Ivan where he had hidden his wealth. Sheremetev replied that his treasure lay where Ivan could not lay hands on it, for he had already given it away to the poor. The intervention of the new Metropolitan Afanasii was to secure his release in March 1564; over twenty-five high ranking boyars, *okol'nichie* and nobles stood as his sureties, the lower nobles staking their heads and 10,000 rubles. There were no princes among the sureties, only boyars.[4] Eventually Sheremetev took the cowl in the monastery of Beloozero. His lands were seized by the Tsar, but he does not seem to have lived in dire poverty.[5]

If Ivan had been pondering on his future, so had one of his leading generals, Prince Andrei Mikhailovich Kurbsky. He had not been prominent in government or administration but on the battlefield. The Prince was only some two years older than Ivan and could therefore converse with him without overawing the younger man as would Sylvester, and he seems to have shared Ivan's interest in religious and political ideas. He was a man of some culture, who could read and write in Russian and Slavonic and in his mature years he seems to have been familiar with Latin and Greek.[6] He was on close terms with Maksim Grek and many other churchmen. He quoted extensively from the Bible and the Church Fathers in his writings[7] and was a devout member of the

Orthodox Church. One of his ancestors, Prince Fedor Rostislavich, had been canonized in 1463, and Kurbsky prided himself on the fact that his family descended from a son of Vladimir Monomakh older than the ancestor of the princes of Moscow.[8] There was moreover a distant connection between Kurbsky and the family of the Tsaritsa Anastasia.[9]

In 1549 Kurbsky was given the court appointment of *stol'nik* (literally, tableman, at that time one of the young men engaged for instance in serving at the vast state banquets); he was then active in the various campaigns against Kazan' with increasing distinction and was seriously wounded in late 1552. During Ivan's nearly fatal illness, in 1553, Kurbsky did not incur the suspicion of siding with Vladimir of Staritsa[10] and, together with Adashev, accompanied Ivan after his recovery on a pilgrimage to the Trinity monastery and to the St Cyril monastery, thus confirming that he was in favour and in the immediate circle of the Tsar.[11] From September 1553 Kurbsky was again on active service in the pacification of Kazan', and from March 1554 he appears to have been unemployed. He was raised to the rank of boyar in 1556, at the age of twenty-eight, and returned again to active service in highly responsible posts against an expected Tatar attack, before being sent in 1557 to the Livonian theatre of war. Once again he was dispatched, in January 1558, this time to Kaluga, against a Tatar threat, where he was appointed second in command under Shigali on a murderous raid through Livonia, and where Ivan himself visited the army in August 1559. In spring 1560 he was sent back to Dorpat in Livonia for as Ivan wrote to him: 'I am forced by the actions of my military commanders either to lead my forces myself against the Livonians or to send you, my dearly loved one, so that with the help of God you may put fresh heart into my troops.'[12] Kurbsky was again active in Velikie Luki, one of the bases for the conquest of Polotsk, where he was second in command of the rearguard, but he was evidently blamed by Ivan as one of the *voevody* guilty of the failure of the Russian forces at the battle of Nevl' in August 1562. In 1563 he was relegated as commander in Dorpat and left there for more than a year in what was clearly some form of disgrace.

In the early 1560s Kurbsky had been watching with mounting indignation the arbitrariness, illegality and cruelty of Ivan's persecution of the boyars, service gentry and often the common people among their retainers.[13] He had many friends among the supporters of Adashev who were being systematically destroyed. He had visited the Pskov Pechersky monastery earlier, he had even borrowed money from the monks, and was on close terms with a number of them. His view of what was happening in Russia is expressed in a letter to the Elder Vassian Muromtsev of the monastery, probably written between December 1563 and April 1564:

> The mighty called to rule and appointed by God to mete justice tempered with mercy to their subjects and to rule their realm in humility and mercy have, for our sins, become raging bloodthirsty wild beasts. Thus not only do they not spare men of a like nature to themselves, but punish their well-wishers with unheard of tortures and death. It is impossible to describe in fitting language all the ills of this time, because of this insatiable robbery of other peoples' property, and the injustice of the judges and the neglect of the interests of the state.[14]

Kurbsky goes on, in another letter to Vassian, to lament the failure of the ecclesiastics to defend the people against their ruler: 'Where are the prophets who exposed the "unjust rulers"? Where is St John Chrysostom who accused the Tsaritsa of love of gold ? . . . Where are the patriarch and the Saints? In truth there is no one to intercede for us . . .', and he attacks the nobles and the monks who do nothing to defend the Christian folk but are 'choked with their property and their great wealth'.[15]

In a more wide-ranging description of the state of Russia Kurbsky bewails the poor state of the armed forces, deprived of horses and weapons, but also of spiritual food, and of the peasants, forced to sell their children into servitude, and the enormous burden of taxation on the merchants and the poor, who do what he, Kurbsky was about to do, namely 'disappear beyond the frontiers of their native land'.

Sitting in Dorpat, and short of money, Kurbsky may well have been approached by, or himself have initiated, contacts with Lithuanian emissaries, to prepare for his reception in Lithuania. He would need money, land and position and therefore he attempted to negotiate terms with King Sigismund beforehand. Russian and Soviet historians differ greatly in their accounts of the reasons for Kurbsky's ultimate decision to flee, but nearly all concur in speaking of him as a traitor, and some even call him an apostate, which he was not. Their standpoint seems greatly to depend on when they wrote, and whether they were strongly patriotic in their views. Traitor to Ivan Kurbsky certainly was, though by the sixteenth century the concept of treason had been somewhat eroded and treachery to a person was already not the same as treason to one's country.

What finally induced Kurbsky to make his bid for freedom at a particular time is not known. There is a story that in 1563 he had heard that Ivan was to disgrace him, and as he could not bear a shameful execution after all his long service, he asked his wife what she would prefer: should he die or should they separate forever? His wife refused to contemplate his death, whereupon, with bitter tears, he said goodbye to her and to his son, and on 30 April 1564 he climbed over the walls of the citadel of Dorpat to join the twelve service gentry companions who were fleeing with him. He did not see his wife and nine-year-old son again. Together with his mother they perished in prison later that year.[16]

This suggests that the decision to leave, though probably long prepared, was taken suddenly, and Kurbsky successfully made his way, without being intercepted, to the Livonian-held fort of Gel'met, which suggests that he had accomplices. He left his books and his other belongings behind in Dorpat, but took away twelve trunks of goods of various kinds, loaded onto at least three horses. He had tried again, and failed, to borrow money from the monks at the Pskov Pechersky monastery. But when he appeared before the Livonians in Gel'met, he had 300 Polish zlotys, 30 ducats, 500 German thalers and 44 Moscow rubles in his bag, a very large sum for the time, most of it in foreign currency and probably received from Sigismund, and also his sapphire seal ring.[17] He had received at some date letters and a safe conduct from Sigismund Augustus, but to what must have been his rage and dismay, they did not serve him. On arrival at Gel'met, held by Livonians, he was detained, his gold was stolen and he was transferred under arrest to the castle of Armus. There the Livonian noble servitors stripped him of his fox fur hat and confiscated his horses, and he was not given the promised support until some time after he arrived at Wolmar which was in Polish-Lithuanian hands. In July Sigismund granted him lands in Lithuania and Volhynia, and eventually also the castle of Kowel that had belonged to his mother Bona Sforza.

Ivan later charged Kurbsky with fleeing merely out of 'fear just of an angry word from the Tsar',[18] but in a letter to his envoys in Lithuania the Tsar stated that he had had the intention of punishing the prince as a traitor and accused him of plotting against the Tsaritsa Anastasia and his children. Punishment in this context meant death and though later Ivan withdrew his remarks, and said he meant only to deprive Kurbsky of his honours, his positions and his lands, Kurbsky had from the start assumed the worst.[19] On a different level, Ivan argued that Kurbsky should have been willing to take on the burden of the Tsar's guilt and be

sacrificed for him, just as the Tsar took on his shoulders the guilt of the
Russian people, including of course Kurbsky's.

From Wolmar Kurbsky wrote a letter to the Tsar, which is one long
accusation couched in language such as had never been used to the god-
given ruler before. In some 1,500 burning words, in high rhetorical style,
designed to be declaimed aloud, and permeated with biblical terms and
images, Kurbsky accused Ivan of having abandoned his role as the most
illustrious personification of the Orthodox faith: 'If you have understanding, may you understand this with your leprous conscience – such
a conscience as may not be found even among the godless peoples. . . .
Wherefore O Tsar have you destroyed the strong in Israel, and subjected
to various forms of death the *voevody* given to you by God?'[20] He goes
on to accuse the Tsar of spilling the blood of his nobles on the threshold
of churches, of using unheard of torments and persecutions and death
against those who have served him, accusing them falsely of treachery
and magic.[21] He reminds Ivan of all the services he has performed for
him:

> My blood spilt like water for you, cries out against you to my Lord
> . . . in front of your army have I marched – and marched again and
> brought you brilliant victories. But to you O Tsar, was this all as
> nought; rather do you show us your intolerable wrath and bitterest
> hatred and furthermore burning stoves [one of Ivan's favourite
> instruments of torture]. Think you yourself immortal O Tsar? Or
> have you been enticed into unheard of heresy

and Kurbsky calls on Christ, who sits on the throne of the cherubim at
the right hand of the Almighty, to be the judge 'between you and me'.

Thus Ivan stands accused and brought down to the level of a common
man, who now proceeds to list the injuries he personally has received
from the Tsar, the lies that have been told of him: 'I have been driven
from the land of God without guilt.' Kurbsky excoriates Ivan's misuse of
the 'Angelic Form', namely the monk's robes, 'when he flies into a rage
. . . and forces people to accept the monastic tonsure together with their
wives and little children, and condemns them to everlasting imprisonment in strong monasteries, making the holy places fortresses of hell,
with the approbation of certain accursed and cunning monks'.[22] Ivan, he
declares is surrounded by liars and flatterers, who urge him on to
'aphrodisiacal deeds', to act more viciously than the priests of Cronus,
and he warns Ivan that he has heard from sacred writings that 'a
destroyer will be sent by the devil against the human race, a destroyer

conceived in fornication, the Antichrist'.[23] This was the kind of language which must have made Ivan furious.

Kurbsky's letter was to be conveyed to the Tsar personally by his courier, Vasily Shibanov, but the latter was seized on the way, in Dorpat, and taken to Moscow. Shibanov proved a very loyal servant, and did not betray his master; he only indicated where Kurbsky had concealed some papers which he did intend in fact for Ivan. Shibanov was tortured and finally delivered over to a painful execution.[24]

Ivan received Kurbsky's missive in May 1564. He spent the next two months visiting monasteries and the lands he had just confiscated from the Prince of Staritsa. But he was also obviously meditating his reply to Kurbsky, for it is dated 5 July 1564, and takes up eighty-six printed pages – 'your grandiloquent and big-sounding screed' – as Kurbsky called it. It must have taken a long time to put it into writing with a quill pen, and one may assume therefore that Ivan dictated it at intervals during the preceding weeks. Its composition also required constant reference to the Old and New Testaments and the Church Fathers, on whom Ivan drew extensively, as well as the History of the Destruction of Troy and various other religious and secular works.

Ivan played on every rhetorical string in this remarkable document which was evidently meant to be widely read. He was proud, indignant, angry, mocking, contemptuous, condescending, reproachful, forgiving by turns; he called up historical parallels from the Bible, the gods of Olympus, the Roman Empire of the West and the East Roman Empire. He meandered, covering the same events in various ways and in a more or less angry frame of mind. To bring some order into this chaos it is advisable to break down his letter into its major component themes, which are often repeated and do not appear in chronological order. Broadly speaking Ivan covers his childhood, his relationship with Prince Kurbsky, the tyranny of Sylvester and Adashev, and the plotting and treachery of the boyars in supporting Vladimir of Staritsa and destroying Anastasia. He also discusses the nature of his powers as Tsar. But he begins with the most damning accusation against Kurbsky that he could call upon, that the Prince was a renegade, a *krestoprestupnik*, or breaker of his oath on the cross – a particularly heinous offence in Russia – the next step being apostasy.

The pages dealing with his childhood supply the only existing evidence on the years between 1533 and 1547, which are alleged to have marked Ivan's character so deeply, because of the neglect he suffered and the disrespect, even insolence, with which he – the Grand Prince – was treated by the boyars, particularly after the death of his mother in

1538.[25] Unfortunately for the historian it is difficult to swallow his portrayal whole, since he was undoubtedly capable of distortion, invention, misunderstanding and deliberate lies. His account of his childhood is in fact the least verifiable of the autobiographical portions of his letter, because it cannot be checked against any other source.[26]

The reproaches directed at Kurbsky are interspersed with long digressions comparing Kurbsky's conduct with that of specific biblical or historical figures or reflections on the exercise of political power: 'Let us now consider this – who is vainglorious? Am I, in that I order my servants (*raby*) who are subjected to me by God, to carry out my wishes? Or are you, in that you reject my dominion, established at God's behest, and your yoke of servitude, and like masters order me to do your will?'[27]

The 'masters' were of course the priest Sylvester and Aleksei Adashev. 'Now at this time, that cur, Aleksei, your chief, who was in our court, and I don't know by what means got himself promoted from usher' was raised, writes Ivan, 'from a dungheap to serve with magnates'. And Sylvester too was chosen to care for Ivan's spiritual welfare, but he 'trampled his priestly vows underfoot . . . and all that appertains to service with the angels at the altar', though he seemed to have begun in a righteous manner. Yet when Ivan 'saw in the holy Scriptures that it is right to submit to good preceptors' . . . he obeyed Sylvester willingly, but through ignorance, for the sake of spiritual counsel. But Sylvester was carried away by power like Eli the priest.[28] And this 'ignoramus' of a priest, joined with Aleksei Adashev in friendship and together they imposed their rule on Ivan, met in secret to plot against him, 'deeming Ivan incapable of judgement' and 'taking the splendour of our power from us'. Ivan then accuses Sylvester of distributing lands and villages, scattering them in the wind in an unbefitting manner, appointing his and Adashev's supporters to important positions, even taking from the Tsar the power to decide on the rank of his boyars:[29]

> When they had all things entirely in their power according to their will, then, without asking us aught, as though we did not exist, did they make regulations and take measures according to their will . . . And so neither in external affairs, nor in internal affairs nor in the smallest and pettiest things, even in shoes and sleeping, was anything according to my will . . . and we remained as it were a child.[30]

Ivan's accumulated hatred of Sylvester is manifest, together with his distrust of nameless boyars, and particularly of 'that dog', Adashev. It was Sylvester who had advised that Ivan should be lord only in words, and that Kurbsky and the priest should rule. Yet God had made Moses the ruler and Aaron the priest, and when Aaron tried to rule, he led the people away from God. Then came Joshua son of Nun, and the judges held sway until the time of Eli the priest, when disaster struck, and all Israel was conquered. 'Do you not see', wrote Ivan, 'how priestly power is incompatible with tsarist authority?'[31] It was Sylvester, too, who was responsible for the fact that the struggle to pacify conquered Kazan' lasted seven years. And it was Sylvester who secretly supported the idea of raising Vladimir of Staritsa to the throne. Finally Sylvester, together with Adashev, 'stirred up great hatred against our Tsaritsa Anastasia and likened her to all the impious Tsaritsas; as for our children, they were not even able to call them to mind'.[32]

Then, modulating to a new key, Ivan accused Kurbsky of failing in his military duties, seeking financial advantages, and running away from the fighting, indeed deserting. There are hints of a sense of guilt at his own military failure in Ivan's accusations, a failure which is also implicit in a letter from Sylvester to Prince Alexander Gorbaty-Shuisky written in spring 1553, after Ivan's near fatal illness. In this letter the priest praises Gorbaty-Shuisky for manifesting more courage than Ivan in the battle for Kazan', in which the latter 'showed himself fearful of the foe'. Indeed, Ivan had spent much time in prayer before the first attack which took place without him.[33] Ivan also referred to the 'well wishers' named by Kurbsky, who, 'having placed me like a prisoner on a ship ... conveyed me with very few people through the godless and most un-believing land' where he could easily have lost his life. This is probably the incident Ivan refers to a few pages later, in this same letter, when Russian stores were lost in a storm on the Volga and, according to Ivan, Kurbsky wanted to return home, after only three days.[34]

There is again a curious touch of familiarity in Ivan's attitude to Kurbsky, which suggests that they had once been on close terms. It is not unrelated to the Tsar's resentment at the Prince's alleged treatment of Anastasia. He makes an odd reference to 'one single little word', presumably uttered by Anastasia, which made her 'rank as worthless' in the eyes of the boyars, and enabled them to prevent her from going on the pilgrimages which might have saved her life. There is a somewhat confused acccount of an incident which evidently occurred between the Tsar and the *voevoda* in which Kurbsky, together with two other boyars, gave judgment against Ivan, in some dispute over land, in which Ivan was concerned, perhaps on behalf of his son. In a second, later, letter to Kurbsky, written in 1577, the Tsar bitterly returns to this incident: 'with what insult to me did you arbitrate between Sitsky and Prozorovsky! And how you examined me as though I were a villain'. It is certainly strange for a subject to decide against the interests of his all-powerful lord in a matter of property.

In a later letter, written in 1577, Ivan brought up another grievance: Kurbsky had evidently bought some trifling presents ('all kinds of adornments') for the daughters of Prince Kurliatev, 'but for my daughters, a curse for the peace of their souls. But enough of that. It is not possible to enumerate all the evils you have inflicted on me.'[35] In another context Ivan argued that if he had committed 'small sins' it was because '... there is no man without sin only God alone'; and if his false friends had misled him, and he had been lax in his religious observances, and had indulged in 'games' this was merely indulgence in human weakness on his part.

In other ways one senses that Ivan had been familiar with the life and movements of Kurbsky in the past. In a reference later in the same letter of 1564 to Kurbsky's opposition to the war in Livonia and his evident reluctance to depart for the front there, Ivan writes that he had to send more than seven messengers after the Prince who took to the field grudgingly, and who at that time was 'in our patrimony of Pskov for your own needs and not because we sent you there', as indeed Kurbsky was, trying to borrow money from the monks of the Pskov Pechersky monastery. And how Sylvester and Adashev, 'and all of you', had opposed waging this war, and given the Livonians a year's truce in which to prepare themselves for a fresh campaign.[36]

But Ivan emphasized that he had done Sylvester no harm – nor had he harmed his son, the *d'iak* Anfim (which was true). But as for the laymen, Ivan punished them according to their guilt. Kurbsky, however, Ivan argued, was forsworn, and for the sake of the delights of this world he had betrayed Orthodox Christianity and his lord, like Judas, for the sake of gold, betrayed Christ. He denied that executions had taken place in churches; all the treacheries he had suffered from were known to the whole world, even the barbarian peoples, and there were eyewitnesses, traders and ambassadors who came to Russia. In Ivan's conception of the world, it was for Kurbsky to sacrifice his life, and accept death for himself and his family because of his oath of allegiance,[37] in the service of the Tsar, and this alone could ensure him a holy death.

Ivan accused Kurbsky of inciting foreign peoples against him – with some justification in the case of Poland–Lithuania. Ivan then makes a somewhat unusual comparison between Kurbsky's 'martyrs' and Antenor and Aeneas, the 'traitors' of Troy.[38] 'To turn light unto darkness I do not endeavour, and that which is bitter I do not call sweet. Is this then light or darkness for servants to rule?' With these words Ivan approaches the kernel of his political conflict with Kurbsky, namely his demand to rule unquestioned and unopposed over all his servants, whereas Kurbsky praises the rule of servants over their masters. 'If a Tsar's subjects do not obey him', writes Ivan, 'then never will they cease from internecine strife. The habit of seizing things for oneself is indeed evil! . . . hitherto Russian lords (*obladateli*) were questioned by no man, they were free to reward and punish their subjects, and they did not litigate with them before any judge.'[39]

Ivan does not claim that Russian *samoderzhavye* or sovereignty is something new which dates from his coronation as Tsar.[40] He begins in the name of the Holy Trinity to trace the story of the emergence of the Orthodox Christian realm of Russia owing to divine intervention:

> And as the words of God encircled the whole world like an eagle in flight, so a spark of piety reached even the Russian kingdom. The sovereignty (*samoderzhavstvo*) of this truly Orthodox Russian kingdom (*tsarstvo*) by the will of God comes down from the great Tsar Vladimir, who enlightened the whole Russian land with holy baptism.

The term *samoderzhavsto* is used here to describe the origin and nature of God-given power, not the way in which it is used.[41] All kings by the grace of God were only too well aware of the moral and physical limits on their capacity to enforce their will. What Ivan is stating categorically is that Russia was a 'sovereign' kingdom (an 'autocracy') as far back as the conversion of Vladimir to Christianity, that is to say an independent polity, recognizing no overlord, and ruled by a Tsar with absolute authority over his subjects.

Moreover Ivan was a sovereign by birth, he had not conquered his kingdom, or taken it by rape, he had inherited it, and was thus born to rule. (He did not regard Elizabeth I of England as being a 'sovereign born', for she did not inherit her power, but was raised to the throne by the English 'estates', or, in Ivan's words, 'The English people expelled king Philip of Spain from the kingdom and made you queen.'[42]) His own power was justified by St Paul: 'for there is no power ordained that is not of God. Whosoever resisteth the power, resisteth the ordinance of God.' As for the Russian sovereigns, they themselves from the beginning have ruled all their dominions, and not the boyars and not the magnates; whereas Kurbsky would only approve if it were rule by 'a certain priest'. There is nothing in these statements of Ivan's to differentiate the *nature* of sovereign power in Russia from that theoretically exercised by his contemporaries Francis I of France or Henry VIII of England, though its *extent* was different: the latter might have to pay more attention to institutional limitations. The right to reward his servants and to punish them (by death if he felt so inclined) was fully used by Henry VIII.[43] But in all these kingdoms, the ability to enforce a decision lagged well behind the consciousness of the right to make it. And even the right to make a decision could be limited by moral considerations, for the Tsar was responsible before God for the spiritual welfare of his subjects, and his right to decide could be lost if he acted like a tyrant. Even Joseph of Volokolamsk had stated that this was so,[44] and the East Roman deacon, Agapetus, had set out the principle that rewarding and punishing should be carried out in accordance with the laws of God. Though the Tsar's power was unlimited, because no one could set limits to it, yet the Tsar himself had to submit to the law.

The same principles were to be found in the *Secretum secretorum*, the mirror of princes, of Middle Eastern origin, well known throughout Europe, of which a Russian version existed, translated from the Hebrew. It was presented as the philosopher Aristotle giving advice to Alexander the Great, and among other axioms it warned Alexander not to give priority to mortal things over the eternal, and to subordinate his rulership to the law, for thus he would be worthy of ruling. 'And he who subordinates the law to his rulership (*tsarstvo*) kills the law.'[45]

'How pray can a man be called sovereign if he himself does not rule?' was Ivan's refrain.[46] Still obsessed by the encroaching sway of Sylvester, Ivan declaimed against priestly intrusion: 'And is this befitting for a tsar: when he is struck on the cheek, for him to turn the other cheek? Is this the supreme commandment?' Referring to the internecine warfare of Russia's princely past he laments, 'Woe unto the house over which a woman ruleth; see you then that the rule of many is like unto the folly of women, for even if men are strong and brave if they are not under one authority they will behave like foolish women.'[47]

But what did *samoderzhavstvo* mean to Ivan as he settled himself more comfortably on his throne? Did he begin to think not just of absolute power, but of unlimited power (*neogranichennaia*) which was not merely God-given but God-like power? The formula: 'I am free to reward and free to punish' was not invented by him, and evidently reflected a well-established approach used and accepted by many of the Russian appanage princes before him. But he went beyond this affirmation because of his psychological need to have his way at once and without meeting any obstacle, whether verbal or physical, whether moral or spiritual. His right to inflict disgrace (*opala*) was unconditional, independent of any judicial procedure. In contrast with Kurbsky's insistence on 'free will' and freely given service, Ivan did not believe that man was free, not even in Paradise. Had not God forbidden him to eat of the fruit of the tree of the knowledge of good and evil?

Much has been written about the nature of Russian absolute government, ever since the imperial ambassador, Sigismund von Herberstein coined his famous formula: in Russia, 'the will of the lord is the will of God' and the powers of the Russian sovereign over his people are greater than in any other country. Herberstein was a very perceptive and knowledgeable German, but his remarks should not be taken in isolation, without reference to any other contemporary polity, nor to possible bias in his sources. He did not, for instance, care for Vasily III. There were periods in most medieval societies when royal authority was greater or smaller, exercised with more or less brutality, and Herberstein's remark should be checked against the facts rather than accepted as establishing the facts.[48]

It is more than probable that Kurbsky's desertion intensified in Ivan the need to clarify the theory and extent of his power. As he wrote later, 'whenever the Tsar wanted to investigate and punish his boyars and his officials for their faults, archbishops and bishops and archimandrites and abbots got together with the boyars and the service gentry and the *d'iaki*, and with all the officials and covered things up from the Lord Tsar and Grand Prince.'[49] There were plots against him, or at any rate he believed there were,[50] centred around his cousin Vladimir, whom he had always, and particularly since 1553, viewed as a dangerous rival for the throne, and who was indeed the only one.

The right of the eldest son, and his descendants, to inherit the throne was not long-established in Russia, as indeed in many other European countries.[51] In his efforts to secure the throne for the baby Dmitri in 1553 Ivan cannot have forgotten that he himself had inherited the throne because of his father's success in asserting the principle of lateral succession, namely the priority of the younger son, Vasily, over Dmitri, who was already crowned and anointed as Grand Prince, and who was descended from the elder son, Ivan the Younger,

To what extent the princes and boyars really plotted to dethrone Ivan and replace him with Vladimir of Staritsa which would have inevitably meant Ivan's death, is almost impossible to establish on present evidence, though there were many rumours, and Vladimir's mother, princess Evfrosin'ya was regarded as particularly prone to promote conspiracies in favour of her son. It was easy for any disgruntled boyar or lower servant to denounce a rival as a supporter of Vladimir of Staritsa and be believed; it was also easy for Ivan to believe that Vladimir would be supported by the Lithuanian King Sigismund Augustus and his nobles. At the session of the Polish Sejm held in 1563, the speech from the throne informed those present that the King 'hoped that as soon as his armed forces entered Russia many boyars, and noble generals, oppressed by the tyranny of that monster will voluntarily come over to his Majesty's grace, and become his subjects with all their lands'.[52] There are also frequent hints in the chronicles that Ivan might have regarded some of the Tatar *tsarevichi*, notably the descendants of Tsar Peter of Kazan', Vasily III's brother-in-law, as possible heirs to the throne.[53]

Another deep-rooted Russian tradition acted as a brake on Ivan's effort to achieve total power: the tradition which was still alive mainly among the Gediminovichi and Riurikovichi of Lithuania (and it is referred to in the speech from the throne mentioned above) and to a lesser degree among those serving the Russian Tsar, of deserting as Kurbsky had done, though he claimed to have done so in order to save his life. One has only to look at the list of princes who moved to Russia from Lithuania, and deserted back to Lithuania, or attempted to do so. The Patrikeevs moved from Lithuania in the fifteenth century, and left a large clan of descendants in Russia,[54] some of whom returned or attempted to return to Lithuania. Mikhail L'vovich Glinsky, Tsaritsa Elena's uncle came over to Russia then, dissatisfied with his treatment, attempted to go back to Lithuania and paid the price. Prince Dmitri Vishnevetsky also moved backwards and forwards, and so did the Princes Bel'sky, and many others whose names are not recorded.[55] Now, however, there seem to have been many desertions lower down the ranks of the service gentry, many of whom went over even on the battlefield to the troops of the Commonwealth, doubtless to the dismay of the Tsar.[56]

The principle of family or collective responsibility for a whole range of activities, whether the maintenance of order, the detection and punishment of crime, and the collection and payment of taxes was common to many European medieval societies, and probably had its roots in Germanic law.[57] It was superseded little by little as the state evolved out of the dynastic patrimony and the administration emerged out of the King's household. But family responsibility in the West declined more quickly than in Russia, with a few remarkable exceptions, as paid royal servants took over the administration. The Mongol period prevented any natural evolution in Russia in this field as in so many others, so that collective responsibility lasted much longer. It was not

until the reign of Catherine II that family property ceased to be confiscated by the Crown for the crimes of the father. In the reign of Ivan
collective responsibility was still an integral part of the administration of
the country. It was collective responsibility which kept the borders
secure, and ensured that anyone attempting to escape would be
denounced to the authorities. It was the same system which maintained
a culture of denunciation at all levels of society. Everyone was bound to
report any evidence of treason or disloyalty, or even inefficiency, for the
obvious reason that they would themselves be punished if they failed to
reveal their knowledge of forthcoming treason. It was also collective
responsibility expressed in written surety bonds which kept the boyars
from flight. Under Ivan, collective *political* responsibility justified the
Tsar in executing wives, children, servants and peasants belonging to the
households of those he had disgraced. All levels of society were
affected.[58] And the increasing number of these bonds, involving more
and more people, was clearly resented by the aristocracy and the service
gentry and intensified their discontent.

In turn, when he was confronted with his nobility Ivan felt that he was
caught in a spider's web, spun by the treacherous boyars, who were
linked together by endless marriage connexions but even more
effectively by the net he had woven himself out of the collective sureties,
forcing leading courtiers to put up large sums of money, which in turn
forced them to make common cause if they did not want to be destroyed,
and drew large numbers of service gentry into their orbit. It was a
question of *quis custodiet ipsos custodies*. Ivan believed that the lower
military servitors would thwart the boyars and princes if the latter
plotted against him, but they knew only too well that if they denounced
these supposed plotters, they too would be destroyed – and their
families. And Ivan's suspicious nature led him to believe that the very
fact that his courtiers put up money and agreed to stand surety for a man
whom Ivan distrusted or had disgraced was further proof of the secret
treachery of those who signed the sureties. The practice of demanding
financial sureties to guarantee loyalty worked both ways. It created
guarantees of loyalty to the Tsar, but it rendered it difficult for the Tsar
to single out an individual as responsible for an offence, as distinct from
the kin as a whole.

What made it even more difficult is that important courtiers at the
time of Ivan were drawn from a relatively small number of large princely
family clans – there were 120 Princes Yaroslavsky, 69 Obolenskys, 29
Belozerskys, 25 Rostovskys, 28 Starodubskys who could be expected, up
to a point, to stand together. Among the non-titled boyars there were a

few large clan groups which might be expected to present a common front. Intermarriages between the Tsar's family and princely and boyar families, within princely families, within boyar families, and between princes and boyars rendered the situation still more complex. Ivan was faced by the fact that it was too dangerous for him to bring down a magnate by calling in his sureties, for they would bring too many down with them. At the same time he evidently felt hemmed in by the close network of boyars, priests, courtiers and administrators. Surviving records of collective guarantees of this kind are few, but there were many cases. There are records of at least twelve members of princely and boyar families who fled. Among the ten published surety bonds which are known, the Russian historian Veselovsky has calculated that up to 950 people put up money and guarantees of the loyalty of others, 117 of them twice, sixteen three times, seven four times.[59]

It should be observed that the disciplining of the nobility in this manner was not confined to Russia. Surety bonds and recognizances, 'a terrifying system of suspended penalties', were also widely used in England in the reign of Henry VII. Out of 62 peerage families in his reign some 46 were under various forms of financial threat including the Marquess of Dorset, the Earl of Northumberland and Lord Mountjoy.[60]

Kurbsky was not the only one to flee at this time. One of those who escaped successfully was an officer in the musketeers, of modest noble origin, T.I. Teterin Pukhov, who had enjoyed a brilliant military career but, after the fall of Adashev, fell into disgrace, was forcibly shorn as a monk and incarcerated in a monastery from which he ran away to Lithuania around 1564. After his flight he wrote an insolent letter to the new governor of Dorpat, the boyar Mikhail Iakovlevich Morozov deriding him for sitting, unpaid, in a Russian fort, while his wife and children remained as hostages in the power of the Tsar. Writing to Teterin in September 1577, in 'the refuge of your Tsar, prince Andrei Mikhailovich Kurbsky, in Wolmar, in our ancestral land of Livonia', Ivan who never forgot or forgave anything, taunted him, the renegade-hero, with taking refuge beyond the Dvina, with not a fort to his name.[61] Of course a forsworn monk was an infinitely worse criminal than even a traitor to the Tsar, as Ivan himself recognized in his letter to Kurbsky, where he praised those who had been forcibly tonsured but yet lived to see the light as monks.[62] Skrynnikov makes a striking parallel with more recent times when he says that in the 1560s the flood of immigrants from Lithuania was reversed, and it was now Russians who left for Lithuania, forming a veritable 'Russian emigration' which for the first time in years could defend their interests and their views against the Tsar.[63]

Chapter XI

The Setting Up of the Oprichnina

According to the chronicle, on 3 December 1564 Ivan left for Kolomna, to celebrate the day of St Nicholas there on the 6th. He was making for his palace of Kolomenskoye, accompanied by the Tsaritsa Maria and his sons. According to both the chronicle and two Livonian nobles, Johann Taube and Eilhard Kruse, who had been in captivity in Russia and had then entered Russian service, before the Tsar left Moscow he had ordered the removal from churches and monasteries of many icons, crosses, jewels and plate, embroidered robes and money, indeed of all his treasure. He also collected church ornaments from monasteries and churches in the countryside around Moscow. They were to be loaded onto carts and sledges in the Kremlin.[1]

Ivan then issued a proclamation, 'either inspired by his native suspiciousness or by the suggestion of the devil or by his tyrannical habit', communicating the following to all religious and secular ranks: 'he knew well and had definite information that they did not wish to suffer either him or his heirs, that they were making attempts on his health and life, and wanted to transfer the Russian realm to be ruled by a foreigner; he had therefore summoned them to him in order to hand over his rule to them'. He then divested himself of his Tsarist crown, his sceptre and his robes in the presence of members of all ranks.[2]

The Tsar then summoned all ecclesiastic and civil ranks to attend a service performed by Metropolitan Afanasii while his servants drew up and loaded the sledges he needed in the courtyard. At the end of the service the Tsar emerged from the church and the Tsaritsa appeared at once with the two children, ready dressed for a journey. The Tsar gave his hand in farewell, and blessed all the high-ranking churchmen and the senior boyars, like Prince Ivan Bel'sky, and Prince Ivan Mstislavsky, gathered there, and all the officials and the commanders and the many merchants.

Then the Tsar sat in his sledge with his sons on either side and drove off accompanied by many distinguished boyars such as Aleksei Basmanov, Prince Afanasii Viazemsky and others to Kolomenskoe. The Tsar also ordered a number of boyars, courtiers and officials to accompany him together with their wives and children, and also a contingent of specially selected military servitors, fully armed and with horses and men-at-arms. The Muscovite public was somewhat astonished at the size and solemnity of the procession, and the number of the escort. This was clearly not an ordinary pilgrimage.[3]

The Tsar was confined for a fortnight or so in Kolomna, by bad weather, and then moved on to the Trinity monastery, arriving on 21 December. Thence he moved to Aleksandrovskaia Sloboda. This estate, used intermittently by Vasily III, was now Ivan's preferred residence outside Moscow, used for his hunting expeditions; he had been fortifying it and supplying it throughout the summer of 1564. He sent the Tsaritsa and his children there at the time of the Crimean raid on Ryazan' in October 1564. Some half way between the Trinity monastery and Pereiaslavl' Zalesskii, it was surrounded by estates belonging to the élite of the Russian aristocracy, mainly the princes of Suzdal', such as the Shuisky clan, but also other branches, both princes and boyars, who found it convenient to have estates near the Tsar's favourite residence. The boyars remaining in Moscow were bewildered, and so were the people for they did not understand what was happening. Ivan now sent for those boyars and *voevody* whom he trusted enough to keep them in his service, while those who seemed reluctant to join him were stripped naked and released to make their way back to Moscow in the snow.[4]

Not until 3 January 1565 was a formal communication of Ivan's intentions received in Moscow, addressed to Metropolitan Afanasii, thus indicating Ivan's rejection of the existing government of Russia, the Boyar Council. Even before reaching Aleksandrovskaia Sloboda, Ivan wrote to the Metropolitan and the men of rank that he: 'would go where God and the weather would allow, and give his realm to the traitors, though a time might come when he would demand it back again and would take it'.

Ivan's gesture could be interpreted as an abdication, but he had no intention of abdicating. He was after all responsible to God, as an Orthodox Tsar ruling over Russia, for the spiritual and material welfare of his people. He was preparing to face the boyar aristocracy which had remained behind in Moscow, together with his cousin the Prince of Staritsa, with a choice of which the outcome was determined before hand since he held all the cards: either he was given full power to punish

treason as he saw fit, without regard to the traditional Russian customary legal procedures or the traditional right of intercession of the
Church, or Russia would be condemned to drift, leaderless and rudder-
less, before her enemies. The boyars were to surrender their present
means of circumventing the wishes of the Tsar, sanctified by time and
custom, or be faced with war against their legitimate ruler, supported by
the armed forces and the people of Moscow.

The messages reaching Moscow on 3 January were addressed to the
Metropolitan[5] and to the people of Moscow.[6] Ivan proclaimed his wrath
with the leaders of the Church, the boyars, the service gentry, and the
civil officials who had taken part in treasonable actions and wasted his
substance ever since his boyhood. The guilt of the churchmen consisted,
in Ivan's view, in their efforts to intercede to protect those whom the
Tsar had proclaimed guilty from their just punishment.[7] The guilt of the
boyars and the senior courtiers was broadly characterized by him as
'treason' (*izmena*), a word which covered suspected support of other
members of the Riurikovich dynasty, in the first place Vladimir of
Staritsa, as successors to or indeed rivals of Ivan on the throne; flight to
Lithuania, a supposed intent to fly, any communication with members
of Lithuanian embassies in Moscow to which treasonable intent could
be attributed; support by means of collective suretyships of those whom
the Tsar wished to find guilty and execute; disagreement with the Tsar
on issues of foreign policy such as a critical attitude to the choice of war
in Livonia instead of concentrating all Russian forces against the
Crimean khanate; lack of success in battle which could only be caused
by treason, cowardice, laziness or disputes over precedence. He
explained his future intentions in his missives in which he 'laid' his anger
(*gnev*) on the Metropolitan, the bishops, the heads of monasteries, and
his disfavour (*opala*) on the boyars and courtiers, duma secretaries,
service gentry (*deti boyarskie*) and all lower rank officials.[8]

The missive to the boyars was read out to them (it was probably quite
long – Ivan IV was not laconic by nature) in a meeting in the
Metropolitan's chamber in Moscow. The Tsar specifically accused the
boyars of wasting his treasure and distributing estates to themselves and
their families, of failing to defend Orthodox Christians from their
enemies the Crimeans, the Lithuanians and the Germans (Livonians),
and of evading service. When he wanted to punish any of these traitors,
the church hierarchy, the boyars and the other ranks all joined forces to
'protect them'. Unable in these circumstances to govern, and unwilling
to tolerate such treasonable activity, he felt bound to abandon his realm,
with heartfelt grief, and settle where God willed.[9]

Ivan now extended his appeal for support to the people of Moscow in a special missive to them, which was also read to those who had been allowed into the Kremlin. In it he drove a wedge between high and low. He assured the common people that they, unlike the boyars and high officials, had not incurred his wrath or his disgrace. The Tsar's exclusion of the townspeople from his wrath coupled with his verbal assault on the record of selfish corruption of the boyars served of course to inflame popular resentment and probably led the boyars to fear an outbreak of social unrest. Meanwhile the common people, anxious not to lose the protection of the Tsar and fearing to be delivered over into the hands of the boyars, begged the Metropolitan and the Church Council to petition the Tsar 'not to leave the country and deliver them to the wolves like unhappy sheep with no shepherd, and to protect them from the strong' and they would be the first to demand the destruction of the traitors and evil-doers. 'To whom shall we run? Who will have mercy on us? Who will protect us from attack by people of other races (*inoplemennykh*)? How can a sheep live without a shepherd? How can we live without a lord?' The Tsar had only to name the evil-doers, and they would have to answer for their deeds, for the Tsar had the right and the power to punish and execute.[10]

Ivan had taken care to be escorted not only by armed men, but by the necessary cadres of administrative officials to constitute an effective *dvor* or administration in Aleksandrovskaia Sloboda, while ensuring that the existing administration in Moscow should be deprived of authority and resources. The boyars, officials and service gentry were in despair at the loss of the protection of the Tsar against their enemies, according to the account of the episode given in the chronicle (no doubt thoroughly vetted by Ivan himself).

The aristocracy was taken completely unawares by Ivan's ploy, so much so that they missed the one and only opportunity they were ever given of accepting the Tsar's offer to abdicate. Besides, there was no tradition in Russia (or scarcely anywhere) of legitimate opposition, of contractual relationship between ruler and ruled, and the boyars were psychologically unprepared for the drastic step of formal opposition to the Tsar, the defender of Orthodoxy – proof if any were needed that plotting against the Tsar had not spread its tentacles very deeply into society. The people of Moscow were profoundly dependent on the protection of the Tsar as their religious leader, in an age of religious controversy and dangerous heresies, and as their defender against the mighty . It was scarcely feasible for a deeply devout people to rise against their ruler at a time when he was leading the struggle against the

Protestant and the Catholic heresies on the battlefields of Livonia and Lithuania.[11]

The Metropolitan determined (wise man) to stay in Moscow to govern the city, left without any central authority, and sent Archbishop Pimen and Archimandrite Levkii as his envoys to Aleksandrovskaia Sloboda, with an appeal to the Tsar as 'the chosen lord of the true apostolic faith' to ward off the danger that it might be polluted and even destroyed. The two ecclesiastics set out the same evening, 3 January 1565. They begged, in the name of the boyars, and in their own, that the Tsar should withdraw his anger and his disfavour from them, and should stay in his realm and rule it as he saw fit, and be free to act as he pleased with the traitors and evil-doers, and punish them as he saw fit. If the Tsar did indeed know the traitors, he should name them, for he had the right to punish them as he wished.

The envoys from Moscow reached Aleksandrovskaia Sloboda on 5 January 1565, followed by a long trail of nobles, armed men, merchants, townspeople and the common people of the city.[12] The Tsar received first the ecclesiastics, then the boyars, who were only admitted under guard, into what was now a fortified camp. Only those whom the Tsar called upon were admitted to his presence, starting with the priests, who begged him to lift his anger from them and to forgive the treacherous boyars and 'allow them to see his eyes, and remove their disgrace, and rule his lands as he wished'. The Tsar at last allowed himself to be persuaded and permitted the boyars and the officials waiting outside to enter and 'see his eyes'. The common people were not admitted and played no further part in the proceedings.

The Tsar now made a clear distinction between the Church and the boyars. He would not consult with the boyars, but in view of the entreaty of the Metropolitan, conveyed to him by the two clerics, he decided to return to his throne, and resume his lands, 'but as to how he would take them and how he would rule them he would issue his orders to the Metropolitan and the churchmen'. The boyars and the Council were simply brushed aside, and the Tsar attempted to render them powerless by dividing the Council, keeping some of the senior boyars like Prince I.D. Bel'sky, with him and sending Prince I.F. Mstislavsky back to Moscow, thus limiting their power to act.

Whether Ivan discussed his plans with the boyars he was holding almost as hostages in Aleksandrovskaia Sloboda who can tell, but some unlikely rumours surround the events of these days.[13] There are reports that Ivan genuinely meant to abdicate and to leave his throne to his two sons. According to Schlichting who may well have been an eyewitness,

Ivan pretended that he had grown tired of power and wished to retire to live the life of a monk. Summoning the boyars he said ' here are my sons whose age and capacity fit them for rule'. He urged the boyars to 'let them rule, let them dispense justice and lead you in war' and if untoward events arose they could always call on him, Ivan, for help, 'for he would not be living far away'; he is said to have drafted a will at the time to that effect. The only surviving will of Ivan's is usually held to date from much later, in 1572 (or even 1579), and what is more, in 1565 his sons were scarcely fit to rule or command armies being seven and five years old respectively.[14] Ivan himself set it about that on the death of his father Vasily III, the boyars had intended to deprive him of his throne in favour of Alexander Gorbaty-Shuisky, the senior of the Suzdal' Shuisky princes, a clan descended from a brother of Alexander Nevsky's, which regarded itself as nearer to the Riurikid throne than the House of Daniel of Moscow to which Ivan belonged. He was a military commander of great prestige and wealth, one of the outstanding generals in the conquest of Kazan', related to the Tsar's family through his daughter, who was married to Prince I.F. Mstislavky.[15] And these were the men, Ivan added, that he was forced to see every day.

The conditions on which Ivan agreed to return to Moscow were set out in an *ukaz* which has not survived but is described in the account of the two Livonian nobles, Taube and Krusc.[16] According to them there was a lengthy preamble setting out the treason of the subjects of the grand princes ever since the days of Vladimir Monomakh in the twelfth century, before Ivan stated his terms: he demanded the right to punish traitors as he thought fit, and those who failed to obey him. He could disgrace them and execute them and confiscate their moveable and immoveable property, without any legal process, without the *prigovor* or assent of the boyars in the Council and need pay no regard to the intercession of the church hierarchy.[17] But Ivan had still a further surprise for his people up his sleeve. He declared that he intended to set up an *oprichnina* for himself, carved out of his realm.

Probably not many people understood what the Tsar meant, for *oprichnina* was an archaic word which was used of an appanage granted for life to the widow of a noble or a prince when the rest of her husband's estate was divided between his children.[18] In his *ukaz* Ivan already described those parts of Russia and of Moscow he intended to take into this appanage he was carving out for himself, leaving the rest, the *zemshchina* or 'land', to be governed by the boyars as before. He had taken care to bring with him to Aleksandrovskaia Sloboda,[19] which was now to be even more strongly fortified and was to become his unofficial capital, a contingent of *d'iaki* and minor officials in addition to commanders and a goodly contingent of service gentry who would constitute his new *dvor* or 'court'. Out of these latter, and with some foreign volunteers, a corps of some one thousand men was to be formed as his own private guard. All Ivan's servants had to swear a special oath of loyalty to him, and 'neither to eat nor drink' with any members of the *zemshchina* nor to have anything to do with them, even if they were members of their families. No one can tell how far this injunction was obeyed. In order to pay for these innovations, Ivan imposed an enormous levy of 100,000 rubles on the whole country, already exhausted by the costs of war.[20]

Ivan had now to set about implementing his plan for the *oprichnina*. Early in February, he cleared the way for his return to Moscow by ordering the execution of Prince Alexander Gorbaty-Shuisky (his alleged rival for the throne)[21] together with that of his seventeen-year-old son and his father-in law. The sources do not suggest any particular reason why he should have been charged with treason just at this point, but it will be remembered that he had been the recipient of a letter from the priest Sylvester critical of Ivan's warlike qualities.[22] It is also possible that Ivan wished to get rid of a prominent and respected figure in the noble bastion of Suzdal' (which he took into the *oprichnina*) before embarking on the further purge which he was planning. Gorbaty is alleged, on the basis of the existence, though not the content, of that single surviving letter to him from the priest Sylvester, to have been a supporter of Vladimir of Staritsa, on the grounds that Sylvester was also a supporter of Vladimir, at the time of Ivan's severe illness in 1553.

Father and son disputed who should lay his head first on the block, according to Kurbsky. The father won and the son kissed his severed head before losing his own.[23] This was the end of the senior line of the Shuiskys and the junior lines were represented only by younger men in the 1560s. Ivan sent 200 rubles to the Trinity monastery on 12 February for prayers for the souls of Gorbaty and his son, so that he seems to have been torn between dynastic fear and hatred of a successful military rival, and awareness of a crime against them.[24]

The date of Ivan's return to Moscow is uncertain, but he had returned by mid-February 1565.[25] The tension of these days had made him unrecognizable: he had previously been regarded as a very tall, well set up man, with a fine head of hair, long moustaches and beard, penetrating light eyes and a Roman nose. He had now lost the hair from his head and his beard (it grew again), his eyes were dimmed, his features marked by a gloomy savagery.[26]

Ivan had at first intended to build a new palace for himself within the Kremlin walls, and took over the site of the palace belonging to his cousin Vladimir of Staritsa, which had recently burnt down, thus leaving Vladimir without a dwelling within the Kremlin. But he changed his mind and finally took over a large site outside the walls of the Kremlin, (which had belonged to his brother-in-law, Mikhail Cherkassky[27]), in the Arbat district, to set up his *dvor*, which became a fortified palace, isolated from the *zemshchina*. All those who had dwellings there and were not taken into the *oprichnina* were expelled and sent to find a settlement elsewhere. The common people were unaffected.

The special *oprichnina dvor* outside the Kremlin was a formidable building, with stone and brick walls, lead-covered gates, 'on which were painted lions the eyes of which were set with mirrors; one stood with its mouth open, looking towards the *zemshchina*, the other towards the *oprichnina*'. Between the two was a large double-headed eagle painted black, with extended wings. On the north side there was another large gate with tin-covered iron plates and all the domestic buildings, such as kitchens, storehouses, and the ice houses and cellars, in which doubtless large quantities of sturgeon and sterlet and meat and game were kept. The whole complex, apart from the walls, was built of wood.[28]

Ivan who seemed indeed to be going through a period of intensive fear welling up from deep psychological depths, now turned his attention to other suspected traitors: P.P. Golovin was executed on 4 February and two Kurakin princes and Prince I.I. Sukhovo Kashnin were executed at the same time, one Kurakin prince was forced to take the cowl, and Prince D.F. Shevyrev was impaled, for what offence is not known, possibly for attempting to flee to Lithuania; he is said to have sat on the pole, singing a canon to the Virgin Mary.[29] The property of the disgraced was confiscated.[30] More executions followed, but what most shocked the aristocracy was the cruelty of the methods chosen and the extermination of whole families when adolescents and even girls were executed. The fear that swept through them is illustrated by the case of one of the Obolensky princes, a soldier so distinguished that Ivan had to release him because he needed him, but who could not find a single prince or boyar to sign a surety bond for him and had to fall back on the merchantry.[31]

The most important task before Ivan was the delimitation of his *oprichnina*. This was a major undertaking, involving the division of the country, of the administration and of the armed forces, a division which had to be carried out while at the same time Ivan pursued his foreign policy aims. Though the Tsar had obviously given some thought to it beforehand, he had now to delimit the areas of Russia he proposed to take in, and then set about expelling from them princes, boyars, *pomeshchiki* and even peasants, recruiting new people he judged more reliable, and settling them in these new lands. Obviously he took over the most productive and economically developed areas and the well-established commercial towns, markets and trade routes, though not necessarily the most agriculturally productive (see map on p. 233). But the major fortifications against outside enemies were left to the care of the *zemshchina*.[32]

The area in which the English Russia Company was allowed to operate was also taken into the *oprichnina*, as was the most prosperous part of northern Russia and the capital of salt production, Staraia Russa. The central districts of Russia, Viaz'ma, Mozhaisk, Suzdal', areas thickly settled with gentry estates, were taken over.[33] Suzdal' for instance lost about 80 per cent of its gentry, but it was high on the list of Ivan's unreliable provinces since it was the centre of the powerful, wealthy, though not large Shuisky clan. While many of the Suzdal' princes had served in the Council in the early part of the reign, during the *oprichnina* not one remained and this powerful clan was leaderless.

The corps of *oprichniki* was set up by recruiting a number of princes and service gentry from the upper ranks of the existing court military servitors and taking them to serve Ivan in the court at Aleksandrovskaia Sloboda, and a second, larger contingent of provincial service gentry was recruited from the towns Ivan had chosen to form part of his appanage. Aleksei Basmanov and Prince A.D. Viazemsky were in overall charge of carrying out this operation which involved detailed inquiries into the families, opinions, histories, relationships, marriages and friendships of all potential recruits. The class composition of the recruits to the corps of *oprichniki* has served historians as evidence for Ivan's alleged intention of downgrading the princes and boyars in favour of men of humbler origin. The principal critics of the *oprichnina* who recorded their views, Prince Kurbsky, the nobles Taube and Kruse, and the German mercenary Staden, all describe the recruits to the armed guard and to the special armed forces as being men who sometimes came from humble beginnings or even from the peasantry, and who were allotted lands ranging from fifty to sixty or more *haken* (a Livonian measure of the production of land). This was true of the early days of the *oprichnina*, when Ivan showed a particular hostility towards high-ranking boyars and princes and recruited lower ranking nobles to the Privy Council. But in the early 1570s the trend was reversed and the princes flooded back again.³⁴ The *oprichniki* had to swear an oath of allegiance as follows:

> I swear to be true to the Lord, Grand Prince, and his realm, to the young Grand Princes, and to the Grand Princess, and not to maintain silence about any evil that I may know or have heard or may hear which is being contemplated against the Tsar, his realms, the young princes and the Tsaritsa. I swear also not to eat or drink with the *zemshchina*, and not to have anything in common with them. On this I kiss the cross.³⁵

In order to emphasize their total separateness from the rest of the people, the *oprichniki* wore a special black uniform of coarse cloth over their rich clothes, and rode around with the head of a dog attached to their bridle and a brush fastened to their whip, to symbolize their function: first they barked and bit the enemies of the Tsar and then they swept them out of the country.³⁶

The two Livonians do not spare Ivan in their description of the horrors he inflicted on the people of Russia in order to carry out his plan. From relatively small beginnings, the *oprichnina* expanded in area and depth, and embraced extensive territories, its administration becoming more and more arbitrary, relentless and inhuman. In 1565 Rostov, Beloozero and Vologda were taken over and well-born men were expelled from their ancestral lands, forced to leave even their moveable property behind, and sent to new lands; their wives and children were sent on after them, on foot; in 1566 another eight districts in central Russia harbouring some 12,000 boyars and landowners, of whom only 570 were taken into the *oprichnina*, were cleansed in the depth of winter, forcing noble ladies to give birth in the snow. Any peasant who attempted to assist them on the way was promptly executed. Those who died were left unburied, the prey of dogs, birds and wild animals. Those who had once been rich were left to beg, and those who had been their servants and possessed nothing now sat in their lands and were given as much as ten of them were given previously. And it happened, conclude the two Livonian nobles, as in the old song: 'Where peasants rule, the government is rarely good.'³⁷ Even Ivan himself felt that his new companions were somewhat baseborn.³⁸

There was at this time no shortage of land at the disposal of the Tsar. Apart from confiscated land, there were abundant resources in conquered Kazan' territory. There were several ways of redistributing lands to Ivan's *oprichnina* guard: either by adding to what they already held in a given province from lands of *pomeshchiki* who had been expelled, or by moving them to provinces from which all existing landowners were expelled. Obviously, throughout the country there were wealthy owners of patrimonial lands (*votchiny*) and these too were removed wherever necessary. If they were taken into the *oprichnina*, they kept their patrimonial estates in the *zemshchina*, and were given additional *pomest'ia*. The extent of the upheaval varied from district to district according to the number and size of *votchina* estates, and the extent of the enrolment into the *oprichnina*. The privileged status of the *oprichniki* enabled them to carry out the policy of resettlement with as much brutality as came naturally to each individual, and there were indeed members of the *zemshchina* who dressed up as *oprichniki* in order to benefit from the immunity of the latter and oppress their fellows.

The introduction of the *oprichnina* was accompanied by a veritable orgy of arrests and killings, in which it is difficult to detect a specific policy. Sometimes it seems as though Ivan were singling out those who had been slow to acknowledge his son Dmitri in 1553; at other times it seems his blows were aimed at those who participated in the alleged plot against him by Vladimir of Staritsa in 1563; sometimes they were aimed at more distant enemies, the members of the large Obolensky clan whose alleged misrule, together with that of the Shuiskys during his minority, was not forgotten, and whose disregard for his status as Grand Prince was not forgiven. At first it was the princes of Suzdal' who suffered most; many of whom had achieved the rank of boyar. Many, though not all, of the far more numerous and less significant Princes Iaroslavsky, Rostovsky, and Starodubsky, were expelled from their lands and exiled to Kazan' in the course of 1565, together with a number of untitled boyars and a considerable number of service gentry.[39] Including wives and children it is estimated that some six to seven hundred were exiled to Kazan', with the loss of all their property, to continue their service from new, often very small holdings, often seized from their native owners in the newly conquered lands of Kazan' and granted to the newcomers in lieu of their previous holdings, in order to consolidate the Russian presence in these areas.[40]

Ivan certainly achieved the object of severing the local links uniting a prince or boyar with his 'people'; the people of course sometimes did not survive either, as in the case of P.I. Gorensky, fifty of whose vassals or retainers were hanged with him.[41] Prince Semen Lobanov Rostovsky, who had disgraced himself in 1554,[42] and had been thrown into prison for attempting to flee to Lithuania, had been released and resumed service. In 1565 he was serving as *voevoda* in Nizhnii Novgorod when he was arrested by *oprichniki*, with forty of his retinue. Taken to Moscow by the *oprichniki*, he was killed on the way and his body pushed under the ice; his head was cut off and sent to Ivan in a bag. The Tsar reputedly addressed it: 'Oh head, head, as long as you were alive you shed a lot of blood!'[43] The fates of Gorensky and Rostovsky were a warning of what might befall those who fled to Lithuania. Many boyars too were exiled, or imprisoned, often for connections with disgraced princes. V.V. Morozov, who had arranged for the burial of Kurbsky's servant, Shibanov, was confined to prison as were other members of his family. The surviving relatives and connexions of Aleksei Adashev were rounded up. What shattered public opinion, if this phrase can be used, was not only the massacre of the élite but also the indiscriminate executions of their families and followers.

While Ivan was organizing the *oprichnina*, he was also fortifying Aleksandrovskaia Sloboda, which had now become the place where above all he felt safe. It was gradually expanded, becoming a small town with many painted churches, houses and stone shops and eventually prisons and torture chambers. The Church of the Mother of God shone in many colours and in gold and silver, and every brick was marked with the sign of the cross. Ivan himself lived in a spacious palace surrounded by ramparts and a moat, while the soldiers and officials lived in specially built quarters. No one could enter or leave without Ivan's knowledge.[44]

Ivan never gave any indication of why he set up the *oprichnina*, or of what he hoped to achieve with it. Russian and Soviet historians have in turn never stopped constructing interpretations of his policy, indeed of what are frequently described as his 'reforms' – though if words have any meaning then a reform nowadays implies an improvement on what went before. The effectiveness of an institution must be analysed in relation to its ostensible purpose, particularly in the case of an institution deliberately created by an act of will, as distinct from one which has evolved over time. But since historians have no idea what Ivan intended the *oprichnina* for, they have had to work back to intentions from consequences, a very unsatisfactory method, particularly where the evidence is both scanty and contradictory. The problem of interpretation has been further obscured by the distinction drawn in Marxist scholarship between subjective and objective forces of history, and by the imposition on historical analysis of the anachronistic concept of the class war. Ivan's conscious purpose, whatever it was, may not have corresponded at all with the results he achieved. Judging by what he did achieve, however, he intended to procure for himself a total freedom of action, in every field, so well expressed in the Russian word *volia*. It is a word which denotes total freedom to pursue one's arbitrary will, not freedom under the law.

One must also ask where did Ivan get the idea of setting up part of his realm to prey on the other part, like a cancerous growth, moving around in the body politic, now taking in cities and land and now expelling them, after having stripped them clean. After all, other kings in other countries have been afraid of dynastic rivals for the throne (like King Henry VIII) or of overmighty subjects who had to be cut down to size, or of a solid aristocratic opposition to their policies like that of the barons to King John of England. Other countries suffered from feudal fragmentation, or difficulty in extending royal authority throughout the land; others have suffered from conflict between a rich and powerful aristocracy, a class of military landed gentry, a poor peasantry. Other countries too were burdened by constant warfare, requiring additional resources in men and treasure which had to be extorted from the population. In other countries economic forces were at work leading to changes in the mode of production. But nowhere was the attempt made to solve these problems by the creation and imposition of a duplicate state. Other rulers have instituted reigns of terror but they have not divided the state into two or even three and allowed one part to prey upon another.

There is one possible source for the idea of setting up a special guard of *oprichniki* in the form which it took, namely the Tsaritsa Maria Temriukovna. She was very young when she arrived in Russia, and most Russian authors, as noted above, completely reject the idea that she had any influence on Ivan or that he even liked her.[45] But she bore him a short-lived son, lived with him for eight years, probably shared in some of the court entertainments since Tatar women were not accustomed to seclusion, and accompanied him everywhere. In summer 1564 she went with Ivan on a pilgrimage to Pereiaslavl' Zalesskii, and the monks and other observers there 'were impressed with her modest bearing, religious proclivities, and grasp of affairs'.[46]

The idea that the concept of the *oprichniki* originated with her is first mentioned by one of the German military nobles who briefly served in the *oprichnina*, Heinrich von Staden. He wrote that: 'She [Maria] advised the Grand Prince to choose five hundred harquebusiers from among his people and generously provide them with clothes and money. They were to ride with him daily and guard him day and night.' Ivan followed this advice according to Staden, 'and chose from his own and foreign nations a handpicked order'.[47] Maria's brother, Prince Mikhail

Cherkassky who had been at court in the care of Ivan since 1558 and whose wife was related to Tsaritsa Anastasia, became an important leader of the *oprichniki*.

Ostrowski, who has pursued more than other scholars the notion of extensive Mongol influence on Russian political institutions,[48] does detect the presence of Tatar influence in what he considers to be Ivan's deliberate choice to set up 'a steppe khanate', taking his cue from Genghis Khan and excluding Byzantium in the form of the Orthodox Church and the Boyar Council in favour of an eastern divan.[49] Maria Temriukovna has a bad reputation in Russian folklore; in a song about the death of Anastasia, the first Tsaritsa warns Ivan not to marry a pagan wife, and Maria and her brother Mikhail are made responsible for the introduction of the *oprichnina*.[50]

There are two respects in which Tatar influence could be discerned. One is the setting up of the corps of *oprichniki*, the special guards, which Staden attributes to Maria. According to Vernadsky, Genghis Khan had organized his imperial guards into a corps ten thousand strong, composed of the best soldiers and officers of each unit. 'The guards became the cornerstone of the whole army organization and administration of Genghis Khan's empire.' They had privileges: a private in the guards was considered higher in rank than any commander of an army unit. They were on permanent duty and when not fighting were employed as messengers, ambassadors and administrators.[51] The second aspect in which Mongol influence may be detected is the setting up of an appanage, which featured also in Mongol practice, particularly in relation to the provision of an income for dowagers.

At least one Soviet historian, S.M. Kashtanov, has raised the question whether the extremely favourable treatment of the Tatar princelings by Ivan was a deliberate measure adopted because he felt he could place greater trust in their loyalty, perhaps in part owing to his wife's insinuations. Because the Tatar tsars and tsarevichi (ex-rulers and their sons) were descended from Genghis Khan or from Tatar families which had recently reigned, and were thus dynastically pure, they stood above the unreliable Russian boyars and service princes. Moreover, the tsarevichi had no support in Russian society and depended entirely on the Tsar's favour alone. They could not compete with the Riurikovichi as possible claimants to the Russian throne. This may also explain Ivan's treatment of the descendants of the Grand Prince of Lithuania, Gedimin, the Bel'sky and Mstislavsky princes, who survived all disgraces and continued to be appointed as leaders of the Boyer Council, in turn, replaced at times by Tatar tsarevichi. This in Kashtanov's view explains the extent of the grants of land the Tatar tsarevichi received and the important positions they held. Mikhail Temriukovich Cherkassky was granted what in fact amounted to an old style appanage with all the attendant privileges.[52] Moreover, Ivan showed considerable interest, even affection, for Tatars in his entourage during most of his life and also trusted them as military commanders.

Chapter XII

War in Livonia and the Zemskii Sobor *of 1566*

In one sense war with the Crimeans was Russia's most pressing and constant problem, for the Tatar hordes could conduct their devastating raids from the distant steppes without any warning. They also fluctuated between alliance with the King of Poland–Lithuania (who also used Tatar mercenary troops) and with Russia. Russia, however, had begun to develop a systematic defence against Tatar raids by creating a chain of fortifications along the southern border which remained a feature of Russian life until the annexation of the Crimea in 1783. The first defensive line was along the river Oka, running through Tula and Serpukhov to Nizhnii Novgorod but this was much too near Moscow by the middle of the sixteenth century, and it was supplemented by a line running through a number of towns such as Kolomna, Kashira, Serpukhov and Kaluga. This defensive line consisted of forts manned by cavalry patrols on the alert to detect Tatar movements and protect the settled population. Early in his reign Ivan IV set about strengthening this line and built another one further south, including the new town of Orel, and extending to Alatyr on the River Sura. The total system was about a thousand kilometres long and the line was composed of earthworks, felled trees and palisades, and moats, manned by patrols based on the nearest towns. Ivan himself attached great importance to this defensive network and in the summer of 1565 conducted a lengthy tour of the new towns and inspected the defences.[1] But if Ivan were to embark on a serious campaign against Lithuania, now increasingly supported by the forces of the more powerful Polish army, he needed to cover himself not only against the Crimea but also against both Sweden and Denmark, who both made claims on Livonia.

Meanwhile in Sweden, Gustavus Vasa's long reign had come to end on 29 September 1560 and he had been replaced by his eldest son, Erik XIV, a man who was, intellectually at least, cast in the mould of the

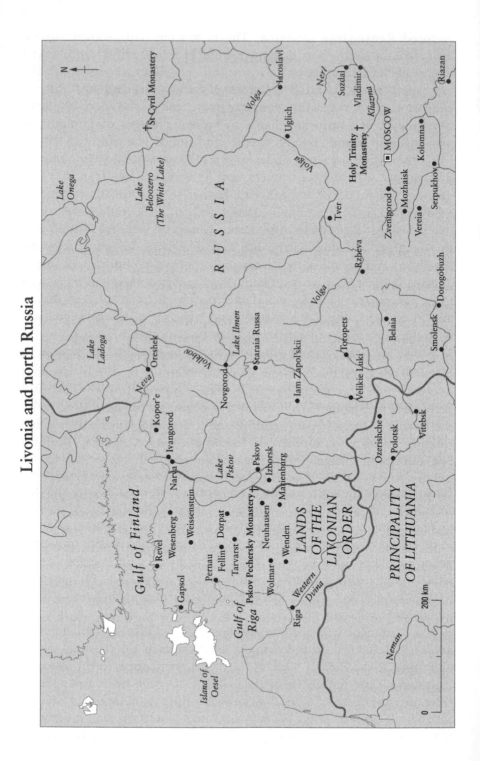

Livonia and north Russia

cultured Renaissance monarch. The new King had recently turned back from a journey to England where Elizabeth, now Queen, had rejected his offer for her hand. It was just as well for, though much the most personable of all her suitors, he was, 'with all his brilliant endowments, a tragically unhappy man, tense and nervous, self-questioning, self-torturing; liable to violent changes of humour; at once suspicious and credulous, cruel and timid. The gem was flawed from the beginning; and under a sharp blow was always liable to disintegrate' – in fact, in temperament he was very like Ivan IV.[2] The accession of Erik XIV introduced a new element into Russo-Swedish relations for, in his communications with Ivan, Erik could start from a much stronger position than his father Gustavus, since his mother was the daughter of a German prince and, like Ivan, he was a king by hereditary right and not by election.[3] Just as Sigismund had refused to address Ivan as Tsar, so Ivan had always refused Gustavus's demand to be acknowledged as his equal and for negotiations between Russia and Sweden to take place directly with the Tsar in Moscow and not with the Governor of Novgorod. Born of a mother of princely rank, Erik was the first Swedish king to demand to be called Majesty, and was very proud of his descent from the Goths.[4]

The new King was determined to achieve Swedish control of Reval which would allow him to dominate both shores of the Gulf of Finland, where Narva, now in Russian hands, had replaced Reval as the Russian staple for the lucrative trade with Russia. In Erik's view his most likely ally among the competing powers was Russia and he negotiated a renewal of the existing truce with Ivan early in 1561, as a result of which Reval accepted the overlordship of Sweden in June 1561. Erik proceeded forcibly to interfere with the trade of the Hansa and other powers through Narva, by seizure of merchant fleets on the high seas, in order to divert the trade to Swedish controlled Reval.[5] An armistice of twenty years was concluded between Russia and Sweden in August 1561,[6] which stabilized their relations and protected Ivan's back. But an event took place in 1562 which was to complicate relations between Russia and Sweden for some time.

Erik's younger half-brother and heir, John, Duke of Finland, was anxious to acquire an independent establishment on the lines of an appanage, and to marry well. He turned his attention to the sister of Sigismund Augustus, Catherine Jagiellonka, she who had refused Ivan's offer after the death of Anastasia not long before. Now, without waiting for the full consent of his brother the King, John took the bit between the teeth and won Sigismund's consent to his marriage to Catherine by being somewhat economical with the truth regarding his political and financial prospects. The marriage took place on 4 October 1562, and outraged Erik. John was arrested, tried and condemned by the Swedish Riksdag for treason. When John resisted, he was besieged in his own castle, taken prisoner and kept locked up in the castle of Gripsholm for five years with his wife. The marriage survived to become a cause of conflict between Sweden and Russia when Ivan decided that he wanted the bride he had lost back.

The situation around Livonia had become more and more complex since the so-called 'Seven Years' War' in the Baltic, between Sweden and Denmark, had broken out in 1563 . Ivan was happy to stand back and let Sweden and Denmark fight it out, but he did not want at that time to alienate Denmark with whom he had signed a treaty in 1562 by which he recognized both Danish annexation of the castle of Sonneburg in Livonia and the King's brother, Duke Magnus, as Bishop of Oesel and Duke of Courland (shortly to be seized by the ex-Grand Master Kettler in agreement with Sigismund Augustus). Erik of Sweden, who needed Russian goodwill for his war with Denmark signed the treaty of Dorpat with Ivan in May 1564 (in Novgorod, as of old), in which Russia recognized Erik's right to Reval and some other castles, while Erik recognized that the rest of Livonia was Ivan's patrimony. But it was not a permanent settlement.[7]

Meanwhile Sigismund had secured a truce with the Crimea for the Commonwealth in 1564/5, during which the Crimeans launched a couple of attacks on Russia, but in 1566 the Sultan called on his Crimean vassal to turn away from attacks on Russia and join in the Turkish struggle against the Holy Roman Emperor in Hungary. The Crimean Tatars, having demanded the return of Kazan' and Astrakhan', were conjuring up the threat of Turkish support, and proposed a two-year armistice in March 1566, provided the Russians paid the usual tribute which Ivan, of course, refused. On the contrary, he carried out a strong demonstration against the Crimeans together with a month-long inspection of the fortifications of the southern border at the end of April 1566.

The Livonian Order had now completely ceased to be an independent factor, though it still had troops in the area. After her conquest of Polotsk, Russia had agreed to sign a truce with Poland–Lithuania until the end of 1563, which later led Ivan to complain that he had been misled into allowing the Commonwealth a breathing space in which to rearm.

In 1563 to 1564 peace talks between Russia and a large Polish–

Lithuanian embassy continued, each side putting forth maximalist claims which were promptly refused by the other. Ivan as usual demanded the return of all the old West Russian lands (Kiev, *et al.*) and the cession of his 'ancestral land', Livonia. The Poles seemed willing to negotiate on the basis of the *uti possidetis* and therefore to cede Polotsk to Ivan. But both sides refused to give way on the real issues which separated them: the Poles insisted on keeping the whole course of the River Dvina and Riga, ceding only a small portion of the land above and below Polotsk, and refused to recognize Ivan's title of Tsar.

The shifting military situation in the Baltic in 1564 and 1565 and the failure of all compromise over the terms of an armistice between Russia and Poland led to the continuation of a war of which both sides were beginning to feel the strain in men and treasure. Ivan now thought up a new plan, namely to recreate the Livonian Order as a vassal state, under its old Grand Master, Wilhelm von Fürstenberg, who had remained in Russian captivity, but whom Ivan respected and had treated well. But Fürstenberg, loyal still to his German overlord, the Holy Roman Emperor, refused the gambit. Spring and summer 1564 saw reverses of the Russian armies in Livonia, notably at the battle of Ula in August, which Ivan regarded as a serious setback, further defections of Russians to Lithuania and clandestine discussions between the nobles in both countries, with or without Ivan's knowledge and approval. The impact of Kurbsky's defection on the Russian attitude in the negotiations with Lithuania must not be underestimated; it had a profound effect on Ivan's attitude to other Russian princes and boyars and increased his suspicions of their loyalty.[8]

The increasing number of executions following on the introduction of the *oprichnina* led eventually to a collective remonstrance on the part of the boyars and princes, including, or possibly led by, the Metropolitan Afanasii, in the summer of 1565. 'They told [Ivan] that no Christian ruler had the right to treat human beings like animals; instead he should fear the righteous dooms of God, who avenges the blood of innocents unto the third generation.' This collective remonstrance must have made Ivan very angry seeing that he had become accustomed to complete submission to his ideas. He was in any case away from Moscow on a pilgrimage, and possibly inspecting his newly acquired confiscated estates from May until the end of July 1565,[9] and seems to have moderated his desire to make a clean sweep of his enemies for a few months. Among those who did suffer in early 1566 was Prince Vladimir of Staritsa.

Always deeply ambivalent towards his cousin, Ivan had already removed all the members of Vladimir's retinue and replaced them by others; he now determined to change all his landholdings, including the principal centre Staritsa, from which he derived his name. These lands were replaced with scattered holdings elsewhere, thus cutting Vladimir's links with traditional supporters in a consolidated appanage. Whether the Tsar suspected his cousin of masterminding a new attempt to dethrone him can only be surmised, but he had certainly deprived him of the means to carry it out.[10]

In April 1566, apparently on the intercession of boyars and service gentry in the *zemshchina* led by the boyar Ivan Fedorov, Prince Mikhail Vorotynsky was freed from his exile in the monastery of Beloozero and allowed to return to Moscow, subject to staggering sureties by five boyars who pledged their heads and fifteen thousand rubles. Much of his enormous estate was returned to him, and he was allowed to maintain his boyars and his military retinue, enabling him to live like an appanage prince.[11]

Though a substantial portion of his patrimonial estates was returned to Vorotynsky, it was still not enough to pay the debts caused by his exile without help from Ivan, which was forthcoming.[12] The way in which Ivan treated Vorotynsky suggests that the Tsar could not make up his mind whether he was an enemy or a friend, whether he needed him as a general or distrusted him as a traitor. Many of the boyars and service gentry exiled to Kazan' were now also allowed to return and received back some land in May 1566 subject also to sureties in which substantial sums of money were put up guaranteeing that the men involved would not flee to Lithuania, and would report any suspicious activities. The advantages of this procedure were that the victims could be allowed back to court, sometimes even to serve in the *oprichnina*.

The time spent in lengthy and fruitless negotiations for peace in 1565 and 1566 coincided with a degree of moderation in Ivan's attitude to the higher nobles and to his servants, though the reshuffling of estates in areas allocated to the *oprichnina* continued apace. During most of 1565 the Tsar did not live in Moscow, but in Aleksandrovskaia Sloboda, which he continued to fortify, and he also started building a fortress in distant Vologda (in *oprichnina* land), on the road to Kholmogory and the White Sea, a more secure refuge in the event of disturbances.

It was here in Vologda that the English Muscovy Company, founded in order to make use of the privileges for English trade granted by Ivan in 1555, had its main base. The Tsar granted the Company the right to trade anywhere in Russia without paying duties or other taxes, and a series of other rights to guarantee its safety and efficiency. The Company was allowed to buy houses in Moscow, Vologda and Kholmogory and a warehouse on a suitable wharf. By 1589, the Company had five houses dotted about the north and it sent its own agents to Russia together with the necessary subordinate staff who often tried to make money trading on the side, and craftsmen and apprentices.[13] The chief agent sometimes acted as envoy for the English Crown; at other times the Queen sent an ambassador of her own.[14] Anthony Jenkinson, who was agent of the Company in 1557, secured the consent of Ivan to explore the possibilities of trade to the Caspian and beyond, and this led eventually to some trading expeditions to Persia. Jenkinson was able to bring back jewels and silks for Ivan which may have established a link between the two men, for Ivan always showed particular confidence in him, even liking for him, in years to come.[15]

In spring 1565 a seven-year truce had been concluded between Russia and Sweden.[16] Meanwhile, relying on their alliance with the Crimean Tatars for peace on their southern boundaries, the Lithuanians had continued to harass the Russian forces on the borders around the Dvina and in Livonia. But in 1566 Lithuania was also faced with war with Sweden in Livonia. The Lithuanian need for Polish military help in the conflicts with both Russia and Sweden pointed to a possible future change in the dynastic constitutional structure uniting the Kingdom of Poland and the Grand Principality of Lithuania about which there was much talk in Vilna. However, talks between Russia and the Commonwealth were soon underway again, because neither side saw a way out of the conflict. On 30 May 1566 a 'grand' Lithuanian embassy arrived in Moscow, led by a great magnate, Iuri Alexandrovich Chodkewicz, brother of the Hetman of Lithuania, and composed of 7 nobles and 10 attendants together with an escort of 850 men, over 12,000 horses, and 56 senior tradesmen in charge of disposing advantageously of the goods the embassy had brought. They were lodged in the Lithuanian House (*Litovskii dvor*), and Ivan, who was at the Trinity monastery, returned on 6 June, when the embassy had settled in. They were given the usual state banquet by the Tsar.[17]

The Lithuanian embassy was the end product of several meetings of the Lithuanian Sejm, in November 1565 in Vilna, and in April 1566 in Beresteisk, which had discussed at length the policy to be followed in the war with Russia in view of the financial exhaustion of the country. It is unlikely that Sigismund expected to achieve peace, in view of the probable rejection of the Lithuanian terms by Ivan, but he might achieve a lengthy truce. Formal talks with Russia began on 6 June, carried out on behalf of Ivan by Vasily Mikhailovich Iur'ev Zakhar'in,[18] a nephew of Tsaritsa Anastasia whose daughter was married to Prince Mikhail Cherkassky, the brother of Tsaritsa Maria (a union of the families of the two Tsaritsas), Prince A. D. Viazemsky and a *duma* servitor, P. Zaitsev, (these last two would become prominent members of the *oprichnina*), I. M. Viskovaty, and a couple of *duma* secretaries.[19] The Lithuanians proposed to partition Livonia with the Russians, with both sides eventually joining to expel the Swedes from Estonia. The Tsar and his advisers took this as an indication of Lithuanian weakness and hoped to win recognition of the Russian right to the whole of Livonia including Riga, simply by ceding Courland, and Polotsk, and some territory around the city to Lithuania, a cession which was considered necessary to protect Polotsk from attack by Russia over the Western Dvina. But the Lithuanians were not prepared to cede control of the waterway of the Dvina and the port of Riga, vital for their economy, and had built a chain of fortified places in Lithuanian territory to defend it.[20]

A meeting of the Russian Boyar Council on 17 June listened to a report by the boyars charged with conducting the talks with Lithuania. Since neither side would give up the claim to Riga, the Council determined to abandon hope of signing a peace treaty in favour of a more limited truce.[21] A proposal that Ivan and Sigismund Augustus should meet in person was welcomed at first by Ivan but no agreement could be reached on matters of etiquette (who was to visit whom at a banquet).[22] Ivan was now asking not only for Dorpat and Narva, but also for the island of Oesel, at present occupied by Denmark. No agreement on the terms of a truce had been reached by 25 June, and the talks, led by V.M. Iur'ev on the Russian side, were adjourned for ten days.[23] At this point the historian Zimin adds: 'it was in order to settle this most important question, that a meeting not just of the Boyar Council but of a *Zemskii sobor* was required, which gave a wider representation to the interests of the Russian ruling class.'[24] The Assembly was to pronounce on two questions: should Russia agree to accept a frontier on the Dvina, as proposed by the Poles, and should Ivan surrender his claims in Livonia?[25]

A gathering of members of some of the various social groups in Russia took place on 28 June 1566, which is usually described by historians as a *Zemskii sobor*, or Assembly of the Land.[26] According to Giles Fletcher, Elizabeth's ambassador to Tsar Fedor in 1588 to 1589, 'Their highest Court of publike consultation for matter of State is called the *Zabore*, that is the Publike assembly.'[27] The intervention of an institution in the negotiations for a truce raises in acute form the problem of what in fact this body was. It is interesting to observe that Karamzin, for instance, in his *History of the Russian State*, which began publication in 1816 does not use the name *Zemskii sobor*; he writes:

> . . . in July 1566 Ivan laid on an unexpected spectacle before Russia: he summoned to the Council of the Land (*zemskaia duma*) not only the highest church dignitaries, boyars, *okol'nichie* and all other high officials, treasurers, clerks, nobles of the first and second rank, but also *gosti* (first rank merchants), merchants, foreign landowners, and submitted the question of the continuation of the Livonian war to their judgment.[28]

Karamzin's description of the meetings and their eventual decisions implies that the various ranks of Russia were all summoned to join in a session of the Boyar Council,[29] or to put it differently, the *Zemskii sobor* formed part of the Boyar Council. The name, *Zemskii sobor*, is an invention of the nineteenth century, at a time when Russians were beginning to write the history of their country and liberal revolutionary movements in many countries were attempting to introduce constitutions establishing representative institutions of many different kinds. These were based on the American and French revolutionary constitutions of 1787 and 1791 or their more recent exemplar, the Spanish constitution of 1812, with which Russian liberals were very familiar since it was one of the most powerful influences on the thought of the northern section of the Decembrist movement in 1825.[30]

Most Soviet historians simply assume that an Assembly of the Land existed in Russia and describe what they take to be its composition, but they rarely provide a rigorous scholarly analysis of its emergence, structure, the nature of representation and of the mandate of representatives, the electoral system, and the political powers (if any).[31] In Zimin's view the decision to call an assembly was expressed in the form of a *prigovor* or ruling by the Boyar Council (of which there is no evidence), and not in a summons by the Tsar.[32] Whereas Skrynnikov, in telling the story of the armistice negotiations, briefly states: 'On 25 June [1566] the talks were broken off, and three days later a special *Zemskii sobor* was called'.[33] Both these historians assume that there was such an institution as a *Zemskii sobor*, which had met before and could be summoned again, and whose consent was advisable, even necessary, on whether to continue to fight to keep Ivan's conquered Livonian ancestral lands. But there was as yet no such institution: it was still in the womb of time.

To begin with, was the body which met to discuss policy in the 1566

Zemskii sobor representative of estates at all?[34] Three hundred and seventy-four people attended. No representative was elected or chosen by any form of electoral process.[35] More to the point, did 'estates' exist in Russia? Society could of course be divided, as almost everywhere, into three categories: those who fought, those who prayed and those who laboured. But this was a sociological classification, not a political one.

Attempts to detect a Western-type feudalism in Russia associated with the name of the nineteenth-century historian, Pavlov Silvansky,[36] failed, in large part because of two features of Russian social development. The first was the absence of a juridical culture in early modern Russia. None of the Russian social groups was legally defined, nor did it have any legal, let alone political corporate rights. The second feature was the broad division of the population into 'service people' and 'taxable people'. Only in the old city republics of Novgorod and Pskov did some memory of a different form of government linger on (and perhaps in Smolensk).

The absence of legal definition of Russian social groups was particularly striking in the case of urban dwellers. The city as a whole was not a legal corporation, nor did it comprise any subordinate legally constituted autonomous institutions such as a town corporation, a mayor and aldermen, or guilds which regulated crafts. There were no chartered boroughs, and town air did not make a man free. Town dwellers too were divided into distinct groups such as the people of the *posad*, the basic trading settlement, who paid taxes, and people attached to monastic estates or service estates, or allodial lands who were also tradesmen or craftsmen or employed in the services of a town, but who did not pay taxes. There were also members of the armed forces like the *strel'tsy*, who participated in trade and crafts, but were not taxable. Among town dwellers there might also be members of the landowning service class, senior officers in the specialist armed forces (*strel'tsy*), etc., the *d'iaki* and central administrative staff and the members of the group who elsewhere would be counted part of the Third Estate, namely the *gosti* or upper ranks of the wealthy wholesale merchants, who were viewed as service people and were not taxed. Such a motley crowd of city dwellers could not easily coalesce and share common political interests, hence Western historians have tended not to regard them as an 'estate'. The memoirs of Staden, for instance, convey the impression that it was relatively easy to pass from one social group to another in a town. The ecclesiastical body constituted a separate social group comprising both regular and secular clerics. They were united by concern for religious values as well as by the consciousness of the problems arising from monastic landownership on a large or a small scale, and came closer to the Western concept of an 'estate', or *Stand*. The generic appellation for these social groups was *chiny*, from which the later word *chinovnik* derives and it did not denote belonging to an 'estate' but to a 'service rank', which could be translated into English as a social 'order'.[37]

Yet to a great extent the Assembly of the Land mirrored the political class, namely the ecclesiastical hierarchy, the boyars, the service gentry, and the small commercial élite. Whether the Assembly met in one chamber or in several, seeing that it signed its depositions in separate curiae, is not known precisely. The summoning of an ecclesiastical council or Church *sobor*, or of a joint boyar and ecclesiastical body, was part of Russian tradition, but it was not a permanently constituted body.[38] Two of the highest ranking hierarchs of the Church *sobor*, for instance, were absent from the Assembly of 1566 possibly for reasons of age or ill-health, including Metropolitan Afanasii. Present were 3 archbishops, 6 bishops, 14 abbots and archimandrites, 3 *startsy* (elders) and a cellarer. Abbots and archimandrites of monasteries were far fewer than those who attended a full Church *sobor* in 1580 devoted to church matters – 14 as distinct from 39 – and the abbots of the most important monasteries were conspicuous by their absence.[39] All told there were 15 Moscow abbots, and 6 from monasteries in the west and northwest to whom the question of war or peace was most relevant. The total came to 32.

The Boyar Council 'present' in the Assembly of 1566 comprised a body of 30, made up of 17 boyars, 3 okol'nichie, 2 treasurers, 1 man serving the boyars in a judicial capacity, 6 *duma* secretaries and 1 *pechatnik* (keeper of the seal), i.e. 17 boyars and 13 non-boyar members. The composition of the boyar presence in a *Zemskii sobor* raises a number of interesting questions about its status and functions or what one might call the constitutional place of the so-called *duma*. To begin with only 17 members of actual boyar rank were present; thus by no means all existing boyars were listed as attending the *Zemskii sobor*, and 14 of the total number of boyars at the time were missing. Many of the absent 14 were on duty as military commanders (*voevody*) or governors (*namestniki*) in various towns; 2 of them were in Moscow but took no part in the *sobor*.[40] There were at the time 2 high-ranking Tatar princes of boyar rank among the senior army commanders, Tsar Simeon Kasaevich (the baptized ex-Tsar of Kazan') and his cousin, Tsarevich Kaibula Akhkubekovich of Astrakhan', who were both frequently in attendance on the Tsar; they seem not to have attended the assembly, at any rate they did not sign the sentence it pronounced. Some of those who took part later became members of the *oprichnina*, like V.M. Iur'ev Zakhar'in, who participated actively in the negotiations with the Lithuanians and died in 1567; some were already in disgrace.[41] At any rate three of the boyars had recently been in disgrace and had only just been restored to their rank, possibly in an effort to conciliate different factions. The absence of as many as 14 boyars from the contingent in the *sobor* undermines the theory that all boyars belonged to the Council as of right and confirms the theory put forward by Sergei N. Bogatyrev, that the analysis of this institution made by the English envoy, Giles Fletcher, in his *Of the Russe Commonwealth*,[42] provides a more perceptive description of the role of the boyar than is usually given.[43] According to Fletcher, there were two kinds of boyars, those who were given the title in a purely honorary form, who were called 'counsellors at large'[44] for they were 'seldom or never called to any publique consultation'. And 'they which are of his [the Tsar's] speciall and privie Counsell indeed (whom he useth daily and ordinarily for all publique matters perteining to the State) have the addition of dumnoy, and are named dumnoy boiaren, or Lords of the [Privie] Counsell, their office or sitting Boarstua dumna'.[45] Clearly the Boyar Council which sat in the Assembly of 1566 did not comprise all the boyars, and was closer to a Close Council, or in English the Privy Council, a socially mixed body including not only boyars but non-boyars such as I.M. Viskovaty, then keeper of the seal (*pechatnik*), N.A. Funikov-Furtsev, treasurer and the Shchelkalov brothers, *d'iaki* from a prominent secretarial family.

Zimin's description of the Boyar Duma in the context of the *Zemskii sobor*, as a body including non-boyars as of right, removes it from the category of a chamber representing boyardom as an estate, a chamber composed of the 'reactionary' aristocracy of birth as a whole, and brings it closer to a constitutionally totally different kind of body, namely a privy council appointed by the ruler both from the aristocracy and the leading non-aristocratic high officials, to advise him and to act in an executive capacity.[46] For a parallel in Western Europe, the English example springs again to mind, if one compares the Council not with the House of Lords but with the English Privy Council. For, though as a separate entity the Tudor Privy Council did not sit in either the upper or the lower House of Parliament, yet the peers sat as individuals in the House of Lords and non-noble members, such as the law officers of the Crown, and senior officials (secretaries) in charge of executive offices, like Sir Nicholas Bacon, Sir William Cecil, and later his son Robert, or Sir Francis Walsingham were elected to the House of Commons.[47]

The perception of the so-called Boyar Duma as an administrative body, a Privy Council rather than a politically representative body, a House of Lords,[48] is bound to modify the notion of the role and powers of the Duma, and its relationship with the Tsar, as defined by many past and present historians of Russia. The Duma is usually portrayed as the soslovnoe or 'estate' organ of the boyar aristocracy, influencing policy and exercising power independently of the Tsar, particularly in the judicial field, in the interests of its own class, and as a legislature.[49] There was, of course, no independent judiciary in Russia, indeed no trained judiciary at all, merely a number of boyars or officials who acted as judges in legal disputes in the *prikazy* and learned the customary and occasionally codified law on the job, in the capital and in the provinces. The Privy Council had no exclusive legislative power: between 1550 and 1572, out of 38 legislative acts, at least 16 laws were approved with the participation of the boyars, hence 22 were not.[50] But the Boyar Council was *de facto* the head of the executive under the Tsar; it was the government, because many of the boyars were heads of *prikazy*, and as such acted also as 'judges' (*sud'i*).

The 204 nobles, or service gentry, present in the Assembly of 1566 included 95 from the first degree (*pervaya stat'ia*) and 100 from the lower degree of the service gentry, most of them belonging to the 1,000 selected servants of the court of the Tsar (*gosudarev dvor*). Many in the second degree were younger sons or as yet unpromoted members of aristocratic families. Of the members of the first degree, more than a third were princes, descendants of the Lithuanian Patrikeevs and other great Riurikovich clans, sundry Obolenskys, Shuiskys, etc. Others were members of prominent old Moscow boyar families not yet promoted, though some were of more modest origin and some 43 were officials (*prikaznye liudi*) of non-duma rank.[51] In the second category there were also princes, but usually of more modest rank. The substantial number of members of princely and boyar families, among the service gentry of the first degree, some of them of very aristocratic family indeed, undermines the traditional Russian historical assertion of the existence of a deep-rooted political conflict between boyars and gentry, with the latter supporting the Tsar's allegedly anti-boyar policy of greater centralization in Russia.

The largest concentration of members of the service gentry from both degrees came from those registered in the towns immediately surrounding Moscow such as Mozhaisk, 12, and Pereiaslavl', 14; Moscow itself produced 16 members. Areas closely concerned with the exploitation and security of the Dvina valley and Polotsk, and the towns along the Western borderland produced a number of members; from Novgorod, there were 21.[52] Zimin confusingly considers that the 42 towns to which members of the service gentry were attached can be considered as 'represented' by them.[53] But service gentry cannot be regarded as 'representing' an urban or mercantile estate, in the absence of any form of electoral process, though they could, of course, in principle represent people not confined to a legally defined social group.[54] But there was no vestige of an election anywhere, no time to call one, and no established procedure.

The urban commercial element numbering 75 is listed as coming from two towns, namely Moscow and Smolensk, and was counted separately: there were 12 *gosti*, the merchant élite, 41 merchants from Moscow, and 22 reputedly from Smolensk, one of the most important trade routes for Russian supplies from the West. However, the 'Smolensk' merchants in Moscow did not come all the way from Smolensk. They were the descendants of the merchants of Smolensk who had been deported to Moscow after the conquest of the city by Vasily III in 1514, had done well and had been awarded a special status as *smol'niane*, ranking after the *gosti* in the capital.[55] The presence of members of the merchantry in the Assembly is not surprising if the purpose was to discuss negotiations for a peace in which commercial issues were bound to be important. Moreover, the whole composition, indeed the very calling of the *Sobor* should be viewed in the context of the presence of the enormous Lithuanian 'great embassy' which had come to Russia in May. Its substantial commercial contingent suggested that trade formed part of its remit.[56]

The sessions of the Assembly lasted from 28 June to 2 July. A number of questions were submitted to the several distinct groups which met and discussed them separately and submitted their opinions separately to the Tsar. The Tsar asked whether he should meet the wishes of the Lithuanians and include the guarantee of the cession to the Lithuanians of the Livonian towns conquered by them in the terms of the peace or even of the truce; and whether he should continue the war for Livonia or not.

According to the language of the time, the ecclesiastics who ranked first were invited to 'give their advice' to the Tsar; the boyars, who ranked below the clergy, were invited merely to 'express their thoughts'.[57] The Church *sobor* recorded its verdict to the effect that it was incumbent on the Tsar to keep Riga (which had still to be conquered), and the lands bordering on the Dvina, but refused to pronounce in favour of peace or war. Presumably to decide on this issue was incompatible with their cloth. The Boyar Council understood clearly that either Russia had to fight to acquire and keep the towns and forts it wanted, or the Poles could build forts threatening Polotsk from their side of the river; and to give up the claim to Riga might, later, endanger Dorpat and Pskov. It objected to a meeting of the two sides, and warned against the danger of the possible political union of Poland and Lithuania which would be unfavourable to Russia. The keeper of the seal, I.M. Viskovaty, was anxious that at least a truce should be obtained. He submitted an independent opinion, suggesting that Lithuania should withdraw from Livonia, while Ivan would give up his claim to Riga and other Livonian towns, on condition that Lithuania undertook not to assist Riga in the event of a resumption of war after the truce.[58] This ludicrous quibble was not likely to take in Sigismund. The Lithuanian embassy was thereupon told to go home, and hostilities were suspended until they had arrived back in their country.[59]

The well-known verdict of the historian Kliuchevsky on the *Zemskii sobor* of 1566, that the Tsar was merely consulting with his own agents, has weighed heavily on Russian interpretations of the subject. Kliuchevsky argued that if the *sobor* represented anything, it represented the capital, where the leading forces in the country were concentrated, and the capital represented the land. Thus a representative attended the *sobor* as his service duty in accordance with his rank or position;[60] the government ordered him to attend a *sobor* as it might send him to any post. There was no fundamental difference between appointment and election. The government could appoint to a post, and if no one was available it could ask for someone to be elected. There was no question of full powers inherent in a deputy. What was required was a person capable of fulfilling the requirements of the government. This interpretation of the nature of elections in the sixteenth century as leading to the choice of a representative who was bound to act in the royal interest because he was an agent of the Crown, ignores the fact that elected members of Parliament in England carried out functions in the localities on behalf of the Crown, for instance as justices of the peace, without necessarily being or becoming agents of the crown. Both Tikhomirov and Zimin reject Kliuchevsky's view because they take 'agent' to mean a person mandated by the Tsar, and therefore committed to defending his policies and not those of his electors. They also, however, rejected Kliuchevsky's interpretation because it did not concord with the Soviet conception of the Russian government as a government by representative institutions (*soslovno-prestavitel'noe*).

Tikhomirov and Zimin, in rejecting Kliuchevsky's view also brushed aside the Slavophile conception of the Tsar consulting with his people to obtain their support, and opted for the view that the people who attended the *sobor* represented the class interests of the social group they sprang from. Yet Kliuchevsky had a clearer vision of the way medieval western European parliamentary systems worked when he rejected a class-based orientation for the sixteenth-century *sobor*, for an 'estate' is not, or not yet, a class. Perhaps the most useful summing up of the debate on the nature of the Russian Assembly of the Land is the conclusion: 'the Sobors were not visualized at the time as popular representative bodies [*Volksvertretungen*]' but as 'forums to ease the government's task by securing the participation of society'.[61]

We have no evidence of what moved Ivan IV to require such a meeting. The military escort of the Lithuanian embassy amounted to over twelve hundred all told, possibly outnumbering the Russian soldiers present in Moscow. Ivan may well have felt the need for the support of the Russian service gentry, of a body representing Russian public opinion, or of the only opinion which was in any way relevant, a body similar in kind to a Lithuanian Sejm, when Lithuania was so powerfully present in Russian territory. It may be that reports of the public deliberations which had taken place in the Sejms at Vilna (November 1565) and Beresteisk (April 1566) influenced him to set up an authoritative rival forum for the consideration of Russian policy. It may be that he genuinely felt the need to win the support of important social groups to continue the war and to deal with its huge financial burden, to which must now be added the levy of 100,000 rubles for the setting up of the *oprichnina*. It is certainly evidence of the Tsar's capacity for political improvisation – already shown in the creation of the *oprichnina*. Maybe he called the Assembly on the advice of his councillors in the Privy Council, some of whom, including those closest to him, were of Lithuanian origin and therefore familiar with the political system prevailing there. For the *Zemskii sobor*, though not yet an institution, was an institution in the making. An ill-defined public assembly had moved from being a body that listened, to being a body that approved, and now in 1566, to a body which discussed and moulded policy.

The historiography of the *Zemskii sobor* has also been powerfully influenced in a different way by the fact that Russian historians began to engage seriously with the history of their own country only in the early nineteenth century. When it really took off Russian intellectual life soon fell into the morass of German romantic philosophy, followed by Hegelianism, economic determinism and eventually populism,

Marxism, Leninism and the class war, which was viewed as the driving force of historical development, even as far back as in the sixteenth century. It is really difficult to discern a class structure at that time, let alone any economic class solidarity in what was a pre-modern economy and a pre-modern social structure, vertically organized into clans, rather than into horizontal layers, and shot through with patronage and clientelism.

Thus because Russia was developing in a way analogous to, if separate from the rest of Europe, and with a time lag of several centuries,[62] historians assumed that it had developed similar institutions, based on the principle of the representation of 'estates': ecclesiastics, aristocracy, nobility, merchantry/townspeople. And thanks to the dominant historical philosophy of the nineteenth century in Russia, estates had to be viewed as the sixteenth-century equivalent of economic classes. But a more modern approach is that consensus was a deeply rooted political system in Russia as elsewhere, that it goes back to an older tradition of the obligation of the King's retinue to provide counsel, and of the King to listen, in the expectation of achieving the outcome of harmony between the participants. The sixteenth-century Russian conception of the polity (it is too early to talk of the state[63]) was not based on ideological struggle conditioned by social interests.[64] It rested on and was represented by the language of medieval symbols which expressed the understanding and acceptance of the rule of a monarch, at that time.[65] In any case parliaments and representative institutions everywhere usually met far too seldom to be able to act as institutions of government.[66]

There is no space here for a thorough analysis of the difference between the English Parliament and the Russian proto-parliamentary institutions, though the comparison with England is in many ways the most fruitful in the sixteenth century, because the English Parliament was more than a representative body, it was also an outgrowth of a judicial court. The 'King in Parliament' was judiciary, legislature and executive, all in one, which was not the case with representative institutions in other countries, and the Commons also had the right to initiate legislation, which no institution had in Russia: 'For to propund bils what euery man thinketh good for the publike benefite (as the maner is in England) the *Russe Parliament* alloweth no such custome, nor libertie to subiects', wrote Fletcher.[67] Parliaments were not instruments of government but of intermittent conflict resolution between clans and factions by means of political bargaining.

Chapter XIII

The Boyar Plot:
1) the Letters to King Sigismund

Events in the summer of 1566 are somewhat confused and overlapping. There was first of all the question of appointing a new Metropolitan, since Afanasii had been given permission to withdraw in spring 1566. But more important was what appears to have been a plot among service gentry present at the *Sobor* of 1566, the Metropolitan, the Master of the Horse, I.P. Fedorov, one of the wealthiest and most prestigious boyars, and the Prince of Staritsa, to force Ivan to abolish the *oprichnina*. The difficulty with political experiments is that they can have unexpected results. Having given the Tsar, at the *Sobor*, the support he needed to continue the burdensome war in Livonia, members of the service gentry took the opportunity, to Ivan's consternation, to press, in a public demonstration, for the abolition of the hated *oprichnina* as a *quid pro quo* for their acquiescence. The evidence of this mutiny is as usual scanty and imprecise and comes from many different quarters.

According to one account, at the *Sobor* of 1566,

> more than 300 members of the 'tyrant's court' met to hold discussions with the Prince, in which they observed: 'Our Lord most illustrious master, why do you order the deaths of innocent brothers . . . you set your retainers upon us as compensation for our service. They kidnap our brothers and relatives, insult, harass, ill treat, ruin and finally kill us.'[1]

An obscure, undated entry in the later Piskarevsky Chronicle confirms that the Tsar, in setting up the *oprichnina*, provoked considerable ill feeling among the service gentry of the *zemshchina*, that

> He divided the towns and he expelled many people from those he took into the *oprichnina*, and from ancestral lands and *pomest'ia*

... and there was great hatred among all the people for the Tsar, and they appealed to him and submitted a petition into his hands about the oprichnina, that it should not be.[2]

And the chronicle continues: 'they started to think of Vladimir Andreevich' (the Prince of Staritsa). The service gentry not only suffered from the executions and confiscations imposed by the *oprichniki* without any legal justification or form, but also from the taxes levied to pay for the costs of the war and the *oprichnina* (though Ivan did quite well out of confiscated lands) and many of them or their relatives had been expelled from their lands and had to resettle elsewhere, which caused great resentment.[3] The fact that Ivan had to some degree abated the persecutions which had accompanied the introduction of the *oprichnina* evidently emboldened the discontented to demand its total abolition, and enough of them were present in Moscow because of the Assembly of the Land to make an effort worth while. There is no evidence of the date on which the boyars and the service gentry submitted the request to Ivan to abolish the *oprichnina* (historians place their petition between 17 and 20 July 1566) but a considerable number of them were promptly arrested.[4]

Some of the prisoners were soon released, though three nobles, V.F. Rybin Pronskii (a boyar), I. Karamyshev (a military servitor) and K. Bundov, who seems to have been a lower rank landowner of peasant origin, were executed. They were all closely connected with I.P. Fedorov, in his capacity of Master of the Horse,[5] head of the *prikaz* concerned with the supply of horses to the court and the armed forces, no sinecure. Fedorov was removed to Polotsk as Governor for the time being, possibly by the intercession of the future Metropolitan Filipp who was a relative. But Ivan's experience of actual open opposition not only from the boyars but from the service gentry, his growing suspicion of Fedorov's loyalty and his permanent suspicion of his cousin Vladimir of Staritsa, coupled with his reliance on his new guards in the *oprichnina*, launched him on a fresh and even more cruel campaign of repression. Some two hundred of the service gentry who had taken part in the demonstration against him were subjected to *torgovaya kazn'* (flogging through the streets with wire whips); servants and attendants of the Metropolitan were arrested and with other prisoners also subjected to flogging through the streets, some had their tongues cut out, some were quartered, some were flayed alive or strips were carved out from their skin.[6] Anthony Jenkinson, the agent of the English Russia Company, writing to Sir William Cecil from Kholmogory where he had just arrived from England, in a letter allegedly dated 26 June 1566, but probably of 26 July, reported:

> Further this Emperor of Moscovia hath used lately great cruelty towards his nobyllyte and gentlemen, by putting to death, whyppinge and banyshynge above four hundred with confiscation of lands and goods for small offence, and specially towards four of theym, viz., one wurryed with beares, of another he cutt of his nose, hys tonge, hys eares and hys lyppes, the third was sett upon a pole and the fourth he commanded to be knocked on the head and putt under the yse in the Ryver.[7]

Jenkinson cannot by 26 June, when he is alleged to have written this letter in Kholmogory, have heard of events in Moscow in mid-July. And yet the description and the figures coincide with what is known from other sources.[8]

Metropolitan Afanasii had not been present at the meeting of the Church Council in the *Zemskii sobor*. He was deeply opposed to the *oprichnina*, had criticized it openly to the Tsar, and had finally laid down the white cowl on 19 May 1566 without seeking the Tsar's permission. The presence of so many abbots and senior ecclesiastics in Moscow at the time may have been due to the need to summon a Church Council to elect a new metropolitan. It was not going to prove easy. Before he became Metropolitan, Afanasii had been Ivan's confessor. He had attempted on several occasions to use the Church's traditional power of intercession for those Ivan wished to destroy. Afanasii had lived up to the role Ivan attributed to him when angry, of acting as an obstacle to the implementation of his will. This irritated Ivan even more than usual at a time when he was in fact using the church hierarchy to communicate with the *zemshchina*, the mainly boyar government of the land which was not incorporated into his own private domain.

The first candidate for the metropolitanate, the Archbishop of Kazan', German Polev, seemed to be a 'safe pair of hands', a follower of Joseph of Volokolamsk, in the style of Makarii, not a fanatic, and acceptable to other trends. Polev came to Moscow but he lasted only two days. As a good churchman he threatened Ivan with damnation unless the Tsar mended his ways, and abolished the *oprichnina*, but he did so 'gently' and in private. However, tactless references to the Last Judgment, with its implication of the immediacy of death and its reference to the tortures of the damned, particularly aroused the timorous Ivan's ire, since he was just as afraid of divine justice as of human rebellion. Polev was promptly told to leave the metropolitan's palace and go back to Kazan'.

The leaders of the *oprichnina* were also opposed to the appointment of a critical metropolitan, and after a second session of the Church *sobor*, the choice of the Tsar and the churchmen now fell somewhat unexpectedly on the Abbot of the Solovki monastery in the White Sea, Filipp Kolychev, in an effort to conciliate the hierarchy, possibly at its insistence.[9] Born in 1507, Filipp had first tried service at court, but in 1537 he left, possibly for fear of implication in the turmoil following on the arrest of Prince Andrew of Staritsa, by order of the Regent Elena, and finally ended up in the monastery of Solovki. He probably attended the Church Council (*sobor*) of 1550 in Moscow, and probably also was well acquainted with the priest Sylvester.[10] Filipp was an excellent administrator and under him the monastery thrived. He belonged to a noble family, a cousin was an *okolnichi*, another cousin was a boyar member of the *Oprichnina* Council, and twelve members of his family were present among the service gentry at the Assembly of the Land. He was also closely connected by family ties with the Staritsky family and with Ivan Petrovich Fedorov, whom the Tsar had, so far, seemed to regard as one of the most able and just of his servants, and who was *de facto* head of the Boyar Council in Moscow in charge of the government in the *zemshchina*.[11] He may indeed have been instrumental in Filipp's appointment. It is also not improbable that Filipp, who was regarded as a man of great integrity and courage, was not unconnected with the protest led by the boyars and the service gentry in the Assembly of the Land and equally it is not unlikely that I.P. Fedorov was behind it, so much so that this period is now viewed as the time of the 'boyars' plot'.[12]

Filipp, not yet appointed metropolitan, demanded, at a meeting of the Church Council that Ivan should abolish the *oprichnina* and declared that unless he did so, he would refuse to be appointed metropolitan. He asked for the prisoners arrested after the recent protest to be released. Ivan controlled his temper and insisted that Filipp should agree to occupy the see as metropolitan and refrain from interfering in anything concerning the *oprichnina*, i.e., he must not indulge in criticism of its activities or of the way in which Ivan ran his 'household'. Filipp may have felt trapped for all we know, for he signed an undertaking in accordance with Ivan's wishes on 20 July, though the right to advise and intercede was restored to him which strengthened his position, and he was duly appointed Metropolitan on 24 July 1566 and enthroned on the following day.[13]

But whatever Ivan may have promised Filipp, the attack by the boyars and the service gentry on the *oprichnina* started him off on a renewed bout of executions and repressions even though the bulk of those immediately arrested seem to have been freed. It is difficult to reconstruct the actual course of events since the main sources differ considerably, not so much about what was said, but about when it happened.

Unfortunately for the new Metropolitan, the Church was divided, some of the hierarchy proving to be closer to the court of Ivan and to the *oprichnina*, such as Archbishop Pimen of Novgorod, Archbishop Pafnutii of Suzdal (in the *oprichinina*), and Evstafii, the Tsar's confessor. Filipp's relations with the Tsar's confessor were particularly tense and he dealt with the problem by imposing a penance on him.[14] But his fate was now to be bound up with one of the most dangerous plots against Ivan – in Ivan's mind – and one of the most awful periods of terror the Tsar launched against his people.

As always in the reign of Ivan sources are scarce, confusing and contradictory, and it is difficult to determine what actually happened, in what chronological order, and how events were connected with each other in the crisis of the years 1567 to 1572. But taking everything into consideration, it is evident that the conflict between Ivan's conception of his role as Tsar and that of the majority of the court and the upper ranks of the armed forces reached its greatest intensity in this period. The open denunciation of the *oprichnina* by the bulk of the service gentry present at the July meeting in 1566 must have outraged Ivan and may have even upset his mental stability. He had never been openly challenged in such a way before by such a large contingent of his subjects. Many passages in Ivan's letter to Kurbsky, of 1564, reflect his conviction of the supremacy of his unlimited God-given power, and his right to reward and punish according to his will all those who disregarded his orders, failed in their duty to him on the battlefield, broke their oath of allegiance to him, betrayed him and the Orthodox Church and attempted to, or succeeded in, fleeing to Lithuania. It was the difference between *samoderzhavstvo*, traditional sovereignty, and *neogranichennaia vlast'*, or unlimited power, which was at stake. A collective demonstration must therefore have been a severe shock to a highly strung and apprehensive character like Ivan, who lived in a fantasy political world created by himself, the world of *volia*, where there were no limitations on his will or on his actions.[15]

He sought for refuge, and a rest from the tensions which pulled him in all directions, in the serious contemplation of retirement to a monastery and taking the cowl. In 1567 it was the monastery of Beloozero which attracted him. It was far away in the north, safe from attack by either Lithuania or the Tatars. It was also on the road to the port of St Nicholas and safety on board an English ship. In May 1567 he went on a pilgrimage to the monastery during which he held long talks with the abbot and a number of elders, withdrawing into a cell, away from the clamour of the world. In these sessions he openly spoke of his wish to become a monk. And the monks described to him the severities of monastic life, 'and when I heard of this godly life my vile and despairing heart was at once comforted for I had found a divine bridle for my ungoverned heart and a refuge for my salvation'[16] – words which reveal all too clearly Ivan's own awareness, in moments of lucidity, of the instability of his character. The Tsar asked the monks to prepare a cell for him and gave the abbot 200 rubles to furnish it, and in the following years he sent a number of icons for his future use.[17] He also gave the monastery a valuable economic privilege, namely the right to trade without paying customs dues throughout the territory of the *oprichnina*.[18]

In the meantime he incorporated a monastic ritual into life in Aleksandrovskaia Sloboda, where he and the members of his *oprichnina* court wore a monastic garment of his own devising and lived according to a monastic rule (when he felt like it and was there), ringing the bell at 4a.m. for matins and continuing to enforce a strict discipline and observe the hours throughout the day. Ivan acted as the abbot, Prince Afanasii Viazemsky was the cellarer, Maliuta Skuratov the sacristan. Ivan particularly liked to sing and was knowledgeable about church music. Having summoned his 'monks' to the refectory, he would remain standing, perhaps singing 'songs of repentance'[19] while the others ate, and he only sat down to eat when they had finished. After he had completed his religious duties he would attend the torture chambers next door, and then went to bed about 9p.m., where three old blind men told him stories, tales and fantasies about the past.[20] The state of Ivan's mind did not of course escape the attention of the senior boyars around him, and nurtured the perhaps not unwelcome belief that he might be thinking of abdicating.

The verdict of the *Sobor* of 1566 had determined Ivan to continue with the campaign in Livonia, and he now sought to revive his alliance with the King of Sweden, Erik XIV, who was convinced that the leading Swedish families were conspiring against him. By an extraordinary quirk of fate Russia and Sweden were at this time both ruled by men of original character and extreme irascibility, suspiciousness, fearfulness and mental instability. Erik, throughout 1566 and 1567 had alarmed his courtiers by seizing on the slightest pretext to arrest, torture and execute anyone who had seemed to mock him or had failed to serve him properly.[21] And indeed, in July 1566, there had been a secret meeting of indignant nobles in which Erik's youngest half-brother Karl took part.

Erik was also faced with the ongoing war against Lithuania and Denmark, and by the consequences of the treaty of Dorpat of 1564 with Russia.[22] Some minor points of that treaty were still being negotiated when Erik heard that Ivan too wished to reopen the subject and had added a new condition. He now demanded that the King of Sweden should hand over to him the wife of his brother John, Duke of Finland, Catherine Jagiellonka of Lithuania–Poland. Quite what Ivan intended to do with the lady is not clear; the general opinion was that he intended to make her his wife or his mistress (he was after all already married to Maria Temriukovna). People about the court knew of the previous rejection by King Sigismund of Ivan's offer for his sister, and may have seen in his insistence a desire for revenge. It also showed a total disregard for the bonds of Christian matrimony scarcely likely to be endorsed by the Russian or any other Church. It has also been suggested that Ivan intended Catherine to be a hostage in his eventual negotiations with Sigismund Augustus, and that her removal to Russia would serve to create a permanent breach between Poland and Sweden, thus strengthening Ivan's position.[23] At any rate the Swedish council, when consulted, unanimously rejected Ivan's demand to separate John's wife forcibly from him, and deliver her to Ivan.

Nevertheless, the military situation of Sweden seemed in Erik's eyes so parlous that he authorized his envoy, Nils Gyllenstierna, sent to Moscow to complete the negotiations in October 1566, to agree in a treaty signed in February 1567, to hand Catherine over to Russia in exchange for a Russian cession of lands in Estonia more favourable to Sweden. Misled by Erik in this way, in May Ivan sent an impressive embassy, led by Ivan Mikhailovich Vorontsov, to Sweden to fetch Catherine, and made all the necessary arrangements for her reception in Moscow even though the treaty had not been ratified. He thus forced Erik to the wall. Erik did not want to break with Russia, but he found it impossible to carry out his undertaking to Ivan, whereas Ivan regarded the handing over of Catherine as essential to the treaty. Catherine proved loyal to her husband and shared his captivity in the castle of Gripsholm, and Ivan's demand to seize John's legal wife by force could only increase suspicion in Sweden that both Erik and Ivan were mentally deranged.

The Swedish Estates had been called to meet in May 1567 in Uppsala. Before they met a number of Swedish nobles were condemned to death on the grounds of treason. One of Erik's potential rivals, Nils Sture, now returned from Germany, where he had been on a mission for the King, and was arrested. At this point Erik's mental balance broke down completely; first he begged the forgiveness of his enemies, then the insinuations of one of his advisers made him change his mind, and marching into the cell of Nils Sture, on 27 May 1567, he personally stabbed him to death. Rushing away from the scene he ordered the execution of a number of noble prisoners, changed into peasant clothes and wandered around the forests.

For six months Erik let the government slide into the hands of a committee of nobles, who were profoundly shocked that the King himself should assassinate one of their number. Yet he was composed enough in the summer of 1567 to make a remarkable proposal to the Russian embassy which was still waiting to escort Catherine Jagiellonka to Russia. It was communicated most secretly by a Swedish emissary to the interpreter who, in Erik's name, asked the Russian envoys to take the King of Sweden back with them to Russia when they left Stockholm. When asked why Erik wanted to go to Russia he had replied that the King was now afraid of his 'boyars'. The Russian envoys then described the scene in which the King had killed Nils Sture and the diplomatic negotiations caused by the Swedish refusal to surrender Catherine Jagiellonka, and their own anger at the endless procrastination of the Swedes.[24]

The two major enemies in Livonia, Russia and Lithuania, continued their secret plotting against each other, though the exact timing and what they were up to is difficult to establish. Sigismund tried to inspire the Russian aristocracy to act against Ivan while Ivan tried in turn to induce the Lithuanian magnates to help him with his secret dynastic plans. These had now become more urgent since it was becoming obvious that the death of the King, who was seriously ill, would lead to a dynastic crisis in Poland–Lithuania, for Sigismund Augustus was the last of the Jagiellos and had no male heir. Ivan had been attracted for some time by the idea of being 'raised' [elected] to the Lithuanian grand ducal throne, which had become *de facto* hereditary in the Jagiellonian line (the throne of Poland remained elective) and might indeed have remained so had Sigismund Augustus had children. It was his failure even to have male relatives which created the crisis, a nephew, Jan Sigismund Zapolya of Transylvania, whom he had hoped to make his heir, died in 1571. He had not even a daughter, only sisters.[25]

But, as the Polish diplomats had urged in February 1561, when they had turned down Ivan's first suit to Catherine, Sigismund II Augustus was an annointed 'King', not merely a grand prince like Ivan (Sigismund did not of course recognize Ivan's title of tsar), and Catherine was a king's daughter (Sigismund I). Nevertheless Ivan thought that he had a good chance of being accepted as ruler in Lithuania if not in Poland and no doubt this had influenced his original offer of marriage to Catherine Jagiellonka in 1559/60,[26] and also his determination to acquire possession of her person. One of the arguments he put forward was that he wished to secure Catherine 'for the sake of his honour' and in order to stand above the King of Poland, his and the Swedish King's enemy. Had the purely dynastic question been the main issue however, Ivan could well have applied for the hand of the remaining unmarried – and older – sister of Sigismund, Anna, when his wife Anastasia died.[27] This did not escape the Swedish negotiator, Peter Brag, who pointed out to the Russian envoys that if Erik could get hold of Anna, he could arrange for her to be handed over to Ivan. The Russian envoys avoided the trap by the simple argument that they had no instructions to deal with such an important matter.[28]

A distinguished Lithuanian commander, Jan Glebowicz, had been taken prisoner at the Russian conquest of Polotsk in 1563, and before he was repatriated to his country he had bound himself by a written oath to serve Ivan in future by persuading three of the great Lithuanian magnates to agree never to accept a lord from any other dynasty but the Russian, either the Tsar himself or one of his sons.[29] In May 1566, as Ivan was preparing himself for a further campaign in Livonia, a secret messenger arrived bearing a letter from Glebowicz in Lithuania to Prince I.F. Mstislavsky. He was arrested and tortured on his return journey by the Lithuanian authorities; his master, Glebowicz, denied that he planned to desert Lithuania for Russia, but revealed the terms of the oath of loyalty he had sworn to Ivan and admitted that he had agreed to urge a number of Lithuanian magnates to 'serve' Ivan, by persuading them that whenever they might wish to appoint a new ruler they should choose one of his – Ivan's – family, namely himself or one of his children. Glebowicz succeeded in convincing the Lithuanians that he was only thinking of what might happen after the death of Sigismund Augustus, and was acquitted of treason but this episode may have given Sigismund ideas, or led him to take up an idea possibly suggested to him by Prince A.M. Kurbsky. This was the devising of a plot to win over leading boyars of the lands bordering on Lithuania, or Lithuanian in origin, to desert to Poland–Lithuania as Kurbsky had done, with the promise of substantial political and social rewards. Such defections would seriously undermine Ivan's military strength by the loss of his best generals and possibly many of his service gentry who would follow their leaders.[30]

At this point the story becomes almost impossible to disentangle: in the summer of 1567 King Sigismund and the Grand Hetman of Lithuania, Grigorii Chodkewicz, allegedly wrote and sent a series of letters in which they attempted to lure a number of distinguished Russian princes and boyars to desert Ivan and to join with him – Sigismund – in replacing Ivan by his cousin of Staritsa on the throne of Russia. The originals of these letters have not been found so far either in the Lithuanian or the Russian archives, but there is nothing improbable in such letters having been written by or on behalf of Sigismund. It was just the kind of plotting and counterplotting that both Ivan and Sigismund engaged in, but unfortunately there is no evidence that such letters were ever written at all. The agent allegedly carrying the letters from Sigismund and Chodkewicz, a certain Ivan Kozlov, had once been a servant of Prince Mikhail Vorotynsky; he was to travel via Polotsk, where Ivan Petrovich Fedorov was now *voevoda*, after his disgrace in the early summer of 1566. Fedorov had pressed for the liberation of Vorotynsky from captivity in 1566.[31] One of the letters, supposedly from Sigismund, was directed to him. The others were addressed to the two distinguished Gediminovichi, Prince I.D. Bel'sky and Prince I.F. Mstislavsky, and to Prince Mikhail I. Vorotynsky, now one of three senior men in Ivan's Council. The three years he had spent confined in the monastery of Beloozero (see above, Chapter IX, pp. 149–50) and the loss of much of his *votchina* land, might have turned him against the Tsar. They were all great magnates with their own military retinues. However, if the original letters from Sigismund have not been found, the replies to his letters have survived and are published in the records of the Russian Posol'sky Prikaz, or Office of Foreign Affairs.

Sigismund's alleged letters had been supported by a further set of letters to the same recipients allegedly from the Lithuanian Grand Hetman Grigorii Chodkewicz which also have not been found. The replies to letters he supposedly wrote to the four Russian boyars have also been published. All the letters were dated between 2 July and 6 August, the last being those 'from' Fedorov in Polotsk, dated 20 July 1567 to Chodkewicz, and 6 August to Sigismund Augustus.

A careful reading of these eight letters addressed by the Russians to Sigismund Augustus and Chodkewicz leaves one in little doubt that they were all in great part written or dictated by Ivan himself, or under his supervision. Not only do they reproduce the Tsar's language and cast of mind as expressed in his first letter to Prince Kurbsky, they also deal with current political problems. They provide many fascinating glimpses of the mental processes of the Tsar and of the way in which Russian foreign relations were conducted. In the course of the five weeks over which the letters extend Ivan presumably worked on the different replies from his boyars, thus providing some indication of the nature of the alleged plot he was going to have to foil. He was at the same time carrying on the negotiations with Erik of Sweden for a truce.

The letters supposed to have been written to King Sigismund Augustus by the two Lithuanian princes in Russian service are almost identical. They start with an invocation to God, Jesus Christ and the Holy Trinity which is omitted in the translations published in the Soviet Union in 1951.[32] The princes use their full titles as Gediminovich princes of Lithuania, and address the Grand Prince of Lithuania, Sigismund, as 'brother'. In view of Ivan's obsession with the order of precedence between rulers, and in particular with the superiority of rulers by inheritance over those by election, this shows him willing to make use of the Gediminovich princes in his service to denigrate the Gediminovich Grand Prince of Lithuania and King of Poland, Sigismund, in this case hereditary but confirmed by election – and who was indeed descended from a junior Gediminovich line. The titles were used with care, Prince M.I. Vorotynsky, for instance, was not described as a Lithuanian prince – he was after all a Riurikovich, with an appanage and all its attendant privileges on the Russian borders of the Grand Principality. All four aristocrats described themselves as 'boyars of the Council (*sovet*)' of Ivan.

The replies from Bel'sky and Mstislavsky start off by referring to the offers said to have been made to them by Sigismund, out of his compassion for the oppression of all Ivan's people, great and small, and his disapproval for Ivan's disregard for their interests and rank:

> If we [the princes] become your [Sigismund's] subjects, as you wish, our brother, you promise to show us great honour and to make us lords (*gosudari*) in your land, in every way equal to the princes subject to you, and you will return our old appanage lands to us in your grand principality of Lithuania . . . and you want to show this grace not only to us but also to all those we bring to you who are worthy of your service.[33]

Thus far Ivan is referring to what Sigismund is alleged to have written and promised, using the King's language; but the real Ivan now takes over: 'How could you, brother,' he addresses Sigismund in the name of

Bel'sky and Mstislavsky 'write like scoundrels and rascals; it is unworthy of a great ruler to create discord with such absurd letters between rulers, and when you are unable to win by courage, to overcome your enemy like a thief, seizing on him like a snake.' But continues Ivan/Bel'sky, 'the sovereignty of our ruler is protected by God'. He calls the messenger Kozlov a hound, wickedly oozing his poison, who had stupefied Sigismund, just like Eve. 'Our ruler [Ivan] like a true Christian rewards his people according to their worth and service and guards his realm against all evils, punishing all evildoers.'

Ivan/Bel'sky then enters on a discussion of principle, on an argument allegedly put forward by Sigismund, which makes one regret the absence of Sigismund's 'original letter'. In view of the lack of precision of the Russian language in the definition of abstract ideas at that time it is difficult to be certain whether Ivan, when he writes about 'freedom', is referring to free will in the theological sense, or to total freedom of action, the original sense of the Russian word *volia* or *volen*. 'You wrote, my brother,' explains Ivan to Sigismund, in the name of both Bel'sky and Mstislavsky,

> that God created man, and gave him freedom and honour, but what you write is far from the truth. For God created the first man, Adam, and gave him free will (*samovlastie*) and placed a prohibition on him, he was not to eat the fruit of one tree, and when he broke this prohibition, how cruelly was he punished! This was the first loss of freedom, the first dishonour, the first fall from light to darkness, from rest to labouring for his bread, from incorruptibility to corruption, from life to death.[34]

After a further discourse on biblical history, Ivan concludes that in Deuteronomy criminals were cursed unto their death, and this same truth was laid down by Jesus Christ: 'commandment, law and the punishment of criminals'. Ivan/Bel'sky continues: 'See you not that there never was any freedom anywhere and that your letter was far from the truth',[35] and he concludes, 'Was it a good freedom (*samovol'stvo*) that your lords turned you [Sigismund] into a scoundrel setting his hand to such rubbish?'

Ivan, still writing in the name of Prince I.D. Bel'sky, proceeds to justify himself by arguing that Bel'sky had a better claim to the Grand Principality of Lithuania than King Sigismund Augustus; that Bel'sky's grandfather had been forced by Ol'gerd, Grand Prince of Lithuania, to flee his land in his shirt, to seek the protection of an Orthodox ruler

[Ivan III] who had treated him very well.[36] Finally Ivan/Bel'sky suggests that Sigismund should give up to 'us', the Lithuanian princes Bel'sky and Mstislavsky, the Grand Principality of Lithuania and the Russian Land, 'except for those lands which Prince M.I. Vorotynsky will ask you for, and we will live together as Jagiello lived with Vitovt', under the sceptre of the Tsar, who is strong enough to defend us against the Turk and the Tatar and the Holy Roman Emperor.[37]

The letter from Ivan/Mstislavsky is almost identical with the Ivan/Bel'sky letter, though there is one little malicious stab on a sore spot. In his attack on free will Ivan/Mstislavsky adds to what he had written in the name of Bel'sky, 'was it a good freedom (*samovol'stvo*) that your lords (*pany*) separated you from Queen Barbara and poisoned her? And that they reproached you about her? All this is well known to us. And you yourself are always ill, and your health is now poor. All this happened to you because of the free will of your lords.'[38]

Ivan/Vorotynsky's reply to Sigismund is quite different in tone. It does not address Sigismund as 'brother'; it attaches much more importance to the role of the messenger, Ivan Petrovich Kozlov, who it will be remembered had been a servant of Vorotynsky's. It is Kozlov who had reported the various oppressive acts the princes had suffered from in Russia to Sigismund, and induced the King to feel compassion for them,

> for it is inadmissible for a Christian to behave in such a way to the people entrusted to him by God. 'For when God created Man, he did not condemn him to slavery but on the contrary bestowed all blessings on him. It was Kozlov who, like a snake, oozing poison, made you [Sigismund] believe that Mikhail Vorotynsky's father Ivan wanted to desert Russia for Lithuania. But how can this absurd, treacherous invention lead to good? How dares this scoundrel [Kozlov] lie, like a mad dog, about our deceased father? We are not traitors but the faithful servants of free, sovereign power' (*vol'noe samoderzhavstvo*) who have received only favourable treatment from the Tsar. And if our father was disgraced (*byl v opale*) it was because of his own actions, his death came by God's will, and to punish and reward – this is a matter for the lord [a somewhat convoluted explanation of the fact that Vorotynsky's father had in fact been a traitor].

Having perused the offers from Sigismund, Ivan/Vorotynsky rejects them with contempt for the man who made them and the man who transmitted them (Kozlov),

For the free sovereignty of our great lords is not your miserable monarchy; no one tells our great lord what to do, whereas your lords tell you what to do . . . our rulers are placed on their sovereign thrones by the all-powerful right hand of God . . . You, Sigismund, have to obey your lords because you are not native rulers.

Ivan/Vorotynsky now draws on the mythical descent of the Russian tsars from Augustus and Prus, through Riurik, to the present Tsar, free to reward the good and punish the evil. Whereas Sigismund was not free in his actions because he was not a hereditary ruler but a chosen ruler.

You cannot even rule yourself, you have no heirs, who will pay for prayers for you? Your sister Anna is not married, and to whom did you give your other sister Catherine, by the plotting of your lords, was that an equal match? And see, you and your sister Catherine wanted her to marry our great lord! Could you get your own will even in such a small thing?

(Sigismund of course did not want Catherine to marry Ivan.) He, Vorotynksy, was now being offered by Sigismund more than an appanage, a vassal state, on a level with the Prince of Prussia or the Prince of Courland.[39] Ivan/Vorotynsky then lays down his terms, which are the same as Bel'sky's, though Vorotynsky specifies the towns he is to have on the Dnieper, as well as Volhynia and Podolia.

Ivan/Vorotynsky embarks on a further theological discussion (which again is not translated in the 1951 edition of the *Poslaniiu*): 'God is all powerful; he is not subordinate to anyone; he gave himself of his own free will to be crucified to save the world, and you [Lithuanian magnates] keep your lord in captivity – this is not an example of divine love of man but a deception carried out by Antichrist.' Ivan then rejects the right of the Lithuanians to discuss the only begotten Son of God, and to attempt to divide the Trinity.[40] Indeed later on, Ivan/Vorotynsky exclaims: 'is it permitted by God to establish a religion in another's lands when you do not even know religion, not only as forsworn but as an apostate?'

'You wrote', continues Ivan/Vorotynsky to Chodkewicz,

of the unheard of cruelties of our lord [Ivan], of his unjust persecution and merciless anger against us, his Christian subjects, and of the unheard of division by our Tsar of a Christian people into an *oprichnina* and a *zemshchina*, and you proclaim yourself surprised and hurt by this. You say your lord [Sigismund] has only restrained himself from raising his royal hand and sharp sword against our land, because of his conviction that our lord [Ivan] is mentally deranged (*rastlen umom*) and is doing more harm to his country and shedding more blood than your lord [Sigismund]. Your lord has pity on us, as he has shown in his generosity to Prince Andrei Kurbsky, even though his family was not of high standing among us, compared with that of the Vorotynskys, the highest among us, who preserve our laws, and customs, our boyars and our *voevody* in our lands.[41]

Yet later in his letter addressed to the Hetman, Ivan/Vorotynsky, rounds on Chodkewicz, that son of a dishonourable mother, pouring out venom like a scorpion for his devilish and apostate opinions, and declaims against 'what he [Chodkewicz] had written about the division of Russia into an *oprichnina* and a *zemshchina* in his devilish letter' which shows that

he did not understand from the words of such sons of pigs that our lord [Ivan] has no such *oprichnina* and *zemshchina*; we serve wherever he wills for all his tsarish power is in his right hand, he is a sovereign who gives orders to us, not like your lord who obeys you like a subject. Moreover in your country [Lithuania] there is also a *zemshchina* and a court [*dvor*] and crown appanage, and hetmans, and treasurers and other officials. You, Chodkewicz, say that the King has not yet unsheathed his sword against our lands, showing pride, worthy of Satan, proclaiming: I will rise above the stars in the heavens, I will place my throne on the clouds and I will be like the almighty. Thus he will be following the devil like Sennacherib, and Nebuchadnezzar, and Chosroes, and other godless tsars, who want to rule over the Orthodox.[42]

Ivan continues in this strain, at times almost dropping the pretence that he is writing in the name of Vorotynsky, and getting more and more excited at the children of dogs, who do not understand what they say. 'You mentioned the favours bestowed on Andrei Kurbsky', he continues, 'a cur, like you . . . but if he had any sense your lord would not reward such a criminal and traitor. No wonder that having betrayed his master, and fled from the gallows, he came to your feeble-witted lord.' He concludes his diatribe:

for us, princes, it is not fitting to be on brotherly terms with you peasants [or common people – *muzhiki*] but you may send your sons to us and we will show them what favours they deserve. To be under the will of a lord is a good thing for subjects – for where there is no will of the lord set above them, they get drunk and do nothing.

The replies from Fedorov to Sigismund and to Chodkewicz are much shorter and so restrained in tone that Skrynnikov, for instance, thinks that Ivan played no part in their composition.[43] It is probable that they really were written by Fedorov, rather than by Ivan, or that the Tsar played a minor part in their composition. In the letter to Sigismund Fedorov points out that he is an old man, and will be no use to the King as a soldier; his legs are too weak to enable him to conduct girls to Sigismund's bedchamber, and he does not know how to play the clown. What use is Sigismund's offer to an old man like him? There are no references to religion or quotations from the Bible in Fedorov's letter which is the last of the series and is dated 6 August from Polotsk. Similarly Fedorov's letter to Chodkewicz is much more sober in character; he reproaches him for attempting to seduce Fedorov from his allegiance to Ivan, calls him 'brother' and 'Lord Grigorii', though he does use the typical Ivanian insulting language (cur, pouring out your poison like a snake). In general Fedorov speaks a little wearily about his relations with the Tsar over his lands, and warns Chodkewicz against indulging in treason in his old age. Thus unlike the other letters, Fedorov's are so normal and reasonable, so likely to be his, that they do make one believe in the possibility of the existence of a conspiracy.

It is odd that Ivan should have included an accusation levelled against him of cruelty to his nobles in the letter allegedly written by Vorotynsky to Chodkewicz, and particularly odd that he should have mentioned the *oprichnina* and the *zemshchina* seeing that he was very anxious to conceal their very existence from the Lithuanians and gave instructions to Russian envoys to Lithuania accordingly.[44] The whole episode of the letters from the boyars is very difficult to interpret, but the possibility that there really was a 'reverse' conspiracy may explain why the letters were never sent to Sigismund, and may be the reason for the more restrained tone of Fedorov's letters. If the four boyars had really cooperated with Ivan in writing these letters to Sigismund, then it must have been with the intention of making clear to the Polish ruler that they did not intend to take up his apparent offers and to desert the Tsar and go over to Sigismund. If this was so it was a factor to be taken into account by all parties, Sigismund, Ivan and the boyars.[45]

Ivan's increasing disquiet emerges in a conversation with Anthony Jenkinson. The latter had returned to England, probably in October 1566, to obtain new privileges for the Russia Company and to present a request from Ivan to procure 'for our owne vse Saphires, Rubies and apperellinge . . . freely to buy and export any other goods', by which Ivan probably meant armaments, and to allow his merchants to trade free of customs dues in England – as the English traded in Russia.[46] Jenkinson sailed again for Russia in May 1567.

Granted a very private audience on 1 September 1567, Jenkinson was taken along most secret ways in the Oprichnina Palace in Moscow, led by Ivan himself. Only one of the Tsar's advisers, Prince A.D. Viazemsky, knew of the meeting and Jenkinson brought an interpreter. Ivan 'familiarly discoursed our meanynge unto him in such sorte that we have vsed the like familiarytye with none'.[47] On his return to England in November 1567 Jenkinson wrote an account of this meeting, and included an explicit message from Ivan to Queen Elizabeth, in which the Tsar proclaimed his fervent desire for a perpetual friendship between their two countries, and warned her that the King of Poland was not her friend. He also told her that a Polish-Lithuanian spy had been seized (evidently Kozlov) bearing letters from Sigismund to the English merchants in Russia, urging them to assist both the Lithuanian agent, and such Russians as might declare their support for Sigismund, with money and other goods. Kozlov had admitted his treachery when he was seized and tortured to make him confess.[48]

The most secret part of Ivan's communication was an unexpected and unusual request from the Tsar for asylum in England in the event of a rising against him in Russia, and his offer to assist Elizabeth in his turn should she need a refuge against her unruly people. According to Jenkinson, Ivan urged Elizabeth 'that yf any misfortune might fall or chance upon ether of them to goe out of their countries, that it might be lawfull to ether of them to come into the others countrey for the safegard of them selves and their lyves. And this to be kept most seacret.'[49] One may wonder if Ivan had already received news from his embassy in Stockholm about Erik's request for asylum in Russia, for fear of his boyars.[50]

It was to his request for asylum that Ivan attached great secrecy, rather than to his express desire for a full scale offensive and defensive alliance between the two powers, which he also put forward, and which was not in itself startling, even if it was unwelcome to Elizabeth. He also wanted England to provide him with shipbuilders to build seagoing ships. For the time being, though Elizabeth was prodigal with general expressions of goodwill towards Ivan, she attempted to evade any commitment and constantly denied to all and sundry that she supplied Russia with armaments.

Ivan made no mention to Jenkinson of the letters Sigismund was supposed to have written to the Russian boyars or of their supposed replies. He portrayed Sigismund's alleged tampering with the English merchants as a provocation (though he does not use the word) intended to create bad blood between him and the Queen and to make him believe that his nobles were betraying him.

There is no evidence, aside from Ivan's message to Elizabeth, through Jenkinson, that Sigismund had made any approach to the English community in Russia.[51] But Ivan clearly took the threat of internal disorder seriously. In the event rumours do seem to have spread within the country both as regards his intention of taking the cowl and about the possibility of his abdication in favour of his sons, even about his request for asylum in England, thus creating a climate favourable to an attempt by the aristocracy to dethrone him in favour of Vladimir of Staritsa

Discontent in Russia was now evidently rampant. The atrocities Ivan had inflicted on the aristocracy and the service gentry after the manifestation in July 1566 were compounded by the continuing turbulence in the countryside provoked by the activities of the *oprichnina*, the constant changes of landowners, moving some to the *oprichnina*, and some out of it. It is hard to imagine the impact this sizeable migration of landowners, with their families and belongings, from place to place must have had on the armed forces, the countryside and the peasantry. Kostroma was taken into the *oprichnina* in early February/March 1567. There were few princes, and approximately 745 service gentry who were born Muscovites. Yet, just as in Suzdal' some two-thirds of the landowners were moved out, leaving the land unoccupied and uncultivated, so in Kostroma about a third of them had to make way for *oprichniki* who were usually of baser birth.[52] The costs of the Livonian war had been brought up at the Assembly of 1566, and those present agreed to sacrifice their lives and their property to pay for it. Taxes were increased, not only to pay for the expenses of the war but also for the costs of setting up the *oprichnina*, and for fortifying Aleksandrovskaia Sloboda, building the new *Oprichnina* Palace in Moscow and Ivan's bolthole in Vologda – all of which were to be borne entirely by the *zemshchina*.[53]

Military skirmishes continued meanwhile but Ivan decided to abandon the pen for the sword and made plans for a new and more powerful campaign against Lithuania. On 20 September 1567 he left Moscow with his son Ivan, for the Trinity monastery and for the Western frontier.[54] Vladimir of Staritsa joined the Tsar in Tver', and a large force under two of those same senior commanders who had allegedly received letters from Sigismund, namely Mstislavsky and Vorotynsky, but not Bel'sky who remained in charge of the *zemshchina* in Moscow, was due to foregather at Velikie Luki on 26 October, with the object of attacking the forts on the Western Dvina and moving on Riga.

It has been suggested that Ivan attempted a military solution, encouraged by the failure of Sigismund's – and by inference, Kurbsky's – efforts to win over the four boyars and by the boyars' letters of rejection.[55] Similarly, it is assumed that Sigismund had advanced his forces in order to cooperate with the Russian boyars who, he expected, would declare for him. He halted however at Radoshkovichi, a town on the border between Russia and Poland–Lithuania.[56]

Chapter XIV

The Boyar Plot:
2) the Executions of Ivan Fedorov,
Metropolitan Filipp and Vladimir of Staritsa

Sigismund was not in fact pressing for military operations in the autumn of 1567, for he was in the throes of very delicate domestic negotiations for a constitutional union between Poland and Lithuania which he had been pursuing for some time. The King had now reached the conclusion that a closer union with Poland was necessary for the survival of Lithuania, even if the magnates were opposed to it. Quite apart from the problem of the succession which might not have been so urgent – he was only forty-nine – the burden of the war was becoming too much for Lithuania to bear both in terms of manpower and of money, and it was becoming necessary to draw upon the superior financial and above all military resources of Poland. There were considerable differences between the political, military, social and financial structures of the two parts of Poland–Lithuania, which needed to be adapted to a new, joint constitutional order. For instance, the title of prince did not exist in Poland and the Lithuanian Gediminovich princes and imperial princes like the Radziwills wanted a guarantee that their titles would survive in a new regime. At the time the great Lithuanian magnates like the Radziwills exercised far more power than their opposite numbers in Poland. They were therefore less attracted to union than the Poles, for in Poland the numerous lower nobility or gentry were in a stronger political position *vis à vis* the magnates through the Sejm and the local dietines, than their opposite numbers in Lithuania, where the only brake on royal power was the Senate, composed of the landowning magnates.

The question of religion was also divisive. The Lithuanian magnates were often Orthodox, but some, like the Radziwills, were Calvinists; the Poles were mainly Catholic, the towns often Lutheran. In addition, whether Livonia was to belong to Lithuania alone, or to both parties had also to be decided.[1] The period of waiting in Radoshkovichi was used by the King of Poland to air and discuss the many issues which divided

Poles and Lithuanians. The Grand Principality was now faced with war in the South, against the Crimeans, and against Sweden as well as Russia in Livonia. Sigismund proceeded to render the union easier for the Poles by abandoning his hereditary claim to the Grand Principality of Lithuania, which would make the succession elective as it was in Poland, and by ceding to the Crown of Poland the Lithuanian held ex-Kievan lands of Podolia and Volhynia (whence many of the great magnates came) and the palatinate of Kiev, thus depriving Lithuania of nearly half its lands. Lithuania's need for subsidies and military help, and the willingness of Poland to provide it if its political terms were met, brought the two sides together, in spite of the objections of the Lithuanian magnates.

It is also possible that Sigismund was waiting on events in Russia, that he was counting on an uprising against Ivan led by Russian boyars, that he hoped for a response to the letters which he had perhaps sent to them in summer 1567, in spite of the negative tone of the replies dictated by Ivan in July and August, which he had, of course, never, as far as we know, received.[2]

Meanwhile Ivan, with an army led by the Princes Mikhail Cherkassky and Afanasii Viazemsky, arrived on 24 October at the western border, and on 12 November he summoned a military council in his camp at Rzhansk, including his son, Ivan, and his nephew Vladimir, as well as the leading boyars and *voevody*. The evidence of what then happened is extremely exiguous and has to be woven together, often disregarding the dates in the sources, in order to produce a coherent story. Almost all of the evidence moreover is of foreign origin.[3] At the Council the Tsar proposed abandoning the campaign because the siege artillery had fallen behind. The Council supported him and the Tsar and the royal family returned to Moscow. It is possible that Ivan called off his campaign in autumn 1567 for military reasons, or possibly he called it off because he had received fresh reports of a plot by the nobles of the *zemshchina* to dethrone him in favour of his cousin Vladimir of Staritsa.[4] He had after all lived for some weeks in the summer obsessively countering Sigismund's alleged efforts to seduce his boyars. No doubt a constant stream of denunciations convinced a man so fearful and apprehensive of treason and betrayal that he was surrounded by traitors. Moreover, there is no doubt that Bel'sky, Mstislavsky, Vorotynsky and Fedorov were cooperating closely in a number of political and military fields at the time, and if not plotting together, were certainly acting together, knew each other well and some were related.

The alleged letters of the Russian princes and boyars to Sigismund, expressing their continuing loyalty to Ivan, were certainly written at Ivan's instigation – that is if the boyars ever actually wrote them. But one cannot take for granted that the four were planning treason. There does not seem much solid evidence that either Bel'sky or Mstislavsky (both were related to Ivan), who were the highest ranking Russian Lithuanians, entitled to be treated as princes of the blood, were planning to flee, and Ivan evidently thought it worth while to keep their services for the time being. Even M.I. Vorotynsky, who had been in disgrace for three years, was kept on, possibly for his military talents. All three of them figure prominently in the negotiations with the Lithuanians recorded in the Russian Office of Foreign Affairs, so that they evidently had ample opportunity to converse with Lithuanian delegates.

The most mature and experienced, and probably the oldest in the group was I.P. Fedorov, or Fedorov Cheliadnin, as he is often known. He had been *konyushii,* Master of the Horse, an office which had been hereditary in the Cheliadnin family for some decades, and was a member of an ancient Muscovite boyar family of great distinction and vast wealth. He was only a Cheliadnin by marriage, for the family died out in the male line and he had married the heiress. During Grand Prince Ivan's childhood I.I. Cheliadnin, the last of the line, who was Master of the Horse until 1541, had acted as the Grand Prince's tutor, and the boy was brought up in his household. His wife Agrafena had been trusted by Vasily III, and had been Ivan's *mamka* or nanny, before the death of Elena Glinskaia. Ivan Petrovich Fedorov had a chequered career, and became *koniushii* by 1549. Later he was active on military service in Livonia, and in foreign affairs and diplomacy in the 1560s. In 1564 he was one of those who signed and put up money guaranteeing the good behaviour of Prince M.I. Vorotynsky. During the first two years of the *oprichnina,* he was close to Ivan and he was also the senior boyar in charge of the *zemshchina,* in Moscow, when the Tsar was absent.[5] On the other hand, at the time of the plot, he was the *voevoda* of Russian-occupied Polotsk, only some twenty to thirty versts from the Russo-Lithuanian border, and would have been able to assist the envoy Kozlov on the way to Moscow to meet M.I. Vorotynsky and the two Lithuanian magnates in Russian service.

The accounts given by the two Germans, Staden and Schlichting, roughly coincide and they implicate the trusted commandant of Moscow. Tsar Ivan must have known of Fedorov's letter to Sigismund, even if he did not write it or see it. Was there a plot at all, and was it led by Fedorov, or was there only some ill-considered and incautious grumbling? Or was there merely Polish gossip about what would happen when Sigismund died? Or was the whole plot, including the letters, engineered by Ivan himself?[6] Schlichting suggests that something had been planned to take place in 1567, when Sigismund was on campaign. In the first draft of his account of Muscovy, he wrote to the King of Poland that

> some thirty prominent noblemen, with their attendants and servitors, led by Prince [he was not a prince] Ivan Petrovich [Fedorov] pledged themselves in writing to deliver the Grand Prince and his *oprichniki* into the hands of Your Majesty [Sigismund], if Your Majesty would only advance on our country. But as soon as they knew in Moscow that your Majesty had withdrawn your forces [from Radoshkovichi], many lost heart, many hid from each other, and all feared that one of them would betray them. This is what happened.[7]

According to the German *oprichnik* Staden, a plot had developed in the *zemshchina* to replace Ivan as Tsar by his cousin of Staritsa, and it was Vladimir Andreevich himself who betrayed the plot to Ivan, where-upon Ivan cancelled the campaign and returned to Aleksandrovskaia Sloboda.[8]

Thus both in Russia and in Poland the much heralded military campaign of 1567 melted away. Ivan clearly seemed more and more convinced of the existence of a deep-rooted plot but, as so often, bided his time. Fedorov may have been the prime mover in the conspiracy as Schlichting suggests; but it is also possible that he, whose reply to Sigismund was so much more restrained than those of the princes, had no desire to side with Sigismund; he may well have been the reason why the whole plot failed, indeed he may well have been the prime cause for the arrest of Kozlov who had after all originally gone to him in Polotsk. It must be remembered that in 1553 Fedorov was one of the most loyal supporters of the baby Dmitri during Ivan's illness. At any rate his behaviour seems inconsistent.

Indeed, once before, Fedorov had been the target of written approaches from Chodkewicz in Lithuania, when he was governor of Dorpat in Livonia in 1562, and he was then rebuked by Ivan and ordered not to communicate directly with the Lithuanians but to send any communication to the Tsar.[9] And he was reputed to have been one of the leaders of the protest made by the service gentry after the *Zemskii sobor* of 1566. But the boyars may have feared for themselves and given up their plans when Sigismund cut short the campaign against Russia in autumn 1567. Whereupon the plot unravelled, the boyars, the Prince of Staritsa and Duke Magnus of Denmark who was already being enmeshed in Ivan's plans for Livonia, fearing mutual betrayal, gave the Tsar the names of the conspirators.[10]

Fedorov's disgrace became manifest when Ivan started to harass his retainers and confiscate his lands in autumn 1567 without any arrest or trial. He entrusted two of the principal *oprichniki*, Grigory Lovchikov and Maliuta Skuratov, with leading punitive detachments through Fedorov's estates in Kolomna (to which Fedorov had recently been banished) killing large numbers of his retainers and their families.[11] Schlichting charges the *oprichniki* with carting away an enormous quantity of Fedorov's treasure in gold, silver and household goods.[12]

Kurbsky singles out the treatment of Fedorov by Ivan in his *History*:

> And the tsar was so angry with this Ioann [Fedorov] that he not only slew every one of his service noblemen and subjected them to various kinds of torture, but he burned all his towns and villages – he had a very large patrimony – while he himself travelled with his children of darkness, and wherever any of them were found, he did not spare them, nor their wives, nor their little children sucking at their mothers' breasts; and they say that he ordered that not a single animal be left alive.

Kurbsky later adds that he had heard from an eyewitness that Ivan ordered several people in one of Fedorov's estates to be bound and held in the rooms of a number of houses under which barrels of gunpowder were placed and blown up, flinging corpses into the air, to the Tsar's delight. Whereupon, adds Kurbsky, 'he and all his children of darkness [the *oprichniki*], verily like a madman surrounded by raving madmen ... galloped at full rein to gaze upon the mangled corpses of Christians',[13] doubtless shouting *hoyda! hoyda!* a war cry of the wild cavalry of the steppes often used by Ivan.

The persecution of Fedorov and his people was carried out throughout 1567 and early 1568, against a background of increasing tension between the Tsar and the Metropolitan, Filipp. From the beginning Filipp had set himself against the barbarities of the *oprichnina*, though he had sworn an oath not to interfere in its affairs, and at first he tried to persuade Ivan in private, threatening him with the Last Judgment. But in a Church Council, probably in late 1567 or early 1568, he attempted to gather support for the abolition of the *oprichnina*. Filipp was unable to win the backing of all the hierarchy, and he was denounced to Ivan by one of the members of the Church Council, probably Pimen, Archbishop of Novgorod.[14] Ivan, determined to bring him to trial, though many, even in the *oprichnina*, thought that trying a metropolitan was beyond the powers of a secular tribunal. The Tsar sent a deputation to the Solovki monastery to collect evidence against the Metropolitan of misbehaviour in his private, as well as in his ecclesiastical life. The monks do not seem to have been very cooperative and when the deputation departed for Moscow, they – the monks – locked up all the documents and the treasury.

But now there was no holding Filipp back. On 22 and again on 24 March 1568, during the church service in the Cathedral of the Dormition in the Kremlin, the Metropolitan openly attacked the *oprichnina*, just when the Tsar happened to have arrived in the capital with a large military escort. The 'Life of Filipp' (a hagiographic work, written many years later) describes the dramatic scene of the courageous priest challenging the men-at-arms with their naked swords, clothed in the black cloaks of the *oprichniki*.[15] 'Gracious tsar and Grand Prince' proclaimed Filipp,

> how long will you shed the innocent blood of your faithful Christian people? . . . How long is this injustice to last? Tatars and pagans and the whole world can say that all peoples have laws and justice, only in Russia is there none . . . Remember that God may have raised you in the world but you are yet a mortal man, and he will exact payment for innocent blood shed by your hands. The stones under your feet . . . will cry out against you and will accuse you, and the Lord orders me to say this to you, even though death threatens me.

Ivan was so furious that he replied 'I have been too merciful to you, Metropolitan, and to your fellows in my land; I will give you something to complain about.'

Ivan then summoned the hierarchy to defrock the Metropolitan, and execute him. He always prided himself on the serious way in which he approached his responsibilities for the spiritual welfare of his land. The Boyar Council was unable to act, according to Skrynnikov, because it had been weakened by the execution of many of its members and by its division between the *oprichnina* and the *zemshchina*. In any case as the Tsar's council it had no real standing to act on its own. Filipp, without giving up his rank, now withdrew from the palace of the Metropolitan in the Kremlin to the small Greek monastery of St Nicholas outside its walls. On 28 July 1568 a further incident took place at a religious service in the Novodevichi convent when Filipp loudly rebuked members of the *oprichnina* – possibly Moslem Tatars – who, in contravention of the rules laid down in the *Stoglav*, had not removed their skullcaps in the church.

The wave of persecutions which engulfed Moscow touched Filipp closely since the Kolychevs, a Novgorod family, many of whom had been executed, had been followers of the house of Staritsa for many years. Ivan continued to treat his Metropolitan with grudging meanness, and it was Vladimir of Staritsa who gave the Metropolitan lands to support him.[16] He began to be seen as the spokesman for the whole of the *zemshchina*, protesting, if Taube and Kruse and Schlichting are to be believed, against the really outrageously sadistic treatment of men, women and children, and the sodomitical orgies indulged in by Ivan and his *oprichniki*.[17] After Filipp's denunciations in the Cathedral of the Dormition, many of his ecclesiastical followers and servants were arrested; four church elders were beaten to death through the streets – a fact later confirmed in the *Sinodiki*. The followers and men-at-arms of Fedorov were sought out and massacred as were those who had taken part in the *sobor* of 1566 and even many of those who had once been exiled to Kazan' and then allowed to return. The repressions were completely arbitrary, families were arrested regardless of status and dispatched without any form of trial, in some cases by Ivan himself.[18]

When, sometime in September 1568, Fedorov was summoned to Ivan's presence the last gruesome scene was enacted. Ivan ordered Fedorov to don royal garments such as the Tsar himself wore, and forced him against his will to

> take the sceptre and to sit upon the throne where only the Grand Prince sits. The tyrant now stood before his subject, seated on the throne, bared his head and knelt before him saying: 'Now you have what you sought for and strove to obtain – to be Grand Prince of Muscovy and to occupy my place. For the moment you are Grand Prince: enjoy and savour the dominion you have craved.' Then he added, 'since I have the power to seat you I can also unseat you'

and grasping a knife 'he plunged it several times into Ivan's [Fedorov] heart', and all the soldiers present thrust their daggers into him so that 'his stomach and entrails poured out before the tyrant's eyes'. The body of Fedorov was then dragged around the Kremlin and the city of Moscow by the heels and exposed in the middle of the square while his retainers and servants were drowned. In a further series of raids by the *oprichniki* on Fedorov's estates, led by Ivan himself; oxen, cattle and horses were destroyed, as were the wives and children of the men who had been killed. Even the wives of the peasants were stripped naked and driven 'like beasts' into the forests, where they were cut to pieces. Fedorov's wife was either forcibly shorn a nun or killed too.[19] All told between a hundred and twenty and a hundred and fifty of Fedorov's retainers, and some two hundred and ninety of their men[20] perished according to the records of the *Sinodiki*. For instance, 'in the villages of Kolomna, there died 20 people of the Orthodox Christian faith and their names are known to God'.[21] Many women were hanged on the gates of their houses, others cut to pieces and the bits shoved down holes in the ice whence people drew their water supplies.

The massacres of 1567 and 1568, the period of most intense terror since the beginning of the *oprichnina*, were closing in on Metropolitan Filipp, as a distinguished member of his family, M.I. Kolychev, an *okol'nichi*, and three of his sons, shared Fedorov's fate on 11 September 1568. (M.I. Kolychev had been one of the guarantors of Prince M.I. Vorotynsky, and went in person to fetch him at the monastery of Beloozero in 1566.) Meanwhile Ivan had gathered together the Church Council which was to judge Filipp on the very inadequate evidence produced by his investigators in Solovki. The Church Council, with some boyars in attendance, met on 4 November 1567 (while Ivan was still at Rzhansk on campaign) and pronounced Filipp guilty of living an indecent and improper life and ordered him to be dethroned. In fact Filipp did not wait for the verdict. He took off his vestments, surrendered his white cowl[22] and prepared to depart, but Ivan, aware that Filipp had been able to impress his listeners, forced him to remain for the time being in Moscow.

Filipp was concerned not only with the inhumanity of Ivan but also with the political situation in the country, for he admonished the Tsar to give up the division into *oprichnina* and *zemshchina*, and to unite his people. Whereupon Ivan replied brutally, referring to the treason he thought he had detected all around him: 'What have you to do, monk, with our Tsarist councils, do not you see that they want to devour me (*poglotiti*)'.[23] Ivan may have been infuriated by the coincidence of support for Filipp with support for I.P. Fedorov among the boyars.

A year later, on 8 November 1568 (St Michael's Day) a major feast day, when Filipp was again taking the service before a large public, Aleksei Basmanov and Maliuta Skuratov erupted into the church followed by many *oprichniki* and read out the *ukaz* of Ivan on the

Areas incorporated into the *oprichnina*

destitution of Filipp whose vestments were then torn off him. He was bundled into a sledge and taken to the Otroch monastery in Tver' where he was imprisoned in very harsh conditions. At least he was not condemned to be burnt, as he well might have been. A week later the Abbot of the Trinity monastery, Kirill, was appointed Metropolitan. Clerical and secular servants of the defrocked Metropolitan were mercilessly disposed of by the *oprichniki*.

The atmosphere at court must have been tense and grim. One need only consider the effect that the killing and dishonouring of their women, and the murder of their children was bound to have on the dense tissue of the aristocracy and the gentry, united by so many intermarriages. Moreover, Russian aristocratic women were kept in seclusion, and their virtue cherished. That they should be raped, and hanged outside the gates of their husbands' dwellings in the Kremlin must have contributed to the festering atmosphere in Moscow. Though it may well be that Schlichting fantasizes somewhat in his description of the horrors, it is nevertheless clear that Ivan was set on a career of furious destructiveness and uncontrolled barbarity, and the evidence of the *Sinodiki* does support some of Schlichting's description.

The savagery of Ivan's reaction to what he interpreted as a series of conspiracies against him by his nobles may well have been intensified by the news of events in Sweden in the course of 1568. Erik XIV, apparently restored to sanity and to the government of Sweden, did little to conciliate the Swedish aristocracy, particularly by his marriage in July 1568 to his commoner wife, intended among other things to legitimize his son, Gustav, born in January 1568. A revolt against the King began to take form soon after the wedding, led by his two brothers, John and Karl, who in Russian eyes inevitably played the part of *udel'nye kniazia* or appanage princes like Vladimir of Staritsa. By a strange irony, in August 1568 Erik renewed his appeals to Russia for asylum: he was afraid that his brother John, who was still a prisoner in Gripsholm castle, and whose wife Catherine he still planned to send to Ivan, was plotting against him, and he begged the Russian envoys arriving in Sweden to fetch Catherine Jagiellonka to obtain for him assurances that Ivan would send troops to defend him and ships and sailors to transport him. He was already loading his treasure on to a ship in Sweden when Duke Karl forestalled him and swept him off his throne on 28 September 1568, and two days later John III was proclaimed King by the nobility and the army. Only the intervention of Duke Karl saved the envoys of the Tsar from being assaulted and plundered by John's supporters, revolted by the idea that Erik was about to proclaim himself Ivan's

1 The christening of Ivan IV.

2 The coronation of Ivan IV.

3 The execution of boyars near Kolomna in 1546.

4 The wedding of Ivan IV and Anastasia.

5 The fire in Moscow in 1547.

6 Icon of *The Church Militant*.

7 The Emperor John VIII Paleologus from *The Journey of the Magi*, wall painting by Benozzo Gozzoli in the Palazzo Medici Riccardi, Florence. It is discussed together with the icon of *The Church Militant* (plate 6) in pp. 105–6, above, and note 43.

8 The departure of the ailing Anastasia from Moscow in flames.

9 Monastery of the White Lake. Rooms said to have been destined for the use of Ivan IV.

10 A session of the Boyar Council.

11 Ivan IV bids farewell to Richard Chancellor and Osip Nepea on their return to England; they are shipwrecked and Chancellor is drowned; Nepea is received by King Philip, and Queen Mary I sitting behind him.

12 Interpolations in the Litsevaia Chronicle, probably dating from 1569 to sometime before July 1570, and variously attributed to Ivan IV himself or to the *diak* Ivan Viskovaty.

Топтулюсвегоодаскашнблпоонгдрю
цртоiелнисомъкнisтосказалъпрогда
споiего книлшнд рiблизмiкнныi
дiлла · чтогрюцртоiелнисомъкнisто
оумышлiлломнюгiе измiкныiедiлла
вгошетлонiсже ийнмiкнипишогдов
скоисискъшнд рiбн прнiкхлпхiсороню
намнюгоеропо пролитiе ретiань
скоiкоролi iсстоiгорад у пошетра

13 Ivan IV receives the letter from Prince Kurbsky in 1564. He does not transfix Shibanov's foot with his staff as in foreign tales.

14 Peasants cutting wood.

15 Fragment of a winding sheet which may represent Princess Evfrosin'ia of Staritsa.

16 'Russian envoys to the diet of Regensburg in 1576'.

17 Stephen Bathory, Prince of Transylvania, later King of Poland–Lithuania.

18 Sigismund II Augustus, King of Poland–Lithuania.

19 Ivan's shadow looming over Russia (from Eisenstein's film).

vassal.[24] Erik was formally deposed by a Riksdag on 25 January 1569. He was afterwards kept in captivity until he died, probably by poisoning, in 1577.[25] So while Ivan was negotiating for a refuge in England against his traitorous boyars, Erik was again seeking for a refuge in Russia against his.[26]

The overthrow of Erik was followed by a well organized propaganda campaign in Sweden blackening his reputation as a man and as a king. The effect on Ivan of this gross indignity inflicted on a man who, though of base origin in his eyes, was nevertheless a crowned king who could do no wrong, must have contributed to his own alarm at the thought of his nobles plotting against him in favour of his cousin Vladimir, and to his distrust of everyone. There is no written evidence to substantiate such an assumption but it does seem most improbable that Ivan could have been unaffected by the fate of a crowned head at the hands of his brothers and his aristocracy, and so near his own borders. If this could happen in Sweden it could also happen in Russia, and all the more would he need the assurance that Elizabeth of England would grant him asylum. To someone whose psychological make-up was so delicately balanced, someone who was so easily aroused to fear and fury, the fate of Erik was a grim warning, and parallels with his own situation only too easy to trace. He protected himself by taking more territory into the *oprichnina* notably around his refuge in Vologda, which was becoming his main base. He also extended the protection of the *oprichnina* over the activities and houses allotted to the Russia Company.[27] Meanwhile he moved permanently into Aleksandrovskaia Sloboda, abandoning Moscow and his new palace there, and providing the Sloboda with guards who patrolled the roads and refused admittance to anyone without a pass. In Vologda he made use of the services of English builders and shipwrights to strengthen the fortifications and to build the ships in which he would sail, if necessary, to the Solovki monastery on the island in the White Sea with his treasure, before embarking on English seagoing ships on his way to England.

But Elizabeth had refused to take seriously his appeals for asylum. An English ambassador (as distinct from an agent of the Company), Sir Thomas Randolph, had arrived in St Nicholas on 23 July 1568, instead of Anthony Jenkinson, whom Ivan was eagerly awaiting. Randolph reached Moscow only at the end of September 1568 and was kept cooped up in his residence until 20 February 1569,[28] when Ivan at last consented to see him. The really insulting delay in receiving the ambassador (probably due to Ivan's anger at Elizabeth's tergiversation over negotiations for a treaty of alliance) was explained later by Ivan by the prevalence of plague in Moscow at the time, but others have put forward the view that the delay in granting Randolph an audience and allowing him out of his residence was caused by Ivan's desire to conceal from him the outrages of the *oprichniki*, and the executions of his nobles and retainers following one upon another.[29]

As Elizabeth explained to Randolph, and as he explained eventually to Ivan, Jenkinson had expounded to her 'very secretly' Ivan's desire

> to have such a frendship betwext vs, as if eyther of us had cause by any misfortune to seeke refuge out of our owne countreis, that in that case the one might be a defendour of the others cause. To which mater you shall saye that we did think that our said servant Anth. Jenkynson might misconceaue the woords of the said emprour.

Certain that 'thoroughe Gods goodnes allwais shewed to us we have no manner of doubt of the contynuance of our peacable gouernment without danger eyther of our subiects or of any forren ennemys' Elizabeth had evidently found it difficult to grasp that Ivan might think himself to be in danger from his own people and 'we doo think that our said servant [Jenkinson] hath mistaken the intencon of the said emperors speche vnto him'. But the Queen now assured Ivan that

> if any mischance might happen in his estate . . . he shall be frendly receiued into our dominions, and shall find assured frendship in vs toward the mayntenance of all his just causes, in as good sorte as if he had speciall graunts or couenants from vs in that behalfe signed with our hand, and sealed with our seale.

Lord Burleigh, the author of this instruction, had ordered Randolph to pass over in silence any question of an offensive and defensive alliance, of which Jenkinson had spoken, in view of the hostile relations between Ivan and the Holy Roman Empire and other kings (Sweden and Poland–Lithuania presumably). The only object of Randolph's negotiations should be to secure privileges for English trade.[30] Nevertheless, though Burleigh rejected any formal alliance, he did stress that Ivan would find support for the defence of his 'just causes', as though a treaty had been signed, thus creating some confusion in the mind of Ivan as to the real intentions of the English.

Ivan later explained to Elizabeth in a letter of 20 June 1569 that he had made Randolph wait for an interview because the envoy would not speak to his officials and refused to discuss matters of moment but concentrated only on 'merchant affaires'.[31] This was a definite attempt to blame Randolph for the delays which had occurred. During the next four months, Randolph complained of the intrigues against him of various English interlopers, and the interception of his letters.[32] But when the ambassador finally 'saw the Tsar's eyes' on 20 February 1569 he indicated to Ivan that he was authorized to speak on those secret matters which the Tsar had discussed with Jenkinson (i.e., mutual asylum in case of need, alliance and possibly, though the evidence is scanty, the subject of marriage) and presented him with a 'notable great cuppe of silver curiously wrought with verses graven on it'. He was ordered to follow the Tsar to Vologda where further meetings took place in which Randolph defended himself against charges of treasonable activity against the Tsar, spread about by disloyal members of the Russia Company.

Finally, on 20 June 1569 Randolph obtained from Ivan the renewal of the privileges of the Russia Company on extremely favourable terms. For instance, the English law denying the right of English subjects to trade in Russia other than through the Russia Company was accepted as enforceable in Russia.[33] The Russia Company was not given a monopoly of foreign trade with Narva, but it was allowed a house in Moscow and the right to build houses elsewhere, and to employ a small number of Russian servants. In the Vychegda valley it was authorized to search for deposits of iron. All the Company's houses and servants were to form part of the *oprichnina*, and were placed under its jurisdiction. It is possible that Ivan was so generous because he was counting on English support in the war with Poland–Lithuania. After such concessions he must have expected that Elizabeth would give him something in return. But he must also have realized that the power to withdraw his concessions gave him a hold on England.

Randolph then returned to England accompanied by a Russian ambassador, Andrei Grigorievich Savin who, Ivan hoped, would advance the negotiations for a treaty of alliance, which would now be dealt with in England. Savin brought with him the draft of a treaty 'of perpetuall amity' between the two powers, offensive and defensive, providing for mutual armed assistance when demanded, and confirming in broad terms the commercial privileges already granted by Russia to England but extending them to both sides.[34]

In the meantime Ivan had become aware that the overthrow of Erik of Sweden in favour of a prince married to the sister of the King of Poland, and the impending union of Poland and Lithuania, had wrecked his

Livonian policy. He was not strong enough to stand alone against the Commonwealth and he had lost his Swedish ally, at a time when the Khan of Crimea was being urged by the new Ottoman Sultan, Selim, who had succeeded in 1566, to join in a campaign against him.

The Ottomans had for some time been reacting against the growing power of Russia in the southeast and its control of the middle Volga, which endangered the pilgrim route from the East to Mecca and Medina. Moreover, the appearance of Russia on the lower Volga upset the balance between the Ottomans and the Persians, and the Khan of Crimea could prove a valuable ally to the former by claiming the heritage of the Golden Horde on the Caspian Sea and demanding the return of the two Tatar khanates, Kazan' and Astrakhan'. Already in 1564 the Khan of Crimea was claiming that he had many grievances against Ivan which could not be assuaged by many 'skins'.[35] The Russians had abandoned the old Tatar city of Astrakhan' on the right bank of the Volga and had built a new and stronger fortress on an island some ten miles downstream.[36] The main outpost of the Ottomans was the fort of Azak on the estuary of the Don, on the Sea of Azov, a centre of the Turkish slave trade. By the mid-sixteenth century, the Cossacks established on the Lower Don, under the leadership of Prince D. Vishnevetsky, the occasional ally of Ivan IV, began to threaten Turkish trade. But relations with Russia were not as yet sufficiently important for the Porte to embark on direct negotiations and these were mainly – though not exclusively – carried on through the Crimean Tatars.

However, émigrés from Kazan', Astrakhan' and Kabarda in Turkish territory pressed the Sultan to expel the Russians from their lands, with the support of the Khan of the Crimea and other local princes, and the idea began to be talked about of cutting a canal between the Don and the Volga which would enable the Turks to advance by water up the Don from Azov to Perevoloka, cross to the Volga and continue into central Russia or down to Astrakhan', which would then become the base for campaigns against Persia, or into the Caucasus.[37] Selim proved more favourable to the plan than had Suleiman earlier, and serious investigation of the possibilities began. By the beginning of 1568, the decision to embark on a campaign had been taken in the Porte. Ships were built in Kaffa; artillery and detachments of janissaries gathered in Constantinople, together with an army of 15,000 from the Balkan provinces. Military supplies and ammunition, as well as a labour force to dig the canal, were collected in the Crimea, where the Khan, Devlet Girey, was by no means enthusiastic at the prospect of closer control of his policy by the Turks. The Russians were kept fully informed of

Turkish plans through their envoy in the Crimea, Afanasii Nagoi, who was privately informed by the Crimeans of what the Porte was planning, because it did not suit them to see the Ottomans installed in Astrakhan' and dominating the Caspian Sea and the Caucasus. Rumours of the plan to dig a canal spread throughout Europe and aroused much interest.

The Turkish flotilla, bearing the troops, advanced from Azov up the Don in July 1569 and joined the Crimean army in Perevoloka in August, where the Ottomans had planned to start on the construction of the canal. But they had left it too late: the Don was too shallow, and even the portage between the Don and the Volga was too difficult, and the digging proved way beyond the capacity of the force assembled, to the indignation of the Turks. The project was abandoned, and the Turkish and Crimean armies withdrew to lay siege to Astrakhan'. They occupied the old, abandoned town, and the local Tatars were happy to provide the force with river galleys to take them up the Volga. But they made no headway against the new Russian fortress which was well defended by Prince Peter Serebrianovich Obolensky who had his own river forces. The real cause of the failure, however, was the divergence of views between the Turks and the Crimeans who, according to some accounts, did their best to thwart Turkish plans in order to discourage them from making any further attempts on Astrakhan'.[38] So the Turks and the Crimeans finally lifted the siege in September 1569, unwilling to face a long stay in such inhospitable country in winter. The Turks turned away to fight the Venetians, and in April 1571 a peace settlement was concluded by an exchange of letters between the Porte and Ivan, by which Russia agreed to destroy a Russian stronghold on the River Terek in the Northern Caucasus, renounce support for Kabarda, open the road to pilgrims and merchants, and satisfy the Khan of Crimea's claims to the payment of tribute by Russia. Thus, the tribute which Ivan III had refused to pay was now imposed again on Ivan IV.[39] Meanwhile the Crimeans, free from the pressure of their over-powerful ally, could return to the pursuit of their own interests, namely the fight for the recovery of Kazan', and prepare for a new campaign of their own.

Ivan now considered a negotiated solution to the war in the North by attempting to set up a vassal kingdom of Livonia as a Russian protectorate, probably on the advice of the two Livonian nobles, who had entered his service, Johann Taube and Eilhard Kruse, and of Ivan Viskovaty, the head of the Office of Foreign Affairs, who had never been enthusiastic about the Livonian war. A candidate for the new kingdom was easily found in Magnus, the younger brother of King Frederick II of Denmark and ruler of the island of Oesel and the Danish possessions in

Livonia, who had been seeking an establishment for himself, and a wife, for some time.

The Russian embassy sent to fetch Catherine Jagiellonka returned at last from Stockholm without the queen, but with detailed information about the overthrow of Erik in June 1569, though Ivan had undoubtedly been kept in touch by means of couriers.[40] No doubt also the spreading undercurrents from the 'treason' of Fedorov, and particularly Fedorov's pre-knowledge of the existence of the plot of 1567 (if he did really provide Vladimir of Staritsa with a list of conspirators), maintained Ivan in a state of constant agitation. He sent his cousin out of the way, to Nizhnii Novgorod, an important military outpost against the then impending Tatar-Turkish attack, while he prepared his downfall. It was easy to bribe a cook in Vladimir's service to denounce his master for having tried to induce him to kill the Tsar with poisoned fish. Ivan sent for his cousin at once to Aleksandrovskaia Sloboda, outside which he was surrounded by *oprichniki*, commanded by Ivan's henchmen, V.G. Griaznoi and Maliuta Skuratov. They informed the prince that he was no longer the Tsar's brother but his enemy, because he had attempted, not only to seize the crown, but to murder Ivan by bribing the cook to give him poison. As members of the Tsar's immediate family the Staritskys could not appear before a tribunal or even be executed; but Ivan had evidently decided that he could no longer allow Vladimir to threaten his hold on the throne and that he must execute him. After a trivial investigation of the evidence, on 9 October 1569 Vladimir, with his wife and daughter, were brought into the Tsar's presence, and told by the Tsar that they were to drink a cup of poison. At first Vladimir refused as he did not want to commit suicide, which was a sin, but his wife persuaded him to drink on the grounds that it was Ivan who would have to answer for it at the Last Judgment. Both then swallowed the poisoned draught, and their nine-year-old daughter also drank the poison. Ivan issued orders that his aunt, Evfrosin'ya, at the time in a convent in Beloozero, should be brought to the Sloboda and on the way she and twelve of her ladies and five of her servants were suffocated by smoke on board the barge they were travelling on by Griaznoi and Maliuta Skuratov, who seemed to be charged with most of Ivan's dirty work at this time. Neither A.D. Viazemsky, nor A.D. Basmanov nor his son Fedor was involved; possibly their disgrace was already looming in 1569 if they dared to protest against the extent of Ivan's executions.

The many executions are confirmed by the entries in the *Sinodiki* where the cook is named, as well as a fisherman who procured the fish which was allegedly poisoned, and a number of *d'yaki* and nobles in

Vladimir's service. Ivan offered prayers for all of them. He was also surprisingly inconsistent about Vladimir's family. The nine-year-old daughter was forced to die, but Vladimir's son, Vasily, and his daughters Evfimia and Maria by his first wife, who were not present, were spared, and some years later an appanage was returned to the son, Vasily.[41]

Chapter XV
Armageddon

The next event in Ivan's intimate circle which might have had a disturbing impact on his emotional balance was the death, on 9 September 1569, of his Tsaritsa, Maria Temriukovna, the Princess of Kabarda, probably then in her mid-twenties. Nothing is known for a fact about her relationship with Ivan, except that she had a son in 1563, who died when he was only a few months old. Russian and Soviet historians have portrayed her in a very negative light. How could Ivan have been attracted by a savage Tatar, however pretty, wrote Solov'ev,[1] in disregard of how attractive a young Tatar girl could be, particularly to Ivan brought up among Tatars. The boyars are said to have detested her, but again where is the evidence? The presence of high ranking Tatar princes and mirzas at court and in the army was taken for granted in Russia at the time, and they probably participated in the feasts and banquets which Ivan organized for the entertainment of his court (a banquet is a solemn meal for ambassadors, a *pir* is a feast). Many of them converted to Orthodoxy and married into boyar families, and probably there were intermarriages lower down the social scale.

Maria's brother, Prince Saldanliuk (baptized Mikhail) Temriukovich Cherkassky had been in Moscow since boyhood, was taught his letters under Ivan's orders and became a boon companion of the Tsar. He was given lands and powers and treated like an appanage prince, even issuing charters in his own name. He was married to the daughter of V.M. Iur'ev, of the Zakhar'in clan, a cousin of Tsaritsa Anastasia, and he continued in high favour until 1571. His other sister was married to the head of the *zemshchina* for a while, tsarevich Mikhail Kaibulich. Daughter of one of the leading rulers of the Tatars of Kabarda, Maria Temriukovna was related to many local chiefs. In reply to a letter of condolence, on her death, from the Khan's wife, Ivan asserted that in memory of his wife he would care for and protect her relatives as before.

But other local khans who did not feel bound to Russia may have aroused his suspicions.

There is some mystery about Tsaritsa Maria's death – a farrago of rumours, that she died poisoned by the boyars or that she attempted to poison her husband. The common people apparently regarded her as responsible for the change in Ivan's nature after the death of Anastasia.[2] But maybe also that they regarded her, as the *oprichnik* Heinrich von Staden states, as responsible for Ivan's formation of a special guard for himself, well-clothed and well-paid, who should ride with him by day and by night, namely the corps of *oprichniki*.[3] That, during one of his attacks of panic, Maria should have advised Ivan, drawing on her memories of Tatar life, is not unlikely.

There is no reason to suppose that Ivan was not profoundly grieved by the loss of Maria. She may have been responsible for the introduction of more unrestrained feasting at court, with clowns, dwarfs and jesters; she may simply have kept Ivan in a good temper. Her death would in any case have been followed by an investigation (with all the usual tortures) of all the possible uses of poison; if Ivan was fond of her, it may have profoundly unbalanced him, as did the death of Anastasia and, coupled with the fate of Erik of Sweden, may well have intensified Ivan's always present suspicions of the loyalty of his cousin Vladimir of Staritsa. Maria's death also seriously undermined his position in the south where discord had broken out among the various princes of the Kabarda.

Relations with Poland–Lithuania and the Livonian war were going badly. Though the Lithuanian magnates had endeavoured to put off the evil day, a closer union with Poland was now imminent. Only the precarious life of the last male heir of the Jagiellos, the childless Sigismund Augustus II, held Poland and Lithuania together and the final arrangements were worked out in summer 1569. The two parties agreed with much difficulty that Livonia would be jointly owned and ruled by Poland and Lithuania, and they drew up a new constitutional structure for what was to be known in future as the Polish-Lithuanian Commonwealth. The Lublin Sejm lasted from 23 December 1568 to 1 July 1569, and the union finally agreed on was proclaimed on 1 July 1569. It provided for a king elected by both nations, and a joint senate and sejm, elected by *sejmiki* or dietines; and for bishops, commandants and castellans, again finally to be elected in both halves of the Commonwealth. The Grand Principality of Lithuania retained its administrative autonomy, its chancellorship, treasury and armed forces under its own Hetman and officials, and the Lithuanian Statute (the law code revised again in 1566) remained valid in Lithuania and unaffected by the union.

Poland had no law code. Poland benefited, however, by a territorial readjustment within the Commonwealth: exasperated by Lithuanian tergiversation over the union, Podlasie, then Volhynia, and then the Palatinate of Kiev were finally incorporated into the Kingdom of Poland, a *coup de main* by which Lithuania lost over half its territory to Poland, and Poland acquired the Ukrainian problem. There were many difficulties in the implementation of this new constitution but over time the Commonwealth worked out its solutions.[4]

Ivan's foreign policy and military alliances suffered a severe setback as a result of these events, for Sweden, in the person of John III, became a hostile power, while Lithuania was immeasurably strengthened by being able to call on Polish forces much stronger than her own. Moreover, any attempt to secure the crown of Lithuania now implied election to the crown of Catholic Poland too and rendered the diplomatic manoeuvring infinitely more complex.

Was there something in the alleged plot of Vladimir of Staritsa, preceded by the alleged plot of Ivan Petrovich Fedorov, which particularly aroused Ivan's suspicions that Novgorod too might be on the verge of revolt against his rule? The town of Staritsa was on the border of Novgorod land and many of the latter's nobles had a soft spot for Prince Vladimir, possibly because he seemed unlikely to become a threat to them. Novgorod had long ceased to be a centre of old style separatism, because the original Novgorodian citizens had been expelled when it was annexed by Ivan III in 1478, and lands had been granted as *pomest'ia* to incoming Muscovites. The fifteenth-century political tradition had been broken and the city was governed from Moscow. But a new-style Novgorodian 'localism' had developed.[5] Culturally Novgorodians, living in a great centre of trade, arts and crafts, and still in contact with European commerce, were different from Muscovites; they spoke with a different intonation, and above all they still felt a primary allegiance to the traditional form of government by their Archbishop, who had his own boyars and service gentry and wore the white cowl.[6] The Church and the monasteries were extremely wealthy both in treasure and in land.

The Novgorodians were not happy with Ivan's constant warfare, particularly when called upon to fight as far away as Kazan'. They were finding it difficult to pay for the equipment they had to provide for themselves and with the introduction of the *oprichnina* their financial situation only worsened. A number of *pomeshchiki* had been moved out to make room for *oprichniki,* and this caused resentment and reduced agricultural production, making increasing taxes more difficult to pay at a time of harvest failure. A number of *pomeshchiki* had attended the assembly of 1566 and had subsequently been disgraced or killed. Novgorod had been relegated to the *zemshchina* and the land was therefore the butt of the violence of the *oprichniki,* and some of the *pomeshchiki* had perished in the aftermath of the Fedorov affair. There had also been two severe epidemics of plague in the 1560s. The last straw perhaps had been the execution of Vladimir of Staritsa and his family, who were liked in Novgorod where they had a secondary residence.

What seems to have launched Ivan on a furious search for treason was the recapture of the town of Izborsk by the Lithuanians in January 1569. Izborsk was not far from Pskov, and the Lithuanians had entered by subterfuge, disguising their troops in the uniform of the *oprichniki,* and inviting the Russian garrison to open the gates and let them in.[7] They did not keep the town long, but the Russians who had failed to defend it, and were recaptured when the *oprichniki* recovered the town, were beheaded; those who had been taken prisoner by the Lithuanians were executed in July after they were released and repatriated, and the Lithuanian prisoners taken in the campaign were all treated as traitors and executed. So were a number of prisoners held in Moscow.[8] This seemed to arouse Ivan to the idea that the lands of Tver', Pskov and Novgorod were seething with treason, and in March 1569 he turned on their inhabitants and forcibly removed some 450 families from Pskov and 150 from Novgorod to the interior, mostly from the lower orders. He felt justified when he heard later that in Stockholm it was these same lower orders who had opened the gates of Stockholm to Duke Karl in the rising against King Erik.[9] Throughout 1567, 1568 and 1569 executions followed each other in Moscow, or wherever the Tsar was. There was no formal procedure. The Tsar simply gave orders wherever he was, on horseback, in church or in his chamber.

Obviously determined to root out the treason he saw everywhere, by any and every means, Ivan turned on Novgorod in a mood of suppressed rage. He collected a substantial force of *oprichniki,* late in December 1569 and established a cordon around all the post houses between Aleksandrovskaia Sloboda and Novgorod, forbidding all travel on the pretext of the plague. The troops advanced, executing people as they went; records of their progress have been perpetuated in the *Sinodiki*: 'on orders from Moscow, six people; . . . Pskovians with their wives and children thirty people'. The city of Tver', where ex-Metropolitan Filipp was incarcerated in a monastery, was surrounded. Ivan apparently entrusted Maliuta Skuratov with an attempt to conciliate his prisoner, in the hope that Filipp would feel sufficiently vindictive to welcome what Ivan planned to do to the Church and to Archbishop Pimen in Novgorod, and would take up his previous position again. Maliuta visited Filipp in his cell, and asked for his blessing on the punishment to be meted out to his former rival. But Filipp declared that he would take up the metropolitanate again only if Ivan dissolved the *oprichnina*, and threatened to place his malediction upon him. To prevent this disaster, Maliuta seized a cloth to shut Filipp's mouth, and suffocated him. The Abbot of the monastery was told that he had died from the unbearable stuffiness in his cell, on 23 December 1569.

For some five days the *oprichniki* ravaged Tver', sparing neither buildings, property nor human beings. The bodies had their legs cut off before being pushed under the ice on the Volga. (Torzhok had already been dealt with.) The total numbers killed vary according to the source, but one estimate was that some thirty-six thousand perished, including nine thousand who were killed and double that number who died of starvation and disease. All Lithuanian prisoners held there were dispatched.[10] Then Ivan moved on to Novgorod on 2 January 1570 and surrounded the city with a cordon allowing not one soul to escape. Here his first target was the Church. The *oprichniki* descended on churches, monasteries and convents, and arrested several hundred clerics who, four days later, on Ivan's arrival with his special guard of some 1,500 *oprichniki*, were whipped and beaten on the shins (*na pravezh*) to force them to give away their property.[11] *Pravezh* continued for a whole year before the survivors were released since one of Ivan's principal aims in the sacking of Novgorod was to fill up his empty coffers, and indeed by 13 October 1570, 13,000 rubles had reached Moscow.

On Sunday 8 January, Ivan proceeded to the Cathedral of St Sophia, and was met on the bridge over the River Volkhov by Archbishop Pimen, hitherto a loyal supporter of Ivan's, bearing aloft the cross and the icons. Pandemonium now ensued. The Tsar refused to allow the Archbishop to bless him and loudly accused all Novgorodians of treason: he alleged that they wanted to hand over his patrimony of Novgorod to Latins, to foreigners, to Sigismund Augustus. Nevertheless, Ivan was too pious to miss the service for Epiphany, and he attended the mass before sitting down to the banquet specially prepared for him. He then in an access of fury ordered the immediate arrest of Pimen and his boyars. According to Schlichting, Ivan called up his retainers and launched them on the plundering of the Cathedral of Saint Sophia, tore the white cowl from Pimen's head, and had his robes removed. Accusing him of being unfit to be an archbishop, he told him he ought to be a strolling player and that he would find him a wife, at the expense of the clergy then present, who were forced to hand over large sums of money. Ivan then sent for a mare and said to Pimen: 'Here is your bride, bestride her and ride to Moscow where you can be enrolled among the strolling players.' The prelate was mounted facing backwards on the mare, a major ritual humiliation common all over Europe, his feet tied beneath her belly, and driven out of the city with a zither and bagpipes, the accoutrements of a *skomorokh* in his hands as a further humiliation (musical instruments were banned in Russian churches) and escorted to Moscow, to await a trial by a Church Council.[12]

The next day the trial of those accused of treason began in Gorodishche, Ivan's camp outside Novgorod, with all the corresponding tortures (this time with red hot stoves, boiling water, semi-drowning in the Volkhov river) while Ivan's confessor Evstafii and the *duma d'iak* L.A. Saltykov, supervised the looting of the churches and monasteries, and the removal of all valuable treasures. Men, women and children and babes in arms were tortured, tied up, roped together and thrown into the river, and since it was frozen, other *oprichniki* followed on foot and broke holes in the ice to push them under the water. According to one interpretation this form of execution, being pushed under the ice, traditional in old Novgorod, was also used here to signify that the victims were guilty of apostasy, in attempting to hand the city over to the 'Latins', that in drowning them in this way their executioners were sending them straight to hell, identified at times in folklore with the depths of a river. Indeed one victim who was dragged on a rope through the water, and then raised up, when asked what he had seen down below replied that he had been with the evil spirits in hell, and saw the place prepared for the Tsar.[13]

It was not difficult in these circumstances to procure evidence of treason. According to a careful reconstruction of the evidence by Skrynnikov, the *Sinodik* listing Ivan's victims in Novgorod suggests that the principal leader in the city of a movement against Ivan was a boyar named V.D. Danilov. The current tale had it that a dweller in Polotsk had become the servant of an *oprichnik*, then fled back to the Commonwealth and there informed the authorities that treason was being prepared in Torzhok, Tver', Novgorod and Pskov, where the people had sent couriers to Sigismund asking to be taken under his protection. Some kind of treasonable document to this effect had been found in Novgorod and supplied to Ivan. The general trend of this treasonable plot was in line with the supposed earlier attempts at treason of 1567, which had culminated in the execution of Ivan Petrovich

Fedorov. The present plot was in appearance a renewed attempt by Sigismund to induce the treasonably inclined boyars of the *zemshchina* to rise against Ivan, making use of Danilov who had been close to Fedorov, and it lists precisely those towns Ivan had attacked when he embarked on his northern tour: Torzhok, and Tver'. It was now Novgorod's turn and Pskov's was still to come.

Danilov was arrested and a confession that he had planned to go over to Sigismund was finally wrung out of him by torture. Archbishop Pimen was also implicated. Ivan was all the more inclined to believe in the existence of this new plot, for it bore all the signs not only of having been cooked up in Lithuania, but of having been thought up by Prince A. M. Kurbsky, whose sinister hand was seen everywhere by the quivering Ivan. There was clearly a continuing course of rebellion of the spirit, which was mainly confined to words and rumours, but which was being fostered in the Commonwealth with two aims in view: the first was to prevent the accession of Ivan or any of his sons to the throne of Poland in the event of a vacancy; the second was to promote the accession of Sigismund to the throne of Russia in the event of the death of Ivan, of which rumours occasionally floated around.[14] According to the reports of a Venetian diplomat, Gerio, who was in Moscow soon after the destruction of Novgorod, the plot was discovered as a result of the seizure of a courier bearing a treasonable letter. The careful unravelling by Skrynnikov of such evidence as there is points the finger at Lithuanian initiatives instigated by Russian émigrés at a time when Kurbsky's influence in Lithuania was at its highest.[15] But there is no proof.

A detachment of *oprichniki* was sent to Narva, where it looted the goods and property of Russian citizens, and exacted a fine of 8,000 rubles from them by beating them on the calves, apparently leaving untouched the property of non-Russians.[16] Brigands and robbers disguised themselves as *oprichniki* and wandered the countryside raiding and killing.[17]

After looting the churches of Novgorod, including the Cathedral of St Sophia, the great doors of which were removed and taken to Aleksandrovskaia Sloboda, where they still are, the *oprichniki* turned on the nobles and the rich tradesmen, destroying not only their goods but their houses, and finally on the poor townspeople, destroying dwellings, storehouses, barns, food supplies. Coming in the middle of a harsh winter and on top of two epidemics of plague (in 1566/7 and 1570/1) such destruction deprived the population of food which could not be found anywhere else at that time of year, and of shelter. But when Ivan heard that the dead were being salted down in barrels, he rounded on those suspected of cannibalism. Indeed famine and plague, which had already made severe inroads in the 1560s in Novgorod, had contributed greatly to the death toll among those who had not simply frozen to death, and rivers full of dead bodies probably accounted for the spread of cholera.

The total number killed in the devastation of Novgorod, a city of about 30,000 inhabitants at this time, has never been established and estimates vary hugely, ranging from 2,771 given by Schlichting, to 700,000 given by Horsey. Historians now accept that about 2,200 people were deliberately executed, but that many more died as a result of the rampages of the *oprichniki*.[18] The *Sinodiki* did not, of course, contain all the names of the people killed in the devastation of Novgorod, (and their wives and children) but among them 379 are named, including 211 *pomeshchiki* and officials, and 137 members of their families. Among the others were bondsmen, craftsmen and monks.[19] All those belonging in any way to the circle of the Staritsa princes were executed. Many of the senior merchants (*gosti*) and senior *d'iaki* perished, some of them after fiendish tortures in order to extract from them all their treasure. Heinrich von Staden did well out of the ravages of the *oprichnina*. He left Moscow with 1 horse and 2 servants, and returned with 49 horses and 22 carts.[20]

On 13 February Ivan left for Pskov, to continue the good work. He stayed in the Nikol'sky monastery outside the city and was met without the gates by a respectful procession with crosses, icons, bread and salt and other signs of welcome. Abbot Kornilii of the great Pskov Pechersky monastery came to meet the Tsar, but was unable to ward off his wrath. As in Novgorod it fell first on the church hierarchy, of which Ivan was particularly suspicious, since Vassian Muromtsev, the correspondent of A.M. Kurbsky, was a distinguished priestly writer in the monastery, while Abbot Kornilii had for many years composed an anti-Muscovite chronicle of Pskov. One of the Pskov chronicles states that on 20 February 1570 the earthly Tsar dispatched Kornily to the heavenly Tsar.[21] According to a *Sinodik*, some thirty to forty service gentry were executed as well as various monks and elders of monasteries, and a number of officials including a woman, Elena, the mother-in-law of the Governor of Novgorod who rejoiced in the most apposite name of Neudacha (failure).

The Tsar seemed to be particularly enraged at the ecclesiastical hierarchy in Pskov and pillaged it more furiously than elsewhere. But the assault by the *oprichniki* on the city itself did not last long for a reason of which many contemporary versions exist, though many historians –

and others – disbelieve it. There was in Pskov a *iurodivyi*, or holy fool, by name Nikola, so well-known that the Tsar visited him in his cell. Offering him bread and salt, Nikola warned the Tsar: 'you have tortured the people enough. Go back to Moscow, otherwise the horse you rode here will not carry you back to Moscow.' And the holy fool issued many warnings to the Tsar to stop the bloodshed and the ravaging of the holy places. Whether this happened, and whether it had any effect on the Tsar is hard to prove.[22] But it is the kind of intervention which might well have influenced his credulous temperament, and he moved off to Staritsa and thence to Aleksandrovskaia Sloboda.

While these atrocious events were taking place Ivan was continuing his cautious diplomacy to stabilize the situation in the north and build up his defences in the south. An impressive embassy, led by Jan Krotowski and escorted by 718 men and 900 horses, together with 643 merchants and their servants arrived from the Commonwealth on 3 March 1570 and was lodged in the Lithuanian diplomatic palace in Moscow. But the Tsar, explaining that he was tired after having put down disturbances in Novgorod and Pskov, apologized for keeping the ambassador waiting while he rested, and remained shut up in Aleksandrovskaia Sloboda until 4 May. He received the Lithuanian ambassador on 7 May with a number of officials headed by Viskovaty, three of whom would be executed in a few weeks.[23] During the ensuing weeks the two sides discussed terms for an armistice, in a situation rendered tense by a renewal of threats from the Crimean Khan, which required the movement of troops to defend the southern border and the presence of the Tsar himself. Fortunately for Ivan, by 21 May the Tatar troops had been defeated and he was able to return to Moscow, leaving substantial forces and the three senior generals in the *zemshchina*, Bel'sky, Mstislavsky and Vorotynsky, behind. (It is here that the anecdote belongs of the incompetent general, who withdrew before the Tatar attack began and was thrown to a bear to be eaten.[24])

The talks with the Lithuanian envoy were now influenced by news of the illness of King Sigismund Augustus which gave immediacy to the whole question of the succession to his throne. The possibility that Ivan might be considered as a claimant had long been at the back of people's minds, but now, on 10 June 1570, the Polish-Lithuanian envoys openly mentioned the subject to Ivan who replied, 'Our realm is big enough, why should I want yours?'[25] But the news of the declining health of Sigismund Augustus hastened the need for a truce.

However, the presence of a large Polish-Lithuanian embassy in Moscow led to a series of unpleasant and violent diplomatic incidents.

Nowhere in Europe was diplomatic etiquette as yet formally laid down by treaty but certain habits of convenience and courtesy were gradually being formed. They were still often disregarded by, for instance, the Eastern powers (the Ottoman Porte), of which Russia was one. It was also still the practice in the East for embassies to be lodged and fed at the expense of the host country, and to use the opportunity for extensive private trade. This made it easy to put pressure on the visiting embassy by providing inadequate lodging, not enough food, and preventing freedom of movement. In this case the problem was created by a member of the Commonwealth embassy who lashed out at the Tsar's confessor with his whip. He explained in vain that it was an accident, but the Tsar protested at the dishonour to his priest and repaid the Lithuanians in kind by dishonouring the members of the embassy, forcing them, when they obeyed his summons to the Kremlin, to dismount in a lowly place and enter the Kremlin on foot. It ended in an assault by Ivan's *oprichniki* musketeers on the Lithuanians who lost their clothes and hats. Ivan placed a Lithuanian hat on the head of his fool, and told him to kneel in Lithuanian fashion, then showed him how to do so to his favourite cry: *Hoyda, hoyda.* In a quarrel over the value of presents, a thoroughbred horse presented to the Tsar was cut to pieces.[26] Nevertheless, a three-year truce was patched up between the Commonwealth and Russia on 20 June 1570, for Ivan was anxious to get rid of this large Lithuanian armed presence which merely increased the tension over foreign policy. There were close family connexions between Lithuanians and Russians, and it was impossible for Ivan to prevent the two sides from talking unofficially together and indeed plotting, and there was no language barrier. Many Russians opposed the truce with Lithuania on the grounds that the absence of war would untie Ivan's hands and enable him to proceed against his subjects.

The agreement for the three-year truce with the Commonwealth was presented on a salver by Viskovaty to the Tsar for his ratification on 22 June 1570, and the Polish embassy departed at last on 3 July 1570.[27] This embassy was noteworthy for the presence of Jan Rokyta, the Hussite Elder of the Bohemian Brethren, as a chaplain attached to the Polish-Lithuanian embassy, and the dialogue which took place between him and the Tsar on the subject of religion. So convinced was Ivan of his knowledge of theology that he twice at least in his life embarked on a public dispute with a leading representative of a foreign faith. The first was with Jan Rokyta, the second was with the Jesuit, Antonio Possevino, who argued publicly with Ivan on several occasions in March 1582.[28]

Jan Rokyta's debate with Ivan took place on 10 May 1570, just after the Union of Lublin and the creation of the Commonwealth of Poland–Lithuania. The Polish-Lithuanian Protestants at the time were testing the ground in Russia for the possible candidature of Ivan IV to the Polish throne in the event of the death of the King. Rokyta was a very senior, experienced and highly respected elder of the Bohemian Brethren.[29] The request for a debate with the Tsar on Protestantism came from him, and Ivan consented to it rather reluctantly. The surviving documents include the reply by Jan Rokyta to a series of ten questions put to him by Ivan, inviting the Bohemian Brother to explain what he taught the faithful, what was the justification of their faith, and raising a few knotty questions on the issue of justification by faith alone and other matters of ritual or conduct, which separated Lutheranism from Orthodoxy. (Ivan: 'If you say that we are saved by the Grace of God alone, then why say that Christ the Saviour will come to judge the living and the dead according to their deeds?')

While denying that he was a Lutheran, Rokyta asserted in his reply to Ivan that his religion had withdrawn from obedience to the Pope, that miracles were no longer necessary to confirm faith, nor was the intercession of the saints, nor did the Brethren worship idols (icons). His views on marriage were perfectly Pauline.

On the whole this was a very moderate statement. Ivan took some time to write or commission a reply, which was delivered to Jan Rokyta in the name of Parfenii Urodivy, Ivan's *alter ego*.[30] In all probability there were extensive consultations with the Metropolitan or some other knowedgeable clerics, for the document, dated 18 June,[31] though un-mistakably written in Ivan's style ('give not that which is holy unto the dogs neither cast ye your pearls before swine') is a serious attempt to discuss religious differences. It is long and divided into fourteen chapters. The Tsar attacked Luther the man, whom he assumed to be Rokyta's teacher, as one who is savage (*liutorstvo*; there is a pun on the name of Luther here) and accuses him of being the Angel of Darkness, and like Satan, cast out of heaven. He accuses Rokyta of distorting the content of the Holy Scriptures, as usual relying on quotations from the Bible and the Holy Fathers. As one might expect he raises the question of faith versus works and rejects salvation by faith alone. ' But wilt thou know, oh vain man,' he says to Rokyta, ' that faith without works is dead?'

Ivan also rejects the concept of predestination, arguing that pre-destination has been completed at the time of the incarnation and he regards the laws of Deuteronomy as tenets of Judaism. Rokyta's rejection of icons and the veneration of images is countered by the argument that icons represent heavenly forces necessary for human salvation, and not wicked idols. The whole allocution is more imbued with sweet reasonableness than is usual, until Ivan comes to the end, when he accuses Jan Rokyta of corrupt teaching, of being a heretic, a servant of Antichrist, and forbids him ever to preach in Russia.[32]

Meanwhile the new Russian ambassador to England, Andrei Grigorevich Savin, arrived safely in London and was given a ceremonial reception at Tower Wharf on 27 August 1569 by the Lord Mayor and Aldermen, clad in scarlet, and the 'merchants adventurers in coates of black velvet all on horsebacke' who escorted Savin to the Muscovy House. Savin's instructions were to conclude an agreement regarding Ivan's asylum in England, and Elizabeth's in Russia, and to finalize the alliance between the two countries which had been discussed and verbally agreed in general terms by Randolph.[33] No details of the negotiations are known, which dealt both with relations between states (the Russian right to trade freely in England, recruitment of craftsmen etc.) and matters concerning the Russia Company. The difficulties encountered by the negotiators are suggested by Savin's request on 6 May 1570 that the Queen's 'letters of secrit' be written in 'Rousse word for word', and that the Queen should sign and take an oath to the letters and hang her seal on them, and the Tsar would undertake to do the same. Ivan's distrust of English procedure is reflected in his request that the translations into Russian should be made in the presence of his ambassador.[34] Again, in Ivan's name, Savin requested that Anthony Jenkinson should be sent on a 'grand embassy', for he had followed the negotiations from the beginning and 'therefore the Emperour will better creditt his wordes'.[35]

By May 1570 Elizabeth delivered to Savin a formal reply to the demand for an alliance, couched in terms so devious and 'Elizabethan' that it is difficult really to be sure of what the Queen meant. Elizabeth speaks of her acceptance of Ivan's offer of a 'league and confederation', and her decision to accept such a friendly offer as he had made 'so far furth as the treaties and confederations which we have had of long time and received by succession of our progenitors kings of England' would permit her. Hence her existing foreign relations took priority over her 'amity' with Ivan which, she also hinted, was offered in reciprocation for his grant of trade privileges. Yet in the end, her offer was generous: she would enter a friendly and sisterly league with Ivan, which she would keep forever, which league would bind them both to withstand all their common enemies with all their forces, and to help each other against their common enemies, 'as farfurth as the effect of these our letters shall stretche'. The sting again was in the tail: 'And we will not ayde comefort or suffer any parson or potentate to offend you or youre contreys, that we may to our power and by justice with reason stay or impeache', which meant that Elizabeth would attempt to protect Ivan by verbal rather than military means. At the same time a second highly secret letter of the same date repeated Elizabeth' s offer of asylum to Ivan and his 'noble empresse and deare children the princes', signed by the principal members of her Council.[36] Elizabeth refused to commit herself to asking for asylum in Russia in the event of her people rising against her.

Yet in spite of the English commitment to act with Russia against their common enemies, Ivan was still not satisfied that the proffered alliance was precise enough to meet his needs. For Elizabeth, who did not want to be forced to take part in any wars, let alone wars in Eastern Europe, did leave herself a loophole by accepting to assist Ivan insofar only as her assistance did not infringe her engagements with other Christian powers, in fact she would decide whether the treaty applied or not. That the Queen obviously thought agreement had been reached is reflected in her decision not to send an ambassador, whether Jenkinson or anyone else, to Russia to continue talks with Ivan.[37]

Savin returned to Russia bringing with him an important addition to Ivan's court, the physician Dr Eliseus Bomelius who was to play a prominent part, acquire a sinister reputation, and suffer an excruciating death in Russia. He was of German extraction, son of a Lutheran preacher in Westphalia, who was a friend of the English Bishop Bale. He took a medical degree at Cambridge, and was a popular practitioner in English society, but was arrested in 1567 for practising without a licence. He was also skilled in astrology and alchemy. He was released from the King's Bench prison in 1570, possibly because Savin offered him employment in Russia. Lord Burleigh had used his services, and is said to have consulted him on Elizabeth's length of life. He is also said to have arranged that Bomelius should supply him with information about Russia.[38]

While the Tsar was still busy with the Commonwealth embassy and his correspondence with Elizabeth, Magnus of Denmark arrived in Moscow on 10 June 1570 with the approval of his brother, the King of Denmark, and was ceremonially welcomed as King of Livonia. He took the oath of allegiance to Ivan as his overlord and received from him the corresponding charter for the hereditary vassal kingdom of Livonia, in what Ivan termed his patrimony, but which had still to be conquered. These lands comprised ex-Russian, Polish and Swedish conquests in Livonia, and included Riga, which was to all intents and purposes a free city at the time. The new kingdom was to enjoy extensive commercial privileges within Russia for its cities, and a great deal of autonomy, since Russian officials and tax collectors were to be excluded from the land, and Magnus was to commit himself to give modest military assistance to Russia if Ivan himself went on campaign. The kingdom was also to ensure free access for Russian imports and exports to and from the West, Ivan's main object. Magnus's betrothal to the eldest daughter of Vladimir of Staritsa, Evfimia, then still only twelve years old, took place and he was crowned with the crown of Livonia. The treaty between Magnus and Ivan was signed by an *oprichnik*, and by a member of the *zemskii* administration, the *d'iak* V. Shchelkalov, who was already beginning to ascend the ladder to power.[39] In order to win over his new subjects, Ivan declared that he was himself of German origin (the myth of his descent from Prus, the brother of Augustus Caesar), that he liked Germans and wanted to marry his daughters to German princes (he had no daughters at the time). He ordered the release of German prisoners-of-war and the repatriation of Livonian citizens from Dorpat. (One must remember that 'Germans' at this time meant mainly Livonians to the Russians.)

The new King Magnus of Livonia left Moscow on 6 July to embark on the conquest of Reval with 15,000 rubles and 20,000 Russian soldiers at his disposal.[40] In what appears to have been a temporary fit of anger with his sons Ivan even went so far as to promise Magnus the succession to the throne of Russia, humiliating his sons and his people, 'whom he would trample under foot'.[41] But the blandishments of Kruse and Taube did not have the desired effect on the inhabitants of Reval, who mindful of the fate of Novgorod, of which they were well aware, having many connexions with the city, determined to cling to their actual Swedish overlord. They defended the Swedish garrison by pouring water on the battlements which froze to a smooth surface, rendering it impossible for the invading Russian forces of Duke Magnus to climb up.[42] They were finally relieved by the Swedish fleet, so Magnus's realm had still to be conquered.

Meanwhile Ivan still did not think he had uprooted all the offshoots of treason which in his view infected the whole of Russian society and which stretched from Novgorod to Moscow. Against a background of increasing poverty, scarcity and even famine among the people, he continued to seek out any evidence of opposition or treason. The recent diplomatic bickering with the Commonwealth embassy, and the unsatisfactory response from the Queen of England may have reminded the Tsar of many past mortifications. Schlichting provides a horrifying picture of the sadistic and cruel pastimes to which Ivan seemed addicted in 1570 on his return from Novgorod to Moscow, once the Lithuanian embassy had departed on 3 July 1570 and Magnus on 6 July. Archbishop Pimen and hundreds of other Novgorodians suffered the tortures of the damned in Moscow and Aleksandrovskaia Sloboda, with Ivan occasionally taking part. Inevitably some were unable to hold out, and denunciations multiplied. The victims were sped on their way by those waiting in the wings to inherit the positions and the wealth of the disgraced and killed. Viskovaty's brother, Tret'iak, suffered and was killed (with his wife) at the beginning of July, for taking part in the alleged Novgorod conspiracy.[43] His brother could do nothing to save him.

Ivan Mikhailovich Viskovaty, *de facto* the head of foreign affairs for many years, may have brought to a head the suspicions nurtured by the Tsar against his old friends in the *zemshchina*, his brothers-in-arms (and in love, in the case of Fedor Basmanov) in the *oprichnina*, his servants in the government of the country and in the Boyar Council. Viskovaty had been a loyal servant of Ivan's throughout his life including the crisis over the succession of the baby Dmitri in 1553.[44] Throughout many of the succeeding years he had been the head of the Office of Foreign Affairs, and took an active part in all the negotiations with Sweden, Lithuania and Denmark, where he spent some time on a mission in 1553. Though no longer the *d'iak* in charge of foreign affairs (in the *zemshchina*) he was now the keeper of the privy seal (*pechatnik*) and his influence on the formation and execution of foreign policy remained dominant. Most authors agree that he was among those who preferred war in Livonia over war in the south, against the Crimeans, which of course meant that he was fulfilling Ivan's wishes; on the other hand he gave a somewhat confused separate opinion at the *Zemskii sobor* of 1566 which may have aroused Ivan's suspicions. The Lithuanians certainly believed that he was opposed to them.[45] However, there were a number of occasions when Viskovaty had spoken out against policies favoured by Ivan, notably on the painting of icons.[46]

It seems that it was the *d'iak* Andrei Iakovlevich Shchelkalov who built up the case against Viskovaty and Funikov behind the scenes. Now, in mid-July 1570, the two Viskovaty brothers were accused, in the account of the investigation of the Novgorod affair, of having joined with the Novgorod plotters to destroy the Tsar and pass the realm to the Prince of Staritsa. In what seems to have been an incredibly courageous, indeed foolhardy attempt to influence the Tsar, Viskovaty, apparently during an interrogation some time after his arrest, begged him not to shed so much blood, not to exterminate his nobility. Who would choose to live in his realm, to fight for him, if he continued to destroy such numbers of brave men? Ivan replied:

> I have not rooted all of you out because I have not really started, but I intend to make every effort to destroy you so completely that no memory of you will survive. I hope I shall succeed, but if I fail and bring God's punishment upon me, and must give way to my enemies, I would far rather yield to Him in a great matter than appear ridiculous before you, who are my slaves.[47]

But Viskovaty and Funikov were not the only targets.[48] The heads of many other *prikazy* such as the *prikaz* of landed estates (*Pomest'nyi*), the principal office of revenue (*Bol'shoi Prikaz*), the office against brigands (*Razboinyi Prikaz*) were all rounded up.[49] When, where and how the victims were arrested and tortured and where they were kept is not known.

Behind Ivan's savagery there lay a determined push by the members of the *oprichnina*, both aristocrats and service gentry, to eliminate the old princely families, leading boyar families and the leading *d'iaki*, in charge of the government offices and of the administration of the *zemshchina*. There was also a secret vendetta against some of Ivan's original servants in the *oprichnina*, such as Prince A.D. Viazemsky, and the Basmanovs.

The final scene was dramatically enacted on 25 July 1570: 'on the feast day of St James the Apostle' Ivan's executioners prepared the public square, the Poganaia meadow, with twenty huge stakes driven into the ground, joined by transverse beams, and supplied with cauldrons of cold and boiling water. The Tsar then appeared, on horseback, dressed all in black, fully armed, and carrying a bow and arrows and an axe, and escorted by 1,500 mounted *strel'tsy* (musketeers). Schlichting, who was an eyewitness (as were the Livonian nobles Kruse and Taube), describes how some three hundred nobles, in various stages of disintegration, prostration and decrepitude, crawling on their broken legs, were brought before Ivan and his sixteen-year-old son, Tsarevich Ivan Ivanovich. 'Seeing the people were frightened and unwilling to behold a scene of such dreadful cruelty', wrote Schlichting,

> Ivan rode about on his horse telling them not to be afraid, and ordering them to draw near to witness the spectacle. He admitted that he had originally intended to destroy all the inhabitants of the city but declared that he had now laid aside his anger. Whereupon

the people came close to the Prince, who asked whether it was right for him to punish those who had betrayed him? The people shouted 'long live our glorious Tsar' and expressed their approval. The Tsar now had one hundred and eighty-four of the three hundred brought forward and gave them into the custody of nobles who were standing by, saying: 'Here you can have them. I make you a present of them . . . I have no further quarrel with them.'[50]

Vasily Shchelkalov now appeared with a long screed listing the charges. The first to be accused was Viskovaty, who as late as 12 July was recorded as still negotiating with the Lithuanian envoys with the rank of Keeper of the State Seal.[51] He was charged not only with intriguing with Lithuania but with the most unlikely accusation that he had been secretly intriguing with the Ottoman Turks and the Khan of Crimea, inviting them to attack Russia. As he read out each charge Shchelkalov struck Viskovaty on the head with a stick, or whip. The executioners tried to persuade Viskovaty to admit his crimes and beg for mercy, but he denied his guilt, and loudly put himself in the hands of God who would judge both Ivan and himself in the next world. 'You lust to shed my blood, go ahead and drink your fill of the blood of an innocent man. Accursed be you, bloodsuckers, and your Tsar' were his last words. Strung up between the stakes, Viskovaty was cut to pieces. Maliuta Skuratov cut off his nose, another cut off his ears, and at last another, named Ivan Reutov, cut off his privy parts, whereupon he died. But Ivan, suspecting that Reutov had done this out of pity, to hasten his death, shouted to him 'You too will soon have a drink out of the same cup from which he is drinking.' (In fact luckily for him Reutov died of the plague.)[52]

It was now the turn of Funikov, the treasurer, who also hardily proclaimed his innocence and said that 'the tyrant's soul would suffer if he killed guiltless men'. Ivan replied: 'I have not caused or instigated your death nor am I responsible for it. Your associate, to whom you listened [Viskovaty] is the entire cause of your ruin. Even if you had not committed any crime you acted in concert with him, and so you both must die.' Funikov was slowly killed by being doused alternately with icy and boiling water. Several other heads of *prikazy* followed, in some cases with their wives and children; Grigory Shapkin, together with his wife and two children was beheaded by a Prince Vasily Temkin, an *oprichnik*, who laid their bodies at Ivan's feet. Lev Saltykov, who had distinguished himself so greatly in the sack of Novgorod was killed. A total of 116 victims were dispatched in various ingenious ways,[53] some having their ribs torn out, others flayed alive or impaled until finally an old man who could barely walk tottered up. Ivan ran him through with a spear, then stabbed him sixteen times and had him beheaded, before at the end of four hours, he had had enough and withdrew to his palace.[54] In the words of the Russian historian A.A. Zimin, 'The Russian capital had seen many horrors in its time. But what happened in Moscow on 25 July, in its cruelty and sadistic refinement, outdid all that had gone before and can perhaps be explained only by the cruel temperament and the sick imagination of Ivan the Terrible'.[55]

The reprisals were not yet quite over. In the following days, some fifty to seventy prisoners brought from Novgorod were dealt with, together with some eighty of their wives and children.[56] It was evident that the *oprichniki* were being torn apart by their own rivalries, by the prevalence of denunciations of all kinds, and by changes in Ivan's policies in regard to the Staritsky family since the engagement of Duke Magnus to Vladimir's daughter, and by Ivan's own growing distrust of his henchmen. It is around this time that three of the highest ranking members of the *oprichnina* disappeared in circumstances which are not clear but which suggest that they had shown lack of sympathy with Ivan's policies, and in particular that they too had perhaps been involved in plots to hand Novgorod over to the King of Poland–Lithuania and had tried to control Ivan's excesses. According to Schlichting, Prince Afanasii Viazemsky had been a leading light in the *oprichnina* since its foundation, a man so close to Ivan that the Tsar would take medicine from no hands but his. Schlichting, who was in service with Ivan's Belgian physician, Dr Arnold (also Dr A. Lindsay) would be likely to know this.[57] But Viazemsky, in common with the two Basmanovs, seems to have opposed in his heart of hearts (if he had one) the planned destruction of Novgorod. Some *oprichniki* were themselves beginning to think that Ivan was going too far, and there is a suggestion that Viazemsky attempted to warn Archbishop Pimen. Denounced by a client of his, one Lovchikov, for having leaked the Tsar's decision to destroy Novgorod, Ivan ordered Viazemsky's servants to be killed, whereupon the Prince concealed himself for a few days in the house of Dr Arnold (where Schlichting may have seen him). But Ivan succeeded in laying hands on him and submitted Viazemsky to the special daily beating inflicted on debtors, *pravezh*, to extract all his wealth from him, until his body swelled up and he turned to denouncing others in order to bring his torment to an end. At this point in the tale, Schlichting fled Russia and took refuge in Lithuania so that he was unable to provide an eyewitness account of Viazemsky's eventual fate. The German now offered his services to Sigismund Augustus.

Viazemsky does not seem to have been executed, for his name does not figure in a *Sinodik*; he probably died in prison.[58] The names of Aleksei and Fedor Basmanov also disappear about this time, but they were clearly executed for they do figure in *Sinodiki*; Fedor Basmanov was allegedly compelled to execute his own father. Ivan sent 100 rubles to the Trinity monastery for prayers for Fedor Basmanov and eventually returned some of the family's estates to his children,[59] one of whom, Peter, became a strong and effective supporter of the first False Dmitri, and died for it in the Time of Troubles. He may have been cured by the fate of his father of all loyalty to the Riurikovichi. The elimination of the previously all-powerful Viazemsky and the Basmanovs is attributed by Skrynnikov to the intrigues of Maliuta Skuratov and of V.G. Griaznoi, who had once been in the service of Vladimir of Staritsa and then helped in the campaign to destroy him and rose in Ivan's confidence in consequence.[60]

The impact of these terrible days on the people of Moscow was profound. And evidently on Ivan too, for never, after the massacre on 25 July, did Ivan show the same confidence in his 'brothers-in-arms'.[61]

Chapter XVI

Foreign Policy and the Tatar Invasions

While Ivan was conducting the fearsome purge of his armed forces and administration, the horizon on his external relations darkened. Shortly after the overthrow of Erik XIV of Sweden, and his coronation as King of Sweden, John III, in July 1569, had sent an embassy to Russia under Paul Juusten, Bishop of Åbo, to negotiate with Ivan. At first Ivan had proved conciliating, suggesting that he had only asked for John's wife, Catherine Jagiellonka, to be handed over to him because he thought John was dead (which John was unlikely to believe) and he hoped to rescue her from the prison in which presumably Erik had incarcerated her, when he had sentenced his brother to death for his rebellious behaviour.[1]

Juusten arrived in Novgorod on 14 September 1569, after the return to Moscow of Ivan's embassy to Sweden under the boyar V.M. Vorontsov, which had been sent in 1567 to finalize the arrangements made with Erik for the collection and delivery to Russia of Catherine. From the beginning Juusten was faced with the demand that he should negotiate with the Governor of Novgorod and not expect to deal with the Tsar himself, particularly as it could be argued, since the deposition of Erik, that John was not an hereditary king, but an elected king of an inferior kind. The Tsar had been outraged at the news of the attack on his ambassador Vorontsov by John's supporters, and insisted that the Swedish envoys should treat the Governor of Novgorod as 'the brother of their king' which Juusten refused to do. The Russians were then ordered by the Governor to attack the Swedish party, and robbed them of their clothes and boots. They forced them to expose themselves in the streets in their underwear, displaying their buttocks and their private parts; they rifled their belongings, 'penned them like pigs in a sty', and deprived them of food and drink. 'None of us had ever before drunk water to quench his thirst save at times of dire necessity and then as little as possible' wrote Juusten plaintively.[2] Ivan's spokesman made it quite clear that this rough treatment was a reprisal for the Swedish attack on the Russian embassy in 1568.[3] Fortunately for them the Swedes were now dragged 'like captured felons' to Moscow in 1570, thus avoiding a meeting with Ivan who was approaching with the *oprichniki* to launch his assault on Novgorod. They escaped just in time.

When Ivan returned to Moscow, in May 1570, from his punitive expedition against Novgorod, he still refused to receive the Swedish envoys. What is more he soon had a free hand to bully them for he no longer feared a Commonwealth attack in the event of war with Sweden since the conclusion of the three-year truce on 20 June 1570. Yet Ivan's policy, in May and June 1570, when the Swedish envoys were finally received in Moscow by Ivan Viskovaty and Andrei Vasil'ev (both shortly to be executed) is difficult to grasp, for the Tsar now asserted that the 'concessions' he had previously made to Erik were conditioned by Swedish willingness to surrender John's Queen. If 'Sweden were prepared to hand her over immediately', the treaty signed with King Erik in 1567 could be renewed. It seemed as though the Tsar were seeking a breach with Sweden. Summoned for a second interview to the Kremlin on 6 June 1570 and under threat of exile, torture and imprisonment, the Swedish diplomatic mission agreed to negotiate in Novgorod in order to mollify Ivan, but still the Russian secretaries insisted on the surrender of Catherine Jagiellonka as a precondition to any negotiation. What her status was to be now, as before, is never made clear: wife (Ivan was at this moment a widower), mistress, or political pawn? In a later letter of 11 August 1572 to John III himself, Ivan was more open and accused Erik of having wanted to hand Catherine to him 'by deceit', a policy which was followed by his loss of his throne. And then, continued Ivan, 'in autumn they told us that you had died, and in spring that you had been chased out of the land by your brother Karl . . . and now they say that your envoys are coming and that you are in your lordship . . . and that you are besieged in Stockholm and your brother Erik is advancing on you.'[4] In this way the Tsar covered his past negotiations over Catherine with confusion.

Sometime in mid-June 1570 Ivan banished the Swedish delegation to Murom,[5] where they were kept under house arrest in very cramped quarters until November 1571,[6] forced to buy their own food with their depleted supplies of money, and make their own clothes. It seemed that Ivan was determined to secure an acknowledgement of Russian suzerainty over Sweden, by means of the claim that Sweden could only negotiate with the Governor of Novgorod and not with the Tsar, as had been usual in the past, when Novgorod was an independent republic. He argued that Sweden was not in fact a kingdom of equal rank with Russia, but a province,[7] whose status was similar to that of Magnus's kingdom of Livonia, now a vassal of Ivan's.

By the summer Savin arrived in Moscow with Queen Elizabeth's reply to the offer of alliance. Whatever she may have meant, Ivan was obviously so agitated by the terms of her letter that he replied in language such had probably never been used to Elizabeth before. He sent a letter through the interpreter Sylvester on 24 October 1570 in which he recapitulated the whole history of Anglo-Russian relations, accusing the English merchants of dishonesty and complaining that none of the letters he had received from England had been properly sealed with the same seal, but always with a different seal, a method which commanded no confidence between states. He complained that he never received any news of 'Anthonie' or 'Onton' (Jenkinson), who did not accompany Randolph when he had been sent as English ambassador, and that Randolph spoke only of merchants' and boorish affairs, and refused to speak of 'princelie affaires'. Ivan stressed that the reason why he insisted on Jenkinson's return was that he wanted to know if he had spoken to the Queen about the secret matters, i.e. the asylum to be offered to Ivan. In a final rhetorical accusation Ivan declared:

> We had thought that you had been ruler over your lande and had sought honor to your self and profitt to your countrie . . . but now we perceive that there be other men that doe rule, and not men but bowers [boors] and merchaunts . . . who seek their owne profitt of marchauntdize; and you flowe in your maidenlie estate like a maide

Whereupon the irate Tsar withdrew all the trading privileges which he had granted to the Russia Company.[8] The Tsar had not so far connected the negotiations for an alliance with English trade privileges. He was now ready to do so and to exercise pressure on England. There were still moreover differences of style which led to misunderstandings. Whereas Elizabeth might think that a verbal agreement was enough, Ivan needed an agreement in which the Queen committed herself by oath, swearing to every paragraph.[9]

With the passage of time, the war in Livonia was becoming more and more of a burden for both Denmark and Sweden and the third partner, Lübeck was also suffering from the loss of much of her trade to other Hanseatic towns. But Ivan's hopes of Danish support for King Magnus of Livonia were doomed to fail: Frederick of Denmark was not interested in conquering Livonia for Ivan's vassal, even though he was his younger brother. A peace congress, organized behind the scenes by the Emperor Maximilian II, the King of France and Sigismund Augustus negotiated a treaty of peace at Stettin on 30 November 1570,[10] which brought to an end the so-called seven years, Northern War. This was, however, no help to Ivan since it freed all the other powers involved in the war in the Baltic to unite against him. Meanwhile the Russian siege of Swedish-controlled Reval, in Estonia, conducted by King Magnus, was faltering. Denmark of course refused any assistance, and Ivan was too strapped for troops to send any. He had hoped that Magnus would be successful enough to be able eventually to reinforce him against the Tatars. More serious for Ivan was the fact that after the peace of Stettin, the King of Sweden, who could count on the passive support of his brother-in-law Sigismund Augustus, stepped up the war at sea. He interfered with Russian supplies which had been landing freely at Narva, whose trade now almost rivalled that of Riga, while no longer attacking and capturing Danish ships. By the end of March 1571 Magnus gave up the struggle for Reval and abandoned the siege.[11] He was now useless to Ivan. So were the Livonian nobles Taube and Kruse.

The Crimean Khan, no longer hampered by Ottoman policy, was also free to embark on a new campaign against Russia. He began by clearing one obstacle out of the way: he sent his son to attack Ivan's quondam father-in-law, Temriuk, Khan of Kabarda, who was seriously injured and two of whose sons were taken prisoner, while the Khan of the Crimea then turned to cultivate the Khan of the Nogai horde, one of the Tatar tribes of the Caucasus. The main Russian defence forces were stationed on the Oka river under two of the most prominent Russian commanders, Princes I.D. Bel'sky and I.F. Mstislavsky, but in 1570 the Crimeans indulged in only a few skirmishes.

The death of the Tsaritsa Maria in 1569 does not seem at first to have affected Mikhail Temriukovich Cherkassky's position in Russia. The fate of Maria Temriukovna's brother was probably decided early in 1571. Normally he would have been appointed to command one of the main Russian corps in a campaign against the Khan of Crimea, but he disappeared from view. There is a good deal of mystery about when and how he died, and there are stories about Ivan tying up a wild bear on either side of the gate to his house, rendering access very risky, and the odd report of the execution of his sixteen-year-old wife, and her six-month-old son, as early as 1568.[12] Mikhail Cherkassky's death is attributed by two leading historians to the period around May 1571 when the Crimean army was advancing on the Oka river. According to one story, a false rumour spread in the Russian army that Maria and Mikhail's father, Temriuk, had joined Devlet Girey in the invading Crimean army. Mikhail was thereupon given a lower rank in the *oprichnina* army and then 'disappeared without trace'.[13] A more reliable story tells that he was sent to command the forces in Serpukhov and between 13 and 16 May 1571 he was shot down or cut to pieces by harquebusiers belonging to the *oprichnina*.[14]

In 1571 the Russian troops were reinforced by a corps of *oprichniki* commanded by the Tsar himself, which started out for the Oka front on 15 May 1571. Ivan now reaped some of what he had sown: large numbers of Russians deserted to join Devlet Girey's army. They reported that many people had died of the plague in Moscow of late, and that the Tsar had executed large numbers of his people; and that moreover he had few soldiers with him because the bulk of his army was still fighting in Livonia. Meanwhile the Tatar army, numbering variously 40,000 or 200,000 continued its advance on Moscow.[15] One deserter offered to guide the Tatars to a ford which would enable them to evade the watching Russian forces on the Oka, and led them to where only the Tsar with a small *oprichnina* force stood before them. Whereupon Ivan withdrew without fighting, taking refuge in Rostov, whence it was easy to move to Vologda and safety at sea. Or according to Taube and Kruse he ran away without stopping until he reached Yaroslavl'.[16] The entries in the military registers describing this event are very restrained but do not conceal the surprise of their authors at the cowardice of the Tsar.

On 23 May the Crimean army advanced unexpectedly on a Moscow denuded of forces. The Khan stayed in Ivan's palace of Kolomenskoe, on the outskirts, while the main Russian army under Prince I.D. Bel'sky, M.Ia. Morozov, Prince I.F. Mstislavsky and Prince M.I. Vorotynsky was disposed throughout the city, with the *oprichnina* corps in the rear under Prince V.I. Temkin Rostovsky. But there was no defence against the weapon used by Devlet Girey: on 24 May he set fire to the suburbs, a sudden gale blew up and wooden Moscow went up in flames. The intense fire raged for three to four hours and consumed most of the wooden buildings and fortifications, and many of the brick and stone ones. The church bells rang the tocsin all over the town, but one by one they fell silent, indeed fell down. Powder magazines blew up. Thousands of people died suffocated by smoke, including Prince I.D. Bel'sky (who had been wounded in the fighting) and his family, and Ivan's physician Dr Arnold, Schlichting's patron. Horses and livestock, even the lions given to Ivan by Mary and Philip and hundreds of buildings including the new *oprichnina* palace, which had only been erected a few years before, all perished, together with huge supplies of food, fodder and arms. The Tsar ordered the dead or dying to be thrown into the river, but it proved impossible, the river overflowed, creating floods, and all the drinking water was polluted. There were so many bodies that 'the Moscow river could not bear the dead'. The only survivors were in the regiment commanded by Prince M.I. Vorotynsky, safe from the wind on the outskirts of Moscow and defending the city as well as he could from the pillaging Tatars. It took more than a year to clear the bodies according to Horsey.[17]

Again the number of victims has been much exaggerated in contemporary accounts, Giles Fletcher, for example, gives 800,000, when the total population of Moscow was about 100,000. Thousands were captured by the Crimeans to swell their slave trade, and thousands more in the towns and villages they ravaged on their return south.[18] The boyars remaining in Moscow scarcely dared to tell Ivan in Rostov of the disaster. When he heard of it he made the bitter remark: 'They have already burnt Moscow and for ten days they did not dare tell me . . . that is treason indeed.'[19]

Of whom was he afraid? Of the Tatars or of his people? Of the latter, states one historian, relying on the report of the envoy Giles Fletcher, that the Tsar was afraid to fight because he doubted the loyalty of his nobles and his commanders, and feared that they might hand him over to the Tatars.[20] Ivan was furious at the situation into which he had been led by the 'disloyalty and treason' of his men, and by the poor figure he had been made to cut. 'Seven *voevody* marched ahead of me with many men and they said not a word to me about the Tatar forces' he exclaimed.[21] Needless to say there was the usual investigation under torture of those who might be responsible for the failure to warn the Tsar of the many desertions, or for allowing the main Crimean army to catch him unawares.

On 10 June 1571 Ivan was back in Moscow, and received messengers from the Khan of Crimea, who addressed him very discourteously, threatening him, demanding the surrender of Kazan' and Astrakhan', and payment of the tribute as of old, taunting him with running away from Moscow.[22] Ivan felt compelled to receive the messengers politely, dressed in his shabbiest clothes as a sign of mourning; he even invited them to dine and presented them with furs. He ordered his longstanding envoy in Crimea, Afanasii Nagoy, to begin talks with the Khan, Devlet Girey, and was prepared to agree to the placing of Crimean khans in Astrakhan' though with Russian consent. But the Khan rejected Ivan's

terms and seemed determined to continue the war.[23] This most humiliating incident added fuel to Ivan's determination to root out the traitors
in his service whom he now identified with members of the *oprichnina*.
The Tsar was convinced that his separate *udel* was unable to provide
him with the security he needed; first the death of his Tsaritsa Maria, and
now the destruction of Moscow shattered his dependence on the
oprichniki. The forces of the *oprichnina* had not defended Moscow, and
it was M.I. Vorotynsky, a member of the *zemshchina*, who proved the
most competent. Someone would certainly have to pay for such a
disaster, and Ivan turned on the *oprichnina* generals, four of whom were
executed in the summer of 1571 including men he had himself chosen
like, Prince I.D. Temkin Rostovsky. According to Taube and Kruse, the
Tsar's physician, Dr Bomelius, poisoned up to one hundred officials and
officers on his master's behalf.[24]

These executions may also perhaps be related to rumours of a serious
quarrel between the Tsar and the Tsarevich which occurred about this
time and rumbled on, of which many versions survive. Tsarevich Ivan
had not been granted his own territorial title and lands, as tsarevich, on
his majority, unlike Vasilly III in his time. One of his serving boyars may
have been murdered in the same period as Prince Mikhail Cherkassky.
According to Skrynnikov a charge of treason against Ivan Ivanovich was
directed by the machinations of senior *oprichniki*, above all Maliuta
Skuratov, the *oko gosudarevo*, the eye of the lord in Eisenstein's film,
Ivan the Terrible, who had become the Tsar's principal adviser in the
oprichnina after the disappearance of A.D. Basmanov and Viazemsky.
Skrynnikov describes him as the head of Ivan's secret intelligence
(*razvedka*) though no such body can be found in Ivan's *dvor*. But the
images of the various heads of the OGPU, GPU, NKVD, the Iagodas,
Iezhovs and Berias, no doubt floated before Eisenstein's eyes while he
was making his famous film in which Maliuta Skuratov plays a
prominent part. The accusations of treason were mainly aimed at the
remaining members of Anastasia's family, the Iur'ev-Zakhar'ins, closely
related to the Tsarevich Ivan Ivanovich through his mother, and to
Mikhail Cherkassky, through his wife.[25]

The rumours of a quarrel between the Tsar and his son may have
reached Poland in early 1571 through the arrival there of Schlichting.
Apparently the papal nuncio, Vincenzo del Portico, in Cracow, wrote to
the Pope on 3 January 1571 communicating the arrival of a man from
Russia who had referred to the dispute between Tsar Ivan and his son.
This might well have been Schlichting who, as secretary and confidant of
the Tsar's physician, would be able to supply all kinds of private details

about the Tsar's family.[26] The quarrel seems to have led to an open breach between father and son and there were reports that many leading nobles were taking sides. Skrynnikov, who tells this story, also draws on the widespread echoes of the quarrel in popular historical and folk songs about the 'anger of the terrible one', which led up to the eventual death of Ivan Ivanovich at the hands of his father. One of the surviving songs runs as follows: Ivan is thinking how to rid himself of treason in 'stone built' Moscow, and Maliuta Skuratov runs up to him and says: 'Hail to you, Tsar Ivan Vasil'evich, you will not root out treason for centuries: your enemy [the Tsarevich Ivan Ivanovich] sits opposite you.' Whereupon Ivan orders his son to be arrested and taken to the Poganaia meadow, where all the executions had taken place in July 1570. But Nikita Romanovich, the brother of Anastasia and uncle of the Tsarevich, warns Maliuta that the morsel is not for him, and that he will be crushed. In the song, Ivan exclaims, 'You boyars, I will boil you all in a cauldron' (possibly a reference to the fate of Funikov on 25 July in Moscow). Maliuta Skuratov is eventually handed over to Nikita Romanovich to dispose of. In fact of course Maliuta became Ivan's principal executioner, and conducted a veritable campaign of extermination against the Iur'iev clan though Nikita Romanovich survived.[27] Nevertheless, Maliuta did well out of his own marriage with a Shuiskaia and the eventual marriage of his daughter with the young and rising Boris Godunov.

Soon after the death of Maria Temriukovna, Ivan had ordered the organization of a bride-show throughout the country to find him a new wife. In 1570, members of the *oprichnina* toured the country to 'inspect suitable young women, young and old, of high or low degree, write down their names, age and appearance' and bring 2,000 of them to Aleksandrovskaia Sloboda. There is a certain improbability about the number – the same number, 2,000, is always mentioned, all converging in sledges or carriages on Aleksandrovskaia Sloboda – particularly as many families would do their best to evade such a dangerous distinction, if necessary by bribing the *oprichniki*.[28]

The description of the bride-show by the two Livonian noblemen now flies into the realms of fancy:

> when all the girls had been assembled he [Ivan] looked them over, taking almost a year over it He had each girl brought into a house where she was to be most beautifully clothed. Then he entered the room with two or three confidants also dressed up in most elegant clothes, bowed to the girls, exchanged a few words, looked at them

and said farewell ... those who did not please him he used for shameful satisfactions of the flesh, gave them something and married them off to his executioners, or chased them away without pity. There remained 24, and keeping them one after another for some time, he chose 12 out of them, and when we came to Aleksandrovskaia Sloboda on 26 June 1571 he made his final choice, for himself and his son in this manner: they had to remove all their ornaments and clothes and allow themselves to be seen naked without any difficulty or resistance.

His physician, Dr Bomelius, who had the reputation of a magus, was present and he had to 'inspect their urine in a glass and define and explain its nature, qualities and health' (this was a classical method of diagnosis at the time). After this performance Ivan chose one, Marfa Sobakina, for himself, and his son Ivan chose another, E.B. Saburova. The two Livonians conclude somewhat superciliously that they did not think it necessary to describe the barbarous customs used in the Tsar's wedding having already seen and heard them at his previous wedding with Maria Temriukovna.[29] It may be to events at this wedding that Polish envoys were referring when they expressed their shocked surprise at the unseemly and coarse pranks of the Tsar's jester, who crawled about on his hands and knees frightening the respectable *zemshchina* boyars by turning his naked buttocks to them.[30] It was to be the shortest lived of Ivan's many marriages.

While Ivan was making up his mind which of the beautiful ladies he wished to marry he was also trying to wriggle out of the humiliating trap into which he had fallen when he fled from Moscow, and shifted the blame for the burning of the city by the Crimeans onto the shoulders of others, making it clear to the army that they could point their fingers at his generals. For a leader of the defence of true Christianity against the Moslems, his hasty withdrawal did not look too good. Several of his commanders including Prince I.F. Mstislavsky were arrested and admitted that they had treasonably assisted the godless Crimean Khan and were thus responsible for the death of many good men and the burning of the city.[31] But Mstislavsky was only disgraced, not executed, though he was compelled to secure guarantors who pledged their heads and 40,000 rubles. The accusations against him seem undoubtedly to have been concerted with the Tsar. They hung over his head for a few years and he was required to give fresh sureties. But he was soon given a new command, and appointed *voevoda* of Novgorod, where Ivan was now establishing his residence until the Tatar danger had been conjured and where parts of the lands of the city were taken into the *oprichnina*.[32]

Indeed Moscow was uninhabitable. It took months to clear away the debris caused by the fire; merchants and craftsmen were imported from the principal urban centres throughout Russia; in October 1571 depopulated Novgorod had to send 100 families of merchants to Moscow. The city was laid out on a new and different plan, paying more attention to fortifications, but it took a long time to rebuild the Kremlin and the new walls.

Soon after Ivan's betrothal, Marfa began to fail; it was said that her mother had given her a magic potion to ensure her fertility. Ivan went ahead with the wedding in the hope that marriage might improve Marfa's health, and it took place on 28 October 1571 in Aleksandrovskaia Sloboda, while Ivan Ivanovich's wedding followed on 4 November. Maliuta Skuratov was the Tsaritsa's attendant with his son-in-law, Boris Godunov, who made his first appearance on a stage he was to occupy so prominently. Marfa died a few days after the wedding. This was a shattering blow to Ivan, not so much because of the loss of a beloved wife, but because obviously she had been poisoned within a fastness which he considered impregnable and where he was surrounded by his loyal servitors. The machinery of investigation was immediately set in motion and Ivan set about finding a new bride and solving the serious religious problem which now faced him: had he, or had he not been truly married to Marfa Sobakina? Had the marriage been consummated?[33] These were problems which had to be put before a Church Council for ever since the Church Council of 920 in the days of the Emperor Leo VI it had been categorically laid down that no Christian could marry for a fourth time. (This did not stop Leo VI from marrying a fourth wife.)

The Swedish embassy sent in 1569 was still languishing in very straitened circumstances in Murom when at last, starved and ill, after fourteen months in detention, and having lost fifteen of their number to the plague, they were swept off to Klin on 28 November 1571. There Ivan awaited them with his new secretaries of the Office of Foreign Affairs, the Shchelkalov brothers, on the way to Novgorod which was to be his base for renewed war in Livonia and for the attacks he was planning to make on the Finnish coast of Sweden.[34] On 9 January 1572 Ivan addressed the Swedes through the Shchelkalovs in arrogant and undiplomatic language, accusing them of failing to display proper respect to his counsellors, and demeaning his majesty by refusing to open their business to them. The insults allegedly inflicted on his envoy Vorontsov in 1568 were the reasons for their present detention in

Russia, and what was more Ivan was preparing to attack and devastate their country.

On 11 December, a Swedish courier who had been sent to join Juusten in Murom in Russia was ordered to depart for Sweden, to 'urge the king to admit his guilt and beg for forgiveness' and to persuade John III to send fresh envoys to Russia to entreat the Tsar not to invade Finland. On 12 January 1572 they were allowed a brief meeting with the Tsar in the street. The Swedish party fell on their knees, while Ivan gave them a complete verbal account of the past relations between Russia and Sweden, notably the way Juusten's embassy

> chose to negotiate in a manner unlike the one followed by former kings of the Swedish realm . . . We could not brook your insolence . . . It was not us who sent our envoys to fetch the sister of the Polish king, Catherine, but you led us into it by the promises and letters we received from your envoys . . . they told us that John had died, childless, and without heirs. Therefore we asked for his widow to be given to us . . . Believing in your lying tales we sent envoys to Sweden where they were ill-treated and fed like convicts.

Ivan then put forward a series of extremely offensive demands, namely that John should give up any claim to Reval, pay 10,000 Joachimsthaler in compensation for the attack on the Russian envoys, provide 200 or 300 cavalry or infantry when required, surrender any silver mines he might own along the Finnish border, and accept that the Russian Tsar should style himself Lord of Sweden. Thus far Juusten's account of the Russian demands; the Russian version puts it somewhat differently: John should send a model of the Swedish coat-of-arms which would be incorporated in the Russian royal seal – a clear acknowledgement of Russian overlordship.[35]

After further talks in Novgorod, and fervent appeals from the Swedish envoys to the Tsar's sons and to his boyars to intercede for them and protect Sweden from attack by his army, they were received in solemn audience and prostrated themselves to the ground before the Tsar who observed sardonically that 'as a Christian prince and lord he did not require us to throw ourselves to the ground before him'. Ivan continued his previous discourse, reverting to the negotiations with Erik for the surrender of Catherine 'who was then Duke John's widow', an assertion that Ivan and everyone else knew was false at the time and since. Finally Ivan acknowledged that he had given way to the appeals of his sons and would not visit his wrath on Sweden, and would allow the envoys to return to Stockholm, if their King came to his senses and ceded all Livonia to Ivan as his patrimony. If he refused it would be war. Ivan then graciously invited the envoys to dine (it was an excellent repast), himself poured them wine and gave them his hand to kiss.[36] The envoys returned to Stockholm (leaving the unfortunate Juusten behind) where King John contemptuously rejected Ivan's terms and war now broke out on the frontiers between Russia and Sweden in Livonia and on the Finnish border, and was carried on for many years.

As far as relationships with England were concerned the ball was at present in Elizabeth's court. Not only had Ivan revoked, in October 1570, all the privileges he had granted to the Russia Company, in December 1570 he had seized all the company's goods. He explained to Elizabeth that Russia had done without English goods in the past and could do so again. Elizabeth now took the obvious course of complying with Ivan's repeated request to send 'Anthonie' as her ambassador, who was further in the Tsar's confidence than any other Englishman.

Jenkinson, carrying some written, but also secret verbal, instructions, duly arrived in Russia on 26 July 1571.[37] Some of the background to Ivan's displeasure was now discovered by him, namely Savin's ill-natured and unjustified reports of the way he had been treated in England.[38] The mystery of Ivan's demand that Elizabeth's 'Council' should countersign every paragraph addressed by Elizabeth to Ivan was now explained: as Ivan put it,

> as afore this we sent you our nobleman Andrey Grigor'evich Savin about some affair and you transmitted this affair to your councellors and did not treat this affairs yourself because of your maidenly state. And your counsellors set aside this great affair and did deal about boorish merchant affairs and by this cause this affair came to nothing.[39]

In his first dispatch home, Jenkinson painted a very dark picture of the situation he found which is worth mentioning, because he was less xenophobic than most of the English envoys to Russia. He was clearly briefed by English members of the Company in Kholmogory and Vologda. The company had suffered as a result of the behaviour of a number of interlopers, i.e. renegade English who traded in Russia though they were not members of the Company, as a result of which Ivan had admitted other nations to what had previously been an English monopoly. Jenkinson gave a horrifying account of the ravages of the recent famine and plague in north-east Russia, which delayed his messenger and his own journey, and also reported that the Tsar had recently put to death 'by soundry torments' a large number of people, evidently a reference to the executions of July 1570. He described the Russian defeat by the Crimean Tatars and the destruction of much of Moscow by fire as 'a juste punyshment of God for such a wycked natyon'.[40] Presumably because Ivan was busy, Jenkinson did not in fact see him until some eight months after his arrival, on 23 March 1572 in Aleksandrovskaia Sloboda.

Jenkinson was given a proper formal reception with fulsome enquiries after Elizabeth's health, in the presence of Ivan's splendidly attired boyars, who were then dismissed, leaving the Tsar and the ambasssador alone with the chief secretary, presumably Andrei Shchelkalov. Ivan explained that having confided his policy to 'Anthonie' in 1567 he had expected Jenkinson to return as ambassador, but other people had always turned up. Ivan was very gracious to Jenkinson, who, at the banquet, was sent food from his table. After each side had argued its case, but without any decision being taken, Jenkinson was dismissed and told to wait for a reply as Ivan was about to fulfil his Easter obligations. He was sent to wait for Ivan in Tver', and finally saw him again on 13 May 1572 in Staritsa. He was again received formally by the Tsar 'with a riche crowne upon his head' and in the presence of his son and surrounded by his boyars. Ivan explained that his displeasure had been aroused by the failure of Elizabeth to send an ambassador who would be authorized to conclude on his secret affairs at a time when Ivan was ' much grieved' at the evil behaviour of the English merchants. Now he was satisfied with what Jenkinson told him of Elizabeth's disposition, but because the 'princely and secret affaires were not finished to our contentation' he would now 'leave all those matters and set them aside for the time . . . and would renew the privileges of the English merchants', though he did not renew them in full. Jenkinson was offered the imperial hand to kiss and Ivan served him 'to drinke with his own hande'.[41]

Jenkinson left for England in July and had arrived by September 1572. Ivan sent a letter to Elizabeth by him confirming that he was leaving aside 'the business you wrote to us in your secret letter'. Jenkinson departed while Ivan was in daily expectation of a further major assault by the Khan of Crimea, and of news of the death of Sigismund Augustus, which was now known to be imminent. This may have led him to be less exacting in his negotiations with Elizabeth. Clearly relations had been restored to their former harmony, but the reason was the change in Ivan's policy. The Tsar dropped for the time being the proposal for a formal alliance (not much use against the Crimeans). He also dropped the formal demand for mutual asylum in England and in Russia respectively, which Elizabeth would not make as he required it, i.e., for herself. Yet Elizabeth had maintained the position that she would not take the part of his enemies against him and would endeavour to maintain supplies of such goods as England never exported to anyone else, i.e., arms, by the northern route, thus evading the Swedish and Polish privateers off Narva. But Ivan did raise the matter of the report that some English subjects were joining the Swedes in fighting against the Russians.[42] At the same time he was preparing for hostilities with Sweden, by raiding the Finnish coasts, with a force commanded by Sain Bulat, Khan of Kasimov.

Ivan had taken a number of steps to repopulate the devastated city of Novgorod by the forcible resettlement of dwellers from other parts of the old Republic but, after the demotion of Archbishop Pimen, he left it for two years without an archbishop, a very humiliating situation for the city which had a very special relationship with the Church, and where the senior ecclesiastic wore the legendary white cowl. During this period the Tsar removed from the jurisdiction of the house of St Sophia (Novgorod's cathedral) many of the lands of the north which had previously belonged to the Republic of Novgorod and which were now handed over to the bishopric of Vologda in the *oprichnina*. Towards the end of 1571 Archimandrite Leonid, a man already closely associated with the *oprichnina*, was appointed to the see and proceeded to milk it for all it was worth, relying on his closeness to the Tsar, who in turn prepared for his stay in Novgorod by somewhat more yielding treatment of the Church and by the restoration of some of the icons looted in January 1570.[43]

The two Livonian advisers of Ivan, Taube and Kruse, now gave up any hope of success in their aims of achieving, under Ivan's suzerainty, an autonomous Livonian principality through King Magnus, and entered upon secret talks with the Lithuanians. They planned to seize the town of Dorpat in Livonia on 21 October 1571 and hand it over to Sigismund Augustus, in exchange for grants of land and status similar to those they had enjoyed in Russia.[44] Unfortunately for them the rising they organized was put down almost at once by the Russian garrison, and the two men had to flee to Lithuania.

Waiting anxiously in Novgorod for the Crimeans' next move Ivan had greatly impaired the efficiency and the trustworthiness of the *oprichniki* and the armed forces in general by the purge of the bulk of the boyars which he had carried out on the urging of Maliuta Skuratov, and their replacement by mainly younger men of princely families. Taube and

Kruse condemn the young princes surrounding Ivan as a lot of 'good for nothings' (*rotozei*) introduced to spruce up the façade of the *oprichnina* before the foreigners, while the heads of *prikazy* remained mostly unchanged. Skuratov, and his relative Bogdan Bel'sky (no connection with the princely Lithuanian Bel'skys who died out in the fire of Moscow in 1571), continued in charge – 'those disgusting parasites and maniacs', according to Kurbsky, though V.G. Griaznoi was disgraced and deprived of his estates, and then was unlucky enough to be taken prisoner by the Crimean Tatars.[45] To his appeals to the Tsar to be ransomed from captivity, Ivan replied in his usual taunting and sarcastic tone: ' Did you believe it was the same thing to make jokes in the Crimea as when you are eating with me?'[46]

Even the *oprichniki* began to feel uncertainty about their relations with the Tsar, who had begun occasionally to eliminate men who had made exceptionally outrageous and illegal demands.[47] Though Maliuta Skuratov seemed to have become Ivan's principal adviser, both in political and in domestic affairs, the Tsar also relied a great deal on his chosen astrologer, magus and physician, Dr Bomelius. However, the personal policy of Ivan remains perplexing: there was no system in his elimination of 'dangerous' or useless boyars. For instance the brother-in-law of Vladimir of Staritsa, Prince N.P. Odoevsky, one of the Upper Oka princes on the borders of Lithuania, whose sister had been forced to take poison, was promoted in the army, made a boyar and a member of the *oprichnina* Council soon after May 1571. In early 1570 V.A. Buturlin had been executed in Novgorod; his brother D.A. Buturlin was invited to the Tsar's wedding in October 1571.[18]

Returning to Aleksandrovskaia Sloboda in January 1572, Ivan continued to devote much time and thought to warding off the expected renewed attack by the Crimeans, again supported by Ottoman forces, and to strengthening his support or alliances on the Polish-Lithuanian and English fronts, while his forces continued their raids on the Swedish border. In the years 1571 to 1572 the imminent death of Sigismund Augustus caused more and more tension between the powers as different candidates for the succession were considered in advance both in Russia and in the Commonwealth. The great Lithuanian magnates, still smarting under the forcible transfer of Podolia and Volhynia to Poland, before the Union of Lublin, inclined towards a Habsburg candidate, Archduke Ernst, younger brother of the Emperor Maximilian II (favourite nephew and brother-in-law of Philip II and educated largely in Spain) in secret talks in spring 1572. Ernst, aged nineteen, would marry the princess Anna Jagiellonka then aged forty-five (b. 1527), but

Maximilian turned the proposal down, and in any case many in the Commonwealth doubted whether the Empire had sufficient military power to defend it against the Tatar raids in the south which were now merging into a systematic Ottoman assault on south-eastern Europe into which Lithuania did not wish to be drawn.[49] A Russian candidate might provide stronger military support, but the Lithuanians knew enough about Tsar Ivan and Ivan Ivanovich to prefer the Tsar's younger son, Fedor, with many restrictions designed to preserve their rights and freedoms and with a redistribution of the old Kievan lands between the two powers, assuring the lion's share to Lithuania. Sigismund Augustus was anxious to maintain the truce with Russia, and in response to a request from Ivan he sent ambassadors to treat with him in the spring of 1572.

Military problems were superseded by domestic issues while Ivan argued before a Church Council on 28 April 1572 that he had not consummated his marriage with Marfa Sobakina, and that she was still a virgin when she died. There had been no marriage, and thus the prohibition of a fourth marriage did not apply to him. He declared that in view of the discord in the Christian world, and his motherless children he had decided to marry again a fourth time. He took advantage of the death of the Metropolitan, Kyrill, on 8 February 1572, and the fact that the Church therefore had no leader, to persuade the Church Council to give him an exclusive permission to enter on a fourth marriage with Anna Koltovskaia. He was, however, subjected to a penance, namely that he should not enter a church for a year until Easter and after a year he should attend services only at the door with other sinners, remaining on his knees, and only in the third year should he be admitted into the building and be allowed by his confessor to take communion at Easter.[50] There does not appear to have been a bride-show. The new bride may have been included in the previous parade, or may have been presented to the Tsar in some other way. The marriage took place in May 1572, and in June Ivan left for Novgorod where he intended to sit out the impending battle with the Crimeans.

The Khan, with Crimean and Nogai forces, appeared on the banks of the Oka on 27 July 1572. The main Russian corps was placed under Mikhail Vorotynsky, in Serpukhov, and other *voevodas* were drawn both from the *zemshchina* and from the *oprichnina* such as Prince D. Khvorostinin. After fierce fighting in a pitched battle the Crimeans broke through the Russian defences, and Devlet Girey, with the whole Tatar army streamed over the Oka and advanced on Moscow. The pursuing Russians managed to halt them some thirty-five *versts* from Moscow at a place called Molodi. This was clearly no sudden tip and run raid, in the usual Tatar style, but a determined assault with the ultimate conquest of the Lower Volga in mind, supported by a major power, the Ottoman Empire.[51] It was a serious threat, particularly in view of the depleted Russian army, the plague and the famine which had been endemic for the last two years and the general shortage of military and food supplies because of the burning of Moscow. The banks of the Oka River were lined with palisades to shelter the harquebusiers while they fired on the advancing Tatars.[52] The Russian armies were divided into the usual formation of five regiments, and in addition they brought with them a frequently used contrivance, the *guliai-goroda* (walking town), the prefabricated moveable fortress on wheels whose wooden sections were carried on waggons and could be bolted together, and behind which the Russian troops could shelter while they bombarded the enemy with artillery.[53]

Serious fighting began again on 30 July. It lasted several days, with intervals, and was very fierce, much of it hand to hand unlike the usual battles with the Tatars. The Russians were able to set up the *guliai-goroda* which gave shelter to their artillery and harquebus forces against the rain of arrows from the Tatar cavalry. A service noble, from Suzdal', with the very non-Russian name of Temir Adalykin, was able to take the murza Divey, one of the leading Tatar commanders, prisoner. The Tatars replied with a fierce assault and there were heavy casualties on both sides. But Vorotynsky manoeuvred in such a way as to take the Tatars in the rear; he left the *guliai-gorod* to be used by the commander from the *oprichnina*, Prince D.I. Khvorostinin with his gunners and a small force of mercenary Germans, and moved from its shelter to take the Crimean forces in the rear at the same time as Khvorostinin threw himself upon them. The Tatars did not withstand this double assault, two of the Khan's sons were killed and many high officials. Traditionally Vorotynsky is given credit for the victory, though Skrynnikov considers that he was appointed to lead the army only because of his rank, and that the victory was really due to the younger Khvorostinin. But there was another candidate for the honour of achieving victory: the thirteenth-century martyred miracle-worker, Prince Mikhail of Chernigov, whose relics had recently been transferred to Moscow.[54]

Chapter XVII

The End of the Oprichnina, *and the* *Succession to the Polish-Lithuanian Crown*

On 6 August 1572 Ivan received in Novgorod the news of the crushing victory of the Russian forces over the Crimean Tatars and their Turkish allies outside Moscow, in what was in fact a joint *oprichnina* and *zemshchina* operation, and the victory was celebrated with great banquets and rejoicings; 'and on that day the church bells rang all day and until midnight and prayers were sung all night in churches and monasteries'.[1] But the victory had shown up the weakness of the *oprichniki* in the military field.

When and why, and whether, Ivan decided to abolish the *oprichnina* remains unknown. No decree was ever issued winding it up and there is no evidence of Ivan's motives in bringing its activities to an end (or for that matter for starting it up). The theory, which Zimin still espoused in 1964, was that Ivan's primary purpose had been to remedy the 'fragmentation' of the Russian state by eliminating the appanages and their princes, and extending his control over the Church and Novgorod. In fact many of the appanages had already been eliminated under Ivan III and most of the few which remained were in the hands of members of the royal family and many had been set up by Ivan IV himself.[2]

The actual process of winding up the *oprichnina* is hard to follow and historians have long been divided as to whether the old system was fully restored or whether the *oprichnina* continued to exist behind the scenes in the guise of the Tsar's *dvor* or court. Opinion now seems to be that its liquidation was genuine. The court continued, but its staff was much smaller, and the double administration of the country was gradually dismantled. Staden says, for instance, that confiscated estates were restored to their original owners because the Tsar felt they had to be conciliated, that the people from the *zemshchina* 'had resisted the Khan of Crimea, and the Grand Prince could no longer do without them'. He also says that no one was now allowed so much as to mention the name of the *oprichnina*.[3] Certainly the armed forces had suffered grievously under the terror of the last years. Of twenty high ranking commanders who had led the campaign for the conquest of Polotsk in 1563 nine had been executed in the course of the ensuing ten years, including the most distinguished.[4]

Ivan may also have decided to abolish the *oprichnina* because he thought it had outlived its usefulness, because it had already achieved his aims, or because he found that it was not an instrument of unlimited power and that such an unreliable institution could not achieve them. As a fighting force against external enemies it had proved a broken reed and the Tsar had been forced to call upon the older generation of seasoned fighters in the *zemshchina*. He may also have been struck by the fact that it had not served to save his third wife from poison, and therefore that it gave him no guarantee of security.[5]

By autumn 1572 when Ivan embarked on his campaign to put an end to Swedish pretensions, the armed forces were no longer separated into two corps under separate commanders, and officers were united under one command under the overall supervision of the military chancellery.[6] Ivan did not abandon his use of terror. But it was easier to re-establish the unification of the armed forces, even it they were not of their former quality (leaving aside Ivan's own special guard), than to set up a new administration under a body of officials now drawn from both the *oprichnina* and the *zemshchina*, both decimated over the past years. The restoration of lands confiscated from members of the *zemshchina* by *oprichniki* proved difficult and was unprofitable for the new owners who received ravaged and ruined estates from which the peasants had fled.[7] There remained moreover an abyss between the *zemshchina*, the government of the land, and the *dvor*, or court of Ivan, which could not easily be bridged.

The financial strains created by war, plague, drought, taxation and famine were also acute, particularly in the territory of Novgorod and the north-east which had suffered so much from the ravages of the *oprichniki*, the constant shifting around of landowners and the displacement, flight or death of peasants by starvation, illness or brutality. Ivan made himself unpopular by forbidding in October 1572 any form of donation of land to monasteries. It had already been forbidden, evidently in vain, and Ivan himself had broken his own law, but he now revived a prohibition which did not increase his popularity either with the monks or those able to care by donations to monasteries for the future of their souls.[8]

One piece of news reached Ivan unofficially in August which galvanized his foreign policy, and radically changed the political horizon. Sigismund II Augustus had died at last on 19 July 1572 some ten days after the battle at Molodi. His death, which rendered the succession problem in Poland actual instead of speculative, as it had been until now, may have been one of the factors which led Ivan to abolish the *oprichnina*, the existence of which he had always endeavoured to keep hidden from the Poles, on the grounds that his candidature stood more chance as the ruler of a united country than of a divided one. The fate of the Polish throne had presumably been the object of discussion in the court of Ivan but there is little evidence of preliminary planning.[9] The King's death was officially communicated to Ivan in Moscow, in October 1572, by a Commonwealth envoy, F. Voropay, who asked for the prolongation of the three-year truce between their two countries, due to expire in July 1573. The envoys also took the initiative in proposing a candidate for the throne, namely Tsarevich Fedor, in an attempt to block Ivan's election. Ivan then, for the first time, spontaneously put forward his own candidature and tried to dispel the poor impression that his treatment of members of his own court had made on the Poles.

Taking the conduct of diplomacy into his own hands, Ivan urged Voropay to arrange for ambassadors to be sent from the Commonwealth to discuss with him the terms for an offer of the throne. In a very long speech, as usual, Ivan addressed the envoys emphasizing the advantages Lithuania would enjoy from union with Russia, what a good ruler and a strong defender he would prove:

> In your land many people say that I am bad-tempered (*zloi*); it is true, I am cross-grained and angry, but let them ask, with whom am I angry? I answer I am angry with those who behave badly to me, and to those who behave well I would not hesitate to give this chain I am wearing and my clothes.

Ivan went on to account for the reputation for harshness he had acquired by his need to fight against constant treason. It was this perpetual treason which had forced him to deviate from the path he would have followed with his forces in the battle against the Tatars in 1571. As a result he explained, the Tatars threw themselves into Moscow, which could have been defended with 1,000 men, and burnt it. But if the great men will not fight how can one expect the little men to do so? 'Do they not execute traitors in your country?' he asked the Commonwealth envoys. If he were offered the crown he would respect the liberties of the citizens of the Commonwealth and even increase them. They would see how wicked and how kind he could be. He offered an amnesty to those Russians who had deserted Moscow for Lithuania –

> Kurbsky came to you. He deprived him (pointing to his eldest son) of his mother, and me of my wife. And God be my witness, I intended only to deprive him of his boyar rank and his lands, and then forgive him, and had no intention of executing him. But he took fright and fled to Lithuania.

As regards Livonia, added Ivan, 'If I become your lord then Livonia, Moscow, Novgorod, Pskov, it will be all one.' He did not wish one of his sons to be chosen, for they were to him like his two eyes, and anyhow they were too young to stand alone. As regards religion, there were adherents of Martin Luther in the Commonwealth who destroyed icons, and did not want him as their lord. 'But I will say nothing about them because Holy Writ has been given to us not for brawling and quarrelling but for peace and submission.'[10]

At this time Ivan was evidently wishing that he himself should be elected to the throne, but he wanted to cleanse his reputation from the charge of cowardice he had displayed before the battle with the Tatars in May 1571, and also to clear his name of the charge of cruelty towards his boyars. What was not discussed in any of these meetings between Ivan and the envoys was the means by which the government of the two or the three parts of the new united kingdom was to be organized, what relationship there would be, could there be, between the Boyar Council and Ivan's *dvor* on the one hand, and the Commonwealth Senate, Diet and dietines on the other.

One might think that a reputation for ruthlessness and the arbitrary use of power would make Ivan an unlikely choice for the Polish *szlachta* as ruler, but for some years now there had been a substantial rift between the run-of-the-mill nobles in both Poland and Lithuania and their respective magnates who, particularly in Lithuania, conducted themselves oppressively towards the poorer nobles. But Ivan was not prepared to be considered as one of many candidates however distinguished; he wished to be invited, and therefore did not send his own ambassadors to take part in the canvassing at the election *Sejm* in the Commonwealth.

Before he left Moscow, Ivan had another little matter to clear up, the relegation to a convent of his fourth wife, Anna Koltovskaia, which took place in October 1572. Nothing is known of the reasons for the separation.

Back in Novgorod, where Ivan now stayed more frequently, since Moscow, after the fire, was unliveable in, he had to reconstruct his court. Various buildings and palaces were prepared for his use, and huge stables for his horses, necessary for the cavalry ravaging the Finnish coasts in the course of the prosecution of the war against Sweden. But on 6 January 1573 he lost one of his most faithful servants. In the course of the renewed campaign against Sweden which Ivan had promised to John III, a widely vaunted attack on a Swedish held fort in Livonia, Paida, took place, in which King Magnus of Livonia and Sain Bulat Bekbulatovich, the Khan of Kasimov, took part as commanders of substantial Russian forces. The Russian attack was unexpected and the Swedish and Estonian forces were caught celebrating the feast of Epiphany, at the end of the Christmas festivities. The Russians advanced, destroying houses, killing the inhabitants and raping the women, meeting with practically no opposition. But when the local people put up some resistance, Maliuta Skuratov Bel'sky, to give him his full name, was killed. Ivan greeted his loss with grief and anger, and had his body conveyed to the monastery of Iosif of Volokolamsk where his family was buried, with a goodly sum of money to pray for him, and burnt all his Swedish and German prisoners alive.[11] Though never a boyar, Maliuta Skuratov had long been the lynchpin of Ivan's more ruthless and sordid undertakings. Perhaps his last service to Ivan was the drowning of a sizeable number of his subjects in the river Volkhov in unknown circumstances.[12]

The Boyar Council, which was now again united, was reconstructed in 1573 and consisted of fifteen boyars and six *okol'nichi*, an unusually large number, but it was soon to be reduced. Five boyars had come over from the *oprichnina*, including the distinguished military commander, Prince N.R. Odoevsky, brother of Vladimir of Staritsa's poisoned wife, uncle of her dead child. Nine boyars had belonged to the *zemshchina*. Until recently the senior member of the Council, though never a boyar, had been a baptized Tatar, Prince Mikhail Kaibulatovich, son of the one-time Khan of Astrakhan' (who was married to a Sheremeteva and hence a cousin by marriage to the Tsarevich Ivan). He had recently died and the senior boyar was again the indestructible Prince I.F. Mstislavsky. Prince M.I. Vorotynsky was also a member together with the boyars M.Ia. Morozov and N.R. Iur'ev Zakhar'in (Tsaritsa Anastasia's brother, Nikita Romanovich). The other hero of the defeat of Devlet Girey outside Moscow in July 1572, Prince D.I. Khvorostinin, was an *okol'nichi* who had served in the *oprichnina*.

The generals who had been victorious in summer 1572 over the hordes of Devlet Girey did not enjoy their status for long. Vorotynsky and Odoevsky were sent south to man the frontier on the banks of the Oka river against a possible resurgence of the Crimean army. It did not come but in May or June 1573 the two generals together with a third distinguished military figure, the boyar Mikhail I. Morozov, were executed in mysterious circumstances. Vorotynsky had had a chequered history: not only had he already once been disgraced in 1562 and lost his ancient appanage lands on the Lithuanian border (though he was granted different lands when he returned to favour in 1566)[13] but he had also been one of the princes involved in the mysterious episode of the letters allegedly written to Sigismund Augustus, in 1567, coinciding with the treasonable plot attributed to Ivan Fedorov, letters which the Tsar had possibly drafted himself in the name of his boyars.[14] Though he had been mainly responsible for the decisive Russian victory over the Crimeans in 1572, Ivan clearly did not trust Vorotynsky, and perhaps did not like him. His appanage had provided him with an income but also with a substantial retinue of service gentry. He was apparently an imposing figure and a respected military commander, responsible for devising the efficient system of frontier guards which protected the Russian borders against deserters and immigrants. After his great victory, Ivan restored to him the title of *sluga* or servant of the Tsar which he had borne as had Ivan Petrovich Fedorov in his time, and he became leader of the Boyar Council, while Mstislavsky was temporarily discredited for having admitted to betraying Russia to the Crimeans in 1571.[15]

Some time in spring 1573 the three commanders were arrested. Morozov was executed at once in Moscow together with his wife and two sons.[16] Kurbsky, writing in the 1570s, states that a servant of Vorotynsky's had denounced his master to Ivan, saying that he wanted to bewitch the Tsar and accusing him of procuring whispering women to cast a spell over him.[17] Vorotynsky had replied with dignity: 'I have not learned, oh Tsar, nor have I received the custom from my ancestors, to practise magic and to believe in devilry.' Whereupon he was tied to stakes, and roasted between two slow fires, then after this lengthy ordeal in which Ivan himself is said to have taken part, he was removed to the prison in the monastery of Beloozero, expiring on the way. Odoevsky was tortured in a different but equally horrible way and died at once. V. Veselovsky suggests that they were charged with some offence against military directives.[18] Other reports suggest that they had been in touch with the Crimeans in order to betray Russia. And there is evidence of a constant flood of denunciations from servants or bondsmen, obtained under torture directed by Ivan himself, charging these three distinguished warriors against the Crimean Tatars with having secretly indicated to the enemy the way to elude the Russian troops. That the denunciations were made after Ivan had already executed his generals did not deter the Tsar from pursuing his inquiries.

Kurbsky states that Ivan was moved by the desire to abolish the appanages and confiscate the wealth of these boyars, and this seems the most probable explanation for these executions though not for the cruel forms they took. They may well have been connected with Ivan's ultimate policy of eliminating any trace of 'appanage' holdings, particularly on the Lithuanian border. Bel'sky's appanage had been confiscated when he had attempted to flee to Lithuania in 1562 but he had been saved by the intervention of Metropolitan Makarii, and by a substantial collective surety. When he died, with all his family, in the fire in Moscow all his lands were escheated to the Crown. The far wealthier Mstislavsky was persuaded – or perhaps volunteered – to be put forward as the scapegoat for the defeat of the Russian army by the Crimeans in 1571. The collective guarantees for him were signed by the whole of the Holy *Sobor*, and 274 service gentry of various ranks. At any rate Mstislavsky did not suffer for his intrepidity which was widely known.[19]

However there is another element to this mysterious incident. For some time Dr Eliseus Bomelius had been acquiring a great influence over the Tsar. Kurbsky follows his account of the death of Vorotynsky with a diatribe against the practice of magic in the Tsar's family, going back to his father Vasily III and that 'law-breaking wife of his [Elena Glinskaia]' who sought wicked magicians everywhere to render them fertile, sending hither and thither for sorceresses, to Finland and among the wild Lapps, and he condemns this sinful behaviour, for 'there are no spells without denial of God and without agreement with the devil'.[20] By coincidence, it was on 11 November 1572 that a brilliant star, a supernova, suddenly appeared in the constellation of Cassiopeia, and sent the whole world of astrologers rushing for their stargazing instruments. The star was visible in London to John Dee and in Denmark to Tycho Brahe, and no doubt in darkest Russia it would shine with great brilliance. Bomelius was, of course, an astrologer and he would be asked to interpret the meaning of this apparition for a public which believed in magic and witchcraft.

The references to witchcraft might be regarded as inventions of the prejudiced Kurbsky were there not other sources which mention the extent of the influence of Bomelius on Ivan and the prevalence of rumours of sorcery at court. Horsey calls Bomelius a 'cozening imposter, doctor of physic in England, a rare mathematician, magician'; Ivan had inquired of him 'What years Queen Elizabeth was of, what likely of success there might be if he should be a suitor unto her for himself.' He was 'much disheartened because he had two wives living . . . but presently puts his last wife into a nunnery to live there as dead to the world'.[21]

Horsey is slapdash and haphazard; he confuses dates and often fantasizes. Yet there is usually a kernel of truth in what he reports and these words may have some truth in them. It is generally assumed that Ivan never aspired to the hand of Elizabeth herself but only – and that was in the 1580s – to the hand of a relative of hers. Yet there are obscure references in the reports of Anthony Jenkinson in the 1560s to the intensely secret matters (see above, Chapter XVI, p. 273) he was reporting on, which may possibly have included a marriage proposal to Elizabeth herself at a time when Ivan was actually a widower. After all, Ivan 'magnified himself, his person, his wisdom, greatness and riches above all other princes', why should he not, like Erik XIV of Sweden in his time, offer for the hand of the sole reigning queen in Europe? This is a much more convincing secret matter than an alliance or an offer of mutual refuge in each other's country in the event of risings against them. And in October 1572 Ivan had got rid of his new wife, Anna Koltovskaia, by sending her to a convent, as Horsey reports.

Both the Tsar and the magnates of the Commonwealth had had time to reflect on the problems which might arise as a result of the death of Sigismund Augustus. The Lithuanian magnates still favoured Tsarevich Fedor, but some of them feared that the Polish nobility might make their own independent approach to Ivan himself. The various groups in the Commonwealth were divided not only by social and religious background, but by the future status of the Ukrainian lands which Sigismund Augustus had ceded from Lithuania to Poland in 1569, and which the Lithuanians wished to recover. Much of the manoeuvring was carried out in secrecy, because under the terms of the Union of Lublin, election to the Lithuanian grand princely throne implied a future election to the royal Polish throne.

Ivan reacted cautiously at first, fearful that election to one throne only might lead to war, but he expressed the desire to continue the talks.[22] Whereupon towards the end of February 1573 a new Lithuanian embassy, led by M. Haraburda, arrived in Novgorod in response to the Tsar's request, with a safe conduct from Ivan. The Lithuanian magnates, well informed about Ivan's activities in Russia through their diplomatic connexions, constant contacts with Russian émigrés, notably Kurbsky, and the extensive range of pamphlets and broadsheets published in

Germany on the sufferings of the Livonians (and the Russians), were horrified at the thought of a tyrant like Ivan on the throne of Lithuania. It is around this time that Kurbsky's *History of the Grand Prince of Moscow* was written, as part of the prince's own campaign against Ivan.[23] The Lithuanian magnates now decided to propose that Tsarevich Fedor should be immediately adopted as heir and should occupy the Lithuanian throne (the Union of Lublin was frequently disregarded at this time); the Tsar himself and both his sons should swear, in writing, to observe the Lithuanian liberties and a perpetual peace should be signed between the two powers to secure which the Russians would have to cede Novgorod and return Polotsk and Smolensk and a few other places to Lithuania. The Tsar should endow the future King of the Commonwealth with a suitable number of goodly properties, and the future Russian ruler of Lithuania would also have to convert to Catholicism.

In talks with the Tsar the suggestion of a separate election to the grand princely throne was dropped, but Haraburda underlined the difficulties that would face Ivan as ruler of both Russia and the Commonwealth. He would need to travel constantly between them; justice would be suspended in the Commonwealth for long periods, since courts could not sit in the absence of the King; treason might break out behind his back when Ivan was out of Russia, and it would be difficult for him to hold on to distant lands like Kazan' and Astrakhan'. And in any case he could not be crowned until he had been converted to Catholicism. Hence the best Russian candidate would be Tsarevich Fedor whose absence from Russia would not affect its government.

The Lithuanians clearly conceived that the projected union between Lithuania and Russia would endow Russia with lands (i.e., the whole Grand Principality of Lithuania) for which Lithuania should be compensated with lands ceded by Russia. They were in fact ultimately striving to avoid the union of the two crowns under one effective ruler and believed that they had ensured it by the choice of the inadequate Fedor, who at that time was in any case only sixteen (b. 1557).[24] There does not seem to have been any very intensive discussion of the nature of the political union between the two powers which would inevitably follow on the choice of a ruling sovereign, like Ivan, and a neighbour at that, as King of Poland–Lithuania, a problem which would not arise in the case of mere princes like the Archduke Ernst of Habsburg or Henri de Valois, whose name had now entered the lists, or indeed of Tsarevich Fedor of Russia. Haraburda again succeeded in negotiating a further prolongation of the truce between the two powers, which suited Ivan who was still energetically pursuing his vendetta against John III of Sweden.[25]

But these conditions put forward by Haraburda, speaking for the Lithuanian magnates, came as a shock to the Tsar.[26] In reply, he declared that he saw no point in reducing the lands of what was to become his own Crown by ceding Russian lands to himself as the new King of Poland–Lithuania, particularly if the Commonwealth might not continue to belong to his dynasty, or be joined with Russia in an elective monarchy. In any case Fedor was too young to reign alone and Ivan did not propose to let him go. In one of his fits of arrogance, Ivan declared:

> We know that the Emperor and the King of France have sent [messengers] to you, they are not an example for us, for apart from us and the Sultan of Turkey there is no lord in any single state whose dynasty has been in power uninterruptedly for two hundred years; that is why they demand to be treated with deference; and we have been lords of our state since the days of Augustus Caesar at the dawn of time as everyone knows. The crown of Poland and the Grand Principality of Lithuania are not naked (*golye*) and one can survive there, and our son is not a maid who needs a dowry.

Reverting to one of his ancient grievances Ivan continued: 'if the lords of the council in the Commonwealth want our friendship let them first of all write out our Tsarish title in full, because we have inherited this title from our ancestors, and did not take it from strangers'. Ivan now insisted again that if Fedor should die and leave heirs they should inherit Lithuania and Poland, and if Fedor did not have children, Poland and Lithuania should remain with his, Ivan's, dynasty – in this running counter to one of the basic tenets of the Polish-Lithuanian constitution, namely the right to elect their King. As regards a perpetual peace between the two realms, it could be arranged on the following conditions: Polotsk and its surroundings and Courland would go to Lithuania, and Livonia, including Riga, to Moscow, with the frontier on the Dvina.[27]

Should the Commonwealth elect the son of the Holy Roman Emperor, continued Ivan, we are prepared to live with him as with our son Fedor. But I know, Ivan told the Lithuanian envoy Haraburda, that some in Poland wish me to be King. Haraburda again pointed out the difficulties of journeying from country to country, and the problems of joint defence. On the next day, the Tsar repeated that he would like to reign over all three states, spending some time in each of them. The

Commonwealth would have to accept the titulature proposed by Ivan, namely first the kingdom (*korolevstvo*) of Moscow, then the crown of Poland and the Grand Principality of Lithuania which would stand as one and defend themselves against all enemies; and Kiev was to be ceded to Russia and be added to the Tsarist titulature, in the correct place, before Vladimir.[28] As ruler, Ivan would be called 'by the grace of God, Lord, Tsar and Grand Prince Ivan Vasil'evich of all Rus' and of Kiev, Vladimir, Moscow, King of Poland and Grand Prince of Lithuania, Grand Prince of Russia, of Great Novgorod, Tsar of Kazan', and Astrakhan', followed by a list of the Russian, Polish and Lithuanian provinces (*oblasti*) according to their seniority, and Polotsk and Courland would be joined to Lithuania, while Livonia would go to Russia. There was also the ticklish problem of precedence should Tsarevich Fedor be elected to the throne of the Commonwealth. Where would he stand in relation to his father the Tsar of Russia? Who would take precedence?

Ivan concluded by asserting the right of the new, Russian, ruler of the Commonwealth to build orthodox churches and appoint ecclesiastics, and should he wish to retire to a monastery in his old age, then the whole land, including the Polish-Lithuanian lords, would choose a successor from among his sons. And if, said Ivan, the Grand Principality of Lithuania alone wished to elect him as ruler, this would suit him even better, Russia could be joined to Lithuania as Poland and Lithuania had been joined. The Lithuanian lands annexed to Poland in 1569 should be returned to Lithuania, except for Kiev. And if they elected him to the Grand Principality of Lithuania alone, let them not fear Poland, he would reconcile the two countries. Moreover, he himself needed to marry, and his two sons were nearly of marriageable age;[29] let the Poles and Lithuanians allow their girls to be examined as possible brides, for it was the Russian custom to choose a wife among their subjects. However, Ivan had also at one stage suggested that he was getting old and would find it difficult to govern three large realms; it would be more peaceful for him if the Poles and Lithuanians elected the Archduke Ernst, and signed a perpetual peace with Russia.[30]

Whether Ivan really wanted the Polish-Lithuanian crown, or thought that his election was a practical possibility is open to question. His remark to Haraburda that he would prefer to be elected by the Lithuanian principality alone, without Poland, is revealing. 'But tell the lords of the council,' he added, 'not to elect a Frenchman as king, for he will be more inclined to favour the Turks, than the Christians; and if you, the Lithuanians, elect a Frenchman, then I will have to think about you.' Subsequently two members of Ivan's *dvor*, and the two brothers Shchelkalov who headed the Office of Foreign Affairs told Haraburda that Ivan would take care of (i.e. restrain) Poland if the Lithuanians agreed to act alone.[31]

The situation was unusually complicated owing to the number of options which seemed open to the various contenders. Ivan could manoeuvre in such a way as to be elected Grand Prince of Lithuania alone, or King of Poland as well. The Lithuanian rank-and-file nobles, of whom many were Orthodox and some were Protestant, were anxious to throw off the predominance of the Lithuanian magnates, secure in their huge estates and their oligarchic powers. They were therefore willing to consider the election of Ivan, which would enable them to draw on the larger resources of Russia in the constant struggle against the Tatars in the Ukrainian lands of the south and in the struggle to recover from Poland the Ukrainian lands which had been lost to the Polish Crown in 1569.[32] The magnates would only elect a Russian Tsar provided his powers were limited. Fedor would not only have to convert to Catholicism, he would also have to buckle to and study Polish, German, Italian and Latin,[33] and would receive Polotsk and a few other important forts, as Ivan ironically put it, as 'his dowry'. The Polish rank and file nobles, who were opposed of old to Habsburg authoritarianism and less familiar with Ivan, hoped to secure from the Tsar a stronger defence against the Tatars and their supporters the Turks on their southern border. A Habsburg would be of little use to them for the Emperor was in no position to defend Poland against the Turks, and his election would immediately bring down the wrath of the Ottomans on their heads – the example of the fate of Hungary was before them. Moreover the presence in Ivan's new kingdom of large numbers of Lithuanians of the same religion and speaking more or less the same language as Russians might place the Poles in a position of inferiority.

The King of Sweden, John III, with his Polish wife, seemed to offer the Commonwealth another choice, but again, Sweden was a minor power and did not have the military strength to stand up to the Tsar. There remained yet another candidate, Prince Henri of Valois, Duke of Anjou, younger brother of King Charles IX of France, now ruling, and of the latter's devotion to the catholic religion he had given recent proofs on St Bartholomew's Eve in 1572. But Henri of Anjou could promise an alliance with the strongest power in Europe, able to protect Poland against Turkish attack by military, naval and diplomatic means.

The various options were discussed at length in a war of pamphlets in which the Tsar was accused of atrocities, of being a tyrant by nature, incapable of guaranteeing the Polish and Lithuanian liberties of his new subjects. And the Tsar in turn feared, or said that he feared, that the Poles wanted his son Fedor only in order to seize him and hand him over to the Turks in order to achieve peace with them.[34]

Ultimately Ivan was not prepared to send ambassadors or envoys to canvass for him; he asserted the superiority of his rank by demanding to be invited, and refusing to mix with other candidates at the Polish *Sejm*,[35] which was summoned for January 1573. On 19 April Haraburda, who had returned from Novgorod, read out the Tsar's reply to the Lithuanian proposals. They came as a surprise to the Lithuanians: the Tsar's refusal to allow the settlement of poor Polish and Lithuanian nobles along the borders of Russia, and the demand for the cession of Kiev indicated that he intended to tear up the Union of Lublin, and to secure separate election to the Lithuanian grand princely throne. Ivan thus lost all his support in the *Sejm*. So the convocation turned to France and on 11 May 1573 proclaimed Henri of Anjou King of Poland and Grand Prince of Lithuania. But the new King was forced to sign a series of conditions, the *pacta conventa*, which guaranteed all the changes introduced into the Polish-Lithuanian constitution in the last four years, the right of all the nobles to take part in the free election of the King, and the regular convocation of the *Sejm*.[36] The Confederation of Warsaw imposed on Henri a settlement of the religious question almost unique at the time: 'We promise . . . that all of us of differing religions will keep the peace between ourselves and shed no blood.'[37]

But Anjou's election suited neither Ivan nor the Emperor Maximilian II, who were both suspicious of the amicable relations existing between France and the Ottoman Empire. This brought about a common front between Ivan and Maximilian who wrote to the Tsar bemoaning that the French King had killed several thousand of his subjects.[38] Ivan sent a messenger to Vienna urging Maximilian not to allow Henri of Valois to pass through imperial lands on his way to Poland. There were discussions between the two powers of a partition treaty by which Ivan would keep Lithuania and Maximilian Poland.[39] Similarly Ivan urged the King of Denmark, Frederick II, to place obstacles in the way of Henri's journey to Poland.[40] But Henri made his way to Poland in time and on 21 February 1574 he was crowned in Cracow. A few months later he had also become King of France, on the death of his brother Charles IX, and he fled in secret, on the night of 18/19 June 1574, from Cracow back to Paris. In law he was of course still the elected king of Poland. He was formally deposed only in May 1575, having failed to return within the year's grace granted to him.

Was Ivan disappointed at his failure to win the election? With his exalted view of the rights of a Tsar it is highly unlikely that he would ever have accepted the kind of limited sovereignty offered to him, and he certainly made it clear that while he would accept election for himself, on his death the crown of the Commonwealth should go to one or other of his sons by hereditary right, which spelled the end of election to the throne. Moreover there remained an enormous gap in the attitude to religion of the respective sides.

Ivan had stated his wish to be crowned by a metropolitan, not by an archbishop, and he was also prepared to embark on a discussion about the nature of the theological issues which separated Russia and the Commonwealth. He had demanded that in the event of his death in the Commonwealth his body should be returned to Russia in order to be buried according to Orthodox rites. But the extent of religious freedom he would in practice have been prepared to tolerate is not at all clear, and would have fallen well below the Polish imposition of religious toleration on Henri of Valois.

The news of Henri's flight back to Paris was formally communicated to Ivan in August 1574 by envoys from the Commonwealth who, at the same time, again procured a prolongation of the truce until 15 August 1576. But the Tsar had probably already received the news, and the talks about a successor to the Polish-Lithuanian crown seemed to pick up more or less where they had left off before the election of Henri, but with an even greater variety of candidates. They now included the Bohemian magnate Wilem Rozmberk (the patron of the English magus, John Dee), Alfonso II of Este, Duke of Ferrara, as well as some pretenders who had appeared in the first round like Ernst of Habsburg, and who might now be manoeuvred into leading a coalition of Russia, Poland and the Holy Roman Empire against the Ottomans. Though the magnates were unlikely to support Ivan there was some backing for his candidature again among lower Polish nobles who had derived little benefit from the brief reign of Anjou, and among the 'Ruthenes' or in modern terminology the lower rank Orthodox Belorussian and Ukrainian elements.

But all was not exactly peaceful around Ivan in Russia at this time. The repercussions of the watering down of the *oprichnina* and of the death of Maliuta Skuratov were still being felt. Ivan needed to restructure the *dvor* and he was evidently finding it more and more difficult to recruit people, either because he distrusted them or because they were reluctant to serve him. The new favourite at court was Prince B.D. Tulupov Starodubsky who was made an *okol'nichii* in 1573, and brought with him a number of members of his family; several members of the Kolychev family (to which Metropolitan Filipp had belonged) were promoted.[41] Both Tulupov and V.I. Umnoi Kolychev played an active part in the negotiations over Ivan's pretensions to the Polish throne. The Godunovs had not yet reached the degree of influence which later was to be theirs. D.I. Godunov had been appointed Chamberlain (*postel'nichii*) in charge of all Ivan's domestic arrangements, but also of all the inquiries into treason against the Tsar which had previously been conducted by Maliuta Skuratov. The children of his deceased brother, Boris and Irina, were left to his care, and grew up at court together. The return of Nagoi from Crimea in 1573 had introduced a new piece into the complicated court factions: the inquiry into the alleged treasonable relations between Prince I.F. Mstislavsky and the Crimeans had been revived and a number of the Prince's bondsmen, now freed from captivity in the Crimea, were arrested, tortured and of course admitted the criminal relations of Mstislavsky with the Crimeans in 1571.[42] The boyar had again been forced to give sureties for his behaviour and subjected to harassment.

No mention was made of a bride-show, but some kind of wedding ceremony took place in January 1575, without the approval of a church council, and without the crowns, between Ivan and his fifth wife, Anna Vasil'chikova, about whom very little is known.[43] Soon after, his two sons were also married: Ivan Ivanovich was now twenty and married for a second time; Fedor was married to Irina Godunova. The usual tensions over precedence blew up between Umnoi Kolychev and Tulupov, and D.I. Godunov and the rising favourite, his nephew Boris Godunov. Tulupov's estate in Staritsa was confiscated and granted to Boris Godunov some time before August 1575, and Tulupov, with several members of his family and a number of other nobles, most of whom had occupied prominent positions at Ivan's wedding with Anna Vasil'chikova, were executed (Tulupov apparently impaled) on 2 August 1575, together with a relative of the previous Tsaritsa, Anna Koltovskaia.[44] The Tulupov clan was practically exterminated.[45]

It seems as though Ivan felt just as circumscribed by boyars opposing his will in his personal *dvor* as he had felt before he instituted the *oprichnina*, and in the mid 1570s his anger turned also on the ecclesiastical hierarchy and on the monastic order. It will be remembered that in October 1572 he had issued a proclamation forbidding nobles to make any grants of land to monasteries. The question does arise: in whose interests was he acting? It has been suggested that this policy suited the boyars who would now be prevented from frittering away their estates on the Church. Yet here too Ivan's anger now seemed to be directed against all the great monasteries which he had patronized and admired in the past.

A missive which the Tsar wrote to Abbot Koz'ma of the Beloozero monastery in 1573 is couched in his most inflammatory biblical style. It is worth quoting to illustrate the curious convolutions of his mind. He opens with the usual invocation for forgiveness for his many sins:

> Alas for me a sinner, woe to me in my despair, Oh me, in my foulness . . . it behoves you, our masters to illuminate us who have lost our way in the darkness of pride, who are mired in sinful vanity, gluttony and intemperance. And I, a stinking hound, whom can I teach, what can I preach, and with what can I enlighten others? Myself always wallowing in drunkenness, fornication, adultery, filth, murders, rapine, despoliation, hatred and all sorts of evil-doing.

Quoting St Paul, Ivan then addresses the monks: 'You believe that you can lead the blind, that you are a light to those in the darkness, that you can preach to the ignorant, teach the young . . . How is it then that teaching others you do not teach yourselves? How, preaching to others, do you remain unworthy?' He advises the monks to turn to the teaching of St Cyril, the founder of the monastery. He reminds them how, some time ago, he had met with a number of monks in a cell and had explained to them his desire to withdraw from the noise of the world and be shorn a monk.[46] 'Hearing of your godly life my despairing soul and filthy heart were filled with joy . . . And it seems to me, in my despair, that I am already half a monk . . . And I have already seen how the many ships of my soul, agitated by fierce storms, have found a safe harbour.' Ivan continues with many quotations from fathers of the Church, and reminders of the feats of the holy martyrs[47] culminating with the sufferings of St John Chrysostom at the hands of the Empress Eudoxia. Much of this eloquence was formulaic, but in Ivan's case a good deal of it was felt, and was a necessary part of the creation of his role as a religious guide and father of his people. Ivan pointed the moral: the monks too should suffer as Christ had done and should not be led astray after silver like Judas.

At the same time Ivan vented his spleen upon the hapless Sheremetev brothers. The burden of Ivan's accusations against the monks was that they had allowed Ivan Sheremetev major and a companion of his to evade the rules of monastic life, to indulge in keeping servants, having their own kitchen and eating abundant food. The boyars who had entered the monastery had introduced into it their own worldly and luxurious ways and were corrupting the spiritual life. 'You are not their teachers, they are yours!' exclaimed the Tsar. He was particularly angered because a tombstone had been set up on the grave of Prince Vladimir Vorotynsky, the brother of Mikhail, but not on the grave of St Cyril. The Tsar gradually wound himself up and became more and more angry at the thought of these boyars who had not abided by monastic rules, concentrating his attack on Sheremetev. He complained that until recently the rule of the house was to observe perfect equality between boyars, bondsmen and trading peasants, a *kholop* was equal to a Bel'sky, whereas now there was no brotherhood. The letter goes on to accuse Sheremetev of being responsible for the abandonment of the practice of religious procession on the required occasions and of the general austerities of the rule, on the pretext of illness. Finally, washing his hands of the monks' neglect of decency and honour, he exclaimed contemptuously: 'Serve Sheremetev on golden dishes and do him honour as to a Tsar – it is your affair . . . do as you wish, it is not my concern, draw up your rules with Sheremetev, don't bother me any more with this for I will not reply.' Calling down the blessing of the Mother of God and of Saint Cyril on the monks, he concluded in sarcastic mode: 'And to you, gentlemen and fathers, we bow our head to the ground.'[48]

It is in this context that one must place the final downfall of Archbishop Leonid of Novgorod, who had succeeded in reconciling the Tsar with the city after the burning of Moscow, though the sources are somewhat confused and scanty. Archbishop Leonid had of course maintained close connexions with the leaders of the *oprichnina* and to that extent was tarred with the same brush. Just as Ivan got rid of his closest followers in the *oprichnina*, so now he turned on Leonid, who was summoned to Moscow some time in August 1575 and brought before a religious council for judgment. Ivan prepared the ground by organizing at the same time an investigation into the doings of Metropolitan Antony and the Bishop of Krutitsa, who were apparently charged with drinking. Thus deprived of any support, Leonid was now accused of a whole array of crimes: treason, maintaining secret correspondence with agents of the King of Poland–Lithuania, sending treasure abroad, minting money, buggery, bestiality, sodomy and keeping witches.[49] Leonid's enormous fortune was confiscated by Ivan, eleven of his servants hanged 'and his women witches shamefully dismembered and burned'. Much of the evidence for the trial of Leonid is provided by Jerome Horsey, the only one to mention the fate of his witches, and his account is confirmed by a surviving note in a *Sinodik* commemorating 'in Novgorod 15 women said to be witches'.[50] Leonid was sentenced to life imprisonment in a dungeon on bread and water and died in October 1575. It is his death which has given rise to many legends about bears being set on to kill condemned friars, and the even better known account of a Pskovian Chronicle of Leonid being sewn up in a bear skin and thrown to the dogs.[51]

Four days after the downfall of Leonid, Protasii V. Iur'ev Zakhar'in, an *oprichnik* who had been attached for years to the *dvor* of the Tsarevich Ivan Ivanovich, was executed. Having begun to harbour suspicions of his eldest son and of the relatives of the Tsaritsa Anastasia, the Tsar now turned on the Iur'ev Zakhar'in family, and even on Tsaritsa Anastasia's brother, the long lasting Nikita Romanovich whose property was ravaged. In November 1575 several prominent boyars and a number of prominent *oprichniki* were executed. One of the recently arrived envoys from the Holy Roman Emperor, Daniel Prinz von Buchau, reported that 'Not long before our arrival, in autumn 1575, he [the Tsar] killed forty nobles who had apparently for a second time plotted against his life.'[52] Probably closest to Ivan now stood Bogdan Ia. Bel'sky, the nephew of Maliuta Skuratov, of modest family, who had been a body servant of Ivan's for fifteen years and who rose steadily in his service.[53] A number of younger Shuisky princes also appeared at the court of Ivan including Vasily Ivanovich, the future Tsar.

War with Sweden continued and had also proved disappointing to Ivan. John III had twice detained Russian envoys and refused to negotiate with Ivan until the Bishop of Åbo and the Swedish embassy sent in 1569 were allowed to return to Sweden. Ivan continued to bombard John III with very rude letters: he accused him of writing his name before that of Ivan which was indecent because Ivan's brother was the Holy Roman Emperor, and he refused to call John 'brother' for in honour Sweden was inferior: 'You say Sweden is the patrimony of your father ... and whose son was he, and was your grandfather on the throne?' Ivan then went back over the whole story of his relations with Erik XIV again and his demand for Catherine to be handed over, because he believed her husband had died, and, out of kindness, as she had no children, he had offered graciously to take care of her and allow Erik to deal directly with him and not through the governor of Novgorod. Our only intention, he continued, for the first time admitting that he proposed to regard John's wife as a hostage, was to give her back to her brother Sigismund Augustus in exchange for Livonia and there would then be no bloodshed:

> They hid you [John] from us, for had we known you were alive
> would we have asked for your wife? . . . There is no need to say
> more, your wife is with you, nobody wants her, and what a lot of
> blood has been shed in vain for lack of one word from her. It is not
> worth talking any more about this nonsense, and if you want to
> talk, we won't listen to you; do you what you want with your wife,
> no one is making any attempt on her.[54]

Ivan continued in this vein for a further eighteen printed pages, going
back to the days of Russian relations with King Magnus of Sweden.

The stalemate in the war with Sweden led Ivan to take up the idea of
a truce, and he sent an envoy with a written message; but the Swedes
were now cautious about receiving missives from Ivan, and John refused
to read it and insisted on handing it to one of his nobles in case it was
too offensive. This led to renewed quarrelling: 'You have come to
Sweden', said the Swedish magnate to the Russian envoy, 'and you must
do what our king tells you.' To which the Russian courier replied, 'I have
come to your land and I will obey the orders of my lord.' When told he
would receive no rations, he replied, 'Very well, I will starve to death.'
The episode ended in a brawl, and again John refused to let the Russian
envoy go until the two Swedish interpreters who were still detained in
Russia were released. Ivan now found a new excuse: the interpreters
were being detained to teach Russian children Swedish. John refused to
send an embassy and declared that he had not sent the interpreters to
Russia to teach Russian children, but to carry out his orders. In such
circumstances agreement over peace terms was impossible to reach and
the only thing achieved was a further truce from 20 June 1575 to 20 July
1577.[55]

Whether the disappearance of the supernova in Cassiopeia in
November 1774, with its underlying implications of cosmic instability,
affected the general state of mind in Russia is not known, but the Tsar
took up again with the English envoy, this time D. Sylvester, his request
for a refuge in England. He now asked for a declaration which should
be countersigned by Elizabeth's whole council. Evidently he no longer
believed in her power to rule alone and in her sole word.[56]

It may also have been the cumulative effect on his unstable temperament of these mortifications which led Ivan to the most startling and
inexplicable venture in his reign. Or it may have been the fear induced
by portents in the sky threatening the life of a king. His solution for his
spiritual turmoil was to escape from his throne and set up a scapegoat,
a substitute tsar who could take his place and become the object of

divine wrath or of public hatred and suspicion, a barrier against those who attempted to oppose his will. In fact it has been suggested that his physician Bomelius had inspired the Tsar with such fear for his life, in view of the adverse astrological signs, that he installed a surrogate tsar as a lightning conductor, to receive the blows of fate in his stead.[57]

Whom did he choose? As Vasily III had looked around for a trusted lieutenant and possible heir among his Tatar friends, having faith in the baptized Tsarevich Peter who then died, in 1521, so did Ivan now place his faith in a baptized Tatar.[58] The most prominent tsarevich at that time, Sain Bekbulatovich, had entered Russian service around 1562. He was a grandson of Akhmat, Khan of Astrakhan', and thus a Genghisid. He inherited or was granted the Tatar khanate of Kasimov which had formed part of Russia since the reign of Vasily II, and served Ivan as a military commander at a time when there were fewer Tatar tsarevichi because many of them had died. He had been a most active and success-ful general in the war in Livonia and with Sweden on the Finnish front, and around July 1573 he was baptized under the name of Simeon. With the death of Prince Mikhail Kaibulatovich, the Tatar tsarevich who had been the senior member of the Council in 1575, Simeon became the most prominent tsarevich in Russian service. What is more he was the nephew of Maria Temriukovna, which made him a nephew of the Tsar, and Ivan now married him to a daughter of Prince I.F. Mstislavsky, Anastasia, who was herself descended from a daughter of Tsarevich Peter and a daughter of Ivan III. Simeon Bekbulatovich was as well bred as a Tatar tsarevich could be.

Chapter XVIII
Grand Prince Simeon Bekbulatovich

According to a laconic entry in the Military Registers, the Lord Tsar and Grand Prince appointed the Grand Prince Simeon Bekbulatovich to be Grand Prince of Russia, in autumn 1575, while Ivan IV remained Prince of Moscow (Kniaz' Moskovskii).[1] He also kept the titles of Tsar of all Russia, Tsar of Kazan' and Astrakhan', and the lordship of Livonia, creating immense confusion at the time and since. There is great uncertainty, because of the loss of records, about Ivan's intentions and about which powers he handed over to Simeon and which he kept, and how long this interlude lasted. As Grand Prince of Russia, Simeon was head of the *zemlia*, that is the government of the land. He could and did issue charters in his own name, though not many have survived so that it is difficult to know with what matters he concerned himself. The charters which have survived deal mostly with grants of land to monasteries. On the other hand Ivan continued to be in total control of relations with foreign powers.[2] According to Jerome Horsey, an eye-witness of these events who, however, wrote up his recollections some time later, Simeon was crowned in the Cathedral of the Dormition in the Kremlin, but as Horsey reported, 'with no solemnity nor consent of peers'.[3]

The unreliability of Horsey's reports is confirmed by Ivan's own language to Daniel Sylvester, previously the interpreter of the Russia Company, now its agent. Sylvester reported to London on 29 January 1576, that Ivan had told him, speaking in Russian because he was aware that Sylvester knew it well, that he still awaited a firm decision from Elizabeth on his renewed demand for asylum. He was dissatisfied with the priority she gave to merchant affairs, and offended by her refusal to place Russia and England on an equal footing by herself demanding asylum in Russia, 'that she makyth daynty to requiar the like of us'. He reproached Elizabeth for her scruples in fulfilling his wishes, seeing that he had granted her merchants, 'who are as free as in England', freedom of trade throughout Russia. Unless she agreed to all his requests he would drop the whole matter, and transfer his trade to the Venetians and the Germans. And he added that

> though we have told you that we seemed to have raised another to our throne and have in this way bound ourselves and others, yet this matter is not final, and we have not resigned from our realm to the extent that we would be unable when convenient to take up our rank again for it is not yet confirmed, and we shall act in this matter as God orders us because he [Simeon] is not yet confirmed by a rite of coronation or appointed by popular choice, but only by our permission. And see, seven crowns and their sceptres are still in our hands with the other tsarist ornaments belonging to the realm, and with all the treasure belonging to each crown.[4]

Moreover, Ivan hinted, he could now fall back on his new friend the Emperor Maximilian.[5] However, what still perplexes and divides historians is where did Ivan get such a strange idea from, and to what extent did it imply a restoration of the *oprichnina*?

In what concerns the first question, there are authors who regarded Ivan's policy as merely 'a political masquerade'.[6] Some thought that he believed that by resigning the Russian crown he might improve his chances of obtaining the crown of Poland–Lithuania, others that he was concerned with relations with the Crimea. Other historians argue that Simeon was enthroned as Grand Prince as a result of a meeting of an 'assembly of the land', which allegedly took place in 1575, which was summoned with the aim of secularizing church lands and was riven by violent disagreements on policy between the aristocracy, the church hierarchy, current boyars and previous members of the *oprichnina*. But alas there is no evidence that a meeting of this non-existent body took place at any relevant time though there may have been a meeting of the Church Council.[7] According to Giles Fletcher's later attempt to explain Ivan's policy as a financial operation,[8] when Ivan placed Simeon on the throne, he instructed him to annul all the charters which he, Ivan, had issued, conceding tax exemptions, and then to return them in exchange for substantial payments. Kashtanov, a specialist in this field, argues however that there was no systematic policy during the year of Simeon's rule in relation to charters granted to monasteries. Some of them were cancelled, but other charters were granted, including charters to monasteries signed by Ivan as Grand Prince of Moscow.[9] Of those signed by Simeon many were destroyed after his removal, as well as other documents emanating from him, as though they were not worthy to survive because they had not been issued by a genuine grand prince.[10] It is noteworthy that in foreign relations Ivan was entitled Tsar as before.[11]

One historian again located the origin of the idea of stepping down from the throne in the oriental tale of Barlaam and Josaphat, as told in the eighth century by St John Damascene and well known in Russia.[12] It has also been referred to in connexion with the origins of the *oprichnina*. However, one element in this tale does reflect an Indian origin, namely the suggestion that the physician and magus Bomelius, or perhaps witches, had produced a horoscope for Ivan showing that in the years 1575/6, a Grand Prince of Russia was to die; the prophecy could be painlessly voided by ensuring that he, Ivan, was not Grand Prince in that year.[13] But another way of evading it was to take refuge in England, hence the renewal of discussions between Ivan and Sylvester in autumn 1575 and winter 1576 on the mutual offer of asylum by both parties.[14] Bomelius was notorious as an astrologer, and was generally regarded as an evil sorcerer who exercised a harmful influence on the Tsar. Recent heavenly manifestations – the appearance and disappearance of the new star, the supernova, in Cassiopeia in 1574, and the appearance of a blazing comet, commonly believed to herald the death of a ruler, and visible to the naked eye in 1577 might indeed frighten the credulous Ivan.[15] The setting up of a substitute Tsar may also have been a means of preparing for the government of Russia during Ivan's disappearance into English asylum. Horsey reported seeing a large number of ships built in Vologda by English craftsmen, and one Pskovian chronicle carried reports of Ivan's intention to flee to England, allegedly inspired by the evil witch Bomelius.[16]

To yet others Ivan IV was moved by fears that his son and heir was plotting behind his back to overthrow him. Some chronicles suggest that Ivan promoted Simeon Bekbulatovich because he suspected the Tsarevich Ivan Ivanovich of intriguing against him.[17] But as a Pskov chronicle put it, 'It is not right, Lord, for you to appoint a man of a foreign race (*inoplemmenik*) in place of your own children to the realm (*gosudarstvo*).'[18] Yet, if his son were really plotting against him, Ivan might well consider it wise to prepare an heir to fall back on, namely a Tatar prince. On a quite different level, it has been suggested that Ivan was so disgusted with the failure of the *oprichnina* to protect him and his people against the last Crimean invasion that he deliberately chose to humiliate Russians by appointing a Tatar to rule the land. Simeon was after all a nephew of his dead wife, Maria Temriukovna.[19] Yet Ivan's execution of a considerable number of courtiers in autumn 1575, including his favourite Tulupov, suggests that he was suffering from one of the periodic fits of panic which led to outbursts of sadism. The heads of the beheaded were thrown into the courtyards of magnates like Prince I.F Mstislavsky, Ivan Sheremetev minor and the Metropolitan Antonii.[20]

In his later work, the historian Zimin rejected all these theories and merely echoed the opinion of a member of the imperial embassy, Daniel Prinz, in his report to the Emperor Maximilian II, who had stated that Ivan was motivated by contempt for the baseness of his subjects,[21] an opinion which was confirmed by Daniel Sylvester who reported Ivan as mentioning 'The perverse and evill dealinge of our subjects who mourmour and repine at us, for gettinge loyaull obedience they practice against our person. The which to prevent we have gyvene them ouer unto another prince to governe them but have reserved in our custodye all the treasure of the land.'[22] Finally, the elevation of Simeon Bekbulatovich was in no way the result of an individual caprice of the Tsar; according to rigidly Marxist Soviet historians, it followed the inevitable laws of historical development (*zakonomernost'*).[23]

The most far fetched interpretation of the raising of Simeon Bekbulatovich to the rank of Grand Prince of all Russia is that of Skrynnikov himself which must be touched upon. He argues that in 1565, when the people allowed Ivan to establish the *oprichnina*, they gave him full legal powers to struggle with boyar treason. By abolishing the *oprichnina* Ivan had deprived himself of these full legal powers, and would therefore be acting without the sanction of the law if he attempted to reintroduce a regime of terror, a policy which would inevitably arouse the strongest opposition in the Boyar Council and in the church hierarchy: 'On this occasion he obtained the necessary legal authority not from the Council but from someone he had himself placed above the Council and the *zemshchina* as a whole, namely Simeon Bekbulatovich.' Having awarded Simeon the title of 'Grand Prince of all Russia', Ivan 'obtained without difficulty from Simeon his permission to introduce a regime of exception'.[24] This circular argument is not at all convincing. Finally, was the abdication of Ivan and the raising of Simeon Bekbulatovich to the throne a means of restoring the *oprichinina* in a different form?

Ivan's first public action after the institution of Grand Duke Simeon (as far as we know for there is very little direct evidence about the timetable of events), was to send a letter to the new Grand Duke begging for his permission as his overlord to recruit a number of service gentry from the principalities ruled over by Simeon and incorporate them into his new *udel* or appanage.[25] So the division between *oprichnina* and *zemshchina* was partly recreated but it did not correspond to the old territorial and administrative division and the name *oprichnina* was dropped because of its unhappy connotation and replaced by *dvor* or court. Indeed it was forbidden on pain of death to use the old word. There were no *oprichniki*, though Ivan set up his own guard of armed pages (*ryndy*) and his own regiment, tax collecting and local judicial authorities, thus acting, as earlier, in complete disregard of the policy attributed to him of 'centralization'. The bulk of the aristocracy remained with Tsar Simeon, while the courtiers and military in the service of Ivan were mainly of lower social origins.[26] The *prikazy*, both in the *udel* of Ivan and in the *zemshchina* were staffed by *d'iaki* distributed among functional and geographic offices, assisted by some mercantile elements. The nucleus of the lands Ivan chose for himself lay in the north, around Novgorod and Pskov, and the route to the White Sea, and his favourite residence now became Staritsa, the city of his murdered cousin. This may be explained by the fact that so soon after the destruction of Moscow by the Crimean Tatars in 1571 the city still remained uninhabitable, at least by him. The population of this once thriving and busy town had been reduced to some thirty thousand according to one source.

Ivan was in fact concentrating his energies and his forces with the intention of reviving the Livonian war and bringing it to a satisfactory conclusion. Hence his choice of residence, nearer the centre of the future campaign, though he moved around a great deal. And there remained the problem of finding a king for Poland–Lithuania.

Henri of Anjou had fled but he had not abdicated. Unless he returned by May 1575 new elections would have to take place. A strong movement in favour of a Habsburg candidate now developed both among the Polish Catholic hierarchy and senators and among the Lithuanian magnates who for different reasons considered that this would benefit their orders. But there were as before profound divisions between the aims of different social groups within the Commonwealth. The arguments had all been gone over before, but they revived again, with not very many variations. The Polish *shliakhta*, or nobility, was deeply anti-Habsburg and anti-German, and more inclined to a Russian candidate, possibly even Ivan IV, whom they viewed as better able to protect Poland against Ottoman or Crimean invasions than the Habsburgs had proved. The Polish magnates, and the princes of the Church inclined more to support the Emperor Maximilian II or his son, the Archduke Ernst, or even Maximilian's brother Ferdinand. The run-of-the-mill Lithuanian nobles also supported a Habsburg candidate. The Emperor Maximilian II was more favourably regarded than Archduke Ernst as a candidate for the throne by many in Poland–Lithuania, because as Holy Roman Emperor he would be unable to come often to the country in person, and would therefore be forced to delegate the administration to the local magnates.

The Lithuanian magnates inclined to a Russian candidate but preferred Fedor Ivanovich to his father, for they were more aware than the Poles of the peculiarities of Ivan's character. Some placed their hopes in a triple alliance between the Empire, Russia and the Commonwealth against the Ottoman Empire. The Lithuanians also protected themselves by sending Ivan copies of the *pacta conventa* signed by Henri of Anjou in 1572 as an indication of the terms he, Ivan, would have to agree to, because he was not a *dedich* of the land, i.e., not descended from native-born ancestors. These were terms quite unacceptable to Ivan, and he did not send his envoys to the *Sejm*, as a result of which he was not in fact represented at all in the discussions. He may of course have been held back by the considerable uncertainty which remained about the status of Henri of Anjou until his formal abdication.[27]

Unwilling to make use of established diplomatic channels, Ivan and his advisers, now Afanasii Nagoy, Andrei Shchelkalov, who had donned the mantle of Viskovaty and the *d'iak* Ersh Mikhailov, made use of a young Polish noble, Krishtof Graevsky, in Russia on a commercial mission, as an unofficial channel, in order to communicate the Russian views directly to the Poles.[48] Graevsky, when the Tsar received him on 6 April 1575 (before the appointment of Simeon Bekbulatovich) in Aleksandrovskaia Sloboda, urged Ivan to cease negotiating with the Lithuanians and to negotiate with the Polish nobles; he proposed a meeting in Kiev to iron out problems, after which the Tsar could proceed through Kiev and Volhynia to his coronation in Cracow. Through the young Pole Ivan stressed his desire to be crowned by a metropolitan, not an archbishop and insisted, as before, on the granting of precedence to his title of Tsar, reigning in Kiev which should be ceded to Russia, over the title of King of Poland and Grand Prince of Lithuania, as well as on granting hereditary rights to inherit the Commonwealth crowns to the Russian dynasty – conditions which had already been communicated to the Lithuanian envoy M. Haraburda in 1573.[29] This suggests that Ivan may have contemplated the removal of the Russian capital from Moscow to Kiev. The political institutions of the three crowns, namely the Senate of the Commonwealth and the Boyar Council should be fused, and Ivan would call a special gathering to discuss religion and religious toleration. The support of the Commonwealth nobles would be sought by promising to grant them lands in the empty territories of Russia.

These conditions implied a rejection of those subscribed to by Henri of Anjou. The Tsar insisted on maintaining a hereditary right to the Polish-Lithuanian crown, and refused to recognize its elective quality, except within his own dynasty; he refused to swear to observe the conditions laid down by both Catholics and Protestants in Poland–Lithuania as Henri of Anjou had been compelled to do, in the famous formula put to him in Paris: *si non jurabis aut non regnabis*. But the Poles, particularly the leaders of the Protestants, clung to their right to worship as they chose as 'free citizens of a free republic'.[30] This gave Ivan an opening to claim the same freedom for himself and to reject the condition that he must convert to Catholicism, unless he were convinced, in an open debate, of its superior merits as a faith. As a result confusion reigned in the *Sejm* and the supporters of a Russian candidature remained divided between Ivan and his son Fedor. Graevsky himself was unable to report on his talks with Ivan, for he was arrested on his passage through Lithuania by the magnates opposed to a Polish-sponsored Russian candidature. While in captivity in Lithuania Graevsky modified his account, emphasizing the concessions made by Ivan, and notably the intention he allegedly harboured to unite Russia with Poland as Jagiello had united Lithuania with Poland, which he then transmitted through his brother Peter.[31]

Ivan it seems was always fearful of a snub, and thus he sent no 'great ambassadors' to Warsaw, though he sent a 'minor' envoy in November 1575 who appeared before the *Sejm* and reiterated Ivan's reluctance to change his terms.[32] His delaying tactics led some of his supporters in Poland to think that he did not really want the Polish-Lithuanian crown, or that he wished to postpone a decision until the Poles and the Lithuanians appealed to him and accepted his terms. For the time being the only remaining serious candidates were the Archduke Ernst, and the Emperor Maximilian himself.

Relations between the Emperor and the Tsar had become cooler since the Russian invasion of Livonia. Remnants of the Livonian Order had appealed in the past to the emperors for help against the invaders from Poland–Lithuania, Russia and Sweden, help which had not been forthcoming. Nevertheless Livonian deputies appeared regularly at meetings of the imperial Diet, and though the Emperors (Ferdinand I and Maximilian II) could do little to assist them, they nevertheless attempted to give the province at least moral support. The interregna in Poland opened up fresh diplomatic perspectives to both powers though it must be stressed that the information on which their policies were based was very deficient, and their envoys were at times unreliable or misleading.

There had been a renewal of some complex negotiations between the Tsar and the Emperor even before the election of Henri of Anjou to the throne of the Commonwealth. A certain Magnus Pauli,[33] a merchant resident in Brandenburg, who may have been an agent of King Magnus of Livonia, had devised a scheme the purpose of which remains unclear. He embarked on a journey to Russia in November 1572, ostensibly as an envoy from the Emperor, bearing a letter from him dated 20 November 1572 and was detained in Riga by the Lithuanian magnate Jan Chodkewicz, then commandant in Polish Livonia, in an effort to foil an understanding between Russia and the Holy Roman Empire. By the time Pauli was freed from arrest, and went on to Novgorod, arriving on 11 July 1573, Henri of Anjou had already been elected to the crown of the Commonwealth, so that it only remained for Pauli to convey what he alleged was imperial policy to the Tsar. Pauli saw Andrei Shchelkalov, and Ivan now expressed the hope of seeing the Archduke Ernst on the throne of Poland, for when all was said and done, the Habsburgs were more likely than a French prince to oppose the Tsar's ultimate enemy, the Ottoman Sultan. Pauli in turn outlined a policy which was only to be implemented two hundred years later: he proposed in Maximilian's name and without any authority from the Emperor[34] the partition of the Commonwealth, the crown of Poland going to the Emperor and the Grand Principality of Lithuania to the Tsar, while the two powers would be united in a common front against the Ottoman Empire.[35]

Diplomatic cooperation between the Tsar and the Emperor had been rendered more likely by the election of Henri to the throne of the Commonwealth, since it was known to all that France was allied in spirit with the Ottomans. The Porte, indeed, alerted to the Emperor's support of Russia, had been willing even to allow Henri of Valois to travel to Poland through Istanbul.[36] After Henri's flight back to France, the Tsar and the Emperor again acted together (with the backing of the Lithuanian magnates, not the Poles). Pauli, whose actual status remains shrouded in mystery, returned to Vienna in summer 1573, while Ivan sent a courier, Skobel'tsyn, at the same time to Maximilian to confirm that 'either our son will be in that land [Poland] or your son will be there'. In December 1574 Pauli carried a message from Maximilian to

Russia to prepare the way for a 'great' imperial embassy, and Ivan now began to prepare measures for the proposed alliance against the Porte by cultivating the Cossacks of the Dnieper River and urging them to ravage the Crimean lands adjoining them. Ivan's hand was strengthened by the appearance in Russia of the *voevoda* of Moldavia, Bogdan Aleksandrovich, exiled by the Turks. He was accompanied by a considerable armed force and a number of Danubian nobles. Ivan granted his kinsman a handsome appanage in Tarusa on the Oka.[37]

The next few months saw much coming and going of envoys to the Commonwealth until, in November 1575, the electoral *Sejm* began its sessions and listened to the various contendants: the imperial envoys, Count Hans Cobenzl and Daniel Prinz, stopping in Cracow on their way to Russia, praised the qualifications of the Archdukes Ernst and Ferdinand, their knowledge of Czech (so close to Polish) and Latin. King John of Sweden put forward the original proposal that if he were not elected then the sister of King Sigismund Augustus, Princess Anna Jagiellonka should be elected, citing as an example of a woman on the throne Queen Elizabeth of England, who had raised the kingdom of England to such heights. Anna Jagiellonka knew the language and the customs of the people. Too old for childbirth, she could appoint her nephew as her heir, the only remaining Jagiello, namely Sigismund, the son of King John III of Sweden, and of Sigismund Augustus's sister Catherine Jagiellonka (who in addition to Polish, spoke Swedish and enough Latin, Italian and German). The Turks sent an envoy advising the election of a Pole, or of Stephen Bathory, Prince of Transylvania, the Sultan's vassal, who sent a spokesman to the *Sejm* to proclaim his own merits, and who promised to keep the peace with the Turks and the Tatars and to recover from Russia the lands Poland–Lithuania had lost to her, at his expense. Finally the Duke of Ferrara, Alfonso II of Este, promised to send scholars and artists to the Academy of Cracow, and to educate 500 young Polish nobles in Italy at his expense if he were elected. Ivan sent no envoys and made no offers or promises.[38]

Relations between Maximilian and Ivan became tense again largely as a result of the inefficiency of their envoys, Pauli and Skobel'tsyn, who were quarrelsome, and dwelt on points of etiquette such as the imperial refusal to call Ivan 'Tsar'. The long awaited imperial embassy headed by Hans Cobenzl von Prosseck and Daniel Prinz arrived at last on the Russian border in November 1575, and in Dorogobuzh on 15 December. But the presentation of the embassy's credentials was postponed while Ivan carried out his religious duties for Advent. This perturbed the imperial envoys, who had already attended the electoral

Sejm in Warsaw, and knew that time pressed, but they refused to open talks until they were properly received. That the Russian spokesmen nevertheless proved willing to embark on negotiations was explained by Ivan: so many people whom he suspected were merely merchants had represented themselves as his envoys in recent years that he was taking precautions in advance. Evidently Ivan had heard something about Pauli's missions, allegedly in his name, but there were other examples of such impostures.[39] However the imperial ambassadors still refused to open their budgets until they had been properly received, and not until early January did the Tsar leave Moscow for Mozhaisk, possibly because Moscow was not yet a fit place in which to receive imperial ambassadors. On the 22 January 1576 the embassy was welcomed by a solemn entry into Mozhaisk, escorted by 2,000 musketeers, and the envoys were given a formal audience on the following day by Ivan, surrounded by hundreds of courtiers and '24 councillors sitting to his right and left'. There followed the usual inquiries after the health of their respective lords and the exchange of presents, then a lavish banquet which lasted for six hours. Ivan and the Tsarevich wore splendid robes, and jewelled crowns which they took off for the meal in order to eat more at ease. The reception of the imperial ambassadors was both lavish and magnificent.[40]

The Emperor asked Ivan to support the candidature of his son Ernst in Poland and to bring peace to Livonia and Lithuania. But, responding to the pleas of the Livonians at the recent Diet in Regensburg, he also demanded the return of Livonia to the Empire, thus ensuring the failure of the negotiations since Ivan expected no such demand and would not give up Livonia. The talks between Russia and the imperial envoys were not concerned only with Poland but also with the previous discussions about possible joint action against the Porte and above all with what was dearest to the papal heart, namely the conversion of Orthodox Russia to Rome. Both Cobenzl and Prinz were convinced (and tried to convince the Pope) that the conversion of Russia would not be a difficult undertaking because there were already great similarities between Catholicism and Orthodoxy, much more than between either and Lutheranism.

Meanwhile Ivan again underestimated the importance of sending his own 'great embassy' to Warsaw; he sent a minor envoy to talk to the Senate and to ask for a safe conduct for yet another courier, but he also addressed a series of missives to important magnates and senators in Poland entrusted to yet another envoy, Novosil'tsev, though this time Ivan did ask for a safe conduct for a 'great embassy'. But these lowly

Russian envoys were vulnerable: hostile Lithuanian magnates easily managed to intercept their journeys, detain them and make them arrive too late in Warsaw to campaign for the election of Ivan.[41] Thus Novosil'tsev was not able to distribute his missives to the important Polish magnates and Ivan's case went by default.

The Russian talks with Cobenzl in Mozhaisk went no better. The imperial envoys were not interested in securing the throne of the Commonwealth for Ivan but for the Archduke Ernst; and they insisted that Ivan surrender his claims to Livonia. They promised to make Ivan Emperor of European Turkey, and to negotiate an alliance with Archduke Ernst as King of Poland–Lithuania, together with the Emperor, the Pope, the King of Spain and other Christian monarchs in order to throw the Turks out of Europe. 'What did a couple of cities in Livonia and Lithuania mean compared to the empire of the East?' asked Cobenzl rhetorically. Ivan clung rather to the idea of leaving Poland to the Archduke and acquiring Lithuania and Livonia for his son Fedor but in any case all these hopes and plans for the future fell by the wayside when it was learnt that, tired of waiting, the Polish-Lithuanian senators led by the Polish primate, who supported the Habsburgs, had proceeded to elect the Emperor Maximilian II King of Poland on 12 December 1575. This spelled the end of the mission to Russia of the imperial ambassadors, who left Mozhaisk after eight days. Ivan, however, kept negotiations alive by sending his own envoys with the imperial envoys back to Vienna.[42] Since Maximilian's election was contested, and not unanimous, it led to an immediate upsurge of politicking in favour of other candidates. The Polish nobles in particular refused to accept an Austrian king and gradually united around Stephen Bathory, the Prince of Transylvania, provided he married Anna Jagiellonka, who had the advantage of having inherited substantial lands and valuable goods from her mother Bona Sforza and her brother King Sigismund Augustus. Stephen Bathory had moreover recently won a substantial victory over a Turkish force which provided him with funds and enhanced his reputation.

Stephen Bathory was a typical Renaissance figure: well-educated (he had visited Padua[43]), intelligent, a successful and experienced soldier, and a good linguist. He had been elected Prince of Transylvania on the death of the previous prince, Jan Sigismund Zapolya, the nephew of Sigismund Augustus II who, the latter had hoped, would one day inherit the Jagiello crowns in Poland–Lithuania, but who had died too soon. Stephen Bathory was a practising Catholic, but accustomed to tolerate other faiths in his Transylvanian principality. A Hungarian himself, he was anti-Habsburg, which suited the Poles. His principality was theoretically under Ottoman suzerainty, which rendered him suspect, but the Turks, after their disastrous defeat in the great naval battle of Lepanto on 7 October 1571, were turning away from the European field of expansion and therefore losing interest in the minutiae of the diplomatic world in eastern Europe. The death of Sultan Selim III in 1574 and the accession of Murad III confirmed the change of orientation in Turkish policy. The emergence of such a stirring character as Stephen Bathory among the candidates for the Polish throne was bound to galvanize the elections and he knew how to cultivate the most important political figures in both halves of the country and set about doing so.

The anti-Habsburg Poles, led by Jan Zamoyski, called a fresh *Sejm* for 18 January 1576, and in the absence of any effective opposition from Maximilian's camp, Bathory was elected and his election ratified on 1 February. So now there were two kings of the Commonwealth. But Maximilian did not appear. Preparations began at once for Bathory's coronation and his marriage to Anna. He arrived in Cracow in April and was crowned in May 1576. Ivan accepted this situation calmly. He does not really seem to have grasped that the election was final, that the Polish voters had disregarded his wishes as expressed to their envoys, and had voted without paying attention to his discussions with Cobenzl and Prinz. Moreover the weakness of Maximilian's position would render his own support more valuable to the Emperor; he might even be successful in pushing through the plan of partitioning Poland–Lithuania between the two empires.

The first envoys of Bathory, as King, to Ivan were met with contumely. The Tsar remained seated as he inquired after Stephen Bathory's health. From whom, he asked the envoys, was their Prince descended? How had they been treated in previous diplomatic negotiations, as princes of Transylvania and subjects of the King of Hungary? He did not give the envoys his hand to kiss and sent them no food from his table. And he refused to call Stephen brother since his rank was no higher than that of a Mstislavsky, or a Bel'sky or a Trubetskoi, who served the Tsar. Marriage to Sigismund Augustus's sister gave him no rights and indeed Poland–Lithuania belonged to Ivan as his patrimony (*votchina*) now that no male descendants of the Jagiellos were left.[44] It has been argued that his contempt for Stephen Bathory led Ivan to regard him as a weakling, incapable of fighting to recover the whole of Livonia for Poland–Lithuania, and to believe that he would be easily out-manoeuvred in any peace negotiations which might arise.[45] Bathory in turn saw that war against Russia to gain the whole of Livonia was essential in order to consolidate his position in the Commonwealth but he needed to postpone it until he had succeeded in asserting his personal authority.

Meanwhile the Tsar continued his preparations for the implementation of the other aspect of the projected Russo-imperial alliance, namely the attack on the Ottoman Empire, and the planned assault on the Crimean Tatars with the help of the Zaporozhian Cossacks.[46] Maximilian in turn prepared to summon a Reichstag in Ratisbon[47] in November 1576 to ask the German princes for assistance in winning his Polish crown against Stephen Bathory, and he informed Ivan in September that he would shortly be sending a 'great embassy' to conclude a formal alliance. But the forty-nine-year-old emperor's health had begun to give way and, on 12 October 1576, he died. His son Rudolph had already been elected King of the Romans and as emperor he carried on with the negotiations with Ivan but he had no intention of embarking on a major war, which would distract his attention from his intellectual activities. Nor did he intend handing over Livonia to the Tsar, or allowing his widowed sister the Queen of France (quondam wife of Charles IX) to be married off to Ivan. The Tsar however still hoped to recruit Rudolph to fight against Stephen Bathory for the crown of Poland, to assist him in obtaining Livonia and at least, if he did not acquire Poland–Lithuania, to ensure that he did acquire the Kievan inheritance.[48]

In late November 1576 Ivan again addressed a letter to Maximilian (of whose death he had not yet heard) warning him to keep out of Livonian affairs, since the province belonged to him. In the Tsar's opinion, in view of the dangerous situation of Europe as a result of the elevation of Bathory, a Turkish vassal, to the throne of Poland, the minor matter of Livonia should be allowed to drop. Moreover Ivan was still not convinced that the legally elected King of the Commonwealth was not Maximilian. In his military expeditions into Livonia during the interregnum he had been careful not to touch Polish-Lithuanian occupied lands. While Bathory was struggling to impose his authority in Poland and above all in Danzig, where he had to contend with Habsburg opposition, Ivan with substantial forces and accompanied by the Grand Prince of all Russia, Simeon Bekbulatovich, had advanced against the Swedish forces in Livonia in February 1576 and occupied the port of Haapsala on the coast north of Riga (warfare in Livonia was not included in the general truce between Russia and Sweden which had been renewed for two years in 1575). Sweden was driven back almost everywhere and barely held on to Reval, which was the object of a fierce attack in which Ivan Vasil'evich Sheremetev (minor) was killed. But the city defended itself to the point of forcing the Tsar to give up the siege in March 1577. The death of Maximilian was a blow to Danzig which lost its royal overlord and imperial protection, but the city continued to struggle against Bathory who now settled down to a siege. However at the end of 1577, the city secured reasonable terms from Bathory and swore allegiance to him,[50] thus freeing him to campaign in Livonia.

Again, for reasons which are not at all clear, Ivan now decided to bring to an end the reign of Simeon Bekbulatovich. Quite when this happened cannot be precisely determined, though it probably occurred in the summer of 1576.[51] Simeon was granted the cities of Tver' and Torzhok as his appanage and proceeded to rule there enjoying all the prerogatives of an appanage prince of old while continuing to serve in the armed forces of Ivan as one of his senior commanders.[51] At the same time in order to strengthen his high command the Tsar appointed a number of new high-ranking boyars and military commanders from the *zemshchina* to his *dvor*, including Prince I.F. Mstislavsky's son, Fedor Ivanovich, who now embarked, as a boyar, on the long career which would take him right through the Time of Troubles.[52] Some time, too, in the course of 1576 and 1577 Ivan's wife Anna Vasil'chikova died, though nothing is known of the circumstances.[53] He had not married her in a formal church ceremony, and his wedding with his next wife, Vasilisa Melent'eva, the widow of a *d'iak*, took place merely 'with a prayer' and lasted only a short time for, in the expressive Russian phrase for a death from natural causes, 'she died of her own death'.[54] Fortunately too, his old enemy Devlet Girey died on 29 June 1577 thus relieving Ivan's anxiety about his southern frontier.

The year 1577 saw the opening of a new Russian campaign in Livonia based on Pskov. The King of Sweden sent envoys in 1576–7 to Moscow instructed to draw out the truce negotiations while Sweden re-armed, but on 13 July 1577, Ivan with 30,000 troops and the Tatar cavalry under Simeon Bekbulatovich marched out to attack not Sweden, but the lands occupied by Poland–Lithuania in southern Livonia. His substantial conquests, extending to the gulf of Riga,[55] led Ivan to write one of his admonitory letters to Prince Polubensky,[56] the Polish vice-gerent in Polish occupied Livonia, on 9 July 1577. Polubensky was a member of a Russian family which had emigrated to the Commonwealth and he had been a successful general in the service of Sigismund Augustus. Indeed it was Polubensky who organized the raid on Izborsk when the Lithuanians were admitted to the Russian fortress, disguised as *oprichniki*.[57]

As usual with Ivan, the letter began with a long exposition of biblical history, drawing on the Apocryphal book of Enoch, and ranging from the Creation, through Adam, Abraham and Isaac, to the Tower of Babel, explaining how when mankind multiplied it turned away from God, and government was given over to the devil. Hence came torturers and rulers and tsars, like the first Nimrod, who started on the Tower of Babel and everywhere different kingdoms sprang up, leading to evil governments. Ivan continued to describe how God had protected the Israelites but again they had fallen away and asked for a king, whereupon God gave them Saul. The moral of this diatribe was that his ancestors, Augustus Caesar, who ruled the whole universe, and his brother, Prus, whose descendant in the fourteenth generation, Riurik, ruled in Russia, had persecuted the followers of Christ. But Jesus Christ did not turn a deaf ear to their prayers and fulfilled his promise: 'I shall be with you until the end of the world', and sent the great Constantine, from whom the sceptre passed through Vladimir to Iaroslav and to Ivan as ruler of Livonia. Alexander Nevsky is then drawn in, as well as Dmitri Donskoi, victor over the Hagarenes, and Ivan invited the Polish commander, who disposed of some four thousand troops, to arrange for the departure of his forces from the Tsar's patrimony, in which case they would not be molested.[58] He hoped to achieve a peaceful withdrawal of the occupying forces, and distributed letters to the fortified castles in his way promising safe conducts to those who departed in peace. Many of the small Polish-Lithuanian garrisons in Livonian cities did in fact surrender.

By August the Russian forces had captured the port of Pernau, and reached the Dvina and the outskirts of Riga. Dünaburg capitulated on 9 August and the Russians, meeting with resistance, stormed the town of Chistvin; the garrison and the townspeople were savagely exterminated. Ivan may have felt himself so near to total victory that he no longer needed to conciliate the Livonians. It was the greatest advance he had ever achieved. He took the opportunity to send a letter to the town council of Riga, informing its citizens that he had sheathed his sword, and awaited their submission.[59]

However, Ivan's puppet king, Magnus of Denmark proved both a selfish and a broken reed; he now claimed some eighteen captured towns for his kingdom, including many which had surrendered to Ivan, thus driving the Tsar into an absolute fury. He sent a detachment to Kockenhausen[60] which had surrendered to Magnus, the town was destroyed and the garrison killed. Magnus was now playing his own hand. He declared that he was acting with the approval of both the Emperor (Rudolph) and the Tsar, which outraged Ivan, for Magnus was taking the credit for the conquest of the towns captured by Ivan and assuming that they were going to be his share of the booty. Magnus also occupied Wolmar where the Polish commander Polubensky was taken prisoner, but he was dislodged by Ivan's troops on 1 September and the garrison massacred. Magnus was shut up with his followers for five days in an old roofless barn, sleeping on straw and then told to take himself off to his island of Oesel. The Livonians who had sworn allegiance to Magnus were executed, and the citizens of the towns sold off to the Tatar troops.[61] It was the end of Magnus's dream of a Livonian kingdom though not yet of his career.

It was from Wolmar that Ivan, in 1577, addressed the second of the letters he composed to Prince Andrei Kurbsky, doubtless remembering that it was from there that Kurbsky had addressed his first bitter accusations against the Tsar in 1565.[62] From Wolmar Ivan also addressed a number of letters to Bathory and Jan Chodkewicz, the Polish commandant in Livonia (who had allegedly been playing a double game with Ivan all this time) inviting them to leave Livonia without a battle. 'There is not a place' wrote the Tsar, in our Livonian land, 'where not only the hooves of our horses, but our own feet have not stood, not a river nor a lake from which we have not drunk.'[63] The letters are less insulting then his previous productions, there is a sense that the Tsar is writing more in sorrow than in anger, perhaps encouraged by his victories to be magnanimous to sinners, though he is one himself.[64] Accordingly, Ivan proposed peace to Bathory on condition that he cede the whole of Livonia to Russia, including the unconquered city and port of Riga. This implied that Ivan was giving priority to Riga over Reval, for, from every point of view – climatic, commercial, military and naval, Riga was clearly preferable, though also liable to be ice-bound for at least three months of the year. Ivan's peace terms and other letters which he now drafted, for instance to the town council of Riga, were handed to Polubensky to deliver to Stephen Bathory, after the Lithuanians who had surrendered to Ivan himself had been entertained and showered with gifts at a great feast on 10 September 1577. To Bathory Ivan expressed himself brusquely, but he set out to charm Chodkewicz, addressing him as 'brave and wise and stately', and referring to his previous feats of arms. His attitude has been interpreted as arising from the belief that Bathory was but a lowly plaything in the hands of the Lithuanian magnates, who would do what he was told by them. Hence it was more important to woo Chodkewicz than the new King,[65] in order to persuade the Commonwealth troops to withdraw from Livonia.

At the end of summer 1577 Ivan had achieved most of the objectives of his present campaign. Of all the major Livonian towns in the Eastern Baltic only Reval and Riga were not his. But his success was too good to last. By the end of 1577 Bathory was freed from anxiety over Danzig, and could concentrate on war with Russia, and he was an authoritative military leader commanding a better army than Ivan. An armistice was concluded between the Emperor Rudolph and the Porte, and Ivan appeared to agree on a three-year armistice with Poland, though since the texts signed by the two parties were entirely different (Livonia and Courland were both attributed to Russia in the copy signed by Ivan) in fact the armistice did not take place.[66] Ivan now became diplomatically increasingly isolated.

In the autumn of 1577 Ivan had ordered an assault on the Polish held Livonian town of Wenden (Kes') but, ominously, the levy of service gentry did not turn up, there were many *netchiki*. The Russian troops under the command of Prince I.F. Mstislavsky conducted a four-week siege in early 1578 which proved unsuccessful and the arrival of Russian reinforcements in May achieved no result. A second attack on Wenden was launched by a substantial Russian force in September 1578, but it was driven off by a much smaller combined force of Poles, Swedes and Germans. Many prominent Russian generals were killed or taken prisoner, and there were heavy Russian losses both in men and armaments.[67] It was a serious setback for Ivan, among other reasons because it was the result of a joint action between Swedish and Polish-Lithuanian forces, which had not cooperated hitherto.

According to some historians Ivan took his revenge on the Livonians, and on the other Germans dwelling in Moscow in the quarter generally known as 'Narva and Dorpat', where the original Livonian inhabitants of these two cities had been allowed to settle when they were expelled from their homes in Livonia at the Russian conquest some eighteen years before. They had also been allowed to establish one (two, according to some sources) Lutheran churches. (This was the origin of the later 'German quarter'.) The Tsar, his son, and a detachment of troops, all dressed in black, unexpectedly arrived, some time in winter 1578, and, with the order 'plunder but do not kill', they set about looting and destroying the property of the inhabitants, leaving many stripped naked in the cold weather, as a result of which many lives were lost.[68] A number of Scots who had been taken prisoner when acting as mercenaries in the forces of John III of Sweden were also in the settlement and Horsey did his best to rescue them, and indeed convinced Ivan to take many of them into his service.[69]

At a *Sejm* held in February 1578 in Warsaw the decision had been taken by the Commonwealth, and its new King, to proceed against Russia itself rather than against the Crimeans, since the reward for the former was Livonia, but what could be obtained from the Crimeans? Taxes had been voted accordingly, and during the interval while both sides prepared for future military operations, exchanges of envoys took place marked again by fierce disputes over precedence which prevented all formal discussions.[70] In the relief of Wenden, the collaboration between Sweden and the Commonwealth opened up a new horizon, though no active alliance emerged between them for the conduct of the war against Ivan in Livonia.[71] Meanwhile, on 5 November 1578 the Porte made peace with the Commonwealth in order to concentrate on war with Persia, and used its good offices to arrange an armistice between the Khanate of Crimea and the Polish Lithuanian kingdom in September 1579, thus freeing the Khan to assist the Porte in the war with Persia but also freeing the Commonwealth from fear for its southern border.

The correspondence between Ivan and Bathory was reminiscent of the language used between John III and Ivan, which was still conducted at low levels unknown between crowned heads. 'You have sent your missive to us . . . full of the barking of dogs' wrote Ivan in 1573 to King John, who refused to be treated as a vassal, or to negotiate with Ivan only through the Governor of Novgorod.

> You write your name before ours, but our brothers are the Emperor of Rome and other great rulers, and you cannot call them brother for the land of Sweden is below them in honour as we shall prove shortly . . . tell us whose son was your father Gustav and what was the name of your grandfather . . . did he sit on a throne, and with which rulers was he brother and friend? If you want to put on the muzzle of a dog and bark at us, we shall not reply, for barking is beneath a great lord.[72]

Similarly, Bathory refused to use the title of 'Tsar' in addressing Ivan, and mocked his pretensions to descend from the Roman emperor Augustus, which outraged the Russian boyars. 'We have cleared our Livonian patrimony and it is improper for you to invade it, for they have plucked you from your principality to reign in Poland and Lithuania but not in Livonia' declared the Tsar to King Stephen. To Commonwealth envoys who arrived in January 1579 Ivan demanded the cession of Livonia, Courland and Polotsk as well as Kiev and many other towns.

He now claimed them on genealogical grounds, because the princes of Lithuania were descended from the Rogvolodovichi of Polotsk, i.e. they were Riurikovichi, 'brothers' of Ivan, and therefore the Polish crown and the grand principality of Lithuania, on the death of the last descendant of Jagiello, were now his patrimony. The princes of Galicia (Russian princes in south-west Russia of old) and the kings of Poland were equal, 'while no one had ever heard of the principality of Transylvania!'[73] The offended Commonwealth envoys pointed out that King David of Judea had been of lowly origin, but Ivan ordered his officials to reply that 'David was chosen by God, not by man; listen to Solomon speaking as the Holy Spirit: woe to the house where a woman reigns, and woe to the city where many reign'.[74] Ivan reproached the envoys for having elected a lowly prince, unworthy of being treated fraternally. In many of Ivan's written and verbal communications at this time a triumphal tone underlies his assurance that at last Russia has achieved her aims and has conquered Livonia and access to the sea. But the Russian defeat at Wenden in February 1578 led the Tsar to consider embarking on peace negotiations by an exchange of 'great ambassadors', to be conducted while continuing with the war. There remained the problem of relations with Sweden. John III continued grimly to hold on to Reval, and to the hope of conquering Narva.

Chapter XIX
Peace Negotiations

Around April 1579 Ivan, then in Aleksandrovskaia Sloboda, fell seriously ill.[1] He summoned the senior church hierarchy and the Boyar Council to his bedside and proclaimed his son Ivan his heir. He also addressed the Boyar Council urging its members to find means of entering on peace negotiations with Stephen Bathory. He had already drafted a will, perhaps several times, but the only surviving text of any of his wills is an undated copy, made early in the nineteenth century, of an eighteenth-century copy of an earlier copy of a sixteenth-century original, and historians are not unanimous about when exactly Ivan may have dictated it, if it is in fact genuine.[2] Some believe that he wrote this will between 6 and 17 August 1572, after the victory over the Khan of Crimea, news of which reached him in Novgorod on the 6th. Another theory holds that the Tsar wrote his will earlier in the summer of 1572, when he was sunk in gloom and fear over his possible defeat by the Crimeans, and believed he might have to take refuge in some other country. Bearing in mind his morbid imagination it is not unlikely that he saw himself being borne away, loaded in chains, as a prisoner of the Khan or even of the Sultan. The dating of the will can to some extent be determined by the mention of bequests to his wife, Anna Koltovskaya, which must have been made before Ivan repudiated her and sent her to a monastery in October 1572.[3] However, Anna's surname is not mentioned in the will, she is only referred to as Tsaritsa Anna, so that the legacy might well have been to her successor, Tsaritsa Anna Vasil'chikova.

The draft will gives some idea of Ivan's frame of mind whenever he dictated it, whether in 1572 or in 1579.[4] It was probably written by Andrei Shchelkalov and like nearly all of Ivan's writings it is extremely verbose, quoting extensively from the Old and New Testaments. In a long prologue, Ivan describes himself as the worst sinner on earth, the most abject of mortals, 'defiled of soul and corrupt of body', whom even the Levite passed by. He had surpassed Cain and was like unto Esau, corrupt of reason and bestial in mind. His head was defiled by the wish and desire for improper deeds, he had discoursed on murder and fornication, wrath and indignation, he had indulged in insatiable rapine and inner murder, gluttony and drunkenness, plundering of others' wealth. He begs Christ to bind up the sores of his spiritual and bodily wounds and have mercy on him, in a paraphrase of the Lord's Prayer.[5] In language of great eloquence since it is based on the Bible, Ivan beat his breast and proclaimed his message commanding his children to love one another, to hold firmly to the Orthodox faith, to be just to their servants, 'and upon those that are evil you should place your disfavour, not hurriedly, but after consideration, not in wrath' – an injunction he rarely carried out himself, but which is an echo of an injunction in the Domostroi. His son Ivan Ivanovich was enjoined to protect his brother Fedor, so that he should not complain that he had not been given his own principality, and Fedor should not ask for one.

Yet, after quoting at length from St Paul on love Ivan draws attention to the apostle's words: 'But if any provide not for his own . . . he hath denied the faith and is worse than an infidel.' The copyist who produced the unsatisfactory version of the will which survives, indulges occasionally in marginal comments which have a certain flavour. When Ivan speaks of wandering about his lands in exile, the copyist notes that because of his fear of revolts the Tsar preferred to live in Staritsa or in Aleksandrovskaia Sloboda; or he notes: 'Here he [Ivan] evinces once more his terror of being deprived of the throne.' Evidently he was fully aware of the nature of Ivan's paranoia.

After further lengthy quotations from parables in the New Testament, Ivan gets down to the division of his kingdom, leaving the Russian regalia and the Russian kingdom to Ivan Ivanovich, as well as the city of Moscow, which he does not divide between his sons as had been usual in the past; nor does he dissipate the heritage from Vasily III and Ivan III. But he does allot a large number of estates to Fedor, creating a very substantial appanage for his younger son. The list of Ivan's lands provides interesting evidence of the extent of the confiscation of estates from a number of princes both before and after the *oprichnina*. One of the main problems in dating the will is the Tsar's bequests of lands to Prince Mikhail Vorotynsky, to replace those which he had confiscated, a bequest which would obviously be superseded by 1573, when the prince was executed.[6]

It is possible, however, that the surviving copy of the will is a draft which has been returned to and altered many times and which does not in any way represent a completed document. In that case the existing copy could well be dated after 1572, particularly as it confirms Ivan's vassal, King Magnus as owner of a number of towns in Livonia which were not conquered by Russia until the campaign of 1577. Magnus was now betrothed to Vladimir of Staritsky's second daughter, Maria, after the eldest had died of the plague. He would have to repay a large advance made to him by Ivan to help him to conquer his vassal kingdom, and if he left Livonia or Russia his lands would revert to the tsarevich Ivan Ivanovich.[7]

There is one reference to the *oprichnina* in the will: 'And that I set up an *oprichnina*, it is now according to the will of my children Ivan and Fedor, let them do what suits them best, a model is ready for them.' Had Ivan already abolished the *oprichnina* when this will was drafted? It refers to the *oprichnina* in the past, but it is impossible to tell. Evidently Ivan still thought that having their own appanage, with their own armed forces and guards might also be necessary for his children.[8]

Ivan's will may coincide in time with another perplexing document attributed to him, namely the 'Kanon to the Dread Angel, the voevoda', attributed to Parfenii the Holy Fool, and dating from either 1572 or 1573, at any rate from a time when Ivan was seriously ill according to later reports. Or the will and the illness may belong together in 1579.[9] So may the prayer, which maybe reflects Ivan's despair at the loss of Polotsk (see below). In May, Ivan had moved to the monastery of Volokolamsk, before continuing to Novgorod on 27 June 1579 and his thoughts may have turned to his fate in the next world.[10] The prayer is sad and gloomy, composed in a moment of the fear of death, and sent to all in the hour of death: 'Use this prayer every day', warns Parfenii the Yurodivy:

> Let the angel pray for me, may I be able to repent of my evil deeds, and cast off the burden of my sins. I have far to go with you, fearsome and dread angel, do not frighten me in my powerlessness . . . give me to drink from the cup of salvation . . . leave me not alone . . . Most Holy Queen by your grace relieve me of the burden of my sins.

The prayer continues in this form, appealing now to the dread angel (who is never mentioned by name), now to the Holy Virgin Mother of God, and now to the King of the Heavens, to forgive the sinner. It is a moving prayer, couched in the traditional, poetic language of church devotion.

The Russian defeat at Wenden led the Tsar to consider embarking on peace negotiations by an exchange of 'great ambassadors', to be conducted while continuing with the war. Bathory too still continued desultory peace talks. But now that he was free from the complications of Danzig, he was determined, as part of the process of establishing his authority, and possibly his dynasty, to obtain the whole of Livonia for his new kingdom, and on 26 June 1579 he formally declared war on Ivan.[11] Until then, Russia had been at war with Livonia, but Poland–Lithuania had not declared war on Russia in spite of the Russian conquest of Polotsk. At the same time, however, Bathory issued a remarkable challenge to Ivan, calling on him to settle their differences by single combat – a most unusual procedure in the annals of sixteenth-century royal behaviour, but typical perhaps of Polish or Hungarian notions of chivalry, a touch of Catholic bravado in a monarch anxious to consolidate his throne. Bathory protested against Ivan's refusal to treat him as a sovereign of equal rank, and declared his intention to seek reparation for the injury done to him by the Tsar on the Tsar's body, since he did not wish to harm the latter's subjects, as Christians, whose freedom he was anxious to preserve.[12]

Bathory expounded his policy in an exhortation to the people of Russia, explaining that he did not want to shed their blood, that his only enemy was the Tsar, and that he wanted the latter to suffer personally for what he had inflicted on others. The gesture was not unprecedented. In 1527 and again in 1528, the Emperor Charles V issued a similar challenge to single combat to the King of France, Francis I who, in Charles's view, had failed to honour his word, given to Charles on his release from captivity in Madrid after the battle of Pavia (1525), and return to captivity in Spain. The challenge was issued in writing, and the meeting was to take place on the River Bidassoa, on the Franco-Spanish border. Francis, however, ignored the herald sent with a safe conduct for him, thus demonstrating that he was no gentleman.[13]

Bathory's attempt to draw a distinction between the Tsar and his people, his effort to 'bring them freedom and law'[14] provoked a response from the Tsar. The reply to Stephen Bathory's challenge, dated some time in August 1579, which Ivan planned to issue in answer to his manifesto was never delivered; however a late archive copy suggests that Ivan appealed for the support of the various ranks of the nation, starting with the church hierarchy, possibly in a *Zemskii sobor*, but modern scholarship does not support this view.[15]

Both sides now prepared for war. Collecting his army proved difficult for Ivan because again many refused to respond to his appeal but he was able to gather a force estimated at between 30,000 and 40,000, including some 6,000 Tatar cavalry, and in June he moved from Novgorod to Pskov which was to be his headquarters. Meanwhile Bathory had also been planning his campaign. He collected an army of some 40,000 men, drawing troops from both Lithuania and Poland and recruiting mercenaries from Germany and Transylvania. Instead of advancing into exhausted and ravaged Livonia, or on Pskov, which would leave his rear unguarded, the King planned to advance first on Polotsk which lay on the River Dvina and would guarantee both supplies and communications. Ivan had expected Bathory to attack Livonia, since the war was about Livonia, and not about Russian-occupied Lithuania, and was taken by surprise when the King appeared before Polotsk in August 1579. Polotsk was on the road to central Russia and, though well garrisoned, was not strongly fortified, since its walls were of wood. Neither Ivan, nor his generals, F.I. Sheremetev and Prince F.I. Mstislavsky (son of Ivan Fedorovich), reached Polotsk in time to relieve it. The fighting was extremely fierce but the besieged city finally surrendered and on 1 September 1579 Bathory entered it. To him it was a recaptured Lithuanian city: the great church of St Sophia was preserved for the Orthodox, and land was set aside for a new and imposing Catholic church.[16]

The loss of Polotsk was a profound psychological shock for Ivan. Its conquest had been a landmark on the road to the realization of the idea of Moscow as the heir of Kiev, and had been accompanied by religious rhetoric and widely accessible religious symbolism. It was the Tsar's *votchina* and after its conquest it was included in his *titl*; it was after all Riurikovich land.[17] Prince I.F. Mstislavsky's proposals to recover Polotsk, with the help of Ivan's two sons, were waved away with contumely by the Tsar who beat Mstislavsky with his staff and called him an old dog, full of Lithuanian spirit, who wanted to place his sons in danger.[18]

Karamzin accused Ivan of cowardice, or refusing to give battle. Zimin and Skrynnikov think he was suffering from shock.[19] More modern authors have stressed that he did not have sufficient knowledge of strategy and tactics to plan a campaign and simply no longer had the means to assemble an army. Already in 1579 many of the service gentry had refused to attend the Tsar's summons to war; and supplies of all kinds were lacking after the fierce fighting and the depopulation due to plague and starvation which had afflicted northern Russia and Livonia. Moreover Ivan had found himself forced to fight a war on two fronts, against the Commonwealth to the south west, and against the Swedes in Estonia to the north, where a Tatar-led assault on Narva had failed.

In fact the loss of Polotsk, after sixteen years in Russian hands, seems to have broken Ivan's spirit. He believed that his military failures were the punishment of God, and Russian prisoners in summer 1580 reported that he had summoned the Metropolitan and the bishops and had asked their forgiveness for his sins (including his many marriages?), and humbled himself before God.[20] Indeed it was probably not military factors alone which led to Ivan's failure in the field.

There was a good deal of military innovation in eastern Europe in the sixteenth century. But military change was related to climate and geography. The horse was still essential for steppe warfare, but both Polish and Russian armed forces increased their commitment to infantry and gunpowder in this period. Ski-troops were known both in Sweden and in Russia. Bathory had introduced in the Commonwealth a medium-weight cavalry force, which could manoeuvre more easily than the Western heavily armoured cavalry, but the Russian cavalryman remained the light-weight horseman suitable for fighting against the Tatars. The Russians were superior to the Poles in artillery and both sides used infantry extensively, relying on firepower.[21] The Commonwealth superiority in the campaigns of 1579 to 1580 lay in its cavalry, but probably also in the generalship of its commanders and the better training of its forces. The Russians did not dispose of sufficient infantry to maintain garrisons in conquered towns and castles. They were unable to consolidate their victories.[22]

Though trade continued with England in the late 1570s both through the White Sea and through Narva, in spite of the dangers from Polish and Swedish privateers, diplomatic relations, while Ivan was on campaign, were allowed to decline. Daniel Sylvester, after his last meeting with Ivan, on 29 January 1576, in which the Tsar had expressed his dissatisfaction with the tone of Elizabeth's messages, which had shown a 'kynde of haughtynes in our systar moved tharto by th'abasynge of our selfe towards her', had returned to England. Ivan had hinted that he might if necessary seek asylum with his good friend the Emperor Maximilian instead of in England, and that he would remove England's trade monopoly and open it to the Germans and Venetians.[23] Sylvester returned to Russia but the Queen's reply which he carried never reached Ivan, for the English envoy's life was dramatically cut short in Kholmogory, where he was killed by lightning as he was trying on his new court clothes of yellow satin, and his whole house was burnt down.[24]

Ivan was still anxious to communicate with England, and he now approached Jerome Horsey to act as his messenger. Always game for an adventure, Horsey embarked on what could have been a dangerous mission, travelling by land, carrying a letter from Ivan to Elizabeth hidden in a 'wooden bottle filled with aqua-vitae to hang under my horse's mane', clothed in his shabbiest garments and with four hundred Hungarian ducats in gold sewn into his boots. He left some time in 1580 (he does not give the date), well attended as far as the Livonian border, where his difficulties began. But his luck held: when he was arrested on the Danish-held island of Oesel, the governor spoke to him privately, and discovered that Horsey had befriended his daughter who was a captive in Russia. Thereafter Horsey was sped on his way, and finally arrived in England where 'I opened my aqua vitae bottle and sweetened the emperor's letter as well as I could', though the Queen remarked on the scent when she read it.

It was for him a very successful mission: the Queen gave him her picture and her hand to kiss. More important, Horsey returned with thirteen company ships loaded with copper, lead, powder, saltpetre, brimstone and other things useful for war, and paid for with nine thousand pounds in ready money, clear evidence that England was providing Ivan with military supplies, whatever Elizabeth might have said to the Emperor.[25]

After the loss of Polotsk, Ivan was too discouraged to undertake any military activity and it is possible that two events combined to dishearten him. It may be that sometime after the loss of Polotsk he concluded that his Dr Bomelius was a traitor and decided to execute him. There is some suggestion that Bomelius tried to persuade Ivan not to take action against the Poles. The most detailed account of his downfall is given by Horsey, but he gives no date and does not say where the events he describes took place. He links Bomelius's downfall with the disgrace of an unnamed archbishop of Novgorod, probably Leonid, which actually happened in 1575. It is more likely that Bomelius's disgrace was connected with an attempt by him to leave Russia, with his ill-gotten gains sewn into his clothes. He was caught and brought back, tortured on the rack and with wire whips, and having confessed to many crimes, and incriminated many people, the Tsar sent orders for him to be roasted on a spit and, as Horsey describes it, 'I pressed among many others to see him; cast up his eyes naming Christ; cast into a dungeon and died there.' Horsey regarded him as a wicked man, and a 'practicer of much mischief, and . . . an enemy always to our nation', who had 'deluded the emperor, making him believe the queen of England was young, and it was very feasible for him to marry her'.[26]

Possibly Ivan's susceptibility to occult influences may in this period have been particularly stimulated by the great comet of 1577, which was visible from Peru to China, came closest to the earth on 10 November and disappeared at the end of January 1578. One astronomer described it 'as a huge shining spherical mass which vomited fire and ended in smoke' with a huge long tail, curved over itself, of a burning dark reddish colour. Other astronomers forecast great changes in the weather and in politics, and many of the observations made caused an upheaval in the previous cosmology, for the new comet had evidently appeared not between the earth and the moon, where comets were supposed to travel, but beyond the moon. A second comet was visible from October 1580 to January 1581 and they were regarded as manifestations of heavenly wrath, of danger to mankind, and particularly to princes. Tycho Brahe reported that the comet of 1577 had first appeared in the astrological eighth house or house of death, and that it foretold a great mortality among mankind. Ivan must have seen the comet, and in all probability Bomelius would have interpreted its significance. According to another source, even before war broke out several wonders happened:

> A comet appeared which without doubt foretold many misfortunes for Russia. Then there was thunder in a cloudless sky on Christmas Day and a thunderbolt hit the splendid palace in Aleksandrovskaia Sloboda and destroyed part of it; lightning turned all sorts of precious things into ashes, entered the bedroom, threw down from the bed a list of Livonian prisoners of war . . . condemned to death. Ivan grew pale, and awaited great changes in his fate.[27]

This must have been enough to unsettle the Tsar.[28]

Inevitably Ivan now turned to diplomacy, and in September 1579, in Pskov, he attempted to interest the *voevoda* of Vilna, then N. Radziwill the Red, in opening peace talks. But he accompanied this opening with a most insulting letter directed to Stephen Bathory, accusing the King of adopting Kurbsky's treasonable ways, and still 'asserting his will to win'. Ivan declared that the Polish King's 'Latin' faith was only 'half Christian', that of his nobles Lutheran, and that now a new heresy had appeared in his country, Arianism (by which he presumably meant anti-Trinitarianism). God would not give victory to such people, who were not even Christian.

Yet again, however, this letter may not have been sent and was perhaps only a safety valve for Ivan's overwhelming rage and resentment at his powerlessness.[29] Meanwhile, in summer 1580, Bathory renewed the offensive, again taking the Russians by surprise by attacking neither Pskov nor Smolensk, but Velikie Luki, a minor but strategically placed

Russian town lying between the two. Couriers travelled again between the two warring parties, but it led to nothing. The Russian loss of Velikie Luki, which fell to the Poles on 5 September 1580, and the defeat of another Russian force two weeks later by the Poles, together with a further Swedish assault in Karelia forced Ivan to think seriously of peace negotiations with the Commonwealth, but he did not wish to suffer the humiliation of being the first to open the subject formally, nor did Stephen Bathory, who categorically refused to open negotiations even for the exchange of prisoners.[30]

Ivan now embarked on a wide ranging diplomatic ploy, which reveals that though he may not have been a good general, he understood very well how to muddy the European diplomatic waters. He had lately showed himself more amenable to discussion, and sent proposals for the renewal of talks between Russia and the Commonwealth in November 1579 and January 1580. He called a meeting of the Boyar Council, on 25 August 1580, in Aleksandrovskaia Sloboda, to discuss the situation. The result of these consultations was the dispatch of a messenger first to Vienna, then on to Rome. Leontii Istoma Shevrigin, who left on 6 September, was a mere courier (*gonets*), belonging to the lowest diplomatic rank in the Russian service, which enabled him to travel without ostentation, and therefore with greater safety, since he was less likely to attract attention and be intercepted. He was charged with a letter from Ivan proposing to join the Emperor Rudolph II in an alliance against the Ottomans and, in order to enable him to do so, inviting the Emperor at the same time to bring pressure to bear on Bathory to make peace with Russia, on terms which would allow Ivan to keep at least four Livonian fortresses.[31]

But Ivan was proposing an even bolder venture. Shevrigin was to continue on to Rome and pick up the threads of earlier soundings from the Vatican, throwing out hints of a possible acceptance of the supremacy of the Pope by the Russian Orthodox Church, an aspiration which had been high on the agenda of the popes ever since the Council of Florence in the fifteenth century.[32] Ivan hoped thus to win time and to encourage the Pope, then Gregory XIII, to mediate a peace or a truce between Russia and the Commonwealth, a thoroughly original proposal running counter to all previous Russian dealings with the Papacy.[33] Since travel by land was too dangerous for a Russian envoy, Shevrigin travelled by sea from Pernau in Livonia to Lübeck, and collected there an Italian interpreter, Francesco Pallavicino, to add to his escort of a German interpreter, Wilhelm Popler. He arrived in Prague at the beginning of January 1581, and was lodged in the accommodation unflatteringly allocated to 'Turks and Muscovites', who were evidently treated on the same footing.

The Emperor Rudolph received Shevrigin on 10 January 1581, but showed no interest at all in his proposals for an alliance against the Turks and for the improvement of trade, nor in the timber of sables offered to him as a gift. The fate of Livonia was in the hands of the Imperial Diet, Shevrigin was told, and he was treated in Prague much as the foreign envoys were treated in Moscow, left in isolation. His request for a passport to Venice was promptly granted if only to get rid of him. The Russian party arrived in the Adriatic on 13 February 1581.

In contrast with his reception in Prague, the Venetian regents received the Russian courier with great pomp and ceremony, and showed him everything, including their formidable naval armament. But alas they did not know that Shevrigin's letter of credentials to them from the Tsar, solemnly read aloud, was a forgery. Since he had no credentials to present to the Serenissima, Shevrigin, with admirable presence of mind, had composed a message from the Tsar in his own hand, and added the seal taken off a letter to the Elector of Saxony to make it convincing. In the letter, he had called himself 'ambassador' not courier, hence the ceremonial treatment he received in Venice (and later in Rome) as distinct from Prague. The episode is explained by the fact that Ivan at this time had no idea that Venice was an independent republic, and believed that the Serenissima was a mere province belonging to the popes, while the Office of Foreign Affairs in Moscow had no idea of the correct form of address to use to the Doge.[34]

Shevrigin, having dropped a few hints about how welcome trade with Venice would be in Moscow, now made tracks for Rome where he arrived on 24 February 1581. Here too he was received with great public ceremony and escorted to the Palazzo Colonna, where he was to reside, and lavishly entertained. Presumably because of the difficulty over religion, the Pope granted the envoy only a private audience, on 26 February, when Shevrigin kissed the Pope's slipper, and on his knees read out the letter from Ivan. This was couched in Ivan's usual terms, in which he described Bathory as no better than a Moslem and the creature of the Sultan. The Pope set up a commission to study Shevrigin's letter which conveyed the Russian perspective on the military situation in the east, and by implication, the Russian need for peace, and requested the Pope to send an ambassador to Moscow to discuss military operations against the Ottoman Empire and a truce between the Commonwealth and Russia. Needless to say, the Poles used their influence in Rome to counter the Russian proposals. But the Pope decided to allow discussion with Ivan on matters of religion and only afterwards to discuss possible military cooperation against the Turks.[35]

The Pope appointed Antonio Possevino as his ambassador.[36] Possevino was a highly regarded Jesuit, experienced in international negotiations, notably in Sweden, where he had succeeded in converting John III to Catholicism. He was an able champion of the Counter Reformation, and before his departure for Russia he immediately embarked on a thorough study of all the known literature on Muscovy, notably Herberstein, Giovio, Cobenzl, whom Possevino met later in Graz and questioned about Russia; perhaps also Prinz von Buchau, and also perhaps Schlichting, a copy of whose *Brief Account* was now available in the Vatican in Latin.[37]

In the instruction prepared for Possevino, the Pope offered to negotiate a peace between Ivan and Stephen Bathory which would lead on to the alliance against the Ottomans Ivan was so keen on. But for it to be solid, it had to be agreed upon within the bounds of the Church, which alone held the key to union, the Roman Catholic Church. Let the Tsar read the decrees of the council of Florence, let him send new ambassadors to the Pope. Shevrigin could also give a positive papal reply to the Russian proposals for commercial relations between Venice and Moscow, but the ultimate aim was a crusade against the Turks and the Union of the Churches. On 27 March 1581, Shevrigin left Rome on his return journey to Russia, accompanied by Possevino.

In the interval Ivan had not only been engaged with public concerns. In the course of 1576/7, his tsaritsa, Anna Vasil'chikova, had died, and in 1578/9, he had embarked on his sixth 'marriage', this time with a reputedly very handsome widow of modest rank, Vasilisa Melent'eva, possibly the widow of a *d'iak* who had served in Livonia.[38] One authority, R.G. Skrynnikov, has stated categorically that Ivan never chose a bride because he was attracted to her but that his marriages were all negotiated by powerful boyar interests at court. The one exception he admits is Vasilisa, who was reputed to be very presentable and handsome, *uriadna* and *krasna*, 'such as you do not find among the girls, brought in for the Tsar to look at'. The marriage did not last long, for Vasilisa died the following year 'of her own death'.[39] But it coincided with the period of Ivan's greatest military successes. As usual, without mourning Vasilisa for long, the Tsar 'married' as his seventh wife, on 6 September 1580, Maria Fedorovna Nagaia, the niece of Afanasii Fedorovich Nagoi, who had played a prominent part in Ivan' s counsels ever since his return from the Crimea. By this match Nagoi increased still more his weight in the boyar councils within Ivan's court. In the same year, Ivan Ivanovich, who had already been compelled to divorce two wives, chose and married a third, Elena Federovna Sheremeteva.[40]

Meanwhile Possevino and the courier Shevrigin advanced on Venice, where they were received by the Doge and the Council of Ten. Possevino expanded on the papal policy of war against the Porte, which met with no response from the Venetians, who had no wish to compromise their lucrative trade with the East. Shevrigin was limited to his written instructions which dealt only with trade. After a brief stay in Prague, where the Emperor Rudolph treated the mission with complete indifference, the two diplomats parted company, Possevino proceeding to Poland and Shevrigin, again avoiding the Commonwealth, travelling home by sea through Lübeck. Shevrigin was an extremely uncongenial companion for the erudite Jesuit. He was after all an uneducated man, with a certain peasant shrewdness about money, lacking all artistic susceptibility, indifferent to the glories of Rome, and according to Possevino mainly concerned with making a good bargain in the sale of the goods he had brought with him.

Stephen Bathory accepted without demur the offer of the mediation of the Pope. He had previously been sounded by the nuncio in Poland on the creation of a vast anti-Turkish coalition and showed no enthusiasm for the present plan to include Russia in the alliance. His main aim at the time was to obtain the whole of Livonia for his new kingdom (which he hoped one day to make hereditary). He provided the necessary passports for Possevino, though he had many reservations about the sudden enthusiasm of Pope Gregory XIII for Ivan IV. By the beginning of June Possevino was in Warsaw, making contacts with the Queen of Poland, Anna Jagiellonka, with the Chancellor, Jan Zamoyski and with every influential person, and then proceeded to Vilna where Bathory had his headquarters.[41]

It was a time when all kinds of strange rumours about Ivan's camp were swirling around Poland, to the effect that Ivan's sons were in open disagreement on policy with their father; even Fedor Ivanovich was said to have parted company with him. A nephew of Maliuta Skuratov, Daniil Bel'sky, fled to Lithuania. Prince I.F. Mstislavsky was once again disgraced, and forced to swear publicly, with his two sons, that he would not flee to Lithuania and that he would not surrender Russian towns. It was precisely these kinds of rumours which encouraged Stephen Bathory to embark on a new campaign and to refuse any concessions to Ivan. The Tsar, meanwhile, was gradually climbing down, agreeing to hand over the whole of Livonia, if only he could keep Narva and receive back Velikie Luki and a few other towns, and trying to persuade Bathory not to carry the war deeper into Russian territory.[42]

The King received Possevino on 17 June in Vilna[43] and, already inclined to favour the Jesuits, he was won over by the obvious openness of Possevino and, particularly, by his assurances that the Pope would always incline more to a devout Catholic than to a dissident ruler with a doubtful reputation. Both parties agreed to wait for the return of the envoys whom Bathory had sent to Russia recently, with his final terms. Possevino would accompany the King to Disna, a fort on the junction of the river of the same name with the Dvina, and await Ivan's reply there. The journey took nine days, during which the King, his Chancellor, Zamoyski, and the priest confirmed the extent of their agreement on most issues, and Possevino showed the papal brief to the King. In turn Bathory, the soldier, gave some very sensible advice to Possevino to the effect that Ivan would never embark on a war against the Ottoman Turks, because the distances were too great and the terrain too difficult.[44]

Bathory's terms were now the cession of the whole of Livonia, a substantial monetary contribution, and the destruction of a few Russian border forts.[45] Ivan, through his envoys, rejected them outright. When they arrived at Disna Possevino called on the Russian envoys, where they had camped outside the Polish fort with their escort of 200 men, but they only repeated that they were bound by their written instructions. Asked why they had changed their replies, they answered: 'A new testament replaces an old one.' To all intents and purposes the talks broke down, since the Russian envoys were not authorized to negotiate, so Possevino prepared to leave for Moscow, for which passports had already been requested.

Meanwhile the two sovereigns took the opportunity to indulge in one more ill-tempered exchange of insults and name-calling, initiated by Ivan, on 29 June 1581. Writing as a ruler by the grace of God, and not 'elected by a noisy assembly of men', Ivan reminded Bathory of his past concessions and contrasted them with Bathory's utter refusal to yield any ground, in fact to negotiate; he reproached him with behaving in an unchristian manner, rejecting solutions agreed upon so that Christian blood should not be shed. Asking for indemnities, declared Ivan, was a Moslem custom, not practised between equal Christian sovereigns, even Moslems did not impose them on each other. Bathory negotiated like a Moslem, leaving no time even for Russian envoys to arrive. Bathory had broken the sworn promises to previous ambassadors, which his predecessors had made (all listed by name, going back to the days of Ol'gerd and Jagiello); he had taken Russian traitors such as Kurbsky into his service; he had seized Ivan's city of Polotsk by treachery. The

Tsar accused the Commonwealth troops, with some justice, of committing atrocities on the battlefield, of disembowelling the most noble and removing their fat and bile (*zhel'ch*) like dogs, as though to use it for witchcraft. It was not for Christians to rejoice in blood and killing, and behave like barbarians.[46]

Polish arrogance seemed particularly to have outraged Ivan, and he continued to inveigh against Bathory for thirty-two printed pages.[47] The most interesting aspect of this particular missive is that Ivan is already refuting the arguments that might be put to him on the Union of Churches, as though afraid of what the mediation of the Pope might produce. He states that 'the popes and all Romans and Latins declare that the Latin and Greek faiths are the same' as has been enacted at the Council of Florence, when Isidore was there as Metropolitan. If the Pope agrees, then there is no need for conflict between us – and presumably no need for papal supremacy, which was the sticking point.[48]

Bathory's reply, written by his Chancellor and confidant, Jan Zamoyski, was the most insulting letter the Tsar ever received. Zamoyski spent a week on it, and arranged to distribute it widely in Europe.[49] He answered Ivan's letter point by point, mocking his so-called descent from Roman emperors from east or west, and proclaimed it useless to argue with 'someone who did not know the laws of Christian countries, only his own wild and savage ones'. Ivan was, if anything, descended from the Greek tyrant '*Fiest*' (Thyestes who was served his own roasted children by his brother Atreus at a banquet); Ivan had destroyed not just two children but a whole city, Novgorod, and could be compared with Cain, Pharaoh and Herod. Not only was he cruel, he was a coward, and concluded Zamoyski, 'The poor hen, faced with the falcon and the eagle covers her chick with her wings, while you, two-headed eagle, hide yourself.' He looked on the Tsar as Satan, the Prince of Darkness.[50] And how dared he reproach Bathory with being a Turkish vassal, he who had 'mixed his blood with that of Islam [a reference to the Tsar's wife, Maria Temriukovna], whose ancestors had licked mare's milk on the manes' of Tatar horses, and served as mounting blocks for the khans of Crimea when they bestrode their horses!' And Bathory repeated his dramatic call to decide the issue by single combat between himself and the Tsar. 'If you refuse, you will prove that there is no truth in you, no royal, no manly dignity, not even that of a woman.'[51]

More and more convinced of Russian weakness, Stephen Bathory launched his third campaign against Russia on 20 June 1581, from Vilna, at a time when Ivan had to divert troops to defend himself against a Nogay attack. The Polish King's target now was the important and extremely well fortified city of Pskov, described admiringly by the King's secretary as: 'A big city, it is like Paris.'[52] He had an army of some 47,000 including German and Hungarian mercenaries, while the garrison of Pskov consisted of some 6,000 harquebusiers and 3,000 cavalry, and its walls extended for nine kilometers with forty towers. It was defended by Prince I.P. Shuisky, whose father, Prince P.I. Shuisky, a distinguished general, had been killed in action in 1564 at the battle of the River Ula.

Meanwhile on 21 July 1581, Possevino and his party of twelve left the Polish camp and started out on the difficult journey to Staritsa where Ivan was residing, passing through Smolensk, where Possevino had to avoid being manoeuvred into attending an Orthodox church service, though he was allowed to visit churches and monasteries.[53] He was met in Staritsa with the usual ceremony and the gift of a splendid black horse, and his audience was fixed for 20 August. Escorted by service gentry in cloth of gold, courtiers and large numbers of troops, Possevino was received by Ivan sitting on a throne two feet above the ground, wearing a gold tunic artistically interwoven with jewels, rings, a silver sceptre, necklaces, one with a cross two-foot-long. On his head was a glittering jewelled tiara, somewhat larger than the one worn by the Pope. The papal gifts were then produced. They were in good taste, including a rock-crystal cross inlaid with gold and containing a splinter of the True Cross – but less apposite was a beautifully bound volume of the decisions of the Council of Florence in Greek, which Possevino thought no one at the court could read. There was also a gift for the Tsaritsa Anastasia Romanovna, since no one in Rome knew she had died long ago, and that Ivan was now on his seventh wife.

The first negotiations took place before the banquet, with two councillors, and the *d'iak*, Andrei Shchelkalov, and a few others. Progress was slowed down by the Russian practice by which the boyars referred back to the Tsar whenever a hitch occurred, and then returned with long scrolls, from which they read aloud, reciting all the Tsar's titles on every occasion.[54] The usual banquet followed, with the usual display of silver on a buffet, which Possevino regarded with the contempt of a good Jesuit, after which he and the priests with him withdrew, refusing to join in a drinking bout.

Talks began at once, lasting over six sessions, and concentrated around three issues, which implied concessions on both sides: Bathory's insistence on acquiring the whole of Livonia, including Reval (then in Swedish hands) and Narva (then in Russian hands); Ivan's insistence on keeping Narva and recovering Russian towns conquered by Bathory;

and Possevino's *basso continuo* on the subject of the Union of Churches and the eventual alliance against the Ottoman Turks which, if victorious, could lead to an eastern Christian empire for Ivan.[55] The religious question was, however, firmly kept out of bounds by the Tsar. But unfortunately for Ivan, who hoped to keep Sweden out of the mediation at that time (and for Bathory, who did not want to share Livonia with Sweden), John III of Sweden was encouraged by the Commonwealth's assault on Pskov to launch a lightning attack against Narva, which fell on 4 September 1581, with an appalling massacre, followed by assaults on Ivangorod, Yam and Kopor'e, the last of which fell on 14 October.[56] This was a real blow to Ivan for it meant the end of the hope of commercial expansion in the Finnish Gulf and direct access to the Baltic Sea and it also made diplomatic bargaining much more difficult for him.

Possevino offered to return to Stephen Bathory's camp to re-open discussions with the King, an offer which Ivan accepted with alacrity after the loss of Narva. But he did not reduce his terms for peace, though he agreed to allow the subjects of the Papacy and Venice to trade through Russia with Persia, and even to bring a Catholic priest with them; however the request to build a Catholic church was too much and was turned down flat. On 9 September Bathory's reply to Ivan's long letter arrived, longer and more discourteous than any Ivan had written.[57] But Bathory was held back by the failure of his forces to make any headway against the indomitable defenders of Pskov, where women as well as men (and the icon of St Dmitri) manned the walls in a defence of their city which has become legendary in Russia. Bathory who had hoped Pskov would fall easily was not even able to conquer the great Pskov Pechersky monastery, and by 1 December, the King left the siege to be conducted by Jan Zamoyski and returned to Vilna. His failure before Pskov rendered him more willing to discuss peace just as it stiffened Ivan's resolution not to abandon Russian towns and persuaded him to demand the cession of more towns in Livonia, and to threaten not to send any more envoys to talks with Bathory. But he climbed down, proposed a truce of seven years to Possevino, and agreed to call Bathory 'brother' in the interests of the cessation of bloodshed between Christian peoples, though in his usual sardonic way, he explained that he did not know who this brother was, where he came from, and how he came to be King of Poland.[58]

The renewed intensity of the fighting between the Commonwealth and Russia led also to a renewal of the correspondence between Ivan and Prince Kurbsky. The Prince had sent a brief reply to Ivan's 'bombastic and long-winded' letter of 5 July 1564. He was particularly scathing about Ivan's obscure references to 'beds and body-warmers . . . and other old wives tales' which would arouse astonishment and laughter. 'I do not understand what you want from us,' he exclaims, 'having killed so many people already.' He introduces a new concept into the discussion, suggesting that it was not befitting chivalrous men (*muzhem rytserskim*) to belch forth unclean and biting words. The use of the word 'chivalrous' may reflect the expansion of Kurbsky's acquaintanceship with western noble culture.[59]

There was no reply from Ivan to Kurbsky until the letter he wrote in July 1577 from Wolmar, through Prince Alexander Polubensky. Though at this time Ivan's hopes of victory were riding high, his language is less aggressive than in many of his other letters. As usual he dwells on his sinfulness, and his trust in the mercy of God. He reverts to the ambitions of Sylvester and Adashev, and of course Kurbsky, to 'see all the Russian land under your feet' and urges that it was not he who was corrupted, but those who sought to evade his power, and took all power and lordship from him, so that in fact he ruled nothing. He goes over a number of very personal past incidents, and accuses Kurbsky of having wanted to give power to Vladimir of Staritsa. The key to his thought is a quotation from the book of Job: 'I have gone to and fro in the earth and walked up and down on that which is below the heaven and that which is below the heaven have I brought beneath my feet.' He accuses Kurbsky of thinking that he would have the whole of Russia beneath his feet. But he himself had now ridden over all the roads, to and from Lithuania, and the hooves of his horses had been everywhere. Even in Wolmar, whence Kurbsky had written to him, Ivan had now caught up with him. 'And we have written all this to you, neither boasting nor puffing ourselves up – God knows; but we wrote to remind you to mend your ways, that you might think of the salvation of your soul.'[60]

Chapter XX
The Truce of Yam Zapol'sky

The financial extremes to which Ivan had now been reduced led him to examine his resources again. A meeting of the Church Council, jointly with the Tsar and all the boyars, was called for the beginning of 1580 which passed a resolution on monastic lands. The text has survived in two forms, one of 15 January 1580, the other of 15 January 1581. In the preamble it was stated that the Council had met in view of the fact that the Crimeans, Nogays, the King of Lithuania, the Livonians and the Swedes were determined to exterminate the Orthodox religion. Moreover many monastic lands had become derelict because of the drunkenness and improper way of life of the monks and the military servitors had become impoverished as a result of lack of land and labour and were unable to serve. It was therefore resolved that the monasteries should keep the land acquired before 15 January 1580, but that all payments made thereafter for prayers for the dead should be in cash. Monasteries were neither to buy land, nor to lend money on it. The ownership of monastic lands by princes should be examined by the Tsar, and princely lands owned by monasteries should be confiscated.[1]

This resolution seems to be a very moderate tidying-up process, by which the rights of monasteries to own land are confirmed, but their right to acquire land is limited. It favoured all secular landowners, without distinguishing between the various types, at the expense of the church holdings, but there was no question of the wholesale confiscation of church lands. Evidently Ivan did not feel it advisable to tackle the Church head on. On the other hand Horsey gives what he calls a verbatim translation of the text of Ivan's original attack on the Church hierarchy at the Council, for its greed and rapacity, its accumulation of property 'by witchery, enchantments and sorcery'. He quotes Ivan, 'thundering out his thrasonical threats' to the clerics for the horrible sins they committed of 'oppression, gluttony, idleness and sodomy and worse, if worse, with beasts'. He referred also to Ivan's frequently felt desire for the dissolution of the monasteries in order to return the land to the nobles to whom it originally belonged, thus creating a 'fair commonwealth', as Henry VIII had done in England. (English Protestants were particularly critical of prayers for the dead in Russia because the Orthodox Church did not believe in Purgatory, therefore prayers served no purpose.[2]) One may surmise, however, that Horsey's frequently expressed contempt for Russian monasticism is colouring his judgment of the Russian political scene on this occasion.

The turmoil about church lands was related to the far more serious subject of the agricultural crisis in north and central Russia. The causes were many: the ravages of the *oprichnina*, the casualties of war, the flight of the peasant population, harvest failures, increasing taxation, epidemics, rising prices and famine. In the Novgorod area, the cadastres of 1580 registered in some places a reduction of population to 7 per cent of what it had been before the *oprichnina* and the Livonian war; in the city itself the population was reduced to 20 per cent of what it had been before Ivan's destructive raid of 1570. In the Shelonskaia fifth of Novgorod 91.2 per cent of the homesteads were empty. In the centre of Russia the figures were similar; the peasants had simply deserted to the outlying districts. Taxes mounted steadily. Even the English merchants were asked for a contribution of 1,000 rubles in 1580, 500 in 1581.

It is this devastation which has led to a debate among historians on whether an *ukaz* was issued in the early 1580s introducing what is known as the 'forbidden years'. Traditionally the peasants could leave their masters to seek another master around St George's Day in the autumn, when the harvest had been gathered in and the dues paid. But there is evidence that this right was suspended around 1580/1, 1582/3 and in other years in the decade 1580 to 1590, in order to curtail the loss of manpower caused by the departure of peasants to new lands, with the consequent decline of agricultural production, and the consequent inability of the service gentry to equip themselves for war. The 'forbidden years' are regarded as the first step in the introduction of serfdom, hence the interest in discovering if and when they were actually enacted. A careful sifting of the evidence suggests that forbidden years were indeed introduced in this decade, not every year but haphazardly, and not in an organized, nationwide way. It was a policy that undoubtedly led eventually to the development of serfdom, for the next step after forbidding the departure of the peasants was to hunt them down if they did depart illegally, and bring them back forcibly, however long ago they might have fled.[3]

Faced with this serious crisis there was all the more reason to bring the war to an end, and by autumn 1581 Ivan had resigned himself to the loss of Livonia, and given up his hope of winning a port on the Baltic. At a farewell audience to Possevino he addressed him:

> Antonio, go to King Stephen; greet him in my name and treat for peace in accordance with the Pope's instructions. After you have done this be sure to come back to us, for you will always be welcome, both because of the Pope and because of the loyal and devoted services you are rendering to our cause.

There was a further exchange of presents; Possevino received valuable sables which he only reluctantly accepted, and then used in order to ransom some prisoners. Seeing that Possevino and his companions were busily converting anyone they could speak freely to, Ivan was clearly showing great self control in adversity.[4] The Tsar then left for Aleksandrovskaia Sloboda.

The escorts who were to accompany Possevino back to the camp of the King of Poland outside Pskov were given strict orders not to let him travel through Novgorod, perhaps so that he should not see the ravages Ivan had caused there, perhaps because he could not count on its loyalty. On 5 October the priest arrived at Bathory's camp before Pskov. The failure of the Polish assault on Pskov had undermined Polish morale and the army was beginning to feel the strain of the campaign in the worsening weather, with no tents to shelter the soldiers from the snow.

Yet if both sides needed peace, neither Ivan nor Bathory was willing to be the first to climb down, and both were feeling a certain distrust in Possevino who seemed to be putting the interests of the Papacy before those of the belligerents in his anxiety to achieve the peace essential for the building of a coalition against the Ottoman Empire.

Possevino set out before the King the peace terms he had received from Ivan and it was decided to seek the latter's consent to adjourn the discussions to the village of Kiverova Gora, near Yam Zapol'sky, some 100 miles from the Polish camp. A month was to pass before Ivan's agreement was received and the talks finally began in the new location. The two parties lodged some distance apart, in tents or extremely primitive and ill-heated huts, and met in the smoky hut allotted to Possevino.[5] This was the first major diplomatic conference between Russia and a Latin power, in which the diplomatic conventions which had been maturing in the West played a formal part.[6] The full powers granted by Ivan to his envoys were rejected by the Poles as inadequate, and certainly Ivan's brief acknowledgement that his envoys 'spoke for him' was very incomplete compared with the elaborate list of powers granted by Bathory to his envoys. The Russians argued that this was the way they had always granted powers to their envoys, and they saw no need to change them. Possevino succeeded in winning both sides over to beginning formal talks without waiting for a solution to the problem of the extent of the Russian powers.

The manoeuvring between the two sides began with Bathory demanding the whole of Livonia, and Ivan rejecting his demand, but ceding ground little by little, and adding to the forts he would be prepared to surrender, while Bathory agreed to return some Russian forts and towns (Velikie Luki for instance) still in Polish hands. A difficulty arose over Possevino's demand to allow the King of Sweden to be a party to the negotiations. This did not suit Ivan who had every intention of going to war with Sweden after concluding peace with the Commonwealth in order to recover Narva, whereas Bathory was, on the contrary, anxious to have Sweden included in the peace as a means of forcing the Swedes to refrain from extending their conquests in what he regarded as his Livonia. Thus Ivan's envoys stressed that their instructions did not mention Sweden, and they could not discuss the matter.

As the talks went on, it is clear from Possevino's journal that he was throwing his weight into the Polish scale. He had expressly assumed that Poland was the victor in the conflict and Russia the vanquished, hence it was the right of Bathory to state his terms first, and Bathory never wavered from the demand for the whole of Livonia, and for the exclusion of any mention of the province in the titulature of the Tsar, in order to prevent the Tsar from ever making any claim to Livonia on the ground that it had once been his. Possevino was of course aware that the inclusion of Sweden in the peace served Polish ends.[7] However the Russians pointed out that as the Swedes were not present there was no one to negotiate with, and moreover they could not cede the whole of Livonia to Bathory since they did not in fact possess it, an argument which they later used the other way round.

Arguments over which forts were to be ceded were interspersed with threats to break off the negotiations, with Possevino doing his best to keep the parties engaged, and at times almost driven to violence in order to force an agreement. The problem of the release of prisoners also led to recrimination. The Russians proposed that both sides should release them all; the Poles proposed a 'one for one' release (a soldier for a soldier, an officer for an officer). The Poles also demanded the release of merchants and of the Livonians held in Russia since the beginning of the war,[8] while the Russians asked the Poles to cease kidnapping Russian peasants and taking them to Lithuania.

Possevino, on his own initiative, also interfered in the question of the Tsar's title, which was crucial in many respects. The Russian delegation had failed to obtain the use of the title 'Emperor' or 'Tsar' in the text of the treaty; Possevino tried to dissuade them on the grounds that such a title could only be granted by the Pope. He took the opportunity to raise again with the Russians what seemed to him a far more important question in a manner which reflects the gulf separating the two sides, both as to the meaning of words and as to the perception of status. Possevino explained that the title of 'single Emperor of the Christians' had been brought to the West at a time when 'the Byzantine emperors began showing less loyalty to the Catholic Church than they should'. If the Grand Prince wanted to enjoy a valid title and a legitimate dignity, he should negotiate with the Pope, like the rest of the Christian rulers, who were well aware that the acquisition of two Tatar principalities did not justify a title such as 'the other Caesar', which meant emperor or king. 'If the Prince tried to call himself Caesar everyone would know that this title meant only Tsar', not Caesar and that it was an oddity borrowed from the Tatars in an effort to approximate to the title held by other Kings.'[9] The Russian envoys replied with the usual formula, that the imperial title had been granted by the Emperors Honorius and Arcadius (AD 384–423) to Grand Prince Vladimir, a reply which Possevino brushed aside as nonsense, because they had lived 500 years before the Grand Prince. But the envoys explained that they meant a different Honorius and Arcadius, who had lived at the same time as Vladimir (980–1015). The Russians then asked Possevino as mediator to use the titles 'Tsar of Kazan' and Astrakhan' in the treaty as these titles were much more important than any of the forts to be ceded to Bathory, but again Possevino rejected this request on the ground 'that the kings of Poland could never be induced to allow Christians to call a Christian ruler by a Tatar or Turkish title like "Tsar of the Tatars"'. It is clear from the discussion that neither Possevino nor the Poles had a clear conception of the origin and meaning of the word 'Tsar', and the Russians, who did have a clear conception of what they meant by it, were not strong enough or knowledgeable enough to formulate and press their own conception clearly.[10]

It was now already New Year 1582, and maybe because all were weary, cold, uncomfortable, suffering from frostbite, and lacking in food supplies, general agreement was reached on 5 January 1582, the fourteenth session of the negotiators. But there was still plenty of opportunity for dispute over the manner of implementing the stipulations of the eventual treaty, the return of supplies of arms and ammunition from the fortresses to be surrendered by each side, the escorting of Orthodox priests and their ecclesiastical impedimenta back from Livonia and Lithuania to Russia, and of course the exchange of prisoners. But a new crisis which the Tsar had himself created, which is dealt with below, led to a speeding up of the negotiations. Relations were eased when a letter was received from him containing a much fuller definition of the powers he was granting to his representatives. But though the Tsar might be a novice in the established ways of diplomacy he was unexpectedly skilled in all its tricks (or his advisers were).

When almost all details had been agreed, and the draft treaty was being examined clause by clause, Ivan's envoys suddenly demanded the inclusion of a clause to the effect that he was also ceding Riga and Courland, which of course he did not possess. But therein lay the crux of the matter. By ceding these two territories in the treaty, he implied that they were his to cede, therefore that he was their legitimate owner and might on some other occasion have the right to ask for them back. Possevino saw through the manoeuvre, threatened the Russian delegation with the breaking off of the negotiations by Bathory, and persuaded the Russians to withdraw this new demand. Nor did another Russian ploy succeed, namely a demand for the inclusion of the statement that the fortresses ceded to Bathory amounted to a reduction of the Tsar's total patrimony, which could also serve as the ground for a claim to that part of Livonia he had not surrendered to Bathory. Possevino worked his magic again, and finally on 15 January 1582 the treaty was signed.

The treaty specified that there would be a ten-year truce between Russia and the Commonwealth, and that Ivan ceded the whole of Livonia in his possession, Polotsk and a neighbouring fort on the left bank of the Dvina, Velizh; Bathory returned to Russia all the other Russian forts conquered by the Commonwealth and did not ask for an indemnity. Ivan was given the title of 'Tsar'' in the Russian text of the treaty but not in the Polish copy. Other outstanding minor problems were left for later consideration. There was no mention of Russian relations with the Papacy, or of the Ottoman Empire.

This was the end of Ivan's great dream of a Baltic empire and access to a usable port, which had cost so much blood and treasure. Russian efforts to hold on to the coast were hampered by the need to send troops to Kazan' to defend it against a Tatar attack, and the Tsar was now reduced to a mere toehold on the Baltic, around the mouths of the Neva, possession of which was eventually confirmed to him in the Russo-Swedish truce of August 1583.[11] But the Tsar knew only too well that Livonia in Polish hands would cut him off from contact with the West and confine him to the northern sea route again, and the building of Archangel as Russia's northern port was set in hand at once. The land route, passing through Commonwealth territory, was at the mercy of the King of Poland–Lithuania.

Possevino intended to go back to Moscow to report to Ivan, and left Kiverova Gora on 14 February. But in the meantime a tragedy of major proportions had overwhelmed Ivan. He had been made to feel in his own flesh what he had so often inflicted on others. His son, Ivan Ivanovich had died in Aleksandrovskaia Sloboda, in November 1581, and what is worse, had died at Ivan's own hand. This may well have hastened his acceptance of a humiliating peace, his feeling that there was nothing worth fighting for any longer. A brief flash of rage at some obstacle to his will, and he had lashed out with his staff at the head of his son, and within a few days Ivan Ivanovich was dead and his pregnant wife had miscarried.

Ivan Ivanovich was reputedly a handsome, well made young man. Horsey describes him as a 'wise, mild, and most worthy prince of heroical condition, of comely presence . . . beloved and lamented of all men'.[12] Elsewhere, Ivan Ivanovich is described as 'shining with wise sense'.[13] Not only was he literate but he is reputed to have written a Life of St Antony of Siisk in 1578 and a eulogy of the same saint in 1580.[14] Antony had apparently been a friend of his mother the Tsaritsa Anastasia. But most of the foreign writers about Russia regarded him as a chip off the old block; Ivan Ivanovich had only too often been present in the torture chamber with his father, at the boisterous festivities in Aleksandrovskaia Sloboda, even at the terrible executions of July 1570. One of the least reliable foreign writers, who was never in Russia and plagiarized others, Guagnini, records that Ivan Ivanovich, 'filius truculentissimis moribus', used to trample on the bodies of the executed, 'piercing their heads with the sharp point of his staff'.[15] He was now married to Elena Sheremeteva, and Ivan did not like the Sheremetev family. It will be remembered that Ivan Sheremetev major had been arrested, tortured, and finally took refuge in the monastery of Beloozero as the monk Iona, and it is to him that Ivan's letter of 1573 to the monks refers.[16] Another brother, Nikita, had been executed. I.V. Sheremetev minor was suspected by Ivan of treasonable relations with the Crimean Tatars, but he had restored his reputation by dying under the walls of

Reval in 1577. There remained the youngest brother, Fedor, the father of Elena, the wife of the Tsarevich Ivan Ivanovich, who had been captured by the Lithuanians in 1579, in itself a possible disguise for desertion, and who was reputed to have sworn allegiance to Bathory.[17]

Karamzin quotes many different versions of a serious quarrel between Tsar Ivan and his son Ivan when the latter reproached his father with pusillanimity, and asked for the command of an army to drive the Polish-Lithuanian forces away from Pskov. In another version, a gathering of service gentry in Vladimir demanded that Ivan Ivanovich should be put in charge of the armed forces in place of his father, to drive the enemy out. Ivan began to quake, thinking that his son and his subjects were rising against him, went out to the people, threw off his crown and the purple, proclaimed that he did not want to rule over a rebellious people, spelled out all the great deeds he had done for them, and shouted out to the people: 'Choose another tsar for yourselves, who will be able to rule you!'[18] But there is really no evidence to support these stories, and it seems most improbable that Ivan would have killed his son in an outburst of rage at his demand to be put in charge of reviving his father's failing military fortunes.[19]

By far the most probable cause of the quarrel is the one given by Possevino, who had access to many people at court and to much court gossip, whose interpreter had been in the service of Ivan Ivanovich, who knew his doctor, and who arrived back in Moscow only two months after the death of the Tsarevich, when news was still fresh. According to Possevino, the Tsar came upon his pregnant daughter-in-law resting upon a bench in her private apartments, clad in only one garment instead of the three which were *de rigueur* with Muscovite ladies of good family. He rebuked her and boxed her ears, whereupon Ivan Ivanovich, on hearing the clamour, rushed in to his wife and attempted to defend her, calling out to his father: 'You thrust my first wife into a nunnery for no good reason; you did the same thing with my second, and now you strike my third, causing the son in her womb to perish' (clearly a report dating from after the event). Elena then miscarried and was delivered of a stillborn baby. It is of course also perfectly possible that the Tsarevich was deeply opposed to his father's irresolution over the war with the Commonwealth, but it is impossible to tell whether this really caused his death. The Tsar's physician, Dr Johann Eyloff, a Fleming and said to be an Anabaptist, was sent for to attend the injured man, and Possevino's evidence, dating from so soon after the event, is more convincing, particularly as he was acquainted with the physician and could communicate with him in Latin.[20] In a later letter to her envoy in Russia

Queen Elizabeth inquired how it had come about that the physician she had sent to Russia 'had not been admitted to the Tsarevich and been given the chance to save him'. She might have been worried for his fate, but in fact he had not arrived in time.[21]

Ivan sent for his one time brother-in-law, Nikita Romanovich Iur'ev Zakhar'in, in a letter of 12 November 1581 in which he stated that his son had fallen ill and was now at death's door.[22] At the funeral, Ivan followed the bier of his son on foot, wearing the Russian form of mourning, black and ragged clothes, with hair growing wild, and without the skull cap normally worn by nobles. Ivan put off his crowns and jewels and fine clothes. The Tsar was overwhelmed with grief; he could not sleep and got up at night, scratching the walls of his chamber with his nails.[23] Apart from the enormity of the sin he had committed in murdering his son, he was appalled at the succession problem he had created. Ivan Ivanovich had left no heir, Fedor Ivanovich was incompetent to rule, and there seemed to be no likelihood of his wife Irina successfully carrying children to full term.[24] No doubt this disaster, caused by himself, weighed terribly on Ivan's spirits from now on, and it must have affected his willingness to make peace.[25]

It was also around this time that rumours of Ivan's plan to seek asylum in England, which could not be kept secret and was true, began to circulate again, arousing much adverse feeling against the Tsar. But since the dramatic death of Daniel Sylvester and the adventurous journey of Horsey, Ivan had been too busy with the war against Stephen Bathory to concern himself with his relations with England, and no letters survive for the next five years. However, the Russian loss of Narva in May 1582 rendered the northern sea route more important to the Russia Company as well as to Ivan, and after achieving the truce with Poland–Lithuania, he may have considered it advisable to reopen negotiations with England in order to provide himself with an ally and an escape route should war break out again.

In England too there was more willingness to negotiate, though Elizabeth herself might not be willing to conclude. She had become more involved in the Dutch revolt in the Netherlands, and had no wish to be entangled in any military complications elsewhere in Europe. Denmark was however raising difficulties with Russia by insisting that English ships trading with St Nicholas, though they did not pass through the Sound, should nevertheless pay the Sound dues imposed by Denmark, which controlled both shores of the entrance to the Baltic Sea. Either that, or Denmark would assert her sovereignty over the open North Sea and demand payment and saluting by dipping the flag when sailing in the waters which separated the coast of Norway from the sea of Iceland, thus again controlling the trade of the Russia Company and the export trade from Russia.[26] Not only was Elizabeth concerned by Danish pretensions, but she was also anxious to recover for the Russia Company the monopoly of trade with Russia which she had previously enjoyed, which was regarded in England as a reward for having discovered the northern route to Russia, and which was now being breached by the Dutch, who were being allowed to trade to the north with the full consent of Ivan.

F. Pisemsky was appointed Russian ambassador to Elizabeth, together with a *d'iak*, and ordered on 19 May 1581 to open negotiations to create an alliance against the King of Poland–Lithuania, to procure money and military supplies to continue the war (at the time of writing it was not yet over) and to find out if there was a widow or maid, of princely descent, who could make the Tsar a suitable bride. Pisemsky was to inquire about her height, complexion and measurements, to procure a portrait of her, on wood and on paper, and to discover the degree of her relationship to the Queen and the extent of her family. Should the Queen ask why, Pisemsky was to reply that the Tsar was thinking of marrying, that at present he was only inquiring and that if Elizabeth sent an ambassador to Russia the affair could be concluded there. And should the English ask how could Ivan marry if he were already married, Pisemsky was to reply: 'Our Lord sent to many countries when he wanted a wife, but it did not work out, so he took to himself a boyar's daughter.' But if the Queen's relative was of good birth, and stately appearance (*dorodna*) and worthy of such a great affair, 'He would put away his wife and he would engage himself to her and explain that a proper wooing (*svatovstvo*) was not necessary between crowned heads.' The bride must be christened (meaning that she would have to be re-baptized into the Orthodox religion), together with all her attendants 'if they wanted to live at court'. If the English asked about the relation of any possible children to Tsarevich Fedor and his descendants, Pisemsky was to explain that it was not possible to disregard the latters' claims, and if they asked whether appanages would be granted to the lady he was to reply 'what appanages?' If Pisemsky was not allowed to see the lady, or was refused a portrait, or if the lady were reluctant, he was to return home. Pisemsky's instructions were given to him by Bogdan Bel'sky, the Tsar's then favourite and, odd though it may seem, by Afanasii Nagoi, the uncle of the Tsar's present wife, Maria, as well as by the *d'iak* Andrei Shchelkalov.

The physician sent by Elizabeth, Dr Atkins, known in Russia as Dr

Roman Elizarov,[27] served as the channel through which Ivan made inquiries as to the availability of a widow or a young woman, who might make him a suitable bride, closely related to the Queen, belonging as he put it to an 'appanage' family, which was interpreted as being descended from an Earl. The good doctor came up with the name of Lady Mary Hastings ('Khantis', or 'Astis'), who was the Queen's niece on the mother's side and daughter of an 'appanage prince', the Earl of Huntington ('Khuntintinsky').[28] Pisemsky arrived in England in September 1581, and was received by Elizabeth, at her most charming, in Windsor in November. But the Queen was in no hurry, and was not perhaps quite sure about the stability of Ivan's government. 'Is your country in its usual state,' she asked, 'or is there some agitation among your people?' Pisemsky replied that those who had been unsteady in their loyalty were now firmly in the Tsar's hand and were serving him properly.[29] Still Elizabeth failed to embark on any discussions, possibly waiting for news of the outcome of the peace negotiations being conducted by Possevino. Pisemsky was urged to entertain himself by hunting deer, but explained rather crossly, that it was the middle of one of the great fasts of Russia and there was little point in killing deer when you could not eat it.

Finally, in mid-December, formal talks began, and again it was clear that Elizabeth would not move from her previous stance: she would not agree to an unconditional alliance, but reserved to herself the right to decide whether Ivan's cause was just, and nevertheless insisted on the concession of a monopoly of the northern trade, and the repayment of what the English traders considered unwarranted taxation (the 1,500 rubles raised for the war). The Queen's tone reflected a perception that Ivan's need was greater than hers, and that therefore she could make demands: 'That if this may be perfourmed her ma——ty . . . can lett passe all that is past . . . and be again Ivan's firm friend.'[30] Ivan refused outright to grant exclusive English access to the port of St Nicholas on the grounds that he was free to welcome all foreign ships to his ports; he did not accept that this was a concession due to England for having discovered the northern route, but thought that the exclusive reduction to a 50 per cent tax on imports served the purpose.

Elizabeth did consent however to Ivan's request to send an ambassador, and she made the not very happy choice of Sir Jerome Bowes, a xenophobe of impatient temper. Towards the end of May 1583, Pisemsky was finally allowed a glimpse of Lady Mary Hastings, in the Lord Chancellor's garden. Pisemsky gazed at her, and remarked 'it is enough', then walked away.[31] Elizabeth had felt some compassion for her niece, and she now backpedalled on the marriage, and instructed Bowes to try to dissuade the Tsar from pressing it on the grounds of Lady Mary's poor complexion and bad health, and her reluctance to leave her friends. She also embarked on a new policy by offering to mediate between the Tsar and the King of Sweden at a time when peace with Sweden was not at all desirable for the Tsar.

Meanwhile Possevino, who had arrived in Moscow on 14 February 1582, left for Rome in March. In the interval he had discussed a whole range of little problems left over from the peace negotiations, and his own wider views on encouraging the formation of a coalition of Russia, the Commonwealth, the Empire and the Papacy against the Ottoman Turks under the military command of Stephen Bathory; indeed he seems even to have envisaged the conquest of Russia by the Commonwealth, and of course its conversion. Bathory, however, was more interested in the conquest of Russia than in war with the Porte and losing his amicable links with the Sultan, who was after all the overlord of his principality of Transylvania, and with whom he shared a deep hostility to the Habsburgs. For Ivan, however, a truce was a truce, not a peace, and he was by no means resigned to the idea of abandoning his claims to Livonia and Polotsk. Meanwhile he drew back on the idea of a coalition and an anti-Turkish crusade. It was probably not so much a diplomatic ploy[32] as recognition that Russia was not fit for a renewed campaign, particularly when a truce with the Crimeans had just been achieved. Nor can he have had any sympathy with any of Possevino's more wide-ranging plans – if he was aware of them. Let all the European powers agree to launch a crusade against the Ottomans and then send their ambassadors to him, inviting him to join them, was his response

In spite of his indifference to plans for a crusade against the Ottomans, the world in which the Tsar acted, thought and felt was permeated at every turn by religion, and his day was taken up with religious services, and his life with pilgrimages This is an aspect of sixteenth-century Russia which the contemporary secular mind finds most difficult to grasp, particularly when it was associated with the breach of every known religious commandment. Ivan prided himself on his knowledge of the Old and New Testaments, other sacred books, and religious history and debate, derived from manuscript copies of separate books of the Bible and the Apocrypha, collections of miscellaneous religious writings and homilies, psalters, chronicles and chronographs copied in monastic scriptoria and sold in monasteries, and eventually from the first Slavonic printed Bible of 1581.[33]

It is interesting to contrast Ivan's attitude with that of Possevino in

1582. The Jesuit father was determined to use his talents and to embark on a public religious debate with the Tsar, to prove the greater authenticity of Roman Catholic dogma. But his efforts were undermined by his arrogant and condescending behaviour and, as he well realized, by the reports of the Russian envoy who had been sent in 1580 to Vienna, Venice and Rome. Shevrygin had informed Ivan about many external aspects of Roman ritual and behaviour in the world, which would prove highly offensive to Orthodox Russians. When Possevino was finally able to embark on his first religious debate with Ivan – for there were three – in the great hall in the presence of the boyars and 100 nobles, on 21 February 1582, Ivan greeted him courteously and pointed out that as he had not much longer to live (he was fifty-two), and the Day of Judgment was approaching, he could not change his religion, but let Possevino say what he wished. Possevino assured the Tsar that he did not want to propose any changes in the Greek religion, but rather to urge the Tsar to 'embrace it in its pristine form' which would lead to the union of the Western and Eastern Churches. He also reminded the Tsar that the Metropolitan of Kiev and all Russia, the Greek, Isidore, at the Council of Florence in 1439, had acknowledged the union of faiths, but he presumably forgot or did not know that the Metropolitan was arrested and deposed for it.

As in the debate with Jan Rokyta, Ivan replied that he did not want to discuss matters of faith in case he offended Possevino. But his reply to the Jesuit was very acute: 'I do not believe in the Greeks. I believe in Christ.' He did not consider the union of the Christian Churches to be necessary before the conclusion of an alliance between the powers against the Turks, and he would allow Catholics to enter Russia and to worship, but only in private. Tsar and ambassador were both somewhat at sea over the date of Russia's conversion. Ivan said that Russia had been converted when the Apostle Andrew passed through Russia on the way to Rome; Possevino replied that Italy had been Christian for 1,200 years before Russia ever heard the name of Christ.

Ivan admitted that the Orthodox Church recognized some of the popes, but many had led evil lives. Yet again the two differed on the succession to the Papacy, and Possevino suspected that Ivan had been briefed by an 'Anabaptist doctor' in English pay (almost certainly the Flemish Dr Eyloff). When he heard the Tsar exclaim: 'The Roman Pope is no shepherd', in a furious voice, Possevino asked why then had the Tsar asked for the Pope's help to make peace with Poland? Whereupon 'the Prince flew into a rage and stood up from his throne' and all expected him to strike the priest. But he calmed down, and in a clear attempt to turn the whole discussion aside he concentrated on superficial questions, derived from the information he had received from Shevrigin: Why was the Pope carried in a chair? Why did he wear a cross on his slippers? Why did he shave his beard? And why does he pretend to be God?

The questions caused uproar, but even when Possevino again tried to reply simply to them, the Tsar took up other superficial issues, notably the fact that Catholics allowed their crosses to hang down below the belt, a practice regarded as sacrilegious in Russia, or that the Pope shaved his beard (which Possevino strongly denied; he was himself bearded). Fortunately the uproar left no ill feeling, but to make sure, Possevino took the precaution of giving the sacraments to his companions, 'and fortified them with relics of the Saints in case the Muscovites should harm them'. The Russians now laid a little trap for Possevino, intending to manoeuvre him into attending an Orthodox church service. He was able to evade it, and on his return to the council chamber, he and his fifteen associates intoned the Te Deum in thanks for their escape. But he did not depart without leaving a long written document containing a 'brief, clear, and firm refutation of the Errors of the Greeks and the Muscovites'. It was a draw.[34] But it cannot be said that any of the participants distinguished himself for real intellectual mastery of the subject. All we learn is that Ivan was willing, in principle, to allow members of other faiths to practice their religion in private, but that he might destroy their chapels if the fit took him, as in the case of the German church in the Livonian suburb in Moscow.[35]

The Tsar, in fact, proved responsive to all Possevino's requests for commercial concessions, but was adamant in refusing the slightest concession regarding religious toleration and the building of Catholic churches.[36]

On 14 March 1582, Possevino left for Rome accompanied by Iakov Mol'vianinov, envoy to the Emperor, the Pope, and Venice. The only person who benefited from this mission was probably Possevino, whose stature as a diplomat rose with every step, though he did not actually achieve any of his ultimate hopes. Fulfilling his self-appointed task of shepherding the Russian party, and aware of the existence of a substantial Greek colony in Venice, Possevino personally prevented the Russians from attending a service in San Giorgio degli Schiavoni, the church allocated by the Serenissima to the Orthodox. The visit of the Russian party to the baths in Padua left an impression of riotousness not unlike that of Peter the Great's stay in Sir John Evelyn's house in Deptford. From the beginning Possevino had been anxious to shelter the

Russians from the full impact of the high Renaissance paintings which adorned churches and palaces with nude Saint Sebastians and Virgins suckling the infant Jesus, and had tried to confine the party to a secluded residence where only paintings in Fra Angelico's style were displayed. But it was not possible, and the Russians, shocked by, and contemptuous of, the licentiousness of the Catholic capital were also caught up in affrays when stones were thrown at them. At the papal reception Possevino felt himself obliged to force the Russian ambassador physically to take off his sable hat and to kneel and kiss the cross embroidered on the Pope's mule. The Russians were offended because they were not invited to a banquet by the Pope, as was the Russian practice. Ivan's mission to Rome proved a complete waste of time and money.

Charged with Elizabeth's instructions, outlined above, Sir Jerome Bowes and Fedor Pisemsky sailed for Russia on 22 June 1583, and arrived on 23 July; Bowes was attended by 'five English dvoriane' and an escort of forty-one. The details of this diplomatic episode can be followed in the report on his mission by Pisemsky, and in the equally full report by Bowes, or 'Kniaz' Ieremei', as he is styled in the Russian report.[37] As usual in Russia, Pisemsky got off to a good start, travelling at once to Moscow, while Bowes was kept at Kholmogory for five weeks. In his report, Bowes indicates that he had discovered during this waiting time the intrigues of a number of Dutch traders, who had bribed leading Russian officials, and secured the backing of three of them, Bogdan Bel'sky, Nikita Romanovich Iur'ev Zakhar'in, and the influential *d'iak*, Andrei Shchelkalov, often called 'Chancellor' in English reports, as head of foreign affairs.[38]

Bowes was not given a formal audience until October, but it was then very lavish indeed, with a large armed escort, a train of nobles clad in cloth of gold, 'rich furres, their caps embroiderd with pearle and stone'. From the very beginning one can note the tone of irritation underlying Bowes's speeches, a determination not to be pleased. He refused to allow Shchelkalov to take from him and deliver to the Tsar the letters written by Elizabeth, saying 'that her Majesty had directed no letters to him'. When Ivan asked him what the Queen had said about the marriage with Lady Mary, Bowes replied: 'Nothing. She waits for you to speak and give me a message for her.' The Tsar replied, 'We want to take her unto ourselves, but what has the Queen said about her changing her faith to mine?' To this Bowes replied: 'Mary is not well, she is very ill and I believe she will not change her faith, and see, she is a Christian.' Ivan answered: 'I do not want to talk about religion, any princess who marries me must first be baptized in our Christian faith, it is clear that you came here to refuse us and we will speak no more with you.' And he blamed Dr 'Roman' (Robert) Atkins for creating confusion, for telling him about this girl, which was why he had written to the Queen. Following his instructions to discourage Ivan's marital hopes, Bowes replied that the Lady Mary was the most distant of all the Queen's nieces, she was ill, her complexion was rough, she was not handsome, she had suffered from smallpox and there were ten maidens who were more closely related to the Queen. Ivan asked to hear about them, whereupon Bowes replied that he had no instructions from the Queen and therefore could not name them.

After this unpromising beginning, the talks on an alliance proved no more satisfactory. Ivan criticized Elizabeth for refusing to support him unless an army had actually already been sent against him. He expected Elizabeth to become his ally against Poland–Lithuania and Sweden, though not Denmark, and in a fit of anger against Bowes he exclaimed to him that 'he did not reckon the Queene of England to be his fellow'. Bowes exploded, and 'tolde him that the Queene his Mistress was as great a prince as any was in Christendome . . . Yea quoth he [Ivan], how sayest thou to the French King and the king of Spaine? Mary, quoth the ambassador, I holde the Queene my Mistresse as great as any of them both' and moreover the Queen's father had had the Emperor in his pay. Ivan replied that were 'Bowes not an ambassador he would throw him out of the doores', whereupon the party broke up.

Yet Ivan did not hold his language against the English ambassador, indeed he seemed rather to view it as an admirable proof of his loyalty to his mistress, and supplied Bowes with a greatly increased quantity of food and drink. He still held to his determination to marry an English wife, though Maria Nagaia had given birth to a son.

In further talks with the boyars, Bowes, striking while the iron was hot, obtained a number of favourable decisions in pending suits, such as the repayment of the taxes amounting to 1,500 rubles and compensation for a robbery.[39] But no progress at all was made with the treaty, and Bowes's efforts to secure confirmation of the English trade monopoly met with considerable hostility in Russia, now that Russia had been approached by France and by traders from the Spanish Netherlands. Ivan's increasing familiarity with international diplomacy was also leading him to resist England's efforts to maintain Russian isolation. The boyars now demanded that Russian envoys to the West and European envoys to Russia should be allowed to travel freely through England and the North Sea to Russia, while England refused point-blank to allow representatives of Catholic powers to pass through her territory. Ivan agreed to the exclusion of envoys from the Papacy but not to the exclusion of envoys of other powers. As the boyars put it: 'Faith is not an obstacle; your Lady is not of the same faith as our Lord, but our Lord wishes to be in friendship and brotherhood with her.'[40]

Bowes, having failed to obtain what he wanted from the boyars, now demanded, through Dr Atkins, a private interview with the Tsar. But when Ivan received him, he denied that he had made any such demand, while insisting that in all his other posts he had always spoken directly with the ruler, and not through an intermediary. Ivan replied shortly that it was not the Russian custom for the Tsar to negotiate in person with envoys (indeed it was not the custom anywhere, *pace* Bowes). Ivan could not get any information out of Bowes regarding the Queen's ten nieces, and the Tsar spoke to him about nothing else. Bowes even put forward a kind of bargain: let Ivan restore all their privileges to the English merchants and the Queen would join him against the Lithuanians and the Swedes; let him send ambassadors with this message and they could examine the ladies together. But the English ambassador backed down when asked to commit himself to English assistance in Ivan's recovery of Livonia. Elizabeth was pious he said, and had already refused the offer of the crowns of the Netherlands and France. Was Livonia really Ivan's ancestral land? Ivan responded angrily that he was not asking Elizabeth to be a judge between him and the King of Lithuania, as he referred to Stephen Bathory, but that she should be his ally against him. Talks between the two had reached a dead end.[41]

Chapter XXI
The Death of Ivan

The death of his eldest son in November 1581 finally broke Ivan's spirit. The Tsar seemed to have lost the will to control the machine of government, to discipline the boyars surrounding him, and he began to redress some at least of the injuries he had caused. He took steps in 1582 to punish false denunciations.[1] He forgave some of those in disgrace, and tried to save the souls of those he had dispatched unshriven to their deaths by sending sums of money to monasteries for prayers for their souls. The *Sinodiki* which list his victims were begun at this time as part of his repentance: seventy-four names were included in the first list sent to the Simonov monastery in Moscow, seventy-five in the second sent to Solovki; in May 1582 the Pskov Pechersky monastery received the order to pray for seventy-five victims, which included some of the most prominent executed in the early days of the *oprichnina*, such as Prince Alexander Gorbaty-Shuisky and Ivan Petrovich Fedorov, executed in 1565 and 1569. The Monastery of St Cyril at Beloozero received 2,000 rubles to pray for the Tsar's son, Ivan Ivanovich, and a hail of gold descended on monasteries for prayers to be said for some three thousand victims, including the many 'whose names were known only to God'. According to the cynics among historians, this was designed primarily to pave the way for the Church to support the unopposed ascension of Fedor Ivanovich to the throne on the death of his father.[2] And Ivan's remorse for his many executions did not extend to releasing his many prisoners from their jails. It relieved the dead more than the living.

Ivan IV had suffered a serious illness, about which almost nothing is known, in the late 1570s, and it is generally assumed that ever since then, or perhaps even before, he had suffered from a spinal condition which made movement very painful, so that he had to give up riding and be carried in a litter.[3] As early as 1572, when he stopped outside

Novgorod to talk to the Swedish envoy, Juusten, Bishop of Åbo, whom he had so badly treated, he was in a carriage and not on horseback.[4] Yet in 1578, when the Tsar and his son Ivan ravaged the Livonian colony, 'Narva and Dorpat' in Moscow, they were on horseback.[5]

There is one eyewitness account of Ivan's death, but not perhaps a very reliable one, namely Jerome Horsey's. Nevertheless, Horsey had no particular self-interest to serve in lying about the circumstances of Ivan's death, and there is therefore little reason to distrust his account of the Tsar's last day – though he does not give the date, which was 18 March 1584.

On the day of his death, Ivan was carried as usual in his chair to his treasury chamber, called for precious stones and jewels to be brought, and proceeded to lecture those about him on their properties and virtues. Taking coral and turquoise stones on his hand and arm, Ivan declared, according to Horsey: 'I am poisoned with disease; you see they show their virtue by the change of their pure colour into pall; declares my death.'[6] (Turquoises were supposed to change colour in the presence of poison.) In the afternoon Ivan looked over his will (no text survives, but he is said to have left the crown to his son Fedor and the appanage of Uglich to his son Dmitri), ordered his physician and his apothecary to attend him to the bath, and then sent for a report from his witches, because the day foretold for his death was coming to an end. But he was warned that there was still time, for the day only ended when the sun went down. In the afternoon he went to the bath, 'solaced himself and made merry with pleasant songs as he useth to do'. He then went to bed, well refreshed, in his loose gown, shirt and linen hose, and sent for a chess board. Bogdan Bel'sky and Boris Godunov stood by the bed. Suddenly Ivan fainted and fell back. The apothecary sent for marigold and rose-water, for the physicians, and for Ivan's confessor. 'In the mean he was strangled and stark dead' (sic), writes Horsey, and added that an attempt to save him was made, to still the outcry. But it was too late. Horsey does not mention any effort to tonsure Ivan as a monk at the time, and he died without the last rites. But his confessor did hurry in to clothe him afterwards in the 'angel's form' as a monk, under the name Iona.[7]

There are many other versions of Ivan's death, most of which assume that he did not die naturally. Pastor Oderborn's *Life of the Grand Prince of Moscow*, published in Latin in 1585, very soon after Ivan's death, reports that the Tsar had been seriously ill for a long period, during which he could neither speak, eat nor drink, and his body was covered with maggots. He called out for his son Ivan, who was of course already dead. But Oderborn tends to exaggerate wildly, he was not present, and his account does not correspond with Horsey's who on this occasion seems more reliable.

Was Ivan murdered? Did Horsey's account imply that Bel'sky and Godunov had hastened his end? It is not clear from his words.[8] If the Tsar was 'strangled' or suffocated, the two men would have had to act together, for to act alone would have been impossible without being detected. The crux of the issue is what did Horsey mean by 'he was strangled'? Did he mean stifled or suffocated, or actually throttled by some outside agency, or did he mean that Ivan choked, on food perhaps, or as a result of poison taken in the bath, a perfectly possible cause of death?

There are many descriptions of the Tsar by foreign visitors to Russia, and they coincide on a number of physical and psychological traits. An autopsy was carried out on his bones, which were exhumed in the year 1963, together with those of many other members of the tsarist family, from sarcophagi in the Archangel Cathedral. The exhumation of his body, moreover, provided an opportunity for the pioneer Russian expert in facial reconstruction, M.M. Gerasimov, to produce a 'virtually real' bust of Ivan which does suggest the real man, with the eagle nose of the Paleologues, the high brow, sensual mouth and dominating countenance which one would expect. His eyes have been described both as small, and as large; they were light-coloured, bright, and flickered rapidly from place to place. The imperial envoy, Prinz von Buchau, describes Ivan in 1575 as very tall, strong and full-bodied. His hair and beard were long and thick, and rusty black; like most Russians, Prinz added, he shaved his head. He was so given to anger that he would foam at the mouth like a horse, and seem beside himself.[9] Horsey, who had seen him often, wrote that he was a 'goodly man of person and presence, well-favoured, high forehead, shrill voice; a right Scythian, full of ready wisdom, cruel, bloody, merciless; his own experience managed by direction both his state and commonwealth affairs' (though Horsey did think Russia was too large for 'one regiment'). Others spoke of his looking like an 'angry warrior'. It was also frequently remarked that he had an excellent memory and a quick, sardonic, wit. He certainly enjoyed dramatizing his clashes with his boyars, and with foreign envoys.[10] Did he smoke? In 1575 Prinz von Buchau presented Ivan, as a gift from the Emperor Maximilian II, with a pipe for smoking the herb hitherto unknown in Russia, namely tobacco, procured for him by his Spanish cousins.[11]

Very little, if anything, is known about Ivan's medical history. As a small child he seems to have suffered briefly from a boil, or possibly a carbuncle, on the back of his neck, if one accepts the simplest explanation – from scrofula, if one accepts the most far-fetched portrayal of the physical and mental constitution of the Russian ruling house.[12]

The Tsar is believed, by modern medical opinion, to have suffered from spondylosis. The disease leads to the formation of osteophytes along the spine, which may press on the nerves as they leave the spinal cord. This condition may, though not necessarily, cause intense pain. But there is no evidence other than the state of Ivan's bones that he suffered in this way. However, it is assumed by many historians that he did so.[13] Since 1963 there have been further medical and chemical analyses which have been pondered over at length by Russian and American experts.[14]

The possibility that Ivan was poisoned has also been talked about because in the autopsy carried out in 1963 on the skeletons of Ivan and other members of the tsarist family, mercury and arsenic have been found in varying quantities, ranging from 12.9 mg of arsenic per 100 gm of bones (Princess Evfrosin'ya of Staritsa) to 8.1 mg of arsenic per 100 gm of bones (her granddaughter Maria Vladimirovna of Staritsa). This seems to confirm that the child Maria Vladimirovna was indeed forced to drink poison and that Evfrosin'ya was poisoned and not suffocated by smoke (see above, Chapter XIV, pp. 240–1). The quantity of mercury was also higher than the maximum tolerated in the human body: 0.10 mg per 100 grams of bones, in the case of Evfrosin'ya, 0.2 mg per 100 gm of bones in the case of the child Maria. However, the amount of arsenic was really considerable and this seems the likelier poison as it would be quick-acting in such quantities. Of the remaining figures none provides convincing evidence for poisoning, except that Prince Mikhail Skopin Shuisky, the nephew of Tsar Vasily Shuisky, who was murdered during the Time of Troubles, had 0.13 mg of arsenic in his bones, and was probably poisoned. In all cases there was more arsenic than mercury. In the case of Ivan IV himself, the amounts of arsenic and mercury are very low (As. 0.15, Hg 1.3), and the level of mercury (Hg 1.3) is the same as in the body of his son Ivan Ivanovich.

The figures for mercury found in Ivan's bones do not suggest that he suffered from syphilis and was subjected to the intensive mercury steam treatment, at the time the main remedy in use. He may have taken mercury compounds medicinally or in the form of calomel (mercurous chloride) for some other illnesses, which may have led to intense bouts of uncontrollable rage.[15] If he did indeed suffer great pain from osteophytes, and if indeed Bomelius was a Paracelsian, he may well have been treated with opium or laudanum to keep pain under control. Poppy seeds are mentioned twice in the available records of the pharmacy which supplied the Tsar. He is also reputed to have drunk large amounts of alcohol, a painkiller which leaves no trace.

What kind of medicine did the physicians in Russia dispense? Needless to say physicians were all foreign, mainly from Germany or the Netherlands. The first English-trained physician (though actually a Westphalian) who seems to have left a really lasting impression both on Russians and on foreigners at the court of Ivan IV, was Bomelius, who practised from 1569 to 1579. These years were particularly critical for the development of medicine in Europe and in England, for it was at this time that medical theories, founded on the traditions derived from Hippocrates and Galen, and their many disciples in the Eastern Roman Empire, in the Arabian world and in Europe, were seriously challenged by the theories of the maverick Swiss physician and alchemist Paracelsus (*c.* 1490–1541). Traditional medicine was based on the four elements, earth, air, water and fire, corresponding to cold, dry, wet, and hot, to the planets, Saturn, Venus/Jupiter, the Moon and Mars, and to phlegm, yellow bile and black bile, and blood. If the balance between these 'humours' was disturbed a 'distemper' occurred, which had to be remedied by restoring the balance.

But the tempestuous Paracelsus was an alchemist, at a time when the boundary between alchemy and chemistry was not yet defined, with his own cosmology and mystical theology.[16] He rejected the humoural medical theories of his predecessors, and replaced them in the field of medicine with a theory based on the study of nature, and a *materia medica* which included chemical products designed to cure particular ailments. For Paracelsus the primary substances were mercury, sulphur and salt, but he introduced others such as antimony, zinc and alcohol.[17] One form in which mercury occurred and was extensively used was *mercurius dolcis*, or calomel. Paracelsus was the first to produce laudanum, the alcoholic tincture of opium, which became the principal treatment for pain.[18]

The university medical establishments in most countries closed ranks against what seemed to them the extravagancies of Paracelsus. But the royal and princely courts proved more open, particularly in Germany and in northern Protestant courts, and possibly in southern Europe (where the Greek Fioravanti was based) though it was the court of Catherine de' Medici which first patronized these new ideas.[19] In England John Dee was familiar with Paracelsian ideas, and so was Queen Elizabeth, while Burleigh asked Dee to transmute base metal into gold for him.[20] In view of these circumstances it seems not unlikely that Dr Bomelius ended up in the King's Bench Prison in 1567 not just for practising without a licence from the University of Cambridge where he claimed to have studied, but for being a Paracelsian.[21]

Like so many other sixteenth-century rulers, Ivan was fascinated by alchemy, by the power to transmute base metal into gold, and by the properties of precious stones, which constituted the obverse side of Renaissance scientific rationalism. The main source of the knowledge of alchemy in sixteenth-century Russia was the *Secretum secretorum,* in its Russian version, which contained sections on the magical properties of stones and on alchemy, including a recipe on how to make gold.[22] Ivan also believed profoundly in witchcraft and, to protect himself from the machinations of his courtiers and his enemies, he sent for many witches 'out of the north, where there is a store between Kholmogory and Lapland', as Horsey puts it. The favourite, Bogdan Bel'sky, had now, according to Horsey, turned against his master, 'this Heliogabalus', and was told by astrologers and witches that the stars were against the Tsar who would die by a specific date. Ivan was, however, carrying on his normal life, and had made arrangements to receive a Polish envoy in the near future. But at the beginning of March 1584 the Tsar had issued orders to a number of monasteries to pray for the restoration of his health.[23]

There is no doubt that the situation at the Russian court after the death of Ivan Ivanovich was such as to justify the suspicion that the Tsar's death was not natural.[24] Ivan himself was terrified of death, and took the witches' forecast of its imminence seriously. Bogdan Bels'ky, considered by many to have been the Tsar's minion, was supervising the dispensing of remedies by the apothecary's pharmacy. At this time, the doctors associated with it were Eyloff, the Netherlander, said to be an Anabaptist, and the English Dr Atkins. The kind of substances dispensed in the pharmacy are mentioned in a few surviving orders which it received from Bogdan Bel'sky, dating from 1581 to 1582, and they are exclusively herbal, including seeds of the red poppy, i.e., opium.[25] Could herbal concoctions have been used to poison Ivan? If so, then Bogdan Bel'sky was the best placed to procure them since he was in charge of the pharmacy and he ordered whatever remedies the doctors prescribed. According to one story, Boris Godunov had particular reason to fear Ivan's wrath, since he had been present when the Tsar had mortally wounded his son, and he had tried to defend the Tsar's daughter-in-law from physical assault by Ivan.[26]

The heir to the throne was now Fedor, with his 'silly smile', but it was clear to all that he was too simple-minded to rule. On the other hand he was devout, kind and popular with the common people. His accession would be bound to lead to a struggle for power on any regency or boyar council, between his maternal relatives, the Iur'ev Zakhar'ins, above all his uncle, Nikita Romanovich, also popular with the people, and the relatives of Fedor's wife Irina, namely the family of Boris Godunov, a favourite of Ivan's, whose star seemed lately to have been declining.[27] But there was another complicating factor: the existence of young Tsarevich Dmitri, supported by his maternal relatives in the Council of the *dvor*, the Nagoys, who might try to take advantage of the incapacity of Fedor in order to seize power on behalf of the child Prince. It is also assumed that the Nagoys and the Godunovs were alarmed at Ivan's plan to marry Lady Mary Hastings, a marriage which might lead to the birth of further heirs who could displace the Nagoys because Lady Mary was of higher rank.[28] But it seems more probable that they did not regard such a marriage as likely to take place.

During the last years of Ivan's reign, the governing élite was divided between the Boyar Council, dominating the 'land' or the *zemshchina*, and the Tsar's Council in the court or *dvor*. The Boyar Council comprised the solid and wealthy group of boyars, Princes Mstislavsky, father and son, and Nikita Romanovich Iur'ev Zakhar'in, who were closely related by marriage, and had survived through thick and thin for over thirty years in Ivan's close entourage. There was also a number of well established boyars (Saburov, Fedor Sheremetev), and the two Shchelkalov *d'iaki*.[29] The *dvor* Council included as senior boyar Prince F.M. Trubetskoy (also from the Upper Oka princes), two members of the Shuisky clan, Dmitri Godunov and his nephew Boris, two members of the Nagoy family and Bogdan Bel'sky. Several other Shuiskys and Trubetskoys also served in more junior posts. Ivan's council also comprised a larger number of representatives of the lower aristocracy, closely interrelated and coordinating their activity. The key figure was the favourite, Bogdan Bel'sky.[30] Thus there were two candidates for the throne, Fedor and Dmitri, and at least three candidates for power, Nikita Romanovich, Boris Godunov and Bogdan Bel'sky. In the background were the small number of *d'iaki*, the efficient secretaries of *prikazy*, who managed the administration and organized the supply and movement of troops. Little is heard about them in foreigners' accounts, other than those who dealt with foreign affairs, such as Viskovaty until 1570 and, after him, the Shchelkalov brothers.

If Ivan died by the hand of man, then it was not, as far as one can tell, by traceable poisoning but by suffocation or strangulation without leaving any evidence. Moreover, though many may, at that particular time, have wanted to murder Ivan, this does not mean that he was murdered. He was more than ever hedged by the divinity which protects a king, and it is very unlikely that the boyars surrounding him would break through such a spiritual barrier, since they had not done so before. The 'sacralization' of the Russian monarchy implicit in the assumption of the title of anointed Tsar was already powerful enough to influence both rulers and ruled against an attack on a tradition in the making.[31] The balance of the evidence is that the Tsar died by choking, or of a sudden heart attack after some months of illness.

The question of how the Tsar died leads back to the question of how he lived. Was Ivan unbalanced? Was he mad? Did he indulge in Heliogabalian orgies? Are the tales true that he deflowered hundreds of maidens, forced noble ladies to get out of their carriages and lift up their skirts while he and his men-at-arms rode jeeringly by? Did he really carry fifty ladies about with him to satisfy his needs on his travels? Did he really have fat priests sewn up in bearskins and thrown to the dogs?[32] What are the sources for these stories? And how do they fit in with the stories of sadistic massacres?

It is necessary to distinguish between different types of atrocities. There is the slaughter of men, women and children which forms part of war. Most of these massacres were written about by Ivan's enemies, the Livonians and the Lithuanians, and were blamed not only on the Tsar but on Russians (and Tatars) in general. They were described in horrible detail in flyleafs and illustrated books printed in Germany. But there was little difference in the degree of horror between the atrocities perpetrated by Russians, Germans, Lithuanians, Poles, Tatars or Turks, or indeed in warfare anywhere at that time. Of a different nature are the barbarities of Ivan's raids on his own people, the devastation of Novgorod, Tver', and many other towns carried out by the *oprichnina* which are well attested by both Russian and foreign sources. And of still a different nature are the torture and execution of Ivan's personal enemies, those whom he regarded as traitors. Here, too, there are Russian sources like some of the chronicles, and many foreign sources, though evidently foreigners who wrote after having lived in Russia and served the Tsar are more likely to be well-informed.

Most of the stories about dishonouring women, even anonymous ladies of high rank, come from foreign sources, Taube and Kruse, Schlichting, Staden, Horsey, Oderborn and the Livonian authors who wrote in German. The many illustrations are all in books printed in Germany and the Netherlands, and are therefore propaganda.[33] This does not mean that all that is alleged is quite untrue, but that only the naive or the wishful thinker will accept that all these stories are true. So many belong in the world of a sick imagination like the lucubrations of the Marquis de Sade, or in that of turning a quick pfennig. The reality of war in Livonia and Russia, of Crimean raids, and of the ravages carried out by the *oprichniki* on the Russian population, was bad enough without being inflated by the gruesome fancies of disordered minds.

An interesting example of the kind of distortion which occurs as a result of the formulaic exaggeration of atrocities is provided by one specific incident of which four different foreign descriptions exist, two by Protestants, one by a Catholic. This is the raid inflicted by the Tsar and his son Ivan on the German (Livonian) Suburb in Moscow in 1578. Johann Boch, the author of one of these accounts, was a Catholic from Antwerp, travelling on some kind of roving mission, probably from the Governor of the Spanish Netherlands, with a safe conduct from Ivan. Suffering from serious frostbite he was cared for in the suburb by the Tsar's surgeon, possibly Bomelius at that date.

Then came Ivan's raid on the suburb, in which Boch was stripped, beaten and forced to flee, until he was rescued and taken to the home of the then apothecary. In the course of the raid, the inhabitants of the suburb were beaten up and stripped of their clothes and possessions, according to Boch's account, in spite of the Tsar's proclaimed edict: 'Plunder but do not kill.' The second account, by Pastor Oderborn, a Protestant, who was not an eyewitness, describes how the Tsar mocked the unfortunate people of the suburb (who, he said, were mostly women and children) and then 'the tyrant, blind with rage, driven by barbaric savagery and maddened with hatred for the German race' moved among them, and when the young maidens protested at being raped, Ivan ordered them to be beaten, have their nails pulled out, tore out their tongues, then 'ran them through with glowing stakes'. All this while the young women invoked the name of Jesus. Horsey (another Protestant) says that Ivan set a thousand gunners on the young women to strip them naked, deflower and rape them or kidnap them. Then as usual, Horsey acted the knight errant and rescued and clothed a few of the young women who got away to the English house. Margeret was a French mercenary in the Time of Troubles, who wrote much later, from hearsay. He concentrates more on the causes of the raid and merely states that the inhabitants were driven out, naked as babes, and their homes pillaged. His religion is not known.[34]

It is possible to study the various accounts of Ivan's cruelty, discard some of the most extravagant tales, and concentrate on the evidence of events for which several different sources exist. There are several Russian sources for the introduction of the *oprichnina*; there are records of the transfer of *pomeshchiki* from one area to another; the persecution of the aristocracy is described in the correspondence between Ivan IV and Kurbsky which conveys very vividly the human qualities of the participants in the Russian drama,[35] and the religious and moral values of Russian society even if all the events described are not to be implicitly believed in. And some of the events described by Kurbsky are confirmed elsewhere. The assault on Novgorod is attested to in many sources. The executions in July 1570 in Moscow also.

Most important of all, how did these dreadful events fit into Ivan's own life? What do we really know about him? It is generally assumed that he had an unhappy childhood, losing his father at the age of three and his mother at the age of eight, and being left to the tender mercies of uncaring boyars. But the only evidence for the casual carelessness with which he was treated comes from Ivan himself, in his first letter to Prince Kurbsky in 1564, which is already deeply coloured by his sense of umbrage at the failure of those around him to treat him with sufficient deference, and which was in any case written when he was well over thirty years old. All that we know, from Russian sources, of his early life, is that he was a rackety young man, and that there are tales of an early taste for torturing birds and animals and a tendency to abuse his power in dealing with adults.

The impact of the fall of Constantinople on Russian culture is often mentioned, but the impact of the advance of Ottoman power in southeast Europe is but rarely touched on, because it had little effect on western European culture. Yet this was extremely unsettling for Russia which might well be next on the list, and was now completely cut off from the cultural contact with Greece and central Europe which had existed until the Ottoman conquests of the fifteenth and sixteenth centuries. Travelling to and from the great Orthodox centre on Mount Athos had become dangerous and expensive. Transit for Russian embassies to the Holy Roman Empire, to Vienna or Rome, depended on the fluctuating suzerainty of the Ottoman Empire, which was exercised with a certain flexibility over the intervening powers, until the final assault under Suleiman the Magnificent.

Ivan's childhood was not normal by the standards of the child-centred education of the twenty-first century, but it was not so different from that of other young princes. He lacked a male role model, maybe, yet so little is known of his childhood that who knows what influences were brought to bear on him? There must have been some tension between his status as a grand prince by the grace of God, already from the age of three, and his status as a minor, subject to rule by graceless boyars. It was also a solitary childhood, particularly after the death of his mother in 1538, but there may have been a gleam of affection and warmth in his relations with his brother. Iuri Vasil'evich is usually described as deaf and dumb, and almost always as feeble-minded. The latter may not have been true. Ivan's constant and apparently affectionate care for his brother makes one wonder whether there was some form of communication between them. Iuri was always treated with consideration as befitted his status; he was even at times left in charge in Moscow while Ivan was away (though no doubt someone else carried out any public duties).

Nevertheless, Ivan's coronation, his marriage, and his first steps in power and war reflected no outstanding abnormality, as against the general run of young European princes, the Valois princes in France, Edward VI of England, Don Carlos of Spain.[36] Possibly in his attitude to the Moscow fire of 1547 Ivan may already have shown some of that apprehension which was to develop into attacks of outright panic. And already in the various campaigns against Kazan' he showed his understanding of his dual role as Tsar and spiritual father in his concept of leadership in time of war. His first real breakdown came with the death of Anastasia in 1560. Many authors have stressed this caesura in Ivan's life, starting with Karamzin. It is already to be found in three early seventeenth-century writers, who are very critical of Ivan.[37] Many historians have rejected what they consider to be Karamzin's romantic approach and preferred to see in Ivan a boor with no feelings, tied up in an arranged marriage. Yet there is no doubt that the thirteen years of Ivan's marriage to Anastasia were the most peaceful and harmonious in his life, and there is one touching phrase in a letter to Kurbsky of 1577, which suggests that she remained alive in his memory: 'Why did you separate me from my wife?', he wrote. 'If only you had not taken from me my young bride (*iunitsy moeia*) then there would have been no sacrifices to Cronus.'[38]

It was after Anastasia's death that Ivan broke out into wild debauchery, and seems to have given way to homosexual leanings. His wife's death not only injured his happiness, it was an affront to his power. He had lost someone who belonged to him, whom he was used to (and Ivan was clearly uxorious as his later life showed), who formed part of his enclosed world. Her loss, though it was not sudden, undoubtedly unbalanced him, and aroused the incipient acute paranoia which led him to see enemies everywhere and to blame them for poisoning his wife – and his next two wives as well. He may or may not have loved Anastasia, but he needed her love, and he may have felt bereft, as though he had lost his mother all over again. The external signs of increasing paranoia were the savage persecution of the Adashev clan, and the widening circle of the disgraced boyars.

Marriage with Maria Temriukovna in August 1561 may have calmed Ivan down for a while. Success with the conquest of Polotsk in 1563 was followed by the death of his brother Iuri, and not long after that of Metropolitan Makarii. This could well have led to a sense of increasing loneliness, with no one left with whom to share his childhood memories. Probably the most serious shock Ivan suffered, and it was a shock to his imperial pride, was the defection of Prince Kurbsky in April 1564. The nature of their relationship undoubtedly needs further study. Taking all their correspondence together, there are several occasions on both sides when a degree of emotion pierces through the anger. In Kurbsky one can detect the emotion of loyalty and allegiance betrayed; an underlying suggestion of friendship betrayed is particularly evident in Ivan's last letter to Kurbsky, when he justifies himself to the Prince for having opposed the efforts he attributed to him to place Vladimir of Staritsa on the throne in his stead. 'Did I ascend the throne by robbery or armed force? . . . I was born to rule by the grace of God . . . I grew up upon the throne. And why should Prince Vladimir be lord?' All this, argues Ivan, took place because Kurbsky was self-willed: 'If only he had not sided against Ivan and with the priest [Sylvester]'. He ends up with a psychologically most revealing assertion: 'You began to oppose me and betray me still more, and I therefore began to oppose you more harshly; I wanted to subdue you to my will – and you in recompense – how you defiled and outraged the sanctity of the Lord',[39] a reference to Kurbsky's campaigning on behalf of Stephen Bathory against Orthodox Russia. Ivan could not forgive Kurbsky for not having submitted to his will, for only the Tsar might have a will and a subject should submit to the death.

But the life of drink, debauchery, religion and sadism which Ivan embarked upon with the institution of the *oprichnina*, his withdrawal to the privacy of Aleksandrovskaia Sloboda and the repercussions of the execution or exile of many of his most prominent generals just when the war with Poland–Lithuania in Livonia had broken out, precipitated a fresh crisis.

In Ivan's first letter to Kurbsky, of July 1564, paranoia is already reinforced by megalomania, and Ivan reacted by setting up the *oprichnina* as a further guarantee of security. But it failed him, and left him unprotected from his external enemies with the death, he believed by poisoning, of his second wife, Maria Temriukovna, in 1569. Whether her death affected him emotionally is hard to tell, but certainly the suspicion that she died by poison within his refuge at Aleksandrovskaia Sloboda must have caused him considerable dismay. In the meantime Ivan was overwhelmed by the news of the overthrow of Erik XIV in Sweden, a King with whom he had been negotiating what amounted to the kidnapping of Catherine Jagiellonka, the wife of Erik's brother John. The insult of the refusal of his offer of marriage by Catherine ten years before was still festering and could only be cured by some resounding revenge. Erik had been betrayed and imprisoned by his nobles, the kingdom handed over to his brother John. Was this not a foretaste of what Ivan could expect to happen between him and Vladimir of Staritsa? The attack on Novgorod and the execution of 'traitors' in Moscow may well have been a means of eliminating those who might treat him as Erik XIV had been treated. Then in autumn 1571 came the death by poisoning of his third wife Marfa Sobakina.[40] She died not long after the fearsome Crimean raid on Moscow where so much of the city was destroyed. Was it in the context of her death that he wrote the 'Kanon' in the name of the holy fool, Parfenii, in which he appeals to the Archangel Michael to grant him a gentle death in his despair, and not to frighten him, to give him time to repent, and also appeals to the Holy Mother of God to intercede for him, and let him be taken to a place of peace?[41]

But Ivan was becoming more and more unstable and it is at this stage that he finally lost all control and began to hit out savagely in every direction. Paranoia advances with age and he was now approaching forty. The death of his three wives was proof that he was not all-powerful, he could not even protect his own family, and this led him to lash out against all those who surrounded him, seeking both revenge and safety. Underlying signs of a severe personality disorder were emerging. Ivan recognized no limits on his power, not only in theory but in fact; he recognized no abstract moral standard by which his deeds could be measured. No one could oppose him. All he did was right and necessary because he did it, because he was like God.

Ivan could also at this time become sly, manoeuvring to catch potential enemies out, losing all sense of right and wrong provided he succeeded in obtaining convincing evidence of treason. It is at this stage that in his relations with foreign powers Ivan becomes more and more resentful of those who fail to address him as Tsar, and dwells more and more frequently on his descent from Prus, the brother of Augustus. This overweening belief that his power was from God is often attributed to the education in 'autocracy' he allegedly received from Makarii, who certainly believed that Ivan ruled by God's grace. Yet the right to reward and to punish had been claimed already by Ivan III, and the theory behind his power, and that of Queen Elizabeth, was the same, for as she put it, 'The Queen's Highness is the only supreme governor of this realm. . . . as well in all spiritual or ecclesiastical things . . . as temporal.'[42] But Ivan had reached the stage when he had no sense of measure in the way he used power, which for him was not merely absolute but unlimited.

So Ivan became personally responsible for the death of Ivan Fedorov Cheliadnin, because he believed the latter had 'wanted to be tsar'; and for the death of his cousin Vladimir of Staritsa, his wife and nine-year-old daughter, because he was his cousin and might be his heir even though Ivan Ivanovich was already fifteen years old, and for the thousands who died in Novgorod because of his fear of treason, however he defined it. What remains inexplicable is the dreadful scene in the Poganaia meadow on 25 July 1570. It was a theatrically staged play of horror and revenge, on people who until a few days before had been Ivan's closest collaborators, and who were not his rivals for power, but his loyal servants. They were suddenly and cruelly exterminated, notably Viskovaty and Funikov. At this time too Ivan turned on three of the early leaders of the *oprichnina*, Viazemsky and the two Basmanovs, and got rid of them.[43]

In his behaviour and in his letters to Kurbsky, Ivan shows a complete inability to see any point of view but his own, to feel any compassion for those he feels the need to destroy, and an incomprehensible indifference to wives and children. It has been suggested that this last attribute of his character was conditioned by the existing Russian tradition of regarding the clan or the *rod* as joined in a collective guilt for serious crimes such as treason. There was also perhaps another motive for the total extermination of a family, namely that its ability ever to act against the Tsar would be cut short. The same consideration applied to the refusal to let important nobles marry. But Ivan's ruthlessness went beyond these fairly common defences. He wished to ensure that there would be none left to pray for the dead.

Yet Ivan was completely inconsistent in his attitude and in his decisions. Several times I.F. Mstislavsky was compelled to procure huge financial sureties to guarantee his behaviour, but he married twice, had two sons, and outlived the Tsar. (He was of course not a Riurikovich.) While M.I. Vorotynsky, after a really distinguished military career, during which he was once in disgrace for a number of years, saved Moscow from the Tatars, and two years later died in agony, but left more than one son.[44] It is impossible to trace a consistent policy in the Tsar's attitude to his courtiers, other than the almost automatic appointment of relatives of his wives to posts at court, and their almost equally automatic disgrace or execution when the wife died or was repudiated. Historians have spent much time trying to trace factional struggles, but in the long run favourites came and went in total disregard of policies.

There is one factor that may have appeared to the Tsar as particularly threatening, and that is the existence of a solid wedge of aristocrats, mostly princes, closely interrelated by marriage, and also by the tightly knit network of suretyships, which stood up against him, and which he eventually relegated into the *zemshchina*. Marriage was certainly a close bond between clans, but suretyship represented an even closer network of relationships. The only thing that remains inexplicable is the lack of evidence that these financial bonds were ever called in by the Tsar.[45] The system of *krugovaia poruka* protected the Tsar from the princes and the boyars, but it also protected the princes and boyars from the Tsar. The whole of society remained tied up in a cat's cradle of bonds.

Why did Ivan's courtiers tolerate such appalling treatment? Why did they not kill him? This question has been passed over by some historians who argue that Ivan was merely an illiterate figurehead, manipulated by powerful courtiers leading factional groups. Yet it does not seem probable that from the 1560s onwards, the powerful boyars in the *zemshchina* would have tolerated the savage repressions carried out by the *oprichniki* – the murders of Gorbaty-Shuisky, Ivan Fedorov, Vladimir of Staritsa, Metropolitan Filipp – if these were merely the result of the decisions of men acting in Ivan's name. Such horrors had to have behind them the authority of an anointed and charismatic ruler, and from what is known of Ivan's personality from many different sources, the Tsar was an imposing and dominant, even charismatic, figure, and his intellectual capacity was unaffected by his psychological disorder. The imperial envoy, Prinz von Buchau, and Possevino, for instance, are much more penetrating and less severe in their judgments of Ivan than the English Fletcher, a Puritan, who never saw the Tsar. Bowes, or Turberville, were typical English xenophobes, though Jenkinson and Horsey show more perceptiveness, but their reports are often discarded as uninteresting precisely because they are not so critical. They were more able to discriminate between what Ivan was and what he did.[46]

One historian has suggested that to Ivan's contemporaries, his tyranny and cruelty represented the torments of Hell associated with the Last Judgment. Hell was associated not only with fire but with water, the bottom of a fiery lake or of an icy river. This explains the use of drowning as a method of execution and in this sense the Tsar's violence was understandable to the people who lived in the same religious framework

Chapter XXII
Ivan's Legacy to Russia

The confusion which still exists over the interpretation of Ivan's reign provides one of the most obvious examples of the nefarious influence of ideology over historical writing. The portrayal of Ivan's reign has been distorted almost from the very beginning, though one may fairly exclude Karamzin, the first professional Russian historian, who was also intellectually honest, if a romantic at heart. He saw Ivan IV first as the handsome young man with his loving and gentle wife, kept to the straight and narrow path by his upright friend Adashev, and by the stern priest Sylvester. But when his wife died, according to Karamzin, the Tsar gave way to the evil trends in his character and became a demon.

This was not a satisfactory explanation of the role of Ivan IV in Russian history for it failed to provide a political and moral justification for his cruelty by pointing to the positive benefit his policies brought to the land and the people. Hence theories had to be devised, according to the intellectual fashions current at the time, which made it possible to interpret events as having been planned with a view to well defined and positive outcomes. The latest of these fashions, which prevailed in the nineteenth century and throughout most of the twentieth, posited the existence of a powerful aristocracy in Russia, bound to oppose the development of tsarist absolutism in defence of its own power base. It was selfish and reactionary, placing its own interests before those of the 'nation'. This theory led to the elaboration of a systematic interpretation of Russian history in which the reactionary princely/boyar aristocracy clung to its vast old 'appanages' with all their privileges, in opposition to the centralizing state and the progressive nobility or service gentry, which both supported and depended on the Crown, and was anxious to fulfil the national objectives of territorial expansion. The Tsar's despotism was necessary in order to achieve the victory of the state (under the Tsar) and the service gentry, over the boyars.

This historical interpretation current in the period from 1940 to the 1970s, under the overall supervision of Stalin,[1] has come under attack in subsequent years,[2] largely because the evidence to sustain it was lacking, and with the slackening of central party control over the intellectual life of the USSR there could be occasional divergences from the historical party line.[3] Indeed, a closer study of the source material led historians to conclude that there was no evidence for this supposed 'struggle' between aristocrats and service gentry over policy, for concealed centripetal forces were acting in a way independent of their presumed class interests. Both aristocrats (princes and boyars) and service gentry accepted the unification of the land under the sole government of the Tsar, and the merging of service tenure and allodial property in land which was taking place and in which they all saw some advantages. Some Riurikid princes, who had survived in sufficiently strong clans might still hanker after their old appanage status, but the pervasive systems of partible inheritance, and suretyship and collective responsibility acted as a barrier against any private initiatives, in an increasingly complex polity, and the monopoly of lucrative service drew the aristocracy and service gentry together.[4]

At a deeper level it has been suggested that though Russian political culture placed no institutional limits on the Tsar's power, it did place intangible and ill-defined moral and religious limits on his exercise of his power, which both he and the people understood. This explains how Iosif of Volokolamsk could at the same time stress the prerogatives of the Tsar, and call on the people to refuse their allegiance to an unrighteous Tsar, a Tsar *muchitel'* or tormentor.[5] There is in fact no incompatibility between a strong ruler and limitations on power, for if he is strong the ruler will know how to manipulate power and make use of the 'constitution' to the full. D. Rowland sums up the political culture in Russia as one in which the Tsar's prime duty is to carry out God's will, as the mediator between God and his people, and make himself responsible for their salvation. If he does not fulfil this duty his people have the right to withdraw their allegiance. There are no limits on the Tsar's right to punish the wicked in pursuance of their salvation. The ruler entrusted with the power to punish needs *groza*, the ability to inspire awe and fear, by the exercise of cruelty if need be.[6]

On the other hand government proceeds by consensus and not by the formation of factions based on support for particular policies favouring different groups or classes. Allegiance is not affected by policies so much as by faith that the Tsar is the true shepherd of the people.

It is also the case that we tend to exaggerate the executive power available to an absolute monarch in medieval times. Kings could be absolute in the sense of *solutus a legibus*, not bound by the laws, which they, or their predecessors, had in any case made. But the power of the executive was very weak compared with what it is today, and the reach of the government in a country as vast as Russia made the exercise of close control of individual activity impossible in the age of the horse.

Throughout his reign Ivan pursued a number of policies with more or less success. One of them was the aim of reducing the powers and holdings of appanage princes, a policy which had already been energetically followed by Vasily III. It was also becoming evident that the tradition of consensus between the Crown and the aristocracy survived, with the aim of achieving a greater integration of disparate principalities and societies which had so much in common. There is no doubt that though his attacks were unsystematic and fuelled by personal hatred and distrust of individual princes and boyars, Ivan reduced the capacity of the remaining wealthy Riurikid princes to present any challenge to his hold on the throne and to act together against him. Though his first target seems to have been the princes, yet he also bridled the wealthy non-princely boyars, and by introducing a perpetual reshuffle of lands, to and from the *oprichnina*, he prevented the establishment of local links between the aristocracy and a possible military following. There were not very many candidates, for the great Gediminovich families did not present a serious challenge and could be allowed greater freedom. But the russified descendants of the Lithuanian Patrikeevs, and the Obolenskys, Shuiskys and particularly Vorotynskys and of course Ivan's cousin Vladimir of Staritsa were hamstrung or destroyed.

By centralization, or unification as it is preferable to call it, Ivan was clearly not aiming at a centralized administration, controlled by a central government and a central bureaucracy, because a literate substructure did not exist, nor the necessary legal knowledge to create it. It meant above all the extension to all parts of the realm of the recognition of one single supreme, ultimate, lawful authority manifesting itself in many ways and delegating the administration of justice, revenue raising and defence to paid or unpaid partners at many social levels, often by means of the system of suretyship. Ivan IV was more successful than many of his contemporaries in Europe in achieving this unified authority.[7] In Russia there was one law (the *sudebnik* of 1550), one currency, one religion, one set of weights and measures, one language, and a unified army command. There were still of course *terrae irredentae*, the lands of Kievan Rus' under Polish-Lithuanian rule, and Russia was beginning to absorb lands inhabited by members of other races and religions, though not to an extent which altered the basic composition of the nation.

During the thirty-four years after his coronation Ivan enormously extended the territory ruled over by Russia by the conquest of Kazan' and Astrakhan' and by pushing forward the settled and defended territory in the south. Advance into Siberia from the northeast of Russia, in pursuit of furs and salt, had been a private venture of the Stroganov family but as they extended their trading expeditions into the lands of the Ob' river basin they needed their own armed force and recruited a Cossack, Yermak, part soldier part brigand, to lead it. Starting out in 1582, as a private adventurer Yermak (like so many of the Spanish conquistadores) was at first successful but then lost his life in a counterattack from the Khanate of Siberia. The Russian state then took over the enterprise and, from then on, Russia advanced steadily into western Siberia.

During some twenty-seven years of almost continuous warfare in Ivan's reign, the armed forces were modernized and their supply improved regardless of cost and of the strain placed on the population. Most striking was the proliferation of fortified towns and fortresses, often manned by Cossack hosts, forming carefully planned and laid out defence lines which after 1571 guarded the heartland of Russia against the devastating Crimean slave raids.[8]

Entirely negative, however, was the impact of Ivan's economic policy designed to extract as much money as possible from the people, largely the peasants, to pay for his wars, for the *oprichnina*, for his extension of the defence lines in the south. The non-military contributions had risen in value from 2.16 roubles to 6 roubles per annum between 1505 and 1584; the military obligations rose in value in the same period from 3.07 to 38.45 roubles per annum, per *sokha* in both cases.[9]

The economic crisis which bedevilled the last years of Ivan's reign affected agriculture and trade equally. The contrast between the flourishing state of central and north west Russia at the beginning of his reign and the appalling desolation in the 1580s is well known. Hugh Chancellor, on his first visit, described the country between Iaroslavl' and Moscow as 'well replenished with small villages which are so well filled with people that it is wonder to see them. The ground is well stored with corn . . . you shall meet in a morning seven or eight hundred sleds coming or going thither [to Moscow]',[10] and all foreigners comment on the incredible cheapness and abundance of food in the country. War, casualties, plagues and famine, Crimean raids, taxation, the extension of the *pomest'ie* system which deprived the peasants of land, change in the method of payment of *pomeshchiki* from central state payments to individual exploitation of the land, the obligation to bring an armed and mounted *kholop* to battle as a military slave, and the depredations of the *oprichnina* in the ensuing twenty-five years, had depopulated the country, which became so impoverished that it could provide neither the manpower nor the money for the continuation of the war in Livonia. The figures are staggering: around Pskov, over 85 per cent of the homesteads were deserted in 1585, around Novgorod figures rose to 97 per cent. In the area around the Oka river deserted holdings numbered up to 95 per cent. Monastery lands suffered just as much as *pomest'ia* or allodial lands. Little by little the population had fled, to the valley of the northern Dvina, east to the wilds of Siberia, south to the *dikoe pole* or wild field, the steppe lands which separated Russia from Crimean territory.[11] Many were lost to the new defence establishments in the south, others could now flee over the Volga or to Siberia. The impossibility of maintaining the cultivation of the *pomest'ia* by the cavalry force, as peasant labour disapppeared, led inevitably to the increasingly frequent suspension of the peasants' right of departure and the approach of enserfment.

The capriciousness and cruelty of Ivan's rule, coupled with the destructiveness of the whole idea of the *oprichnina*, served only to delay the evolution of the concept of the state, of the separation of Tsarist power and property from public power and property, and of the development of independent state institutions. As long as Ivan incarnated the state in his own person, independent political or social institutions could not exist.[12] In this respect the absolute power exercised by tsars differed from the absolute powers of western rulers, in that in Catholic Europe, the monarch was bound by laws which regulated his sphere of action, and that therefore institutions with an independent existence could take root.[13]

This explains why a body like an assembly of the land failed to acquire consistency in Russia as the collective voice of the people, let alone as an institution representing different social layers – which it would be misleading to call classes. Russian historians have contributed to the confusion about the existence of Russian political institutions in the sixteenth century because they use words which do not designate accurately the social formations they attempt to describe. Contemporary historians, notably Skrynnikov, often speak of the existence of 'noble corporations' (*korporatsii*) in sixteenth-century Russia, a formula which conveys the impression of an association given coherence in action by legally defined structures and powers. No such bodies existed in Russia, hence they could not be represented by political institutions. The Assembly of the Land remained an *ad hoc*, non-elected group, until Russian society was faced with the inescapable dilemma of the end of the dynasty, in 1598, and had to improvise a political procedure to give legitimacy to the succession to the Crown by borrowing from the well attested practices of the Polish-Lithuanian Commonwealth and the Holy Roman Empire.[14] It proved stable enough, in the conditions of the Time of Troubles, to provide a precedent for future political action with the Assembly of 1613. Similarly, the idea of a boyar *duma* as a repre-sentative body, as part of a 'legislature' (there are many references to it as a 'parliament' by contemporary English visitors to Russia and present-day Russian historians) is quite erroneous, for the Tsar's Council comprised members of more than one 'estate' and its function was not to represent the interests of a social estate, but to advise the Tsar.

The reign of Ivan typifies a period of political experimentation in Russia, with the Tsar trying at the beginning to find means of carrying on a dialogue with his people, experimenting with the convocation of different types of *ad hoc* meetings, some of them deriving from church councils, some of them going back to the tradition of the *veche*. Some administrative and judicial tasks were delegated to the members of the provincial élite. This period of experimentation ended in the despotism of the *oprichnina*, while the boyars and the service gentry made use of the opening provided by Ivan in 1566 to establish their own dialogue with the Tsar, but were unable to give it permanence. Ivan's reign thus hindered the development of political institutions in Russia and retarded their growth. The government was not separated from the court, nor was the state separated from the ruler, the *gosudarstvo* from the *gosudar'*.

Finally, it can be argued that Ivan's way of conducting foreign policy delayed the acceptance of Russia into the European states' system on equal terms. The rejection of Renaissance and Reformation culture and thought, and of any attempt to master Latin or European languages outside the confines of the *prikazy* or government offices, left Russia dependent on foreign intermediaries for the conduct of foreign affairs. The drive of the English members of the Russia Company supplemented the linguistic weakness of Russia in dealings with England. Both Jenkinson and Horsey seem to have acquired a working knowledge of Russian. Many of the more humble members of the English colony undoubtedly did so. The availability of German translators also facilitated relations with the Holy Roman Empire, but otherwise it seems that the diplomatic relations of Russia in the reign of Ivan developed by fits and starts. Contacts with the East and the Tatar world, the Ottoman Empire, and the Balkans survived as leftovers from the days of the Eastern Roman Empire. But the war for the Baltic opened up a new sphere of diplomatic activity for Russia in the West in which Tsarist diplomacy was often out of its depth through ignorance of the human and historical geography of Europe, and of the diplomatic forms of the Latin world, insofar as they had crystallized at that time. Central to Ivan's conduct of foreign policy was the demand for the recognition of his title as Tsar, not as a step in the *translatio imperii*,[15] a policy which really played very little part in Ivan's conception of his imperial role, which was limited and oriented towards the West, towards equality of status with the Holy Roman Empire, and did not imply ruling over other nations.[16] The increasing insistence on his descent from Prus, the mythical brother of the Emperor Augustus, served to give added length to past Russian history, and is linked to his claim to equality with the Holy Roman Emperor. His pride in his alleged descent from *nemtsy* is designed to underscore his claim to Livonia as part of his ancestral heritage, as a descendant of Riurik, descended in turn from Prus, not to argue that he is a foreigner in Russia. *Nemets* (dumb) does not necessarily mean German. *Nemtsy* from Portugal discovered America. Ivan's concept of 'empire' is not that of ruling over other nations, but is dynastic, based on descent.[17]

Yet Ivan's diplomacy suffered from his growing megalomania, his contempt for rulers who were not hereditary (like the King of Sweden or the King of Denmark, or eventually Stephen Bathory) or for powers whose rulers were not 'sovereign' but were forced to listen to the wishes of their subjects, like Queen Elizabeth I. Similarly, he expected 'great' embassies to be sent to him; he must be sought after and did not take the initiative. This is most noteworthy in the negotiations over the succession to the Crown of Poland–Lithuania, which leave one with the impression that Ivan did not really want the crown for himself, foreseeing the difficulties he would experience in establishing his authority over a political system totally alien to him and divided in religion, and uncertain about winning it for his younger son. In general Russian diplomacy suffered from ignorance of the outer world and its ways, and of languages.

The combination of the despotism of the Tsar, the ravages of war, and the demoralization and havoc created by the *oprichnina* served also to delay and even prevent the opening up of Russia to the intellectual and spiritual movements which had been manifested in the

West, the Renaissance, the Reformation and the Counter Reformation. The whole period from 1453 to 1598 is one of extreme
fermentation of minds and spirits in Russia, which was far more
profoundly affected by the fall of Constantinople than western
Europe and by the ensuing advance of Ottoman power and Islam into
the Danubian basin – even if this advance was compensated for by the
conquest of Kazan'. It was an event with both spiritual and political
consequences for a country only just emerging from the overlordship
of the Golden Horde.

Meanwhile, diplomatic relations with the Holy Roman Empire and
the principalities of the Danube basin, even if under Ottoman
suzerainty, all brought Russia nearer to west European culture. Yet the
long years of single-minded concentration on war for the Baltic – from
1558 to 1582 – accompanied by the terror, left Russia with neither the
intellectual nor the spiritual energy to embark on a wide-ranging
intellectual opening to western culture and technology. The moral and
material resources available for cultural development were concentrated
rather on advances within the range of traditional Orthodox culture.
Russia did not link up at all with the European intellectual system; it
remained outside the network of universities and schools, springing up
in western Europe, and even in the New World, which were in any case
based on Latin.

Neither the state, in the person of Ivan IV, nor the Church, whose
international aura had been somewhat dimmed by the fall of its spiritual
capital into non-Christian hands, and which clung still to the theory of
the divine nature of the ruler, could tolerate the development of
independent thought. Thus knowledge of the various theological
currents which flourished under the name of the Protestant Reformation
was very superficial. Russians met with Protestantism in England,
Sweden, Livonia, and to some extent Poland–Lithuania, and with
Catholicism in the Commonwealth, and the Church of Rome remained
the ultimate political and religious rival.[18] Anglicanism was perceived as
a variety of Lutheranism. Much has been made of the discussion
between Jan Rokyta and Ivan IV on Lutheranism and between Possevino
and the Tsar on Catholicism, but it is really time to recognize that
neither of these debates was carried on at a particularly high intellectual
level.[19]

Paradoxically, the aspect of Renaissance culture which dominated the
court of Ivan, sustained by Ivan's paranoia, was the world of the occult,
based on alchemy, magic, witchcraft, and astrology, together with some
aspects of the carnavalesque culture of misrule which existed in other

countries and which in Russia was the province of the *skomorokhi*, wandering entertainers who incurred the severest condemnation from the Orthodox Church. The *Litsevoi svod* or illuminated sixteenth-century Chronicle contains a version of the *Alexander Romance*, with a miniature of the wizard king of Egypt, Nectanebus and his magic wand, the real father of Alexander the Great by Olympias, and by implication, in the tale, an ancestor of Prus and the dynasty of Riurik.[20]

One of the intellectual and moral trends which had contributed massively to the cultural flavour of the Middle Ages in the West, the ideal of chivalry, was totally absent in Russia.[21] However meretricious much of this ideal may have been, against the background of the ruthless medieval wars and the Crusades, nevertheless the ideal flourished in court society and it contributed to a slow, European-wide process of civilization of manners and behaviour, and particularly to an increasing appreciation of the role of educated women in society. Paradoxically, however, a resemblance between the members of the *oprichnina* and the orders of chivalry has occasionally been detected.[22] It is possible that the parallel is rather with the military orders of Spain, though who knows whether the Order of the Dragon, founded by Sigismund, King of Hungary, later the Emperor Sigismund, at the end of the fourteenth century, of which Vlad Ţepeş Dracul I became a member, was not the model.

The final blow which Ivan inflicted on his country was the destruction of the dynasty by the political murder of his cousin Vladimir and one of the latter's children, and the accidental killing of his childless eldest surviving son, at a time when dynastic continuity was a principal guarantee of prosperity and stability. The succession of Ivan's younger son, Fedor, postponed the disaster until the latter's childless death in 1598, when for the first time a tsar was elected. Ivan must have turned in his grave at the spectacle of an elected tsar on his throne.[23] But however serious the crisis created by the arrival on the scene of the first False Dmitri, it would not have been so disastrous for Russia had Boris Godunov not died when he did, or had his capable son been a grown man, able to seize the reins of power.

There remains the problem of the significance of Ivan's reign for the spiritual and moral quality of the Russian people. At the beginning of his reign, the young Ivan seemed to display some of the inspiring qualities of the young warrior kings and princes of the West, Henry V, Jean sans Peur, Charles VIII, the young Henry VIII, an image which lasted until after the conquest of Kazan'. In the 1550s he showed some aspects of an astute and prudent ruler, in a period which saw the enactment of some constructive measures. Then came the domestic tragedy of 1560, and what was probably the first of many severe bouts of paranoia, which completely overthrew the balance of the still young Tsar. The cruelty and sadism which were unleashed on the governing élite eventually spread in widening circles throughout the country in an orgy of debauchery, culminating in outbursts of torture and atrocities.[24]

The general obsession with Hell and the tortures of the damned in the Christian world of the West and the East at this time should not be forgotten. This is the age of Hieronymus Bosch, Botticelli's drawings illustrating Dante's *Inferno* and endless portrayals of the most ingenious and painful torments which can be devised by human imagination, painted on church walls and icons in both Orthodox and Catholic Europe. And these events are echoed in folk-tales with a superimposed grim humour.[25] In addition to the torments of Hell, most countries, west or east, suffered from extremely cruel wars and punitive systems. The *chevauchées* of the Black Prince in France during the Hundred Years' War, the raids of the *écorcheurs* in the service of Louis XI of France, the execution of prisoners in the Wars of the Roses, the horrors of Anglo-Scottish border warfare, or of the conquest of Ireland; and in a different field, the flames of the Spanish and Roman Inquisitions, the rule of the Duke of Alba in the Netherlands, the execution of Catholics and heretics in England, the burning of Savonarola, Miguel Servet and Giordano Bruno, the Massacre of St Bartholomew's Day, and the savage repression of the Pilgrimage of Grace under Henry VIII and of the Rising of the Northern Earls by Elizabeth I, all bear witness to an intensification of cruelty not perhaps unrelated to religious conflict, at a time when people believed they were fighting for their salvation.[26]

Such a moral climate was bound to lead to a festering and corrupt morass of fear and suspicion. Even without making use of the often partisan memoirs of the foreign writers on sixteenth-century Russia, merely confining oneself to the *Sinodiki* and the various Chronicles as sources,[27] even those inured to the horrors of the twentieth century cannot but be appalled at the numbers of men, women and children ('whose names were known only to God') who were sacrificed to the demon of fear by the paranoid Tsar. The mentality of fear and suspicion that he deliberately cultivated both in the *zemshchina* and in the *oprichnina*, or *dvor*, contributed to the culture of denunciation implicit in the system of *krugovaya poruka* or collective suretyship.[28] It conceals behind a dense shadow the nature of the policies pursued by the Tsar.

One should pause a moment to consider the effect of such a human haemorrhage on a society in which the élite was extremely closely inter-related by common descent from the dynastic founder, and by intermarriage.[29] Men killed in battle or in the torture chamber, or executed, women dishonoured, many struck down without religious rites, left unburied, their bodies thrown to the dogs, children massacred we know not how – what hatreds must have consumed a society in which the executioners and the executed were bound so closely to one another and in which surviving depended on stepping on the bodies of one's friends and relatives. The lack of evidence about individuals renders it difficult to reconstruct personal relationships, but a few tentative suggestions may be made.

Take the case of Peter Basmanov, who fought gallantly for Boris Godunov until the Tsar died, in 1605. Either because of a precedence dispute, or because he had not forgiven the deaths of his father Fedor and his grandfather Aleksei at the hands of Maliuta Skuratov, Ivan's chief executioner, whose daughter Marfa was Boris Godunov's wife, Peter Basmanov now transferred his support from young Tsar Fedor Borisovich, and espoused the cause of the first false Dmitri.[30] Similarly, Prince Ivan M. Vorotynsky, the son of Prince Mikhail Ivanovich, the victor over the 1572 Tatar attack on Moscow who was executed in 1573, may well have provided information to the *d'iak* Ivan Timofeev, who was close to the Vorotynsky clan, about the horrors of the destruction of Novgorod.[31] The violence which subsequently marked the Time of Troubles in the seventeenth century has its roots in the reign of Ivan IV.[32] Not many people have expressed themselves so openly and so critically in the seventeenth century as Ivan Timofeev, but what he wrote is evidence that people knew and had not forgotten.

At this point one must come to grips with the roots of Ivan's cruelty and his ability to impose it on his people throughout a long reign. In the first place there is his justification for the emphasis on punishment in his conception of the role of a Tsar. Ivan has left plenty of material in letters, instructions, recorded speeches on which to base such an analysis, but it must be recognized that evidence of his thought and activity must always be slightly suspect. It is almost certain that he did not write his long tirades himself, but dictated them over time to clerks who remain unknown, and they have survived mainly in manuscript copies. In the case of the letters allegedly from the four boyars written in 1567 the scribes may well have been employees of the Office of Foreign Affairs.[33] But nothing is known about Ivan's private secretariat, or scriptorium, except that it must have existed in view of the constant activity in the organization and supervision of warfare, internal government, and foreign affairs, all of which were still conducted in his own *dvor*.[34] There is enough similarity in the cast of mind, the expressions used, the choice of the lengthy quotations from the Bible and the Apocrypha, the *Velikii Chetii Minei*, and other religious sources such as the Pseudepigrapha, to convince the reader that we are not faced here with seventeenth-century forgeries. It is also impossible to find a convincing substitute for the Tsar, someone who could have been responsible behind the scenes for the letters from the four boyars of 1567, in which Ivan actually speaks of himself as 'mentally deranged', or the letter to the Lithuanian Prince A. Polubensky of 9 July 1577.[35]

It is mainly in relations with foreign rulers and envoys that Ivan's arrogance as an hereditary monarch and his claim to descend from the brother of the Emperor Augustus, Prus, is proclaimed. However, the religious dimension of Ivan's personality cannot be ignored. The extent to which it pervades letters written as part of the conduct of foreign affairs is striking. Fundamental to Ivan's conception of his role as Tsar was his responsibility for the eternal salvation of his people, for which he would be called upon to answer at the Last Judgment, which in Russian goes by the more dramatic name of *Strashnyi Sud*, Doomsday, the Fearful Judgment. It is to this aspect of his role as Tsar that his people responded, for they too needed to feel the judgment of God in the judgment of the Tsar.

Ivan derived his ideas of sovereignty not merely from the Eastern Roman Empire but from the Old and New Testaments. It may well have taken some time for him to work out a consistent justification for his extreme interpretation of his sovereign rights. The first stage in the process is made clear in his first letter to Prince Kurbsky, in which he stresses his right to reward and punish his subjects, and in which he begins to reveal the mental processes which lead him to the conclusion that he is surrounded by treason. This is based on what he sees as his betrayal by his subjects, as reflected by the refusal of some of the boyars to swear allegiance to his son Dmitri in 1553; the death, clearly by poisoning, of Anastasia, the boyars' objection to his debauchery and wild way of life after her death, culminating in the flight of Kurbsky. At this point, in his first letter, Ivan also articulates his complaints against Sylvester and Adashev, again justifying himself by accusing them of betraying him and depriving him of his power.[36]

The sadism and cruelty of the regime, imposed by Ivan IV and his henchmen, are given added authority by the religious overtones and symbolism which the Tsar's particular form of mania had taken. The ritual he had introduced in Aleksandrovskaia Sloboda in which he played the main role in a parody of a monastic order is described at length by Taube and Kruse, though we do not know for how long he carried on with it.[37]

By then Ivan was launched on the policy of the *oprichnina*, which gave him a free hand to organize repression. Within his *udel*, or appanage, he was sole master, but the *udel* itself was the instrument of control and oppression throughout the rest of the country. It could no longer be regarded as a tool for imposing a particular policy (e.g., centralization) by fighting *against* something, or someone, but as a way of fighting *for* something. This view, was first put forward by V. Kobrin, who argued that Ivan was fighting *for* unlimited power, for total, arbitrary power over his subjects.[38] Much depends on the meaning which is attached to the words *samoderzhavie* and *samovlastie*.

Samoderzhavie, usually misleadingly translated as 'autocracy', was not at this time part of the official titulature of the Tsar. Again, the Austrian envoy, Prinz von Buchau is illuminating. After the enunciation of all the territories of which Ivan was Tsar, and over which he ruled, Prinz von Buchau adds: 'To this title he often adds the name of "monarcha", which in the Russian language, which is, like the Greek happy in its constructions, is successfully translated by the word samoderzhets, which means he who governs alone.' The emblem of the Grand Prince Ivan Vasil'evich, continued Prinz von Buchau is: 'I am subject to no-one except Christ, son of God.'[39] *Samovlastie* is closer in meaning to arbitrary will, and to 'free will' in the theological sense, and Ivan claims that Man does not enjoy free will since even in the Garden of Eden there was at least one prohibition: eating of the fruit of the tree of knowledge of good and evil. Nevertheless, it was *samovlastie* that Ivan wanted and claimed, 'unlimited power'.

Priscilla Hunt has argued that Ivan's self-justification was founded on the concept of sacred kingship developed by Metropolitan Makarii *after* the Tsar's coronation in 1547. This was an official 'wisdom theology' which enabled Ivan to live out the dual 'image of Christ' on earth with two bodies, one human and one divine, by expanding the divine until it absorbed the human. It enabled him to commit widescale atrocities in his role of Christian ruler, because he was engaged in purifying the world of sin. And it was adopted in order to compensate for the paranoia which seized him intermittently, and to justify measures seen as self-protective. Ivan, as ruler, lived on a higher plane than other men, defined not only by his role as Tsar, but by his role as like unto God himself. In no way therefore can the *oprichnina* be explained away as required by objective political or social causes

Priscilla Hunt has specifically pointed to some of the origins of Ivan's thought in her exploration of a source which seems particularly fruitful, namely the *Velikii Chetii Minei* put together by Metropolitan Makarii, which contained, *inter alia*, the treatise 'On the Celestial Hierarchies' of the Pseudo Dionysius the Areopagite, as well, incidentally, as the Epistle to Filofei on the Third Rome and the tale of Barlaam and Josaphat. Other sources of Ivan's conception of his role are found in Revelations, in the Apocrypha, the Slavonic Book of the Secrets of Enoch (2 Enoch) and in the iconography of the period, for the Tsar is also the Lord of Hosts and the Archangel Michael, the ultimate judge, the instrument of cleansing destructiveness.[40] In Ivan's interpretation, the two bodies – human and divine – are joined, thus superseding the conception of Agapetus of two separate bodies, and following rather the idea of the Areopagite on the union of the two bodies in one, proceeding through repentance and prayer to divine grace.[41]

This last expression of the nature of Orthodox spirituality explains the form taken by so many of Ivan's verbal interventions in spiritual matters. The exaggerated depiction of his sinfulness, a medieval topos, in his letter to the Abbot of the Beloozero monastery in 1573, and the lengthy prologue to his will, believed to date from summer 1572 or 1579,[42] show him wallowing in repentance, not for his atrocities, but for what the Church would regard as sins, blasphemy, fornication, the anti-world of the *skomorokhi*. This repentance was a necessary preliminary to inflicting punishment on those who betrayed him.

Already in the campaign against Kazan', the young Tsar had taken on the role of spiritual leader more than military general, by attending religious services and following the precepts of Metropolitan Makarii from a distance. We do not know enough about his presence on the battlefield to know whether he was consistent in his behaviour, but there is sufficient evidence about his participation in one of his major campaigns during the Livonian war to reconstruct the spiritual dimension. The Tsar's role was not that of the warrior, he would do little fighting. But he was responsible for the moral purity of the host under his command, and his constant concern for it was expressed by sending for both religious relics and magicians. The same spirit of religious commitment was noticeable in Kazan' and in the victorious campaign against Polotsk in 1562 to 1563 which is more fully described in the Chronicle than any other of Ivan's campaigns. There is a suggestion that

Ivan was urged onwards by an upsurge of Lutheranism in Polotsk, against which he had to fight as the Orthodox Tsar.

The intensity of Ivan's drive on Polotsk is reflected in the religious rhetoric in the Chronicles and in the working documents of the campaign. The central religious objective of Ivan's crusade was symbolized by the cathedral of Saint Sophia in Polotsk, the third cathedral of that name in Russia after Kiev and Novgorod. Unfortunately, both Hunt and Bogatyrev speak of the symbolic creation of analogies between the 'king and the state', in the ideology developed by Ivan which articulated the likeness of the ruler to the second person in the Trinity. But it is difficult to accept the existence of such an objective concept as the 'state' in Ivan's understanding of the relationship between the ruler and what he ruled over. He was physically and spiritually one with his realm, united in a profounder symbiosis than the patrimonialism which is often attributed to him. He brought together the human and the divine, which authorized him to act to purify the world of sin, using divine violence. He was an incarnation of this union, which gave moral authority to everything he did and placed him on a par with God.[43]

It was this self-identification of Ivan with the idea of sacred violence which opened the way for the Tsar's belief in the purificatory value of his cruelty, and enabled him to accept as divine in origin the sadism which made life a hell for his subjects. He needed it in order to cleanse both himself and his people from sin. He expresses this notion in so many words in his first letter to Kurbsky: 'If you are so righteous and pious . . . why have you feared an innocent death? . . . that is the will of God – doing good to suffer. If you are so righteous . . . why do you not permit yourself to accept suffering from me, your froward master and so inherit the crown of life?'[44]

It was also the quality of Ivan's firm conviction in his God-given duty of rewarding and punishing his people that induced in them the acceptance of the duty of obedience to the divinely powerful Tsar, to whose judgment they submitted as though it were the Last Judgment.

In his power to decide their fate, Ivan was not like God, he tried to be God. His reign is a tragedy of Shakespearean proportions.[45] His cruelty served no purpose, and as Ivan Timofeev wrote, 'The killers filled our land with blood . . . every place was so filled with the bodies of the dead that the animals which ransack the ground, and swim in the water, and fly in the air were unable to devour their corpses, for they were all more than replete.' Kliuchevsky, who seized upon this aspect of the Tsar, compared him with Samson, who brought down the columns of the temple of Gaza upon himself.[46] But Prince Kurbsky and Timofeev (and I) see him as Lucifer, the star of the morning, who wanted to be God, and was expelled from the Heavens:[47]

> How art thou fallen from heaven, O Lucifer, son of the
>   morning! How art thou cut down to the ground . . .
> For thou hast said in thine heart, I will ascend into heaven, I
>   will exalt my throne above the stars of God . . .
> I will ascend above the heights of the clouds; I will be like the
>   most High.
> Yet thou shalt be brought down to hell, to the sides of the
>   pit . . .

Isaiah 14: 12–15

Abbreviations

Notes

FOREWORD

1 See for instance the works of S. Platonov, M.N. Pokrovsky, and more relevant to the present those of, among others, A.A. Zimin, S.O. Schmidt, D.N. Al'shits, V. Kobrin, R.G. Skrynnikov and B. Floria. They all begin their main works with lengthy, serious, if sometimes idiosyncratic, chapters on the evolution of the historiography of Ivan IV.

2 For a full account of the career of S.F. Platonov, see the Introduction by John T. Alexander to his *Boris Godunov Tsar of Russia*, ed. and tr. by I. Rex Pyles, Academic International Press, Gulf Breeze Florida, 1973.

3 A. Yanov, *The Origins of Autocracy – Ivan the Terrible in Russian History*, University of California Press, Berkeley and London, 1981.

4 The very anti-German film Aleksandr Nevsky was withdrawn from public showing after the signature of the Molotov-Ribbentrop Pact in August 1939.

5 See Maureen Perrie, *The Cult of Ivan the Terrible in Stalin's Russia*, Studies in Russian and East European History and Society, Basingstoke and New York, Palgrave, 2001.

6 Ibid., p. 154

7 In a meeting to discuss part II of the film with Stalin, Molotov, Zhdanov, Cherkasov, the actor who played the part of Ivan IV, and Eisenstein, at the end of February 1947, Cherkasov explained that the film would end with the words: 'Na moriakh stoim i stoiat' budem' to which Stalin replied; 'that's what happened and even more'. See G.B. Mar'yamov, *Kremlevskii tsenzor: Stalin smotrit kino*. Moscow, Kinotsentr, 1992, pp. 83ff, at p.90. Zhdanov objected to Cherkasov's beard as too long.

8 Ibid., p. 89.

9 Perrie, p. 173.

10 See S. Bogatyrev, 'Oprichnina A.A. Zimina, ed. A.L. Khoroshkevich', in *JGOE*, 52, 2004, no. 2, pp. 279–82.

11 G. Hoff (G. Khoff), *Erschreckliche, greuliche und unerhoerte Tyranney Iwan Wasiljeviec*, 1582.

12 See under Hugh Graham in the bibliography.

13 A. Käppeler, *Ivan Groznyj im Spiegel der ausländischen Zeitschriften seiner Zeit, Ein Beitrag zur Geschichte des Westländischen Russlandsbilde*, Bern/Frankfurt am Main, 1972.

14 Edward L. Keenan, *The Kurbskii-Groznyi Apocrypha. The Seventeenth-*

Century Origin of the "Correspondence" Attributed to Prince A.M. Kurbskii and Tsar Ivan IV, Harvard University Press, Cambridge, MA., 1971.

15 'Muscovite Folkways', *The Russian Review*, 45, 1986, pp. 115–81.

16 In a posting on the Early Slavic Studies Internet channel.

17 See the evidence of Possevino on their manner of negotiating, in which discussions were recorded on scrolls and the boyars took them back to Ivan and read them to him.

18 See *SIRIO* (*Sbornik imperatorskogo russkogo istoricheskogo obshchestva*), 71, introduction. The letter allegedly from the fourth boyar, I.P. Fedorov, was probably written by Fedorov. See below, Chapters XIII and XIV.

19 Henry VIII did not like the physical chore of writing either. Writing with a goose quill must have been a much more slow and tedious performance than with a ball-point pen.

20 For those who read Russian see R.G. Skrynnikov, *Perepiska Groznogo i Kurbskogo, paradoksy Edvarda Kinana*, Leningrad, 1973; see also the extensive discussion in his *Tsarstvo Terrora,* St Petersburg, 1992, pp. 10ff, ch. I, 'Istochniki', which also analyses the foreign sources, such as Taube and Kruse, Staden, and Schlichting. In English, I include a selection in chronological order: C.J. Halperin, 'A Heretical View of Sixteenth-Century Muscovy'. Edward L. Keenan: the Kurbsky-Groznyy Apocrypha', *JGOE*, 22, 1974, pp. 162–86; by the same author, 'Keenan's Heresy Re-visited', *JGOE*, 28, 1986, pp. 482–99; idem, 'Edward Keenan and the Kurbskii-Groznyi Correspondence in Hindsight', and Edward L. Keenan, 'Response to Halperin, "Edward Keenan and the Kurbskii-Groznyi Correspondence in Hindsight"', *JGOE,* 46, pp. 376–403, 404–15; Professor Halperin's articles cover works by many authors, survey the discussion from many angles and he refers to a vast amount of further literature in his footnotes. For a recent Russian discussion see V.V. Kalugin, *Andrey Kurbsky i Ivan Groznyi,* Moscow, 1998, pp. 157–8, 252–3 and passim.

21 This could of course be called imperialism.

22 See Isabel de Madariaga, 'La monarquía rusa, una monarquía compuesta?' in *Las Monarquías del Antiguo regimen, monarquías compuestas?*, ed. Conrad Russell and Jose Andres Gallego, Editorial Complutense, Madrid, 1996.

23 The German equivalent is much more accurate: *Selbstherrscher*.

CHAPTER I The Historical Background

1 The role of the Scandinavian Vikings in the formation of the Russian principalities is now accepted in Russia, but more attention has been paid to the possible influence of the Mongols on Russian political culture than to the possible influence of the Vikings, or the Ottomans, at any rate in the work of Western historians. See in general S. Franklin and J. Shepard, *The Emergence of Rus 750–1200*, Longman, London, 1996.

2 See N. de Baumgarten, 'Généalogie et mariages occidentaux des Rurikides russes du Xe au XIIIe siècles', *Orientalia Christiana* IX, no. 35, 1927, pp. 5–94; and 'Genealogy of the Riurikids in the period covered by the Primary Chronicle' in S.H. Cross and O.P. Sherbowitz-Wetzor, *The Russian Primary Chronicle*, Laurentian Text, Medieval Academy of America, Cambridge, Mass., 1953, p. 298.

3 I shall use the word Mongol until the final overthrow of the Golden Horde in 1480 as more convenient, using Tatar thereafter.

4 See map on pp. xii–xiii.

5 M. Roublev, 'The Periodicity of the Mongol Tribute as Paid by the Russian Princes During the Fourteenth and Fifteenth Centuries', *Forschungen zur*

Osteuropäischen Geschichte, Osteuropa Institut an der Freien Universität
Berlin, Otto Harrassowitz, Wiesbaden *(FOG)*, 15, pp. 7–13.

6 At the other end of Europe, in the Christian Spanish mountain kingdom of
Asturias, the Moslem invaders were also known as the Hagarenes *(Agareños)*.

7 A share in the empire allotted to a member of the Golden Kin.

8 See J. Martin, *Medieval Russia, 980–1584*, Cambridge University Press, 1995,
pp. 239ff, for an intelligible account of a very confused situation.

9 C.J. Halperin, *Russia and the Golden Horde: The Mongol Impact on Russian
History*, London, 1987, pp. 59–60.

10 V.A. Kuchkin and B.N. Floria, 'Kniazheskaia vlast' v predstavleniakh tverskikh
knizhnikov XIV–XV vv' in *Ot Rima k tret'emu Rimu (Moscow, 1989)*, IX
*Mezhdunarodnyi seminar istoricheskikh issledovanii 'Ot Rima k tret'emu
Rimu'*, Moscow 1995, p. 188.

11 This may be the origin of the bride-shows (see Chapter II) held in Russia to
choose brides for the grand princely family; but it is usually held that this
practice comes from the Eastern Roman Empire. However, Runciman thinks
the Byzantine bride-shows may have had a steppe origin (S. Runciman,
quoted in D.G. Ostrowski, *Muscovy and the Mongols: Cross-cultural
Influences on the Steppe Frontier*, Cambridge University Press, Cambridge
1998, p. 83).

12 J.I. Fennell, 'Princely Executions in the Horde, 1308–1339', FOG, 38, 1986,
pp. 9–19. 'Appanage' princes are the descendants of Riurikids who inherited
sovereign rights over a principality or part of a principality.

13 C.J. Halperin, op. cit., p. 111 and n. 28, stresses that many of these genealogies
must be rejected, notably that which ascribes Tatar origin to Boris Godunov.

14 The Russians had been officially converted to Orthodox Christianity from
Constantinople in 988 in the reign of Vladimir I (predictably canonized later,
like St Stephen of Hungary and Good King Wenceslas).

15 Gedimin (Gediminas in Lithuanian), Grand Prince of Lithuania, 1316–41, is
regarded as the founder of the Lithuanian dynasty.

16 All Lithuanian princes descended either from Gedimin or from Riurik except for
the Radziwills, who were given their princely title by the Holy Roman Emperor
Maximilian I; there were no native Polish princes and all their titles were
imperial.

17 The Livonian Order was the remnant of two Germanic Military Orders, the
Livonian Order of the Sword and the Teutonic Order, in which many of the
knights had been converted to Lutheranism; the Order had to a great extent
disintegrated, but its control of the Finnish Gulf and the Gulf of Riga made its
lands into desirable conquests. It was a dependency of the Holy Roman Empire.

18 The central diets and the local dietines.

19 B.N. Floria, *Russko-pol'skie otnoshenia i baltiiskii vopros v kontse XVI–
nachale XVII vv.*, Moscow, 1978, pp. 23ff.

20 See D. Strémooukhoff, 'Moscow, the Third Rome: Sources of the Doctrine',
repr. in M. Cherniavsky, ed., *The Structure of Russian History: Interpretive
Essays*, New York, 1970, pp. 108–25; see also M. D'iakonov, *Vlast'
moskovskikh gosudarei: Ocherk iz istorii politicheskikh idei drevnei Rusi do
kontsa XVI veka*, St Petersburg, 1889, repr. Mouton, The Hague, 1969, pp.
66ff.

21 V.A. Kuchkin and B.N. Floria, 'Kniazheskaia vlast' v predstavleniakh tverskikh
knizhnikov', in *Ot Rima k tret'emu Rimu*, p. 186; 'zhaleiu kogo khochu,
kaznuiu kogo khochu,' are the words used by Boris Alexandrovich.

22 See L.A. Dmitriev, *Literatura drevnei Rusi: Khrestomatia*, St Petersburg,1997,
pp. 174–6.

23   The influence of the Byzantine deacon Agapetus (early seventh-century) on the order of the coronation of Ivan IV will be dealt with in Chapter IV.

24   V.O. Kliuchevsky, *Sochineniia: Kurs russkoi istorii*, 8 vols. vol 2, Moscow, 1957, p. 123: 'samoderzhets … at that time did not signify a ruler with unlimited power within his realm, but a ruler free from any external control and paying tribute to no one.' See also I. de Madariaga, 'Autocracy and Sovereignty' in *Politics and Culture in Eighteenth-Century Russia: Collected Essays,* London and New York, 1998, pp. 40–56; J. Lehtovirta, *Ivan IV as Emperor: The Imperial Theme in the Establishment of Muscovite Tsardom*, Turku, 1999, p. 69, n. 1; Marc Szeftel, 'The Title of the Muscovite Monarch up to the End of the Seventeenth Century', *CASS*, 13, nos 1–2, 1979, pp. 59–81. According to Szeftel, *autokrator*, the Greek original of *samoderzhets*, means 'a sovereign monarch holding his power directly from God, and not by delegation of any other ruler'. See also G. Elton in the *New Cambridge Modern History*, Cambridge University Press, 1958, vol. II, *The Reformation*, p. 234, on Cromwell's theory of the empire of Henry VIII: as 'the civilian concept of imperium existing in any polity whose ruler did not recognise a superior on earth, and which he called the "empire of England" i.e. imperium, was not concerned with authority over other nations but over his own'.

25   See Shevchenko, op. cit., p. 80.

26   Quoted in his own words by N.M. Karamzin, *Istoria gosudarstva Rossiiskogo,* 12 vols, St Petersburg, 1892, VII, p. 140 and notes, p. 61, n. 410, from the *PSRL*, II, pp. 205, 206, 213.

27   See Shevchenko, op. cit., passim, for a fascinating pursuit of Agapetus through the Tale of Barlaam and Josaphat, the 'Admonition on Good Rulership also addressed to Boyars, Bishops and Abbots, and becoming to Monks', to Chapter 16 of Iosif Volotsky's *Prosvetitel'* ('The Enlightener') Shevchenko, op. cit., pp. 88ff. Agapetus indeed served as an ideological source for writers of very different ideas, often without attribution.

28   S.F. Platonov, *Ocherki istorii smuty v moskovskom gosudarstve XVI–XVII vv,* St Petersburg, 1910, pp. 96–7, though to my mind he goes too far in linking Ivan's patrimonial rights to Moscow's championship of the national Russian cause, and thus embodying an 'absolute and democratic power'. R. Pipes, in *Russia under the Old Regime*, London, 1974, puts forward the same theory from a more Weberian point of view. But he does not consider that other European monarchs, such as William the Conqueror and Louis XIV, were also residuary owners of all the land in their realms.

29   See e.g., R.O. Crummey, *The Formation of Muscovy, 1304–1613*, Longman, London and New York, 1987, passim.

30   A.A. Zimin, *Formirovanie boiarskoi aristokratii v Rossii vo vtoroi polovine XV – pervoi treti XVI v*, Moscow, 1988, pp. 143ff. Among Riurikids these princes included the Vorotynskys and Odoevskys; among Gediminovichi, the Mstislavskys, Bel'skys, Trubetskoys, etc.

31   The post of *koniushii* (Master of the Horse or High Constable) is sometimes treated as hereditary, but if so appointments were very unsystematic. The title is sometimes translated 'equerry', but seeing that the holder was in charge of the horses for the court and the armed forces, it was a much more important task.

32   See Chapter II, p. 36–7. The first Russian prince to be created by a tsar was Prince A.D. Menshikov by Peter the Great. The second was Prince A.A. Bezborodko by Paul I.

33   Zimin, *Formirovanie*, on whom I have largely drawn in these pages: see pp. 19ff and entries under the various families. In common with aristocracies elsewhere at this time mortality was very high and families often died out naturally.

34 On the tradition of giving advice see S.N. Bogatyrev, *The Sovereign and His Counsellors: Ritualised Consultations in Muscovite Political Culture, 1350s–1570s*, Helsinki, 2000.
35 Zimin, op. cit., p. 18.
36 S. von Herberstein, *Zapiski iz Moskovii*, Moscow, 1988, p. 120.
37 Kliuchevsky, op. cit., p. 123.
38 Compare the Russian titulature with that of the Holy Roman emperors or Philip II of Spain, not precisely parvenus.
39 S.M. Solov'ev, *Istoria Rossii s drevneishikh vremen*, III, Moscow, 1961–5, pp. 135–6. The full text is: 'We by the grace of God are lord of our lands from the beginning, from our first ancestors, and were placed here by God, both our ancestors and ourselves, and we pray God that he should grant to us and our children to the end of time [*i do veka*] to be there as we are now rulers in our land and to be placed above this we did not wish and do not wish.' Quoted in N.V. Sinitsyna, 'Itogi kontseptsii "Tret'ego Rima"' in *Ot Rima k tret'emu Rimu*', Rome and Moscow, 1993, pp. 16ff.
40 Despina was the title given to Zoe (Sofia) by the many Greeks and Italians in Moscow. It is the feminine of *despotes*.
41 S.M. Solov'ev, *Istoria Rossii*, III, pp. 55ff; V.O. Kliuchevsky, *Sochinenia: Kurs russkoi istorii*, II, pp. 120ff.
42 P. Pierling, *La Russie et le Saint Siège: Etudes diplomatiques*, 2 vols, Librairie Plon, Paris, 1891, vol. I. The bride was inspected on Ivan III's behalf.
43 For a description of Sofia's journey see Robert M. Croskey, *Muscovite Diplomatic Practice in the Reign of Ivan III*, Garland Publishing Inc., New York and London, 1987, pp. 240ff. Other Paleologus marriages took place at this time, notably between the daughter Maria of Andrei Paleologus and Prince Vasily Mikhailovich of Vereya. Ibid., p. 246.
44 E. Skryzhinskaia, *Barbaro i Kontarini v Rossii – k istorii italo-russkikh sviazei*, Leningrad, 1971, p. 204; 'Pouchenie Vladimira Monomakha' in Cross and Sherbowitz-Wetzor, *The Russian Primary Chronicle*, p. 37.
45 Herberstein, *Zapiski iz Moskovii*, p. 66.
46 Solov'ev is wrong.
47 Solov'ev, *Istoria Rossii*, vol. III, p. 58.
48 Kurbsky's *History of Ivan IV*, tr. and ed. J.L.I. Fennell, Cambridge University Press, 1965, p. 3.
49 For more information on Maxim Grek see Chapter II.
50 Solov'ev, III, p. 59.
51 Ibid.
52 Elena is usually known in Russian as Elena Voloshanka, i.e. Elena of Wallachia, but her father was Stephen the Great of Moldavia.
53 A summary of the state of play in 1961 will be found in Appendix A in J.L.I. Fennell, *Ivan the Great of Moscow*, Macmillan, Glasgow, 1961.
54 It is noteworthy in view of the later connection of Elena of Moldavia with the alleged Judaizers that Mikhail Olel'kovich's sister Yevdokia was the wife of Stephen of Moldavia and Elena's mother. (Fennell, *Ivan the Great*, Appendix E, descendants of Vasily I.)
55 W.F. Ryan, *The Bathhouse at Midnight*, Pennsylvania State University Press, 1999, p. 16, and n. 55, which refers to a number of studies by Moshe Taube.
56 Gennady used the services of Dmitri Gerasimov, who had resided in Rome for some years and played an important part in the transmission of Western culture to Russia, Nicholas Bülow, the Grand Prince's physician (and astrologer), and the translator from Latin, the monk Benjamin, a Serb or Croat Dominican in his service.

57 R. Tsurkan, *Slavianskii perevod Biblii*, St Petersburg, 2001, pp. 188ff. The translation was based on Greek texts, on the Vulgate, and also on the German edition of Cologne, 1478, and on some Hebrew originals. See also Alastair Hamilton, *The Apocryphal Apocalypse: The Reception of the Second Book of Esdras (4 Ezra) from the Renaissance to the Enlightenment*, Clarendon Press, Oxford, 1999, for an explanation of the numbering of the books of Esdras. 2 Esdras was important as a source of prophetic interpretation, notably of the advance of the Turks, one of the signs of the end of the world, together with the books of Daniel and Revelations. Among the admirers of the book of Esdras were Pico della Mirandola, and those who sought to reconcile Judaism with Christianity (Hamilton, op. cit., p. 9ff).

58 Croskey, *Muscovite Diplomatic Practice*, pp. 238ff.

59 In addition to Croskey, see L.A. Iusefovich, *Kak v posol'skikh obychaiakh vedetsia*, Moscow, 1988.

CHAPTER II The Reign of Vasily III

1 Solov'ev, *Istoria*, III, p. 63.

2 For the wills of Ivan III and Vasily III see Robert Craig Howes, *The Testaments of the Grand Princes of Moscow*, Cornell University Press, Ithaca, NY, 1967. Ivan III may have had a stroke.

3 Ivan III had left his brother Andrei the Elder to die in prison in 1493; Ivan's two younger sons were kept by their brother Vasily in prison in Pereiaslavl' in chains, where they both died. They could of course have become rivals for the throne. Henry VIII's policy of eliminating possible Yorkist claimants to his throne in England provides a parallel.

4 See Martin, *Medieval Russia, 980–1584*, p. 248.

5 It was regarded as wrong to shed the blood of a member of the ruling family, but starvation supplied a practical alternative.

6 Louis XII, King of France from 1498 to 1515, also divorced his wife, a daughter of Louis XI, in order to marry Anne of Brittany in 1499.

7 N.A. Kazakova, *Ocherki po istorii russkoi obshchestvennoi mysli, pervaia tret' XVI veka,* Leningrad, 1970, pp. 116–18, and p. 210. The sources on Vasily's marriage are extremely confusing since chronicles have been edited to please Vasily by portraying Solomonia as asking him to repudiate her and send her to a monastery.

8 See D.G. Ostrowski, 'Church Polemics and Monastic Land Acquisition in Sixteenth-Century Muscovy', *SEER*, 64, no. 3, 1986, pp. 355–79. Ostrowski argues very cogently against the existence of 'church based' parties, and suggests that the concept took hold so easily in the later historiography because 'it conveniently paralleled the conservative vs liberal political arguments of the late nineteenth century'. The arguments bandied back and forth in Russian historiography do suggest some of the worst excesses of kremlinology of the 1950s and 1960s.

9 For a general outline of his life and works see Jack V. Haney, *From Italy to Muscovy: The Life and Works of Maxim the Greek*, Wilhelm Fink Verlag, Munich, 1973; see also R.G. Skrynnikov, *Sviatiteli i vlasti*, Leningrad, 1990, pp. 143ff.

10 See L.E. Morozova, 'Ivan Groznii i publitsisty XVI veka o predelakh i kharaktere tsarskoi vlasti' in *Ot Rimu k tret'emu Rimu*, pp. 236–51, at p. 237. Morozova assumes that this means Maksim Grek was a supporter of government by representative institutions; government by 'council' does not enter her horizon, though the word used by Maksim Grek is '*sinklit*'(Council, from the Greek).

11 See V. Val'denberg, *Drevnerusskie uchenia o predelakh tsarskoi vlasti*, Petrograd, 1916, p. 258.
12 Ibid.
13 Skrynnikov, *Sviatiteli i vlasti*, who calls it a club, pp. 141ff.
14 See Haney, op. cit., pt I, section 3, pp. 64ff.
15 G. Alef, 'Das Erlöschen des Abzugsrechts der Moskauer Bojaren', *FOG*, 10, Berlin, 1975, pp. 7–74, at p. 66.
16 Skrynnikov, *Sviatiteli i vlasti*, p. 142.
17 Herberstein, *Zapiski*, pp. 105–6, who adds that though Vasily liked Maksim, the latter vanished and was probably drowned. He was not, but he did die in prison.
18 See J.J. Scarisbrick, *Henry VIII*, Methuen, London, 1983, p. 350 for the Act of Supremacy passed by Parliament in 1534 allowing Henry to appoint any successor at any time by letters patent or by will.
19 Marc Szeftel, 'Joseph Volotsky's Political Ideas in a New Historical Perspective', *JGOE*, 13, 1965, pp. 19–29.
20 Skrynnikov, *Sviatiteli i vlasti*, pp. 150–52.
21 Ibid., and see also Herberstein, *Zapiski*, p. 87 and n. 235. Needless to say, the Chronicles are silent on an episode casting such an unpleasant light on Vasily. Solomonia is portrayed as anxious in every way to please her husband. The editors of Herberstein argue that Metropolitan Daniel was not concerned in the divorce because he was a supporter of Iuri Ivanovich, Vasily's brother and heir to the throne, and thus did not care whether Vasily had children or not.
22 V.D. Nazarov, 'Svadebnye dela XVI veka', *Voprosy istorii*, 1976, no. 10, pp. 116ff, at pp. 121–2 publishes an order from the Grand Prince to S.I. Lyatsky to investigate carefully that a potential bride should not be related in any way, however distant, to the Shcheniatev and Pleshcheev clans, thus suggesting that political considerations weighed heavily in the choice of bride. The Shcheniatevs were descended from the Patrikeev clan, which had been disgraced in 1499. See also Zimin, *Formirovanie*, pp. 33ff.
23 A.A. Zimin, 'Sluzhilye knyaz'ia v russkom gosudarstve kontsa XV-pervoi treti XVI v.' in *Dvorianstvo i krepostnoi stroi Rossii XVI–XVIII vv*, Moscow, 1975, pp. 28–56.
24 Herberstein, *Zapiski*, pp. 69 and n. 135; p.188 and variants; and n. 698.
25 H. Rüss, 'Elena Vasil'evna Glinskaja', *JGOE*, 19, 1971, pp. 481–98, genealogical chart at p. 487. The sister of Peter Raresh's wife married Ivan Vishnevetsky, and was the mother of Dmitri Vishnevetsky, the Lithuanian prince who played a big part in the cultural world of Russia and Lithuania. Rüss rejects the idea that Elena Glinskaia had a Western education on the grounds that she was too young when she came to Russia to benefit from it.
26 See M.N. Tikhomirov, 'Stranitsa iz zhizni Ivana Peresvetova' in *Rossiiskoe gosudarstvo XV–XVII vekov*, Moscow, 1973, pp. 70–73. This may also cast a light on Ivan Peresvetov's admiration for the *voevoda* of Moldavia (see below, pp. 88–90). See also article by Tikhomirov, 'Petr Raresh i Ivan Groznyy' in *Omagiu lui P. Constantinescu*, Iasi cu prilejui impliniri, Bucharest, 1965, in Russian; and S. Simionescu, 'Les Relations de la Moldavie avec les Habsbourgs pendant le règne de Petru Raresh, 1527–1538, 1541–46', *Revue romaine d'histoire*, XVII, no. 2, April–June 1978, pp. 455–67.
27 Karamzin, *Istoria*, VII, ch. 3, pp. 112ff.
28 L.A. Dmitriev, ed. and tr., 'Skazanie o kniaz'iakh Vladimirskikh', in *Literatura drevnei Rusi. Khrestomatia*, St Petersburg, 1997, pp. 283–95.
29 See Dmitriev, op. cit., n. 35, pp. 283ff. The story goes on to describe the destiny of Gedimenik's various sons, one of whom is Jagiello, eventually King of

Poland. Scenes from the Tale of the Princes of Vladimir were incorporated in the frescoes which decorated the chapel in which the tsar's throne was installed in the Dormition Cathedral in the Kremlin. (E. Etkind, G. Nivat, I. Serman, V. Strada, eds, *Histoire de la littérature russe*, Fayard, Paris, 1992, vol. I, p. 173.)

30 See for instance Brutus in England, Francus in France and Hercules in Spain. Perhaps the most picturesque is the claim that the grand dukes of Lithuania were descended from Nero, though some people held that the Lithuanians were descended from Englishmen who fled their country after the battle of Hastings.

31 C.J. Halperin, 'The Russian Land and the Russian Tsar: The Emergence of Muscovite Ideology, 1380–1408', *FOG*, 23, Berlin, 1976, pp. 7–103, at p. 77, quoting the monk Akindin to Grand Prince Michael of Tver', 'you are tsar, lord prince, in your land'.

32 Herberstein, *Zapiski*, p. 16.

33 Rüss argues that Herberstein got most of his information from circles hostile to Vasily and Elena, which accounts for his negative attitude to the Grand Prince; Rüss, 'Elena', pp. 481ff.

34 See Marshall Poe, 'What did Russians Mean When They Called Themselves Slaves of the Tsar?', *Slavic Review*, 57, no. 3, 1998, pp. 585–608.

35 There were also of course prisoners of war who had been enslaved.

36 I am grateful to Dr Jonathan Shepard for permission to use an unpublished seminar paper given at a meeting of the Society for Court Studies on 14 October 1998 and for further written communications on the subject of ceremonial in the East Roman Empire, which to my mind is undoubtedly closer to the Russian in every way, including the use of clothing, than Mongol ceremonial. On usage in Western languages see *servus* (Lat. slave) and *servus* (Austrian German: 'your servant', friendly greeting).

37 Zimin, *Formirovanie*, p. 289.

38 Skrynnikov, *Tsarstvo terrora*, St Petersburg, 1992, pp. 78–9. It is not clear whether Andrei was an older or younger brother of Alexander. In the entry 'Rossia' in the *Granat encyclopaedia* he appears as older than Alexander, in Brokhaus and Efron under 'Alexander Nevsky' he appears as younger.

39 See Nancy Shields Kollman, *Kinship and Politics: The Making of the Muscovite Political System, 1345–1547*, Stanford, 1987.

40 This discussion is largely taken from Zimin, *Formirovanie*, pp. 306ff, and N.A. Kazakova, *Ocherki po istorii russkoi obshchestvennoi mysli*, p. 285.

41 There was no procedure for ennoblement in Russia until the reign of Peter I. But the concept of the 'well-born' existed and applied to descendants of princes and boyars and of landowners in general whether of allodial estates, which ranked higher, or of service estates, which were more frequent. Service gentry were in principle offshoots of well-born families, but not always.

42 S.O. Schmidt, 'Kniga A.A. Zimina, "Reformy Ivana Groznogo"', in *Rossia Ivana Groznogo*, Moscow, 1999, pp. 91–102, at p. 96.

43 Skrynnikov, *Velikii gosudar' Ivan Vasil'evich*, 2 vols, Smolensk, 1993, I, p. 109.

44 Zimin, *Formirovanie*, pp. 296ff.

45 See V.A. Kivelson, 'The Effects of Partible Inheritance: Gentry Families and the State in Muscovy', *Russian Review*, 53, 1994, pp. 197–212.

CHAPTER III Ivan's Birth, Childhood, Adolescence, Coronation and Marriage

1 I. Thyret, 'Blessed is the Tsaritsa's Womb: The Myth of Miraculous Birth and Royal Motherhood in Muscovite Russia', *Russian Review*, 53, no. 4, 1994, pp. 479–96.

2 Karamzin, *Istoria*, VIII, ch. 1, p. 119.
3 E. Keenan, 'Ivan IV and the "King's Evil": *Ni maka li to budet?*', *Russian History*, 20, nos 1–4, 1993, pp. 5–13. Russian rulers did not touch for the King's Evil.
4 The texts of the wills of Vasily III have not survived, but a testamentary 'writ' (*zapis*) dated 1523 exists. See R. Craig Howes, *The Testaments of the Grand Princes of Moscow*, p. 50 and pp. 299ff.
5 Skrynnikov, *Tsarstvo terrora*, pp. 81ff, discusses the different opinions among historians on the nature of the Regency Council and the appointments to the Duma.
6 Karamzin, *Istoria*, VIII, ch. 1, p. 119.
7 *PSRL*, XIII, pt 2, p. 410; Vasily's wound was dressed with a mixture of wheat, honey and baked onion, in what used to be called in English a poultice. There were rumours that he wanted to retire to a monastery before his final illness, and it is noteworthy that the one he is said to have chosen was the monastery of St Cyril of Beloozero, where Vassian Patrikeev had been exiled and which was the centre of Nil Sorsky's teachings. Skrynnikov, op. cit., p. 66, points out that once shorn, if Vasily survived, he would be unable to reign as Grand Prince. See also the dramatic deathbed scene described by Karamzin, *Istoria*, VII, ch. III, pp. 105ff.
8 Ibid.
9 One is reminded of the speedy way in which Henry VIII removed all possible Yorkist claimants to the throne, including eventually the aged Countess of Salisbury, niece of Edward IV, who was beheaded in 1540 in the aftermath of the Pilgrimage of Grace.
10 The rumour is still current today, and tests have been made for the presence of mercury on her bones and hair. H. Rüss in 'Elena Vasil'evna Glinskaja' is very critical of Herberstein's negative portrayal of Elena Glinskaia and does not believe she was poisoned, see passim. He also argues that conflict with the boyars was held in check as long as Telepnev Obolensky was in power.
11 I have drawn largely on Karamzin, *Istoria*, VII, ch. 3, pp. 5574ff. and 597ff., for the account in these pages.
12 *The Correspondence between Prince A.M. Kurbsky and Tsar Ivan IV of Russia, 1564–1579*, tr. and ed. by J.L.I. Fennell, Cambridge University Press, 1963, pp. 75ff.
13 D.B. Miller, 'The Coronation of Ivan IV of Moscow', *JGOE*, 15, 1967, pp. 559–74; L.A. Iusefovich, *Kak v posol'skikh obychaiakh vedetsia*, p. 102, quoted from Antony Jenkinson.
14 See Kurbsky, *Correspondence*, p. 74, n. 2; the phrase is used by Ivan to convey confusion.
15 Ibid., pp. 75ff.
16 N.S. Kollman, in 'Pilgrimage, Procession, and Symbolic Space in Sixteenth Century Russian Politics', *Medieval Russian Culture*, II, ed. M.S. Flier and D. Rowland, University of California Press, 1994, pp. 163–81, attempts a 'social anthropological' analysis of these journeys. But like those of Queen Elizabeth I, they were often caused by the need to consume local produce on the spot and to clean up the living quarters vacated by princes and servants.
17 Karamzin, *Istoria* VIII, p. 19, n. 153.
18 A.I. Ivanov, *Literaturnoe nasledie Maksima Greka*, Leningrad, 1969, pp. 147ff, nn. 216 and 217. L.E Morozova, 'Ivan Groznyi i publitsisty XVI veka', in 'Ot Rima k tret'emu Rimu', p. 237, holds to the idea that Maksim Grek favoured a monarchy limited by representative estates (*soslovno-predstavitel'naia monarkhia*), because he argues in favour of a conciliar monarchy, i.e. a

monarchy in which the monarch rules with a *sinklit*. The two concepts are totally different.

19 B.N. Floria, *Ivan Groznyi: Zhizn' zamechatel'nikh liudei*, Moscow, 1999, p. 18.

20 Not only in Russia; barons, knights and men-at-arms employed clerks or clerics for this work in medieval England.

21 See above, pp. 28–9 and n. 28.

22 See Dmitriev, *Literatura drevnei Rusi*, pp. 236–46.

23 M.J. Trow, *Vlad the Impaler: In Search of the Real Dracula*, Sutton Publishing, Stroud, 2003. See also M. Cazacu, *L'Histoire du Prince Dracula en Europe centrale et orientale*, Librairie Droz, Geneva, 1988, for Matthias Corvinus's part in blackening Vlad Ţepeş's reputation.

24 For the modern Russsian text see Dmitriev, op. cit., pp. 241ff.

25 Jerome Horsey in *Rude and Barbarous Kingdom: Russia in Accounts of Sixteenth-Century English Voyagers*, ed. L.E. Berry and R.O. Crummey, University of Wisconsin Press, 1968, referred to in future as Horsey, *Travels*.

26 For a fuller discussion of the *Secretum secretorum* see Chapter X, p. 169. I am grateful to Professor W.F. Ryan for allowing me to make use of an unpublished lecture on apocalyptic literature in Russia and of the MS of his translation of the *Secretum secretorum*.

27 The Italian version of the *Iliad* by Guido de Columna was available in Russia by the end of the fifteenth century: see Kalugin, *Andrei Kurbsky*, pp. 60 and 96. I owe this reference to the kindness of Professor Ryan.

28 M.V. Kukushkina, *Kniga v Rossii v XVI veke*, St Petersburg, 1999, p. 45.

29 Kurbsky, *Correspondence*, p. 27.

30 Kurbsky, *History*, pp. 11ff.

31 It is difficult to know what to believe with these tales, which show people led like lambs to the slaughter. See Kurbsky, *History*, pp. 12–13, and n. 1 and Schmidt, *Rossiya Ivana Groznogo*, pp. 323ff., at pp. 331–3. Reports were current according to the Chronicles that Ivan suffered from ungovernable rages, 'like a lion'.

32 The copies of the *Velikii Che'ti Minei* for the month of December, in *Pamiatniki slavyano-russkoi pis'mennosti, izdannye arkheograficheskoiu kommissieiu: Velikii Chet'i Minei*, Moscow, 1–5 December, 1901; 18–23 December, 1907, contain extensive excerpts from the writings of Greek Church Fathers in Slavonic and from a debate between a Jew and an Orthodox Christian, Arkhiepi (Orthodox) and Orkan (Jewish).

33 See P. Hunt, 'Ivan IV's Personal Mythology of Kingship', *Slavic Review*, 52, 1993, no. 4, pp. 769–809. Hunt notes that Ivan made use of materials to be found in the *Great Menology*. See p. 809.

34 Dmitriev and Likhachev, eds, *Pamiatniki literatury drevnei Rusi XVI veka*, I, Moscow, 1985, pp. 550 and 635. The poem quoted is at p. 551.

35 Makarii, though he was a priest, was put in charge of the government in Moscow while Ivan was in Kazan' for the campaign. There are also occasions in which Ivan 'beats his forehead' to Makarii.

36 See Boris Uspensky, *Tsar i patriarkh: Kharisma vlasti v Rossii* (*Vizantiiskaia model' i ee russkoe pereosmyslenie*), Moscow, 1998, p. 31 and n. 53.

37 See the section 'Letopisets' in 'Iz velikikh miney – Chet'ikh Makaria' in Dmitriev and Likhachev, op. cit., p. 479.

38 A derivation which Karamzin, for instance, rejects.

39 It should be noted that anointing the emperor was not traditional in Byzantium but came in with Baldwin of Flanders, the first Latin emperor, in 1204; the first Western ruler to be anointed was Pepin le Bref. See Uspensky, *Tsar i patriarkh*. Herberstein remarked that Vasily III '*se regem et dominum totius Russiae vocat*',

i.e. he used *tsar'* as equal to 'king', which in Russian is actually *korol'*. V.I. Savva, *Moskovskie tsari i vizantiiskie Vasilevsy*, Khar'khov, 1901, p. 284, n. 3.

40 The Jesuit Possevino, who was in Russia to mediate the peace with Poland in 1582, translates *'hospodar' i tsar'* into Latin as *'sen'or i imperator'*. V. Podzhi (Poggi), 'Ioann Pavel Kampana i Ivan Groznyi' in *Ot Rima k tret'emu Rimu*, pp. 272ff.

41 For the further development see my article, 'Tsar into Emperor: the Title of Peter the Great', reprinted in my *Politics and Culture in Eighteenth-Century Russia: Collected Essays*, London and New York, 1998, pp. 15–39.

42 See E.V. Barsov, *Drevne-russkie pamiatniki sviashchennago venchania tsarei na tsarstvo, v sviazi s grecheskimi ikh originalami: S istoricheskim ocherkom chinov tsarskago venchania v sviazi s razvitiem idei tsaria na Rusi*, Moscow, 1883. For a full discussion see Miller, 'The Coronation of Ivan IV of Moscow', *JGOE*, 15, 1967, pp. 559–84.

43 I have already explained my reasons for preferring to translate *samoderzhavie* as 'sovereignty' in pre-nineteenth-century contexts.

44 I.M. Sokolova, '"Monomakhov tron" pervogo russkogo tsaria: Zamysel i forma' in *Rossia i khristianskii vostok, vypusk* 1, Moscow, 2001.

45 Miller, 'The Coronation of Ivan IV of Moscow', p. 568.

46 Val'denberg, *Drevnerusskie uchenia*, pp. 59–61. Val'denberg points out (p. 56) that the formula (from Justinian), *'quod principi placuit legis habet vigorem'* was found in the documents of the Office of Foreign Affairs no earlier than 1673. It is worth noting that many of the writings of Agapetus were known and quoted, without acknowledging the author, by many monks and prelates in Russia, and even by Ivan IV himself. See Ihor Shevchenko, 'A Neglected Byzantine Source of Muscovite Political Ideology', *Harvard Slavic Studies*, II, 1954, reprinted in M. Cherniavsky, ed., *The Structure of Russian History: Interpretive Essays*, pp. 80–107, at p. 87. There are seventy-two so-called hortatory chapters by Agapetus, of which Chapter XXI is the most often quoted in Russian texts, with no acknowledgement. The whole work is dedicated to the Emperor Justinian, and evidently played an important part in Russian political thought. There is an English translation by Canon Thomas Paynell (from the Latin) dated 1546, and a French translation by King Louis XIII, Paris, 1612 (Shevchenko, p. 106, n. 124).

47 Val'denberg, *Drevnerusskie uchenia*, p. 277, comments that this thought has never been so clearly stated as by Maksim Grek. The passage was probably written by Makarii himself and reflects his ideas, or it may have been a later interpolation.

48 Skrynnikov, *Velikii gosudar'* I, p. 139.

49 Uspensky, *Tsar i patriarkh*, p. 44

50 Val'denberg, op. cit., pp. 278–81, p. 292.

51 Letter sent to all the districts (*pyatiny*) of Novgorod around 12–18 December 1546. Karamzin, *Istoria*, vol. VIII, ch. 3, note 164, p. 21.

52 Solov'ev, III, p. 432. In these same terms 150 years later Peter I would summon young noble children to a *smotr* to be inspected for military service. Henry VIII's rapid search for a replacement for Jane Seymour (d. 24 October 1537) has some characteristics of a bride-show. 'Nine women were seriously considered, several more glanced at, and five of them required to sit for portraits.' Henry at one point proposed that 'a bevy of French ladies' should be brought to him at Calais for him to make his choice. It was not French practice, said Francis I of France, to 'send damsels of good birth to be passed in review like horses for sale'. Scarisbrick, *Henry VIII*, pp. 355ff.

53 There is a suggestion that Anastasia had already been chosen because her name

is included in the version of the coronation ritual published in *Drevniaia rossiiskaia vivliofika*, 1774, pt 7, pp. 4–35. See Ya. N. Shchapov, 'K izucheniu "china venchania na tsarstvo Ivana IV"' in *Ot Rima k tret'emu Rimu*, pp. 213ff.

54 Karamzin, *Istoria*, VIII, notes, p. 22, n. 165: *'blagopoluchnye dni'* is the phrase used by Karamzin, quoted from *Drevniaia rossiiskaia vivliofika*, pt 14, p. 227.

55 Karamzin, *Istoriya*, VIII, p. 2, n. 165.

56 The nearest we come to it is an article by S.O. Schmidt dating from 1954, and it may well be that the sources no longer exist on which to base such a study. See Schmidt, 'Pravitel'stvennaia deiatelnost' A.F Adasheva', repr. in *Rossiia Ivana Groznogo*, Nauka, Moscow, 1999, pp. 50–84.

57 See Iusefovich, *Kak v posol'skikh obychaiakh vedetsia*, ch. 6, *passim*. The Ottoman sultans adopted much of the preceding East Roman ceremonial. In Poland–Lithuania the thrones in Cracow and Vilna were placed in the middle of a wall.

58 The tale of the prince's son Josaphat converted by the hermit Barlaam, based on the life of the Buddha, was very popular in Russia. See *St. John Damascene, Barlaam and Josaphat*, ed. G.R. Woodward and H. Mattingley, London, 1914.

59 N.I. Kostomarov, *Ocherk domashnei zhizni i nravov velikorusskogo naroda v XVI i XVII stoletiakh*, Moscow, 1992, pp. 176ff.

60 See Schmidt, 'Issledovanie N.N. Zarubina, "Biblioteka Ivana Groznogo i ego knigi"' in *Rossia Ivana Groznogo*, pp. 404–19, for a survey of the question of Ivan's library in 1978, and for references to later studies.

61 The uncertainty about the whereabouts of any remaining books which might have belonged to Ivan has led to the proliferation of legends such as the existence of a subterranean library in which treasures from Constantinople, brought by Sofia Paleologa, were buried to protect them from fire. For a survey of the state of knowledge see W.F. Ryan, 'Aristotle and Pseudo-Aristotle in Russia' in *Pseudo-Aristotle in the Middle Ages: The Theology and Other Texts*, ed. W.F. Ryan et al., Warburg Institute Surveys and Texts, XI, London, 1986, pp. 115ff.

Chapter IV The Era of Aleksei Adasher

1 See D. McCulloch, *Tudor Church Militant: Edward VI and the Protestant Reformation*, London, 1999; by a stroke of irony the portrait of Edward VI which prefaces this work is in the Hermitage Museum in St Petersburg.

2 See description in the Kazan' chronicle, *PSRL* XIX, p. 43.

3 Skrynnikov, *Sviatiteli i vlasti*, p. 170.

4 A.A. Zimin, *Reformy Ivana Groznogo*, Moscow, 1960, p. 296.

5 Skrynnikov, *Tsarstvo terrora*, p. 92.

6 Ibid.

7 It is not surprising that an old woman should have been cast for the role of a witch.

8 This account is put together from a number of different sources, including the interpolations in the Tsarstvennaia kniga chronicle (*PSRL*, XIII, 2, pt, 2), which according to some authors are by Ivan IV himself, see Skrynnikov, *Velikii gosudar'*, I, pp.140–41; *Tsarstvo terrora*, p. 93 (though other authors disagree); and Ivan IV's letter to Prince A.M. Kurbsky, see Kurbsky, *Correspondence*, pp. 81–2.

9 D.S. Likhachev and Ya. S. Lur'e, eds, *Poslania Ivana Groznogo*, Moscow-Leningrad, 1951, p. 523; from Ivan's speech at the meeting of the Stoglav council in 1551.

10 Kurbsky, *Correspondence*, p. 81. Ivan's relations with Prince A.M. Kurbsky will be dealt with in Chapter X below.

11 Karamzin, *Istoria*, VIII, pt 2, pp. 63ff and nn. 177, 178, bases himself on Kurbsky's *History* and on Ivan's own words in the meeting of the Church Council (Stoglav) in 1551.

12 A.I. Filiushkin, *Istoria odnoi mistifikatsii: Ivan Groznyi i izbrannaia rada*, Moscow, 1998, suggests that this speech was probably made by Makarii, and not by Sylvester, pp. 37ff.

13 See A.A. Zimin, 'O sostave dvortsovykh uchrezhdenii Russkogo gosudarstva kontsa XV i XVI v,' in *Istoricheskie zapiski*, no. 63, Moscow, 1958, pp. 180–205. The structure and status of these appanages ruled by *dvortsy* can be compared to the palatinates in England.

14 Quoted from S.V. Bakhrushin, 'Izbrannaia rada Ivana Groznogo', *Istoricheskiie zapiski*, no. 15, Moscow, 1945, pp. 45ff, in A.S. Usachev, 'Obraz tsaria v srednevekovoi Rusi', *Drevniaia Rus'*, *Voprosy medievistiki*, Moscow, 2001, vyp. 3 (5), pp. 93–103.

15 In the term preferred by Kivelson, 'The Effects of Partible Inheritance'.

16 Skrynnikov, *Tsarstvo terrora*, pp. 78–9.

17 'frankpledge – the system by which every member of a tithing was answerable for the good conduct of, or the damage done by, anyone of the other members,' *OED*.

18 In England, Henry VIII abolished the suretyships imposed by Henry VII on great nobles.

19 See the essential article by H.W. Dewey and A.M. Kleimola, 'Suretyship and Collective Responsibility in Pre-Petrine Russia', *JGOE*, 18, 1970, pp. 337–54, particularly at pp. 343ff, which follows suretyship down through various social levels.

20 H.W. Dewey, 'Political *Poruka* in Muscovite Rus', *Russian Review*, vol. 46, 1987, pp. 117–34, at p. 118. See also, as regards denunciation, H.W. Dewey and A.M. Kleimola, 'From the Kinship Group to Every Man His Brother's Keeper: Collective Responsibility in Pre-Petrine Russia', *JGOE*, 30, 1982, pp. 321–35. These two articles and the one by Dewey and Kleimola in n. 19 above provide in my view by far the most illuminating analyses of the early Russian relationship between state and society.

21 Not many are known to have enjoyed this title: Prince D.I. Bel'sky, a Gediminovich, who spent most of his life campaigning; Prince Alexander Borisovich Gorbaty-Shuisky, a prominent soldier; Ivan Petrovich Fedorov Cheliadnin, who was not a prince; and later Prince M.I. Vorotynsky, who was a soldier. On *sluga* see Schmidt, *Rossiya Ivana Groznogo*, p. 96.

22 Sir Francis Walsingham was described as a '*d'iak*' in the dispatches of F. Pisemsky from London in the 1580s. See *SIRIO*, 38, passim. He would have been delighted! See in general Schmidt, 'D'iachestvo v Rossii serediny XVI veka' in *Rossia Ivana Groznogo*, pp. 103ff., at p. 109.

23 See I. Gralia, *Ivan Mikhailov Viskovaty*, Moscow, 1994, p. 462, for a list of *d'iaki* and clerks in the 1560s in the Office of Foreign Affairs. There were two principal *d'iaki*, who were members of the Council, and four ordinary *d'yaki*; there were thirteen clerks and eleven translators, not counting translators from Eastern languages and Polish.

24 I would argue that the English gentry provided through its younger sons, the universities, and the Inns of Court a social class similar to a *noblesse de robe*. However, in an unpublished article, 'Entail and Noble Power in Early Modern Europe', which he has kindly allowed me to refer to, Professor H.M. Scott has pointed out that entail (*mayorazgo, Fideicommiss* etc.) was not in the sixteenth century as yet widely or firmly established throughout Europe. The first systematic attempts occurred in Spain in the early sixteenth century.

25 There is some evidence that strategies of avoidance of the impoverishment following on the division of estates had been worked out by the lower service gentry, but the assault on the landholdings of the aristocracy was severe in the reign of Ivan IV. See V.A. Kivelson, 'The Effects of Partible Inheritance'. See also Chapter XXI.

26 *PSRL* XIII, pt 2, p. 131.

27 See above, Chapter II, p. 32.

28 Skrynnikov, *Tsarstvo terrora,* pp. 98–9.

29 Schmidt, *Rossiya Ivana Groznogo,* p. 55.

30 Ibid., p. 58.

31 Ivan suggests that he had been promoted from a very lowly position. Ibid., p. 56.

32 Ibid., p. 56 and n. 6. From Russian *spat'*, to sleep, and *postel'*, bed.

33 See, for example, the works of D. Starkey or R.J. Knecht on the structure and influence of the court in sixteenth-century England and France. No such detailed studies have been produced in Russia. They did not fit into the Marxist paradigm.

34 Zimin, *Reformy,* p. 312; cf. Schmidt, 'Pravitel'stvennaya deyatel'nost' A.F. Adasheva' and additions by I.I. Smirnov, *Ocherki politicheskoi istorii Russkogo gosudarstva 30–50kh godov XVI veka,* ANSSR, Moscow-Leningrad, 1958, pp. 212–31.

35 Ivan's first letter to Kurbsky, see Kurbsky, *Correspondence,* pp. 13ff.

36 A.A. Zimin, *I.S. Peresvetov i ego sovremenniki: Ocherki po istorii russkoi obshchestvennoi mysli serediny XVI veka,* ANSSR, Moscow 1958, p. 42.

37 See her portrayal in Eisenstein's film *Ivan the Terrible.* But this suggestion is a late interpolation in the Tsarstvennaia kniga, itself a later chronicle. Ibid., p. 44. A comparison between what Zimin wrote in 1958 and what he wrote later is very instructive. According to Zimin in 1958, Sylvester was a supporter of Prince Vladimir of Staritsa, of the non-possessors, and was supported by boyars and supported them; he was engaged in the early 1550s in a constant 'struggle' with hostile forces at court, namely the possessors led by Metropolitan Makarii. The evidence for this portrayal is derived from interpolations long after the event in the Chronicles. The atmosphere in Zimin's account in *I.S. Peresvetov i ego sovremenniki,* pp. 46ff is redolent of the struggles of the 1950s in Moscow between different factions in the Party and the nomenklatura. The language is the same, and recalls the language of kremlinology.

38 Ivan seems to have been impressed with the wickedness of Manasseh, for he reverts to him in his first letter to Kurbsky. For the discourse see D.N. Al'shits, *Nachalo samoderzhavia v Rossii: Gosudarstvo Ivana Groznogo,* Leningrad, 1988, pp. 65–6. See also Floria, *Ivan Groznyi,* pp. 26–7.

39 I am not suggesting that corporal punishment was not extremely severe, but so it was elsewhere at the time.

40 C.J. Pouncy, ed. and tr., *The Domostroi: Rules for Russian Households in the Time of Ivan the Terrible,* Cornell University Press, Ithaca and London, 1994, pp. 143–4. The tale that a Russian wife does not believe her husband loves her unless or until he beats her, as related by Herberstein, has been disputed by a later traveller, Olearius.

41 A.A. Zimin, 'Sostav boyarskoy dumy v XV–XVI vekakh', *Arkheograficheskii ezhegodnik, za 1957,* Moscow, 1958, pp. 41–87, at p. 63, remarks that for a long time after the disgrace of Prince S. Rostovsky there were few changes among the boyars. According to Skrynnikov, *Velikii gosudar',* 1, p. 207, the only magnate to have incurred disgrace in the period 1550–59 was Rostovsky, see p. 113, below.

42 See Thyret, 'Blessed is the Tsaritsa's Womb'.

43 K.G. Holum, *Theodosian Empresses: Women and Imperial Dominion in Late Antiquity*, University of California Press, 1989, ch. II, 'Aelia Eudoxia Augusta', pp. 48–78, at pp. 70ff.
44 Kurbsky, *History*, pp. 19ff.
45 Quoted from the Russian historian E.A. Belov by Anthony M. Grobowski, '*The Chosen Council' of Ivan IV: A Reinterpretation*, New York, 1969, pp. 139ff. at p. 142.
46 Quoted in Grobowski, op. cit., pp. 2ff., from V. Sergeevich, *Russkie iuridicheskie drevnosti*, St Petersburg, 1900, II, pp. 366–9. The names of members given include Sylvester, Adashev, Prince A.M. Kurbsky, Prince Dmitri Obolensky Kurliatev, Prince Semen Lobanov Rostovsky, Mikhail, Vladimir and Lev Morozov, Metropolitan Makarii and 'several presbyters'.
47 Zimin, 'Sostav boyarskoi dumy v XV–XVI vekakh', pp. 41–70.
48 Nancy Shields Kollman, *Kinship*, passim.
49 Grobowski, '*The Chosen Council*', Addenda, pp. 147–55. Grobowski does not believe that the Chosen Council was the same as the Blizhniaia Duma, he simply does not believe it existed at all. He also states that the term 'Blizhniaia Duma' is not found in the sources until the seventeenth century.
50 Kurbsky, *Correspondence*, pp. 45ff.
51 Grobowski, '*The Chosen Council*'.

CHAPTER V The 'Government of Compromise'

1 See Schmidt, 'Pravitel'stvennaia deiatel'nost' A.F. Adasheva', pp. 50ff.
2 See Chapter VI.
3 Zimin, *Reformy*, passim.
4 Karamzin, *Istoria*, VIII, pt 3, pp. 64–5, and p. 24 of notes, n. 182. See also S.O. Schmidt, 'Sobory serediny XVI v.' in *Istoria SSSR*, no. 4, 1960, pp. 66–92. According to L.V. Cherepnin, 'Zemskie sobory i utverzhdenie absoliutizma v Rossii' in *Absoliutizm v Rossii XVII–XVIII vv.*, ed. N.M. Druzhinin, Moscow, 1964, pp. 92–133, Ivan introduced a powerful element of demagogy into proceedings in view of the acute class contradictions between various feudal classes, in order to prevent a recurrence of the riot in Moscow and to rally the forces of the ruling class.
5 Zimin, *Reformy*, pp. 325–6.
6 Ibid., p. 326, suggests that this was the first step in defining the privileges of the noble class (as distinct from the aristocracy).
7 A useful general survey of the development of representative institutions will be found in A.R. Myers, *Parliaments and Estates in Europe to 1789*, Thames and Hudson, London, 1975.
8 See A.E. Pollard, *The Evolution of Parliament*, London, 1964, and Myers, op. cit. The presence of Makarii on this occasion is confirmed in L.V. Cherepnin, ed., *Pamiatniki Russkogo prava IV*, Moscow 1956, pp. 575–6.
9 Zimin, *Reformy*, pp. 325–6, 'Soslovno-predstavitel'naia monarkhia'.
10 Skrynnikov laments that 'legislation' in Ivan's Russia did not take legal form, but simply appeared in the form of orders. This was at times also the case in parliamentary England, where by no means all legislation came before Parliament in the sixteenth century (see J. Guy, 'The Privy Council: Revolution or Evolution' in C. Coleman and D. Starkey, eds, *Revolution Reassessed: Revisions in the History of Tudor Government and Administration*, Oxford, 1986, pp. 59–86). It was possible to issue laws by proclamation in England. S.N. Bogatyrev notes that of thirty-eight laws enacted in Russia between 1550 and 1572, sixteen were decided on 'with the consent of the boyars' (*The Sovereign*

and His Counsellors, p. 79). But of course the implication is that twenty-two Acts did not need the consent of the boyars, though they might have had it.

11 See Myers, op. cit., for parallel developments in Serbia and Bulgaria, where representative institutions failed to develop before the Ottomon conquest. In Latin Christendom they were widespread from the early Middle Ages. The influence of the Catholic religious orders on the development of constitutional thought and practice is analysed by Leo Moulin, 'Policy-Making in the Religious Orders', *Government and Opposition,* 1, no. 1, October, 1965, pp. 25–54.

12 C. Given-Wilson, *The English Nobility in the Late Middle Ages: The Fourteenth Century Political Community,* Routledge & Kegan Paul, London, 1987, pp. 177–8. See also R.F. Treharne, 'The Nature of Parliament in the Reign of Henry III', *English Historical Review,* IXXIV, 1959.

13 But see Chester Dunning, *Russia's First Civil War,* Pennsylvania State University Press, 2001, pp. 92ff, who downplays the importance of the election of Boris Godunov to the throne, and states that it took place after his coronation in 'a sham zemskii sobor'.

14 G. Vernadsky, *The Tsardom of Moscow, 1547–1682,* V, pt 1 of *A History of Russia,* Yale University Press, New Haven and London, 1969, pp. 33–4, quoting E.F. Maksimovich in 'Tserkovno-zemskii sobor 1549 goda', in *ZRNIB,* 9, 1933, pp. 1–15. See also Bogatyrev, *The Sovereign and His Counsellors,* pp. 137ff for discussion of the origin and nature of the *zemskii sobor* and for the suggestion that Makarii introduced the notion of a church *sobor* (a well established institution) into the government of the state.

15 Aleksei Adashev does not figure in the list of heads of *prikazy* in 1549 in Filiushkin, *Istoria odnoi mistifikatsii,* pp. 50–51, and he appears for the first time in the list for 1550 as a *kaznachei,* or treasurer, which may have implied that he was in charge of the Tsar's personal effects, and papers in the bedchamber. These government offices and their locations had various names at various times: *palata* (chamber), *dvorets* (modern tr. is palace, but better 'court'), *izba* (bureau), *prikaz* (office); there is no indication of the kinds of buildings they were housed in.

16 Schmidt, *Rossia Ivana groznogo,* p. 55.

17 E.g. Smirnov, in *Ocherki,* pp. 222ff, who also doubted that Adashev and Sylvester would actually work together in a government office.

18 Filiushkin, *Istoria odnoi mistifikatsii,* pp. 56ff.

19 M.V. Kukushkina points out that a copy of the 1550 code was first discovered by V.N. Tatishchev, Petrine statesman and historian, in 1734. In a note on the MS Tatishchev says that the Grand Prince, seeing the great extortion prevailing in the judicial process, had ordered the towns each to send one good man, who, together with the boyars, *okol'nichie* and *dvoretskie,* were to produce a new code. *Kniga v Rossii,* pp. 68–9. See also Zimin, *Reformy,* p. 350, n. 2.

20 Kukushkina, *Kniga v Rossii,* p. 109.

21 Zimin, *Reformy,* p. 351.

22 It has been suggested that there was an intermediate code of Vasily III's, but this has been rejected by Soviet experts. See *Pamiatniki prava perioda ukreplenia Russkogo tsentralizovannogo gosudarstva, XV–XVII vv,* ed. L.V. Cherepnin, Moscow, 1956, p. 231.

23 I have drawn extensively on H.W. Dewey, 'The 1550 *Sudebnik* as an Instrument of Reform', *JGOE,* 10, 1962, pp. 161–80. Dewey argues that the *Sudebnik* was not really effective, as it was overtaken by the lawlessness of the *oprichnina.*

24 See the interesting comparison by S.N. Bogatyrev, 'Administrativnye sistemy Tiudorov i Riurikovichei: Sravnitel'nyi analiz', *Zerkalo istorii: Sbornik statei,* ed. N.I. Basovskaia, Moscow, 1992, pp. 74–84.

25 But see above, n. 10.
26 That the code was regarded as an essentially practical document is confirmed by the fact that some fifty MS copies have survived, whereas only one copy of the code of 1497 still exists. Kukushkina, *Kniga v Rossii,* p. 73.
27 See '*Stoglav*', n. 33 below.
28 Ivan attempted to send delegates to the Council of Trent, but the Polish-Lithuanian government did not allow them free passage through the Commonwealth.
29 Skrynnikov, *Sviatiteli i vlasti,* p.173, suggests that the questions were drafted by Sylvester and Aleksei Adashev; the evidence of Sylvester's participation is all internal, but it is not improbable that he was involved.
30 Skrynnikov, op. cit., pp. 172ff; Skrynnikov states that copies of speeches by Ivan have been preserved among the papers of the *Sobor,* the main burden of which is criticism of the dereliction of duty by the boyar government.
31 I am drawing, among other sources, on P. Bushkovitch, *Religion and Society in Russia, Sixteenth and Seventeenth Centuries,* Oxford University Press, New York and Oxford, 1992.
32 Ivanov, *Literaturnoe nasledie Maksima Greka,* pp. 170–71 mentions that Maksim Grek thanks Makarii for sending him money, complains of the persecution he has suffered by the deprivation of his books and personal comforts and is sending some writings on church teachings.
33 See '*Stoglav*' in A.D. Gorsky, ed., *Rossiskoe zakonodatel'stvo X–XX vekov,* 10 vols, Moscow, 1985, II, *zakonodatel'stvo perioda obrazovania i ukreplenia Russkogo tsentralizovannogo gosudarstva,* n. 242ff. and N.V. Sinitsyna, *Maksim Grek v Rossii,* Moscow, 1977, pp. 155–8.
34 Gorsky, *Zakonodatel'stvo, Stoglav,* p. 267. It is worth noting that Ivan finished his appeal to those present with the words: 'I ia vam ottsem svoim i s brateiu i s svoimi boyary chelom b'iu', i.e. he 'beats his forehead' to his 'father' with his brothers and boyars.
35 See Jack Kollman, 'The Stoglav and Parish Priests', *Russian History,* 7, 1980, pp. 65–91, and Gorsky, *Zakonodatel'stvo, Stoglav,* pp. 269 and 438.
36 Gorsky, op. cit., pp. 290–91.
37 It was *de rigueur* for donors of sums of money for prayers for the dead to donate sufficiently to provide for a feast on the name day of the person concerned. See seminar paper by L. Steindorff, in Professor Hughes's seminar series, at SSEES in the Centre for Russian Studies on 'Death and Immortality in Russian Cultural History', 2001–2002 in 2002, on the very large number of feast days entered in *Sinodiki* for the commemoration of the dead. The monks must have been feasting every second day throughout the year.
38 Gorsky, op. cit., p. 210, and see for a second example, p. 420, a miniature of the Church *Sobor* of 1555.
39 It should be noted that wearing beards was normal throughout Europe at this time.
40 Gorsky, op. cit., p. 426, pp. 440–41. These replies are usually attributed to Sylvester.
41 Ibid., p. 426. But see Zimin, *Reformy,* p. 474, miniature of Ivan IV from the Kazan' Chronicle, mounted, crowned and beardless, but with a faint moustache, rather like the young Peter I.
42 Gorsky, op. cit., pp. 437–8. The editor of the *Stoglav* comments that this was regarded as necessary because the common people often married six or seven times. So, of course, did Ivan IV eventually.
43 Ibid., p. 333, ch. 60; see also pp. 338ff, chs 60, 64, 65, 66. On the Donation of Constantine see below.

44   See Horst Jablonowski, *Westrussland zwischen Wilna und Moskau*, E.J. Brill, Leiden, 1961; V.O. Kliuchevsky, *Istoria soslovii* v Rossi, repr. by Academic International, p. 133; and S.B. Veselovsky, 'Poslednye udely v severovostochnoi Rusi', *Istoricheskie Zapiski*, no. 22, 1947, pp. 101–31 at pp. 113ff. According to Zimin, *Formirovanie*, p. 143, these princes were known as service princes as distinct from appanage princes, and they had no claim to the grand princely throne.

45   From 1714 Peter I paid salaries to officers and men, but did not deprive officers of the landed estates originally granted to enable them to serve.

46   Veselovsky, 'Reforma 1550g. i tak nazyvaemaia tysiachnaia kniga', *Issledovania po istorii oprichniny*, Moscow, 1963, pp. 77–91.

47   A.V. Chernov, *Vooruzhennye sily russkogo gosudarstva v XV–XVII vv.*, Moscow, 1954, pp. 46ff.

48   R. Hellie, *Enserfment and Military Change in Muscovy*, University of Chicago Press, 1971, pp. 156–7.

49   For information about this somewhat obscure character see W. Philipp, *Ivan Peresvetov und seine Schriften zur Erneuerung des Moskauer Reiches*, Königsberg (today Kaliningrad), 1935; A.A. Zimin, comp., and D.S. Likhachev, ed., *Sochinenia I. Peresvetova*, Moscow and Leningrad, 1956; and Zimin, *I.S. Peresvetov i ego sovremenniki*, Moscow, 1958.

50   The use of 'Wallachia' to describe Moldavia is frequent at this time.

51   For a very knowledgeable discussion of the Russian army and armament see Lt. Col. Dianne Smith, Xenophon Group International, 24 January 1984, 'The Sixteenth-Century Muscovite Army'. (www.xenophongi.org/rushistory/muscovy/htm).

52   On Peter IV of Moldavia see above, pp. 31–2 and below n. 59.

53   Lt. Col. Dianne Smith, op. cit.

54   The German '*Gerechtigkeit*' conveys more exactly the many meanings of '*pravda*'.

55   'The Tale of Prince Peter IV of Moldavia' in Zimin and Likhachev, *Sochineniya I. Peresvetova*, p. 189.

56   Zimin and Likhachev, *Sochinenia I. Peresvetova*, p. 167.

57   Ibid., p. 153.

58   M.N. Tikhomirov, *Rossiiskoe gosudarstvo XV–XVII vv*, Moscow, 1973, pp. 70ff.

59   See also A.L. Iurganov, 'Idei I.S. Peresvetova v kontekste mirovoi istorii i kul'tury', *Voprosy istorii*, no. 2, Moscow 1996, pp. 15–27; Lehtovirta, *Ivan IV as Emperor*, pp. 239ff.

CHAPTER VI The Conquest of Kazan'

1   See J. Pelenski, 'The Origins of the Official Muscovite Claims to the Kievan Inheritance', *Harvard Ukrainian Studies,* I, 1977, pp. 29–52.

2   The khans of Kazan' and of the Crimea had to be chosen from among the descendants of Genghis Khan.

3   See G. Vernadsky, *The Mongols and Russia*, vol. III of *A History of Russia*, Yale University Press, New Haven, 1953, p. 431 for the ancestry of Kasim.

4   Skrynnikov, *Velikii Gosudar'*, I, p. 180 lists apart from the 'tsarstvo' of Kasimov, the appanages of Iur'ev and Romanov, and lands held by baptized Tatars in Zvenigorod.

5   Ibid., p. 181. *Kormlenie*, it will be remembered, was a form of living off the income and produce of a particular town or province.

6   *PSRL*, XIII, no. 2, p.1, 1506.

7   See Tikhomirov, 'Petr Raresh i Ivan Groznyi'.
8   See the careful analysis by Lehtovirta, *Ivan IV as Emperor*, op. cit., pp. 91ff. But see also P. Mansel, *Constantinople: City of the World's Desire, 1453–1924*, Penguin, Harmondsworth, 1997, p. 50, for the hint by Patriarch Theoleptus in 1516 that a 'Russo-Byzantine empire might be created'.
9   See D.N. Bantysh Kamenskii, *Obzor vneshnikh snoshenii Rossii po 1800 god*, Moscow, 1902; see also on the diplomatic relations of Poland–Lithuania with Russia and of Russia with the Nogai Horde, Crimea and the Porte the relevant volumes of *SIRIO*, i.e. 35, 59 and 71, and 41 and 95. There is an excellent overview in Hans Übersberger, *Österreich und Russland seit dem Ende des 15 Jahrhunderts*, vol. I: 1488–1605, Wilhelm Braumüller, Vienna and Leipzig, 1906.
10 Iuzefovich, *Kak v posol'skikh obychaiakh vedetsia*, pp. 51ff. Iuzefovich comments that a similar attitude is found in the Manchurian rulers of China, which leads me to speculate whether the habit of speaking of oneself in derogatory terms which Herberstein and others so disapproved in Russia originates far back in Mongolian/Chinese custom. Iuzefovich provides a perceptive and entertaining survey of Russian diplomatic practice in pre-Petrine days.
11 Ibid., p. 82.
12 The word 'international' was coined by Jeremy Bentham.
13 Garrett Mattingly, *Renaissance Diplomacy*, Penguin Books, London, 1965, p. 26.
14 It is noteworthy that in Mattingly's excellent survey this is the only mention of the Orthodox world in connexion with the development of diplomatic practice.
15 See in later chapters the difficulties which arose between Russia and Sweden in this respect.
16 N.A. Kazakova, '"Evropeiskoi strany koroli": Issledovania po otechest-vennomu istochnikovedeniu' in *Sbornik statei posviashchennykh 75-letiu S.N. Valka*, Moscow, 1964, pp. 418–26. There are fourteen copies of this document attached to various collections or chronicles. Kazakova argues that it cannot be dated earlier than 1506, when Ferdinand of Aragon became king of both Aragon and Castile – but in fact he never did. On the death of Queen Isabel the throne of Castile went to her daughter Joan the Mad.
17 See A. Bérélowitch, *La Hiérarchie des égaux: La Noblesse russe d'ancien regime XVIe–XVIIe siècles*, Seuil, Paris, 2001, pp. 352ff. Sir Jerome Bowes, whose relations with Ivan IV could not have been worse, was told by the Tsar: 'I doo not esteme the Queen your mystris for my fellow; ther bee that are her bettars, yes her worstars, wheruntto answering as I thought fytt (wheche no was vnreasonable) he told me in furye hew would throwe me owt of the doores and bad me gett me home'. G. Tolstoy, *England and Russia: Rossia i Anglia, 1553–1593*, St Petersburg, 1875, p. 232.
18 Mattingly, op. cit., p. 17.
19 Iuzefovich, *Kak v posol'skikh obychaiakh vedetsia*, pp.138ff. The display of large quantities of plate on 'buffets' at official banquets was also practised by Henry VIII. See Alison Weir, *Henry VIII: King and Court*, Jonathan Cape, London, 2001, p. 74.
20 Iuzefovich, op. cit, pp. 96ff; cf. *SIRIO*, 38, p. 171.
21 A first cousin is called *dvoiurodnyy brat* (brother of the second birth) or *brat* (brother), for short, which can create confusion.
22 *Muzhichi rod, ne gosudarski*, 'of peasant birth and not of lordly descent', and for the king of Denmark see I. Hofmann, 'Posol'stvo I. Gofmana v Livoniu i russkoe gosudarsto v 1559–1560', *Istoricheskii Arkhiv*, no. 6, Moscow, 1957, pp. 131–42, at p. 138.

23 I have translated 'vozovoditel' as coachman. Iuzefovich, op. cit., pp. 17–18.

24 Ostrowski, *Muscovy and the Mongols*, ch. 8, pp. 164ff., discusses possible Tatar derivations of the title tsar, but I do not find him convincing.

25 Imperialism as an ideology is put forward by two very different authors, each in his own way: G. Hosking, *Russia: People and Empire, 1552–1917,* HarperCollins, London, 1997; and D. Ostrowski, *Muscovy and the Mongols*.

26 The word 'state' is recorded for the first time in English in 1538; the Russian situation is more complex, because the word state in use today, 'gosudarstvo' in the sense of 'Staat' or 'Etat' as allegedly used by Louis XIV, for instance, in the phrase 'L'état c'est moi,' was first used in Russian in the first surviving will of Ivan IV dating from 1572 (or possibly from 1579). It then referred to his realms, the lands he ruled over, or in German his *Herrschaft*, English 'Lordship', French *seigneurie*, Spanish *señorío*. See below, Chapter XXI.

27 Ostrowski in *Muscovy and the Mongols* implies that this irredentism did not exist spontaneously at the time, that it was fostered by a particularly warlike Church under Metropolitan Makarii, and that Ivan III had even been capable of inciting the Crimeans to attack and destroy Lithuanian-occupied Kiev. This is true, but this is a pre-nationalistic era, and the same indifference to nationality and at times even to religion is evident in border warfare between Scotland and England, and in the wars between Christians and Moslems in medieval Spain. The claims of a dynasty come before those of a non-existent nation, let alone a state, and often of a Church.

28 Professor Averil Cameron has kindly confirmed that the name Byzantium for the Roman Empire of the East only came into use in the mid-sixteenth century.

29 See also the stimulating discussion of Ivan as Holy Emperor and as Universal Emperor, in Lehtovirta, *Ivan IV as Emperor*, pp. 273–347. which I find most convincing.

30 See for instance D. Loades, *The Tudor Court*, Headstart History, London, 1992, p. 29: 'The Kings of France had been recognised as "Emperors in their own kingdom" since the Bull *Per Venerabilem* of 1202, not so the kings of England.' Since the reign of King John, England was under the suzerainty of the Pope.

31 This was of course also the motive for the Reconquista. I have been struck by the lack of understanding of religious passion shown by a number of historians. Religious belief as a factor in the history of a people is barely mentioned, in spite of the vital importance of 'salvation' in both the Christian and the Moslem faiths. In contrast see Lehtovirta, *Ivan IV as Emperor*, p. 327, who does not consider Tatar khanates in the relevant period as impressive models for Russian tsars.

32 Notably, Pelenski, Ostrowski and Halperin. See Pelenski, 'Muscovite Imperial Claims to the Kazan' Khanate', *Slavic Review*, XXVI, 4, 1967, pp. 559–96.

33 *PSRL*, XXIX, *Letopis' nachala tsarstva*; *Kazanskaia istoria*, ed. G.N. Moiseeva, Leningrad, 1954, pp. 75–8.

34 Quoted in Mansel, *Constantinople*, p. 25.

35 Karamzin, *Istoria*, vol. VIII, ch. 3, pp. 74ff.

36 I am drawing on Kurbsky's description of the battle in which he took part, which may well be inaccurate, since he wrote it some twenty-five years after the event, but which nevertheless is very vivid. See Kurbsky, *History*, pp. 27ff.

37 Ibid., p. 53.

38 See the description by the Danish envoy Uhlfeldt of the Russian habit of turning one's naked buttocks to face spectators as a gesture of contempt. 'Puteshestvia v Rossii datskogo poslannika Iakova Uhlfeldta v 1575', tr. by E. Barsov from the Latin in *Chtenia*, 1883, pt 1, pp. 14, 16.

39 According to Karamzin it is now that the title of *sluga* was awarded to the *voevodas* A.B. Gorbaty-Shuisky and M.I. Vorotynsky; Karamzin, *Istoria*, VIII, ch. 3, p. 90 and notes p. 39, n. 262.

40 I have taken this description of events from Karamzin, *Istoria*, VIII, ch. 4, pp. 85ff.

41 Ibid., VIII, ch. 3, pp. 79ff.

42 *PSRL*, XIII, no. 2, pp. 214ff, 1553–4.

43 For a reproduction of the icon and commentary see O.I. Podobedova, *Moskovskaia shkola zhivopisi pri Ivana IV*, Moscow, 1972, pp. 22ff. For a different perspective and an imaginative and knowledgeable discussion of the portrayal of Ivan as 'emperor' see Lehtovirta, *Ivan IV as Emperor*, pp. 184ff. The icon is large (144 cm by 396 cm). There is a family likeness between this icon and the painting called the *Journey of the Magi*, very different in tone, by Benozzo Gozzoli, in the Palazzo Medici-Riccardi in Florence, dating from the mid-fifteenth century, in which the Emperor John VIII Paleologus, whose first wife, Anna, was a daughter of Grand Prince Vasily I, is escorted on his way to the Council of Ferrara/Florence, followed by the Three Kings. He is of course the elder brother of Thomas, Despot of Morea, father of Ivan IV's grandmother Sofia. It is not beyond the bounds of possibility that Sofia might have described the painting; nor is it at all unlikely that Maksim Grek, who had doubtless visited the Palazzo Medici, as it then was, had seen it in Florence. In both the icon and the Renaissance painting, the figures are richly dressed and embellished with gold ornaments, and surrounded by the upright lances above and the horses' legs below marching in uniform and rhythmic formation. The crown of the principal horseman is not the usual radiate crown given to a Russian tsar.

CHAPTER VII The Dynastic Crisis of 1553

1 *PSRL*, XIII, no. 2, pt 1, supplement to Nikonovskaia, pp. 524ff; and *PSRL*, XXIX, Aleksandro-Nevskaia letopis', pp. 212ff.

2 It is often stated that Sylvester was Ivan's confessor. This is not so.

3 According to Veselovsky, the interpolations were either dictated by Ivan or written under his supervision; according to modern research, the interpolations were made in the late 1570s or maybe even later. See S.B. Veselovsky, 'Interpoliatsii tak nazymaevoy tsarstvennoi knigi o bolezni tsaria Ivana 1553g', in his *Issledovania po istorii oprichniny*, Moscow, 1963, pp. 255–91.

4 Most of this account is taken from Veselovsky's 'Interpoliatsii' and his article 'Poslednie udely', pp. 109ff. The dating of the interpolations has been discussed at length by Russian historians (D.N. Al'shits, N.E. Andreyev (Cambridge), I. Gralia, A.A. Amosov, V.V. Morozov and many others). I am very grateful to Dr S.N. Bogatyrev for his help in steering my way through the difficulties of dating the sources. The first to swear allegiance were the senior boyars, many of them related by marriage or by clan, such as I.V. Sheremetev bol'shoi (senior), M. Ia. Morozov, D.R. Iur'ev Zakhar'in (the Tsaritsa's brother), V.M. Iur'ev Zakhar'in (her cousin), the gentleman of the bedchamber, Aleksei Adashev, the chamberlain (*postel'nichii*), Ignatii Veshniakov, and the *d'iak* Ivan M. Viskovaty.

5 Skrynnikov, *Velikii gosudar'*, I, p. 192.

6 Floria, *Ivan Groznyi*, p. 68. Kurbsky, *Correspondence*, Ivan to Kurbsky, 1564, at p. 95.

7 See Carolyn Pouncy, ' "The Blessed Sil'vestr" and the Politics of Invention in Muscovy, 1545–1570', *Harvard Ukrainian Studies*, vol. XIX, 1995, pp. 549–72.

8 Veselovsky, 'Interpoliatsii', pp. 284ff. It was also possible that Vladimir of

Staritsa recollected the fate of his father, Andrei, who had been arrested and kept imprisoned by the Regent Elena on the death of Vasily III to make sure that he would not overthrow his nephew, the young Ivan IV (Floria, op. cit., p. 70).

9 Veselovsky, 'Interpoliatsii' in *Issledovania po istorii oprichniny*, p. 284.

10 Ibid., pp. 290.

11 'i byst mezh boyar bran' velik i krik i shum velik' (and there was much loud shouting and cries and great noise among the boyars) (Aleksandro-Nevskaia Letopis', *PSRL*, XXIX, p. 213).

12 Ivan Petrovich Fedorov was entitled to call himself Cheliadnin through his marriage to a member of that family. Zimin, *Formirovanie*, p. 169, and Zimin, *Oprichnina Ivana Groznogo*, Moscow, 1964, pp. 276ff, for his career.

13 Account put together from Floria (*Ivan Groznyi*), Skrynnikov (*Tsarstvo Terrora*), Veselovsky, op. cit., Gralia, and Filiushkin (*Istoriia odnoi mistifikatsii*, pp. 77ff).

14 Gralia, *Ivan Mikhailov Viskovaty*, pp. 101–2.

15 A new rank, duma noble; actual date of its introduction uncertain.

16 Grobowski, '*The Chosen Council*', appendices. V.I. Vorotynsky had died.

17 Kurbsky, *Correspondence*, pp. 96–7.

18 The figure of Ivan Viskovaty is very prominent in the miniatures illustrating the Tsarstvennaia kniga, which suggests that this chronicle was probably put together in the scriptoria of the Office of Foreign Affairs, under his eyes. Gralia, op. cit., pp. 109–9.

19 See Kurbsky, *History*, pp. 77ff. It is on this journey that Ivan met Vassian Toporkov, nephew of Iosif of Volotsk, who advised the Tsar not to appoint advisers wiser than himself. In my view far too much weight has been attached to this superficial remark (Floria, *Ivan Groznyi*, p. 73).

20 Floria, op. cit., p. 83.

21 For details of this complex story see N.E. Andreyev, 'Ob avtore pripisok v litsevykh svodakh Groznogo', 'O dele d'yaka Viskovatogo' and 'Ioann Groznyy i ikonopis' XVI veka', repr. in *Studies in Muscovy: Western Influence and Byzantine Inheritance*, Variorum Reprints, London, 1970; see also Pouncy, '"The Blessed Sil'vester"', pp. 556ff. (cf n. 24 in which Sylvester writes to Makarii, 'Ivan Viskovatyy wrote to you, gosudar' which is translated as 'sovereign'!)

22 Floria, op. cit., p. 79ff.

23 *Stoglav*, article 98, pp. 373–4 and 496; see also Zimin, *Reformy*, pp. 375–6.

24 I. Gralia argues that at this point Ivan, deeply disappointed by Makarii's defence of church ownership of lands, freed himself from his authority and surrounded himself with advisers of his choice, led by Adashev. In a very negative portrayal of the Metropolitan, he charges Makarii with interfering in secular matters, usurping for himself the role of final arbiter. Gralia, *Ivan Mikhailov Viskovaty*, pp. 133ff. He seems very biased to me and hence not entirely convincing on this issue.

25 The entries in the Nikonovskaia and Tsarstvennaia Chronicles date from the late 1560s.

26 The words *rab*, and *rabinya* are usually translated 'slave', but this gives a wholly incorrect impression of the actual sense conveyed at the time.

27 Filiushkin, *Istoria odnoi mistifikatsii*, p. 80.

28 Filiushkin gives the names of the individual members, ibid., p. 91.

29 Among them were several of the Rostovsky princes, and the Princes Shcheniatev, Kurakin, Pronsky, Nemoi and Obolensky. Some of the traitors had been denounced by Ivan Petrovich Fedorov, on whom see Chapter XIV.

30 Floria, *Ivan Groznyi*, pp. 82ff.

31 Skrynnikov, *Velikii gosudar'*, I, p. 207; *Tsarstvo terrora*, p. 119. Semen Rostovsky is said to have lost his rank of boyar, but I have never seen any mention of any other such loss of rank.

32 Filiushkin, op. cit., p. 80, analyses the different accounts of 1553, 1564, 1570 and 1580.

33 Gralia suggests that Ivan was already turning against the Metropolitan, pp. 132–46; and see n. 24 above.

34 The Tsarstvennaia Chronicle and the Piskarevskaia Chronicle (*PSRL*, XIII, no. 2 pt 2, PSRL, XXXIV). The former is quoted in Carolyn Johnston Pouncy as an epigraph to her article, '"The Blessed Sil'vestr"'.

35 Floria, *Ivan Groznyi*, p. 117; Floria states that he was in fact in charge of Russian foreign policy.

36 L.V. Cherepnin, ed., *Pamiatniki russkogo prava*, IV, Moscow 1956, *prilozhenia*, pp. 576ff., 'Voprosy Ivana IV Metropolitu Makariu, soderzhashchie proekt gosudarstvennykh reform', and pp. 592ff., for text in modern Russian.

37 Ibid. The editor points out that parts of this proposal were carried out in the *ukaz* of 11 January 1558.

38 Ibid., question 10, 'O vdovykh boyariniakh'. But the question applies to *deti boyarskie* (service gentry). The disregard of personal choice compares not too badly with the practice of the Court of Wards in England.

39 See Smith, 'The Sixteenth-Century Muscovite Army', passim, and Chernov, *Vooruzhennye sily*, pp. 43ff.

40 For the quotation from the code of service see PSRL, XXIX, Letopis' nachala tsarstva. Skrynnikov, *Tsarstvo terrora*, pp. 103ff.

41 The failure to impose many of the central authority's decrees throughout the country illustrates how thin was the administration on the ground and how slow was the process of unification.

42 A.N. Kurat, 'The Turkish Expedition to Astrakhan' in 1569 and the Problem of the Don-Volga Canal', *SEER*, XL, 94, December 1961, pp. 7–23.

43 Vasily III had experienced difficulty in sending envoys to Charles V and to Ferdinand of Habsburg, and was also prevented by Sigismund I of Poland–Lithuania from developing his relations with Peter Raresh of Moldavia. Übersberger, *Österreich und Russland*, pp. 267ff. For the Sound tolls, see Chapter VIII, n. 7.

44 Ibid., pp. 289–307. Karamzin, *Istoria*, VIII, ch. 3, pp. 70ff and p. 28ff. of notes, starting at p.25, which has additional details on Schlitte.

45 Quoted in Karamzin, op. cit., vol. VIII, ch. 3, notes p. 62, n. 479.

46 The *Bona Speranza*, under Sir Hugh Willoughby, was eventually found, with all the crew frozen to death where they sat or lay.

47 Roast swan was also a gourmet dish at the English court. See Weir, *Henry VIII*, p. 68. Cygnets were particularly tasty.

48 Berry and Crummey, eds, *Rude and Barbarous Kingdom*, pp. 24ff. The same 'buffets' were used in the English court for the same display of silver, see Weir, op. cit., pp. 49–50.

CHAPTER VIII **The War in Livonia and the End of the 'Chosen Council'**

1 According to Filiushkin, *Istoria odnoi mistifikatsii*, pp. 127ff, it had been formally decided around 1555 that the next campaign after the conquest of Astrakhan' would be against Crimea, for which anti-Moslem allies would have to be sought, such as Poland–Lithuania. A courier had already been sent in 1554 to Vilna to discuss a possible alliance, 'so as to free Christianity from the hands of Islam' ('ot besermenskikh ruk'), but nothing came of these talks.

2   Iuzefovich, *Kak v posol'skikh obychaiakh vedetsia*, pp. 16ff.
3   I have drawn extensively on E. Donnert, *Der livländische Ordensritterstaat und Russland: Der livländische Krieg und die baltische Frage in der europäischen Politik 1558–1583*, Berlin (GDR), 1963; and M. Roberts, *The Early Vasas: A History of Sweden, 1523–1611*. Donnert tends to stress the welcome and assistance the Russian troops received from the native Latvian and Estonian peasants against the Germans of the Order.
4   Roberts, op. cit., p. 155.
5   These claims dated back to the fifteenth century and were founded on the theory that the Livonians paid tribute in exchange for the permission to settle on land which was Russian until it was conquered by the Knights of the Sword in the thirteenth century. See Floria, *Ivan Groznyi*, pp. 124ff, and Filiushkin, op. cit., p. 125.
6   There is an interesting footnote to this episode: since the original charter was granted in England under Philip and Mary it extended to Philip's subjects in the Netherlands, who took immediate advantage to trade 'at the Corelian mouth of the Dvina'. They continued to do so up to 1587, much to the indignation of Queen Elizabeth. Tolstoy, *England and Russia*, pp. viii–ix.
7   A tax imposed by Denmark on shipping passing through the Sound or narrow channel which controlled the entrance to the Baltic Sea.
8   Floria, op. cit., p. 132.
9   Skrynnikov, *Tsarstvo Terrora*, pp. 130–31; *Sbornik imperator skogo istoricheskogo obshchestva*, St Petersburg (SIRIO), 129, pp. 7ff.
10 Roberts, op. cit., pp. 155–6.
11 T.S. Willan, *The Early History of the Russia Company, 1553–1603*, Manchester University Press, 1956, pp. 12ff. and 52ff. but see T. Esper, 'A Sixteenth-Century Arms Embargo', *JGOE*, 15, 1967, pp. 180–96.
12 See Martin, *Medieval Russia*, pp. 306ff., for a discussion of relations between Russia and Lithuania at this time.
13 Donnert, op. cit., pp. 42ff and 223–4.
14 Filiushkin, op. cit., p. 132; *PSRL*, XIII, pt 2, pp. 292–3; XXIX, p. 265.
15 Roberts, op. cit., p. 159.
16 See p. 124 above.
17 Roberts, op. cit., pp. 161–2, where the author gives a delightful account of the negotiations and details of the possible commercial implications of such a marriage.
18 *SIRIO*, 59, diplomatic relations with Poland–Lithuania, p. 570; Alfer'ev's account of 8 March 1558, p. 572. See also Floria, *Ivan Groznyi*, p. 132.
19 Mainly based on Filiushkin, *Istoria odnoi mistifikatsii*, pp. 126ff.
20 'Zatem zakhotela za nego zamuzh', Filiushkin, op. cit., p. 145.
21 See Filiushkin, op. cit., pp. 145ff; Donnert, op. cit., pp. 46ff. Donnert suggests that the armistice was the work of Adashev, who was more in favour of attacking the Crimean Tatars than of war in Livonia. But where is the evidence?
22 Skrynnikov, *Tsarstvo terrora*, p. 133.
23 Kurbsky, *Correspondence*, pp. 98–9.
24 Floria, *Ivan Groznyi*, pp. 132–3. See also Zimin, *Reformy*, pp. 471–5, on differing views at Ivan's court, including differences between Adashev and Viskovaty.
25 See Schmidt, 'A.F. Adashev i Livonskaia voina' in *Rossia Ivana Groznogo*, pp. 246–9, where the author suggests that Adashev preferred negotiated solutions to war.
26 On Sylvester, see S.B. Veselovsky, 'Po povodu trilogii tov. Kostyleva, i

voznikshei o nei polemiki' (August 1943), in *Tsar Ivan Groznyi v rabotakh pisatelei i istorikov*, Moscow, 1999, pp. 7–34, at p. 27.

27   Gralia, *Ivan Mikhailov Viskovaty*, p. 257 and n. 312.

28   Ibid., p. 116, slightly modified.

29   Filiushkin, *Istoria odnoi mistifikatsii*, pp. 148–9.

30   Kurbsky, *History*, pp. 149 and 151; see also Skrynnikov, *Tsarstvo terrora*, p. 133, n. 35.

31   Schmidt, 'Pravitel'stvennaia deiatel'nost' A.F. Adasheva', pp. 50ff. For a detailed account of the family and career of A. Adashev see Filiushkin, op. cit., Appendix, pp. 281–308.

32   Schmidt, op. cit., p. 55, quoted from the early seventeenth-century Piskarevsky Chronicle (*PSRL*, XXXIV, p. 181) in which Sylvester is described as governing Russia and sitting with Adashev in the Office of the Master of Requests.

33   Kurbsky, *Correspondence*, p. 13.

34   Schmidt, op. cit., p. 61.

35   Grobowski, '*The Chosen Council*', Addenda, pp. 147ff.

36   See Zimin, *Reformy*, p. 328, where the Chamber of Requests is described as an appeal court and a body exercising powers of inspection over all other government institutions.

37   Adashev was not involved in the first period of reforms in 1547–52, when the Iur'ev Zakhar'ins dominated the government.

38   Filiushkin, *Istoria odnoi mistifikatsii*, p. 305, n. 29.

39   Owners of estates in Novgorod were not considered of sufficient rank to take part in high government office; they could not belong to the ruler's court (Floria, *Ivan Groznyi*, p. 136).

40   Filiushkin, op. cit., pp. 300–1.

41   Quoted in Filiushkin, pp. 178–9, from the diary of A.I. Turgenev in 1837.

42   See Skrynnikov, *Tsarstvo terrora*, pp. 157–8; Veselovsky, 'Sinodik opal'nykh tsaria Ivana Groznogo kak istoricheskii istochnik', in *Issledovania po istorii oprichniny*, pp. 354–5, notes that neither Aleksei nor Daniil and his son were mentioned in Ivan's *Sinodiki*.

43   Filiushkin, *Istoria odnoi mistifikatsii*, pp. 323–4.

44   Zimin, *I.S. Peresvetov i ego sovremenniki*, p. 46.

45   The timing of these events is extremely confused. Kurbsky says that Adashev was banished from the sight of the Tsar without a trial to the fortress of Fellin. Since he was only there for a very short time in late August/September this very unlikely meeting of the Council must have taken place in summer 1560. See Kurbsky, *History*, p. 159.

46   Pouncy, in ' "The Blessed Sil'vestr" ' p. 563, states that there is no authentic sixteenth-century source confirming the existence of the Church Council allegedly called to judge Sylvester and Adashev for their role in the death of the Tsaritsa Anastasia.

47   This account is reconstructed from Kurbsky's *History*, pp. 153ff.; Skrynnikov, *Tsarstvo terrora*, pp. 136ff.; Grobowski, '*The Chosen Council*', pp. 98ff., and *Tsar Ivan i Silvestr: Istoria odnogo mifa*, tr. from the English by Israel and Irina Rabinovich, London, 1987; and Filiushkin, op. cit., pp. 309ff.

48   See Kurbsky, *Correspondence*, Ivan to Kurbsky, pp. 12ff. See Chapter X below for a full discussion of the correspondence.

CHAPTER IX The Death of Anastasia and Ivan's Second Marriage

1   PSRL, XIII, pt 2, p. 327.

2 Ibid., p. 328. This is the account given in the chronicle, but there are historians who regard Ivan IV as incapable of any human emotion.
3 Anne Boleyn suffered several miscarriages because of Henry VIII's lack of consideration.
4 Kurbsky, *History*, pp.153–4; Karamzin, *Istoria*, VIII, ch. 5, p. 195.
5 The use of poison at Ivan's court has been the subject of intensive discussion on the H-Early Slavic discussion group on the internet. A communication dated 24 September 2002, from Sergei Bogatyrev, summarizes the evidence used by D. Babichenko, 'Kremlevskie tainy: 33-i element', in *Itogi*, no. 37 (327), 17 September 2002, pp. 36–39, based on material provided by T.D. Panova, Head of the Archaeological Department of the Moscow Kremlin Museum. (www.h-net.org/~ess/), 24 September 2002. I do not find the evidence for wholesale poisoning convincing.
6 Veselovsky quotes with bitter irony the scenes in Kostylev's novel on Ivan IV where the Tsar, a touchingly tender father, treats his wife as an equal, whispers confidential political information into her ear, asks her advice on the appointment of generals, complains that he is not understood, in fact behaves like a sensitive and liberal 'intelligent'. Veselovsky, *Tsar Ivan Groznyi v rabotakh pisatelei i istorikov,* Moscow, 1999, p. 30. As Pushkin put it, you cannot harness a horse and a quivering doe together to a chariot.
7 Karamzin, *Istoria*, vol. IX, notes, p. 5, n. 28, from one of the MSS of the Synodal Chronicle.
8 Kurbsky, *Correspondence*, pp. 192–3; 'sacrifices to Cronus' is an ambiguous reference to Saturnalia: Cronus killed and ate his own children. 'Sacrifices to Cronus' is also used by Kurbsky to describe victims of Ivan's executioners.
9 Karamzin, op. cit., IX, notes pp. 1ff., quoting from several Chronicles.
10 *PSRL*, XIII, pt 2, p. 325, 'i o sem gosudariu skorb' byst' ne malaia'.
11 Ibid., p. 329, year 1560. Henry VIII inspected six portraits before choosing Anne of Cleves as his wife. Scarisbrick, *Henry VIII*, p. 355.
12 Because of the marriage between Sofia Vitovtovna and Grand Prince Vasily I.
13 *SIRIO*, 71, pp. 1ff. Solov'ev, III, *Istoria Rossii*, ch. 6, pp. 572ff.
14 Karamzin, *Istoria*, VIII, ch. 1, pp. 22–3.
15 Reconstructed from Russian diplomatic accounts in SIRIO, 71, pp. 1–46, and Donnert, *Der livländische Ordensritterstaat*, pp. 228ff.
16 See PSRL, XIII, pt 2, p. 283, describing the arrival of a group of Circassian (Kabardian) princes wishing to enter Russian service.
17 Ibid., p. 333; Karamzin, *Istoria*, IX, ch. 1, pp. 23–4.
18 Zimin, *Oprichnina Ivana Groznogo*, p. 90. Zimin suggests that Glinsky may have opposed a Tatar marriage.
19 Horsey, *Travels*, p. 264. It has been suggested that the marriage with Maria was encouraged by the Iur'ev Zakhar'ins because the young Prince Mikhail Temriukovich, her brother, was married to a Iur'ev Zakhar'in niece of Anastasia's.
20 Floria, *Ivan Groznyi*, p. 139.
21 Solov'ev, op. cit., p. 702.
22 Karamzin, op. cit., IX, ch.1, p. 29.
23 Skrynnikov, *Tsarstvo terrora*, p. 178.
24 Kurbsky, *Correspondence*, pp. 9–10.
25 Kurbsky, *History*, p. 167. The reference to Manasseh, Fennell points out, is in 2 Chron. 33. Note also Kurbsky's reference to free will.
26 Ibid., p. 155.
27 Those who remember Eisenstein's film of Ivan the Terrible will recall the scene.
28 Guagnini, based on A.A. Schlichting, 'A Brief Account of the Character and Brutal Rule of Ivan Vasil'evich, Tyrant of Muscovy', pp. 204–67. There

is little point in discussing whether Ivan was or was not a homosexual. He was evidently bisexual and there is really nothing surprising about that. Russians were frequently considered to be addicted to sodomy and one of the articles in the *Stoglav* which attached significance to the wearing of beards was specifically devised as a guard against this vice in monasteries.

29 Zimin, *Oprichnina Ivana Groznogo*, p. 92.
30 See also G. Alef, 'Bel'skies and Shuiskies in the XVIth Century', *FOG*, 38, Berlin, 1986, pp. 221–40.
31 Zimin, *Oprichnina Ivana Groznogo*, p. 478.
32 Ibid., p. 99. Veselovsky, 'Poslednye udely' pp. 113ff.
33 *Vedro*, pl. *vedra*, pail, Russian liquid measure; Bastr: A kind of wine, known in English as bastard from the Bastardo grapes from Portugal. Information kindly supplied by Professor W.F. Ryan.
34 Karamzin, op. cit., IX, ch. 1, p. 28 of notes, n. 145. Veselovsky, op. cit., p. 127, suggests that because both the Vorotynskys were exiled with their wives and families, Ivan's grievance was not of a service nature but possibly an accusation of witchcraft.
35 Kurbsky, *History*, p. 183. However, it is also striking that the Church accepted the forcible tonsure of the faithful. The Kurliatevs were later executed.
36 Esper, 'A Sixteenth-Century Russian Arms Embargo', passim.
37 Zimin, *Oprichnina*, p. 102
38 See S.N. Bogatyrev, 'Battle for Divine Wisdom: The Rhetoric of Ivan IV's Campaign against Polotsk', in E. Lohr and M. Poe, eds, *The Military and Society in Russia 1450–1917*, E.J. Brill, Leiden, 2002, pp. 325–63.
39 Karamzin, op. cit., IX, ch. 1, p. 25.
40 Zimin, *Reformy*, p. 101.
41 N.S. Stromilov, 'Aleksandrovskaia Sloboda', *Chtenia*, bk 2, pt VI, 1883, pp. 1–118.
42 Veselovsky, 'Poslednye udely', p. 115; Karamzin, op. cit., IX, ch. 1 p. 14, n. 86.
43 But Skrynnikov in *Sviatiteli i vlasti* says she was forcibly shorn a nun, p. 196. See also Skrynnikov, *Tsarstvo terrora*, pp. 162–3.
44 Skrynnikov, *Tsarstvo terrora*, p. 175.
45 Zimin, *Oprichnina*, p. 103, n. 2.
46 Karamzin, op. cit., IX, ch. 1 p. 14, nn. 84 and 85.
47 The printing in Church Slavonic of various ecclesiastical texts (books of hours, psalters, service books etc.) had already begun in Lithuania, initiated by Francis Skarina of Polotsk, and copies were widespread in Russia. Kukushkina, *Kniga v Rossii*, pp. 151ff.
48 Ibid., pp. 164–5.
49 The grave of Archbishop Vasily of Novgorod, the first to wear the cowl in Russia, was opened in 1946 and the white cowl was found.
50 Skrynnikov, *Tsarstvo terrora*, p. 179; *PSRL*, XXXIV, Piskarevsky Chronicle, pp. 190ff.
51 S.O. Schmidt, 'Mitropolit Makarii i pravitel'stvennaia deiatel'nost' ego vremeni' in *Rossia Ivana Groznogo*, pp. 239ff. The Tale of the White Cowl probably originated in the circle of Archbishop Gennadii of Novgorod, and may have been written by Dmitri Gerasimov, his agent in Rome. See A.V. Kartashev, *Ocherki po istorii russkoi tserkvi*, I, YMCA, Paris, 1959, pp. 389ff.; for a translated partial text see S.A. Zenkovsky, ed., *Medieval Russia's Epics, Chronicles and Tales*, New York, 1963, pp. 267ff. Schmidt says that a new approach to the study of Makarii is necessary, as after his death his personality and his achievements were often distorted.

52 Schmidt, op. cit., p. 245.

CHAPTER X Tsar Ivan and Prince Andrei Kurbsky

1 See Kurbsky, *History*, pp. 2–3, and pp. 181–2 for dancing in masks and drinking to the health of the Devil. And see W.F. Ryan, *The Bathhouse*, pp. 38–9 and pp. 46–7 for more general remarks on Christmas and Midsummer festivities with cross-dressing, mumming, wearing masks, etc.

2 Karamzin, *Istoria*, IX, ch. 1, pp. 13ff. see also Kurbsky, *History*, pp. 180ff. They were both killed on 31 January 1564. See also Schlichting, 'A Brief Account', p. 215, n. 43.

3 Schlichting, op. cit., pp. 216–17.

4 Skrynnikov, *Tsarstvo terrora*, p. 180.

5 See Kurbsky, *History*, pp. 207–9. The Sheremetevs are not mentioned in the *Sinodiks*. See Veselovsky, 'Sinodik opal'nykh', in *Issledovania*, p. 471. Ivan men'shoi (minor) was killed in battle much later. Skrynnikov does not accept the reliability of Kurbsky.'s description (op. cit., p.189, n. 34).

6 His ability to read and write is disputed by E. Keenan, and his ability to write in Cyrillic characters by Inge Auerbach. Historians of Russia as distinct from literary experts mostly reject Keenan's theories, see, for example, most recently, V.V. Kalugin, *Andrey Kurbsky i Ivan Groznyy*, Moscow 1998, pp. 18ff. There is no need here to go into the arguments pro and con., but see ibid., pp. 157–8, 252–3 and Foreword, p. xxx.

7 Kurbsky wrote a number of religious works which were eventually published in Lithuania.

8 Kurbsky, *Correspondence*, p. 265. A fourteenth-century ancestor of Kurbsky's was known as Vasily Groznyi, Grand Prince of Iaroslavl', another example of the positive use of Groznyi. See *Skazania Kniazia Kurbskogo*, ed. N. Ustrialov, 3rd edn, St Petersburg, 1868, pp. viiff. K. Stählin, *Der Briefwechsel Iwans des Schrecklichen mit dem Fürsten Kurbski*, Leipzig, 1921, p.8.

9 See for a sensible survey of Kurbsky's early life, N.E. Andreyev, 'Kurbsky's Letters to Vassian Muromtsev', reprinted in *Studies in Muscovy, Western Influence and Byzantine Inheritance*, Variorum Reprints, London 1970, pp. 414–36.

10 However, it is worth noting the opinion of Catherine II on this point. In the Hermitage copy of the MS of the correspondence Catherine notes: 'It is clear that Andrei Mikhailovich Kurbsky was among those who refused to take the oath to his young son when Ivan was ill, because he distrusted the Zakhar'ins, and wanted the Staritsa prince to rule because he was a good general', Stählin, op. cit., p. 8. Kurbsky himself denies this: 'Indeed, I did not think of this, for he in truth was not worthy to rule', Kurbsky, *Correspondence*, pp. 211–13.

11 Kurbsky is not mentioned in Filiushkin's detailed study of those close to Ivan in 1553–4, but this may be because he was a soldier (*voevoda*) and not in court service, Filiushkin, *Istoria odnoi mistifikatsii*, p. 85.

12 Kurbsky, *History*, p. 137: 'abo sam itti . . . abo tebya, lyubimago moego, poslati . . .' This does suggest that there was a degree of affection between the Tsar and Kurbsky; it is unlikely that the prince simply invented this phrase, nor that he forgot it.

13 Attempts to reconstruct Kurbsky's motives and actions have been made by a number of historians; I am basing myself largely on Skrynnikov, *Tsarstvo terrora*, Andreyev, Schlichting, Floria, and Auerbach.

14 Andreyev, op. cit., p. 431.

15 This is considered by Andreyev as possibly meant to apply to theTsaritsa Maria Temriukovna.

16 *Skazania Kniazia Kurbskogo,* ed. N. Ustrialov, Appendix.
17 Skrynnikov, op. cit., pp.184–5; Skrynnikov suggests that the money represents payment by Lithuania to Kurbsky for services rendered.
18 Kurbsky, *Correspondence,* Ivan to Kurbsky, p. 23. All quotations from the correspondence are taken from this edition though I have very occasionally diverged from Fennell's text.
19 *Skazania Knaza Kurbskogo,* ed. N. Ustrialov, pp. vii–xix. See also Kalugin, *Andrei Kurbsky,* p. 340. Kurbsky attempted to recover his belongings and there is a list of them in the Lithuanian archives including the sapphire ring which he recovered and lost again.
20 'Strong in Israel' is a phrase frequently used by Kurbsky to describe the virtuous boyars at the Russian court. According to W.F. Ryan, it originates with the Song of Solomon 3: 7 where the guards around Solomon's bed are described as 'of the valiant in Israel' (King James's Bible; 'sil'nykh izraelevykh' in OCS Bible). The image of Russia as the new Israel was the source of many edifying tales which could be put before the Tsar such as the Biblical models of Joshua and Gideon.
21 It is possible that Kurbsky was afraid that he was going to be accused of heresy and magic practices, which would undoubtedly have meant torture and death.
22 According to Fennell, in Kurbsky, *Correspondence,* p. 8, note 2, this is a marginal note in some copies of the text.
23 The reference to the priests of Cronus suggests that Kurbsky is alluding to the 'Saturnalia' indulged in by Ivan, with their pagan connotation.
24 The capture of Shibanov gave rise to a romanticized tale of the faithful servant, who intercepted the Tsar outside the palace in the Kremlin to announce his mission; Ivan leant forward and ordered Shibanov to read Kurbsky's missive out loud, leaning in the meantime on his pointed staff with which he pinned Shibanov's foot to the ground. Shibanov remained motionless in spite of the pain. *Poslania Ivana groznogo,* ed. D.S. Likhachev and Ya. S. Lur'e, ANSSR, 1951, notes to the letter to Teterin, p. 585.
25 They are also used by Kurbsky himself in his later *History,* pp. 9ff., who ascribes Ivan's evil character to his conception, 'in transgression and concupiscence' and goes on to describe his cruel tendencies as a boy.
26 I have of course drawn on it in my account of his childhood, but with some caution.
27 Kurbsky, *Correspondence,* p. 127.
28 Eli was the father of Samuel, Samuel 1: 1–3.
29 A reference to the Tsar's decisive voice in matters of *mestnichestvo.*
30 Ibid., p. 91.
31 Ibid., p. 49. Did Adashev and Sylvester really dictate to Ivan what shoes he should wear?
32 A reference to the Empress Eudoxia, who had opposed St John Chrysostom; and also perhaps a reference to Kurbsky's failure to buy presents for Ivan's children, see note 37 below. Kurbsky, *Correspondence,* p. 95.
33 See above, ch. VI, p. 103. See also C. Pouncy, ' "The Blessed Sil'vestr" ', p. 555.
34 Kurbsky, *Correspondence,* p.p 93 and 115, n. 5; *PSRL,* XIII, pt 2, pp. 205 and 501.
35 Ibid., p. 191.
36 For the truce, see Chapter VIII, above, p. 130. It is worth repeating, as I am using Kurbsky's letter so extensively, that I do not accept Professor E. Keenan's view that the Kurbsky–Groznyi correspondence is a seventeenth-century forgery (see Foreword). I do not, for instance, see how a seventeenth-century forger of this correspondence could know that Kurbsky was on a private visit to Pskov at precisely this time. See Kurbsky, *Correspondence,* p. 119.

37   For a perceptive analysis of the ideological gulf separating Ivan and Kurbsky, see Inge Auerbach, 'Die politische Vorstellungen des Fürsten Andrej Kurbski', *JGOE*, Bd 117, 1969, pp. 170–86. Her discussion ranges beyond the dialogue of 1564, and will be returned to later.

38   Ivan would be familiar with the story of the *Iliad* in various versions including the History of the Destruction of Troy.

39   Kurbsky, *Correspondence*, p. 106, 'vol'ny byli podovlastnykh zhalovati i kazniti, a ne sudilis' s nimi i ni pered kem'.

40   Ibid., pp. 12–13, Ivan to Kurbsky.

41   There is a difference which is often overlooked between absolute legislative power and absolute executive power.

42   Floria, *Ivan Groznyi*, p. 111.

43   Henry was able to use parliamentary Acts of Attainder to dispose of his enemies, which he had no difficulty in steering through Parliament. See for instance the execution of Anne Boleyn and her 'lovers'.

44   See above, ch. I, p. 13.

45   'Taina Tainykh', ed. and tr. R.D. Bulavin, *Pamiatniki literatury drevnei Rusi, konets XV – pervaia polovina XVI veka*, Moscow, 1984, p. 543. That Ivan was acquainted with this text is suggested by his remark to Kurbsky, *Correspondence*, p. 143, ' Where will one find a just man who has grey eyes? For your countenance betrays your wicked disposition', a direct reference to a warning in the *Secretum secretorum* not to trust a man with grey eyes. An alternative reading gives *zekry* for *sery*, which is closer to pale blue, see Kurbsky, *Correspondence*, p. 143 and n. 4.

46   Ibid., 'build' p. 47.

47   Ibid., pp. 59–61. Eccles. 10: 16; Is. 3: 12; and Ecclesiasticus 25: 24.

48   One little incident is revealing: Herberstein heard that when Russian envoys returned from abroad, all valuable gifts they had been given by the rulers to whom they had been accredited were confiscated for the Tsar. This had happened to two envoys and their secretary who had received heavy gold necklaces and chains, Spanish gold coins and other valuable presents from Charles V, and from his brother Ferdinand, and when they returned to Moscow the Grand Prince deprived them of the chains, and gold and silver goblets and most of the Spanish coins. 'When I asked one of these envoys', writes Herberstein, 'whether this was true, one of them, fearing to betray his master, firmly denied it, and the other said that his master merely asked him to bring the imperial presents so that he could see them.' Later writes Herberstein, 'One of these men avoided me, trying to avoid telling a lie if he continued to deny this story, or the danger of accidentally admitting its truth.' The determination to interpret Vasily's justified decision to see at least, maybe even to sieze, what were probably actually presents to him as a tyrannical abuse is based on prejudice. The presents which the envoys took abroad with them were provided by the Tsar, and it was tsarist financial policy to monopolize all gold and silver and particularly all coins (*Zapiski o Moskovii*, p. 74).

49   Quoted by Floria, *Ivan Groznyi*, p. 146.

50   And so do many historians on very little solid evidence, e.g. the assumption that Vladimir of Staritsa must have wanted to be Tsar.

51   Henry VIII had enacted a law entitling the King to name the heir to the throne, after the death of his bastard son, the Duke of Richmond, which is an anticipation of the similar law passed by Peter I of Russia in 1721. The succession was fairly irregular throughout Europe in the sixteenth century as many dynasties died out.

52   Floria, *Ivan Groznyi*, p. 147.

53 It is noteworthy that much later Boris Godunov feared that Tsar Simeon Bekbulatovich (see below, ch. XVIII) who was related to both Ivan and Maria Temriukovna could be a rival Tsar to him, and allegedly had him blinded to disqualify him for rule.

54 See for the descendants of the Patrikeevs, A.A. Zimin, *Formirovanie boyarskoy aristokratii ...*, pp. 30ff. They included the Golitsyns, Bulgakovs, Shcheniatevs, Kurakins, and many others. Evfrosin'ya of Staritsa was a descendant of the Patrikeev clan.

55 See, for a general discussion, O.P. Backus, 'Treason as a Concept and Defections from Moscow to Lithuania in the Sixteenth Century', *FOG*, 15, pp. 119–44. Nor was it, as R. Pipes suggests, equivalent to apostasy since there were many Orthodox princes and churches in Lithuania and indeed the daughter of Ivan III had married King Alexander of Lithuania–Poland who was a Catholic.

56 Floria, *Ivan Groznyi*, p. 147

57 See the extremely useful survey by Horace W. Dewey and Ann M. Kleimola, 'Suretyship and Collective Responsibility in pre-Petrine Russia', *JGOE*, 18, 1970, pp. 337–54. This article, together with a second one by the same authors referring more particularly to criminal responsibility, 'From the Kinship Group to Every Man His Brother's Keeper: Collective Responsibility in Pre-Petrine Russia', *JGOE*, 30, 1982, pp. 321–35 are absolutely fundamental for the understanding not only of administration in sixteenth- and seventeenth-century Russia but also of the way things worked at all levels of society. I disagree with the authors, however, where they state that 'The principle of collective responsibility emerged as one of the key tools of authoritarian rule in Russia.' I do not think it emerged specifically with authoritarianism in mind. It emerged in many countries including Russia as a means of ensuring that certain necessary public functions would be performed in a period in which there was no state organization to see to it, indeed in which the state did not yet in fact exist, and in which such functions were carried out by nobles, gentry, peasant elders, etc., however inadequately. Cf. the concept of frank-pledge in England.

58 See for instance the execution of Kurbsky's servant Shibanov (above, p. 164 and n. 24) and the later execution of Fedorov's servants.

59 See Veselovsky, 'Pobegi za granitsu i poruchnyye zapisi' in *Issledovania*, pp. 118ff. for a careful analysis of the social situation at court.

60 See J.R. Lander, 'Bonds, Coercion and Fear', in *Florilegium Historiale, Essays presented to Wallace K. Ferguson*, Toronto University Press, 1971, pp. 327–67. Bonds and recognizances had existed intermittently in England under Henry V and Henry VI. Under Henry VII sums involved ranged up to £10.000. ' Among peers Henry VIII cancelled at least forty-five recognizances imposed by Henry VII during the first year of his reign and one hundred and thirty more over the next five years.' In Scotland a different system flourished by which nobles bound themselves to each other, but not to the king, for the fulfilment of given obligations. See J. Wormald, *Lords and Men in Scotland, Bonds of Manrent 1442-1603*, Edinburgh University Press, 1985.

61 *Poslania Ivana Groznogo*, p. 389.

62 Ibid., pp. 17, 291.

63 Skrynnikov, *Tsarstvo terrora*, p. 188.

CHAPTER XI THE SETTING UP OF THE OPRICHNINA

1 *PSRL*, XIII, pt 2, pp. 391ff. See also 'Poslanie Ioganna Taube i Elerta Kruze', Iohann Taube und Eilhard Kruse', ed. M.G. Roginsky, *Russkii istoricheskii zhurnal*, 1922, pp. 8–59. I have only been able to make use of a Russian

translation which may distort the meaning of sixteenth-century words, for instance the word *soslovie* is used, which only began to be used in the nineteenth century. The suggestion that Ivan stripped the monasteries and churches of Moscow of their icons and treasure is rejected by Roginsky (op. cit., p. 14). I propose to use both the standard description of events in the chronicle, as supervised by Ivan himself and that produced by Taube and Kruse, who were eye-witnesses, trying of course to whitewash their own roles in Russia, but where their interests were not involved, usually reliable. Heinrich von Staden who served Ivan for a number of years refers in his *The Land and Government of Muscovy*, ed. and tr. by T. Esper Stanford, 1967, to 'an insurrection', presumably in Moscow, in December 1564, which led Ivan to leave Moscow (p. 18). There is no confirmation elsewhere of this insurrection.

2   The text in the Chronicle is somewhat different but conveys the same meaning. A speech is not mentioned but a letter dated 3 January 1565 describes the treason of the boyars and Ivan's anger with the ecclesiastical hierarchy, the boyars and all his servants. This was because during his youth they had robbed him right and left, taken no care of Orthodox Christianity and had refused to fight against the Crimeans, and the 'Tsar and grand prince, out of the great pity in his heart, and not wanting to tolerate their treasonable activities is leaving his state and will go where God disposes'.

3   Zimin, *Oprichnina*, pp. 127ff. There is some inconsistency in the chronology of events as described by Taube and Kruse who also imply that Ivan was aware of a rejection of himself and his heirs (see also Skrynnikov, *Tsarstvo*, pp. 213ff.). But N.I. Kostomarov, according to Zimin, p. 131, suggests that some kind of *Zemskii Sobor* was sitting in that autumn and that Ivan failed to put his policy through, and fearing a revolt he left Moscow. According to him, the story of the people coming to appeal to Ivan to return to his capital was a later invention inserted into the Chronicle but does not reflect what actually happened. See also S.O. Schmidt, 'K istorii soborov XVI v', *Istoricheskie Zapiski*, 79, 1965, pp. 120–51.

4   This is rather an exaggeration, as in January they would all have died. The most likely meaning of this tale is that they had to leave behind any ceremonial robes and headgear they were wearing.

5   It is not clear whether there were two missives to the Metropolitan. One is more likely but there is a considerable discrepancy between the Chronicle and the account of Taube and Kruse.

6   Zimin, *Oprichnina*, p. 131, seems to accept that this was a *Zemskii Sobor*. This seems again a confusion between an institution and an occasional public gathering.

7   Zimin, *Oprichnina*, p. 130, suggests that the boyars' guilt was indicated by their willingness to sign surety bonds in large sums of money to protect each other.

8   These missives have not survived, but their content is known from the summaries in the chronicles.

9   Floria, *Ivan Groznyi*, pp.176ff. Floria suggests that this missive was probably very much longer than what has survived in the chronicle and might have been in the nature of a manifesto. For Skrynnikov it is an answer to Kurbsky's letter of April 1564. There is also an echo in Ivan's words according to the chronicle of what he allegedly said several days earlier as reported by Taube and Kruse.

10 *PSRL*, XIII, pt 2, pp. 392–3.

11 Ibid., p. 180.

12 It is the procession of the people of Moscow led by Pimen and Levkii as portrayed in Eisenstein's film which so impressed the mayor of London, Ken Livingstone, as to make him identify himself with a man so loved by his people

as Ivan the Terrible. According to Albert Schlichting, Ivan declared that he was bowed down by the weight of ruling, wanted to give it up and live a holy and monastic life in solitude (quoted in Zimin, *Oprichnina*, p. 130, n. 1). Schlichting was a Pomeranian who had been captured in battle and remained in Russian captivity for seven years. He knew Russian and German and found work as translator for Ivan's foreign physician. He fled Russia in 1571 and wrote his 'A Brief Account of the Character and Brutal Rule of Ivan Vasil'evich Tyrant of Muscovy', and a shorter 'News from Muscovy concerning the Life and the Tyranny of Prince Ivan', both of which were translated from a Latin copy and published by H. Graham, *Canadian American Slavic Studies*, IX, No. 2, Summer 1975, pp. 204–72, with very useful notes. The original was probably in German; a Latin MS has survived, now in Harvard University, but the Latin version which was prepared in 1572 for the Vatican seems to have disappeared.

13 Skrynnikov, passim, suggests that Ivan addressed a meeting of the Boyar Council in Aleksandrovskaia Sloboda. I find this unconvincing.

14 Skrynnikov, *Tsarstvo terrora*, pp 208–9. But see Schlichting, 'A Brief Account . . .', p. 218. Seeing that Schlichting's account was written in late 1570 the story of the abdication was probably remembered in a distorted form. The will will be dealt with later, see below, Chapter XIX.

15 Skrynnikov, *Tsarstvo terrora*, p. 240; cf. Kurbsky, *History*, p. 47. Taube and Kruse, 'Poslanie loganna . . .', pp. 33–4 who however call him Cheliadnin Barbatta, an evident confusion between Fedorov Cheliadnin and Gorbaty-Shuisky.

16 Taube and Kruse, op. cit., pp. 32 and 34. They mention a certain Garbato, evidently a distortion of Gorbatov, as having been accused by the Tsar of conspiring to place himself on the throne.

17 Floria, *Ivan Groznyi*, p. 193; see also Staden, *Land and Government*, p. 17, who attributed to the Metropolitan the power to take a prisoner sentenced to death from a jailer and set him free.

18 The word was derived from *oprich* meaning 'besides' or 'except', i.e., set aside, and was akin to *krome*.

19 See above, p. 175.

20 Floria, *Ivan Groznyi*, p. 183.

21 See above, note 16.

22 See above, Chapter X, p. 166.

23 Kurbsky, *History*, pp. 185–6.

24 Zimin, *Oprichnina*, p. 134, note 4.

25 Taube and Kruse, 'Poslanie loganna . . .', give 8 January, Zimin, *Oprichnina*, gives 2 February and Skrynnikov, *Tsarstvo terrora*, 15 February.

26 Karamzin, *Istoria*, IX, ch. 1, pp. 50–1.

27 Mikhail Temriukovich, brother of Maria.

28 Staden, *Land and Government*, pp. 48ff.

29 Zimin, *Oprichnina*, pp. 136–7 points out that both Taube and Kruse and Kurbsky (*History*, p. 183) relate this incident; it is possible that he incurred the particular wrath of Ivan as a member of the Obolensky clan. See Skrynnikov, *Tsarstvo terrora*, p. 242, for details of the extermination of this clan.

30 Note that in England the property of those executed on a bill of attainder passed in Parliament was also confiscated. This loophole was extensively used by both Henry VII and Henry VIII.

31 Skrynnikov, *Tsarstvo terrora*, p. 243.

32 Ibid., p. 218.

33 In Suzdal' 612 service gentry were serving in the regiments, in Mozhaisk 486, in Viaz'ma 314. Skrynnikov, *Tsarstvo terrora*, p. 221.

34   S.N. Bogatyrev, *The Sovereign and His Councillors*, p. 217.
35   Taube and Kruse, 'Poslanie loganna . . .', p. 35.
36   Ibid., p. 38 .
37   Ibid., p. 36. The two have an interest in painting the scene in particularly black colours, but there is enough evidence to show that they were not far wrong.
38   Likhachev and Lur'e, eds, *Poslania Ivana Groznogo,* Ivan to Vasily Griaznoi, 1574, pp. 371–2.
39   See Skrynnikov, *Tsarstvo terrora*, pp. 247ff. for a list of the Iaroslavskys, Rostovskys, Starodubskys, Obolenskys, untitled boyars and *pomeshchiki* who were expelled to Kazan' in 1565.
40   It is noteworthy that Kurbsky who belonged to the Iaroslavsky princes was outraged by the confiscation of the lands of some of them. In 1603 Prince D.M. Pozharsky, the future hero of the Time of Troubles, petitioned Tsar Boris Godunov about the lands confiscated from his grandfather who had been exiled to Kazan', ibid., pp. 245 and 252.
41   Skrynnikov, *Tsarstvo terrora*, p. 262, note 25.
42   See above, Chapter VII, p. 113.
43   Ibid., p. 221.
44   Karamzin, *Istoria*, IX, ch. 3, p. 53.
45   Notably Platonov who is positively scathing about the notion. On the other hand Floria, writing in 1999, points out that according to all the evidence, Ivan 'fell for' Maria, *Ivan Groznyi*, p. 139.
46   Quoted by H. Graham, in Schlichting, 'News from Muscovy . . .' p. 263, note 175.
47   Staden, *Land and Government*, pp. 17–18. The social composition of the *oprichiniki* as given by Staden differs somewhat from that given by most Russian historians, in that he says it was drawn from the *strel'tsy*, who were not gently born. He also stresses the presence of foreigners.
48   See his *Muscovy and the Mongols, Cross-Cultural Influences on the Steppe Frontier. 1304–1589, passim.*
49   Ostrowski, *Muscovy and the Mongols*, pp. 102–3. Ostrowski also attributes to Mongol influence the 'introduction of the principle of collective guilt' practised by Ivan. I regard this as much older, and derived from the principle of collective responsibility inherited from Germanic, not Mongol, law. See above, p. 171. But perhaps the Goths also derived it from the steppe?
50   See Maureen Perrie, *The Image of Ivan the Terrible in Russian Folklore*, Cambridge University Press, 1987, pp. 73ff.
51   G. Vernadsky, *The Mongols and Russia*, pp. 28–30. The Mongol Imperial Guard bears a distinct resemblance to Peter the Great's guards regiments. But B.Vladimirtsov (*Obshchestvenyi stroi Mongolov: Mongolskii kochevoi feodalizm*, Leningrad, 1934) and particularly the study by A.E. Hudson of Kazak social structure in 1938 mention a social group which Hudson describes as 'bodyguards, friends or companions, recruited from sons of high officials, known as the nokod, who were free, usually of high birth and were bound by a purely personal oath of allegiance to the khan whom they served'.
52   An alternative source has been proposed by V.I. Koretsky, the only historian ever to my knowledge to ask where the idea of the *oprichnina* came from. He suggests that Ivan derived it from the Buddhist Tale of Barlaam and Josaphat, eastern in origin, but respected in Russia as it was supposed to have been written by St John Chrysostom. In the story a king has a son who converts to Christianity. A wise man proposed to him to divide his kingdom with his son, and see who succeeded best, each in his own religion. The king does so, and in his cities Josaphat 'destroyed idolatrous temples and built a temple for

Christ and converted his people and his name outshone that of his father'. Whereupon the king renounced idolatry, abdicated his kingdom and made a holy end. Josaphat in turn called an assembly of the people, and now that his father was no longer there to oppose him, declared his intention to abdicate and lead a life of holiness. Ivan knew the story for he mentions it in his letter to Kurbsky, but there does not seem to be any real parallel between his *oprichnina* and *zemshchina* and Barlaam's division of his country.

CHAPTER XII War in Livonia and the *Zemskii Sobor* of 1566

1 R. Hellie, *Enserfment and Military Change*, pp.175ff.
2 The quotation is from Roberts, *The Early Vasas*, p. 201.
3 I have drawn extensively on Roberts, *The Early Vasas* in these pages.
4 Ibid., p. 201.
5 The commercial considerations involved in the Baltic wars of the 1560s ranged widely, involving the Hansa and Lübeck, Danzig, the Dutch, the Poles, Swedes and Danes and the Russians. The story is too long and complicated to retell here.
6 Negotiations took place between the Swedish envoy and the Governor of Novgorod in accordance with Ivan's refusal to recognize the King of Sweden as an equal and receive his envoy in Moscow. W. Kirchner, *The Rise of the Baltic Question*, Greenwood Press, Westport, Conn., 1970, p. 177, note 64.
7 Roberts, op. cit., pp. 233–5.
8 Donnert, writing in 1954, postulates a deep gulf between the treacherous boyars who opposed the war in Livonia and the military servitors loyal to Ivan, and also posits the existence of a powerful group around Metropolitan Afanasii striving for the overthrow of Ivan and his regime. Russia, in Donnert's view, was on the verge of a civil war which paralysed her military effort. *Der livländische Ordensritterstaat*, pp. 50ff.
9 Schlichting, 'A Brief Account', p. 217. Graham gives the year 1564 for this collective protest; elsewhere it is dated 1565.
10 Floria, *Ivan Groznyi*, pp. 205–6.
11 Skrynnikov (*Tsarstvo terrora*, p. 273), who also points out that the signatories of the sureties for Vorotynsky give an indication of the grouping of boyars and nobles opposed to the *oprichnina*.
12 Floria, *Ivan Groznyi*, pp. 201–2.
13 See T.S. Willan, *Early History of the Russia Company*, passim.
14 See Esper, 'A Sixteenth-Century Russian Arms Embargo', pp. 180–96, for a lucid account of the commercial problems underlying the war in the Baltic, and in particular for a refutation of the generally held idea that the embargo was instrumental in preventing Russia from importing weapons without which she would be unable to defeat her enemies in the Baltic. In the sixteenth century there was no generally agreed definition of what constituted 'war supplies' or contraband of war. Queen Elizabeth was accused by the Senate of Cologne in 1561 of exporting arms to Russia and denied it indignantly. In 1560 King Sigismund wrote to Elizabeth threatening to stop the trade to Narva because 'the Muscovite was an enemy to all liberty under heavens'. Esper, p. 191. See also Willan, op. cit., p. 63: 'The evidence [of Ivan's demand for arms] comes largely from those who opposed the sending of arms to Russia and from Elizabeth's denials.'
15 Willan, op. cit., pp. 56ff.
16 Zimin, *Oprichnina*, p. 153; PSRL XIII, pt 2, p. 396.
17 SIRIO, 71, p. 26. Prince M.I. Vorotynsky sat at the high table with Prince I.D. Bel'sky and Prince I.F. Mstislavsky.

18   V.M. Iur'ev Zakhar'in became a prominent member of the *oprichnina*.
19   S.N. Bogatyrev, 'Blizhniaia duma v tret'ei chetverti XVI v. I, 1550s, II, 1560–1570, III, 1571–2', *Arkheograficheskii ezhegodnik za 1992*, Moscow 1994, pp. 119–33; *za 1993*, Moscow 1995, pp. 94–112; *za 1994*, Moscow 1996, pp. 64–89.
20   See Floria, *Ivan Groznyi*, p. 203 and *PSRL*, XXIX, 'Aleksandro-Nevskaia letopis', *prodolzhenie*, pp. 350–1, said to reflect the views of Ivan himself.
21   This is called a *komissiia* by Zimin, but there is no evidence of the existence of a commission nor discussion of what a commission was in the Russian context. For a more detailed account of the negotiations see the article by A.A. Zimin, 'Zemskii sobor 1566 g', in *Istoricheskie zapiski*, no. 71, 1962, pp. 217–23.
22   One wonders whether the idea of a personal meeting, at which King Sigismund should visit and be entertained by Tsar Ivan in his camp, who would thus grant him a lower personal status than his own, was influenced in any way by recollections of the meeting of Henry VIII of England and Francis I of France on the Field of the Cloth of Gold.
23   M. N. Tikhomirov, 'Soslovno-predstavitel'nye uchrezhdenia (zemskie sobory) v Rossii XVI veka', *Voprosy istorii*, no. 5, 1958, pp. 217–35; A.A. Zimin, 'Zemskii Sobor', in *Istoricheskie zapiski*, no. 71, 1962, pp. 217–33.
24   Ibid.
25   Zimin, 'Zemskii Sobor', in *Istoricheskie zapiski*, no. 71, 1962, pp. 220–1. Ivan would receive Polotsk and sixteen towns (forts?) on the Lithuanian bank of the Dvina, fifteen forts on the Russian side of the river, Riga, four other towns in Polish hands and all Livonian territory then occupied by Russia.
26   *PSRL*, XIII, pt 2, 2, Tsarstvennaia kniga, p. 402.
27   G. Fletcher, *Of the Russe Commonwealth*, ed. R. Pipes, Harvard University Press, Cambridge, Mass., 1966, p. 22.
28   Karamzin, *Istoria*, IX, ch. 1, pp. 73ff.
29   The official chronicle also does not mention a *zemskii sobor*.
30   See M. Raeff, *The Decembrist Movement*, Prentice-Hall, Englewood Cliffs, NJ, 1966, and my 'Spain and the Decembrists', *European Studies Review*, III, 2, April 1973, pp. 141–56.
31   Comparative studies of the *Zemskii sobor* and Western assemblies of estates have been undertaken in Russia by Latkin, Chicherin, Kliuchevsky, Tikhomirov and many others.
32   Zimin, *Oprichnina*, pp. 162–6.
33   Skrynnikov, *Tsarstvo terrora*, p. 267
34   The word usually used in Russian for a fully fledged institution of a parliamentary type is the clumsy formula *soslovno-predstavitel'noe*, 'representative of estates'. This is very unwieldy, both in English and in Russian. I propose shortening it to 'representative'. I am relying in these pages partly on Kliuchevsky, *Istoria soslovii v Rossii*, St Petersburg, 1918; Academic International reprint 1969, M.M. Tikhomirov, 'Soslovno-predstavitel'nie uchrezhdenia v Rossii XVI v', in *Rossiiskoe gosudarstvo XV–XVII vekov*, Moscow 1973, pp. 42–69, and Zimin, 'Zemskii Sobor 1566g.', as well as the standard histories by Kliuchevsky, Zimin, Skrynnikov and Floria. The literature on the subject of the *Zemskii sobor* in Russian is too vast to list.
35   Corresponding in this respect to the Elizabethan House of Commons, where according to J.E. Neale, there were no party politics, and election implied not choice of a candidate but approval. J.E. Neale, *The Elizabethan House of Commons*, London, 1976, pp. 65ff.
36   For a general discussion of the topic of 'estates' in sixteenth-century Russia see G. Stökl, 'Gab es im Moskauer Staat Stände?', in *Der Russische Staat im*

Mittelalter und Früher Neuzeit, Franz Steiner, Wiesbaden, 1981, pp. 146–67; also Cherepnin, 'Zemskiye sobory' in Druzhinin, ed. *Absoliutizm v Rossii*, pp. 92–133.

37 This very sketchy outline is based partly on J.M. Huttle, *The Service City, State and Townsmen in Russia, 1600–1899*, Harvard University Press, Cambridge, Mass., 1979, pp. 1–21.

38 Stökl, op. cit., pp. 147 and 151.

39 The Trinity, Spaso-Iaroslavsky, Spaso-Efim'ev (Suzdal'), Nizhnii Novgorod, Pskov Pechersky monasteries.

40 Those who signed the boyar *prigovor* included I.D. Bel'sky, I. F. Mstislavsky, I.V. Sheremetev, major and minor, M. I. Vorotynsky, V.S. Serebrianoi, N.R. Iur'ev Zakhar'in (Anastasia's brother), I.Y Chebotov, I.M. Vorontsov, M.Y. Morozov, V.M. Iur'ev Zakhar'in, V.D. Danilov, V.Y. Maly Trakhaniot, and S.V. Iakovlev. I.P. Fedorov also signed the *prigovor*, though he does not figure on the list of those present. Zimin, *Oprichnina*, p. 196, note 4.

41 Zimin, *Oprichnina*, pp. 192ff.

42 See the text and variants in I. F. Berry, ed., *The English Works of Giles Fletcher, the Elder*, University of Wisconsin Press, Madison, 1964.

43 The text edited by R. Pipes in 1966 is the 1591 English edition, but it refers to additions and variants in the Lloyd Berry edition.

44 In the last years of Henry VIII councillors 'at large' 'were excluded from the Privy Council but were sworn councillors nonetheless'. Guy, 'Privy Council', in *Revolution Reassessed*, ed. Coleman and Starkey, pp. 59–86. Guy concludes that 'what counted was the Crown's ability to advise those whom it preferred not to attend Parliament, Privy Council or Star Chamber to stay away' (p. 82).

45 Quoted from S.N. Bogatyrev, 'Tsarskii sovet v sochineniakh Dzh. Fletchera i V.O. Kliuchevskogo', in *V.O. Kliuchevsky. Sbornik Materialov, vyp.*1, Penza, 1995. The author points out that Kliuchevsky had adhered to the idea of a privy council composed of *duma* boyars as distinct from ordinary boyars in his early work on foreigners in Russia (1866, sixteen years before his *Boiarskaa Duma* appeared) but subsequently revised his ideas to conform with the predominant juridical concept of history, which postulated that every boyar had a right to sit in the *Duma* (pp. 46 7), and that 'By its nature the Boyar Duma was a legislative institution ... a constitutional institution with broad influence but without a constitutional charter...' (quoted by Bogatyrev, p. 235, from *Boiarskaia Duma*).

46 Bogatyrev, 'Blizhniaia duma v tretei chetverti XVI v.', part II, 1560–1570.

47 See Bogatyrev, 'Administrativnye sistemy Tiudorov i Riurikovichei' in *Zerkalo istorii*, ed. Basovskaia. Bogatyrev suggests an analogy with the Tudor Privy Council as restructured in the 1540s after the execution of Cromwell.

48 Not that the Lords were a representative body, since the peers did not represent others but attended in person.

49 See, e.g., Skrynnikov, *Velikii gosudar' Ivan Vasil'evich*, I, p. 411.

50 See Bogatyrev, *The Sovereign and his Counsellors*, p. 79. Some members of the English Privy Council could act as judges in Star Chamber. See Guy, 'Privy Council', and the Privy Council could act as an ultimate court of appeal, but rarely did so. See Neale, *Elizabethan House of Commons*, p. 9.

51 The forty-three officials are sometimes counted in with the representatives of the *dvoriane*, which seems logical since they came mainly from middle or lower noble families or even clerical families like Anfim, the son of the priest Sylvester, a *d'iak* in Smolensk. See Skrynnikov, *Tsarstvo terrora*, pp. 268ff; Zimin, *Oprichnina*, pp. 167ff.

52 Zimin, *Oprichnina*, pp. 172–3 provides a complete list.

53 From which he draws the conclusion that the principle of the compulsory representation of the towns did not exist.
54 M.N. Tikhomirov, *Rossiiskoe gosudarstvo XV–XVII vv*, Moscow, 1973, pp. 55ff.
55 J. Martin, 'Mobility, Forced Resettlement and Regional Identity in Muscovy', in *Culture and Identity in Muscovy, 1359–1584*, ed. A.M. Kleimola and G.D. Lehnhoff, *UCLA Slavic Studies*, New Series, Moscow,1997, pp. 431–49.
56 Zimin, *Oprichnina*, p. 176.
57 Tikhomirov, *Rossiiskoe gosudarstvo*, pp. 53–4; PSRL XXIX, *Aleksandro-Nevskaya letopis'*, pp. 350–1.
58 Zimin, *Zemskii Sobor 1566 god*, p. 222.
59 Ibid., p. 351.
60 Kliuchevsky uses the bureaucratic phrase 'po dolzhnosti', see his *Sochinenia*, vol. II, *kurs russkoi istorii*, part 2, Lecture XL, pp. 383ff.
61 J.L.H. Keep, 'The Decline of the Zemsky Sobor. Afterword', in *Power and the People, Essays on Russian History*, Boulder Col., 1995, pp. 82 and 73ff. for a summary of the debate among several historians, and notably J. Torke, on the question of the existence of genuine representative institutions in Russia.
62 S.M. Kashtanov in 'O tipe russkogo gosudarstva XIV–XVI vv', in *Chtenia pamiati V. B. Kobrina: Problemy otechestvennoi istorii i kul'tury perioda feodalizma*, Moscow, 1992, p. 86, had put forward the view that though Russia was following the general economic path taken by other countries in Europe, it was seven to eight centuries behind, and that it was vital to take this backwardness into account in any comparative approach. Quoted in S.N. Bogatyrev, '"Smirennaia groza." K probleme interpretatsii istochnikov po istorii politicheskoi kul'tury Moskovskoi Rusi', in *Istochnikovedenie i kraevedenie v kul'ture Rossii. K 50-letiu Sigurda Ottovicha Schmidta. Istoriko-arkhivnomu Institutu*, Moscow, 2000, pp. 79–93.
63 The word 'state' (*gosudarstvo* in modern Russian) is often used interchangeably with 'empire' (*tsarstvo*) or realm.
64 See Inge Auerbach's illuminating analysis of Kurbsky's political conceptions, which were probably typical of a Russian aristocrat, in 'Die politische Vorstellungen . . .', *JGOE*, 117, 1969, pp. 177–83.
65 I am paraphrasing here the very perceptive article by S.N. Bogatyrev, cited in n. 15, at p. 80.
66 See Neale, *Elizabethan House of Commons*, p. 417 for a list of Elizabeth's Parliaments. In the course of a reign lasting forty-seven years there were thirteen sessions of Parliament. The rest of the time Elizabeth managed without.
67 Fletcher, *Of the Russe Commonwealth*, p. 23. His use of the word Parliament has misled many a Russian. In general the mixture of Herberstein and Horsey on which his work is based leads to odd remarks.

CHAPTER XIII The Boyar Plot: 1) the Letters to King Sigismund

1 Schlichting, 'A Brief Account', *CASS*, IX, 2, p. 248. And note 140.
2 Piskarevsky Chronicle, *PSRL*, XXXIV p. 190: Zimin, *Oprichnina*, p. 203: 'o oprichnine, chto ne dostoit semu byti'.
3 There is very little evidence of what they did indeed think, but Skrynnikov quotes a letter of 20 December 1566 from a German trader in Nuremberg, quoted by Karamzin, which referred to the discontent of the nobles. *Tsarstvo terrora*, pp. 288–9 and note 63.
4 Skrynnikov, *Tsarstvo*, p. 298 suggests that the demonstration took place while

the Lithuanian embassy was still in Moscow and that Ivan hastened their departure so that he could deal with it.

5 The functions of the *koniushii* are stated to be head of the *prikaz* concerned with horses according to the dictionary of the Russian language of the eleventh to the seventeenth centuries. It would be, as in other countries, an extremely important function in a society in which the horse was the only means of transportation and locomotion.

6 See Skrynnikov, *Tsarstvo terrora*, pp. 294–5, drawing on Schlichting for details and some of the names of the condemned; far smaller figures (fifty *dvoriane*) are given in Skrynnikov's earlier *Sviatiteli i vlasti*, 1990; Schlichting, 'A Brief Account', pp. 248–9. Taube and Kruze, 'Poslanie Ioganna . . .', pp. 42–3. Kurbsky also gave the figure of 200.

7 E.D. Morgan and C.H. Coote, eds, *Early Voyages and Travels in Russia and Persia by Anthony Jenkinson and Other Englishmen*, Hakluyt Society, London 1886, vol. I, pp. 186ff. Jenkinson is probably referring to the same incident quoted above, p. 207. He adds that Ivan also arrested all the families of the victims, made a hole in the river and drowned them all. This adds to the confusion since it is not easy to make a hole in a river in June. However there is considerable doubt about the date of this letter for, though Jenkinson does end it with the words: 'from Kholmogory this 26 of June 1566', in a later report he states that he embarked on 4 May for St Nicholas and arrived on 11 July, and in Moscow on 23 August. The editor has added a footnote to the effect that Jenkinson evidently wrote July for June by mistake in this second letter, whereas from the context it is much more likely that the editor's dating is wrong and that the date 26 June, added by him, should be corrected to 26 July 1566. This makes it possible for Jenkinson to be referring to the repression after the *sobor*. See Morgan and Coote, op. cit., vol. II, pp. 186 and 189. Anthony Jenkinson says that these events were also witnessed by his servant Edward Webbe, aged twelve. Webbe wrote a brief account of his many adventures which included his capture by the Crimeans during the fire in Moscow in 1571, and a period as a slave in Kaffa, from which he was ransomed, and later as a galley slave in Turkey. See E. Webbe *His Travails*, London, 1590, pp. 3ff.; Webbe says that some eighty-three Danish prisoners taken aboard a 'freebooter' (privateer) at Narva in 1570 had been impaled, 'spitted upon powles as a man would put a Pig unpon a Spitte and so vij score were handled in that manner' (p. 19). He adds that Ivan also arrested all the families of the victims, made a hole in the river and drowned them all.

8 Prince P.M. Shcheniatev, a leading general, already arrested, was very cruelly put to death in August 1566, and the names of four of those who were executed for protesting after the *sobor*, are known (see above, p. 207 and see P.A. Sadikov, *Ocherki po istorii oprichniny*, reprint. Mouton, The Hague, 1969, p. 29; Skrynnikov, *Tsarstvo terrora*, p. 294 and note 96). Shcheniatev had also offended by taking the cowl without asking permission of the Tsar a few years before. This had been forbidden in 1565.

9 Floria, *Ivan Groznyi*, p. 208.

10 Karamzin, *Istoria*, IX, ch. 1, p. 59, supposes that Sylvester exercised considerable influence on Filipp's image of Ivan. But it is not certain that Sylvester ever went to Solovki.

11 See Staden, *Land and Government*, p. 20. He signed the sentence of the boyar curia in the Assembly of 1566 in third place after Bel'sky and Mstislavsky, Skrynnikov, *Tsarstvo terrora*, p. 292.

12 Skrynnikov, *Tsarstvo terrora*, p. 294.

13 See in general Zimin, *Oprichnina*, pp. 240ff. These conditions were duly

recorded in a *Zapis o postavlenii Filippa*, signed by some of the archbishops (Pimen of Novgorod but not German of Kazan').

14 Skrynnikov, *Tsarstvo terrora*, p. 217.

15 Kurbsky, *Correspondence*, Ivan's first letter to Kurbsky, passim. One must remember that it had been written only three years before.

16 'Ivan IV', in 'Poslanie v Kirillobelozerskii monastyr', in Likhachev and Lur'e, eds, *Poslania Ivana Groznogo*, pp. 352–3

17 Floria, *Ivan Groznyi*, p. 214.

18 Skrynnikov, *Tsarstvo terrora*, p. 341, note 31; Sadikov, 'Iz istorii oprichniny', p. 210.

19 'Stikhi pokaiannie' ('I came into this vale of tears, as a naked boy, and naked will I depart . . .') in Dmitriev and Likhachev, eds, *Pamiatniki literatury*.

20 Taube and Kruse, op. cit., pp. 38ff. Some of this applies to a slightly later time.

21 Roberts, *The Early Vasas*, pp. 225ff. In the years 1562 to 1567 the Swedish high court issued more than 300 death sentences for an enormous range of serious and trivial offences; many were not carried out but were commuted for heavy fines. Extra-judicial torture was widely used to obtain the names of accomplices in cases of sedition. It is generally believed that torture was prohibited by common law in England at this time, but see Clifford Hall, 'Some Perspectives on the Use of Torture in Bacon's Time and the Question of his "Virtue"', *Anglo-American Law Review*, XVIII, 1989, pp. 289–321 on the frequent use of extra-judicial torture in England.

22 See above, Chapter XII, p. 192.

23 Zimin (*Oprichnina*, p. 261) suggests that Ivan thought a marriage with Catherine would entitle him to become heir to the Polish–Lithuanian throne.

24 *SIRIO*, 129, no. 12, *stateinii spisok* of the boyar Ivan Mikhailovich Vorontsov, 20 July 1567 to 4 June 1569, at pp. 134ff.

25 Sigismund Augustus had been both elected and crowned before the death of his father Sigismund I. Floria, *Russko-Pol'skie otnoshenia*, p. 32.

26 Such an outcome was even hinted at in negotiations at the time between the Russian and the Polish envoys. *SIRIO*, 71, pp. 31ff.

27 She was then over forty and eventually married Stephen Bathory when he was elected King of Poland in 1577.

28 *SIRIO*, 129, pp. 153–6, 11 July 1567, the Russian account of negotiations with the Swedish envoys.

29 *. . . niotkuda pana sebe dostat' ne khoteli krome ego roda to est' ego samogo i detei ego.*

30 Skrynnikov, *Tsarstvo terrora*, pp. 307ff. Was it a coincidence, Skrynnikov asks, that not long before, in February 1567, the large crown estate of Kowel was bestowed by Sigismund on Kurbsky? The deed of grant referred to the oppression of a Christian people and to the cruel *panovania* ('rulership') by Ivan which led people to flee to Lithuania where they were lavishly rewarded by the King.

31 See Zimin, *Oprichnina*, p. 274.

32 Likhachev and Lur'e, ed. *Poslania Ivana Groznogo*. In the 1951 edition the letters are printed in sixteenth-century Russian, with a translation into modern Russian which, not surprisingly in view of the date of publication, leaves out the references to God, Jesus Christ, the defence of the Orthodox religion etc. They are also printed in *SIRIO*, 71 (see under dates). I do not see who but Ivan could have written them, at any time, nor who could have faked them in the seventeenth century and why.

33 Likhachev and Lur'e, *Poslania Ivana Groznogo*, Prince I.D. Bel'sky to Sigismund, pp. 417ff.

34 Ibid., but here I have drawn on both the original old Russian text, pp. 241–8, and the translation into modern Russian, pp. 417–21.

35 Ibid., p. 419. In a commentary on these letters, Ia.S. Lur'e suggests that the 'freedom' mentioned by Ivan must be the concept of free will used extensively in religious debate at the time, particularly by the Catholics (pp. 510–11). However it is clear that Ivan is referring to freedom of action, but it is difficult to be precise in view of the large number of different words used at the time (and today) to express freedom. The *Poslania* were published in 1951, just before the Doctors' Plot, which may have induced a certain discretion in the treatment of the topic.

36 The grandfather of I.D. Bel'sky had fled Lithuania in 1482 because of the persecution of the Orthodox by the Catholics; his great uncle fled in 1499 with all his lands. I.D. Bel'sky had secured a safe conduct from the Polish–Lithuanian King to flee back in 1562.Ibid., Notes, pp. 669–70.

37 Jagiello was Grand Duke of Lithuania, and married Jadwiga, heiress of Poland in 1386, thus becoming also king of Poland. Whereupon his cousin Vitovt disputed the succession with Jagiello, and emerged as Grand Prince of Lithuania until his death in 1430.

38 The marriage of Sigismund Augustus to Barbara Radziwill was very unpopular, and she died a few months after her coronation. She is said to have been poisoned at the instigation of her mother-in-law, Bona Sforza.

39 Both were ex-princes of military orders of chivalry, the Prince of Prussia of the Teutonic Order and the Prince of Courland of the (Livonian) Order of the Sword.

40 *Ustanavlivat' zakon dlia chuzhogo gosudarstva'*, see *SIRIO*, 71, p. 497. Paragraphs omitted in the 1951 translation.

41 The use of the phrase '*rastlen umom*' either by Ivan himself or by Vorotynsky, raises an important point. In Ivan's letter dated 1577 to Kurbsky, (*Correspondence*, p. 187 at p.188) Ivan writes: 'You write that I am mentally deranged', using almost these same words: 'Yaz rastlen razumon' as he used in the letter from Ivan/Vorotynsky to Chodkewicz. Skrynnikov, *Tsarstvo terrora*, p.309 suggests that this may indicate that Ivan believed Kurbsky to have written the letters from Sigismund to the boyars, and that they therefore existed. But he adds that Kurbsky never in fact used this phrase, only Ivan, so we are none the wiser. It is of course extremely unlikely that a boyar (or a *d'iak*) in the Office of Foreign Affairs would have written about Ivan as 'mentally deranged' to a foreigner, let alone a Russian. Only Ivan himself could do it.

42 Isaiah, 14, 5. 4 onwards. The pot calling the kettle black.

43 Skrynnikov, *Tsarstvo terrora*, pp. 308–9.

44 Likhachev and Lur'e, *Poslania Ivana Groznogo*, p. 675, note 18. In the instructions to envoys, they were told to say: 'we know nothing about an *oprichnina*; the lord decides who is to be near him and who is to be far away'; see also *SIRIO*, 71, pp. 331, 593, 597, where the letters are printed.

45 See Donnert, *Der livländische Ordensritterstaat und Russland*, pp. 236ff.

46 Tolstoy, *England and Russia*, p. 34, 10 April 1567. There is some confusion about the date of Jenkinson's visit and whether he made one journey or two to Russia in 1566/67. See articles by H.R Huttenbach, ' Antony Jenkinson's 1566 and 1567 missions to Muscovy from unpublished Sources', *CASS*, vol. 9, no. 2, Summer 1975, pp. 179–203. Huttenbach argues that Jenkinson returned to England in autumn 1567, before the sea route became impossible and sailed again to Russia in the spring. He bases his case on the supposed existence of a missing letter from Queen Elizabeth which can only be fitted in by postulating an unmentioned journey by Jenkinson. On the problem of dates see also note 7 above.

47 This interview is not mentioned in any of the contemporary dispatches because its subject was so secret, and it is referred to for the first time in a personal note sent by Ivan to Jenkinson's interpreter, and later himself an envoy, Daniel Sylvester, printed in Tolstoy, op. cit., pp. 179ff. No. 39 and No. 40, dated 29 November 1576.

48 Likhachev and Lur'e, *Poslania Ivana Groznogo*, pp. 417ff, at p. 422, from Prince I.D. Bel'sky. According to Jenkinson, Tolstoy, op. cit., p. 26, and to the Polish chronicler Martin Belskii, Kozlov was seized and impaled. Zimin, *Oprichnina*, pp. 267–8.

49 Tolstoy, op. cit., p. 38, Jenkinson, November 1567; Ivan expected to hear Elizabeth's reply by St Peter's day (29 July or another St Peter?).

50 See above, pp. 213.

51 Sigismund had written to Elizabeth directly to explain his interference with navigation to Russia, not only because of its effect on him but because it affected religion and the whole of Christianity. See Tolstoy, op. cit., pp. 30–3, three letters of 13 July 1566, 13 March 1568 and 6 December 1569.

52 Soviet historians e.g. Zimin, reject the assertion that the service gentry taken into the *oprichnina* were of baser birth, but both Staden and Schlichting assert that they were men of little substance and no personal qualities. Staden was a German and not precisely savoury.

53 S.A. Kozlov and Z.V. Dmitrieva, *Nalogi v Rossii do XIX veka*, St Petersburg, 1999, conveniently sums up taxation policy (pp. 28ff).

54 Donnert, op. cit., pp. 236ff.

55 A Russian embassy to Poland–Lithuania and a Polish-Lithuanian embassy to Moscow had continued useless discussions on terms for a truce, which are recorded in *SIRIO*, 71, pp. 521–54 and 554–63. Donnert, op cit., at p. 236, argues that the fact that his boyars refused to go over to Sigismund was considered by Ivan as a great victory over Kurbsky's treasonable efforts to win over Russian nobles to Sigismund's side.

56 It is near Minsk, and now in Belarus.

CHAPTER XIV The Boyar Plot: 2) the Executions

1 See H.E. Dembkowski, *The Union of Lublin – Polish Federation in the Golden Age*, Columbia University Press, New York, 1982, pp. 82ff. and for the financial burden on Lithuania, pp. 119ff.

2 Ibid., pp. 117ff.

3 See e.g. Staden, *Land and Government*, pp. 20ff, where the chronology is all wrong.

4 *SIRIO*, 71, p. 563. Skrynnikov, *Tsarstvo terrora*, p. 316, suggests that the real reason for the withdrawal was news of a new plot in the *zemshchina*, led by Fedorov, which Ivan had received. Schlichting, 'A Brief Account', p. 317, also mentions the plotting of the boyars, declaring that some thirty committed themselves in writing. See also Floria, *Ivan Groznyi*, p. 218.

5 Zimin, *Reformy,* pp. 277–9.

6 Ibid., Staden, *Land and Government*, pp. 19–20.

7 Schlichting, quoted from Skrynnikov, *Tsarstvo terrora*, p. 317. Schlichting's dating of the event to 1567 is correct. He also suggests that the conspiracy was betrayed by Vladimir of Staritsa himself, who obtained the names of the conspirators from Fedorov, and the other boyars and passed them on to Ivan. See also Floria, *Ivan Groznyi*, p. 217.

8 Staden, *Land and Government,* pp. 21 and 24

9 Zimin, *Oprichnina*, p. 274, note 1.

10 Skrynnikov, *Tsarstvo terrora*, pp. 308ff and 319. Schlichting states that the great Russian nobles were completely disunited and that Staritsky, Mstislavsky and Bel'sky asked Fedorov for a list of the conspirators on the grounds that others might wish to join, and then handed it over to Ivan. Indeed. Skrynnikov suggests that this was a *provokatsia* by Ivan, deliberately making use of Staritsky to ensure betrayal of the plot. See Schlichting, 'News from Muscovy', pp. 271–2 and Schlichting, 'A Brief Account', pp. 222–3, note 59.

11 Graham's note 61 on Schlichting, 'A Brief Account', p. 223.

12 Schlichting, 'A Brief Account', p. 223.

13 But did Kurbsky get his information by reading Schlichting's account in Poland, or even personally from him?

14 Skrynnikov, *Tsarstvo terrora*, p. 325. Skrynnikov argues that the Church Council was not supported by the Boyar Council.

15 Ibid., pp. 325–6.

16 Ibid., p. 324.

17 Taube and Kruse, 'Poslanie loganna . . .', pp. 39–41. The authors accuse Ivan of having the sixteen-year-old wife of his brother-in-law, Mikhail Temriukovich Cherkassky and her six-month-old son killed, laying the bodies in the yard of his palace where her husband was bound to pass by her body every day, but his dating seems rather unlikely. On 19 July 1568 Ivan sent his henchmen to collect as many women and girls as they could, of all classes, throw them into waggons and remove them from Moscow (probably to Aleksandrovskaia Sloboda); he then chose a few for himself and left the others to his *oprichniki*, and for six weeks he roamed around Moscow, burned and killed animals and everything that breathed. The women had to run around naked after chickens and were then shot. When he had finished with them, they were put back in the waggons and those who had survived were sent home to their husbands. There are echoes here of the harassment of Fedorov's lands and people, and a number of fantasies seem to have been merged together. But for once a date is given.

18 See Skrynnikov, *Tsarstvo terrora*, pp. 529ff., for a list of the killed which includes many retainers of Fedorov. Some were killed with swords or an axe; the lower orders were blown up with gunpowder. See also Taube and Kruse, 'Poslanie loganna . . .', pp. 40–1.

19 Skrynnikov, *Tsarstvo terrora*, p. 337. This was the end of the Cheliadnins

20 Schlichting, 'A Brief Account', pp. 224ff and see note 67; Taube and Kruse (p. 40) report that Ivan ordered his brother-in-law Mikhail Temriukovich Cherkassky to cut up his treasurer Khoziain Iur'evich into little pieces together with his wife and sons and two daughters, and to leave them lying in the open. (This sounds like a confused echo of the tale that Mikhail Temriukovich's wife and daughter were killed and left lying in the open.)

21 Staden confirms Schlichting's and Kurbsky's account with the addition that the naked peasants' wives were 'forced to catch chickens in the fields' (p. 21). One is sometimes led to wonder whether Staden read Schlichting's 'A Brief Account', and particularly whether Kurbsky had access to it in Lithuania in view of the similarity of their reports. But the *Sinodiki* do confirm much of what they write. See above all the careful summary by Skrynnikov, *Tsarstvo terrora*, pp. 529ff, where he gives three accounts of the extermination of Fedorov's people, and places Fedorov's death on 11 September 1568. Those killed are not always mentioned by name, but just lumped together as e.g. 'twenty of Fedorov's people'; in a number of cases their nameless wives and children are included. Many had their hands cut off and presumably died as a result, since on 11 September 1568 twenty-six people are stated in a *Sinodik* to have died as a result of this amputation.

22 On the white cowl, see Chapter IX.
23 Skrynnikov, *Tsarstvo terrora*, p. 327, quoted from the life of the Metropolitan Filipp, dating from the 1590s and written in the Solovki monastery. See ibid., p. 324 and n. 159. Archbishop German Polev of Kazan', who had once protested to Ivan about the *oprichnina* was one of the few to support Filipp. Zimin, *Oprichnina*, p. 250.
24 Roberts, *The Early Vasas*, p. 239, footnote. However, according to Russian accounts their envoys were manhandled and robbed in Sweden.
25 Ibid., pp. 236ff.
26 *SIRIO*, 129, pp. 164 and 197.
27 Skrynnikov, *Tsarstvo terrora*, p. 352 who argues that this enabled Ivan to benefit from the capital of the English company for his *oprichnina* activities. There is no evidence of such investment in Russia by the Russia Company and it seems highly unlikely.
28 Morgan and Coote, *Early Voyages*, I, p. xlix.
29 Tolstoy, *England and Russia*, p. xxiii; it is possible that Ivan may also have been affected by the calumnies circulated in Moscow by interlopers against the agents of the Russia Company.
30 Ibid., pp. 43 and 44ff., 26 June 1568, delivered February 1569.
31 Ibid., pp. 68, the Tsar to Elizabeth, 20 June 1569; pp. 71ff., contemporary translation into English of Ivan to Elizabeth of 20 June 1569.
32 Willan, *The Early History of the Russia Company*, p. 104.
33 Ibid., pp. 107–9; Morgan and Coote, op. cit., II, p. 184.
34 Willan, op. cit., pp. 112ff; Morgan and Coote, op. cit., II, pp. 280–3 and Tolstoy, op. cit., pp. 74ff. It is not clear whether Savin negotiated only with the Russia Company or also with the English government. Ivan was worried about the accuracy of the translation of documents from English in the original which he insisted on, into Russian, and there was correspondence on the question between Cecil and the Russia Company, Tolstoy, op. cit., pp. 82–4. The draft treaty and the permission to the Russia Company were both written in Russia and carried to England by Savin (ibid., p. 90).
35 Floria, *Ivan Groznyi*, p. 260.
36 Kurat, 'The Turkish Expedition to Astrakhan' in 1569', *SEER*, 40, no. 94, December 1961, pp. 7–23. See also for the Turkish background, A. Bennigsen and C. Quelquejay, 'L'expédition turque contre Astrakhan en 1569', *Cahiers du Monde Russe et Soviétique*, 8, Paris, 1967, pp. 427–46.
37 There was also a plan to cut a canal at Suez (Kurat, 'The Turkish Expedition to Astrakhan' in 1569', p. 13, note 27, from the Ottoman Archives).
38 Floria, *Ivan Groznyi*, p. 262.
39 The tribute continued to be paid until the reign of Peter the Great.
40 Skrynnikov, *Tsarstvo terrora*, p. 355.
41 In contemporary German flyleafs and brochures Staritsky is often called the Tsar's brother; so he is in Russian sources because in Russian a cousin is a 'brother of second birth' (*dvoiurodnyi brat*). Ivan can thus be accused of fratricide. See A. Käppeler, *Ivan Groznyj im Spiegel der ausländische Zeitschriften seiner Zeit. Ein Beitrag zur Geschichte Westlichen Russlandsbilde*, Bern and Frankfurt am Main, 1972. Vasily Vladimirovich Staritsky died in 1574.

CHAPTER XV Armageddon

1 See above, Chapter IX.
2 According to some authors, after the fall of Sylvester and Adashev.

3　Staden, *Land and Government*, pp. 17–18.
4　See Dembkowski, *The Union of Lublin*, and particularly Chapter IX, pp. 175ff. Titles were also reaffirmed. There were no Polish princes, but the Lithuanian Gediminovichi, like the Riurikovichi, were all princes.
5　To use Bogatyrev's word.
6　See above, Chapter IX, pp. 155–6.
7　Staden, op. cit., p. 32.
8　Schlichting, 'A Brief Account', p. 258.
9　*SIRIO*, 129, pp. 124ff.
10　See Skrynnikov, *Tsarstvo terrora*, p. 363, who observes that the figure of 90,000 is given in the text of Taube and Kruse edited by Roginski, but the more accurate edition is that of G. Hoff, published in 1581 in Germany which I have not been able to consult.
11　A particular form of corporal punishment used to force debtors to pay their debts.
12　Schlichting, 'A Brief Account', p. 236 and see Taube and Kruse, 'Poslanie Ioganna . . .', p. 49 and Floria, *Ivan Groznyi*, pp. 240ff.
13　Floria, *Ivan Groznyi*, p. 240. Schlichting, 'A Brief Account', p. 236.
14　Floria, *Ivan Groznyi*, pp. 43–5. I have drawn extensively on Skrynnikov, Floria and on the German witnesses, Staden, Schlichting (in Hugh Graham's translation and notes) and Taube and Kruse in this account.
15　Skrynnikov points out that Kurbsky was also highly regarded in Vienna at this time and was negotiating with Maximilian II through the Abbé Cyrus for a Russo/Habsburg alliance against the Porte. Nothing came of it. See Ia. S.Lur'e, 'Donesenia agenta Maksimiliana II abbata Tsira o peregovorakh s A. M. Kurbskim v 1569', *Arkheograficheskii ezhegodnik za 1957*, Moscow, 1958, p. 456.
16　Schlichting, 'A Brief Account', p. 238; Zimin, *Oprichnina*, p. 300, note 4. Floria, *Ivan Groznyi*, p. 242, adds that new evidence of the events in Narva has recently been found in a German pamphlet, apparently by an eyewitness.
17　According to Staden, *Land and Government*, p. 32, many *oprichniki* went north as far as the White Sea and requisitioned the daughters of rich merchants and peasants in the name of Ivan. One may wonder if this is not rather an attempt to fulfil orders from the Tsar to arrange a bride-show for him after the death of Maria Temriukovna.
18　R.G. Skrynnikov, *Oprichnyi terror*, Leningrad, 1969, pp. 27–30; Zimin, *Oprichnina*, pp. 300ff.
19　Skrynnikov, *Tsarstvo terrora*, p. 369.
20　Staden, *Land and Government*, p. 121.
21　Skrynnikov, *Oprichnyi terror*, p. 374, Karamzin, *Istoria*, VIII, notes, p. 103, note 485, gives various versions and dates for the death of Kornily, one of which says that Ivan himself beheaded Kornily having met him outside Pskov.
22　Skrynnikov, *Oprichnyi terror*, p. 375 rejects the influence of Nikola on the Tsar, and attributes the escape of the city to the fact that Ivan had already before removed several hundred families and distributed them in various towns. But the legend of Nikola lived and thrived in the Chronicles of Pskov.
23　*SIRIO*, 71, pp. 630ff. The envoys were given a banquet at which Mikhail Temriukovich was present on 7 May (pp. 639–40).
24　Zimin, *Oprichnina*, p. 432, note 2.
25　*SIRIO*, 71, p. 677.
26　Skrynnikov, *Oprichnyi terror*, pp. 395–6.
27　Zimin, *Oprichnina*, p. 436.
28　See below, Chapter XIX, p. 319.

29 Not all the documents have survived, and I am relying here on V.A. Tumins, *Tsar Ivan's Reply to Jan Rokyta*, Mouton, The Hague, 1971, and L. Ronchi de Michelis, *Ivan il terribile – Jan Rokyta, disputa sul protestantesimo*, Claudiana editrice, Turin, 1979. I see no reason to assume that either of them hoped to convert the other. See Tumins, op. cit., p. 479 for the translation into English of the report by Rokyta on Ivan's questions and Rokyta's replies.

30 Parfeny Urodivy is the name under which the Canon of the Dread Angel, attributed to Ivan himself was written and circulated. See below, p. 319.

31 Tumins, op. cit., p. 15. Ivan was in a hurry to get rid of this embassy which was holding up his projected executions held on 25 July 1570.

32 Ibid.

33 Willan, *Early History of the Russia Company*, p. 112.

34 Tolstoy, *England and Russia*, pp. 85–6. It should be noted that the spelling of the English letters follows no rules.

35 Ibid., p. 85, 6 May 1570.

36 Ibid., pp. 90ff., no. 25, 18 May 1570, no. 26, same date. The letter is endorsed as seen by Elizabeth's councillors, who sign it on the back, and sealed with the privy seal. The translation by Daniel Sylvester is also sworn to be a true copy.

37 Ibid.

38 *Dictionary of National Biography*. It is also possible that Bomelius got into trouble with the medical establishment in Cambridge, still strongly opposed to Paracelsian medicine.

39 Skrynnikov, *Oprichnyi terror*, p. 399.

40 Käppeler, *Iwan Groznyi*, p. 128.

41 Skrynnikov, *Oprichnyi terror*, p. 430; Shcherbachev,' Kopengagenskie akty otnosiashchiesia k russkoi istorii', in Soobshchil Yu. N. Shcherbachev, *Chteniya*, II, p. 34.

42 Floria, *Ivan Groznyi*, p. 258.

43 They both appear in a *Sinodik*; according to Schlichting, Tret'yak's wife was summoned before Ivan, who ordered his retainers to strip her; they then tied a rope around her and dragged her off to the river to be drowned. Schlichting, 'A Brief Account', p. 253.

44 On his disagreement with Sylvester in 1553, on religious grounds, see above, Chapter VII, p. 12.

45 Floria, *Ivan Groznyi*, pp. 248–9 quotes a letter from Ostafy Volovich, a Lithuanian magnate, in which he states that Viskovaty had always been unfriendly and difficult to deal with.

46 See above, Chapter VII, p. 112.

47 Schlichting, 'A Brief Account', p. 272, and H. Graham's comment in note 207.

48 According to one historian, Funikov had been the last to swear allegiance to the baby Dmitry in 1553; he might also have been incriminated by Prince S. Rostovsky, under torture. Was there indeed a link between the executions of 1570 and the appearance of loyalty to the baby Grand Prince in 1553? See Filiushkin, *Istoria odnoi mistifikatsii*, pp. 79–81. And was there a later link between the publication of A. Malein's translation into Russian of Schlichting's account in 1934, and the onset of the Stalinist terror?

49 Floria, *Ivan Groznyi*, pp. 248–9. See also p. 251 on popular legends of common people standing up against the Tsar's terror.

50 Schlichting, 'A Brief Account', pp. 259–50.

51 *SIRIO*, 71, p. 747.

52 Schlichting, 'A Brief Account', 261–2. There are various descriptions of the execution of Viskovaty, each more horrible than the last.

53 Schlichting gives a total of 122, Staden, 130, the Piskarevsky Chronicle, *PSRL*, XXXIV, 120. See Skrynnikov, *Oprichnyi terror*, p. 403.
54 Taube and Kruse (op. cit., p. 51) agree on many things with Schlichting in their description of the horrors of 25 July in Moscow.
55 Zimin, *Oprichnina*, p. 437.
56 The deaths can most conveniently be followed in the study of the *Sinodik* in Skrynnikov, *Tsarstvo terrora*, pp. 529 and 540ff.
57 Dr Arnold was a Belgian physician who came to Russia under English auspices. He is known under various names, often as Dr Arnold Lindsay. H. Graham, introduction to Schlichting, *News from Muscovy*, pp. 206–7.
58 Schlichting, 'A Brief Account', pp. 240–1, notes 116 and 117 by Hugh Graham. Floria accepts Staden's account that Viazemsky died in prison in chains (*Ivan Groznyi*, p. 35) so does Skrynnikov (*Oprichnyi terror*, p. 405); Graham says that he was alive in 1594/5.
59 Floria, *Ivan Groznyi*, p. 253. These were not public executions.
60 Skrynnikov, *Oprichnyi terror*, pp. 376–7.
61 Floria, *Ivan Groznyi*, p. 253.

CHAPTER XVI Foreign Policy and the Tatar Invasions

1 Roberts, *The Early Vasas*, pp. 255–6.
2 H.F. Graham, ed. and tr., 'Paul Juusten's Mission to Muscovy', *Russian History*, 13, no. 1, 1986, pp. 41–92. Juusten also reports that 'Some 11,000 girls beautifully dressed and adorned (as we were told) came to Novgorod and after 25 October set out for Moscow escorted by some thirty-four persons'. Graham considers the number too high even for Ivan's lust, but this is obviously a reference to the organization of a bride-show, after the death of Maria Temriukovna, which took place on 12 June, while the Swedish embassy was in Novgorod. The figure is clearly wildly exaggerated, but to my mind it always is, and 11,000 may be an echo of the virgins of St Ursula in Juusten's mind. The usually mentioned figures, 1,500 or 2,000, come from a foreign source, Herberstein, who is probably mistaken, and every one else has copied him. This ties in with a report from Staden (see below, Chapter XV, note 18).
3 Ibid., p. 64, note 58 for the official report by the envoy V.M. Vorontsov in Moscow of the efforts made by Duke Karl to stop the looting of their property and to compensate them.
4 T. Chumakova, ed., *Ivan IV. Sochinenia*, St Petersburg, 2000, pp. 116–18.
5 *SIRIO*, 129, p. 190.
6 Graham, op. cit., pp. 71ff.
7 Roberts, op. cit., pp. 256.
8 Tolstoy, *England and Russia*, no. 28, pp. 106ff., no. 28, p. 110. It has been suggested that Ivan is referring to Elizabeth menstruating but the original Russian text does not bear out that suggestion. 'Boorish' is the translation made in England for the Russian *muzhichii*.
9 This was made clear later in May 1575, 'Instruction to Mr Sylvester', Tolstoy, op. cit., no. 38, pp. 160ff.
10 Roberts, op. cit., pp. 252ff.
11 Both Skrynnikov and Floria report on the scandalous behaviour of the Russian *oprichnina* troops in Estonia during the siege of Reval.
12 See above, Chapter IX. It is impossible to determine the date of this execution, but it is attributed by Taube and Kruse (op. cit., pp. 39–41) to 1568. See also Zimin, *Oprichnina*, pp. 460–1. Skrynnikov (*Tsarstvo terrora*, pp. 543 and 545) includes Mikhail Cherkassky's name in the *Sinodik*, in an undated paragraph,

under the heading 'executions in the *oprichnina*', and again in the year 7060 (1571).

13 Floria, *Ivan Groznyi* p. 267; Skrynnikov, *Tsarstvo terrora*, pp. 425, 433–4 and 543. Mikhail Cherkassky figures in the *Sinodik* probably because Ivan discovered that the rumour about his father was not true. Skrynnikov states that he was shot by *oprichniki* between 16 and 23 May 1571. Taube and Kruse (op. cit., p. 54) say that he was impaled. Zimin, *Oprichnina*, pp. 460–1 suggests that Ivan got rid of Mikhail's wife and son as the latter might have been a rival for the throne of Russia as the nephew of a tsaritsa, indeed of two tsaritsas, Anastasia and Maria. Seeing that two of Ivan's sons were living this seems to disregard any hereditary claim.

14 Skrynnikov, *Tsarstvo terrora*, p. 434.

15 Zimin, *Oprichnina*, p. 453; Staden (*Land and Government*, p. 77) says that 30,000 Nogais were in Devlet's army.

16 Taube and Kruse, op. cit., p. 52. In general the Tatar armies evaded pitched battles and preferred skirmishes, advances and sudden withdrawals.

17 Horsey, *Travels*, p. 272.

18 S.M Seredonin, *Sochinenia Dzhilsa Fletchera kak istoricheskii istochnik*, St Petersburg, 1891, pp. 75–6. Giles Fletcher was sent as English ambassador to Russia in 1588. See his *Of the Russe Commonwealth*, p. 65, ob.

19 Skrynnikov, *Tsarstvo Terrora*, p. 427.

20 Floria, *Ivan Groznyi*, 264; Fletcher, op. cit., p. 65; Floria agrees with Fletcher.

21 Skrynnikov, *Tsarstvo terrora*, p. 426.

22 According to another account Ivan received the Crimean envoys in shabby sheepskins and explained that the Crimeans had left him too poor to pay tribute. Ibid, p. 426. (See also the agreement with the Ottoman Turks, above, Chapter XIV, p. 239 and L. Hughes, *Russia in the Age of Peter the Great*, Yale University Press, New Haven and London, 1997, p. 50.)

23 Skrynnikov, *Tsarstvo terrora*, p. 446.

24 Zimin, *Oprichnina*, p. 462.

25 Ibid., p. 432; see also Taube and Kruse, op. cit., p. 22 who point to Ivan's new doctor, Bomelius, as the instigator of the new terror. See also ibid., Roginski's, introduction, p. 22. There is a rumour that Ivan poisoned Maria who, it will be remembered, died on 6 September 1569. There is possibly here again a connexion with rumours that Ivan was then contemplating marriage with Elizabeth, and she would certainly not have accepted if he were married. See *Calendar of State Papers*, Elizabeth 1566–8, no. 2414, Randolph to Cecil, 12 August 1568.

26 It may well have been at this time that Portico commissioned a Latin translation of Schlichting.

27 Skrynnikov, *Tsarstvo terrora*, pp. 431–2; B.N. Putilov and B.M. Dobrovol'sky, eds, *Istoricheskie pesni XIII–XVI vekov*, Moscow, 1960, p. 655. M. Perrie, *The Image of Ivan the Terrible in Russian Folklore*, Cambridge University Press, 2002, pp. 209ff. where translations of two versions are published, with a very perceptive commentary.

28 Taube and Kruse, op. cit., p. 55. Staden has an obscure and undated report of *oprichniki* being sent out to 'requisition the daughters of all the rich merchants and peasants in unfortified settlements, pretending that the Grand Prince wanted them in Moscow. If a peasant or a merchant gave money, his daughter was excluded from the list as though she were not pretty' (*Land and Government*, pp. 32–3).

29 Taube and Kruse, op. cit., p. 55.

30 Skrynnikov, *Tsarstvo terrora*, p. 431.

31 Mstislavsky was denounced by a Tatar tsarevich in Russian service who had attempted to desert to Devlet Girey. Skrynnikov, *Tsarstvo terrora*, p. 429.

32 Floria, *Ivan Groznyi*, pp. 267–8.

33 It is likely that it had, as the whole point of holding the wedding when Marfa was ill was that semen was regarded as a cure for female ailments (not only in Russia).

34 Graham, 'Paul Juusten's Mission', *Russian History*, 13, no. 1, 1986, p. 78.

35 Ibid., pp. 76ff., and notes, and *SIRIO*, 129, pp. 216–18; see also Skrynnikov, *Tsarstvo terrora*, pp. 445–6.

36 Graham, 'Paul Juusten's Mission' pp. 81ff. See also S.N. Bogatyrev, *Pavel Juusten, Posol'stvo v Moskoviu, 1569–1572*, Helsinki, 2000, pp. 153ff. Before Juusten returned to Stockholm the Shchelkalovs and one of the boyars inquired of him about the age and appearance of John III's remaining sister, Elizabeth, and suggested that the new Swedish envoys should bring a portrait of her when they came.

37 Morgan and Coote, *Early Voyages*, II, pp. 297–8.

38 See account in R. Hakluyt, *The Discovery of Muscovy, 1589*, Cassell, London and New York, 1904.

39 Tolstoy, *England and Russia*, pp. 148ff., for the Russian text dated 20 August 1574 which refers back to 1570; at p. 150: 'a ty to delo polozhila na svoikh boyarakh a sama esi dlia devecheskogo chinu togo dela ne delala'. English text pp. 153ff.

40 Morgan and Coote, op. cit., II, pp. 335–8.

41 Tolstoy, op. cit., pp. 128ff. and 140ff.; Willan, *Early History of the Russia Company*, pp. 117ff. R. Hakluyt, *The Principal Navigations of the English Nation*, II, Dent, 1936, pp. 136ff., dated after July 1572. Jenkinson had also raised a number of specific problems of the Russia Company (unpaid debts, arrests of interlopers, compensation for losses in the fire of Moscow). Not all were granted and in any case they were left for discussion with the secretary.

42 Willan, op. cit., pp. 123ff. These were probably Scotsmen.

43 Skrynnikov, *Sviatiteli i vlasti*, pp. 247ff.

44 Taube was given a barony. Was he the ancestor of the legal historian?

45 A.M Kurbsky, *Correspondence*, p. 243.

46 Likhachev and Lur'e, eds, *Poslania Ivana*, p. 193.

47 Skrynnikov, *Tsarstvo terrora*, pp. 456–7. Staden, *Land and Government*, p. 35.

48 Skrynnikov, *Tsarstvo terrora*, pp. 436–7.

49 Dembkowski, *The Union of Lublin*, pp. 197ff.; Floria, *Russko-Polskie*, pp. 46–7.

50 Floria, *Ivan Groznyi*, p. 275. Solov'ev, *Istoria Rossii*, III, p. 703. There is some doubt whether Ivan actually fulfilled these requirements, which were in any case lifted while he was on campaign. But see also A. Possevino, *The Moscovia of Antonio Possevino, SJ*, tr. H. Graham, University of Pittsburg, 1977, p. 48, who states that Ivan was no longer taking communion in 1582 as he was under a penance imposed on him for marrying four times. Karamzin says Koltovskaia was the daughter of a merchant, but this is denied by other historians who say she was the daughter of a minor noble.

51 Floria, *Ivan Groznyi*, p. 282. Ivan had sent an envoy to Constantinople in April 1571, making certain concessions to Turkish demands and demanding in return that the Crimeans should cease attacking him. A Turkish reply was received in December 1572, in which the Sultan demanded the cession of Astrakhan' to him, of Kazan' to the Khan of Crimea, and that Ivan should become the Sultan's vassal. It came too late.

52 Staden, op. cit., p. 53.

53 R.I. Frost, *The Northern Wars, 1558–1721*, Longman, London, 2000, p. 50.; for a description see Skrynnikov, *Tsarstvo terrora*, pp. 447–8, and Floria, *Ivan Groznyi*, pp. 281ff.
54 Ibid., pp. 282–3.

CHAPTER XVII The End of the *Oprichnina*, and the Succession to the Polish-Lithuanian Crown

1 S.B. Veselovsky, 'Dukhovnoe zaveshchanie tsaria Ivana, 1572', in *Issledovania po istorii oprichniny*, Moscow, 1963, pp. 302ff.
2 See below for a fuller discussion. Zimin, *Oprichnina*, pp. 478ff. points out that Ivan IV thought he had completed the unification of Russia and therefore no longer needed the *oprichnina*. Zimin censures Ivan for building the unity of Russia on the bones of so many of its people, mired in despotism and violence. On centralization see, for instance, award of an appanage to Bogdan Aleksandrovich of Moldavia when he was expelled from his throne by the Ottomans in 1574.
3 Staden, *Land and Government*, p.130. Skrynnikov (*Tsarstvo terrora*, p. 9) also concludes that the weakening of the army led to the abandonment of the terror.
4 R.G. Skrynnikov, *Rossia posle oprichniny*, Leningrad, 1975, p. 8.
5 Veselovsky, *Issledovania po istorii oprichniny*, pp. 292ff. at p. 300: 'Chto daet genealogia dlia ponimania nekotorykh sobytii . . .'.
6 I have drawn largely on Zimin, *Oprichnina* and his *V Kanun groznykh potriasenii*, Moscow, 1986; Skrynnikov, *Rossia posle oprichniny;* Veselovsky, *Issledovania po istorii oprichniny*; and A.P. Pavlov, *Gosudarev dvor i politicheskaia bor'ba pri Borise Godunove*, St Petersburg, 1992, to reconstruct the events of the 1570s.
7 Staden was one of those who lost his estates. See *Land and Government*, p. 130.
8 Skrynnikov, *Rossia posle oprichniny*, p. 13.
9 Planning of a sort had taken place in the Commonwealth. Particularly in 1570 to 1571, when a rumour was circulating that Ivan had died. Sigismund wrote to N. Radziwill the Red warning him not to allow either of Ivan's sons to succeed to the Polish-Lithuanian throne. Talks between Lithuanian magnates and the Habsburg party hoping for the election of the Archduke Ernst of Habsburg also continued, and the candidature of Kurbsky was even contemplated by Sigismund Augustus. See Floria, *Russko-pol'skiye,* pp. 44–6 and note 44.
10 Solov'ev, III, pp. 620–3.
11 Karamzin, IX, 1, p. 137.
12 Skrynnikov, *Sviatiteli i vlasti*, p. 250.
13 See above, Chapter IX.
14 See above, Chapter XIV.
15 See above, p. 269, and see Skrynnikov, *Tsarstvo terrora*, p. 475. The inquiry into Mstislavsky's alleged treasonable contacts with the Crimeans rumbled on for a number of years, conducted by A.F. Nagoi who seems to have replaced Maliuta Skuratov in the role of investigator of possible treason.
16 Zimin, *V Kanun*, p. 11.
17 On casting spells by whispering, see Ryan, *In the Bathhouse at Midnight, ad indicem*. M.I. Vorotynsky died on 12 June 1573 according to Zimin, 'Sostav boyarskoi dumy', p. 73, n. 380.
18 Veselovsky, *Issledovania po istorii oprichniny*, p.120. Kurbsky, *History*, pp. 197ff.
19 Veselovsky, 'Poruchnye zapisi', in *Issledovania po istorii oprichniny*, pp. 123ff.; see also Zimin, *Oprichnina*, pp. 463ff. for 1571.

20 Kurbsky, *History*, pp. 201–3: Kurbsky goes on to explain that with the help of magicians and sorceresses, two sons were born from Vasily's 'foul seed', one of them so savage and bloodthirsty that he exceeded even the evil Nero, and the other one, just as strange and wondrous, born without mind, memory or speech.

21 Horsey, *Travels*, pp. 279–80. The Pskov Chronicle of 1570 describes Bomelius as a 'savage witch and evil heretic' (Brockhaus and Efron, *Encyclopaedia*, under Bomelius; Skrynnikov, *Tsarstvo terrora*, p. 484).

22 Floria, *Ivan Groznyy*, pp. 52ff.

23 Ed. and tr. by J.L.I. Fennell, Cambridge, 1965. This is Zimin's dating and politically the period after the death of Sigismund Augustus seems likely, but there is evidence that incidents which occurred after 1573 are included in the text.

24 Floria, *Russko-Polskie*, pp. 49–51; Skrynnikov, *Tsarstvo terrora*, pp. 469ff.; Solov'ev, III, ch. 6, p. 619.

25 V. Novodvorsky, *Bor'ba za Livoniu mezhdu Moskoviu i rech'iu pospolitoiu 1570 1582*, St Petersburg, 1904, p. 14.

26 Floria, *Russko-Polskie*, pp. 52–3.

27 Solovy'ev, III, ch. 6, pp. 624–5.

28 I am not convinced by Pelenski's article, 'The Origins of the Official Muscovite Claims to the Kievan Inheritance', which does not seem to me to understand dynastic as distinct from nationalist ideas.

29 Ivan Ivanovich had already repudiated his first wife and sent her to a convent.

30 Solov'ev, III, ch. 6, pp. 626ff.

31 Ibid., for a long summary of the talks.

32 See above, Chapter XIV, p. 225–6.

33 Novodvorsky, op. cit., p. 18.

34 Floria, *Russko-Polskie*, p. 55.

35 Solov'ev, III, ch. 6, p. 631 ('tiazhelo emu bylo unizit'sia do iskatel'stva').

36 Frost, *The Northern Wars*, p. 41.

37 J.H. Elliott, *Europe Divided, 1559–1598*, Fontana, London 1968, pp. 232ff. The nearest case of an act of toleration was the edict passed by the Transylvanian diet in 1571.

38 Karamzin, *Istoria*, IX, 1, p.149 and notes p. 90 note 434.

39 Novodvorsky, op. cit., p. 17; cf. Karamzin, op. cit., 3, pp. 148–9.

40 'Russkie akty Kopengagenskogo gosudarstvennogo arkhiva', *Russkaia istoricheskaia biblioteka*, XVI, p. 103, no. 28, 31 July 1573, asking Frederick in his name and that of Maximilian to close the Sound to Henri of Valois.

41 Skrynnnikov, *Rossia posle oprichniny*, p. 19.

42 Ibid., p. 11. See also Ivan's question regarding those taken to the torture chamber: 'who among our boyars betrays us? Kolychev, Tulupov, Mstislavsky, Fedor Trubetskoi, Ivan Shuisky?' Ibid., note 31.

43 Ibid., p. 19, note 25 where the author states that I.F. Kolychev and his wife acted as the principal *druzhki* (friends) of the bride at Anna Vasil'chikova's wedding to Ivan, and nineteen Kolychevy are recorded as playing some part in the ceremonies. There is some doubt about the date. See discussion in Zimin, *V Kanun*, p. 14. Solov'ev, III, 6, p. 703 and note 136, regards Anna Vasil'chikova and Vasilisa Melent'eva, Ivan's sixth wife, as concubines. He states that they were not called 'tsaritsa'.

44 Zimin, op.cit., pp. 12ff, and see notes 40 and 41.

45 Skrynnikov, *Sviatiteli*, pp. 251ff.

46 See above, pp. 211–12.

47 Examples of martyrdom are the refusal to eat pork, or the refusal to eat meat on a fast day.

48 Ivan Groznyi, *Sochinenia*, ed. T. Chumakova, pp. 145–168: 'chelom b'em do zemli'. The letter takes up twenty-three printed pages! Priscilla Hunt ('Ivan IV's Personal Mythology') regards this farewell as expressing humility.

49 Horsey, *Travels*, pp. 292–3. Horsey suggests that Bomelius had denounced Leonid – possibly as a rival witch. Skrynnikov, *Tsarstvo terrora*, p. 494.

50 Horsey, op. cit. pp. 292–3; Skrynnikov, *Rossia posle oprichniny*, pp. 16ff; Skrynnikov, *Svatiteli i vlasti*, pp. 255ff.

51 Zimin, *V Kanun*, pp. 32–3. Various versions and dates are given for his death. I have followed Zimin.

52 Prinz von Buchau, 'Nachalo i vozveshchenie Moskovii', tr. from the Latin by A. Tikhomirov, *Chteniya*, III, p. 29.

53 According to A. Possevino, 'Missio Moscovitica', tr. and ed. by H. Graham, *Canadian American Slavic Studies*, VI, 3, Fall, 1972, p. 49.

54 Ivan Groznyi, *Sochinenia*, ed., T. Chumakova, pp. 120–38.

55 Solov'ev, III, 5, pp. 641ff.

56 Tolstoy, *England and Russia*, pp. 159 .

57 Or it may be that Ivan thought he would be in a better position to acquire the Polish crown and actually rule in the Commonwealth if he was not ruling in Russia.

58 Zimin, *V Kanun*, p. 26 suggests that Vasily only decided to marry a second wife after the death of Tsarevich Peter, whom he had regarded as his heir, in the absence of children of his own.

CHAPTER XVIII Grand Prince Simeon Bekbulatovich

1 Skrynnikov, *Tsarstvo terrora*, p. 485.

2 Ivan's formal title now became Prince Ivan of Moscow, Pskov and Rostov, Staritsa and Dmitrov; but he also held on to Riazan, and some of the Novgorod lands were annexed to his appanage. See Skrynnikov, *Rossiia posle oprichniny*, p. 25.

3 Horsey, *Travels*, p. 275 (probably written after Fletcher's *Of the Russe Commonwealth* was printed). Peers is taken to mean members of the Boyar Council, Skrynnikov, *Tsarstvo terrora*, p. 485. However I do not accept Skrynnikov's conception of the Boyar *duma* as 'the representative organ of the boyar aristocracy', nor does the English notion of peers and a peerage apply to Russia. And Ivan told the English envoy Sylvester that Simeon had not been crowned.

4 The words 'appointed by popular choice' do not ring true of Ivan, since no Russian ruler had ever been appointed by popular choice; it is possible that Sylvester inserted them precisely because he was more aware of the role performed by representative institutions in other countries. On the other hand it is possible that Ivan did use them, since he was at that time very much aware of the role of a representative institution in the election of a ruler as in Poland. The seven crowns are Moscow, Kazan', Astrakhan', Riazan, Tver', Novgorod and Pskov, the most recent acquisitions of the House of Moscow; the crowns frequently reposed on a bench next to the Tsar.

5 Tolstoy, *England and Russia*, 29 January 1576, pp. 186–8 at p. 188.

6 Zimin, *V Kanun*, p. 35, attributed to V.O. Kliuchevsky.

7 V.I. Koretsky, 'Zemskiy sobor 1575 g. i postanovlenie Simeona Bekbulatovicha Velikim Kniazem vseia Rusi', *Istoricheskii Arkhiv*, 2, 1959, pp. 148ff. Koretsky argues that just as in foreign policy Ivan had used a put-up figure, King Magnus, so in internal policy he was sheltering behind a dummy, Tsar Simeon (p.149). Skrynnikov, *Tsarstvo terrora*, pp. 484–5 rejects the view that there was a meeting of a *Zemskii sobor*.

8 Fletcher, *Of the Russe Commonwealth*, pp. 42–3. It is possible that Fletcher believed that Ivan was moved by financial considerations all the more easily because he was as strongly in favour of the confiscation of the lands of the Russian Church as he was of the confiscation of the lands of the English Church.

9 See S.M. Kashtanov, 'O vnutrennei politike Ivana Groznogo v period velikogo kniazhenia Simeona Bekbulatovicha', in *Trudy Moskovskogo gosudarstvennogo-istoriko-arkhivnogo instituta*, Moscow 1961, p. 427.

10 Ibid., p. 429, note 18. See also P.A. Sadikov, 'Iz istorii oprichniny', in *Istoricheskii arkhiv*, 1940, III, p. 169, note 1 on the destruction of Simeon's charters.

11 Kashtanov, 'O vnutrennei politike . . .' p. 430; when Ivan and Simeon were mentioned together Ivan' s name continued to appear first on documents, note 23.

12 Woodward and Mattingly, eds, *St John Damascene, Barlaam and Josaphat*. See also A. Pypin, in 'Istoria Varlaama i Iosafata', *Ocherk literaturnoi istorii starinnykh povestei i skazok russkikh*, St Petersburg, 1857, p. 124, who states that many copies of this tale were known to have existed in various libraries, though the anecdotes in the story often circulated separately. The story is also told later of the Persian Shah Abbas I, whose death at a specific time was foretold. The Shah abdicated in favour of a craftsman for the few doom laden days mentioned in the prophecy, then resumed his power and executed his double. See P.A. Sadikov, *Ocherki po istorii oprichniny*, Moscow/Leningrad, 1950, p. 38.

13 Skrynnikov, *Rossia posle oprichniny*, p. 36.

14 Tolstoy, op. cit., pp. 183ff.

15 On the supernova and the comet, see B. Woolley, *The Queen's Conjuror: The Science and Magic of Dr Dee*, HarperCollins, London 2001, pp. 161ff. Tycho Brahe noted that the comet's tail pointed northeast, 'where it would "spew its venom" over the Muscovites and Tartars'. Maybe Bomelius thought so too. See also Ryan, *The Bathhouse*, pp. 374–5.

16 Skrynnikov, *Rossia posle oprichniny*, p. 21, and notes 78 and 79.

17 Skrynnikov, *Tsarstvo terrora*, p. 494; see also his *Rossia posle oprichniny*, pp. 20ff. Ivan Ivanovich was already in his twenties, and was given no independent command. Such a suspicion explains Ivan's persecution of the Iur'ev Zakhar'ins at this time. See Chapter XVII, p. 295.

18 Quoted in Skrynnikov, *Tsarstvo terrora*, p. 495.

19 In spring 1578 Kambulat Idarovich, a brother of Temriuk, now the Senior Prince of Kabarda visited Moscow, and left behind his son, a first cousin of the Tsaritsa Maria, who converted to Orthodoxy, entered Russian service and eventually as Boris Kambulatovich Cherkassky, married a daughter of Nikita Romanovich Iur'ev Zakhar'in, Tsaritsa Anastasia's brother. See Zimin, *V Kanun*, pp. 52–3. It should be remembered that Ivan's mother was descended from a leading non-Genghisid Tatar warrior, Mamay.

20 Skrynnikov, *Rossia posle oprichniny*, p. 33.

21 Daniel Prinz von Buchau, op. cit., p. 29.

22 Tolstoy, op. cit., pp. 179–80, note of Ivan's speech to Daniel Sylvester, Moscow, 29 November 1575. Sylvester says that the interview took place in the 'howse of Oprisheno' to which Ivan had moved on leaving the Kremlin and which was in the Arbat. It had presumably been repaired after the fire of 1571.

23 Skrynnikov, *Tsarstvo terrora*, pp. 508ff.

24 Ibid., p. 485. Kashtanov had put forward a similar kind of argument in 1961 ('O vnutrenney politike . . .', p. 440). The role of Simeon Bekbulatovich was dual, he argued. Ivan had put him forward but had also to guard against him.

'Only such a dialectical dualism in the role of Simeon can explain the internal contradictions of the policy of Ivan in 1575–6' and the rapid demotion of Simeon.

25　Likhachev and Lur'e, eds, *Poslania Ivana Groznogo*, letter to Simeon Bekbulatovich, pp. 195 and 372.

26　For a detailed analysis of the personnel and the lands taken in to the *udel* of the Grand Prince of Moscow (Ivan IV) during the 'reign' of Simeon Bekbulatovich, see the study by S.P. Mordovina and A.L. Stanislavskii, 'Sostav osobogo dvora Ivana IV v period "Velikogo Kniazhenia" Semena Bekbulatovicha', *Arkheograficheskii ezhegodnik za 1976*, Moscow, 1976, pp. 153–92.

27　See Floria, *Russko-Pol'skie otnoshenia*, pp. 93ff. for discussion of various view points.

28　Ibid., pp. 98ff., and by the same author, 'Artikuly skazannyye cherez Krishtofa Graevskogo – vazhnyi istochnik po istorii russkoy vneshnei politiki 70-kh godov XVI veka', in *Arkheograficheskii ezhegodnik za 1975g*, Moscow, 1976, pp. 334–8.

29　Floria, *Ivan Groznyy*, p. 325.

30　Ibid., p. 327.

31　Floria, *Russko-Polskie otnoshenia*, pp. 102–3.

32　Zimin, *V Kanun*, p. 22.

33　See Übersberger, *Österreich und Russland*, pp. 404ff. on the unreliability of Magnus Pauli as a Russian envoy. He is nevertheless quoted by Floria, *Ivan Groznyy*, pp. 332ff., as confirming to Ivan Maximilian's plans for an anti-Turkish alliance between Russia, the Commonwealth and the Habsburgs (it is not clear whether the Empire is meant or only the Habsburg lands).

34　This is stated by Übersberger, op. cit., pp. 407 and 409, but Floria in *Ivan Groznyi* assumes that Pauli was speaking with the Emperor's full authority.

35　Ibid., p. 331; Floria speaks of the actual partition of the Commonwealth, but a few lines further he waters down his language and speaks merely of a division of spheres of influence. Übersberger, op. cit., pp. 408–9, argues that partition runs counter to the whole trend of Maximilian's Polish policy and is an invention of Pauli's; he is critical of the interpretation of Novodvorsky in *Bor'baza Livoniu*, pp. 16ff.

36　Übersberger, op. cit., pp. 396ff. It is during this period that Kurbsky proposed an anti-Turkish alliance between Russia, the Commonwealth and the Empire, through the Abbé Cyrus, the imperial representative in Warsaw. See Lur'e, 'Doneseniya agenta Maksimiliana . . .'. Nothing came of it.

37　Tikhomirov, *Rossiskoe gosudarstvo*, pp. 72–3.

38　Solov'ev, pp. 632–3.

39　Übersberger, op. cit., p. 443, and note 1 for examples of two such impostors.

40　See Hans Cobenzl's account in *Chtenia*,1876, IV, pp. 1–20, where it is printed under the title 'Donesenie o Moskovii Ioanna Pernstaina', ed. O. Vodiansky. There is no mention of the presence of Tsar Simeon at the banquets or political discussions.

41　The Papal nuncio at this stage favoured the election of Ivan in the belief that he could be moved to accept the authority of the Pope in exchange for the title of Emperor of Constantinople, once he had of course conquered that city. Übersberger, op. cit., p. 446.

42　Cobenzl, op. cit., pp. 1–20.

43　There is apparently no record of his having studied at the University, See G. Gömöri, 'Where was Istvan Bathory Educated? Or the Genesis of a Legend', *SEER*, vol. 80, no. 3, 2002, pp. 483–6.

44　Floria, *Ivan Groznyi*, p. 340.

45 Ibid.
46 Ibid., p. 334.
47 Ivan sent a delegation to this Reichstag which is the subject of a well known illustration of Russian boyars.
48 Übersberger, op. cit., pp. 460ff.
49 Solov'ev, III, p. 648.
50 For a consideration of the issues involved see Zimin, *V Kanun*, pp. 41ff. As late as 1580 however, when Ivan was dividing his troops for the campaign of that winter, the military registers mention 'the departure to the Lithuanian border of the baptized Tatar tsarevich Grand Prince Simeon Bekbulatovich and Boyar I.F. Mstislavsky', so that Simeon was still being given his title. Solov'ev, III p. 657.
51 Zimin (*V Kanun*, p. 41) quotes Horsey's extremely muddled description of the demotion of Tsar Simeon. He confused it with the famous request of the people to Ivan to return from Aleksandrovskaia Sloboda to Moscow in 1565. Horsey's easy use of the term 'act of parliament' to describe popular demand to the Tsar to return has proved particularly confusing since it has led some historians to assume that a *Zemskii sobor* was called in autumn 1576 to approve the demotion of the Tatar tsar. The final status of Simeon has been variously described as no more than that of an ordinary *pomeshchik*, and that of an appanage prince.
52 Ibid., p. 47.
53 V.B. Kobrin, 'Sostav oprichnogo dvora Ivana Groznogo', *Arkheografcheskii ezhegodnik za 1959*, Moscow, 1960, p. 167
54 Kobrin, 'Sostav oprichnogo dvora', p. 134. However Solov'ev refers to a report that Vasilisa's husband was executed by an *oprichnik*, and that the Tsar sent her to a convent in Novgorod on 1 May 1577, because her eye wandered to someone else, whom the Tsar executed (III, vol. 6, p. 739. note 136).
55 I have come across no mention of Ivan ever seeing the sea. It would be interesting to know what impact it had on him.
56 Polubensky is described as a descendant of Palemon, a legendary ancestor of the Lithuanian princes, related to Nero, who fled from Rome to the Niemen and founded the Lithuanian nation. *Poslania Ivana Groznogo*, pp. 374ff.
57 Prince Alexander Polubensky belonged to a branch of the Trubetskoy clan which had left Russia, entered Polish–Lithuanian service and fought against the Russians. See Kurbsky, *Correspondence*, p. 186, note 1.
58 *Poslania Ivana Groznogo*, pp. 374ff. Ivan addresses Polubensky as 'Palemonova roda', or 'poloumnogo roda' (half-witted) because he had not had the wit to keep what he had conquered.
59 Floria, *Ivan Groznyy*, p. 344.
60 Kukonos.
61 Floria, *Ivan Groznyi*, pp. 343, using Baltasar Russow.
62 Kurbsky, *Correspondence*, pp. 187–97, dated 1577. It was probably sent to Kurbsky via Polubensky, when he returned to the Commonwealth. See below, Chapter XXI for further discussion.
63 Zimin, *V Kanun*, p. 50. Ivan expresses the same idea in his letter to Kurbsky.
64 Kurbsky, *Correspondence*, pp. 187–97.
65 Floria, *Ivan Groznyi*, pp. 344–5.
66 Zimin, *V Kanun*, p. 52
67 Solov'ev, III, p. 646. See also Floria, *Ivan Groznyi*, pp. 350–1; Roberts, *The Early Vasas*, p. 263.
68 Zimin, *V Kanun*, p. 53. See the account of Johann Boch, who was staying in the foreign quarter, in Graham, ed., 'Johann Boch in Moscow'.

69 Horsey, *Travels*, pp. 288–9.
70 Solov'ev, III, p. 649. Floria, *Ivan Groznyi*, suggests that the Russian envoys succeeded only in misleading Ivan by suggesting that Bathory had not been accepted as king in Poland, hence only a few Lithuanian troops would follow him; the people really wanted the Tsarevich Fedor Ivanovich. Unfortunately Floria provides no footnotes so that the source cannot be checked (ibid., p. 352).
71 Roberts, op. cit., p. 263.
72 *Poslania Ivana Groznogo*, pp. 337–50, 'Vtoroe poslanie Shvedskomy koroliu Ioganny III, 1573'. Ivan's letter takes up thirteen printed pages.
73 Solov'ev, III, 6, p. 648.
74 Ibid., the quotation is from Ecclesiasticus (Jesus of Sirach).

Chapter XIX Peace Negotiations

1 Zimin, *V Kanun*, p. 54. Skrynnikov, *Rossia posle oprichniny*, p. 45, note 22 and p. 90 and note 18. Floria found a report of Ivan's illness of 3 April 1579 in the Jan Zamoyski archives in Poland. Ivan's health is also mentioned in the *Vremennik Ivana Timofeeva*, ed.O.A. Derzhavina, Moscow and Leningrad, 1951, p. 174 in the context of the Tsar's fondness for foreign doctors.
2 Howes, *Testaments of the Grand Princes of Moscow*, pp. 304ff.
3 Veselovsky, 'Dukhovnoe zaveshchanie Tsaria Ivana 1572' in *Issledovaniia po istorii oprichniny*, pp. 302ff. Zimin, *V Kanun*, p. 8 and note 6. Metropolitan Antoni, who is mentioned in the will, was appointed in May 1572, and remained in office until 1581, thus mention of his name does not help to establish the date.
4 This is the date suggested by A.L. Iurganov, in 'O date zapisania zaveshchania Ivana Groznogo', *Otechestvennaia istoria*, 6, 1993, pp. 135–41.
5 A will usually began with a reference to the testator as 'a sinful poor slave of God', any other sins having been confessed to the private chaplain before undertaking such a solemn act as making a will.
6 The ultimate destiny of Vorotynsky's lands is very complicated and the details are not relevant here. See B.Yu. Belikov and E.I. Kolycheva, 'Dokumenty o zemlevladenii kniazei Vorotynskikh vo vtoroi poloviny XVI – nachale XVII vv', in *Arkhiv russkoi istorii*, vyp. 2, Moscow, 1992, pp. 427–46.
7 Ivan also lists many towns and villages which had belonged to his brother Prince Iuri and which he had made over to the latter's widow, Princess Ul'iana, which were to remain hers for her life.
8 Howes, op. cit., p. 173, my translation from the Russian version of Ivan's will.
9 The Kanon was edited and published by D.S. Likhachev, who attributes it to Ivan in *Issledovania po drevnerusskoi literature*, Leningrad, 1986, pp. 372–3. It is reprinted in modernized Russian in Ivan Groznyi, *Sochinenia*, pp. 139ff.
10 Zimin, *V Kanun*, p. 248, note 41.
11 The message was sent by his courier Lopatinsky. Zimin, *V Kanun*, p. 55. There were also very secret talks about the King divorcing Anna Jagiellonka in order to marry again and produce an heir.
12 Floria, *Ivan Groznyi*, p. 352. Solov'ev does not mention this incident.
13 See Alfonso de Valdés, *Diálogo de Mercurio y Caron*, Bk II. Valdés was Charles V's secretary at the time. He was also a close friend of Johannes Dantiscus, the Polish ambassador to the court of Charles, and kept him well informed of the incident. I am grateful to Professor M.-J. Rodriguez-Salgado for advance information from her forthcoming book, *Monarch of the World. The International Politics of Charles V*, Yale University Press. See also R.J. Knecht, *Francis I*, Cambridge University Press, Cambridge, 1982, pp. 211 and 214–16.

14 Zimin, *V Kanun*, p. 55; as I write the US-led coalition is doing the same in Iraq. There is nothing new under the sun.
15 Zimin, *V Kanun*, pp. 55 and 258, note 47. The archive copy dates from 1626.
16 Karamzin, IX, 5, pp. 188–9.
17 See D. Rowland, 'Biblical Military Imagery in the Political Culture of Early Modern Russia: the Blessed Host of the Heavenly Tsar' in M.S. Flier and D. Rowland, eds, *Medieval Russian Culture*, II, University of California Press, Berkeley, 1994, pp. 182–212; see also Bogatyrev, 'Battle for Divine Wisdom', where the author underlines the emphasis on the symbolic significance of the recovery of the cathedral of Santa Sophia in Polotsk, which had its origins in Kiev–Constantinople.
18 Zimin, *V Kanun*, p. 57.
19 Ibid.
20 Floria, *Ivan Groznyi*, p. 358
21 See the very useful article by Lt Col. Dianne Smith, 'The Sixteenth-Century Muscovite Army'.
22 See Frost, *The Northern Wars*, pp. 28–9.
23 Tolstoy, *England and Russia*, p. 183. See above, Chapter XVIII, pp. 298–9.
24 Horsey, *Travels*, pp. 289–90. Again an evil omen for Ivan?
25 Ibid., pp. 294–8. Horsey also saw Francis Walsingham, and Leicester, and was evidently very well received. It is possible that he executed some commercial commissions for both Leicester and Walsingham. No doubt the Queen enjoyed the story of his journey, which makes very good reading.
26 Ibid., pp. 292–3. See Staden, *Land and Government*, pp. 123–4; Taube and Kruse, 'Poslanie loganna . . .', p. 54; J. Hamel, *England and Russia*, London, 1854, pp. 98–9; Zimin, *V Kanun*, p. 258, note 56; it is possible that some of this took place in Pskov, since Bomelius is mentioned briefly in a Pskovian chronicle as being there with Ivan. He is described as a *lyutyi volkhv* (savage magician) (ibid., p. 58). Jerome Bowes, ambassador from Elizabeth to Ivan in 1583, secured the repatriation of Bomelius's widow, Jane Ricards; see note to the effect that Bomelius was 'rosted to death in Mosco' in 1579 in R. Hakluyt, *Principal Navigations of the English Nation*, p. 259.
27 Karamzin, IX, notes, p. 127, note 603, quoting Oderborn's report of the comet and his many exaggerations.
28 I am grateful to Mrs G. Learner and Peter Hingley, Librarian of the Royal Astronomical Society, for having guided me to the relevant literature on comets: C.D. Hellman: *The Comet of 1577: its Place in the History of Astronomy*, Columbia University Press, New York, 1971 edition; D.K. Yeomans, *Comets, A Chronological History of Observation, Science, Myth and Folklore*, Wiley, Chichester, 1991, pp. 33ff.; Gary W. Kronk, *Cometography, A Catalog of Comets*, I, Cambridge University Press, Cambridge, 1999, pp. 317ff.
29 Floria, *Ivan Groznyi*, p. 353. The Russian reply has only fairly recently been found, states Floria, but in any case it was not sent as fighting broke out.
30 Skrynnikov, *Rossia posle oprichniny*, pp. 50–1.
31 Pierling, *La Russie et le Saint-Siège*, II, pp. 3–5. I shall be drawing extensively on this work in this chapter. See also Floria, *Ivan Groznyi*, p. 364, who argues that Ivan was responding to an imperial decision to ban the export to Russia of lead, tin and copper, essential for armaments.
32 For the earlier papal soundings in Russia see Pierling, op. cit., I, passim.
33 See for instance, A. Tourguéniev, *Historica Russiae Monumenta*, I, St Petersburg, 1841, p. 258, Caligari (nuncio in Warsaw) to Cardinal Commendone, in Rome, 3 July 1579, on the Polish Catholics' hope that the Muscovites would accept the Catholic faith, and pointing out that if Ivan were

offered the title of King, the King of Poland–Lithuania would still be better off as Ivan's title would be lower in rank and later than his. Evidently Caligari did not realize that Ivan would notice this too!

34 Pierling, op. cit., II, pp. 12ff. It was Antonio Possevino who later discovered the truth about this episode. Shevrigin's letter to the Doge is in the Venetian archives, while the Doge's reply to Ivan was 'lost' by Shevrigin on the return journey.

35 Ibid., pp. 17ff., for the discussion of Ivan's letter in the Vatican and the resolution of 6 March 1581. Shevrigin, in his report to Ivan, left out the detail about kissing the Pope's slipper and kneeling before him.

36 For details on Possevino see H. F. Graham's introduction to 'The Missio Muscovitica' of Antonio Possevino, pp. 437–77, partly based on information from Possevino's travelling companion, Father John Paul Campano; and see also Possevino, *The Moscovia of Antonio Possevino*, which deals in more details with Possevino's actual negotiations in Russia.

37 Pierling, op. cit., II, p. 42.

38 Karamzin, IX, notes, pp. 116–17, note 554, states that a bride-show was held, and then quotes Bathory's Polish secretary, G. Heidenstein, who gives a very fanciful description of the procedure.

39 Possibly in childbirth? See Skrynnikov, *Rossia posle oprichnina*, pp. 99–100, and notes 56 and 57.

40 Daughter of Fedor V. Sheremetev.

41 Pierling, op. cit., II, pp. 53–5.

42 Zimin, *V Kanun*, pp. 62ff and 71–2; Floria, *Ivan Groznyi*, p. 361.

43 The delay was due to the funeral of Bathory's brother, Christopher, Prince of Transylvania.

44 Ibid., pp. 55–65

45 Pierling, op. cit., II, p. 69.

46 There were atrocities on both sides, but the Russian atrocities are better documented because of the flood of printed and illustrated propaganda issuing partly from Poland and partly from printing presses in Germany.

47 See *Poslania Ivana Groznogo*, pp. 390–415; Ivan IV, *Sochinenia*, pp. 186–219.

48 Ibid. Floria, *Ivan Groznyi*, pp. 363–5, argues that this missive is not really aimed at Bathory but at the Papacy and above all the Empire, and is designed to show that the Polish King supports the Ottomans and will not support an anti-Turkish coalition, and is appealing to some of the magnates in the Commonwealth who previously had supported the Emperor.

49 It exists in Polish, Russian and Latin versions.

50 The letter was circulated together with the work of Guagnini (based on Schlichting) and that of Taube and Kruse. See Floria, *Ivan Groznyi*, p. 367; Pierling, op. cit., II, pp. 77–9.

51 Ibid.

52 Zimin, *V Kanun*, p. 73.

53 *Pamiatniki diplomaticheskikh snoshenii*, X, p. 53, instruction to the *pristav* meeting Possevino at the Polish border, 29 July 1581. There is frequently a discrepancy between the accounts of Possevino and the Russian sources.

54 Pierling, op. cit., II, p. 87.

55 Ibid., Pierling suggests that Bogdan Bel'sky who, with Nikita Romanovich Iur'ev Zakhar'in, led the negotiations offered a financial inducement to Possevino which was indignantly brushed aside.

56 Roberts, *The Early Vasas*, pp. 263–4.

57 Possevino,' 'Missio Moscovitica', p. 462.

58 Pierling, op. cit., II, 94; *Pamiatniki diplomaticheskikh snoshenii*, tom. X, cols

206–35. Ivan writes to Possevino explaining their correspondence, more in sorrow than in anger and with his usual sarcasm over twenty-nine printed columns. The text was translated for Possevino. He accuses Bathory of taking Polotsk by treachery, having suborned his captains to let the Lithuanians in, and at the end he introduces a new claim to the lordship of the East and the West. It is a long process of self-defence and slightly mad.

59 Kurbsky, *Correspondence,* pp. 181–5.
60 Ibid., pp. 187ff.

CHAPTER XX **The Truce of Iam Zapol'sky**

1 Zimin, *V Kanun*, pp. 59–60.
2 Ibid. Skrynnikov argues that this resolution echoes the policy enacted in 1572, but Zimin, *V Kanun*, p. 60, argues that the decree of 1572 only forbade acquisition of land by large monasteries for prayers for the dead, whereas the decree of 1580 corresponded to the interests of the service gentry and the state treasury, and in any case it was not put into effect because of the war. Horsey is probably referring to the *ukaz* of 1581 for he refers also to Ivan quoting Possevino's insistence on the restoration of papal supremacy. He also states that Ivan raised 300,000 marks sterling by this means. See Horsey, *Travels,* pp. 382ff. See also Skrynnikov, *Rossia posle oprichniny*, pp. 73ff. who compares Horsey's memoirs with the official resolution.
3 This is a very abbreviated summary of a very complex question, based on Zimin, *V Kanun*, pp. 64ff.
4 Possevino, 'Missio Moscovitica', pp. 462–4. Father Campano was to return to Rome, while Possevino's other companion, Father Drenocki, a Croat, was to remain in Russia until Possevino returned. Drenocki was held very closely while in Moscow, and was unable to proselytize.
5 Possevino has left a description of the place and a journal of the twenty-one sessions over which the negotiations stretched, from 13 December to 15 January 1582. See Possevino, *The Moscovia of Antonio Possevino*, pp. 106ff.
6 See Mattingly, *Renaissance Diplomacy*, passim.
7 Pierling, op. cit., II, p.110. Pierling attempts to clear Possevino of the charge of bias, but inevitably, committed as he was to the defence of the Papacy, he found it difficult to be completely objective, though he lodged with the Russian delegation at Kiverova Gora.
8 Possevino, *The Moscovia of Antonio Possevino*, pp. 128–9.
9 Ibid., pp. 128–9.
10 It should be pointed out that this did not refer to the concept of 'Moscow the Third Rome' which played no part in the negotiations, nor as far as I can see in any negotiations.
11 Skrynnikov, *Rossia posle oprichniny*, pp. 61–2.
12 Horsey, *Travels,* p. 300.
13 Quoted from the 'Stepennaya Kniga' Chronicle by Karamzin, IX, notes, p. 28, note 609.
14 Tsar' Ivan Vasil'evich Groznyi, *Dukhovnie pesnopenia i molitvoslovia,* Obshchestvo sviatitela, Moscow, 1999, pp. 186ff.
15 Karamzin, IX, notes, p.128, note 608.
16 See above, p. 293.
17 Skrynnikov, *Rossia posle oprichniny*, pp. 92–3.
18 Ibid. The source is Oderborn, quoted in Karamzin.
19 See Perrie, *The Image of Ivan the Terrible,* pp. 76ff., and for the actual text of one of the songs about the Tsar and his sons, in English translation, see pp. 209ff.

20 G.V. Zharinov, 'Zapisi o raskhode lekarstvennykh sredstv 1581–1582', *Arkhiv russkoi istorii*, 4, 1994, pp. 103–25. An English apothecary, John Frensham and a physician, Dr Robert Atkins arrived in Russia, highly recommended by Queen Elizabeth, just too late to attend the Tsarevich, on 15 November 1581.
21 Tolstoy, *England and Russia*, p, 194, A Memorial for Her Majesty, May 1582.
22 Zimin, *V Kanun*, p. 265, note 30.
23 Possevino, *Moscovia of Antonio Possevino*, pp. 12ff.
24 Irina did give birth to a daughter, Feodosia in 1592 who lived very briefly. Horsey, as usual full of gossip about his own important activities, says that on one of his visits to England he was charged with consulting physicians in Oxford, Cambridge and London to procure their advice on matters of 'conception and procuration of children', for Irina Godunova. The relevant words are written in English but in cyrillic in the original text. Horsey, *Travels*, p. 319. His tactlessness in this field contributed to his final disgrace at the Russian court.
25 Pastor Oderborn (who was never in Russia) reports a rumour that at the time of the death of the Tsarevich, Boris Godunov had been in the room when Ivan attacked his son. He had intervened to restrain the Tsar, and had in turn been beaten and even injured by the irate monarch. Ivan had apparently not forgotten and was harbouring a grievance against his favourite, which might have led him to exclude Boris from any regency council. See Floria, *Ivan Groznyi*, p.389.
26 Willan, *History of the Russia Company*, pp. 157ff.
27 Solov'ev, *Istoria*, III, pp. 677ff. See also 'Stateinyi spisok' of F. Pisemsky in *Zapiski russkikh puteshestvennikov XVI–XVII vv.*, N.I. Prokof'ev and L.I. Alekhinoi, eds, for F. Pisemsky's official report of his mission to England.
28 Ibid., Pisemsky, 'Stateinyi spisok', pp. 220ff., at pp. 264ff.; *SIRIO*, 38, correspondence with England, pp. 1ff. The negotiations were to be carried on with Bogdan Bel'sky, the Tsar's closest adviser, and Afanasii Nagoi, the uncle of the Tsar's present wife.
29 Tolstoy, op. cit., p. 194, Memorial of May 1582; Willan, op. cit., pp. 161ff.
30 Willan, op. cit., p. 163.
31 See Prokof'ev and Alekhina, eds, op. cit., pp. 67ff. In the meantime the Tsaritsa Maria Nagaia had given birth to the Tsarevich Dmitri.
32 As Pierling assumes, op. cit., II, pp. 163ff.
33 Kukushkina, *Kniga v Rossii*, pp. 165ff., printed in Ostrog.
34 Possevino, *The Moscovia of Antonio Possevino*, pp. 67ff. Possevino submitted two further memoranda on the differences between the Orthodox and the Catholic Churches to Ivan, see ibid., pp. 80ff., and a work on the English breach with Rome, to counter the book in which the Anabaptist heretic had tried to 'prove that the Pope is Antichrist' ibid., pp. 97ff.
35 See above, Chapter XVIII, p. 314.
36 Ibid., pp. 163–4; *Pamiatniki diplomaticheskikh snoshenii*, X, cols 277ff.
37 For Bowes, see Hakluyt, *Principal Navigations of the English Nation*, II, p. 251, 'A brief discourse of the voyage of Sir Jerome Bowes . . . in the yeere 1583'; for Pisemsky see *SIRIO*, 38, pp. 104ff.
38 Hakluyt, op. cit., II, p. 253: their names are given as Mekita Romanovich and Andrew Shalkan. The Dutch trader was apparently from Antwerp in the Spanish Netherlands, and known as Ivan Beloborodov.
39 Drawn from Hakluyt, op. cit., II, pp. 255f.; *SIRIO* 38, 104ff.; Solov'ev, III, pp. 678ff., Tolstoy, op. cit., pp. 201ff. (Bowes is asked to procure the return of John Frensham, the apothecary, to England, in which he was successful.)
40 Solov'ev, III, p. 680.
41 Ibid., pp. 681ff.; Denmark had been bought off by Elizabeth who had privately

agreed to pay for the right to sail through allegedly Danish waters to the White Sea, instead of paying the Sound dues. Willan, op. cit., pp. 158–9.

CHAPTER XXI The Death of Ivan

1 V.A. Rogov, *Istoria ugolovnogo prava, terrora i repressii v russkom gosudarstve XV–XVII vv*, Moscow, 1995, pp. 156–7 (cf. law of 1582 on false denunciations mainly by *kholopi*).
2 Skrynnikov, *Rossia posle oprichniny*, pp. 97–8.
3 Early Slavic Studies Internet. http://www.h-net.org/~ess/ 24 September 2002, posting by Sergei Bogatyrev; Horsey, *Travels*, p. 304 reports that Ivan was being carried.
4 Graham, ed. and tr., 'Paul Juusten's Mission to Muscovy', *Russian History*, 13, no. 1, 1986, p. 81. Graham, ed. and tr., 'Johann Boch in Moscow', *Russian History*, 13, No. 1, 1986, pp 93–110, note 5, where Ivan is described as being on horseback.
5 Ibid.
6 See W.F. Ryan, 'Alchemy and the Virtues of Stones in Muscovy', in *Alchemy and Chemistry in the 16th and 17th Centuries*, ed. P. Rattansi and A. Clericuzio, Kluwer, Dordrecht and London, 1994, pp. 149–59. See also Horsey, op. cit., pp. 304–5. Ivan declared his aversion to the diamond: 'It restrains fury and luxury and abstinacy [abstinence] and chastity.' Horsey writes in a headlong way, leaving out many pronouns, which makes him difficult to follow at times.
7 Ibid., p. 306. The angel's form is the monk's robe. V.I. Koretsky, 'Smert' groznogo tsaria', *Voprosy istorii*, No. 9, 1979, pp. 93–103. Koretsky quotes a Moscow Chronicle of 1591, and also the *Vremennik Ivana Timofeeva*, 1951, pp. 15 and 178, where Timofeev actually names Godunov and Bel'sky as the criminals. See Ivan Timofeev, *Vremennik*, ed. and tr. O.A. Derzhavina, Moscow-Leningrad, 1951. Dr Eyloff was charged with providing the poison. He was not only the Tsar's physician but traded on his own account in a big way.
8 Jerome Bowes said later that Ivan died of a surfeit, and he could have died as a result of choking over food.
9 Prinz von Buchau, 'Nachalo Rusi, i vozvyshchenie Moskovii,' p. 28.
10 Zimin, *V Kanun*, pp. 98ff. Horsey, op. cit., pp. 310 and 313.
11 Iuzefovich, *Kak v posol'skikh obychaiakh vedetsia*, p. 49.
12 Boils are frequently caused by vitamin B deficiency. But see Keenan, 'Ivan IV and the "King's Evil"', pp. 5–13.
13 Advice from Dr S. Sebag Montefiore.
14 See the lengthy correspondence on the Early Slavic Internet, following posting referred to in note 3 above.
15 Abraham Lincoln suffered from violent outbursts of rage, which were eventually attributed to 'blue pills' of mercury compounds, which he had been prescribed; they ceased when he gave up the pills on becoming President.
16 His real name was Theophrastus Bombastus von Hohenheim. His adopted name signifies 'beyond Celsus' (an early Roman writer on medicine). For an introduction to his theories and his influence see H.E. Midelfort, *Mad Princes of Renaissance Germany*, University of Virginia, 1994, pp. 9ff.
17 'Paracelsus made opium, mercury, lead, sulphur, iron, arsenic, copper sulphate and potassium sulphate a permanent part of the pharmacopoeia'. Quoted from P.H. Kocher, 'Paracelsian Medicine in England: the First Thirty Years (1570–1600)', *Journal of the History of Medicine*, II, 1947, pp. 451ff. at p. 452, note 2.

18 Fax from Beverley Berry to Dr S. Sebag Montefiore, 8 March 2002.
19 H. Trevor Roper, 'The Court Physician and Paracelsianism', in *Medicine at the Courts of Europe, 1500–1837*, ed. V. Nutton, Routledge, London and New York, 1990, pp. 79–94.
20 Woolley, *The Queen's Conjuror*, p. 104 and passim.
21 *Dictionary of National Biography*, Bomelius, Eliseus or Licius. He was highly thought of by Philipp Melanchthon, which strengthens the connexion with Paracelsus.
22 See above, Chapter XX.
23 Zimin, *V Kanun*, p. 267, note 59. Ivan Timofeev, in his *Vremennik*, suggests that Bel'sky was now Ivan's homosexual partner. Quoted by D. Rowland, 'Did Muscovite Literary Ideology Place Limits on the Power of the Tsar (1540–1660s)?' *Russian Review*, 49, 1990, p. 133.
24 Isaac Massa reports that he was poisoned by Bogdan Bel'sky, who supervised Dr Eyloff, then in charge of the pharmacy. See his *A Short History of the Muscovite Wars*, ed. and tr. by G.E. Orchard, University of Toronto Press, Toronto, 1982, p. 21. Koretsky, 'Smert' groznogo tsaria', p. 100.
25 Zharinov, 'Zapisi o raskhode . . .', pp. 104–25; among the many herbs and spices listed are cloves, cardamom, cinnamon, asparagus, saxifrage, pumpkin, water-melon, cucumber, mint, parsley.
26 Zimin, *V Kanun*, p. 98 quotes a report by the unreliable Oderborn to the effect that Ivan had tried to rape (*ovladet'*) Irina, and when she resisted he urged Fedor to repudiate her for sterility.
27 V.I. Koretsky, 'Smert' groznogo tsaria', pp. 95ff. gives various rather highly coloured accounts of the alleged poisoning of Ivan IV, by Irina, on behalf of Bel'sky and Godunov, but the evidence is not very reliable.
28 Yet Horsey also implies that Boris Godunov and Bel'sky were both perturbed at this possibility.
29 The head of the *zemshchina* was Prince I.F. Mstislavsky, now, according to Zimin (and Horsey) over eighty years old: he was more probably in his sixties. His first wife had been a daughter of Gorbaty-Shuisky, executed in 1564, his second wife a daughter of V.I. Vorotynsky, who died naturally but belonged to the group of Upper Oka princes viewed with deep suspicion by Ivan. The wife of Nikita Romanovich was a sister of Mstislavsky's Vorotynskaya wife. See Zimin, *V Kanun*, pp. 108–9.
30 Pavlov, *Gosudarev dvor . . .* pp. 27ff.
31 V.M. Zhivov and B.A. Uspensky, 'Tsar i Bog: semioticheskie aspekty sakralizatsii monarkha v Rossii', in *Iazyki kul'tury i problemy perevodimosti*, ed. B.A. Uspensky, Moscow, 1988, pp. 55ff.
32 Horsey, *Travels*, pp. 283–4.
33 Kappeler, *Ivan Groznyj*, passim.
34 See H.F. Graham's comparison, in his 'Johann Boch in Moscow', pp. 106ff; for Oderborn, see p. 108; Horsey, op. cit., p. 299 and J. Margeret, *Un Mousquetaire à Moscou*, ed. A. Bennigsen, Paris, 1983, pp. 56–7.
35 I have already briefly explained in the Foreword the reasons why I do not accept Professor Keenan's theory that this correspondence is a seventeenth-century forgery.
36 It has been suggested in modern Spanish historiography that Don Carlos suffered from autism. I am grateful to Professor M. Rodríguez Salgado for the information. Edward VI received a good, strictly Protestant, education but he seems to me to have been extraordinarily impervious to the execution of his uncles, and a young religious fanatic.
37 Rowland, 'Muscovite Literary Ideology', p. 133 specifies Ivan Khvorostinin, Simon Shakhovskoy and the author of the *Khronograf* of 1617.

38 Kurbsky, *Correspondence,* pp. 186ff. Ivan's letter written in Wolmar around September 1577.
39 Ibid., Ivan to Kurbsky, p. 193: '*Ia khotel vas pokoriti v svoiu voliu* . . .'.
40 See, for a very perceptive account of Ivan's mental processes, R.O. Crummey, 'New Wine in Old Bottles? Ivan IV and Novgorod', in *Russian History,* 1987, 14, pp. 61–76.
41 As usual with Ivan the language of prayer is very eloquent, and he draws on many sources, including the Pseudepigrapha (books which do not even form part of the Apocrypha). *Ivan Groznyi – Sochinenia,* ed. T. Chumakova, p. 1.
42 Act of Supremacy, 8 May 1555 (Elton, 'The Reformation', p. 273). See also King James I, quoted in Crummey, 'New Wine in Old Bottles?' Many historians will disagree with me here, but that is because they believe in the existence of a political system called autocracy. I do not. I hope my readers will note that I have not used the word so far in this book. As for the word 'autocratic', it belongs to the world of *Alice Through the Looking Glass.*
43 I do not find convincing the suggestion that the Basmanovs and Maliuta Skuratov might have been ruling Russia in Ivan's name. When the time came Ivan disposed of the first two easily, and Maliuta remained close until his own death. See Crummey, 'New Wine in Old Bottles?', p. 71. Ivan was perfectly capable of ruling and taking decisions, though he might often take the wrong ones.
44 Mstislavsky and Nikita Romanovich had both signed a vast surety bond for M.I. Vorotynsky when he was released from captivity in 1567, but they refused to act as witnesses to his will in 1570. Was this because they suspected him of plotting? Was he denounced to Ivan and then killed?
45 I have not seen one single reference to the calling in of a surety bond, though Ivan was chronically short of money.
46 In this discussion, in addition to sources mentioned in previous footnotes I have drawn upon a large variety of Russian and Anglophone sources, notably, S.N. Bogatyrev, 'Povedenie Ivana Groznogo i moral'nye normy russkogo obshchestva XVI veka', in *Studia Slavica Finlandensia,* XI, Helsinki, 1994, pp. 1–20; idem, 'Groznyi Tsar ili groznoe vremia? Psikhologicheskii obraz Ivana Groznogo v istoriografii', *Russian History,* 22, no. 3, Fall 1995, pp. 285–308; Crummey, 'New Wine in Old Bottles?', pp. 61–76; R. Hellie, 'What Happened? How Did he Get Away With It? Ivan Groznyi's Paranoia and the Problem of Institutional Restraints', *Russian History,* 14, 1987, pp. 199–224; Lehtovirta, *Ivan IV as Emperor.* To sum up my own view, I find the interpretations of Kliuchevsky, and Veselovsky most convincing among older historians and of Crummey, Bogatyrev and Lehtovirta among contemporary historians writing in English.

CHAPTER XXII Ivan's Legacy to Russia

1 See M. Perrie, *The Cult of Ivan the Terrible in Stalin's Russia,* Palgrave, London, 2001; Professor Perrie deals with both the Stalinization of Russian history and the Stalinization of Ivan the Terrible, and with several novels as well as Eisenstein's film.
2 Notably by V.B. Kobrin, *Ivan Groznyi,* Moscow, 1989.
3 I find profoundly moving two brief remarks by Zimin quoted by A.L. Khoroshkevich in the preface to the second edition of his *Oprichnina Ivana Groznogo* (1964), which came out in 2001: 'I (Zimin) wrote the Oprichnina in one breath. The whole of it. To the end (probably in half a year).' Khoroshkevich adds, 'He was afraid that he would not be able to publish it in that short period of semi-liberation from the previous Stalinist dogmas.' 'A donkey's hide sticks to the skin – tearing it off costs blood' (p. 5).

4   Though it no longer applies today, 'it was a common maxim of medieval writers that "royal service ennobles"'. See Given-Wilson, *The English Nobility in the Late Middle Ages,* p. 17.

5   See Rowland, 'Muscovite Literary Ideology', pp. 125–55. It will be remembered that *muchitel'* is also the Russian translation for the Greek *tyrannos.*

6   See the way in which this is portrayed in the tales of Vlad Țepeș (see above, Chapter III, pp. 44–5).

7   Fragmentation was much greater in Spain and France at this time. The German-speaking lands remained fragmented until 1870.

8   For the harmful effects of this intensified defence policy on the *pomeshchiki,* and other kinds of military servitors of different social ranks, and the multiplication of cossack hosts, see Dunning, *Russia's First Civil War,* pp. 47ff.

9   See tables in M.D. Zlotnik, 'Muscovite Fiscal Policy, 1462–1584', *Russian History,* 6, pt 2, 1979, pp. 243ff., at pp. 252–3. The *sokha* was a measure of taxable land. There were also increasingly heavy commercial duties. Monasteries often enjoyed considerable immunities, but during the period of the *oprichnina* the situation became chaotic.

10   Hakluyt, *Principal Navigations and Discoveries of the English Nation.*

11   See J. Blum, *Lord and Peasant in Russia,* Princeton, 1961, pp. 249ff.

12   See the perceptive remark of Stökl, in 'Die Würzeln des Modernen Staates in Osteuropa', pp. 255–69 at p. 265. 'It is not accidental that the modern word for "state" in Russian derives its origin from "Land of the Lord" (Land des Herrn, Herrschaft) in the sense of "Grundherrschaft"'. Elsewhere Stökl has argued, as have others, that the notion of state only really arose after the extinction of the dynasty, when the separation between the ruler and the land became obvious.

13   I have borrowed from R.J. Knecht, *Francis I,* p. 19. But it must be said that they might not necessarily survive, e.g., the closure of the monasteries in England or the Revocation of the Edict of Nantes in France.

14   The election of a new dynasty by a representative assembly was a new departure in the politics of the succession to the crown in monarchies which had become hereditary. Dunning argues in *Russia's First Civil War,* p. 93, that the Assembly and the election of 1598 took place after Boris Godunov had been crowned Tsar.

15   Moscow the Third Rome is a concept of importance in relation to the Orthodox world of eastern Europe. As far as western Europe was concerned, the first Rome dominated politics and religion.

16   See Lehtovirta, *Ivan IV as Emperor,* pp. 358ff. The author points out that Ivan was never portrayed with a halo, and was never called holy. There is now however an embryonic attempt to portray him as a saint.

17   See ibid., pp. 327ff.

18   The Donation of Constantine dates from the early ninth century, in the Papacy of Sylvester II, and had allegedly been issued by the Emperor Constantine to Pope Sylvester I in AD 327, granting the Popes spiritual supremacy and temporal dominion over the Christian world. Sylvester II was the last Roman Pope to be recognized by the Orthodox Church. The Donation was often made use of during the Middle Ages to support papal claims, though it was attacked as a forgery by Lorenzo Valla in 1440. The incorporation of the Donation in the *Stoglav* in 1555, probably by Metropolitan Makarii, when the Russian Church may already have realized that it was a forgery (through Maksim Grek) was part of the defence of the Russian Church against any encroachment by the Tsar in Russia. See A.D. Gorsky, *Rossiiskoe zakonodatel'stvo X–XX vekov,* II, pp. 333ff and pp. 465–6.

19   See above, Chapter XV, pp. 251ff. and Chapter XX, pp. 346ff.

20 Ryan, 'Alchemy and the Virtue of Stones in Muscovy', p. 226. Ryan also quotes Horsey's description of Ivan's staff, which was inset with magical stones. See the Tale of the Princes of Vladimir in Dmitriev, *Literatura drevnei Rusi,* pp. 283ff.

21 Contrast the painting of the seventeenth-century surrender of the Russian General Shein to the Polish army, lying with his generals face down, flat on the ground outside Smolensk, reproduced on the cover of Frost's *The Northern Wars,* with the portrayal of the surrender of Breda to the Spanish commander, Spinola, by Velázquez.

22 Review by A. Filiushkin in *Kritika,* 3.1., 2002, pp. 89–109, of A.L. Yurganov, *Kategorii russkoi srednevekovoi kul'tury,* Moscow, 1998.

23 I find it strange that there is still so much confusion about the right of succession of the Riurikid heirs to the Russian throne. The dynasty which had died out in 1598 was not that of Alexander Nevsky, the founder of this particular branch, but that of the Danilovichi of Moscow who, as all the Riurikides knew, was junior for instance to the Shuiskys who had a better right to the all-Russian throne (and knew it). Nikita Romanovich Iur'ev Zakhar'in had no claim at all. He was not a Riurikid, he was merely the brother-in-law of Ivan IV, just as Boris Godunov was the brother-in-law of Fedor. The Lithuanian Gediminovichi (Mstislavkys, and the extinct Bel'skys) also had no claim to the throne. The Riurikides were not very consistent about the succession, hovering between descent by father to son, and brother to brother. But they knew quite well who were the rank outsiders. See the reference in *Vremennik Timofeeva* to Timofeev's links with Mikhail Skopin Shuisky (D. Rowland, 'Towards an Understanding of the Political Ideas in Ivan Timofeev's *Vremennik*', *SEER,* 62, no. 3, pp. 371–99, at p. 375).

24 The clearest account of the systematic elimination of princes is in Grobowski, 'The Chosen Council', pp. 104ff.

25 See Perrie, *The Image of Ivan the Terrible in Russian Folklore,* pp. 96–101, and see also her reference to the sadistic imagination of the seventeenth century in the context of the Time of Troubles in her *Pretenders and Popular Monarchism in Early Modern Russia,* Cambridge University Press, Cambridge, 1995, pp. 137–8.

26 For European practice see *inter alia* the Constitutio Criminalis Carolina, issued by the Emperor Charles V for the Holy Roman Empire, and fairly mild by the standards of the time. See also R.J. Evans, *Rituals of Retribution. Capital Punishment in Germany, 1600–1987,* Oxford University Press, Oxford, 1996, pp. 27–108; E. Peters, *Torture,* Basil Blackwell, Oxford, 1985. Perhaps England suffered relatively less, for after the battle of Bosworth no wars were fought by invaders on its own territory in this period.

27 The illustrations to the *Litsevoi Svod* are also a harrowing source of evidence of (unidentified) executions in the presence of the young Tsar, and in some cases of the Tsaritsa also. See for instance endpapers of Skrynnikov, *Tsarstvo terrora.*

28 Much has been written about the effect of the all-pervading culture of denunciation in the world of the Gestapo, the KGB, the Stasi, *et al.*

29 According to Skrynnikov, *Tsarstvo terrora,* p. 259, Ivan recognized descent from Grand Prince Vsevolod 'Big Nest' (d.1212) as giving the right to sit in the Tsar's Council.

30 Dunning, op. cit., p. 183. Petr Basmanov's father Fedor is generally supposed to have been Ivan's homosexual partner. He was allegedly compelled by Ivan to behead his father Aleksei. See above, Chapter XV, p. 260.

31 See Rowland, 'Towards an Understanding', p. 378.

32 As foretold by Giles Fletcher, *Of the Russe Commonwealth,* p. 26.

33 See above, Chapter XIII.

34 Prinz von Buchau, 'Nachalo Rusi, i vozvyshenye Moskvy', p. 68: 'They never write their name as even simple people consider it shameful for them to do so.'

35 See Ivan Groznyi, *Sochineniya*, ed. Chumakova, pp. 172ff. for a modern Russian translation. Possevino confirms that Ivan dictated all replies to foreign envoys or rulers (ibid., p. 6). See also Bogatyrev, 'Battle for Divine Wisdom', p. 5, quoting B.M. Kloss on the existence of Ivan's scriptorium in Aleksandrovskaia Sloboda. For the boyars' letters, see above, Chapter XIII.

36 Many Russian and non-Russian authors have written on the mental and psychological state of Ivan IV. Without following them in every particular, I have found the following particularly helpful: on Kurbsky and Ivan, Inge Auerbach; on the process by which Ivan justifies his actions to himself and to his people, Priscilla Hunt, 'Ivan IV's Personal Mythology of Kingship', *Slavic Review*, no. 52, 4, Winter 1993, pp. 769–809; Uspensky, *Tsar' i patriarkh*; Bogatyrev, 'Battle for Divine Wisdom', and 'Groznyi Tsar ili groznoe vremia?'; Lehtovirta, *Ivan IV as Emperor* (a particularly penetrating exposition); A.L. Yurganov, 'Oprichnina i strashnyi sud', *Otechestvennaia istoria*, 3, 1997, pp. 52–75; Crummey, 'New Wine in Old Bottles' (remarkable for straightforward common sense); Rowland, 'Muscovite Literary Ideology'. I have also used V. Lossky, *The Mystical Theology of the Eastern Church*, James Clarke, Cambridge and London, 1973, passim.

37 Taube and Kruse, 'Poslanie Ioganna . . .', pp. 39–40.

38 See Iurganov, 'Oprichnina i strashnyi sud', p. 52.

39 'Nemini subjectus sum quam Christo filio dei', Prinz von Buchau, op. cit., p. 62. The word 'tsar' he adds is of Scythian provenance. Buchau's original text is in Latin and has been translated into Russian. The English version of *samoderzhavie* at that time was usually 'self-upholder'. Prinz is the first foreigner I have come upon who comments on the true meaning of *samoderzhets*, even if he does not recognize tsar as deriving from Caesar.

40 See Podobedova, *Moskovskaia shkola zhivopisi*, for a development of the portrayal of the wisdom theology in icon painting.

41 Hunt argues that Ivan's first letter to Kurbsky shows that he was familiar with the writings of the Pseudo-Dionysius in the *Velikie Chetii Minei*; see also in *Poslania Ivana Groznogo*, pp. 531–2.

42 See Iurganov, 'O date zaveshchania Ivana Groznogo', pp. 125–41.

43 See Hunt, 'Ivan IV's Personal Mythology of Kingship', passim and Bogatyrev, 'Battle for Divine Wisdom', passim. Both these essays are closely argued and I hope I have done the authors justice.

44 Kurbsky, *Correspondence*, pp. 20–1.

45 Quoted from the film critic, Vsevolod Vyshnetsky, referring to Eisenstein's film, *Ivan the Terrible*, by Perrie, *The Cult of Ivan the Terrible in Stalin's Russia*, p. 151.

46 Kliuchevsky, *Sochinenia*, II, Moscow 1957, p. 199.

47 Kurbsky, *History*, p. 85; Ivan Timofeev, *Vremennik*, p. 173.

Brief Glossary

boyar, boyaryn'ia	highest rank in aristocracy, usually member of the Council
chashnik	cupbearer
gosudar', gosudaryn'ia	lord, lady
duma, dumnyy	Council, of the Council
d'iak	secretary
dvor	court (of the tsar, or of nobles); also courtyard
dvorets	palace
dvoretskii	major-domo
dvorianin, dvoriane	gentry, noble
gost'	privileged merchant
kaznachei	treasurer
kholop	bondsman
kniaz', kniaginia, kniazhna	prince, princess, unmarried daughter
kormlenie	receipt of maintenance
kravchii	equerry with various duties
namestnik	governor, lieutenant
okol'nichi	attendant on the tsar
pod'iachii	clerk
pomest'ye, ia	estate held on service tenure
postel'nichii	chamberlain
prikaz, izba	government office
rynda	armed page, guard
samoderzhavie	sovereignty
samoderzhets	sovereign, sole ruler, self-upholder (Eng.) *Selbstherrscher* (Ger.)
spal' nik	gentleman of the bedchamber
stol'nik	steward
strelets, strel'tsy	harquebusiers
striapchii	master of the wardrobe and other functions
vedro	pail, liquid measurement
voevoda	commandant, general, senior officer

Select Bibliography

All sources will be mentioned in full in footnotes when first quoted and subsequently with shortened titles.

Al'shits, D.N., *Nachalo samoderzhavia v Rossii. Gosudarstvo Ivana Groznogo*, Leningrad, 1988.

Alef, G., 'Belskies and Shuiskies in the XVIth Century', *FOG* 38 (Berlin 1986), pp. 221–40.

—— 'Das Erlöschen des Abzugsrechts der Moskauer Bojaren', *FOG* 10 (Berlin 1975), pp. 7–74.

Amosov, A.A., *Litsevoi letopisnyi svod Ivana Groznogo. Kompleksnoe kodikologicheskoe issledovanie*, Moscow, 1998.

Andreyev, N.E., 'Kurbsky's Letters to Vasyan Muromtsev', reprinted in his *Studies in Muscovy*, Variorum Reprints, London, 1970, pp. 414–36.

—— *Studies in Muscovy: Western Influence and Byzantine Inheritance*, Variorum Reprints, London, 1970.

Arel, M.S., '"The Lawes of Russia Writte"'. An English Manuscript on Muscovy at the End of the Sixteenth Century', *Oxford Slavonic Papers*, ns 23 (1999), pp. 13–38.

Auerbach, Inge, 'Die politische Vorstellungen des Fürsten Andrej Kurbskij', *JGOE* 117, 1969, pp. 170–86.

Babichenko, D., 'Kremlevskie tainy 33–1 element', *Itogi* 37 (327), 17 September 2002.

Backus, Oswald P., 'A.M. Kurbsky in the Polish Lithuanian State, 1564–83', *Acta Balto-Slavica* 6 (1969), pp. 29–50.

—— 'The Problem of Unity in the Polish-Lithuanian State' (with comments by O. Halecki and J. Jakstas, and reply), *Slavic Review* 22, no. 3 (September 1963), pp. 411–55.

—— 'Treason as a Concept and Defections from Moscow to Lithuania in the Sixteenth Century', *FOG* 15, pp. 119–44.

Bantysh-Kamenskii, D.N., *Obzor vneshnikh snoshenii Rossii po 1800 god*, Moscow, 1902.

Barlow, F., *The Feudal Kingdom of England, 1042–1216*, Longman, London, 1988.

Baron, S., 'Ivan the Terrible, Giles Fletcher, and the Muscovite Merchantry; a Reconsideration', *SEER* 56, no. 4 (1978), pp. 563–85.

Barsov, E.V., *Drevne-russkie pamiatniki sviashchennago venchania tsarei na tsarstvo, v sviazi s grecheskimi ikh originalami; s istoricheskim ocherkom chinov tsarskago venchania v svyazi s razvitiem idei tsaria na Rusi*, Moscow, 1883, reprinted Mouton, The Hague and Paris, 1969.

Bartenev, S., 'Opis stenopisnykh izobrazhenii v Zolotoi Palate' in *Moskovskii Kreml'; v starine i teper'*, Vol. 2, Moscow, 1916.

Baumgarten, N. de, 'Généalogie et mariages occidentaux des Rurikides russes du Xe au XIIIe siècles', *Orientalia Christiana 9*, no. 35 (1927), pp. 5–94.

Belikov, B. Yu, and Kolycheva, E.I., 'Dokumenty o zemlevladenii kniazei Vorotynskykh vo vtoroi poloviny XVI-nachale XVII vv', *Arkhiv russkoi istorii*, *vyp*. 2 (Moscow 1992), pp. 427–46.

Bennigsen, A. and Quelquejay, C., 'L'expédition turque contre Astrakhan en 1569', *CMRS* 8 (1967), pp. 437–46.

Berelowitch, A., 'La Noblesse à la Cour de Michel Romanov', *Revue des Etudes Slaves* 70, no. 1 (1998), pp. 249ff.

—— *La Hiérarchie des Egaux: La Noblesse russe d'ancien régime, Ve–XVIIe siècles*, Seuil, Paris, 2001.

Berry, L.E. (ed.), *The English Works of Giles Fletcher, the Elder*, University of Wisconsin Press, Madison, 1964.

—— and Crummey, R.O. (eds), *Rude and Barbarous Kingdom. Russia in Accounts of Sixteenth-Century English Voyagers*, University of Wisconsin Press, Madison, 1968.

Billington, J.H., *The Icon and the Axe: An Interpretive History*, Alfred A. Knopf, New York, 1966.

Blum, J., *Lord and Peasant in Russia*, Princeton University Press, Princeton, 1961.

Bogatyrev, S.N., 'Administrativnye sistemy Tiudorov i Riurikovichei: Sravnitel'nyi analiz', *Zerkalo istorii: Sbornik statei*, ed. N.I. Basovskaia, Moscow, 1992, pp. 74–84.

—— 'Blizhniaia duma v tre'tei chetverti XVI v. I, 1550s, II, 1560–1570, III, 1571–2', *Arkheograficheskii ezhegodnik za 1992*, Moscow, 1993, pp. 119–32; *za 1993*, Moscow, 1995, pp. 94–112; *za 1994*, Moscow, 1996, pp. 64–81.

—— 'Groznyi Tsar ili groznoe vremia? Psikhologicheskii obraz Ivana Groznogo v istoriografii', *Russian History* 22, no. 3 (Fall 1995).

—— 'Povedenie Ivana Groznogo i moral'nye normy russkogo obshchestva XVI veka', *Studia Slavica Finlandensia* 11 (Helsinki 1994), pp. 1–19.

—— 'Tsarskii sovet v sochineniakh Dzh. Fletchera i V.O. Kliuchevskogo', in V.O. Kliuchevsky, *Sbornik materialov*, *vyp*. 1, Penza, 1995, pp. 45–50.

—— ' "Smirennaya groza": k probleme interpretatsii istochnikov po istorii politicheskoi kul'tury Moskovskoi Rusi', in *Istochnikovedenie i kraevedenie v kul'ture Rossii. K 50-letiyu sluzheniya Sigurda Ottovicha Schmidta, Istoriko-arkhivnomu institutu*, Russian University for the Humanities, Moscow, 2000, pp. 79–83.

—— *The Sovereign and his Counsellors. Ritualised Consultations in Muscovite Political Culture, 1350s–1370s*, Helsinki, 2000.

—— 'A.A. Zimin, *Oprichnina*, 2nd edn revised and expanded, intro. by A.L. Khoroshevich', Moscow, 2001.

—— 'Battle for Divine Wisdom: the Rhetoric of Ivan IV's Campaign Against Polotsk', in E. Lohr and Marshall Poe (eds), *The Military and Society in Russia 1450–1917*, E. J. Brill, Leiden, 2002, pp. 325–63.

—— (ed.), *Pavel Juusten. Posol'stvo v Moskoviu, 1569–1572*, Helsinki, 2000.

Bulavin, D. (ed. and tr.), 'Taina tainykh', *Pamiatniki literatury drevnei Rusi, konets XV-pervaia polovina XVI veka*, Moscow, 1984.

Bushkovitch, P., *Religion and Society in Russia. Sixteenth and Seventeenth Centuries*, Oxford University Press, New York and Oxford, 1992.

—— 'The Life of Saint Filipp, Tsar and Metropolitan in the Late Sixteenth Century', *Medieval Russian Culture*, Vol. 2, ed. M.S. Flier and D. Rowland, University of California Press, Berkeley, 1994.

Calendar of State Papers, Elizabeth, 1566–8, Public Record Office, London.

Cazacu, M., *L'Histoire du Prince Dracula en Europe centrale et orientale*, Librairie Droz, Geneva, 1988.

Cherepnin, L.V. (ed.), *Pamiatniki russkogo prava*, Vol. IV, *Pamiatniki prava perioda ukreplenia Russkogo tsentralizovannogo gosudarstva, XV–XVII vv.*, Moscow, 1956.

—— 'Zemskie sobory i utverzhdenie absoliutizma v Rossii' in *Absoliutizm v Rossii XVII–XVIII vv.*, ed. N.M. Druzhinin, Moscow, 1964, pp. 92–133.

Cherniavsky, M., 'Ivan the Terrible and the Iconography of the Kremlin Cathedral of Archangel Michael', *Russian History* 2 (1975), pp. 5–28.

—— (ed.), *The Structure of Russian History. Interpretive Essays*, New York, 1970.

Chernov, A.V., *Vooruzhennye sily russkogo gosudarstva v XV–XVII vv.*, Moscow, 1954.

Cobenzl, Hans von Prosseg [originally under the name of Pernstein], 'Donesenie o Moskovii Ioanna Pernstaina', *Chtenia v imperatorskom obshchestve istorii i drevnostei rossiskikh pri moskovskom universitete*, Vol. 4, Oct.–Dec., 1876, pp. 1–20.

Coleman, C. and Starkey, D. (eds), *Revolution Reassessed. Revisions in the History of Tudor Government and Administration*, Clarendon Press, Oxford, 1986.

Croskey, Robert M., *Muscovite Diplomatic Practice in the Reign of Ivan III*, Garland Publishing, New York and London, 1987.

Cross, S.H. and Sherbowitz-Wetzor, O.P., *The Russian Primary Chronicle: Laurentian Text*, Medieval Academy of America, Cambridge, Mass., 1953.

Crummey, R.O., *Aristocrats and Servitors: the Boyar Elite in Russia, 1613–1689*, Princeton University Press, 1983.

—— 'Court Spectacles in Seventeenth-Century Russia: Illusion and Reality', in *Essays in Honor of A.A. Zimin*, ed. D. Clarke Waugh, Columbus, Ohio, 1983, pp. 130–58.

—— 'The Fate of the Boyar Clans, 1556–1613', *FOG* (1986), pp. 243ff.

—— 'New Wine in Old Bottles? Ivan IV and Novgorod', *Russian History* 14 (1987), pp. 61–76.

—— *The Formation of Muscovy, 1304–1613*, Longman, London and New York, 1987.

Dembkowski, H.E., *The Union of Lublin – Polish Federation in the Golden Age*, Columbia University Press, New York, 1982.

Denissoff, Elie, *Maxime le Grec et l'Occident*, Paris/Louvain, 1943.

—— 'Maxime le Grec et ses vicissitudes au sein de l'église russe', *Revue d' Etudes Slaves*, vol. 31, nos 10–14 (Paris 1954), pp. 7–20.

Derzhavina, O.A. (ed.), *Vremennik Ivana Timofeeva*, Moscow/Leningrad, 1951.

Dewey, H.W., 'The 1550 *Sudebnik* as an Instrument of Reform', *JGOE* 10 (1962), pp. 161–80.

—— 'Political *Poruka* in Muscovite Rus', *Russian Review* 46 (1987), pp. 117–34.

—— and Kleimola, Ann M., 'Suretyship and Collective Responsibility in pre-Petrine Russia', *JGOE* 18 (1970), pp. 337–54.

—— and Kleimola, Ann M., 'From the Kinship Group to Every Man his Brother's Keeper: Collective Responsibility in Pre-Petrine Russia', *JGOE* 30 (1982), pp. 321–35.

D'iakonov, M., *Vlast' moskovskikh gosudarei: Ocherk iz istorii politicheskikh idei drevnei Rusi do kontsa XVI veka*, St Petersburg, 1889. Reprinted Mouton, The Hague, 1969.

Dmitriev, L.A., *Literatura drevnei Rusi. Khrestomatia*, St Petersburg, 1997.

—— (tr. and ed.), 'Skazanie o kniaziakh Vladimirskikh', *Literatura drevnei Rusi. Khrestomatia*, St Petersburg, 1997, pp. 283 95.

—— and Likhachev, D.S. (eds), *Pamiatniki literatury drevnei Rusi. Seredina XVI veka*, Vol. 1, Moscow, 1985.

Donnert, E., *Der livländische Ordensritterstaat und Russland. Der livländische Krieg und die baltische Frage in der Europäischen Politik 1558–1583*, Berlin (GDR), 1963.

Druzhinin, N.M., *Absoliutizm v Rossii XVII–XVIII vv.*, Moscow, 1964.

Dunning, C., *Russia's First Civil War*, Pennsylvania State University Press, Philadelphia, 2001.

Elliott, John, *Europe Divided, 1559–1598*, Fontana History of Europe, Collins, London, 1968.

Elton, G., 'Introduction, The Reformation 1520–1559', in *New Cambridge Modern History*, Vol. 2, ed. G.R. Elton, Cambridge University Press, 1958, pp. 1–22 or Ch. 7, 'The Reformation in England', pp. 226–49.

Eskin, Yu., *Mestnichestvo v Rossii XVI–XVII vv. Khronologicheskii reestr*, Moscow, 1994.

Esper, T., 'Russia and the Baltic, 1494–1558', *Slavic Review* 25 (1966), pp. 458–74.

—— 'A Sixteenth-Century Russian Arms Embargo', *JGOE* 15 (1967), pp. 180–96.

Etkind, E., Nivat, G., Serman, I., and Strada V. (eds), *Histoire de la littérature russe*, I., Fayard, Paris, 1992.

Evans, R. J., *Rituals of Retribution. Capital Punishment in Germany, 1600–1987*, Oxford University Press, 1996.

Fedotov, G., *Sviatye drevnei Rusi*, Moscow, 1990.

Fennell, J.L.I., *Ivan the Great of Moscow*, Macmillan, Glasgow, 1961.

—— 'Princely Executions in the Horde, 1308–1339', *FOG* 38 (1986), pp. 9–19.

—— 'Ivan IV as a Writer', *Russian History* 14 (1987), ed. R. Hellie, pp. 145–54.

—— *A History of the Russian Church to 1448*, Longman, London and New York, 1995.

Filiushkin, A.I., *Istoria odnoi mistifikatsii. Ivan Groznyi i izbrannaia rada*, Moscow, 1998.

Fletcher, G., *Of the Russe Commonwealth*, ed. R. Pipes, Harvard University Press, Cambridge, Mass., 1966.

Flier, M.S., 'Breaking the Code. The Image of the Tsar in the Muscovite Palm Sunday Ritual', in *Medieval Russian Culture*, Vol. 2, ed. M.S. Flier and D. Rowland, University of California Press, Berkeley, 1994.

—— and Rowland, D. (eds), *Medieval Russian Culture*, Vol. 2, University of California Press, Berkeley, 1994.

Floria, B.N., 'Artikuly skazannye cherez Kristofa Graevskogo – vazhnyi istochnik po istorii russkoi vneshnei politike 70-kh godov XVI veka', *Arkheograficheskii ezhegodnik za 1975 g.*, Moscow, 1976.

—— *Russko-pol'skie otnoshenia i baltiiskii vopros v kontse XVI-nachale XVII vv.*, Moscow, 1978.

—— 'Privilegirovannoe kupechestvo i gorodskaia obshchina v russkom gosudarstve (vtoraia polovina XV-nachalo XVII vv.)', *Istoriia SSSR*, no. 5 (1997), pp. 145–160.

—— *Ivan Groznyi*. Zhizn' zamechatel'nikh liudei, Moscow, 1999.

Folz, Robert, *The Concept of Empire in Western Europe from the Fifth to the Fourteenth Century*, Edward Arnold, London, 1969.

Fomin, S., (ed.), *Tsar' Ivan Vasil'evich Groznyy, dukhovnye pesnopenia i molitvoslovia*, Obshchestvo svyatitelia Vasilia Velikogo, Moscow, 1999.

Forsten, G.V., *Baltiiskii vopros v XVI i XVII stoletiakh: 1544–1648. Issledovanie*, St Petersburg, 2 vols, 1893–4.

Franklin, S. and Shepard, J., *The Emergence of Rus', 750–1200*, Longman, London, 1966.

Frost Robert I., *The Northern Wars 1558–1721*, Longman, London, 2000.

Gemil, Tarsin, 'Les Relations de la Moldavie avec la Porte Ottomane pendant le premier règne de Petru-Raresh (1527–1538)', *Revue Romaine d'Histoire* 17, no. 2 (avril–juin 1978), Bucharest, pp. 291–312.

Given-Wilson, C., *The English Nobility in the Late Middle Ages: the Fourteenth-Century Political Community*, Routledge & Kegan Paul, London, 1987.

Gömöri, G., 'Where was Istvan Bathori Educated? Or, the Genesis of Legend', *SEER* 80, no. 3 (2002), pp. 483–6.

Gorsky, A.D., *Rossiiskoe zakonodatel'stvo X–XX vekov*, 10 vols, Vol. 2, *Zakonodatel'stvo perioda obrazovania i ukreplenia russkogo tsentralisovannogo gosudarstva*, Moscow, 1985,

Graham, H.F. (ed and tr.), 'Missio Moscovitica' of Father Campano', *CASS* 6, no. 3 (Fall 1972), pp. 437–77.

—— (ed. and tr.), 'Johann Boch in Moscow', *Russian History* 13, no. 1 (1986), pp. 93–110.

—— (ed. and tr.), 'Paul Juusten's Mission to Muscovy', *Russian History* 13, no. 1 (1986).

Gral'ia, Ieronym, *Ivan Mikhailov Viskovaty*, Moscow, 1994.

Grobowski, Anthony M., *'The Chosen Council' of Ivan IV. A Reinterpretation*, New York, 1969.

—— *Tsar Ivan i Sil'vestr. Istoria odnogo mifa*, tr. from the English by Israel and Irina Rabinovich, London, 1987.

Guy, J., 'The Privy Council: Revolution or Evolution?' in *Revolution Reassessed: Revisions in the History of Tudor Government and Administration*, ed. C. Coleman and D. Starkey, Clarendon, Oxford, 1986, pp. 59–86.

Hakluyt, Richard, *The Principal Navigations of the English Nation*, Vol. 2, Dent, London, 1936.

Halecki, Oscar, *From Florence to Brest, 1439–1596*, Sacrum Poloniae Millennium, Rome, 1958.

Hall, Clifford, 'Some Perspectives on the Use of Torture in Bacon's Time and the Question of his "Virtue"', *Anglo-American Law Review* 18 (1989), pp. 289–321.

Halperin, C.J., 'A Heretical View of Sixteenth-Century Muscovy. Edward L. Keenan: the Kurbsky-Groznyi Apocrypha', *JGOE* 22 (1974), pp. 162–86.

—— 'The Russian Land and the Russian Tsar. The Emergence of Muscovite Ideology, 1380–1408', *FOG* 23 (Berlin 1976), pp. 7–103.

—— 'Keenan's Heresy Revisited', *JGOE* 28 (1986), pp. 482–99.

—— *Russia and the Golden Horde. The Mongol Impact on Russian History*, Tauris, London, 1987.

—— 'Edward Keenan and the Kurbskii-Grozny Correspondence in Hindsight', *JGOE* 46, no. 3 (1998), pp. 376–403.

Hamel, J., *England and Russia*, London, 1854.

Hamilton, Alastair, *The Apocryphal Apocalypse. The Reception of the Second Book of Esdras (1 Ezra) from the Renaissance to the Enlightenment*, Oxford University Press, 1999.

Haney, J.V., *From Italy to Muscovy: The Life and Works of Maxim the Greek*, Wilhelm Fink Verlag, Munich, 1973.

Heer, F., *The Holy Roman Empire*, tr. Janet Sondheimer, Phoenix Giants, London, 1996.

Hellie, R., *Enserfment and Military Change in Muscovy*, University of Chicago Press, 1971.

—— (ed. and contributor), *Ivan the Terrible. A Quatercentenary Celebration of his Death, Russian History* 14 (1987).

—— 'What happened? How did he get away with it? Ivan Groznyi's paranoia and the problem of institutional restraints', *Russian History* 14 (1987), pp. 199–224

Hellman, C. Doris, *The Comet of 1577: its place in the History of Astronomy*, Columbia University Press, New York, 1971.

Hellman, M., 'Die Heiratspolitik Jaroslav des Weisen', *FOG* 8 (1962), pp. 7–25.

Herberstein, S. von, *Zapiski iz Moskovy*, Moscow, 1988.

Hittle, J.M., *The Service City, State and Townsmen in Russia, 1600–1899*, Harvard University Press, Cambridge, Mass., 1979.

Hoff, G. (G. Khoff), *Erschreckliche, greuliche und unerhorte Tyranney Iwan Wasiljeviec*, Cologne, 1582.

Hofmann, I., 'Posol'stvo I. Gofmana v Livoniu i russkoe gosudarstvo v 1559–1560', ed. Yu.K. Madisson, *Istoricheskii arkhiv*, No. 6, Moscow, 1957, pp. 131–42.

Holum, K.G., *Theodosian Empresses. Women and Imperial Dominion in Late Antiquity*, University of California Press, Berkeley, 1989.

Horsey, Jerome, *Travels*; see Berry, L.E. and Crummey, R.O., *Rude and Barbarous Kingdom. Russia in Accounts of Sixteenth-Century Voyagers*, University of Wisconsin Press, Madison, 1968.

Hosking, G., *Russia: People and Empire*, HarperCollins, London, 1997.

Howes, Robert Craig, *The Testaments of the Grand Princes of Moscow*, Cornell University Press, Ithaca, NY, 1967.

Hughes, Lindsey, *Russia in the Age of Peter the Great*, Yale University Press, New Haven and London, 1998.

Hunt, Priscilla, 'Ivan IV's Personal Mythology of Kingship', *Slavic Review* (Winter 1993), pp. 769–809.

Huttenbach, H.R. (ed. and tr.), 'The Search for and Discovery of New Archival Materials for Ambassador Jenkinson's Mission to Muscovy in 1571–72: Four Letters by Queen Elizabeth I to Tsar Ivan IV', *CASS* 6, no. 3 (Fall, 1972), pp. 416–35.

Huttenbach, H.R., 'Anthony Jenkinson's 1566 and 1567 Missions to Muscovy from Unpublished Sources', *CASS* 9, no. 2 (Summer 1975), pp. 179–203.

Huttenbach, H.R., 'The Correspondence between Queen Elizabeth and Tsar Ivan: An Examination of its Role in the Documentation of Anglo–Muscovite History', *FOG* 24, pp. 101ff.

Iurganov, A.L., 'Idei I. S. Peresvetova v kontekste mirovoi istorii i kul'tury', *Voprosy istorii*, no. 2 (1996), Moscow, pp. 15–27.

—— 'Oprichnina i strashnyi sud', *Otechestvennaia istoria* 3 (1997), pp. 52–75.

—— *Kategorii russkoi srednevekovoi kul'tury*, Moscow, 1998.

Iuzefovich, A., *Kak v posol'skikh obychaiakh vedetsia*, Moscow, 1988.

Ivan Vasil'evich Groznyy, Tsar, *Dukhovnye pesnopenia imolitvoslovia*, obshchestvo sviatitelia, Moscow, 1999.

—— *Sochinenia*, ed. T. Chumakova, St Petersburg, 2000.

Ivanov, A.I., *Literaturnoe nasledie Maksima Greka*, Leningrad, 1969.

Jablonowski, H., *Westrussland zwischen Wilna und Moskau*, E.J. Brill, Leiden, 1961.

Jimenez Landi, A., *Una ley de sucesión y quince siglos de historia*, Madrid, 1968.

Kaiser, D., *The Growth of the Law in Medieval Russia*, Princeton University Press, 1980.

—— 'Symbol and Ritual in the Marriages of Ivan IV', *Russian History* 14 (1987), pp. 247–62.

Kalugin, V.V., *Andrei Kurbsky i Ivan Groznyi*, Moscow, 1998.

Kämpfer, F., 'Russland an der Schwelle der Neuzeit, Kunst, Ideologie und historisches Bewusstsein unter Ivan Groznyj', *JGOE* 23 (1975), pp. 504–24.

—— 'Über der theologische und architektonische Konzeption der Vasily-Blazenniyj-Kathedrale in Moskau', *JGOE* 24 (1976), pp. 481–98.

Käppeler, A., 'Die Letzten Oprichninajahre (1569–1571)', *JGOE* 19 (1971), pp. 1–30.

—— *Ivan Groznyj im Spiegel der ausländische Zeitschriften seiner Zeit. Ein Beitrag zur Geschichte des Westlichen Russlandsbilde*, Bern/Frankfurt-am-Main, 1972.

—— 'Die Moskauer "Nationalitätenpolitik" unter Ivan IV', *Russian History* 1–4 (1984), pp. 263–82.

Karamzin, N.M., *Istoria gosudarstva rossiiskogo*, 12 vols, St Petersburg, 1892, Vols 7–9.

Kartashev, A.V., *Ocherki po istorii russkoi tserkvi*, Vol. 1, YMCA, Paris, 1959.

Kashtanov, S.M., 'O vnutrennei politike Ivana Groznogo v period velikogo kniazhenia Simeona Bekbulatovicha', *Trudy Moskovskogo gosudarstvennogo istoriko-arkhivnogo instituta*, Moscow, 1961, 16, pp. 461ff.

—— 'O tipe russkogo gosudarstva XIV–XVI vv', in *Chtenia pamiati V.B. Kobrina: Problemy otechestvennoi istorii i kul'tury perioda feodalizma*, Moscow, 1992, p. 86.

Kaufmann-Rochard, J., *Origines d'une bourgeoisie russe – XVI et XVIIe siècles*, Flammarion, Paris, 1969.

Kazakova, N.A., ' "Evropeiskoi strany koroli". Issledovania po otechestvennomu istochnikovedeniu', in *Sbornik statei posviashchennykh 75 letiu S.N. Valka*, Moscow, 1964.

Keegan, J.A., *History of Warfare*, Hutchinson, London, 1993.

Keenan, E.L., *The Kurbskii-Groznyi Apocrypha. The Seventeenth-Century Origin of the "Correspondence" attributed to Prince A.M. Kurbskii and Tsar Ivan IV*, Harvard University Press, Cambridge, Mass., 1971.

—— 'Muscovite Folkways', *Russian Review* 45 (1986), pp. 115–81.

—— 'Ivan IV and the King's Evil. Ni maka li to budet?', *Russian History* 20, nos 1–4 (1993), pp. 5–13.

—— 'Putting Kurbsky in his Place, or Observations and Suggestions concerning the Place in the History of the Grand Prince of Muscovy in the History of Muscovite Literary Culture', *FOG* 24, pp. 131ff.

—— 'Response to Halperin, "Edward Keenan and the Kurbskii-Groznyi Correspondence in Hindsight"', *JGOE* 46, no. 3, pp. 76–403, 404–15.

Keep, J.L.L., 'Bandits and the Law in Muscovy', reprinted in *Power and the People. Essays on Russian History*, East European Monographs, Boulder, Colorado, 1995, pp. 87–108.

—— 'The Decline of the Zemsky Sobor' and 'Afterword', in his *Power and the People, Essays on Russian History*, East European Monographs, Boulder, Colorado, 1995, pp. 51–86.

Kirchner, W., *The Rise of the Baltic Question*, Greenwood Press, Westport, Conn., 1970.

Kivelson, V.A., 'The Effects of Partible Inheritance. Gentry Families and the State in Muscovy', *Russian Review* 53 (1994), pp. 197–212.

Kleimola, A., 'Kto kogo: Patterns of Duma Recruitment, 1547–1564,' *FOG* 38 (1986), pp. 205–20.

—— 'Reliance on the Tried and True: Ivan IV and Appointments to the Boyar Duma, 1565–1584', *FOG* 46 (1992), pp. 51–63.

—— '"In accordance with the Holy Apostles", Muscovite Dowries and Women's Property Rights', *Russian Review* 51 (1992), pp. 204–29.

—— and Lehnhoff, G.D. (eds), *Culture and Identity in Muscovy, 1359–1584* (articles therein), UCLA Slavic Studies, New Series, Moscow, 1997.

Kliuchevsky, V.O., *Sochinenia. Kurs russkoi istorii*, Vol. 2, pt 2, Moscow, 1957.

—— *Boiarskaia Duma: Drevnei Rusi*, Moscow, 1909. Reprinted by Europe Printing, The Hague, 1965.

—— *Istoria soslovii v Rossii*, reprinted by Academic International, 1969.

—— 'Sostav predstavitel'stva na zemskikh soborakh drevnei Rusi', *Sochinenia*, Vol. 8, pp. 5–112.

Knecht, R.J., *Francis I*, Cambridge University Press, 1984.

Kobrin, V.B., *Ivan Groznyi*, Moscow, 1989.

—— 'Sostav oprichnogo dvora Ivana Groznogo', *Arkheograficheskii ezhegodnik za 1959*, Moscow, 1960.

—— *Vlast' i sobstvennost' v srednevekovoi Rossii (XV–XVI vv)*, Moscow, 1985.

—— *Problemy otechestvennoi istorii i kul'tury perioda feodalizma*, Moscow, 1992.

Kocher, P.H., 'Paracelsian Medicine in England: the First Thirty Years, ca. 1570–1600', *Journal of the History of Medicine*, Vol. 2, 1947.

Kollman, J., 'The Stoglav Council and Parish Priests', *Russian History* 7 (1980), pp. 65–91.

Kollman, Nancy Shields, *Kinship and Politics. The Making of the Muscovite Political System 1345–1547*, Stanford University Press, 1987.

—— 'Pilgrimage, Procession and Symbolic Space in Sixteenth-Century Russian Politics', *Medieval Russian Culture*, Vol. 2, M.S. Flier and D. Rowland (eds), University of California Press, Berkeley, 1994.

—— *By Honor Bound. State and Society in Early Modern Russia*, Cornell University Press, Ithaca, NY, 1999.

—— 'The Boyar Clan and Court Politics: The Founding of the Muscovite Political System', *CRMS* 23, 18

—— 'The Seclusion of Muscovite Women', *Russian History* 10, pp. 170–242.

Koretsky, V.I., 'Zemskii sobor 1575g. i postanovlenie Simeona Bekbulatovicha, Velikim Kniazem vseia Rusi', *Istoricheskii arkhiv* 2 (1959), pp. 148ff.

—— 'Smert' groznogo tsaria', *Voprosy istorii* 9 (1979), pp. 93–103.

Kostomarov, N.I., *Ocherk domashnei zhizni i nravov velikorusskogo naroda v XVI i XVII stoletiyakh*, Moscow, 1992.

Kotoshikhin, Grigory, *O Rossii v tsarstvovanie Alekseia Mikhailovicha*, St Petersburg, 1906.

Kozlov, S.A. and Dmitrieva, Z.V., *Nalogi v Rossii do XIX veka*, St Petersburg, 1999.

Kronk, Gary, W., *Cometography. A Catalog of Comets, Vol. 1, Ancient to 1799*, Cambridge University Press, 1999.

Kuchkin, V.A. and Floria, B.N., 'Kniazheskaia vlast' v predstavleniakh tverskikh knizhnikov XIV–XV vv.' in "Ot Rima k tret'emu Rimu", pp. 186–201.

Kukushkina, M.V., *Kniga v Rossii v XVI veke*, St Petersburg, 1999.

Kurat, A.N., 'The Turkish Expedition to Astrakhan in 1569, and the Problem of the Don-Volga Canal', *SEER* 40 (94), 1961, pp. 7–23.

Kurbsky, Prince A.M., *The Correspondence between Prince A. M. Kurbsky and Tsar Ivan IV of Russia, 1564–1579*, tr. and ed. J.L.I. Fennell, Cambridge University Press, 1963.

—— *History of Ivan IV*, tr. and ed. J.L.I. Fennell, Cambridge University Press, 1965.

Lander, J.R., 'Bonds, Coercion and Fear: Henry VII and the Peerage', *Florilegium Historiale. Essays presented to Wallace K. Ferguson*, ed. J.D. Rowe and W.H. Stockdale, Toronto University Press, 1971.

Lehtovirta, Jaakko, *Ivan IV as Emperor. The Imperial Theme in the Establishment of Muscovite Tsardom*, Turku, 1999.

Levy, Sandra, 'Women and the Control of Property in Sixteenth-Century Muscovy', *Russian History* 10, pt 2 (1983), pp. 201–12.

Likhachev, D.S., *Issledovania po drevnerusskoi literature*, Leningrad, 1986.

—— and Lur'e, Ia. S. (ed.), *Poslania Ivana Groznogo*, Moscow/Leningrad, 1951. Slavica reprint no. 41, 1970.

Liubavsky, M.K., *Ocherki istorii litovsko-russkago gosudarstva*, Moscow, 1910.

Loades, D., *The Tudor Court*, Headstart History, London, 1992.

Lossky, V.L., *The Mystical Theology of the Eastern Church*, James Clarke, Cambridge and London, 1973.

Lur'e, Ia. S., 'Donesenia agenta Maksimiliana II abbata Tsira o peregovorakh s A. M. Kurbskim v 1569', *Arkheograficheskii ezhegodnik za 1957*, Moscow, 1958, pp. 451–66.

—— *Ideologicheskaia bor'ba v russkoi publitsistike kontsa XV–nachala XVI v.*, Moscow/Leningrad, 1960.

McCulloch, D., *Tudor Church Militant: Edward VI and the Protestant Reformation*, Allen Lane, London, 1999.

Madariaga, I. de, 'Spain and the Decembrists', *European Studies Review* 3, no. 2 (April 1973), pp. 141–56.

—— 'La Monarquia rusa, una monarquia compuesta?'. Las Monarquias del Antiguo regimen, monarquias compuestas?', ed. C. Russell and J.A. Gallego, Editorial Complutense, Madrid, 1996.

—— 'Tsar into Emperor: The Title of Peter the Great', in *Politics and Culture in Eighteenth-Century Russia. Collected Essays*, Longman, London and New York, 1998, pp. 15–39.

—— 'Autocracy and Sovereignty' in *Politics and Culture in Eighteenth-Century Russia. Collected Essays*, Longman, London and New York, 1998, pp. 40–56.

Mansel, P., *Constantinople: City of the World's Desire, 1453–1924*, Penguin Harmondsworth, 1997.

Margeret, J. *Un Mousquetaire à Moscou*, ed. A. Bennigson, Paris, 1983.

Mar'iamov, G.B., *Kremlevskii tsentsor. Stalin smotrit kino*, Kinotsentr, 1992, pp. 69–74, 83–94.

Martin, Janet, *Medieval Russia, 980–1584*, Cambridge University Press, 1995.

—— 'Mobility, Forced Settlement and Regional Identity in Muscovy, 1359–1584', in *Culture and Identity in Muscovy*, ed. A.M. Kleimola and G.D. Lehnhoff, UCLA Slavic Studies, New Series, Moscow, 1997, pp. 431–49.

Massa, Isaac, *A Short History of the Muscovite Wars*, ed. and tr. Edward Orchard, Toronto University Press, 1982.

Mattingly, Garrett, *Renaissance Diplomacy*, Penguin, London, 1965.

Midelfort, H.C. Erik, *Mad Princes of Renaissance Germany*, University Press of Virginia, 1994.

Miller, D.B., 'The Coronation of Ivan IV of Moscow', *JGOE* 15 (1967), pp. 559–84.

—— 'Official History in the Reign of Ivan Groznyi', *Russian History* 14 (1987), pp. 534–41.

Moiseeva, G.N. (ed.), *Kazanskaia Istoria*, Leningrad, 1954.

—— (ed.), *Varlaamskaia beseda*, Leningrad, 1958.

Mordovina, S.P. and Stanislavskii, L.A., 'Sostav osobogo dvora Ivana IV v period "Velikogo Knyazhenia" Semiona Bekbulatovicha', *Arkheograficheskii ezhegodnik za 1976*, Moscow, 1976, pp. 153–92.

Morgan, E.D. and Coote, C.H. (eds), *Early Voyages and Travels in Russia and Persia by Anthony Jenkinson and Other Englishmen*, 2 vols, Hakluyt Society, nos 72–3, Vol. 1, *The travels of Anthony Jenkinson*, introduction, pp. i–clv, travels of Jenkinson, pp. 1–349. Appendix, pp. 355–479. London, 1886.

Morozova, L.E., 'Ivan Groznyi i publitsisty XVI veka o predelakh i kharaktere tsarskoi vlasti', in *Ot Rima k tret'emy Rimu*, pp. 236–51.

Moulin, Leo, 'Policy-making in the Religious Orders', *Government and Opposition* 1, no. 1 (October 1965), pp. 25–54.

Myers, A.R., *Parliaments and Estates in Europe to 1789*, Thames and Hudson, London, 1975.

Nazarov, V.D., 'Iz istorii tsentral'nykh gosudarstvennykh uchrezhdenii Rossii serediny XVI veka', *Istoriya SSSR* 3 (1976), pp. 77–96.

—— 'Svadebnye dela XVI veka', *Voprosy istorii* 10 (1976), pp. 121ff.

Neale, J.E., *The Elizabethan House of Commons*, Fontana, London, 1976.

Nefedov, S.A., 'Reformy Ivana III i Ivana IV: osmanskoye vlianie', *Voprosy istorii* 11 (2002), pp. 30–51.

The Nikonian Chronicle, tr. S.A. Zenkovsky, 5 vols, Kingston Press, Princeton, 1984–9.

Norwich, J.J., *Byzantium: The Decline and Fall*, Viking, London, 1995.

Novodvorsky, V., *Bor'ba za Livoniu mezhdu Moskoviu i rech'iu pospolitoiu 1570–1582*, St Petersburg, 1904..

Ostrowski, D.G., 'Church Polemics and Monastic Land Acquisition in Sixteenth-Century Muscovy', *SEER* 64, no. 3 (1986), pp. 357–79.

—— *Muscovy and the Mongols: Cross-Cultural Influences on the Steppe Frontier, 1304–1589*, Cambridge University Press, 1998.

Pamiatniki slaviano-russkoi pis'mennosti, izdannye arkheograficheskoi kommissieiu, *Velikii Cheti Miney*, 1–5 December 1901; 18–23 December 1907, Moscow.

Pavlenko, N.I., *Dvorianstvo i krepostnoi stroi Rossii XVI–XVII vv: Sbornik statei posviashchennikh na pamiati A. Novosel'skogo*, Moscow, 1975.

Pavlov, A.P., 'Prikazy i prikaznaia byurokratiia, 1584–1605', *Istoricheskie Zapiski* 116 (1988), pp. 187–227.

—— *Gosudarev dvor i politicheskaya bor'ba pri Borise Godunove*, St Petersburg, 1992.

Pavlov-Sil'vansky, N.P., *Sochinenia*, Vol. 1, St Petersburg, 1909, reprinted Europe Printing, The Hague, 1966.

Pelenski, J., 'Muscovite Imperial Claims to the Kazan' Khanate', *Slavic Review* 26 (1967), pp. 559–76.

—— *Russia and Kazan. Conquest and Imperial Ideology 1438–1560*, Mouton, The Hague, 1974.

—— 'The Origins of the Official Muscovite Claims to the Kievan Inheritance', *Harvard Ukrainian Studies* 1 (1977), pp. 29–52.

—— 'The Sack of Kiev of 1482 in Contemporary Muscovite Chronicle Writing', *Harvard Ukrainian Studies* 3–4 (1979), pt 2, pp. 638–649.

Peresvetov, I.S., *Sochinenia*, ed. D.S. Likhachev, Moscow/Leningrad, 1956.

Pernstein or Pernstain *see* Cobenzl.

Perrie, Maureen, *The Image of Ivan the Terrible in Russian Folklore*, Cambridge University Press, 1987.

—— *Pretenders and Popular Monarchism in Early Modern Russia*, Cambridge University Press, 1995.

—— *The Cult of Ivan the Terrible in Stalin's Russia*, Palgrave, London, 2001.

Peters, E., *Torture*, Basil Blackwell, Oxford, 1985.

Philipp, Werner, 'Ivan Peresvetov und seine Schriften zur Erneuerung des Moskauer Reiches', *Osteuropäische Forschungen* NF, Nd. 20, Berlin, 1935.

Pierling, P., *La Russie et le Saint Siège. Etudes diplomatiques*, 2 vols, Librairie Plon, Paris, 1891.

Pipes, R., *Russia under the Old Regime*, Weidenfeld and Nicholson, London, 1974.

Platonov, S.F., *Ocherki istorii smuty v moskovskom gosudarstve XVI–XVII vv*, St Petersburg, 1910.

Podobedova, O.I., *Moskovskaia shkola zhivopisi pri Ivana IV*, Moscow, 1972.

Podzhi, V. (Poggi), 'Ioann Pavel Kampana i Ivan Groznyi', *Ot Rima k tret'emu Rimu*.

Poe, Marshall, *Foreign Descriptions of Muscovy. An Analytical Bibliography of Primary and Secondary Sources*, Slavica, Columbus, Ohio, 1995.
—— 'What did Russians Mean When They Called Themselves Slaves of the Tsar?', *Slavic Review* 57, no. 3 (1998), pp. 585–608.
—— 'A People Born to Slavery', *Russia in Early Modern European Ethnography, 1476–1748*, Cornell University Press, Ithaca, NY, 2000.
Pollard, A.E., *The Evolution of Parliament*, London, 1964.
Possevino, Antonio, 'Missio Moscovitica', tr. and ed. H. Graham, *CASS* 6, no. 3 (Fall 1972), pp. 437–77.
—— *The Moscovia of Antonio Possevino, SJ*, tr. and with a critical introduction by Hugh Graham, University Center for East European Studies, University of Pittsburg, 1977.
Pouncy, C.J. (ed. and tr.), *The Domostroi Rules for Russian Households in the Time of Ivan the Terrible*, Cornell University Press, Ithaca, NY, and London, 1994.
—— '"The Blessed Sil'vestr" and the Politics of Invention in Muscovy, 1545–1700', *Harvard Ukrainian Studies* 19 (1995), pp. 548–72.
Prinz, D., von Buchau, 'Nachalo Rusi, i vozvyshchenie Moskovii,' tr. from the Latin by I.A. Tikhomirov, *Chtenia* 1876, III, Moscow, pp. 1–73.
Prokof'eva, N.I. and Alekhina, L.I. (eds), *Zapiski russkikh puteshestvennikov, XVI–XVII*, Moscow 1988.
Polnoe sobranie russkikh letopisei (Chronicles).
  PSRL IX–XIV *Nikonovskaia* or *Patriarshaia*
  PSRL XIII, 2, pt 1 Supplement to *Nikonovskaia*
  PSRL XIII, 2, pt 2, *Tsarstvennaia kniga*
  PSRL XIX, *Kazanskaia*
  PSRL XXIX, *Letopis nachala tsarstva; Aleksandro-Nevskaia letopis*
  PSRL XXXIV, *Piskarevskaia*
Putilev, B.N. and Dobrovol'sky, B.M. (eds), *Istoricheskie pesni XIII–XVI vekov*, Moscow, 1960.
Pypin, A., 'Istoria Varlaama i Iosafata', *Ocherk literaturnoi istorii starynnikh povesti i skazok russkikh*, St Petersburg, 1857.
Raeff, M., *The Decembrist Movement*, Russian Civilization Series, Prentice-Hall, Englewood Cliffs, NJ, 1966.
Roberts, M., *The Early Vasas: A History of Sweden, 1523–1611*, Cambridge University Press, 1968.
Rodriguez-Salgado, M-J., *Monarch of the World. The International Politics of Charles V*, Yale University Press, New Haven and London, forthcoming.
Rogger, H., *National Consciousness in Eighteenth-Century Russia*, Harvard University Press, Cambridge, Mass., 1960.
Rogov, V.A., *Istoria ugolovnogo prava, terrora i repressii v russkom gosudarstve XV–XVII vv.*, Moscow, 1995.
Ronchi, Michelis L. de, *Ivan il terribile – Jan Rokyta, disputa sul protestantesimo*, Turin, 1979.
Roublev, M., 'The Periodicity of the Mongol Tribute as Paid by the Russian Princes during the Fourteenth and Fifteenth Centuries', *FOG* 15, pp. 7–13.
Rowe, J.G. and Stockdale, W.H. (eds), *Florilegium Historiale. Essays Presented to Wallace K. Ferguson*, University of Toronto Press, 1971.

Rowland, D., 'Muscovite Political Attitudes as Reflected in Early Seventeenth-Century Tales about the Time of Troubles', Ph.D dissertation, Yale University, 1976.

—— 'The Problem of Advice in Muscovite Tales about the Time of Troubles', *Russian History* 6, pt. 2 (1979), pp. 259–83.

—— 'Did Muscovite Literary Ideology Place Limits on the Power of the Tsar (1540s–1660s)?', *Russian Review* 49 (1990), pp. 125–55.

Royal Historical Society, *Transactions*, 'The Eltonian Legacy', in Sixth Series, Vol. 7, Cambridge University Press, 1997.

Runciman, S., *Byzantine Civilization*, E. Arnold and Co., London, 1932.

Rüss, H., 'Elena Vasil'evna Glinskaja', *JGOE* 19 (1971), pp. 481–98.

—— *Herren und Diener*, Beitrage zur Geschichte Osteuropas, Bohlau Verlag, Cologne/Weimar/Vienna, 1994.

Russian Primary Chronicle. Laurentian Text, ed. S.H. Cross and O.P. Sherbowitz-Wetzor, Medieval Academy of America, Cambridge, Mass., 1953.

'Russkie akty Kopengagenskogo gosudarstvennogo arkhiva', *Russkaia istoricheskaia biblioteka* 16, no. 28 (31 July 1573), p. 103.

Ryan, W.F., 'Aristotle and Pseudo-Aristotle in Russia', in W.F. Ryan *et al.* (eds), *Pseudo-Aristotle in the Middle Ages: the Theology and Other Texts*, Warburg Institute Surveys and Texts, 11, London, 1986, pp. 115ff.

—— 'Alchemy and the Virtues of Stones in Muscovy', in *Alchemy and Chemistry in the 16th and 17th Centuries*, ed. P. Rattansi and A. Clericuzio, Kluwer, Dordrecht and London, 1994.

—— *The Bathhouse at Midnight*, University Park, Pennsylvania State University Press, 1999.

—— *The Secret of Secrets. An Historical Survey of Magic and Divination in Russia*, forthcoming.

Sadikov, P.A., 'Iz istorii oprichniny', *Istoricheskii arkhiv* 8, 1940.

—— *Ocherki po istorii oprichniny*, Moscow/Leningrad, 1950, reprinted Mouton, The Hague, 1969.

Savva, V.I., *Moskovskie tsari i Vizantiiskie vasilevsy*, Khar'kov, 1901.

Sbornik Imperatorskogo Russkogo Istoricheskogo Obshchestva, St Petersburg *see* SIRIO.

Scarisbrick, J.J., *Henry VIII*, Methuen, London, 1983.

Schlichting, A.A., 'A Brief Account of the Character and Brutal Rule of Ivan Vasil'evich, Tyrant of Muscovy', tr. and ed. H. Graham, *CASS* 9, no. 2 (1975), pp. 204–67.

—— 'News from Muscovy concerning the Life and the Tyranny of Prince Ivan, conveyed by the Nobleman, Albert Schlichting', tr. and ed. H. Graham, *CASS* 9, no. 2 (1975), pp. 267–72.

Schmidt, S.O., 'Sobory serediny XVI v.', *Istoria SSSR* 4 (1960), pp. 66–92.

—— 'Pravitel'stvennaia deiatel'nost' A. F. Adasheva', Reprinted in *Rossia Ivana Groznogo*, Nauka, Moscow, 1999, pp. 50–84.

—— *Rossia Ivana Groznogo*, Nauka, Moscow, 1999.

Sergeevich, V., *Russkie iuridicheskie drevnosti*, St Petersburg, 1900.

Shchapov, Ia N., 'Kizucheniu "China venchania na tsarstvo Ivana IV"', in *Ot Rima k tret'emu Rimu*, Rome/Moscow, 1995, pp. 213–25.

Shcherbachev, Iu. N., 'Kopengagenskie acty otnosiashchiesia k russkoi istorii.

Soobshchil Iu. N. Shcherbachev: 2 vols, 1326–1569, 1570–1576; *Chtenia* no. 255, 1915; no. 257, 1916.

Shevchenko, Ihor, 'A Neglected Byzantine Source of Muscovite Political Ideology', *Harvard Slavic Studies* 2 (1954), reprinted in *The Structure of Russian History. Interpretive Essays*, ed. M. Cherniavsky, New York, 1970.

Simionescu, Stefana, 'Les relations de la Moldavie avec les Habsbourgs pendant le règne de Petru Rareş (1527–1538, 1541–1546)', *Revue Romaine d'Histoire* 17, no. 2 (avril–juin 1978), pp. 455–67.

Sinitsyna, S.O., *Maksim Grek v Rossii*, Moscow, 1977.

Skrynnikov, R.G., *Nachalo oprichniny*, Leningrad, 1966.

—— *Oprichnyi terror*, Leningrad 1969.

—— *Rossia posle oprichniny*, Leningrad, 1975.

—— *Sviatiteli i vlasti*, Leningrad, 1990.

—— *Tsarstvo terrora*, St Petersburg, 1992.

—— *Veliki gosudar' Ivan Vasil'evich*, 2 vols, Smolensk, 1993.

Skryzhinskaia, E., *Barbaro i Kontarini v Rossii, k istorii italo-russkikh sviazei*, Leningrad, 1971.

Smirnov, I.I., *Ocherki politicheskoi istorii russkogo gosudarstva 30–50kh godov XVI veka*, Moscow/Leningrad, 1958.

Smith, Lt-Col. Dianne, Xenophon Group International, 'The Sixteenth-Century Muscovite Army', 24 January 1984, http.www.Xenophongi.org/rushistory/muscovy1htm.

—— 'Muscovite Logistics, 1462–1598', *SEER* 71, no.1 (1993), pp. 35–65.

Sokolov, I.M., *Monomakhov tron. Rossia i khristianskii vostok*, vyp1, Moscow, 2001.

Solov'ev, S.M., *Istoria Rossii s drevneishikh vremen*, Vol. 3, Moscow, 1961–5.

Staden, H. von, *The Land and Government of Muscovy*, tr. and ed. T. Esper, Stanford University Press, 1967.

Stählin, K., *Der Briefwechsel Iwans des Schrecklichen mit dem Fürsten Kurbski*, Leipzig, 1921.

Stelletsky, I. Ya., *Poiski biblioteki Ivana Groznogo*, Moscow, 1999.

Stökl, G., 'Der Moskauer Zemskii Sobor. Forschungsproblem und politischen Leitbild,' in *Der russische Staat im Mittelalter und früher Neuzeit*, Franz Steiner Verlag, Wiesbaden, 1981, pp. 124–45.

—— 'Gab es im Moskauer Staat Stände?', in *Der russiche Staat im Mittelalter und früher Neuzeit*, Franz Steiner Verlag, Wiesbaden, 1981, pp. 146–67.

—— 'Die Würzeln des modernen Staates in Osteuropa', in *Der russische Staat im Mittelalter und früher Neuzeit*, Franz Steiner Verlag, Wiesbaden, 1981, pp. 255–69.

Stremooukhoff, Dmitri, 'Moscow, the Third Rome. Sources of the Doctrine', in *The Structure of Russian History: Interpretive Essays*, ed. M. Cherniavsky, New York, 1970, pp. 108–25.

Stromilov, N.S., Aleksandrovskaia sloboda, *Chtenia*, Bk 2, pt 6, 1883, pp. 1–118.

Szeftel, M., 'Joseph Volotsky's Political Ideas in a New Historical Perspective', reprinted in his *Russian Institutions and Culture up to Peter the Great*, Preface by Donald W. Treadgold, Variorum Reprints, London, 1975.

—— 'The Title of the Muscovite Monarch up to the End of the Seventeenth Century', *CASS* 13, nos 1–2 (1979), pp. 59–81.

Taube, I. and Kruse, E., 'Poslanie Ioganna Taube i Elerta Kruse (Johann Taube und

Eilhard Kruse)', ed. M.G. Roginsky, *Russkii istoricheskii zhurnal* (1922), pp. 8–59.

Thyret, Isolde, 'Blessed is the Tsarita's Womb. The Myth of Miraculous Birth and Royal Motherhood in Muscovite Russia', *Russian Review* 53, no. 4 (1994), pp. 479–96.

Tikhomirov, M.N., 'Soslovno-predstavitel'nye uchrezhdenia (Zemskie sobory) v XVI veka', *Voprosy istorii*, no. 5, 1958.

—— 'Petr Raresh i Ivan Groznyi', *Omagiu lui P. Constantinescu* – Iasi cu prilejui impliniri, Bucharest, 1965.

—— *Rossiiskoe gosudarstvo XV–XVII vv*, Moscow, 1973.

—— 'Stranitsa iz zhizni Ivana Peresvetova', in *Rossiskoe gosudarstvo XV–XVII vv*, Moscow, 1973, pp. 70–73.

Timofeev, Ivan, *Vremmennik*, ed. and tr. O.A. Derzhavina, ANSSR, Moscow/Leningrad, 1951.

Tolstoy, George, *England and Russia. Rossia i Anglia, 1553–1593*, St Petersburg, 1875

Torke, H.-J., *Die Staatsbedingte Gesellschaft in Moskauer Reich*, E.J. Brill, Leiden, 1974.

Tourguéniev, A., *Historica Russiae Monumenta*, 1, St Petersburg, 1841.

Trevor Roper, H., 'The Court Physician and Paracelsianism', in *Medicine at the Courts of Europe 1500–1837*, ed. V. Nutton, Routledge, London and New York, 1990.

Trow, M.J., *Vlad the Impaler. In Search of the Real Dracula*, Sutton Publishing, Stroud, 2003.

Tsurkan, Roman, *Slavianskii perevod Bibli*, St Petersburg, 2001.

Tumins, V.A., *Tsar Ivan's Reply to Jan Rokyta*, Mouton, The Hague, 1971.

Tyla, A.,'The Formation of Lithuanian Eastern Policy: the Dietine of Rudninkai, September 24–27, 1572', *Lithuanian Historical Studies* 1, Vilnius (1996), pp. 22–38.

Übersberger, H., *Österreich und Russland seit dem Ende des 15 Jahrhunderts*, Band 1, 1488–1605, Wilhelm Braumüller, Vienna and Leipzig, 1906.

Uhlefeldt, J., 'Puteshestvie v Rossiu datskogo poslannika Iakova Ulfeldta v 1575', *Chtenia*, 1883, pt 1, pp. 1ff.

Usachev, A.S., 'Obraz Tsaria v srednevekovoi Rusi, Drevniaia Rus', *Voprosy medvistiki*, vyp. 3 (5), Moscow (2001), pp. 93–103.

Uspensky, B., *Tsar i patriarkh: Kharisma vlasti v Rossii (Vizantiiskaia model' i ee russkoe pereosmyslenie*, Moscow, 1998.

Ustryalov, N. (ed.), *Skazania Kniazia Kurbskogo*, St Petersburg, 1868.

Val'denberg, P., *Drevnerusskie ucheniia o predelakh tsarskoi vlasti*, Petrograd, 1916.

Vernadsky, G., *The Mongols and Russia*, Vol. 3 of *A History of Russia*, Yale University Press, New Haven, 1953.

—— *The Tsardom of Moscow, 1547–1682*, Vol. 5 of *A History of Russia*, Yale University Press, New Haven and London, 1969.

Veselovsky, S.B., 'Uchrezhdenie oprichnogo dvora v 1565 i otmenenia ego v 1572', *Voprosy Istorii* 1 (1946), pp. 86–104.

—— 'Poslednie udely v severovostochnoi Rusi', *Istoricheskie Zapiski*, no. 22 (1947), pp. 1101–31.

—— *Issledovania po istorii oprichniny*, Moscow, 1963.

—— 'Dukhovnoe zaveshchanie Tsaria Ivana 1572', in *Issledovania po istorii oprichniny*, Moscow, 1963, pp. 302–22.

—— *Tsar Ivan Groznyi v rabotakh pisatelei I istorikov*, Moscow, 1999.

—— 'Po povodu trilogii tov. Kostyleva i voznikshei o nei polemiki', (August 1943), *Tsar Ivan Groznyi v rabotakh pisatelei i istorikov*, Moscow, 1999, pp. 7–34.

Vladimirtsev, V., *Le Régime Social des Mongoles*, Paris, 1948.

Vodiansky, O. (ed.), 'The Missions of Pernistan, Pernstein, etc. actually Count Cobenzl and Daniel Prinz von Buchau to Poland, Lithuania and Russia', *Chteniia, Oct–Dec, 1876.*

Volkhovsky, M.G. (ed.), *Domashnii byt russkikh tsarei v XVI i XVII vv.*

Volotsky, Iosif, *Prosvetitel'*, tr. E.V. Kravets, Moscow, 1993.

Webbe, E., *His Travails*, London, 1590.

Weir, Alison, *Henry VIII: King and Court*, Jonathan Cape, London, 2001.

Willan, T.S., *The Early History of the Russia Company, 1553–1603*, Manchester University Press, 1956.

Wood, I., *The Merovingian Kingdoms, 450–741*, Longman, London, 1994.

Woodward, G.P. and Mattingly, H. (eds), *St. John Damascene, Barlaam and Josaphat*, William Heinemann, London, 1914.

Woolley, B., *The Queen's Conjuror. The Science and Magic of Dr. Dee*, HarperCollins, London, 2001.

Wormald, J., *Lords and Men in Scotland: Bonds of Manrent, 1442–1603*, John Donald, Edinburgh, 1985.

Yeomans, D.K., *Comets: a Chronological History of Observation, Science, Myth and Folklore*, Wiley Science Edition, 1991.

Yanov, A., *The Origins of Autocracy – Ivan the Terrible in Russian History*, University of California Press, Berkeley and London, 1981.

Zenkovsky, S.A. (ed.), *Medieval Russian Epics, Chronicles and Tales*, New York, 1963.

Zharinov, G.V., 'Zapisi o raskhode lekarstvennykh sredstv 1581–1582', *Arkhiv russkoi istorii* 4 (1994), pp. 103–25.

Zhivov, V.M. and Uspensky, B.A., 'Tsar i Bog: semioticheskie aspekty sakralizatsii monarkha v Rossii', in *Iazyki kul'tury i problemy perevodimosti*, ed. B.A. Uspensky, Moscow, 1987.

Zimin, A.A., *I.S. Peresvetov i ego sovremenniki. Ocherki po istorii russkoi obshchestvennoi mysli serediny XVI veka*, ANSSR, Moscow, 1958. (Extensive bibliography.)

—— 'O sostave dvortskovykh uchrezhdenii russkogo gosudarstva kontsa XV i XVI v.', *Istoricheskii Zapiski*, no. 63, Moscow, 1958, pp. 180–205.

—— *Reformy Ivana Groznogo*, Moscow, 1960.

—— 'Zemskii sobor 1566 g.', *Istoricheskie zapiski*, no. 71 (1962), pp. 217–35.

—— *Oprichnina Ivana Groznogo*, Moscow, 1964.

—— 'Sluzhilye kniaz'ia v russkom gosudarstve kontsa XV-pervoi treti XVI v', *Dvorianstvo i krepostnoi stroi Rossii XVI–XVIII vv*, Moscow, 1975.

—— *V Kanun groznykh potriasenii*, Moscow, 1986.

—— *Formirovanie boyarskoi aristokratii v Rossii vo vtoroi polovine XV-pervoi treti XVI v*, Moscow, 1988.

—— *Oprichnina*, 2nd ed., A.L. Khoroshkevich, Moscow, 2001.

—— (comp.) and Likhachev, D.S. (ed.), *Sochinenia I.S. Peresvetova*, Moscow/ Leningrad, 1956.

Zlotnik, M.D., 'Muscovite Fiscal Policy, 1462–1584', *Russian History* 6, pt 2 (1979), pp. 243 ff.

Index